ALSO BY PHILIP SHORT

Banda

The Dragon and the Bear: Inside China and Russia Today

Mao: A Life

Pol Pot: The History of a Nightmare

Mitterrand

Mitterrand

A Study in Ambiguity

PHILIP SHORT

THE BODLEY HEAD
LONDON

Published by The Bodley Head 2013

2 4 6 8 10 9 7 5 3 1

Copyright © Philip Short 2013

Philip Short has asserted his right under the Copyright,
Designs and Patents Act 1988 to be identified as the author of this work

First published in Great Britain in 2013 by
The Bodley Head
Random House, 20 Vauxhall Bridge Road,
London SW1V 2SA

www.bodleyhead.co.uk
www.vintage-books.co.uk

Addresses for companies within The Random House Group Limited can be found at:
www.randomhouse.co.uk/offices.htm

The Random House Group Limited Reg. No. 954009

A CIP catalogue record for this book
is available from the British Library

ISBN 9781847920065

The Random House Group Limited supports the Forest Stewardship Council® (FSC®),
the leading international forest-certification organisation. Our books carrying the FSC
label are printed on FSC®-certified paper. FSC is the only forest-certification scheme supported
by the leading environmental organisations, including Greenpeace. Our paper procurement policy
can be found at www.randomhouse.co.uk/environment

Typeset in Dante MT 11.5/14 pt by Palimpsest Book Production Limited, Falkirk, Stirlingshire

Printed and bound in Great Britain by
Clays Ltd, St Ives PLC

For Ging
who made it possible

Contents

Acknowledgements

Books are written for all sorts of reasons. The genesis of this one dates back to the 1980s, when I represented the BBC in Paris and, over the course of ten years, scarcely a day went by without my finding new reasons to thank the tutelary deities for having put me in France at a time when its presidency was in the hands of François Mitterrand – a gifted, devious man, part visionary, part pragmatist, who when he was not shooting himself in the foot could run rings round his political opponents – rather than either of his two worthy but uninspiring predecessors.

To be intrigued by a man, however, is one thing; to write a book about him is another. For a long time my attention was distracted by the lives of two other complicated men, Mao Zedong and Pol Pot. But the project began to take shape one summer after a conversation with Bruno Philip, then the correspondent for *Le Monde* in China, who, through the intermediary of a colleague in India, introduced me to Dominique Hernu, who had married Mitterrand's close friend, Charles Hernu and afterwards worked for Danielle Mitterrand at the Elysée. Dominique proved to be an open sesame, unlocking so many doors that, had I walked through all of them, this book would occupy multiple volumes and still be a work in progress. Through her I met Pierre Avril, Georges Fillioud, Louis Mermaz, Guy Penne, Laurence Soudet and, last but not least, André Rousselet, whose affectionate, ironic and lucid appraisals of his old friend, François Mitterrand, I have found invaluable.

Anne Pingeot put aside her legendary discretion to talk about the man with whom she acted out an extraordinary, and courageous, love story, spanning more than thirty years – the 'heroine of a film which no one will ever see', as their daughter, Mazarine, put it. And, through one of those happy coincidences which come when least expected – a chance encounter one evening on a houseboat on the River Seine with a professor of Renaissance literature, Caroline Trotot, whose uncle turned out to be a friend of Danielle Mitterrand's companion, Jean Balenci – I met the third member of the *ménage à trois* which constituted Mitterrand's 'official' family until the start of his presidency in 1981. He, too, has until now remained silent about the twenty-three years he spent as a member of the Mitterrand household.

Anne Lamouche introduced me to Danielle, with whom I spent many hours, in Paris and at Latche, and whom I found, at the end of her life, at peace with herself and reconciled to the extraordinary roller-coaster ride on which her impossible husband had led her. Mitterrand's niece by marriage, Anne-Marie, offered a characteristically idiosyncratic view of her adopted family, while her husband, Olivier, persuaded his uncle, Jacques, then the last of the four Mitterrand brothers still living, to break his long silence and deliver some choice comments on the misdeeds of his sibling. Olivier's mother, Édith Cahier – Robert Mitterrand's first wife – and her husband, Jacques Maroselli – also provided instructive insights.

Not all are cited here: a book is only as good as the parts that are left out. But all helped to fashion the portrait of a complex, puzzling, exasperating and highly important European leader.

So did Mitterrand himself, whom I met from time to time at the Elysée during his years in power and whom I found, as did many others, intimidating – a trait which he shared with de Gaulle – subtle, stealthy, artful and determined. Many of his contemporaries whom I interviewed in the 1980s also shed light on his character, among them his friend, Georges Beauchamp; his colleagues, Robert Badinter, Claude Cheysson, Edith Cresson, Roland Dumas, Laurent Fabius, Lionel Jospin and Pierre Joxe; his bête noire, Michel Rocard; and his principal right-wing opponents, Raymond Barre, Jacques Chirac and Valéry Giscard d'Estaing – not to mention Jean-Marie Le Pen.

My thanks are due, also, to Hubert Védrine; Gilles Ménage and Georges Saunier of the Institut François Mitterrand; to Pascal Genest and Zénaide Romaneix of the French National Archives; and to Dominique Bertinotti, for their help in making available documentation from Mitterrand's time as President and, in the case of the Institut, from his private papers.

It would be vain, however, for a writer to pretend that a book depends only on himself and his sources. This book, like my earlier forays, owes much to Jack Macrae in New York, to my agents, Veronique Baxter and Emma Sweeney, and to Jacqueline Korn in London. My editor at The Bodley Head, Will Sulkin, nurtured the project through the six years it has taken to bring to fruition and, in the final months, used his blue pencil to good effect, skewering imprecise arguments and infelicities in the text. Stuart Williams and Katherine Ailes showed a merciful understanding of repeatedly missed deadlines, while Beth Humphries waged war on delinquent syntax and punctuation. I am in their debt.

Paris – La Garde Freinet, June 30 2013

Prologue

Other nations have scandals. The French have affairs.

From the Dreyfus Affair, before the Great War, when the country was at loggerheads with itself over the supposed treason of a Jewish officer; to the Stavisky Affair in the 1930s, in which a politically well-connected embezzler 'committed suicide with a bullet which someone fired at him at point-blank range', as one newspaper gleefully put it, bringing down the government of the day; the Bazooka Affair in the 1950s, when Michel Debré, a close aide to France's wartime leader, General Charles de Gaulle, was suspected of complicity in the attempted murder of the French army commander in Algeria; the Affair of Bokassa's Diamonds, in the 1970s, which helped end the re-election hopes of President Valéry Giscard d'Estaing; and the Clearstream Affair, twenty years later, when another French president, Nicolas Sarkozy, threatened to hang a rival 'from a butcher's hook', affairs have punctuated the rhythms of French political life.

They are never fully elucidated, never satisfactorily explained, and leave an odour of malfeasance which continues to haunt the protagonists for the rest of their political careers.

Few affairs in modern French history have been as enduring and insidious as the Observatory Affair, so called because it took place near the gardens of that name in the Latin Quarter of Paris. That year, 1959, the Algerian war of independence was raging. De Gaulle had been called out of retirement by French army commanders who, infuriated by the reluctance of the civilian government to crack down decisively on a rebellion in what was then still officially part of metropolitan France, had threatened a *coup d'état*. He had been given emergency powers and, the previous September, a new constitution had been approved, enshrining presidential rule. The Fourth Republic, with its fragile and ephemeral parliamentary governments, was gone. France found itself catapulted into a new era of republican monarchy.

Among the few mainstream politicians who had voted against de Gaulle's return was François Mitterrand, then among the leaders of the non-communist opposition. Mitterrand was not exactly a rising star, having held government office a dozen times since 1944, when he had become the youngest French minister since the Second Empire of Napoleon III, almost a century earlier. A gifted orator, his devastating put-downs, deceptively casual and often slightly tongue in cheek, masked an innate shyness which he went to great lengths to conceal.

Until de Gaulle's recall, Mitterrand had been regarded, not least by himself, as a Prime Minister in waiting. Subsequently he had been marginalised as the fault line in French politics shifted. Instead of dividing Left from Right, it now separated those who wanted negotiations in Algeria from those who favoured a military solution. To diehard conservatives, who had championed the General's return but had afterwards come to distrust his intentions, Mitterrand epitomised the decadence of the weak civilian leaderships which had sold out French Indochina and seemed to be preparing to do the same in the one imperial stronghold France had left: North Africa. His opponents attacked him as 'anti-national', parliamentary language for a traitor.

That autumn, Paris was alive with rumours of right-wing assassination squads being sent from Algiers by extremist settler organisations to execute political moderates. Louis Mermaz, later Speaker of the National Assembly, remembered it as 'a sulphurous time, threats flying in all directions'. Albin Chalandon, the Gaullist party Secretary-General, spoke of a plot to overthrow the government. Certain politicians, who were judged to be particularly vulnerable, including the former Prime Minister, Pierre Mendès France, were given round-the-clock police protection. In October, one of Mitterrand's closest friends informed him that death lists were circulating in Oran, Algeria's second city: 'Mitterrand's name was listed first and Michelet (the Gaullist Justice Minister) second'. In the summer, plastic explosives were placed outside the door of his apartment but failed to detonate.[1] His wife, Danielle, at home alone with two young children, started getting telephone calls late at night. 'A voice would say, "Does black suit you? I hope so because soon you will wear it for your husband." I told François, but he wouldn't take it seriously. He said it was just cranks.'

Nevertheless, on October 14, Mitterrand asked a trusted friend, Bernard Finifter, to find him a bulletproof jacket. Finifter approached the Director of National Security at the Interior Ministry, Jean Verdier. 'It's a matter of life and death,' he pleaded. But he refused to explain why he wanted it and Verdier turned him down.

The following day, a Thursday, brought more ominous developments.

The right-wing evening newspaper, *Paris-Presse*, led its front page with a melodramatic warning: 'A tragedy is in the making . . . It could be for tomorrow. Already groups of killers have crossed the border from Spain. Those to be executed have been chosen . . . 18 months after [de Gaulle's return to power], we risk seeing the outbreak of a fratricidal internal conflict.' It had been written by a prominent Gaullist MP, who said later that his information had come from two concordant sources in Algeria and that the head of the French counter-espionage service, the DST, had confirmed it.

Mitterrand dined at home that night with Danielle and a group of friends. Afterwards with three companions, he drove to the Champs-Elysées, the great thoroughfare that points like an arrow into the heart of Paris, descending from the Arc de Triomphe to the Tuileries Gardens and the Louvre. They bought *Paris-Presse* at a news-stand and stopped at a café, the *Pam Pam*, to discuss the story over a drink. 'It seems things are coming to a head,' Mitterrand murmured. At his suggestion they drove back to St Germain des Prés on the Left Bank, not far from his home, to have a nightcap at the Brasserie Lipp.

Lipp was, and remains today, a Parisian institution, a meeting place for politicians, philosophers, actresses and bishops, writers and celebrities, from Hemingway and Jean-Paul Sartre to Verlaine and Chagall.[2] Its wood-panelled façade, belle époque floral ceramics, painted Veronese-style ceilings, and mirrors subtly tilted so that its habitués can both see and be seen, have witnessed more than a century of copious Alsatian cuisine, foaming jugs of beer (of which Marcel Proust, when not nibbling madeleines, was said to have been a devotee), flirtatious dalliances and political and literary intrigues.

Mitterrand was a regular. But on this occasion, after greeting a few acquaintances, he told his companions he felt tired and left. Within minutes, he said later, he sensed that he was being followed. Two men in a light green Renault Dauphine kept steadily behind his car. To be sure that his imagination was not playing tricks, he changed his usual route, turning left at the Senate to drive down the eastern side of the Luxembourg Gardens, past the rise that leads to the Pantheon, then southward towards the Observatory, founded in 1667 by the Sun King, Louis XIV. Whenever he slowed down, the Renault did the same.

> Abruptly I turned right into the rue Auguste Comte, accelerating as I did so . . . The other car did the same and started gaining on me. It would be hard for me to explain what was going through my head at that moment, but I knew that whatever happened I had to escape my pursuers. I was familiar with the area and instinctively I veered across the road, jamming on the brakes and coming to a halt between two parked cars. I literally flew out of my seat, raced towards the [Observatory] gardens and jumped the fence, throwing myself face-down in a flower-bed. A volley of shots rang out . . . Then I saw them drive off . . . I had the impression that they gave up trying to kill me when they saw me jump out and run. They shot up the empty car in order to be able to say to their bosses, 'We did it. But there were unforeseen circumstances.'[3]

Mitterrand's car, a blue Peugeot saloon, had seven bullet holes, which the police established had been fired from a Sten gun.

When he finally got back to his apartment, long after midnight, Danielle found him 'shattered . . . He was always reserved – not the kind of man to throw himself into his wife's arms, announcing "I've just escaped death!" . . . But that night he was completely closed in on himself. I couldn't even talk to him. He just stayed in his room.'

Expressions of sympathy poured in from all sides. To many it was a sign that the *ultras*, as the diehard nationalists were called, were losing patience with de Gaulle's regime.[4] Mitterrand had been targeted not because of his liberal views but as a shot across the bows of the government, a warning to the administration that the French settlers in Algeria and their extremist leaders would not sit idly by if the authorities tried to abandon them.

A week later came the *coup de théâtre*.

On October 22, a former MP named Robert Pesquet, who had represented an extreme right-wing party in parliament until the year before, informed the investigating magistrate that the assassination attempt had been faked.

Mitterrand, he said, had approached him earlier that month with a proposal that he simulate an attack 'in order to provoke the destruction of the *ultras* and their organisations'. In return, Mitterrand had promised to help him relaunch his political career. Pesquet said he had played along with the subterfuge because, as a supporter of French rule in Algeria, he wanted to expose Mitterrand as a liar in order to discredit him, and all those like him, who favoured negotiating with the rebels. He had staged the shooting himself with an accomplice, he added, but in such a way as to ensure that nobody would be hurt.

Summoned by the magistrate to explain himself, Mitterrand denied everything. He said he had encountered Pesquet by chance two weeks earlier and the latter had repeatedly telephoned, asking to see him again. When eventually he agreed to a meeting, on October 14, Pesquet told him that he was linked to a terrorist group which had put Mitterrand on a blacklist to be killed. The former MP had sworn him to secrecy, saying that if his associates learnt that he had betrayed them his own life and the lives of his family would be in danger. He had come to warn Mitterrand, he added, because, whatever their differences about Algeria, he wanted no part in murder. The following afternoon, Mitterrand told the magistrate, Pesquet had contacted him again to tell him the attack was imminent and promising that if he had more information, he would wait for Mitterrand at Lipp that night. But there had been no sign of Pesquet at the brasserie and the next thing he knew his car was being followed.

To the magistrate's inevitable question, 'Why didn't you go to the police?', Mitterrand replied that he had given his word and did not intend to break it.*[5]

There matters might have rested. Pesquet had a history of shady deals that had caused him earlier brushes with the law. Mitterrand kept repeating to his friends, 'It's his word against mine.'

But Pesquet had been cunning.

---

* In Mitterrand's defence, Pierre Mendès France disclosed shortly afterwards that he had been placed in an identical dilemma two years earlier when, following an assassination attempt which injured his bodyguard, a member of the group responsible had come to warn him that another attempt was being planned. 'I would have regarded it as utterly contemptible to put in danger the life of [that] man,' he said. If Mitterrand was at fault for not alerting the authorities, Mendès said, he had been equally so, 'and I wouldn't hesitate to do it again'.

Six hours *before* the attack, he had sent a letter to himself at a poste restante address describing in detail what was to happen. A bailiff accompanied him when he collected it and attested to the time on the postmark. For the press and for public opinion, it followed that Pesquet must be telling the truth. The only possible explanation was that he and Mitterrand had concocted the whole thing together. Overnight, from having been a hero, Mitterrand became a bad joke; at best a naïve dupe, at worst an incompetent trickster whose machinations had come unstuck, deserving, as one newspaper put it, 'not hate, but a certain contempt'.

The trap, for trap it was, had been diabolically set.

Mitterrand in the late 1950s was a savvy, seasoned politician with a national reputation. A serial seducer, with countless conquests to his name, a mark in France not of inconstancy but of virility and savoir-faire, he was controversial, charismatic and secretive. That he could have been bamboozled by an adventurer like Pesquet seemed totally out of character. André Bettencourt, who had known him since they were students together, was quoted in the press describing his 'instinctive distrustfulness and sang-froid'. Mitterrand normally weighed to a nicety the pros and cons of every step he took. Yet he had walked blindly into an ambush which even a neophyte should have seen.

André Rousselet, a long-time member of Mitterrand's inner circle, felt that in the days after Pesquet's revelations, he was close to suicide. François Dalle, a friend since the 1930s, thought the same: 'for a week I spent every day with him, because I wanted to avoid a disaster'. Georges Beauchamp, a colleague from the Resistance, feared a repeat of the Salengro Affair, when, in 1936, a minister in the Popular Front government had killed himself after a campaign of calumny. 'Salengro was on all our minds,' said Roland Dumas, later French Foreign Minister. 'With hindsight, I don't think he would have done it . . . But back then I wasn't so sure.'

Mitterrand believed that his career was finished and that he would never recover. 'He was convinced of it,' a colleague recalled. 'I remember going out for a walk with him. He thought it was all over.' That weekend was his forty-third birthday. Danielle, for the first time since their marriage, saw him weakened. 'I discovered that he was human that day. He was staring into an abyss. For nights on end he paced up and down in the apartment, trying to figure out what to do. It became an obsession.' Years later he spoke of feeling 'as though I were at the bottom of a well'.

Jean-Jacques Servan-Schreiber, who edited the progressive weekly, l'Express, remembered a meeting in his office where Mitterrand, normally the most private and unemotional of men, 'broke down and cried like a baby'. With a handful of exceptions, Servan-Schreiber among them, his political friends abandoned him. Even Henri Frenay, a wartime Gaullist minister who was godfather to Mitterrand's son, Gilbert, told Danielle when she sought his help that he 'didn't want to get involved'.

Salvation, of a kind, came in November, when it was disclosed that, during the summer, Pesquet had approached Maurice Bourgès-Maunoury, a Centre-Right leader and former Prime Minister whose views on Algeria were more conservative than Mitterrand's, with a similar claim that he was to be targeted for assassination. Bourgès, two years older and a more down-to-earth, phlegmatic character, had wisely refused to have anything to do with him. De Gaulle's government had known this for weeks but had kept quiet so as to cause Mitterrand the maximum political damage.[6]

The disclosure fatally undermined his opponents' case against him. If Pesquet had tried earlier to ensnare others, Mitterrand could no longer be accused of having initiated the plot himself. Like a soufflé that collapses once the hot air inside cools, the Observatory Affair began to look like the political silliness it was. Who after all could seriously believe that Mitterrand would turn to a virtual unknown, a political opponent to boot, to simulate an attempt on his life, in which real bullets would be used, at the risk of getting himself killed?* Had he wished to fake a murder attempt, he had plenty of trusted friends from the Resistance who would have been only too glad to help him.

Yet Pesquet's letter, describing exactly how the attack would be mounted, was impossible to explain away. In parliament, Mitterrand insisted 'there was nothing he could not have known or guessed . . . If its contents had not conformed to the use that he wished to make of it, it would never have been divulged.' It was a good try, but it fell

---

* Apart from two groups of neo-Grecian statuary on stone plinths in the centre of the gardens, the area offers no cover. When the police staged a reconstruction of the attack, Mitterrand offered to re-enact his role. The magistrate refused, saying that with live fire it was too dangerous.

short. The letter included details which could only have been agreed in advance.[7]

Fifty years later, Mitterrand's brother, Jacques, then dying of cancer, explained what had really happened. 'He screwed himself completely,' Jacques said. 'It was a trap with many levels. He thought he could benefit from it, yes . . . he thought he could turn it to his own advantage. But in fact he trapped himself.' Pesquet, he said, had begged Mitterrand to help him. He seemed terrified and claimed that he risked being killed if he did not show his bosses that he had at least attempted an attack. It was an approach well calculated to appeal to what André Rousselet called the 'romanesque' side of Mitterrand's nature. When Pesquet insisted that to go to the police would put him in mortal danger, Mitterrand decided to play along. It was a gamble which, if it succeeded, would put him back in the forefront of French political life. 'At that time,' François Dalle remembered, 'no one was talking about him. [De Gaulle was in the spotlight.] Mitterrand needed people to talk about him . . . He was no longer centre stage. So he committed this enormous, fantastic piece of stupidity.'

The Observatory Affair would remain an albatross around François Mitterrand's neck for the rest of his life and beyond. Most French people, on the Left as well as the Right, believe to this day that he instigated the attack himself. In later years, he refused point-blank to discuss it. The result, as Jacques acknowledged, was that he was not believed. 'He never explained completely what had happened. Had he done so, the affair would have been over. But he didn't.' He did not because he could not without admitting that he had lied. That was the beauty of it. Once the trap had closed, there was no way he could ever escape.

The autumn of 1959 was a watershed in Mitterrand's career. As Danielle put it, shortly before her death, 'there was "before" the Observatory, and "after".'

Until then, politically at least, he had had a charmed existence. While still in his thirties, he had held two of the highest posts in government as Interior and Justice Minister. After de Gaulle's return, he and Mendès France had led the challenge from the Left. Now his career was in ruins: everything had to be rebuilt.

The identity of those who had tried to frame him, manipulating

Pesquet from behind the scenes, was never formally established. But the fetid whiff of intrigue, of conspiracies and cover-ups, lingered long after. Although Mitterrand was able, with difficulty, to retain a seat in parliament, he became the whipping boy of the Right, which excoriated him as a symbol of all that it despised. 'Whenever he got up to speak,' Rousselet recalled, 'his opponents would chant, "Pesquet! Pesquet!" . . .'

Old accusations, which he had thought long since laid to rest, were raked up anew. As a student in the 1930s, had he not joined a terrorist group, the Secret Organisation for Revolutionary Action, known as La Cagoule (The Hood)? His role in the Resistance was trashed. Had he not worked at Vichy for the government of Marshal Pétain, which collaborated with Hitler? Had not Pétain awarded him the *francisque*, the Marshal's personal decoration?

Mitterrand had ready answers: half the leaders of the Resistance had worked for Vichy at one time or another, as had many of de Gaulle's own ministers; the *francisque* had been a cover approved by de Gaulle's aides in London. The General himself had described Mitterrand as one of a handful of 'our representatives' responsible for keeping him informed about developments inside France.[8] But that was not what his opponents wished to hear. The orthodox version of wartime history was written in black and white, with no place for shades of grey. It held that the majority of the French people had been patriots; Vichy, a nest of traitors. That the reality might have been more complicated has never been widely accepted in France. In the early 1960s, it was pointless even to try to discuss it.

Politics, however, like other forms of human endeavour, has its arsenal of surprises.

Six years later, in 1965, the same François Mitterrand whose name had been dragged through the mud and whose future had been written off by all but a tiny handful of loyalists, achieved a resounding triumph in the first direct presidential election of the new Fifth Republic. De Gaulle's towering stature at that time meant there was never any possibility of an opposition victory. Mitterrand's achievement was to force him into the humiliation of a run-off, in which the challenger received an unhoped-for 45 per cent of the vote. In 1981, he became France's first popularly elected socialist president, going on to win a second term. By the time he completed his mandate, he had led the

country for fourteen years, longer than any other French Head of
State in modern times, establishing himself in the eyes of French
people of all political persuasions as being with Charles de Gaulle one
of the two defining leaders of twentieth-century France.

They were strange bedfellows.

De Gaulle, the wartime hero, gave France back its pride after the
Nazi Occupation, ended the war in Algeria and took the first, essential steps towards reconciliation with Germany and the making of
post-war Europe. Mitterrand, in peacetime, transformed France into
a modern democratic state, legitimised the Left as a responsible voice
in the nation's political affairs and, together with Helmut Kohl, pushed
Europe towards political union, with a common currency and a reuni-
fied Germany anchored firmly in the West.

One was an austere, granite monument of a man, the self-appointed
guardian of French honour, as strict with others as with himself and
displaying sovereign contempt for all whose moral standards did not
meet his own exacting conception of how men should behave. The
other was an enigma, a bourgeois intellectual from a solidly right-wing
background capable of firing a left-wing crowd into a fervour of
political enthusiasm, an introverted, inspiring figure who transcended
his origins and culture to build a political career on the back of a
working class with whom he had almost nothing in common.

De Gaulle was a good Catholic, devoted husband and father (of a
daughter with Down's syndrome), the incarnation of respectability.
Mitterrand was a lapsed Catholic who spent years in a *ménage à trois*
and then maintained two homes and two families, one legitimate, the
other adulterine.

They were chalk and cheese and, not surprisingly, allergic to each
other. But it was an antipathy based on respect. De Gaulle was twenty-
five years older than Mitterrand, died twenty-five years before him
and left no written record of how he viewed his young challenger.
To Mitterrand, de Gaulle represented 'mastery over oneself, which
meant mastery over history'. After the General's death, he compared
him to Henri IV, the great sixteenth-century King who ended the Wars
of Religion, and Cardinal Richelieu, Chief Minister to his son, Louis
XIII, who laid the foundations of modern Western statecraft. It was
an extraordinary tribute to a man who, for most of his career, had
been his arch-enemy. Yet the panegyric was tempered by distance.

Late in life he penned an appreciation of de Gaulle's 'astonishing sureness of judgement':

> With him, one was in History. One lived it. One made it. I saw that and . . . I admired [him] for being able to rule like that. But I was not tempted to join him politically . . . I could have done so . . . But with de Gaulle there was a certain militarism, a tone which did not suit me . . .

De Gaulle projected a vision of French grandeur. Mitterrand mirrored France in all its imperfections, its turpitudes and tragedies, its cowardice and glory, its weakness and its strength. Both men changed their country profoundly, but in profoundly different ways. De Gaulle reflected its ambitions; Mitterrand, its reality.

They also had much in common. A generation apart, both had been taken prisoner: de Gaulle in the First World War, Mitterrand in the Second. De Gaulle tried repeatedly to escape, but each time was recaptured; Mitterrand succeeded. Both rebelled: de Gaulle against the military hierarchy, Mitterrand against his class; yet even there, the distinction was perhaps less than it seemed. 'De Gaulle,' Mitterrand wrote, 'dared to deny his social class by an act of indiscipline, . . . by breaking with the established order on June 18 1940 . . . when that established order betrayed [his country]'.

Both men radiated a natural authority over those around them. A fellow PoW wrote of de Gaulle in 1917: 'Under a simple, sometimes familiar exterior, he knew how to maintain a distance. All the other [officers] used the informal "*tu*" when they talked among themselves. No one ever used "*tu*" to de Gaulle.' The same could have been written of Mitterrand. No one used '*tu*' to him either.[9]

Both men had an inner solitude, a part of their being that was locked, inaccessible to others, which is one of the characteristics of uncommon leaders everywhere. De Gaulle was nicknamed the *Connétable*, or Supreme Commander; Mitterrand, the Sphinx. Both spent long years in the wilderness, de Gaulle in the 1950s, Mitterrand a decade later. Both used unhesitatingly every weapon in the political armoury. De Gaulle was portrayed as a model of political rectitude but employed a private army of thugs to intimidate opponents, special courts to stifle dissent and state controls on radio and television to inhibit democratic debate. Mitterrand ended those practices, but as

President created an eavesdropping unit to spy on those rash enough to take an interest in his complicated private life.

De Gaulle, like Mitterrand, was a master of the oracular phrase. In Algiers in June 1958, he famously assured French settlers, *'Je vous ai compris!'* ('I have understood you'), words greeted with tumultuous applause. By then he had already decided that the settlers had no future and would have to be abandoned. It would take them another year to realise that his meaning was not what they thought. For de Gaulle such ambiguity was discretionary. For Mitterrand it was systemic. Laurent Fabius, his Prime Minister in the 1980s, wrote perceptively that 'the key to Mitterrand's personality, to his extraordinary success, to his [political] longevity and his energy, the key to the fascination which he exerted on others . . . was his staggering and quite exceptional ambivalence . . . a deep-seated, metaphysical ambivalence which made him view everything as both itself and its opposite, every person as both good and bad, every situation as containing the seeds of both tragedy and hope'.

The French statesman Mitterrand most admired was the seventeenth-century Cardinal Mazarin, preceptor and First Minister of Louis XIV, after whom he named his daughter, Mazarine. Much of what the cardinal wrote in his *Breviary for Politicians* could be taken as a vade mecum for Mitterrand himself:

> Be sparing with your gestures, walk with measured steps and maintain a posture at all times which is full of dignity . . . Each day . . . spend a moment studying how you should react to the events which might befall you . . . Know that how you will appear [to others] will be determined by the way you have fashioned your inner self beforehand. Always keep in mind these five precepts: Simulate; dissimulate; trust nobody; speak well of everyone; anticipate before you act . . . There is scant chance that people will put a good complexion on what you say or do. Rather they will twist it and think the worst of you.[10]

However the saying which fitted him best he attributed to Mazarin's rival, the Cardinal de Retz: 'if you set aside ambiguity, it is always to your own detriment.'

In Mitterrand's later years, in the wake of the Observatory Affair, his secretiveness and mistrust grew more pronounced. Rousselet said the affair 'armour-plated him': he would never allow his instincts to trip him up again.

His ambiguities had begun much earlier. In the 1940s Mitterrand was at Vichy *and* in the Resistance; in the 1950s he was elected to parliament by voters from both Left *and* Right. His personal friends ranged from communists to those who, before the war, had supported fascist groups. Even at his most doctrinaire, as head of the Socialist Party, he rejected ideological constraints. He believed in social justice, he said, which meant that he was on the Left. But he would not allow anyone else's '-ism' to dictate to him what he should think.

Mitterrand's ambiguity was both a strength and a weakness. The ability to see two sides of every issue prevented him from becoming sectarian and provided a framework for coexistence when, in the 1980s, the socialists lost their parliamentary majority and, for the first time in French history, a president from one political camp had to work with a legislature from another.

De Gaulle would have resigned. Mitterrand's predecessor, Giscard d'Estaing, had threatened to leave Paris and spend the rest of his term of office 'inaugurating chrysanthemums' at the Castle of Rambouillet. Mitterrand made the system work. Cohabitation, as it was called, became briefly the new norm. But the same mixture of agility and patience that allowed Mitterrand to fashion compromises and finesse domestic crises inspired in both allies and adversaries wariness and suspicion.

Not least of the ironies of Mitterrand's rule was that, having in opposition denounced the institutions of the Fifth Republic as a 'permanent *coup d'état*', and the manner in which de Gaulle utilised them as an abuse of personal power, he found, once in office himself, that they fitted him like a glove, and in the decade and a half he was President opposed any attempt to change them. They gave him greater powers over his own country than any other Western leader and, like his august predecessor, he used them to the full.

In the mythology of contemporary France, de Gaulle was the man who said no: No to Pétain, No to NATO, No to Britain in the European Community. Mitterrand could say no, too: 'no to de Gaulle, no to the Communists, no to his cancer, no to death,' wrote Franz-Olivier Giesbert. But he said it differently. 'Even as he battled against his final

illness,' Giesbert wrote, 'he never lost the look of a mischievous child.'
Where de Gaulle had been a monolith, Mitterrand was a mystery. His
doctor, in the last months of his life, told him he was a mixture of
'Machiavelli, Don Corleone, Casanova and the Little Prince'. When
Mitterrand enquired, 'in what proportions?', the physician replied
prudently: 'That depends on which day.'

François Mitterrand was a sensualist, an aesthete, a bookworm, a
quicksilver, complicated man, by turns reckless and prudent, passionate
and withdrawn, calculating and intuitive, gifted with unusual intellect
and political acumen. He loved literature as much as politics and at
one time dreamed of becoming a writer, but had the good sense to
recognise that his talents lay elsewhere. So he 'wrote' the story of his
life in actions rather than words. It is a narrative which, like his character, is frequently opaque. De Gaulle took France by the scruff of
the neck and, with a mixture of flattery and fetters, discipline and
self-denial, welded it back together again. Georges Clemenceau, 'the
Tiger', stiffened French spines during the First World War (and in
company with Lloyd George and Woodrow Wilson prepared the
ground for the Second). Mitterrand did nothing comparable. His life
mirrored the contradictions and compromises of the times in which
he lived. Yet he changed the ground rules of French social and political debate in ways more far-reaching and fundamental than any other
modern leader before him, setting the agenda for France, and helping
to shape that of Europe, for a generation to come. It is an agenda to
which the French, like other Europeans, are still learning to adjust.

I

A Family Apart

François Maurice Adrien Marie Mitterrand entered the world, like most children in middle-class homes in those days, on his mother's four-poster bed, with a midwife in attendance. It was four o'clock in the morning on October 26 1916, in the small town of Jarnac, in the Cognac country north of Bordeaux. His father, Joseph, had been appointed earlier that year to the post of stationmaster in Angoulême, the county seat, on the main line from Paris. But his wife, Yvonne, preferred to return to her parents' home at Jarnac, 20 miles to the west, for her numerous confinements. François, like his brother, Robert, a year earlier, and like his three older sisters, was born in his maternal grandparents' house and baptised in the local church. He spent the first years of his life in the family apartment above the station at Angoulême, listening to the puffing and whistling of steam engines as they clattered over the tracks.

In the summer of 1919, Joseph was offered a more senior post with the railways in Paris but, not without regret, turned it down. Yvonne was reluctant to leave, and her father, Papa Jules, who owned a vinegar manufacture, was past retirement age and would one day need a successor. The family moved to Jarnac for good.

Their new home was a spacious three-storey eighteenth-century house adjoining that of Yvonne's parents. They shared a large interior courtyard and garden and faced on to the rue Abel Guy, a stone's throw from the river which gives the *département* of the Charente its name. The town itself is a maze of narrow streets with high stone walls, surrounded by vineyards in rolling countryside, interspersed with wheat fields and woodland. It is far enough south to escape the worst of the northern winter, but not so far as to have to endure heatwaves in summer – an equable, temperate part of France where a month without rain is as rare as a snowstorm. In later life, Mitterrand looked back on 'a luminous childhood' at Jarnac and at Touvent, a hamlet in the depths of the countryside further to the south, where his grandparents had a farm and he stayed for months each year, on the pretext of 'building up his strength', as used to be said at the time, after a bout of peritonitis.

The farmhouse, built on a rise, looking out over the plain, had neither electricity nor running water, unlike their home at Jarnac, where electric light replaced candles and oil lamps when François was five years old. The nearest neighbour was two miles away. Papa Jules and his wife had a cook and a coachman, a nurse for the younger children and a generous helping of maids. When the family drove from Touvent to church on Sundays, they used a carriage-and-four. But for the journey from Jarnac, Joseph had a motor car, in the early days an ancient Chenard & Walcker, which suffered constant punctures, and later on a Ford.

Robert remembered Touvent as 'an enchanted domain', where he and François would roam over the hillsides, hunt for mushrooms, fight mock battles with their sisters and cousins, and spend lazy afternoons by the river where an old mill, invaded by greenery, was on the brink of ruin. 'There I learnt the meaning of the hours, the contours of the days, the seasons,' François said later. 'I accumulated sensations, the feel of the wind, the air, the water, the country roads, the animals.' At Touvent he felt at one with nature, 'going from wonder to wonder . . . The world was being born alongside me. My head was full of the music of natural things . . . Each hour had its scent.' It was a childhood such as Tolstoy and Dostoevsky described in nineteenth-century Russia, a hymn to nature from a time when mechanical inventions had yet to come between man and the soil. It left François with an enduring love of the countryside, of trees, and of long walks in the forest, communing with the world around him.

At Touvent, as at Jarnac, the house was always full. When the family sat down at table, they were rarely fewer than a dozen and often fifteen or twenty. Papa Jules presided. He was the uncontested master of a clan sufficient unto itself, a family circle to which outsiders were rarely admitted and then with a certain suspicion, 'as though they were breaking and entering', as François later put it. All the children knew that Papa Jules was the dominant figure in the family.

François remembered him as a man who 'sparkled'. Strongly built and bursting with ideas, he was a talented storyteller who, when the mood was upon him, would recite ribald fables, inspired by La Fontaine, in the local dialect, *saintongeais*, making the men of the family chuckle and the women blush.

Joseph Mitterrand lived for years in the old man's shadow, and his example made his sons determined never to be put in that position themselves. Not only had he had to wait ten years before Papa Jules, at the age of 76, consented at last to hand over the reins of the vinegar business for which he had given up his career on the railways, but much earlier, when he was in his twenties, his own father had made him abandon his dream of becoming a writer in favour of a 'public service' career, where he had had to work his way up from the bottom, spending the first year with a team of workers pushing freight wagons. Joseph sought solace for his frustrations in religion, his piety exceeded only by that of his wife, Yvonne, who went to Mass at 6 a.m. each day, summer and winter alike, and had resolved as a young woman to 'raise her heart to God four times every hour'.

Beneath his strait-laced exterior, Joseph was a free spirit, 'one of the freest people I have ever known', François would write later. 'He would have loved the bustle of the towns, the movement of ideas. Instead his companions were silence and solitude.' Life had made him 'very introverted, rather cold, sometimes glacial'. His freedoms he kept to himself, taking refuge in a world of reflection which others could not share.

François asked him once what he thought about when they went fishing together. Life is like a river, his father replied. 'At first sight, nothing happens there. The hours follow each other . . . the days . . . and in turn the seasons. But if you look more closely, with eyes which by dint of seeing . . . have been opened, you learn that everything is changing.'

Joseph Mitterrand spoke rarely. When he did, 'he threw out words as though he was casting bait'. Locally he was well-liked and respected, becoming President of the French vinegar-makers' association and a member of the municipal council. But with his children he was reserved, a taciturn, undemonstrative man, who loved them but was too inhibited to show his affection. One of his grandchildren remembered him as 'very severe . . . He kept everything inside'. François had much in common with him:

There were a lot of us . . . eight children and two cousins, all brought
up together . . . [but] I was able to set aside for myself moments of
solitude, because that was what I liked. [Outside the family], I didn't
have many friends of my own age. I was shy . . . I loved words . . .
but I wasn't talkative. [When I was upset], I would walk in the countryside, or go up into the loft . . . and make [imagined] speeches to an
invisible crowd within . . . They used to say I was withdrawn, that I
found it difficult to communicate. In fact I have never felt the need to
open myself to other people . . . I was very calm, very quiet, poking
fun at others rather than being naughty myself . . . I wasn't a child
who laughed a lot or was particularly gay . . .[1]

Something else may also have been at work. As a small child, his
brother, Robert, had fallen seriously ill. The eldest son, born after a
succession of girls, Robert was the apple of his mother's eye. Fifty
years afterwards, François still talked about how, at that time, 'everyone
could only think of my brother and I was left alone in my corner'.
Some in his family felt that he had 'an abandoned child complex',
which explained why, as an adult, he would never abandon a friend.

But that was only one side of his character. His brothers recalled
a different François, who slid down banisters; fidgeted so much in
church that he caused a scandal by falling off his chair; and stubbornly
held his finger a millimetre away from an object he had been forbidden
to touch, insisting that he was not disobedient and was doing nothing
wrong.

What he remembered was a self-image, a recollection of childhood
from which, he once wrote, he would draw strength all his life.

All the Mitterrand siblings had absorbed the values their parents
and grandparents taught them. Robert and Jacques, who was born a
year after François, both remembered the family rules: 'Be discreet
and, in all circumstances, endeavour to control your emotions. Always
remain master of yourself without ever showing your feelings.' Money
was taboo as a subject of conversation, a vulgar thing which in polite
company was not to be discussed.

Yet behind the decorous, old-fashioned façade, it was in some ways
a rather modern household. No child was ever beaten. They could
go to bed when they liked and, apart from mealtimes, when the whole
family ate together, attendance at school and church and other sundry

obligations, were free to spend their days as they wished. It was noisy and boisterous, and if a child wanted to read, he had to learn to shut out the din all around him. 'It wasn't rigorous at all,' Jacques insisted, 'there were a few rules we had to follow, but it was the opposite of strict.' François remembered, 'there was a great deal of freedom . . . I never had to rebel.'

The Mitterrands were different in other ways too. In later life, François would describe his family as being from the *petite bourgeoisie*. They were not. As a teenager in the 1870s, Papa Jules had been sent to Britain to perfect his English, later establishing his own marque of cognac, in partnership with Louis Despas, whose family would subsequently amass a fortune at the head of the Monoprix supermarket chain. Joseph Mitterrand was a classicist, who read both Latin and Greek. His wife, Yvonne, adored reading and gave François his love of books, of which the house was full. Their children went on to careers that other families might envy. Robert entered *Polytechnique*, the French equivalent of Oxbridge or Harvard; Jacques passed through Saint-Cyr, the country's top military academy. The family was markedly right-wing, but more monarchist than reactionary, nostalgic for the Empire yet open-minded by the standards of the time. François later found one of his mother's early diaries, in which she had expressed disgust at the vilification of Captain Dreyfus. 'Such hatred is not Christian,' she had written, 'Christ and the Virgin Mary were both Jews' – hardly a typical right-wing response to one of the watershed issues of the day.[2] Papa Jules even found merit in the Cartel des Gauches, a left-wing coalition which took office in 1924. None of them supported the extreme anti-Semitic nationalism being propagated by men like Charles Maurras, whose movement, Action Française, then a leading force in French political debate, they regarded as anti-clerical.

The family did not belong to the *grande bourgeoisie* either. To the old aristocracy of Jarnac, they were outsiders – 'immigrants', as Jacques liked to say. Papa Jules's family had arrived from Rouillac, all of 10 miles away, a mere half-century earlier. Joseph's parents were from the Limousin, a hundred miles to the east. Still worse, the family was Catholic in a region dominated by Protestants where the wounds of the sixteenth-century Wars of Religion were still raw. The name, Jarnac, entered French history in 1547, when a local Protestant nobleman took the champion of the Dauphin by surprise in a duel.[3]

Twenty years later the Catholics took revenge and proceeded to commit such atrocities as the Protestants neither forgave nor forgot. Nearly 400 years afterwards, François Mitterrand wrote, 'the fire of [those] wars was still smouldering under the ashes . . . Every Catholic [in Jarnac] felt he was suspected of [supporting] the revocation of the Edict of Nantes' – a reference to the decision by Louis XIV, at the end of the seventeenth century, to outlaw the Protestant religion.[4]

So persistent was this legacy that when his older sisters tried to join the local tennis club, most of whose members were Protestants, the Calvinist pastor protested that it was 'not right that Catholics be allowed to play there'. The Mitterrands responded in kind: 'My grandmother [Papa Jules's wife] never set foot in a Protestant house,' Jacques remembered, 'and no Protestant ever darkened her door.'[5]

Such conflicts fuelled the religious fervour that infused the Mitterrand household. 'First and foremost, and before anything else,' Robert wrote, 'we had to practise our religion' – *benedicite* before each meal, vespers every evening. On Sundays the boys sang in the choir and, when they were older, served Mass. Yvonne told her husband that she hoped François would take holy orders: Robert was bound for business or government; Jacques wanted to be a soldier; and Philippe, the youngest son, was set on becoming a farmer. All that was missing was a priest.

François did not discourage her: 'When I was a child, I thought I would be pope or king.'[6]

There was another important matter that set the Mitterrands apart. In Jarnac at that time, the cognac business was what counted and 90 per cent of it was in the hands of Protestant families. Some were local aristocrats. Others, like Thomas Hine, today purveyors of cognac 'by appointment to Her Majesty Queen Elizabeth II', whose cellars, in an elegant white stone mansion on the banks of the Charente, were only a few minutes' walk from Papa Jules's home, had settled in Jarnac in the eighteenth century. Papa Jules's own attempt to break into the trade had failed, leading him to set up his vinegar manufacture. But the *vinaigriers*, as they were called, were a notch down the social scale from the *cognacquiers*, and there was little contact between them. 'There were 25 families in Jarnac who made up the local bourgeoisie,' Jacques recalled, 'and only five of them were Catholic. With a few exceptions, the *cognacquiers* were Protestant. We were neither Protestant nor in the cognac trade. That made us different from the others. We were unclassifiable.'[7]

Édith Cahier, who married Robert, agreed. 'In Jarnac,' she said, 'there were the Mitterrands. And then there was everyone else.'

Some of François's family and friends,[8] notably François Dalle, were convinced that these caste divisions had a lasting influence on his attitude to wealth and those who flaunted it:

> He was exasperated in his youth . . . by those young cretins from the cognac families . . . They couldn't pass their bac, they were hopeless, yet they lived like high-fliers . . . His father had a little vinegar manufacture, with a dozen employees . . . There was no comparison with the immense wealth of the cognac trade. But the intellectual superiority of the Mitterrands . . . was obvious . . . The fatuousness of the moneyed bourgeoisie [there] annoyed him, and he felt it more strongly as he got older.[9]

François himself wrote later of 'the literally brahminical code which governed human relations [in Jarnac]'. He added, however: 'I do not wish to paint in black [a time] that was sweetness and light.'

In September 1926, a few weeks before his 10th birthday, François left the family cocoon and enrolled as a boarder at St Paul's College in Angoulême. At Jarnac the children had gone to a private parish school, which had only two classes, where they learnt the three Rs, and then attended the local elementary school. In the holidays, at Touvent, François studied Latin each Sunday after Mass, under the guidance of the village priest. But school had not been taken very seriously and François and Jacques were often absent. Now all that changed.

An imposing, solidly built, forbidding, grey stone edifice, perched on the ramparts of the old city, gazing out over the plains to the south, the college had some 200 boarders and half as many day boys and was staffed by diocesan priests appointed by the bishop.

The regime was austere.[10] There was no heating in the dormitories, which contained long rows of iron-framed beds, and when the children were awakened at 5.45 a.m., in pitch darkness in winter, there would be ice in the long basin which, like a horse-trough, lined the length of the far wall. They washed quickly in cold water from old-fashioned copper taps, and then made for the chapel, where the angelus was said. Lessons took up eight hours a day, five or six days a week, with two hours for homework and, if the weather was bad, extra study on Sundays. Lunch began in silence, while a priest read an edifying text or pages from the scriptures. Only when the reading was over were the children allowed to talk. The day ended as it had begun, with prayer. Each term they took part in a three-day religious retreat for meditation and bible study.

Those who were disobedient, turbulent or simply lazy risked rustication. But most were brought back into line by the threat that if they persisted, they would be sent to a Jesuit college in the neighbouring Dordogne where conditions were rumoured to be harsher and the discipline still more severe. Apart from holidays and half-term, they were not permitted to leave the college precincts, and could see their parents only on visiting days in a reception room near the gate, which was often more upsetting than not seeing them at all.

For François, it ought to have been a traumatic experience. Apparently it was not.[11] Robert, who had started a year earlier, was there to show him the ropes. He made friends, among them the future poet and polymath, Claude Roy, one year older than himself, of whom he later wrote: 'His sense of literature was more developed than mine . . . What an awakening! What conversations we had! Thanks to him, I entered a . . . world where style was king.' With Roy he discovered *La Nouvelle Revue française*, the literary monthly founded in 1908 by a group including André Gide, as well as more provocative and ambiguous literary figures: Arthur de Gobineau, whose essay on the inequality of races was seized on by the Wagnerians and later by Nazi theorists; and Jacques Chardonne, who later collaborated with the Nazis, but whose 'concise, dyed-in-the-wool French style' Mitterrand would admire all his life.[12]

Another boon companion was Pierre Guillain de Bénouville, the scion of an aristocratic family which had fallen on difficult times, who arrived at the college two years later, accompanied by his elder brother and, to the other boys' amazement, an ecclesiastical tutor. He had the bed next to François and introduced him to the writings of Henry de Montherlant, who exalted manly pursuits and the comradeship of the trenches. Pierre was impetuous and obstinate, a boy who acted faster than he thought. François was contemplative, a dreamer, able to lose himself in a book for hours, offended when others teased him that his head was in the clouds. They became inseparable.

At the college the boys saw their first film, a silent black-and-white epic of the Wild West, in which, Robert noted, 'everyone was either good or bad, never a mixture of the two'[13] – a remark intended less as a criticism of simpleton America than to mark the contrast with European novels, with their complex, often ambiguous heroes and labyrinthine plots. From Colette and Proust, Malraux and Mauriac, whom François was now reading at home, to an early Hollywood western was, after all, quite a leap. Much more daunting was the English language, which, to his chagrin, François never managed to learn, despite being sent to England to study during the holidays.* He and Robert with their cousin, Lolotte, stayed as paying guests at the home of two middle-aged English ladies at Westgate-on-Sea, in Kent, about 20 miles north of Dover. They were won over by English breakfasts; intrigued by the whistling kettle, which signalled the approach of tea; and disheartened by lunch and dinner, 'the indisputable proof twice a day that we had crossed a frontier'. They spent their days at the local tennis club, where they learnt to play on grass courts and marvelled at English good manners – 'the exemplary fashion,' as Robert put it, 'in which the English address one another' – but that was about the extent of their cultural immersion.[14]

François was goalkeeper in the college football team and represented St Paul's in table-tennis tournaments, which he often won. The other boys looked up to him and he acquired a following.

Now that he was a boarder, he was allowed more independence during the holidays. He discovered the joys of bicycling and set out on long solitary rides from Touvent, to discover, as he put it, 'the hidden face of the earth'. He and Robert fished in the Charente for tench and went rowing at a boat club, which had been established by the wealthy English owners of some of the nearby cognac houses. In autumn their father took them hunting for rabbits and for partridges and larks, trapped with the aid of a 'lark mirror' which one of the

* When he was President, this showed through in a certain petulance toward members of his government who spoke English on official occasions, supposedly because they were failing to uphold the use of French but actually because he was irritated that he could not do it himself. He only ever pronounced four words of English in public: 'Happy Birthday, Miss Liberty!', at the centenary celebrations in New York of the Statue of Liberty, which he attended on July 4 1986 at the invitation of Ronald Reagan. The statue was designed and built in France and had been renovated with the help of French technicians.

boys would rotate.* François played chess with his grandfather and, to the old man's delight, soon became a redoubtable opponent.

But the age of innocence was about to end. In 1929, Papa Jules sold Touvent. The Great Depression was looming, he was growing old and he sensed that it was time to put his affairs in order. That was the year he finally let his son-in-law take over the vinegar business. It marked the passing of an era. Years later, François remembered:

> It was my first bereavement. Truly, a bereavement, like the loss of a loved one. They had already started to take the furniture away. My grandmother sat in an armchair in the corner of an empty room. Her eyes were red from crying, and I stood beside her with a feeling of despair. Soon after that [in August, 1931] . . . she died. My childhood was upended . . . It was the first time [death] had touched the circle of those I loved . . . *I grieved all the more because I felt that one day, I wouldn't grieve as much. I thought that time would do its work, life would make me forget, and in that way I would be betraying her.* [Emphasis added][15]

The words are revealing. At fourteen, he was already looking inward, questioning his own reactions, treating with a certain distance even those events which touched him most closely. In the college boy at Angoulême, François Mitterrand, the introspective, complicated, sometimes convoluted thinker, who would be nicknamed 'the Florentine' in an allusion to Machiavelli and Lorenzo de Medici, was beginning to emerge.

His intellectual gifts were not immediately reflected in his school reports. But he did not let that bother him – or, at least, he did not allow it to show. Robert, who was a brilliant student, told their parents that François was not working properly and had come ninth out of nineteen in essay-writing, but that when he had urged his brother to do better, the younger boy had retorted that he was 'quite happy with the place he had'. By his own account François was best at history, geography and French, but paradoxically less good at Latin, which he loved. 'I learnt by heart whole passages from Horace and from

---

* A 'lark mirror' or *miroir aux alouettes* was a wooden board shaped like a bird with outstretched wings, in which pieces of mirror were encrusted, placed on a stake and rotated when a flock of larks was seen, so as to attract them to fly into the hunters' nets. The season lasted from October to mid-November.

Virgil . . . All my books were scrawled over with horizontal and vertical lines to mark the rhythm of the prosody.' In philosophy, his teacher reported, he was 'intelligent . . . though sometimes lacking clarity'. Despite his shyness, he was an accomplished debater, winning the college prize for eloquence and going through to the regional final at Bordeaux.[16] But maths and science did not interest him and he remained a dunce at English. Partly in consequence, he was forced to repeat a year, a setback which wounded his vanity and which he never afterwards mentioned.[17]

In the autumn of 1934, at the age of eighteen, having finally, to his parents' relief, obtained his baccalaureate, François Mitterrand set out for Paris to begin his higher education. Once again his big brother, Robert, was there to give him a helping hand. But this time he found the adjustment more difficult: 'I felt lost, as though I were very small, at the foot of a mountain which I had to climb. I had no identity.' He compared himself to Eugène de Rastignac, the hero of Balzac's great novel, *Père Goriot*, who had come to Paris a century earlier, also from the Charente, determined to make his fortune. But unlike Balzac's hero, he did not see Paris spread out at his feet.

Mitterrand spent the next four years living with other students from the provinces in a hostel in the Latin Quarter run by priests of the Society of Mary, a Catholic denomination from Lyon, who described themselves as 'social Christians'. It was a long, terraced four-storey stone building, dating from the 1860s, when Baron Haussmann had redesigned the city. He enrolled both at the Faculty of Law and the Faculty of Letters, at the Sorbonne, while also studying for admission to the diplomatic section of Sciences-Po, the Institute (or as it was then called, the Free School) of Political Sciences.* It was not unusual at that time to take more than one degree, but literature, law and

---

* In France, then as now, students who obtain the baccalaureate may either go straight to university or spend an additional two years studying for the competitive examinations which determine admission to one of the *grandes écoles*, the top tier of the French educational system where only the brightest students are accepted. Sciences-Po had a status midway between the two. In Mitterrand's time, a one-year preparatory course was required before students could attempt the entrance exam. Today they are selected directly after the baccalaureate.

politics were a high-powered combination. 'He was a bit out of the ordinary,' his friend, Jacques Bénet remembered. 'Those who did that were a kind of elite . . . Not as much as those who were preparing the examinations for one of the grandes écoles [like Polytechnique]. . . but a good level all the same'. François Dalle, with whom he went to the Law Faculty library each morning, was less impressed. 'Mitterrand didn't work much,' he remembered. 'Instead of studying legal problems in the library, he used to read the newspapers. Then in the afternoon he went to the Sorbonne.' But Dalle, too, recognised that the young Mitterrand had something else. He had 'unbelievable culture . . . he stood out from all the rest'.

Politics intrigued him. 'Another phase of my life was beginning,' he said later. 'I opened my eyes to other things, I became interested in the problems of grown-ups.'

In Jarnac, political events had never been a major topic of discussion. At college in Angoulême, François's best friend, Pierre de Bénouville, had been an ardent supporter of the ultranationalist movement, Action Française, which had been outlawed by the Pope, who accused its founder, Charles Maurras, of placing the nation above religion. François was never tempted to join him. 'I was brought up to think of Action Française with horror,' he said later, 'not because it was right-wing, but because it had been excommunicated.'[18] In February 1934, when 30,000 right-wing demonstrators tried to storm parliament, leaving more than a dozen dead and many hundreds injured, his mother had written to Robert that Maurras's supporters were as bad as the Communists.

That did not apply to the Croix de Feu (Fiery Cross) movement of Colonel François de la Rocque, which had been founded in the 1920s as a patriotic league of First World War veterans. Politically conservative but socially liberal, de la Rocque had nearly half a million followers and campaigned for national reconciliation and social progress, including a minimum wage, paid holidays for workers and women's suffrage.[19] The Croix de Feu opposed extremism, whether from Left or Right, and it was its refusal to join the attack on the National Assembly that had caused the failure of the insurrection which Action Française had attempted in February.

Soon after his arrival in Paris, François joined the National Volunteers, the league's youth movement, attending meetings of their local chapter in a café on the Boulevard St Germain and, in November 1934, participating in his first street demonstration.

However it was a student protest, three months later, which won him wider attention. On February 1, the Faculty of Medicine staged a strike, ostensibly to protest against the admission of foreigners who, it was claimed, were occupying places which should have been available for French students. In fact, the protesters were being manipulated behind the scenes by Action Française in order to embarrass the government on the anniversary of the attack on parliament. They carried banners with what they viewed as patriotic slogans, including 'France for the French!', 'Down with the Wogs!', and 'Strike against the Wog invasion!'. After a day and a night of mayhem, the agitation died down. But in the next morning's papers, a photograph of François and his comrades, in the thick of the fray, was on every front page.

His old philosophy teacher at Angoulême, Abbé Jobit, who had also been his confessor, wrote in the college magazine that he had been 'not a little astonished to see in the front rank of the rowdies the face of our friend François'. Yet it was in character. François Mitterrand always wanted to stand out. Moreover the anti-immigrant rhetoric reflected his ideas at the time. In an article for a right-wing newspaper, l'Echo de Paris, he complained that the Latin Quarter had lost its soul. 'A virus has infected it,' he wrote. '[It has become] a complex of colours and sounds so discordant that one has the impression of a Tower of Babel.'

In the winter of 1935 a campaign was launched against a law professor named Gaston Jèze. He was unpopular with the students because he was thought to be excessively strict. He was also one of the first French jurists to protest against anti-Jewish legislation being enacted in Nazi Germany. That alone would have gained him the hatred of the French Right. But Jèze compounded his offence by agreeing to act as legal adviser to Emperor Haile Selassie of Ethiopia, who was pressing the League of Nations to condemn Italian aggression. Ethiopia was then one of only two African states not under colonial rule, the other being Liberia. When courses resumed in January 1936, students linked to Action Française disrupted Jèze's lectures and demanded that he resign. After a two-month stand-off, culminating in street battles with the police in early March, the university authorities caved in and announced that Jèze would be transferred elsewhere.

It was a foul campaign, typical of a time when fascism was rising in the West and Stalin's purges were bloodying the East. The right-wing student journal, *l'Étudiant français*, denounced Jèze as a Jew and, in a reference to Britain's opposition to Mussolini's African ambitions, an 'Anglo-Ethiopian . . . who prostituted his intelligence'. Not to be outdone, *l'Echo de Paris* called him a 'Negroid'.

François would refer to this episode as 'the glorious days of March'.

Did that make him a racist? Not by the standards of the 1930s. At the college in Angoulême, François had befriended African students from the French colonies, inviting them home to Jarnac at Christmas and Easter. Some would remain lifelong friends. Shortly after the Jèze affair, François wrote approvingly, after attending a lecture on Ethiopia, that it was useful 'to know the history of peoples so different and yet so similar to others, for at bottom it is not a man's colour or the look of his hair which give value to his soul'.

So in what way was the campaign against Jèze 'glorious'?

The explanation lay in the image of colonialism in Europe in the 1930s. Hardly anyone then believed that African countries should be allowed, or were able, to run their own affairs. At the college in Angoulême, François and his brothers had listened to missionaries expounding on the dissemination of Christianity and the benefits of colonial rule for less developed peoples. 'Not for a second,' Robert wrote, 'did it ever cross our minds to doubt the usefulness of such an enterprise or the merits of those carrying it out . . . [We felt] a sense of national pride . . . at the large expanses of pink [on the map]'. To Action Française and its allies on the far Right, the Jèze affair was an opportunity to destabilise the centrist government. The students saw it quite differently. 'Since colonialism was thought to be a good thing,' one of them explained, 'we didn't see why Mussolini should be stopped from taking Ethiopia.'* Jacques Bénet, who later married one of François's cousins, offered another reason. 'Some [of us] took

---

* At that time Mussolini enjoyed widespread sympathy in France, where he was seen as a strong, nationalist statesman who had rescued Italy from the chaos that threatened after the First War. French attitudes began to change after 1937, when Italy increased its support for Franco in the Spanish Civil War and began to align itself more closely with Hitler's Germany. But at the time of the Jèze affair, at least in the minds of the French Right, he was the respected and respectable leader of a friendly neighbouring state.

it badly that Britain was trying to tell Italy what to do, when Britain and France both already had their own splendid colonies . . . It seemed unfair, and we asked ourselves what this fellow [Jèze] was up to, trying to forbid Italy to expand.' Nationalism and chauvinism were two sides of the same coin. Even the Marian fathers at the hostel saw nothing wrong in their students protesting against 'wogs'.*

In later life, Mitterrand would be accused of having, as a student, been close to the extreme Right, which in pre-war France was profoundly anti-Semitic. But association is not a proof of guilt. That the young Mitterrand had anti-Semitic acquaintances is not in doubt – indeed, in Paris in the 1930s it was almost impossible not to, so widespread and so widely accepted was anti-Jewish feeling – but there is no evidence of his ever having been actively anti-Semitic himself. On the contrary, he and a friend intervened during a fracas at a café in the Latin Quarter to help a Jewish law student being taunted by a group of young toughs from Action Française. The student, Georges Dayan, eighteen months his senior, was from a long-established family of left-wing Jewish intellectuals from Oran, in French Algeria. He and François became fast friends. For the next forty years, Dayan would be Mitterrand's alter ego.

The same was true of his supposed links to the Cagoule, a terrorist group created by hard-line elements of Action Française after the failure of the attack on parliament in 1934. For years after, opponents would claim that as a young man Mitterrand had been if not a member then at least a sympathiser and even, in the most exaggerated versions, a participant in Cagoulard bomb attacks against the political and financial establishment. The organisation's membership was secret. François's old friend from Angoulême, the turbulent Pierre de Bénouville, now enrolled at the Faculty of Letters and staying at the same Marian hostel, had played a prominent role in it.[20] So had a young man named Jean Bouvyer, who in June 1937 acted as lookout when four other members of the group assassinated Carlo and Nello Rosselli, two Italian anti-fascists who had taken refuge in France. The Bouvyer family was close to the Mitterrands. They spent their holidays near Jarnac – the young people played tennis together and attended

---

* I doubt that there exists a British schoolboy in the first half of the last century and even the 1960s who did not at some point gleefully chant, 'Wogs begin at Calais!'

the same parties. Jean, some months younger than François, would later have a long affair with one of the Mitterrand sisters.[21] His mother, Antoinette, a fanatical royalist who hated with equal vehemence communism and the Republic (which she regarded as essentially the same thing), had taken François under her wing when he had come to Paris to study and he was a frequent visitor to their home.

In January 1938, after learning that Jean had been arrested for his part in the Rosselli murders, François rushed round to offer help. 'Jean Bouvyer . . . is one of my best friends,' he explained to a relative. 'I spent the day yesterday, feeling absolutely shattered, at Jean's parents' home, and accompanied his mother to see the police . . . As you can imagine, the family is distraught. They are bourgeois to the marrow and knew nothing of what was going on.' The last line was true only to a point. Half the leaders of the Cagoule had been regular guests at Antoinette's table, although she may not have known, or wished to know, what they represented.

To François, fidelity to friends, especially those whom everyone else had abandoned, was an article of faith, even when, as in this case, the man concerned was, he admitted, 'a poor wretch, intelligent and cultivated but a terrible whiner, who tends to make a mess of everything he ever undertakes'. In public he maintained that Jean was innocent and visited him frequently in prison.

Soon afterwards he acquired yet another link to the Cagoule. In the spring of 1939, Robert became engaged to Édith Cahier, whose uncle by marriage was none other than the organisation's leader, Eugène Deloncle.

These ties were not fortuitous. François Mitterrand was not a member of the Cagoule or of Action Française, nor was he anti-Black or anti-Jewish. But his milieu and his family connections meant he had friends who were[22] and he could live with that. He dealt with the diversity of his fellow human beings by appreciating their qualities and putting their faults in a box. It left him open to charges of lack of principle and it brought him some strange and ultimately regrettable friendships. But it enabled him to maintain an eclectic range of contacts with men and women whose ideas and attitudes were very different from his own.

Another strand in François's character pulled in a contrary direction.

One of his uncles, Robert, who had died at the age of 20 from tuberculosis, had helped found a lay Catholic movement called Le Sillon ('The Furrow'), which sought to make the Church a force for social justice.[23] Robert had stayed at the same Marian hostel when he had been a student in Paris, thirty years earlier, and had left behind a luminous reputation. François saw himself as following in his footsteps. He joined the Catholic student movement, the JEC (Jeunesse Étudiante Chrétienne), participated in the week-long annual retreat which the Marian Fathers held at Clamart, and became President of the local section of the Society of St Vincent de Paul, of which his father had been a member at Jarnac, carrying out charitable work among the poor. 'The way to teach those around us that Christianity alone can bring about a total renewal,' he wrote to his old confessor, Abbé Jobit, 'is by social action, linked to political action, bound together more and more closely.' But he was not sure that charitable giving was the answer. All too often, he thought, those who set out to help the poor, telling themselves each week that they were making a noble sacrifice, were simply trying to atone for their own wealth and privilege.

The 'social Catholic' François had left-wing friends like Dayan and Louis Clayeux, who in later life became an art critic and a patron of the sculptor, Alberto Giacometti. He admired the Socialist leader, Léon Blum, for his oratory, while detesting his alliance with the Communists in the Popular Front, which ruled France for a year from June 1936, seeing it as a menace which would sap the little strength that remained in the moribund French polity. He was fascinated by the Jewish writer and thinker, Julian Benda, who lambasted French and German intellectuals on both Left and Right as apologists for nationalism, racism and war.

François the right-winger read the *Courrier royal*, the journal of the Count of Paris, the Pretender to the French throne, and in 1939, with several other students, paid a visit to the Count at his residence in Belgium. He listened to speeches by Jacques Doriot, a dissident Communist who had founded the PPF (French People's Party), the closest France had to a fascist movement. Despite the Church's edict against Maurras, he took an interest in the ideas of Action Française and attended a meeting where one of the movement's leaders, Henri Massis, spoke of the need to oppose Germany while supporting Mussolini and the Portuguese dictator, Salazar. Maurras himself, he decided, even if politically beyond the pale, was a great intellectual, a 'magical' writer and 'intransigent patriot'.

In short, at 21, François Mitterrand was still searching for his way. 'Two thirds of my thinking reflected my milieu, which was right-wing,' he said later. 'On one side was the conformism of my family; on the other my own anti-conformism which sprang from a sort of instinct of opposition.' Towards the end of his life, his brother, Jacques, endorsed that judgement. 'The problem with François,' he said disapprovingly, 'was that he was always opposing something.'

Literature competed with politics for pride of place in Mitterrand's affections during his student days and in 1937 and 1938 the former was in the ascendant. He loved the written word better than the spoken – his friend, Jacques Bénet, said later he had 'the sensibility of a novelist' – and maintained a voluminous correspondence with his family as well as contributing articles to *l'Echo de Paris* and to a student journal, the *Revue Montalembert*, often on literary topics. He was a voracious reader, both of the classics – Balzac, Stendhal, Flaubert and Chateaubriand – and of living writers – Mauriac, Gide, Hemingway, Faulkner and, later, Joyce, 'who is so much better [than his contemporaries]'. At one point his favourite novel was *The Brothers Karamazov*; at another he preferred Tolstoy. His brother, Robert, remembered his room at the Marian hostel 'filling up with books'. Friends whom he invited to stay at Jarnac during the holidays would find that he suddenly disappeared to re-emerge hours later having shut himself in his room to read.

At *l'Echo de Paris*, where he became chief of the literary section, he argued that style was as important as the message it conveyed. The result, as his French biographer, Jean Lacouture, has written, was a series of articles that were 'truly mediocre, somewhere between dull and pretentious'. His teacher at Angoulême had been right. For François, at this stage, writing with clarity was a struggle.

These activities left little time for study. François Dalle maintained that he was chronically idle.[24] Nonetheless, at Sciences-Po, where he was admitted in the autumn of 1935, he was awarded his diploma with a *mention bien,* equivalent to an upper second in Britain or *magna cum laude* in the US. In the same year, 1938, he obtained his law and literature degrees, the former also with distinction.[25]

There was a lighter side too. For all François's fulminating against the decline of his beloved Latin Quarter, he played a prominent part in the coterie around Ferdinand Lop, an eccentric Jewish writer in his forties with a shock of reddish hair and a signature broad-rimmed hat, who was part of the folklore of the area. Lop campaigned repeatedly for the French presidency on a platform including the prohibition of poverty after ten o'clock at night; nationalising brothels so as to give whores the status of public servants; extending the main thoroughfare, the Boulevard St Michel, as far north as the English Channel; reducing pregnancy from nine months to seven; and moving Paris to the countryside so that the inhabitants could breathe clean air. François became his Prefect of Police and later his Prime Minister.

Mardi Gras, when he paraded in a mask with a pig's snout; the University Rag; and the Feast of Sainte Barbe, the patron saint of firemen, on December 4, were other highlights of the year. But almost every weekend there were dances at the houses of friends, lunch parties, art exhibitions, evenings at the theatre or the opera, and afternoons at literary salons.

His brother, Robert, loved the social whirl and made a point of introducing him to the leading names of Parisian society. They attended musical evenings on Wednesdays at the home of André Levy-Despas, the founder of Monoprix, whose uncle had been in partnership with Papa Jules. In the spring their father came from Jarnac to present his borzoi, who rejoiced in the name of Orloff, at the Paris dog show. Once a year they accompanied Jacques, who had enrolled at the Saint-Cyr military academy, to the President's ball at the Elysée Palace. 'They needed students from the *grandes écoles* to act as escorts for the young ladies,' Jacques recalled. 'We did not stay long. But we had a free dinner!'

In 1936, François's mother died after a long and painful illness. Papa Jules followed, eighteen months later. But neither affected him as much as the death of his grandmother five years before. 'I grieved,' he wrote later, 'but it was more in the natural order of things.'

On January 28 1938, a Friday, François attended a ball at Normale Sup', one of the most prestigious of the *grandes écoles*, where academics – including a string of Nobel prize-winners – and top civil servants were trained. He had not originally intended to go. But he had had a depressing day and he thought it would cheer him up. It did.

'I saw a blonde girl standing with her back to me,' he told a friend later. 'She turned round. I was rooted to the spot . . . I invited her to dance. I was crazy about her.' The object of his passion refused to tell him her name and left with a friend soon after. But she did say that she was seventeen and a half and was studying at the Lycée Fenelon, not far from the Sorbonne. That was enough. After several days discreetly staking out the school entrance at the close of classes, his patience was rewarded and, keeping at a distance, he was able to follow her home.

Beatrice, as he decided to call her, after the heroine of Dante's *Vita Nuova*, who eats her lover's heart surrounded by a cloud of flame, lived with her parents and two brothers in an apartment on the Avenue d'Orléans, beyond the Observatory Gardens at the southern end of the Latin Quarter. He soon discovered that she took a tram to school in the morning, and walked back with a classmate each afternoon. Two weeks later, bringing with him François Dalle and Georges Dayan to provide moral support, he waited at the terrace of a café in the Boulevard St Michel. As she walked by, he jumped up and reminded her that they had met at the Normale Sup' ball the previous month. Would she and her friend join them for some pancakes? With some hesitation – she had obviously made a vastly greater impression on François than he had made on her; moreover her mother had made her promise not to talk to young men – she allowed herself to be persuaded. She told them her name was Marie-Louise and repeated that she was 'nearly eighteen', but gave away little more. Nonetheless, the ice was broken. His friends found her as bewitching as he did. For the next three months, François would meet her two or three times a week after school and walk with her through the Luxembourg Gardens until they neared her home.

Gradually he learnt more about her. Her name was Marie-Louise Terrasse.[26] Her father, André, was private secretary to Pierre-Etienne Flandin, a leading Centre-Right politician who had once briefly served as Prime Minister. But there could be no question of telling her parents. For despite her sophisticated looks, Marie-Louise was only fourteen years old.

François was head over heels in love and left her in no doubt of his feelings. She was charmed, fascinated, flattered, frightened by the earnestness of her suitor and not sure of her own sentiments at all.

Nonetheless, in May, she allowed him a first kiss. Three weeks later he wrote to her, urging her to make their relationship official:

> If we don't impose our will on [your family] . . . we will lose each other.
> And that I do not want. Why should I not hold on to you, with my
> two hands and with all my soul, since I love you? . . . I know that you
> have always been a little bit afraid of me . . . I do not want those fears
> any more. Would I have stolen . . . your heart did I not firmly intend
> to keep it? . . . We must now envisage the future with clarity . . . It is
> essential to find a way to introduce me to your family . . . If you could
> explain to one of your brothers . . . then I could be introduced through
> him: that would be much more orthodox! [But whatever happens] the
> absolute minimum is for us to make sure that during the summer
> holidays we will be able to see and write to each other.[27]

It was the first of some two thousand love letters he would send her over the next three and a half years. Often he wrote several times a day. His friends became concerned for him. 'He could talk of nothing else,' François Dalle remembered, 'I couldn't take it any more!' Dalle often carried letters between them. 'I must have done that a hundred times! But I was his friend, and he was in such a state of dependence towards this love of his, he was crazy . . . It was mad.'

Every new obstacle which arose merely redoubled his ardour. Marie-Louise became an obsession, a citadel to be conquered. He had never been in love before. He paid court to her with a mixture of romantic yearning and the same dogged persistence that he would bring to a tennis tournament. It soon became overwhelming.

In June, half hoping that her parents would forbid her to see him again, Marie-Louise confided in her mother, Marthe, who was suitably scandalised and ordered her to end the relationship. But François refused to take no for an answer and Marie-Louise, touched, despite herself, by his evident devotion, relented and persuaded her mother to invite him to Sunday morning coffee. Marthe found him charming and gave his suit her blessing.

So began a long saga. Marie-Louise's parents saw him as an ideal future son-in-law. Marie-Louise herself was torn. She recognised François's qualities. But she was a spoiled little princess who adored flirting with boys and had been aware of her physical charms and the power they gave her over men since she was thirteen years old. He was a lovelorn supplicant but she did not feel that he was the man of her dreams. So she kept him at arm's length – 'far enough off to feel herself free; but not so far as to discourage him altogether' – responding to his professions of ardour distantly or not at all. It was as though they were acting out a nineteenth-century novel: 'He would take one step forward, she would go along. He would try a second step . . . and then she would take fright.'

He teased her, often pointedly: 'You deserve, my darling Beatrice, severe punishment. What shall it be? Copy out a hundred times, "I am an unsociable little girl who talks in class and won't talk else-where . . ."' Or on another occasion: 'Disagreeable and most demanding Beatrice, you are making me your slave of the moment, your plaything of the hour!' But above all he kept repeating that she alone gave meaning to his life, and complained piteously when she failed to write back: 'If only you knew how much I look forward to your letters . . .' A month later: 'nothing from you again this morning. Why don't you write? I can't believe your feelings have changed – what can have stopped you sending me a few words?'

In the end his very reasonableness, the solicitude and understanding with which he bore her outbursts of ill temper, drove her to distrac-tion. If only he would yell at her sometimes! But he did not. She realised she did not love him. When he suggested they should become engaged, she refused.[28] In the spring of 1939, she told him that she did not wish to continue the relationship. He replied that he would wait.

Military tensions were rising. In 1934, Japan had occupied Manchuria. A year later, Hitler announced German rearmament in violation of the Treaty of Versailles. Another year later, in March 1936, Germany reoccupied the Rhineland. Some of François Mitterrand's contempo-raries could already see the writing on the wall. For Pierre de Bénouville, two years his senior, 'it was obvious that when the politi-cians led us to give back to the Germans the left bank of the Rhine, we signed off on Hitler's victory . . . Germany had rearmed, and that made the process of war ineluctable.'

François did not see that until two years later. The Spanish Civil War; the Stalinist show trials in Russia; the Axis between Mussolini and Hitler; the German–Japanese anti-Comintern Pact; Italy's punitive massacres in Ethiopia; the start of the Sino-Japanese war, all of which occurred in the following fifteen months, seemed to pass him by. Even his brother Robert, by then an officer-trainee at the School of Artillery, wrote that Paris was 'chloroformed' when it came to the outside world. Not until the *Anschluss,* the German annexation of Austria, in March 1938, did François finally sit up and take notice. Like de Bénouville, he then realised that appeasement was leading France to destruction. A month later he wrote in the *Revue Montalembert*:

> In politics, only two attitudes are conceivable: total surrender or abso-
> lute force . . . Forgetting the axiom that the just must be stronger than
> the strong . . . the countries that won the Great War have rested on
> their laurels, falling asleep in the cardboard fortress erected by their
> treaties. Every time the opponent of yesteryear broke down one of
> their towers . . . they cried: 'thus far, but no further!' . . . But why
> should the one who is strong come so far if he does not intend to go
> further? . . . Each success demands another success . . . Every with-
> drawal is a battle lost. France [and] Britain . . . have 'taken note' of the
> *Anschluss* . . . They have more or less accepted it. 'That's enough,'
> [they say]. 'Don't touch Europe again. Enough blackmail . . . Thus far
> and no further!' It is what you call being in a bad mood. But a bad
> mood has never been a substitute for anger . . . When I see the trium-
> phal arrival of the God of Bayreuth [Hitler] in the land of Mozart, I
> know what sacrilege is being prepared and, despite myself, I feel a kind
> of shame, as if I recognise that I am myself to blame.[29]

For a young man of 21 it was a perceptive analysis and ahead of its time, for it would be another year before the French government of Édouard Daladier and the British, under Neville Chamberlain, would reach the same conclusions. France, in 1938, was still wedded to the doctrine of *'Plus jamais ça!'* ('Never again!'). The memory of the butchery in the trenches was still too fresh and too terrible for people to imagine a new war.

François may have been influenced by his father, Joseph, who even before the *Anschluss* was starting to 'see the future in black'.[30] Joseph Mitterrand had not fought in the First War, but his brother-in-law, Francis Sarrazin, who had been an army doctor, had died in 1917, leaving behind the two young cousins whom Joseph had brought up with his own children. He hated Nazi Germany and wrote to his son, Robert, that Hitler was 'a brute . . . a coarse bastard . . . a beast which should be put down' – terms which, Robert noted in his diary, he had never heard his father use before. When François met André Terrasse that spring, he found he held similar views but despaired of convincing his friends in government of the danger that was looming.

In France, unlike Britain and America, military service was compulsory and, in view of the deteriorating situation in Europe, had been extended from one year to two. After completing his degree, François had intended to join the navy and in January 1938 came fifth in the competitive examination to become an officer in the Merchant Marine. His plan had been to enrol at the College of Naval Administration at Brest.[31] But then Marie-Louise entered his life. If he joined the navy he would be away at sea for two years and unable to see her. He abandoned the idea. Instead he and François Dalle entered the preparatory course for officer cadets at the military college at Saumur,[32] from which they hoped to graduate as sub-lieutenants in the infantry. Both failed ignominiously: Dalle because his puttees came undone on parade and slipped around his ankles, Mitterrand because he botched a question about military theory. 'I don't know what they asked him,' Dalle said later, 'but he was furious.' More than that, his vanity was wounded. Just as he always passed over in silence the year he had had to repeat at the college in Angoulême, so now he put it about that he had decided not to seek a commission, preferring to serve in the ranks.

Even François's brother, Robert, to whom he was probably closer than any other member of his family, did not know that he had flunked Saumur.[33] Nor did Robert know until almost a year later that François had fallen in love.[34] His friends knew; his family did not. He was beginning to compartmentalise his life, organising his friends and relations into separate, overlapping circles. Some were closer, some more distant, some knew one thing, some, another, but only the person at the centre knew everything that each of them knew.

On October 1 1938, German troops occupied the Sudetenland, the German-populated regions of northern and western Czechoslovakia. France and Britain, abandoning their treaty obligations, decided not to oppose the invasion. The previous day, Neville Chamberlain had returned from a conference in Munich with Hitler and Mussolini, proclaiming 'peace in our time!' The French Prime Minister, Édouard Daladier, who had followed Chamberlain's lead, flew back to Paris expecting an icy reception. When instead he was welcomed by rapturous crowds, he is said to have turned to Alexis Léger, the Secretary-General of the French Foreign Ministry, and muttered: 'What fools!'

That month François was assigned to the 23rd Colonial Infantry Regiment at Ivry, just outside Paris. He began training as a private on November 4 and was eventually promoted to sergeant. His best friend, Georges Dayan, was in the same unit, and when they moved to a barracks near Port Royal, within the city proper, they rented a room together as a place to spend days off, becoming so inseparable that their friends nicknamed them Jallez and Jerphanion, after the two student heroes of a series of popular novels by Jules Romains.

Robert noted, with some understatement, that his brother had reservations about military life. Six years later, François explained why:

> To know what you are talking about when you speak of the army, you need . . . to have seen it from the bottom rung of the ladder . . . To find yourself under the control of NCOs with minds as nimble as a battering ram does not make you particularly enthusiastic . ... We found that . . . the main occupation of our peaceable soldiers lay more in frequenting bars than in studying Clausewitz or even dismantling a Hotchkiss machine-gun. To be a soldier, for those of us who were called up in 1938, was to learn how a run-of-the-mill, honest citizen can grow accustomed, in a minimum of time, to filth, laziness, drink, brothels and sleep.[35]

The French army in the 1930s was made in the image of the bourgeoisie which commanded it: cannon fodder on one side, the officer corps on the other. François's brothers, Jacques and Robert, were naturally in the latter category. So were almost all his friends. François himself should have been too, but found himself by chance on the wrong side of the tracks. To François Dalle, it was one more factor, added to the arrogance of the *cognacquiers* in Jarnac, which would lead him later to break with the bourgeoisie. 'His superiors [were] imbeciles,' he recalled. 'His experience of the army was dreadful, [and] made him furious . . . He could not stand the absurd, artificial authority of it.'

In the spring of 1939, attitudes in London and Paris were at last beginning to change. In January – the same month that *Time* magazine voted Hitler its 'Man of the Year' – there were rumours that Germany would invade Holland. Two months later it seized the remainder of Czechoslovakia. Appeasement was plainly not working. That Easter, during a furlough, François accompanied Dalle, his friend André Bettencourt and two other students on a motoring trip around the Low Countries. On the German side of the border river with Luxembourg, a giant stage had been erected and an orchestra played Beethoven. 'The young Germans were stripped to the waist [and] dived in unison into the river,' Dalle recalled. The exaltation of discipline troubled them.

All through that summer, the drumbeat of bad news continued.

Italy occupied Albania. Mussolini and Hitler signed the 'Pact of Steel', under which each undertook to aid the other in the event of war. On August 23, the Soviet leader, Joseph Stalin – alarmed at the failure of Britain and France to honour their treaty commitments; isolated by American neutralism, and by the anti-Comintern Pact between Germany, Italy and Japan – signed a non-aggression treaty with Berlin. A week later German troops invaded Poland.

Britain and France had no choice. On September 3 1939, the Second World War began.

For the next eight months, life continued much as before. The 'phoney war', as it was called, meant that François Mitterrand, together with other young Frenchmen, was mobilised and sent to live under canvas at the front. But for the moment Hitler was busy with Poland and then Denmark and Norway, and Stalin with the Winter War in Finland. Along the Maginot line, a supposedly impregnable barrier of fortified blockhouses which ran the length of the French–German border, 120 British and French divisions remained immobile in the face of 23 from the *Wehrmacht*, numbed by cold and boredom. Chamberlain and Daladier were still in power. Promises of a major offensive to take the pressure off the Poles were quietly forgotten.

Before leaving, François had ridden out by motorbike to the Terrasses' country house at Valmondois, north of Paris, to say goodbye to Marie-Louise and her parents. Despite her decision to end the relationship, they had remained in occasional contact. This time she found him 'sad . . . as though he did not expect to return'. A few days later, just after her 16th birthday, she took a lover. The affair, about which she told no one, lasted only a week, but that was long enough for the young man, a friend of her brother, to fall madly in love with her. History was repeating itself. For her it had been just an adventure; for him it became a passion. But the experience gave her pause for thought, and in October, for the first time since the spring, she wrote to François to enquire how he was. It was the opening he had been waiting for.

The correspondence they now resumed was different from before. Instead of endlessly droning on about love, he told her about life at the front. '[I live] with my feet in the mud, wet clothes and cold up to my neck . . . Everything here is so brutal, inexorable . . .' His section of eleven men, all from different parts of France, among them a Parisian 'who is splendid: a real lout, an anti-militarist with an impossible character', was at a front-line post at Bitche, about three miles from the border, between Sarreguemines and Hagenau in northern Alsace. 'I get on very well with them, even if they are difficult to lead . . . All of them are more or less "moaners", but they work hard. I believe – and I find it touching – that I can count on them. Some class feeling undoubtedly remains [in them], but the devil take class struggle!' In another letter he predicted that he would come through the war feeling 'revolutionary and positive'.

To Marie-Louise's father, André, he wrote that 'apart from the snow which follows the rain, the mud which follows the mud . . . and the fact that, ill-shaven, soaked to the skin, my hands slashed and my body full of aches and pains, I am not living up to the image that the cinema gives of a warrior', everything was going well. Writing to his own family, he was more truthful: 'Beyond the Maginot line,' he told Robert, 'I have seen villages that have been abandoned and pillaged [by our own soldiers]. That story must be told one day.' To Robert's fiancée, Édith, he wrote, 'I am well, but not completely so, for a uniform wounds a person who loves life.' What would be awful, he declared, would be 'to die for values (anti-values) in which I do not believe'. That was why he had decided not to die but to live, to put up with it all and in so doing, to pay a debt: 'What debt? That of idiocy!' Whose idiocy he did not say, but nor did he need to: it was the idiocy of the political and military leaders whose short-sightedness and arrogance had placed France on the road to certain defeat.

Disillusionment with the ruling elite was one more element causing the young François Mitterrand to question the superiority of his own class. Not everyone reacted that way. His brothers, Jacques and Robert, also saw that France was unprepared for war and knew the reasons why, but both remained solidly right-wing. If François was different, it was because he asked more questions and was less willing to accept the conventional explanations with which those from his milieu reassured themselves.

In mid-November, his section was ordered back to the second defence line, about 30 miles from the Luxembourg border, where, he told Marie-Louise, he had 'a real mattress with sheets, and even a candle to read by'. His run of good luck continued. In December, when Robert married Édith Cahier, François managed to get leave. Marie-Louise was in Paris. He waited for her outside the Church of St Dominique after midnight Mass on Christmas Eve and told her he was still passionately in love with her. This time, she did not reject him. Next day, he took her to meet Édith, a vivacious eighteen-year-old to whom she took an instant liking. The two girls became firm friends. Marie-Louise's resistance began to crumble. That night, with André's permission, François took her to Montmartre where they danced until three o'clock in the morning and walked home together in the rain. This time he knew he was winning. Marie-Louise said later that even though she still felt afraid of him, François had dazzled her and her fickleness towards him made her ashamed. François Dalle thought she came round 'because she was forced to. He exerted such pressure of persuasion that in good faith she couldn't do otherwise.' Whatever the reason, by the time he returned to his regiment, they had decided to become engaged.

That winter was brutal. The thermometer fell to − 20 degrees centigrade. The wine ration froze in the soldiers' metal canteens. Mitterrand's section was set to digging trenches, 'a job,' he wrote to Georges Dayan, 'which resembles the punishments inflicted on criminals or those who subvert public order'. When a captain reprimanded him because his boots were not properly polished, he retorted: 'The difference between you and me is that I often have to get mine dirty.'

Years later he still bristled at the memory: 'Those officers who were so full of themselves and spent their days playing cards infuriated us.'

On March 3 1940, François proposed and placed on Marie-Louise's finger a diamond engagement ring. That night André and Marthe hosted an engagement party in their apartment in the Avenue d'Orléans with François's father, Joseph, and most of his brothers and sisters in attendance. Marthe worried that the Mitterrands were above their station. 'François . . . is wealthy . . .' she wrote to her cousin. 'What a gulf there is between his family and ours! [Marie-Louise] will live differently [from us], she will have luxury and ease.' Her intuition was not wrong. François's sisters looked askance at what they saw as Marthe's lack of refinement. And when he gave Marie-Louise a bottle of expensive perfume – it must have cost a fortune, Marthe exclaimed – and sent a bouquet of flowers on the third of each month to mark the day they became engaged, her joy at her future son-in-law's thoughtfulness was mixed with a vague unease.

Had she been able to read her daughter's heart, she would have been more alarmed still. Marie-Louise was radiant. She told her girl-friends how happy she was. When François took her briefly to Jarnac at the end of his ten-day leave, she wrote to her father: 'You can't imagine how good everyone is to me . . . They pamper me like a baby . . . The house is marvellous and the atmosphere extremely nice.' But to her elder brother she confided that she still had doubts. When he asked what they were, she said merely that she still felt very young. But deep down she continued to dream of a man who would set her heart on fire. François was sensible, charming, everything a girl should want. In his letters, he poured out his love: 'How have you bound me so tightly to you? I used to think I was master of my feelings . . . that I was independent, a rebel, and I still am towards everything that is not you . . . Do you realise your power over me? . . . I love you, I love you, I love you.' On the one hand it was what she wanted to hear; on the other, it was exactly what he should not have said.

In April, François's section was transferred to a forward position near the Belgian border, 'not the very front line,' he wrote to Marthe, 'but this time I think it is serious'. Despite efforts to get himself promoted, he was still a sergeant. Georges Dayan had left to join an officers' training course, but his own application had been rejected. He asked Marie-Louise's father, André, who had a post on the General Staff, whether he could help. 'The surest way to get a commission (and perhaps the only one),' he wrote, 'is to have support from high up . . .

[Otherwise] it will be intercepted at the middle levels . . . and there everything goes to the highest bidder.' But to his dismay, his failure at Saumur meant he was once again turned down. 'I shall try to envisage the outcome with serenity,' he told his prospective father-in-law, 'although the position of an NCO in the infantry is scarcely a matter for rejoicing . . . The obscure rolè of a border guard is so thankless and empty that it is hard to think of notions of duty.'

By then, the architects of appeasement were retiring from the stage.

Édouard Daladier had resigned in March. On May 10, it was the turn of Chamberlain, who was replaced by Churchill. The previous night, German forces had occupied Luxembourg, followed by Holland, which capitulated five days later, and Belgium. German armoured columns started crossing the Ardennes in such strength that the resulting tank jam took two weeks to clear. Instead of seizing the advantage, the French General Staff disbelieved its own intelligence. That night François and his comrades heard a continuous, lugubrious rumbling as waves of German planes passed overhead. Next morning, from his observation post on a hillside overlooking the River Chiers, he watched French and Belgian units fleeing before the German advance. Sedan fell on the 14th. Ten days later Marthe told her cousin that she had had news from him. He was 'just back from the front, after a week under machine-gun attack and artillery. They were hand to hand with the Germans . . . The fighting was furious. His regiment has been cited for valour, although 15 of them are going to be punished [for cowardice].' In fact, François's regiment was one of the few which retreated in good order and continued to do so up to the Armistice. At the beginning of June, he was promoted to the rank of staff sergeant, cited in divisional despatches for bravery and awarded the *Croix de guerre* (Military Cross). 'The only one who has really fought is my daughter's fiancé,' Marthe wrote. 'He had to withdraw 200 metres under enemy fire. He [says he] doesn't know how he managed it; he lost everything except his skin and that without so much as a scratch.' By then, at François's urging Marie-Louise had left Paris to join his family in Jarnac. In early June she received a letter from him complaining that he had been wearing 'the same shirt and socks for a month'. She imagined he must have a beard like a fireman.

On Monday, June 10, the French front collapsed. Marthe left Paris next morning to follow her daughter. It was the beginning of a chaotic

exodus which sent millions of people fleeing from the capital, abandoning their possessions as they went. Two days later the Germans
were on the Champs-Elysées.

On 14 June, at Hill 304 near Verdun, where some of the deadliest
fighting of the First World War had occurred, François was wounded
by shrapnel from an artillery shell, which entered near his spine and
lodged in his right shoulder. He remembered it as though in a film:

> I was sleeping in a shell-hole . . . Suddenly at 5 a.m., machine-
> guns and artillery opened fire with a long barrage aimed in our direc-
> tion . . . The Germans marched towards us, singing . . . Our commander
> [Édouard Morot-Sir, a philosophy professor in civilian life] ordered us
> to move towards Dead Man's Hill. The weather was wonderful, and
> as though in tribute to the splendour of that month of June . . . the
> assault troops paused for a moment. Morot-Sir and I had only to stretch
> out our hands to pick the wild strawberries that carpeted the hillside.
> Then a shell exploded above our heads . . . I was knocked out by the
> explosion. Morot-Sir was wounded in the knee.[36]

Having survived five weeks of combat unscathed, he could not believe
that he had been hit. 'The victim acts out a drama,' he said later.
'When I collapsed, bleeding, bruised and in shock . . . I continued to
be an actor. There was a Mitterrand who was whole and safe, who
was watching, with desperation and distress, another Mitterrand who
was wounded. I didn't manage to understand how such a thing could
have happened to me! To me! It choked me, I was so offended . . .'
For three days he was moved from one field clinic to another. At first
a medical orderly pushed him on a stretcher, but the roads were
jammed with refugees, 'whole families, fleeing they knew not where'.
They had carts loaded with 'everything they could take out of their
houses . . . sheets, mattresses, wardrobes, chairs, piles of things spilling
out', pulled by horses and donkeys.

> Then Italian aircraft appeared and machine-gunned the column.
> Everyone threw themselves down the banks and into the fields,
> including my companion, who left me [lying on my stretcher] with
> the comforting words, 'Don't worry, I'll be back!' I remained there,
> immobile, looking up at the sky, watching the planes punching holes

in the road with a rosary of bullets. The alert over, we resumed our wandering. Everywhere we went, there were wounded . . . At Esnes-en-Argonne, surgeons were operating in a cave, amputating arms and legs. I wasn't keen [on that], so we pressed on . . . At Vittel, the civilian doctors had all fled. There were just groans, cries of pain, the smell of blood and pus . . .[37]

Finally Mitterrand was put on a train for the wounded and taken to Bruyères, where his injuries were treated. The whole region was already encircled. After the war he learnt he had been awarded a second *Croix de guerre*, this time for 'magnificent morale and total devotion . . . putting his life on the line from the start of the campaign and, by the force of his example, contributing to the maintenance of the ardour of his section'. On June 21, he was taken prisoner and moved to Lunéville, near the French city of Nancy, where he remained in hospital for a month. Local girls were serving as volunteer nurses. He gave one of them his camera and the photographs he had taken near the front of 'bits of human bodies that had been blown into the trees'. Through her, he was able to get word to his family, and to Marie-Louise, that he had been wounded and captured but was safe. For a time he hoped that he might be demobilised and sent home on the grounds that he was needed in 'industry' (his father's vinegar manufacture), industrial workers being among the categories exempted from deportation. But the subterfuge was too obvious. He and another wounded prisoner began making plans to escape. Before they could do so, they were moved to a transit camp and, at the beginning of August, to Germany.[38]

2

The Captive

In six weeks, four-fifths of the French army deployed against Germany was taken prisoner. More than a defeat, it was a moral and physical collapse which only the French word, *débâcle*, adequately describes: 1.8 million soldiers were captured, more than half of them, like François Mitterrand, in the five days between June 17, when the government, which had fled to Bordeaux, called on the troops to lay down their arms, and June 22, when the Armistice came into effect.

Most were so demoralised that they did not even try to escape from the poorly guarded transit camps set up in France to hold them. 'As good psychologists,' Mitterrand said later, 'the Germans . . . kept us . . . believing that peace was about to be signed and we would soon be sent home. There is no surer prison than hope for the morrow.' Instead, they were sent to PoW camps inside Germany, where they worked as labourers to replace the young Germans who had been drafted into Hitler's war machine. For many it would be five years before they saw their homes again. Only the details of their journey differed: how many days it lasted, how many prisoners were crammed into each freight wagon. Mitterrand's description could have applied to a million others:

> A train awaited us . . . Each of the wagons was supposed to hold 40 men, and we managed that without too much difficulty. We knew by now how to sit cross-legged, at what angle the knees should be bent, how to lie side by side . . . how to use our haversacks as seats, backrests, pillows . . . To keep us out of temptation, the sliding doors were chained shut, but to allow in air and daylight they let us open the shutters . . . We squeezed in without any argument: formalities,

disturbances, comings and goings, discomfort no longer made us lose patience. Our elemental social state had ended such distinctions. All the same, I was astonished at how easily men become accustomed to living the life of the herd, these same men who used to show off so proudly their qualities as individuals . . .[1]

Mitterrand was among the lucky ones. His wagon had the standard load – '8 horses or 40 men' – not 70 or 100 as some of his fellow prisoners endured. The doors were opened once a day for a few minutes for the men to get out and empty their bladders and bowels. No one in Mitterrand's group suffered from raging diarrhoea in a wagon without sanitation, or, if so, he suppressed the memory: others were less fortunate. Nor was he in a convoy which stopped for days on end in the full heat of the sun, the men inside tortured by thirst, on its way to a distant camp in eastern Prussia or Poland: his destination was Stalag IXA at Ziegenhain, near Kassel, in the centre of Germany. Even so, deportation was for all of them 'a moral martyrdom . . . one of the harshest trials of captivity'.

By comparison with the journey, the camp itself was almost a relief. In an account written the following summer, he recalled the night of their arrival:

Stiff and dazed from the monotony of the hours spent at the bottom of the wagon . . . we marched mechanically and in silence the four kilometres to the camp . . . We felt little of the emotion that is supposed to mark the first impressions of exile . . . The only thing in our minds was sleep: to fall into a sleep unencumbered by legs and a mixture of other men's breath, by that clinging fraternity which smells of wet greatcoats. We had so many sorrows, so many hopes and so much weariness to forget, so much of ourselves to bury that first night in Germany, that beginning of a very long night.

When we woke, the sun was already striking obliquely the roofs of the tents . . . The other side of the barbed wire . . . the fields, the woods, the villages were repeating the gestures of yesterday and everyday. People were harvesting, binding the sheaves and setting them up in stooks. Life was playing its game, a game from which for the first time we understood we were excluded.[2]

That first day all the prisoners were searched and deloused. 'Their [personal] effects were put in bags to pass through a disinfection oven before being returned to their owners. The latter, naked, were sent in groups to a room where their heads and pubic hair were shaved, their bodies smeared with a delousing product and then, after a communal shower, they waited, still naked, for their clothes to be brought back.' Mitterrand wrote of it later as a day of 'anxiety' marked by 'displays of misplaced curiosity'. The phrase is intriguing: throughout his life he was prudish, and so disliked nudity that he refused to walk barefoot, even on the beach.[3]

After the preliminaries were completed, they were given their camp numbers. Mitterrand was No. 21176 IXC.[4]

In June 1940, Ziegenhain had held 3,000 Frenchmen and 12,000 Poles, all living under canvas. By the time Mitterrand arrived three months later, the number of prisoners had almost doubled. They were put to work building wooden barracks, and by the end of that year the last tents had disappeared. Life was monotonous but predictable. 'We all wore the same patched and torn clothes, we all ate the same soup,' he wrote. 'We all followed the same daily routine. There was nothing to distinguish between us.' At one level the anonymity was reassuring; at another, he found himself in the midst of an utterly unfamiliar world:

Life in the camp was my first real experience of the social fray. I became acquainted with types of people about whom I knew absolutely nothing; I discovered class reflexes which were foreign to me; I saw the world of my youth fall apart . . . How could it be otherwise when you saw company directors, well-known professors, members of the upper middle classes, going through piles of refuse to lick pieces of dirty paper where a trace of jam or cheese had stuck? . . . At night, when we got back from the worksites, we sat on our pallets and talked till curfew while digging out the lice that congregated in the folds of our clothes. At first the promiscuity overwhelmed me. I felt it marked our final degeneracy. Then I got used to it, as I got used to the open-air latrines, immense trenches disinfected with cresol, at the bottom of which there was sometimes a dead body. We philosophised, cracking lice between our nails, losing ourselves in a dream of the future which compensated our shared misery.[5]

The first weeks had brought other problems. 'The Germans were not brutal,' Mitterrand recalled, 'but they paid no attention to what happened among the prisoners.' Gangs formed. 'It was the rule of the strongest – government by the knife.' Anything of value was extorted. 'It became an achievement to keep . . . your watch or your pen.' At the once-daily food distribution – swede or barley soup, doled out from huge basins, except on Sundays, when there was meat – the gang leaders 'served themselves first, and the rest had to await their pleasure to get a bit of dirty water to survive'. If anyone objected, the knife would be put to use. 'In the early mornings, under the big tents where we slept, there would be a few corpses.'

But then, he wrote later, 'A few bold men stood out from the mass, and with the support of the others put in place the beginnings of an organisation. The violence ended . . . The law of the knife had been curiously replaced by a new law, based on the exactitude with which food was shared out.'[6]

Two of those men took Mitterrand under their wing, winning his lifelong friendship, gratitude and admiration. Roger-Patrice Pelat was two years younger but knew a great deal more of the world. The son of a washerwoman and a soldier disabled during the First World War, he had started work at fourteen as a butcher's boy. From there he joined Renault as a factory worker, became a member of the Communist Party's youth movement and fought in Spain with the International Brigades against Franco. At Ziegenhain he was in charge of the delousing ovens. 'Without him,' Mitterrand said later, 'I would not have survived.' Bernard Finifter was a Jewish tailor of White Russian origin who had been born in Dnepropetrovsk in the Ukraine and fled with his family to Poland and afterwards Germany to escape the pogroms. In Berlin, in 1933, he had earned a living, improbably, as a boxer. After Hitler assumed power, he fled again, this time to France, where he joined the Foreign Legion. He spoke four languages, including German, and was one of the camp interpreters. Mitterrand and he arrived at Ziegenhain on the same day. As they stood next to each other in the queue to register, Mitterrand noticed that in the space for religion, Finifter had written, 'Jew'. He looked at him and said: 'You know how they are here?' Without missing a beat, Finifter replied: 'I know, I've lived here. When they ask me if I'm a Jew – I am. So?' Mitterrand found the Germans respected him. 'He spoke their language perfectly, with a slight Yiddish accent. Reversing the roles, he talked to them high-handedly. He did as he liked.'*

Speaking long after the war, Mitterrand described his months in captivity as the beginning of a fundamental change in his social attitudes:

> Captivity was a great revelation . . . Life within the [prisoner] community marked me deeply. I enjoyed it – I, who am so profoundly individualist! But the biggest shock was when I suddenly realised that the natural hierarchy . . . the society in which I found myself, that of a prisoner-of-war camp, bore absolutely no relation to the hierarchy I had known in my youth. That is when I started to doubt . . . The hierarchy of decorations, diplomas, money, is worth nothing. The scale of true values is different.[7]

Elsewhere he wrote sardonically that 'the old order did not resist swede soup!' It was left to his friend, Georges Beauchamp, to fill in what was between the lines: 'He realised,' Beauchamp said, 'that those from his own class – the notables, the bourgeoisie – often did not behave very well, and that those with humbler origins behaved better.'

But that was with the benefit of hindsight. At the time he was less explicit, simply noting that among 'prisoners united by misfortune, all classes and social differences [were] abolished'.

The PoWs were divided up into 'a multitude of small groups of seven or eight individuals who shared everything – food parcels, chores, the work schedule'. Mitterrand's group included a high-school teacher, two Jesuits and two priests. After the first few months, the Germans realised that if the prisoners were to be kept manageable they would have to be allowed their own activities. Accordingly they authorised a chamber orchestra, a theatre troupe, led by a former luminary of the Folies-Bergère in Paris, and the 'Ziegenhain Temporary University' which organised evening lectures. A library was also opened containing

* André Rousselet, speaking of Mitterrand's relationship with Pelat and Finifter, used the analogy of a spiral staircase: 'When you talked to François Mitterrand,' he said, 'he was always one step above you.' They alone escaped this rule. Throughout Mitterrand's life, they were always one step above him. 'The Stalag was like a primitive society,' Rousselet explained. 'Only force and authority counted. And he wasn't yet equipped for things like that. So they took him under their protection and for ever after there was this one step between them . . . It was like that to the end.'

several thousand volumes 'requisitioned' from a French bookseller in German-occupied Metz.[8]

French prisoners, like British and Americans, were treated in accordance with the Geneva conventions. For Russians and Serbs, it was different. When they began arriving in the camp, Mitterrand remembered, 'they were so exhausted, starved and ill-treated that we tried to smuggle them food. The Germans forbade [it] . . . and beat with rifle butts those of us who disobeyed . . . It soon became quite usual to find corpses on the pathways through the camp – there were so many that we were drafted to load them on to carts . . . In my memory I still see those stiff, light bodies which we grabbed by the arms and legs and threw up over the sides, on top of a pile of their comrades.'

Even for the French, the wind could suddenly turn. A football match organised on Bastille Day ended in chaos when, without warning, German guards in a watchtower shot two prisoners who had left the crowd to relieve themselves and strayed too close to the barbed-wire perimeter.

At the 'Ziegenhain Temporary University' Mitterrand was a prolific speaker, most often on literary topics. Former prisoners remembered him giving talks on *Lady Chatterley's Lover*, on Voltaire, and on more recondite subjects, like the *lettres de cachet* of pre-revolutionary France, which the King signed when ordering the imprisonment of suspected political opponents. He always spoke without notes, resting his hands on the table. His companions nicknamed him 'the Professor'. One, Paul Charvet, noted in his diary:

> He does not talk down to us. I find it admirable that so brilliant a mind can open so willingly to [the ideas of] others, which he takes in and analyses, thereby enriching his own thoughts. To me that is the mark of a generous intelligence. There are only two attitudes which are unforgivable in his eyes: spinelessness and vulgarity. Thus a coward is 'a shoddy person'. He said that in my presence. The tone, the look, the movement of the lips were inflexible. [He shows] the same attitude, though silently this time, when someone walks by and announces that he is answering the call of nature. We all appreciate this constant elegance in the midst of promiscuity.[9]

To those who knew Mitterrand in captivity, there was something about him that was hard to pin down. 'He inspired respect,' one remembered, 'and made it a point of honour to respect others and to be respected by them.' The first impression was usually that he was 'very cold, very distant'. In the camp newspaper, named, more in hope than expectation, *L'Ephémère* (The Ephemeral), which Mitterrand edited, an anonymous contributor likened him to Vautrin, the ruthless and mysterious benefactor of Balzac's Eugène de Rastignac:

> François Mitterrand, like Vautrin, is a man of multiple identities . . . and I suspect him to be in possession of the dreadful secret of a split personality. Like some new Janus, you see him here as the elegant editor of a newspaper, a man of letters, a perspicacious and subtle philosopher; and there as a meticulous, busy medical orderly [working in the camp clinic] . . . But whether [one or the other], we must not forget that François Mitterrand has a personal cult of all that is noble; that is to say, he is ceaselessly consumed by the flames of lyricism, beauty, high-mindedness . . . Make no mistake, he is both honey and sting, like the bee; an ironic wit and a tender heart . . . That allows [him], one might say, to go through life with rose-coloured spectacles . . . But Mitterrand is [also] wise and full of scepticism . . . and through those rose-coloured spectacles he sees everything in black.[10]

The high-flown style, neatly tailored to its subject, offered a perceptive glimpse of Mitterrand at the age of 23. The 'cult of all that is noble' which he affected, terming it an 'elevation of thought which distinguishes the elite', was noticed by others too. A cartoon in *L'Ephémère* depicted him as Dante with a crown of laurel leaves.

He was not always the reserved figure that some of these recollections suggest. Paul Charvet remembered him miming for his barrack-room comrades a skit 'both comical and disdainfully ironic' in which a prisoner went through the motions of sharing out some stolen bread while artfully contriving to keep the best bits for himself.

He was also a talented counterfeiter and during his time at the camp made a dozen or more sets of false papers, both for himself and for others, teaching his companions how to make copies of seals using a half-potato. For whatever else he might do as a PoW, one thing François Mitterrand was completely clear about: he had no intention of spending the rest of the war in Germany. His thoughts, from the first day, were focussed on how to escape.[11]

Military District IX, between the Rhine and the Elbe, included as well as the main camp at Ziegenhain a smaller camp, Stalag IXC at Bad Sulza, 130 miles to the east,[12] and several dozen labour sites or *kommandos*, from which the prisoners were sent out to work among the local community.

In October 1940, two months after arriving at Ziegenhain, Mitterrand and others were moved to Bad Sulza and from there to a village called Schaala, near Rudolstadt on the banks of the River Saale. The *kommando* to which he belonged, No. 1515, was a heterogeneous group of about 250 men, known among the prisoners as 'the intellectuals' because nearly half were priests, teachers or students. Others had fought for the Foreign Legion, like Finifter, or the International Brigades, like Pelat. They stayed in an abandoned porcelain factory which was well guarded, though some of the sites where they worked during the day were not. The food was a little better than at Ziegenhain, but they were all constantly hungry.

For the first few days Mitterrand was employed as a gardener, raking up leaves at a military driving school. Then came two weeks as a road-builder. At other times he cleared snow from railway tracks, worked for a local carpenter, 'cutting rafters, measuring laths and sawing planks', and served as a medical orderly. In November, he was assigned to a team stacking hay for the winter.[13] The section chief, Jean Munier, a farmer's son from Burgundy, a year older than Mitterrand, seeing him sitting idly on top of one of the stacks, yelled at him to do some work. 'If you did as I do,' the younger man coolly replied, 'none of this would be done at all.' Munier was shamefaced: he had forgotten that aiding the Germans was not the prisoners' goal. The two became fast friends.

Mitterrand planned to escape from the hay station. He had discovered that, at the driving school, large-scale maps of Germany were posted along a corridor wall. 'I arranged to go along that corridor as often as possible, and each time I copied one or two square centimetres on to a scrap of paper. I traced an itinerary from Schaala to Schaffhausen on the land border [with Switzerland] . . . After I had pasted all the pieces together, I had a map showing the route to follow,

390 miles long and 12 miles wide.' His comrades saved food for him; one of the Jesuits, who knew how to sew, made a rucksack; and he found an overcoat belonging to a German factory-worker which came down to his ankles, hiding what he wore beneath. In addition, he packed shoe polish – 'because the Germans would have noticed dirty shoes' – and razor blades, to shave.

On March 5 1941, Mitterrand and a companion, Xavier Leclerc, a parish priest from the Allier, in the Massif Central, arrived with the rest of the team at the hay station before dawn. The pair slipped through the barbed wire, crossed a railway line and disappeared into the darkness. Munier and Finifter covered for them and the Germans did not discover their departure until the evening roll call. For three days, they walked across country. 'We followed the trails made by wild boar, because the snow was so deep,' Mitterrand wrote later to Georges Dayan, 'and we slept in hollows made by deer.' But the terrain was too difficult. So they decided to use the roads, walking only at night and hiding in the woods during the day. They started to hallucinate about food. Mitterrand became obsessed by a dish of duck with orange that he had had as a child. When Leclerc fell ill, he went to the nearest village and, pretending to be an Italian worker, used his few words of German to buy some medicine and bread.

After three weeks of rain, snow and mud, they reached the small town of Egesheim, 25 miles from the Swiss border. There they took a wrong turning. It was a Sunday morning, and the faithful were coming out of church: not the right moment for two strangers to be retracing their steps. Captured by villagers armed with staves, they were escorted to the town hall and thence to the district prison at Spaichingen. 'At no other time in my life,' Mitterrand said later, 'did I feel so destitute and alone.' A month later they were returned to Bad Sulza, where they were placed in the disciplinary section, tried by a military tribunal and sentenced to three weeks' bread and water.*

* The night Mitterrand arrived, he heard a familiar voice outside his cell: 'Is that you, François?' It was Finifter, who had escaped shortly after him and had also been recaptured. 'Next morning,' Mitterrand recalled, 'we found ourselves in the wash-room and were able to talk. He told me: "Tonight, you will have a mattress." And that night, a German soldier came in with a mattress and threw it into my cell. The following day, I questioned Bernard. He told me how, after obtaining a cigarette

After that, it was back to Ziegenhain,[14] but under a stricter regime than before. Those who had escaped once were likely to try again.*

Mitterrand confessed much later that he had been desperate to escape 'for a very personal reason': Marie-Louise Terrasse.[15] There were other considerations too. He missed France and resented being deprived of his freedom by a war the duration of which he was powerless to influence. 'Liberty,' he wrote later, 'is like the air you breathe. I needed to breathe.' But that was incidental. The overriding imperative was his separation from his fiancée.

Marie-Louise had written to him regularly during the first months, even though she told her brother and her friends she thought her engagement might have been a mistake. She liked François immensely. But she realised she did not miss him. What she felt was not love but esteem. She tried to hide it in her letters, but by the beginning of 1941 he could see that her feelings were changing. That spring she fell in love, seriously in love for the first time, with a handsome young Polish count named Antoine Gordowski who was in Paris studying architecture. In June she became his mistress. In his far-off camp, Mitterrand sensed that something was broken. Through a fellow prisoner who was being repatriated he sent a letter to her father, André, asking for his help. It was extremely long, sometimes disjointed and in places almost incoherent. Every line breathed a terrible distress:

> I have no illusions: my long absence explains everything . . . But if [she] is becoming more distant towards me, it is not just . . . because she is tired of waiting . . . [It is because] she is growing close to someone else. I sense it, and I suffer from it . . . It doesn't mean that all is lost . . . But there are two conditions . . . That I return quickly, quickly.

---

through the indulgence of his guard, he had grabbed the man's wrist and hissed, looking him straight in the eye, "Now, I'm going to denounce you." The poor fellow saw himself . . . being sent off to the front. He agreed to [Finifter's] conditions: a packet of cigarettes (renewable) and two mattresses, one for himself and the other for me . . . This was at the height of Hitler's power, and . . . the master of the situation was a Jew!' Small wonder that until his dying day Mitterrand regarded Finifter and Pelat as superior beings.

* In 1941, 16,000 French prisoners, one in every hundred, escaped from Germany. For every successful attempt, it was estimated that twenty failed.

And that Marie-Louise has at least the patience to wait a little before embarking on a course which will prevent us ever coming together again.

I am trying to speak reasonably, sir, but believe me, I find it hard. I am too upset . . . to be able to look ahead to the coming days without terrible anxiety . . . I love [her] too much to put my own happiness before hers. Even if I am suffering atrociously, that . . . should be secondary . . . If I no longer have a place in her heart, we can do nothing. My worry is that she doesn't know herself what she wants, where her love lies, and all this will end in a catastrophe of which she will be the victim . . . But what can I do – I who am so far from her? . . . My despair should not weigh in the balance; but I am so afraid she is going to ruin her life . . .

I am asking you for your support . . . At least let her be patient until my return . . . There is nothing I haven't tried in order to be with her again . . . You cannot know how much effort I make every day . . . I love her and she is my whole life. You understand my distress. Everything was going well for me here, I glimpsed that wonderful moment when I was going to find her, never to leave her again – and then suddenly this revelation . . . Do you know what liberation means to us, all that that word contains of repressed affection, friendship . . . joy? And me, I won't even have my poor joy. I do not wish to sway you, but truly our plight is hard. Our youth will have known the glory of being crushed, beaten, derided and enduring a lamentable defeat . . . Yet it would still all be fine if our return were marked by a [new] happiness beginning. But me, I will have none of that . . . I love Marie-Louise. You cannot know how much.[16]

André Terrasse was aghast. But when he confronted Marie-Louise, she fought back: did her parents want her to marry a man she did not love? Her mother, Marthe, called her 'a mad little girl who has been too spoiled'. All André was able to extract from her was a promise that she would take no decision before her fiancé's release.

For Mitterrand, it had been an infernal series of events, each worse than the one before: he had tried, and failed, to escape; he had spent three weeks in the punishment cells; and now his fiancée, his great love, was slipping from his grasp. Despondently, he clutched at straws. He hoped for repatriation as a medical orderly, and, when that failed, as a veteran of the First World War (having faked his identity papers to make it appear he was fifteen years older).[17] He convinced himself that Marie-Louise was misunderstood. 'She needs my support,' he wrote to André. 'She is suffering deeply. We must not add to her pain by . . . doubting her loyalty and the nobility of her feelings.' He asked his brother, Robert, whose regiment had been far from the front when the invasion occurred and was now back in civilian life, to see her and assure her that he would soon be back. Other friends in Paris passed on similar messages.

At Ziegenhain, most of his comrades knew that he had a fiancée and that he chafed at their separation. 'François used to pace up and down the barrack room,' Jacques Biget remembered. 'It drove him crazy when he did not hear from her.' But it was not something he ever discussed. The child who had never felt the need to open himself to others had become a man who locked it all inside. Some of his editorials for L'Éphémère offered hints of his state of mind, but always in elliptical terms. 'Those we love are growing up, getting older, far away from us,' he wrote in August. 'Over our joys and our loves oblivion spreads.' Three months later, he returned to the same theme: 'as month follows month our disappointments pile up, the burdens of absence grow heavier, each of us is thrown back into the rigid path of his own solitude.'

Like many others, he felt that France had turned its back on its prisoners and wished only to forget them:

> Even though the material conditions of camp life respect international conventions . . . what power, what benevolence, will ever be able to dispel . . . the vision of days dying and carrying off our youth – that youth of which our only experience will have been the taste of bitterness? Surely they are taking care of us! . . . Committees, associations, charitable works . . . Oh yes, they are taking care of us! But for every admirable letter from a mother, a wife, a faithful friend . . . how much forgetfulness, silence and neglect, how much lost tenderness? . . . I am afraid that they speak of the prisoners as one speaks of the dead: by singing their praises, speaking highly of them, while thinking that their most important quality is that, above all else, they no longer bother the living.[18]

Adding to the sense of abandonment, to Marie-Louise's infidelity, to war-weariness and the calling into question of long-held social assumptions, in the middle of 1941 Mitterrand underwent a crisis of religious faith. As a student, when many of his friends were questioning their beliefs, his faith had not wavered. But in the camp, when others were taking refuge in religion, he began to doubt.[19]

The priority, however, remained his fiancée. He had to get back to France.

On the afternoon of Sunday, November 28 1941, when the camp guards were allowed to receive visits from relatives outside and security was slightly more relaxed, Mitterrand and two others concealed themselves in a storeroom in the area reserved for the camp administration. When night fell, they crawled out along a roof-beam which projected over an open-air latrine. 'Mitterrand was astride the beam,' one of his companions wrote later, 'when a German soldier, singing and whistling, came in and lowered his pants three feet away. We feared the worst. Mitterrand didn't move. He couldn't even breathe . . . Still whistling, the intruder departed.' They then made their way to a section of the 14-foot-high barbed-wire fence where a newly installed transformer obscured the view from the watchtowers. Wearing stolen German raincoats, they crossed on a wooden ladder laid against the wires and dropped into the ditch beyond. Mitterrand went last. There were guards every hundred metres and frequent patrols. Once safely on the other side, they tried to blend in with the visitors making their way home. One of the three, Pierre Barrin, was spotted. 'The soldiers arrested [him] at gunpoint . . . They started coming towards me. I decided to act as if nothing were happening, dug my hands deep in my pockets and stopped and looked at him as they passed. Our eyes met. He didn't turn a hair.'[20]

When they realised that two other prisoners were missing, the Germans sent motorbike patrols and dog teams in pursuit. Mitterrand hid under a bridge for an hour, with water up to his knees, to throw them off the scent. Then he made his way to the nearest railway station and bought a ticket to Metz, in Lorraine, which Germany had annexed, using money which his brother Robert had sent to him hidden in cigarette packets. He tried twice to cross the border but each time was foiled by German patrols. The second night, half-dead with cold, he took a room in a small hotel. The French couple who owned the place denounced him. He was arrested and sent to a transit camp at Boulay, a country town 15 miles to the east, to await return to Ziegenhain or, perhaps, far worse, to a disciplinary camp in Poland. At Boulay he volunteered to carry boxes to the adjoining German barracks. Early on the morning of December 10, under cover of darkness, he vaulted the barracks fence and ran towards the town centre, where a fellow prisoner had told him he would find a newspaper shop whose owner, a woman, would help him. As he arrived, out of breath, she was just opening the metal shutter. She hid him for two days and then accompanied him to Metz, where he was put aboard a train for the border village of Sainte-Marie-aux-Chênes. As the train slowed, he decided to jump. Ahead of him was a small railway station. When he reached it, he found that he was in France.

His journey was not yet quite over. It was German-occupied territory. The railway workers fed him and put him on a bus to Nancy, where he obtained false papers. From there he took a train to Besançon, further south, jumped again and crossed the demarcation line to what was called the 'Free Zone', controlled by Marshal Pétain's government in Vichy. That night a farmer let him sleep in a hayloft. Still heading south, he made his way towards Lons-le-Saunier, 100 miles north of Lyon, where he had been told he could get his demobilisation papers. On the way he noticed a sign for Mantry and remembered that the family home of his cousin, Marie-Claire Sarrazin, was nearby. When he arrived, she was giving a Latin lesson to a group of local schoolchildren. 'He looked awful,' she recalled. 'The poor man was pale and exhausted, and scared of being caught again.' She and her sister gave him honey and goat's-milk cheese, vegetables from the garden and warm clothes. It was December 15 1941.[22]

3

Schisms of War

The France to which Mitterrand had returned was, in his own word, 'confused'. Not only was the country physically divided – the Germans in the North; the Vichy administration in the South – but there were rival claimants to the role of national saviour: Pétain and de Gaulle.

Marshal Pétain was a First World War hero who, in 1916, had halted the German offensive at Verdun. At the age of 84, when France was once more crumbling before a German attack, he had been called to serve again and, on June 22 1940, approved the signing of an Armistice in the same railway carriage at Compiègne, in Picardy, where the German High Command had surrendered in November 1918. It allowed German troops to occupy Paris and all of northern France as well as the western seaboard as far south as the Spanish border. The remaining third of the country, known as the Free Zone, was to be administered by the French themselves. In theory sovereignty remained French; in practice the Germans had passed on much of the effort and cost of administering the conquered territory to the conquered people themselves. It was one of Hitler's better ideas.

On July 10, parliament had voted Pétain emergency powers. The following day he had proclaimed himself Head of State, notionally over the whole of France but in reality over the area controlled by the rump government which he set up at Vichy, 80 miles west of Lyon.

In 1941 and 1942, the overwhelming majority of French people revered Pétain, both for his wartime role at Verdun and as the man who they believed would preserve whatever was left to be preserved from the cataclysm of defeat. Mitterrand was of that view too. Pétain's device, 'Work, Family, Motherland', copied from the Croix de Feu, came from a monarchist tradition stretching back at least to the 1870s, and his 'National Revolution' promised new institutions which would

serve France better than the unworkable parliamentary democracy
of the discredited Third Republic.

De Gaulle, by contrast, was almost unknown. Mitterrand had heard
his name but little else. 'I learnt in the camp at Lunéville . . . that he
had refused to accept the defeat and had launched an appeal from
London on the BBC . . . Later, at Schaala, we sometimes talked about
[him]. It was enough for us to know that over there was an unknown,
rebel general, who was addressing France . . . We were searching for
a symbolic hero. We didn't know there already was one.'

The prisoners, like most of their compatriots, considered that de Gaulle
and Pétain were fighting for the same cause, albeit, as Mitterrand put it,
'each in his own fashion'. While the Free French upheld the standard of
revolt against Germany, Vichy, they believed, was trying to minimise the
nation's suffering and maintain morale at home. Together they formed
the sword and shield which would get France through the war.

Afterwards history was reshaped to portray the Vichy administration
and all who worked for it as dyed-in-the-wool collaborators, who had
decided that the Nazis would win the war and were determined to
ensure for France a place in the new European order by establishing
a fascist state on German or Italian lines. That was not how it looked
at the time. The United States, Australia, Canada and some thirty other
countries recognised Pétain's government. Even Britain maintained
informal contacts. At the beginning of 1942, the regime was a melting
pot. There were monarchists, churchmen, anti-republican intellectuals,
Nazi sympathisers, bourgeois notables, fanatical anti-Semites, most of
the defeated French officer corps 'which paraded up and down as
though it had won the war', and, more numerous than all the rest,
honest if misguided men and women who believed sincerely that they
were doing what was best for France in a time of need. The one thing
they all had in common was that they were solidly right-wing.

The country was 'neither collaborating nor resisting', Mitterrand
wrote later. 'It was wait-and-see.' Vichy reflected the multiple schisms
which had fractured French society after the defeat of 1940 and the
collapse of parliamentary government that followed. It was 'a little
principality of a pseudo-military character that lived cut off from
reality',[1] one official remembered. Pétain's ministers were forbidden
to visit the administration in Paris that they supposedly controlled
without German permission, which was rarely given. To the majority

of the population, the Marshal was a venerable figurehead and his government largely irrelevant.

Mitterrand decided to go there because, for an escaped prisoner, the Free Zone was the safest place to be and he had friends in Vichy who could help him find a job.

But what kind of country might emerge from the war, and what role he might play in it, he had no idea. At the PoW camp in Ziegenhain he had written that statism, collectivism and socialism were 'just different ways of looking at the same problem: how to prevent (or perhaps encourage) a man to bite his fellows . . . Words ending in -ism solve nothing . . . The only way to improve society is by working to improve oneself.' That was fine in theory, but in practice it did not take him very far. The pre-war political leaders, led by Daladier, disgusted him. But who was to take their place? Pétain seemed the least bad option. Mitterrand regarded himself as a *maréchaliste* rather than a *pétainiste*, supporting the man rather than the regime. At Ziegenhain, as at other camps, there had been a 'Pétainist Circle'. He had refused to join. His fellow prisoners remembered that when a collaborationist priest in the camp had argued that Vichy had preserved French sovereignty, he shot back: 'What sovereignty, when two-thirds of France is occupied and there are two million prisoners? Those are just empty words.'

His closest friends in captivity, Finifter, Pelat and Munier, all had left-wing views. Where did he stand politically? He hardly knew. The schisms traversing France were mirrored within himself.

All the things he had believed in were being called into question – first among them, his relationship with Marie-Louise Terrasse. Robert had visited him at Mantry and tried gently to prepare him for the break which was now inevitable.

François was so thin and debilitated that his brother was able to persuade him to spend Christmas with their friends, the Levy-Despas, who had a house near the citadel in St Tropez, then a small fishing village that was home to a community of artists.[2] But the moment the festivities were over and he could decently leave, he set out for Paris, travelling by way of Jarnac to see his father, his youngest brother, Philippe, and their sisters, who had gathered there for the holidays.

It was a quiet, understated homecoming, whose joy found expression in what was left unsaid. 'When you think there is so much to say to each other,' he wrote later, 'freedom is . . . the silence which overcomes you because it is all too huge, because it is all beyond the understanding of a man. When all is said and done, freedom is perhaps for each of us no more than the possession of silence.'

On January 4 1942, Mitterrand arrived in Paris. He had telephoned ahead for Marie-Louise to meet him and they walked together through the Luxembourg Gardens, where it had all begun, four years earlier. She told him that she admired him, but did not love him and did not want to be his wife. When they reached the Seine, she gave him back her engagement ring. He took it and swung his arm as if to hurl it away, as though to show that since she did not want it, the current could take it, and him, where it would. She thought – wrongly as it turned out – that he had thrown it into the river. She burst into tears and fled.

At Vichy Mitterrand found Robert's father-in-law, Captain (now Colonel) Cahier, who had also been a prisoner in Germany but had been released on the grounds of ill health, and Jacques le Corbeiller, a friend of his sister Colette's husband, Pierre Landry. With their help he obtained a clerical job in a documentation service attached to the Légion Française des Combattants (French War Veterans' Legion). It was not much, but it paid 2,100 francs a month (equivalent at the time to about £11 or US $45), which was more than the lump sum of 300 francs that he had been given as demobilisation pay, and it allowed him to rent a room at a modest boarding house, the Pension Vincent, near the river.[3]

The town was, and remains today, a genteel, slightly faded spa where the bourgeoisie of pre-war days came to take the waters. Mitterrand loathed it:

> Vichy is a dreadful place (not disagreeable, not boring, but ugly) [he wrote to one of his cousins]. There is nothing to attract the eye – bloated, jowly hotels, built in ridiculous straight lines, pretentious villas planted here and there to accord with the doubtful taste of fat women. These watering places should be razed, [otherwise] our imbecile grand-children will think they are beautiful just because they are old.[4]

His boss, Jacques Favre de Thierrens, was a First World War flying ace – 'original, complicated and jovial, intelligent and cultivated' and above all, 'extremely colourful', as Mitterrand described him – who served as an agent for the French army's counter-intelligence service, the Bureaux for Anti-National Activities, and, at the same time, as an 'honourable correspondent' for British intelligence. Like so much in Vichy, the Bureaux had an ambiguous role. Officially they were charged by Pétain's government, with German approval, with tracking down Gaullists, Communists and other hostile elements. But they also served as cover for a clandestine operation to launch the first military resistance networks. Mitterrand's job was to compile deliberately misleading dossiers on potential suspects. 'It was all doctored,' he said. 'Favre . . . told me . . . "I want you to falsify everything" . . . So we wrote complete rubbish.'

It was his introduction to the world of smoke and mirrors in which he would spend the next two and a half years.

The Legion had been set up to merge the various veterans' movements in existence before the war into a vehicle for supporting Pétain. In April 1942, it was taken over by pro-German elements and a year later provided the manpower for the Milice, a collaborationist militia which worked closely with the Gestapo and employed the same methods. Unsurprisingly, given its subsequent reputation, Mitterrand would later insist that he had never worked there.[5]

His first months in Vichy were a time for reflection and self-questioning. In March he moved into a small apartment near the city centre. He read widely, not literature as in the past but books on European history. He told a friend: 'I am taking lessons in English and German . . . There are so many things that I don't know . . . I won't find it all in books, [but] I am trying to give myself a solid foundation.'

In an article later that year, recounting his experiences as a PoW, he offered some tentative conclusions. The defeat in 1940, he wrote, was not just the fruit of 'a regime that was collapsing, men who were useless and institutions emptied of their substance', although all that was true. Its roots went deeper. Germany had been created by a French Emperor, Napoleon, who had welded the principalities into a modern state. France was now paying the price for a century of self-aggrandisement when it had lost touch with reality – 'shedding its blood outside its borders' in 1870 and 1914 – in a misconceived quest for glory that was beyond its means. The result had been a historical cycle of mutual aggression for which France as well as Germany was responsible. He recalled the German carpenter for whom he had worked at Schaala. The man had been wounded at Verdun in 1916 and was an avid collector of Napoleonic memorabilia. 'All the things which united us,' Mitterrand realised, 'were memories of struggle and combat. Napoleon and Verdun formed between us that link of blood which brings nations together instead of separating them.'[6]

That he could formulate such ideas in the middle of the war was all the more striking because, in other ways, he was viscerally anti-German. It was as though he put his long-term vision and the day-to-day reality of living under the Occupation into separate, sealed boxes. At one level he fumed that 'their accent irritated me more than their tanks'; that they were upstarts, 'a nation not even 200 years old'; and that their presence in France was 'a rape [which] seemed to me blasphemous'. At another he understood that something would have to be done to break the nexus which bound the two countries' fates in an endless secular tragedy.

In the spring of 1942, however, he had a more immediate and egotistic concern. What part in this immense drama should he, François Mitterrand, attempt to play? In letters to Marie-Claire Sarrazin, he pondered his future:

> When I think of my destiny, all I find there is uncertainty. The only thing I know is to live outside the usual run of things and as intensely as I can . . . I will go [wherever] I find the taste for risk, but I would not want [my life] to be useless or in vain . . .

> It's better to die while doing something, acting at a moment's notice, accepting all the risks, than to wait for death to come and find you . . . These are stirring times. I do not wish to watch them pass from my window (even if that might be the wisest course . . .)[7]

Mitterrand's sense of being fated to assume an exceptional role was not new. His companions at Ziegenhain remembered him as 'ambitious and proud. He already felt that he stood out from the mass.' In captivity he had daydreamed about ways 'to arouse France not from the outside, but from within', even though he had 'neither the age nor the authority to achieve that'. Now, he told Marie-Claire, he needed to give himself the means 'to satisfy that ambition'. The question, he explained to her, was: 'How can we set France back on its feet?'

That spring he saw two possible ways forward. The first was through

Pétain, to whom he was drawn by his right-wing upbringing and his circle of friends and acquaintances. The second was through the growing number of PoWs who had either been repatriated to France or, like himself, had escaped.

He had seen the old Marshal one afternoon at a theatre and had been impressed, he told Marie-Claire, by his 'magnificent bearing and face like a marble statue'. He wanted Pétain to succeed. The ending of parliamentary government, he thought, was not a bad thing. France needed new institutions, 'something different [from] the old political parties'.[8] But the 'National Revolution', which was to give France back its pride and strength, was 'unfortunately a combination of two words emptied of their meaning'. The Marshal was surrounded by 'the Right of yesteryear', which had rallied to him for its own purposes and 'will inevitably cause us to fail'.

The PoWs offered a very different perspective.

In Paris in January he had run into a friend from his student days, Jacques Bénet, who had also escaped from a German camp. They found they shared a 'PoW mentality', Bénet remembered. Both felt that the prisoners had been forgotten and that they had a 'primordial duty . . . towards them' which made them want to stay in France, rather than going to London to join de Gaulle, whose priorities lay elsewhere. Although Mitterrand never claimed that he went to Vichy in order to promote the PoW cause, it may well have played a part in his decision. Certainly from the moment of his arrival the prisoners were a common thread in much of what he did. Not only was the French Legion, for which he worked, charged with aiding the PoWs, but in March he gave a series of talks on French radio about conditions in the camps. Later that month, he attended a meeting in a café with some forty other escaped prisoners, among them Max Varenne, who had been with him at Schaala, and Jean-Albert Roussel, who worked with Marcel Barrois at the Labour Ministry finding jobs for PoW returnees.

It was with Roussel, at the beginning of April, that he undertook his first act, if not of resistance, then at least of defiance against the Germans. Together with another ex-prisoner, Guy Fric, they disrupted a meeting in Clermont-Ferrand, the chief city of the region, 30 miles to the south, at which a French scientist named Georges Claude, a notorious Nazi sympathiser, spoke in favour of collaboration.

For the next year, Mitterrand's life would run on twin tracks: on one, an official career, surrounded by right-wing friends; on the other, an unofficial and increasingly clandestine existence, working with other ex-prisoners against the Germans and their French allies.

The contrasts were sometimes flagrant. In the same month that he demonstrated against Claude, he wrote to his cousin, Marie-Claire, praising the Service d'Ordre Légionnaire, a pro-Nazi militia set up by Joseph Darnand. Its members, he wrote, were 'carefully chosen, and bound by an oath founded on the same convictions of the heart'.

Was he keeping a foot in both camps? Or, as he maintained later, using his official persona as a cover for resistance activities? The truth is simpler: he was horribly confused. There were moments when he despised Vichy, and others when he came dangerously close to embracing the collaborationists' cause. In the latter vein he justified the return to office of Pierre Laval, Pétain's collaborationist Prime Minister. 'If we think [Laval's] methods are bad, do we really know what they are?' he asked. 'If they allow us to endure, they are good.' What was needed, he thought, was an elite – 'a gathering of men united by the same faith' – to hold the country together. 'Whether Germany or Russia wins, so long as our will is strong, they will handle us carefully.'

The last line is revealing. In the spring of 1942, the Allies' situation appeared desperate. France had been knocked out; all of Europe was occupied or neutral, apart from Britain which was fighting on alone; America had still not sent troops and German armies were in the heart of Russia. It was not necessary to be pro-Nazi to envisage the possibility that Germany would win the war and to wonder what would happen if it did.

In mid-April 1942, Mitterrand resigned from Favre de Thierrens's service, having decided that his presence there served no purpose. After working out his notice he was free by the beginning of May – but not idle. At the Labour Ministry, Barrois had set up a clandestine workshop manufacturing false papers, which were sent to the camps hidden in food parcels. Half a dozen people helped him, all ex-PoWs, including Jean-Albert Roussel, Guy Fric, and Serge Miller, a Lithuanian who was for a time Mitterrand's flatmate. Mitterrand soon joined them, contributing the counterfeiting skills he had learnt at Ziegenhain.[9]

In May a man arrived in Vichy who would exert a decisive influence over Mitterrand's future. Antoine Mauduit was the scion of a wealthy

Parisian family who had given up a comfortable way of life to return to the soil as a peasant. A charismatic, mystical figure, he later joined the Foreign Legion and spent eighteen months in an Oflag, where he vowed that on his return, he would establish a Christian phalanstery to serve as a refuge for escaped PoWs and a centre of resistance against German Occupation. At Vichy, Mauduit met Roussel, who was enthralled by his personality and enthusiastically supported his plan to base the refuge at the fifteenth-century Château de Montmaur, in the Hautes Alpes, 100 miles south-east of Lyon.

On Friday, June 12 Mitterrand and a score of others travelled to Montmaur to spend the next three days discussing how best to oppose the German Occupation. They were a very mixed bunch. Beside Barrois and Roussel, there were Marcel Haedrich and de Gaulle's nephew, Michel Cailliau, who were trying to set up a prisoners' resistance movement; Colonel Gonzales de Linares who was creating a military escape network; and Etienne Gagnaire, an ex-communist trades unionist, who, with Jacques de Montjoye, a factory-owner and follower of the Count of Paris, ran the Prisoners' Action Centre in Lyon, a forum where returned prisoners could discuss the country's political future. Most were meeting each other for the first time. Together the groups they represented comprised not more than a few hundred men.

No firm decisions were taken, but Mitterrand wrote on his return that 'a group has been set up which I believe is destined to have an outstanding future'. He found Mauduit inspiring, 'an extraordinary, engaging character, a man worth following'. Near the end of his life he would say: 'I have not met five men who radiated such authority'.

The refuge which Mauduit created at Montmaur, which he called 'the Chain', attracted men of all classes and beliefs.[10] Mitterrand remembered it as 'a mixture of the Boy Scout mentality, the Christianity of the convent, a spirit of renunciation and militant patriotism.' In the winter of 1942, it would become one of the first *maquis*, or armed resistance bases, in France.[11]

The Montmaur meeting and Mauduit's example were powerful antidotes to whatever collaborationist temptations Mitterrand may have been entertaining earlier in the year. Nonetheless, the twin tracks continued. The day after he got back, he started work at the Vichy administration's Commissariat for Prisoners of War as deputy head of press relations, in charge of the Free Zone.[12] He did his job conscientiously, giving radio broadcasts, speaking at conferences, writing articles, editing a liaison bulletin and vetting everything that appeared about the PoWs in the Vichy-controlled press. 'I like it pretty well,' he wrote at the end of his first week there. 'Either I am overwhelmed with work, which eats up my days, or I have nothing to do . . . so it's balanced.'

The Commissioner, Maurice Pinot de Périgord de Villechenon, from a wealthy upper-class family of industrialists, had been taken prisoner on the Marne in June 1940 and repatriated after fourteen months in an Oflag. He was fiercely anti-German, harboured grave doubts about Pétain, detested the Vichy regime and tried to keep his department apolitical, concentrating on social issues and closing his eyes 'when he did not encourage' the 'parallel activities' of his staff.

In July 1942, Mitterrand spoke to Jacques Bénet about 'launching a resistance movement, recruited among the PoWs', and, with Pinot's blessing, began developing a network of contacts in Prisoners' Mutual Aid Centres, which the Commissariat had started creating in the Free Zone that summer to do social work among the returnees, many of whom found it difficult to re-enter normal life after their captivity.[13] In August he and Marcel Barrois founded the Mutual Aid Centre for the *département* of the Allier, based in Vichy, intending to use it as a cover for future resistance activities.[14]

That month there was another meeting at Montmaur, with many of the same participants. Mitterrand would write later that it marked 'the first organised appearance of the PoW resistance movement'. That was stretching the truth. The participants had appointed a steering committee consisting of himself, Mauduit and de Montjoye – the 'three Ms', as they were called – with a mandate to explore further ways to bring such a movement into being.[15] But that was as far as it went. He was still in two minds about taking the plunge and so, it seems, were many of the others.

Earlier that summer Mitterrand had written: 'If only I had a firm belief in something, nothing would be a sacrifice for me. But what can I do without solid ground beneath my feet before I jump?'

> I recognise in myself a curious mixture of daring and prudence, which I am afraid may average out as what we call weakness. But I am still reluctant to commit myself . . . I think the three months to come will

give me a direction, perhaps they will impose a choice . . . [My problem is that] I am faithful, and that is fatal . . . when one wants to get involved in politics. So I am mistrustful, I won't commit myself unless forced to, because I know that afterwards I won't deviate from the course I have chosen . . .[16]

The three months passed. Nothing changed.

Mitterrand's reluctance to break with Vichy would later be held against him by political opponents who claimed that he turned his coat only after it had become obvious that the Germans were going to lose. Today it is widely acknowledged that the German defeat at Stalingrad, announced by the Soviet High Command on the evening of February 2 1943, marked the crucial turning point of the war in Europe. But that was far from clear at the time. The BBC that night described the three-month-long battle as 'one of the most horrific chapters of the war so far', but neither then nor for months after did anyone speak of a turning point. The German advance had been halted before, outside Moscow in December 1941, only for the *Wehrmacht* to regain the initiative. A year later there was nothing to suggest that that could not happen again. Churchill himself had said in November 1942, after the victory at El Alamein: 'It is not the end. It is not even the beginning of the end. But it is perhaps the end of the beginning.'

In Mitterrand's case, aside from his own anguished uncertainties, two sets of factors were at work.

Throughout 1942, he remained convinced that Pétain, despite his faults and the failings of those around him, offered the best hope of getting France through the war in a state to play an effective role when it ended. To do that would require authoritarian institutions and a powerful elite. Mitterrand had not forgotten the collapse of social barriers in the PoW camps and the uncommon courage of working-class men like Pelat and Finifter. The elite did not have to come from the traditional ruling classes. But to leave the country's future to the common herd was unthinkable. After a visit to a rural district in the Auvergne, he wrote despairingly of the local peasants: 'Poor, ugly little men . . . How can we put back some fire into them? What separates them from pigs, unless it be that they are failures?' He quoted Mauduit as saying, 'it is we, with our blood and heroism, who will [make] . . . sacrifices for the vast masses'.

Like many other returnees, Mitterrand believed that the 'prisoner spirit' of egalitarianism and fair play should be part of whatever social model would be adopted after the war. But at Vichy his patrician instincts dominated and were coloured by the fascist leanings of many of those around him. The circle of officials he frequented – including men like Simon Arbellot de Vacqueur, Pétain's press chief, and Gabriel Jeantet, who edited the Pétainist monthly, *France*, both linked to the pre-war Cagoule; and Jean Delage, who had been his mentor at *L'Echo de Paris* – was drawn largely from the far Right.[17] All of them believed that Pétain was the only rational choice.

The second set of factors was more complicated.

If Pétain's policy of coexisting with the Germans was untenable, the sole alternative was open revolt. That was what de Gaulle urged from London. Some of Mitterrand's friends, notably Pierre de Bénouville, had already taken that course. But in the Free Zone, there were no Germans and therefore no military targets. The three main resistance movements in the South – Combat, led by Henri Frenay; Libération, under Emmanuel d'Astier de la Vigerie; and Franc-Tireur (Sharp-shooter), headed by Jean-Pierre Lévy – carried out intelligence-gathering, published clandestine newspapers, intimidated known collaborators and organised demonstrations and boycotts against the Occupation. To Mitterrand, that did not go much further than what he and his colleagues at the Commissariat were already doing. In the Occupied Zone it was different. Since the spring of 1942, a communist movement, the Franc-Tireurs et Partisans, had been killing enemy soldiers, provoking harsh reprisals against the civilian population. But even there, Resistance activity was limited. In the winter of 1942, some 20–30,000 French men and women, or fewer than one in 700 of the adult, able-bodied population, actively opposed the Germans. There was as yet no regular channel for parachuting in arms, and tensions between de Gaulle's Free French and the British Special Operations Executive (SOE), both of which wanted to control the non-communist Resistance inside France, meant that the weapons supply was sporadic and parsimonious, when it existed at all.

In these circumstances, to go underground was to take a leap into the unknown. A year earlier, Mitterrand had made such a leap to escape from Ziegenhain. But this time there was no Marie-Louise to goad him into action.

A third factor which might have been expected to influence

him – the increasingly blatant complicity of the Vichy administration in the persecution of Jews – had no effect at all.

In October 1940, when Mitterrand was a PoW, Pétain had promulgated decrees excluding French Jews from the civil service, the army, the teaching profession and journalism, and ordering foreign Jews to be interned. In 1941, also before his return, additional decrees extended the list of prohibited professions; authorised, in certain cases, the internment of French Jews; and provided for the confiscation of Jewish businesses. In the Occupied Zone, where similar regulations were in force, Jews were required after June 1942 to wear a yellow star on their clothing.

That summer, at the Germans' request, Laval's police chief, René Bousquet, initiated a systematic round-up of foreign Jews throughout France, which he insisted, as a matter of national pride, be carried out by the French police. Before the war Bousquet had been an unusually gifted provincial administrator, one of the youngest ever recipients of the principal French decoration, the *Légion d'honneur*. He was not pro-Nazi and his motives remain opaque. To some he was utterly cynical, a moral spiv who played both sides in the war, ready to do anything to advance his own interests. To others, perhaps more plausibly, his role in the deportation of the Jews was an extreme case of that perverse reflex which holds that empowering one's own countrymen, even if it is to do the enemy's work, is a way of upholding sovereignty.* The one does not necessarily exclude the other. On July 16 and 17 1942, in what was named Operation Spring Wind, Bousquet's

---

* This attitude was well described in Pierre Boulle's novel, *The Bridge on the River Kwai*, which was the basis for a classic war film, directed by David Lean. In it a British officer, Colonel Nicholson, orders his men to work for the authorities of a Japanese PoW camp in order to maintain morale.

In France, out of an estimated 290,000 Jews before the war, 200,000 were stateless or foreign. Nearly 60 per cent survived, including 90 per cent of those who held French citizenship, a higher proportion than in any other occupied territory with the single exception of Denmark, which had a Jewish population of only 7,000. Apologists for Vichy have claimed that Pétain's policy of collaboration was 'a lesser evil' which saved thousands of Jewish lives because, had the Germans administered France directly, Nazi policies would have prevailed from the start. Others argue that had the French police and administration not collaborated, the manpower of the German occupation force would have been stretched much more thinly and fewer deportations would have occurred. But history is not what might have been: the French State did collaborate and more than 40 per cent of the Jewish population died.

men detained nearly 13,000 foreign Jews from the area around Paris. The following day the first trainload left for Auschwitz.

Towards the end of his life, when Mitterrand was asked about his reaction to these events, his response was chilling: 'I didn't think about the anti-Semitism of Vichy. I knew that, unfortunately, anti-Semites occupied an important place around the Marshal, but I did not follow the legislation . . . We weren't dealing with that. We were concentrating on the plight of the PoWs and the returnees . . .'

In conversations with Elie Wiesel, the Jewish writer and Nobel Peace Prize laureate, who had become a friend, he was a little more forthcoming and, at the same time, misleading. 'When I saw the yellow stars,' he said, 'when I knew the status of the Jews, it contributed to distancing me from a system which accepted that crime.' It was an odd choice of words – 'distancing', not 'condemning' – and in any case he saw no yellow stars until the winter of 1942.[18] Until then the plight of the Jews completely passed him by.

Many others, French Jews included, closed their eyes to what was happening. The Levy-Despas, with whom he had stayed in St Tropez, were Jewish. So was Mitterrand's flatmate in Vichy that spring, Serge Miller. Even among them the anti-Jewish legislation was not a topic of discussion. Throughout Mitterrand's time at Vichy, the fate of the Jewish community was a non-issue. Just as, in the 1930s, when he was a law student in Paris, it had not troubled him that some of his friends were anti-Semitic, so now he contributed articles to Pétainist magazines which published strident anti-Jewish propaganda.[19]

Such attitudes were widespread. Before the war, anti-Semitism was woven into the fabric of continental European societies, no more remarked on than segregation in the southern United States. Some people approved of it; others – like Mitterrand – did not. But almost no one was outraged. Anti-Semitism then, like homelessness today, was part of the landscape.

The Vichy legislation was drawn up in this context. Mitterrand's friend, Jacques Bénet, said later: 'For us – for him as well – it was fatally bound up with German domination. The Germans demanded it.* Since they did it in their country, it was almost normal that

---

* In fact, they did not. The anti-Jewish decrees were enacted, with Pétain's blessing, at the urging of French anti-Semites. In the summer of 1942, Pierre Laval authorised the deportation of Jewish children without the Germans having requested it.

they imposed it here. We had the choice between lumping it and resisting, and we said to ourselves, "all right, we are going to have to lump it".' To Bénet, with hindsight, the situation became intolerable when the large-scale detention of Jews began that summer. However that was a judgement made half a century later. How many French people at the time, other than those whose friends or families were directly involved, felt revulsion at the mass arrests is much harder to know.*

Paradoxically it was Hitler, through the revelation of the death camps, who made tolerance of anti-Semitism impossible in Europe. Confronted with the Final Solution, looking the other way ceased to be an option.

But that was afterwards. It was not until 1945, when Germany surrendered, that the full horror of places like Auschwitz and Belsen became widely known.[20] In the meantime, those who opposed Nazi policies towards the Jews did so not so much from revulsion against the principles of the Vichy legislation as on a personal, case by case, basis, reacting to the distress of individuals they knew and cared about. French schoolteachers concealed the identities of Jewish children in their classes; families protected Jewish neighbours; householders sheltered Jewish friends. The men and women who risked their lives to save Jewish families from the Gestapo and the Milice were not members of the Resistance or de Gaulle's Free French in London.[21] They were the same ordinary citizens that those groups implicitly

---

Mitterrand and Bénet may have believed that Vichy was simply anticipating German wishes, but that was not the same thing as having anti-Jewish measures 'imposed', as Bénet put it, by an outside force.

* The French philosopher, Edgar Morin, himself Jewish and a student at Toulouse in October 1940, said he was 'not particularly struck' by the Vichy statutes against the Jews. Morin went on to join the Resistance and one of his uncles died at Auschwitz. Nonetheless he had only a vague memory of the mass arrests of July 1942. 'If I heard about them,' he said, 'it was some time afterwards.' When nearly fifty former Resistance figures contributed to a lengthy compilation of memoirs of their wartime experiences, only three mentioned the persecution of Jews and just one, Pierre Merli, who was honoured by Israel as one of 'the Righteous', described working actively against it. The journalist, Pierre Péan, who undertook exhaustive researches into the period, noted that among more than a hundred contemporary figures whom he questioned, the subject of the Jews 'was never brought up spontaneously, not even by those who had impeccable Resistance credentials'.

condemned for not taking a stronger stand against the Germans and their allies. The image of collective cowardice during the Occupation was palliated in reality by a multitude of acts of individual courage.

As in the case of Vichy, so in the case of French Jews, history was rewritten to serve the interests of those who came after.

October 1942 found Mitterrand still at the Commissariat for Prisoners of War. In the middle of that month, he and Marcel Barrois were received by Pétain to report on the work of the Mutual Aid Centre in the Allier. Mitterrand would later claim that the prisoners' resistance movement had been formed at this time from the fusion of several small groups led by himself, Mauduit, de Montjoye, and Guy Fric. This was not true. Nothing changed that autumn. Mitterrand continued to believe in the Marshal, while remaining obsessed with his own doubts and demons. 'It has been so long that I have not known who I am,' he had complained to a friend some weeks earlier. He agonised over his loss of religious faith and 'the vanity of my hopes and my struggles'.

At last, in November, the event occurred which, as he had hoped, would 'force' him to commit himself. The Allies invaded North Africa. Three days later, on November 11, the Germans occupied the Free Zone. The myth of Pétain, 'the shield', protecting France from the invader, shattered.

At the beginning of December, a third, inconclusive meeting was held at Montmaur. Once again there was no agreement on how best to move forward. But then, in January 1943, the Prime Minister, Pierre Laval, summoned Maurice Pinot and told him that he was being replaced as Commissioner for Prisoners of War by one of Laval's minions, André Masson. When Pinot refused to resign, Laval dismissed him.

The following day, Mitterrand and most of the rest of Pinot's colleagues resigned en masse. At the time it was an exceptional gesture, which could have ended in all their arrests. Laval toyed with that idea, but then thought better of it. For Mitterrand, the time for self-questioning was finally over: the moment of truth had arrived. He told his cousin, Marie-Claire Sarrazin:

> I don't worry [any more] about what lies ahead. On the contrary, things are looking good – under different forms but all of them rather

cheering – and I am going to lie low for a bit . . . I almost despaired when
I saw that all our work over the last few months had been wiped out at
the stroke of a pen, but my taste for uncertainty – that uncertainty that
carries the seeds of triumph – has won out. This new departure is both
a separation [from what came before] and a coming closer to the things
that remain true. I am starting [again], and not from my point of origin.[22]

His letters that month showed an enthusiasm he had not felt since the
previous summer. On paper he was merely one of the three members
of the 'steering committee' appointed at Montmaur in August, but he
was determined to make that a springboard to a more prominent role.
He established links with the Chantiers de Jeunesse (Youth Worksites),
a national service organisation which Vichy had set up after the
Armistice, and the Compagnons de France, aimed primarily at teen-
agers, which was among the few organised groups at that time to
accept and protect Jewish members. Both movements supported Pétain,
were hostile to Pierre Laval and opposed the Communists and de
Gaulle. Like the Mutual Aid Centres, they were resources which
Mitterrand could use when the nascent prisoners' resistance took wing.

In February 1943, the pieces began to fall into place.

At the beginning of that month, Mitterrand and five others met,
with Pinot's blessing, at an isolated farm near the hamlet of Bellegarde-
en-Marche, 50 miles east of Clermont-Ferrand, where they decided
their first priority should be to sabotage the attempts of the new
Commissioner, André Masson, to mobilise the PoWs behind Laval.
They also discussed the opportunity of military action but decided it
would be premature.[23]

Pinot, meanwhile, had been in touch with Bernard de Chalvron,
one of the co-founders of a Resistance organisation called Super-NAP,
from the initials of Noyautage des Administrations Publiques
(Infiltration of the Public Administration), which placed informers in
senior government posts in Vichy and in Paris. That month, Pinot
and de Chalvron met General Georges Revers, one of the leaders of
the ORA, the Organisation de résistance de l'armée (Army Resistance
Organisation), formed by dissident army officers after the Occupation
of the South. Pinot introduced Mitterrand and it was agreed that he
should act as the public face of the future prisoners' movement
because, as de Chalvron put it, there were 'obvious political reasons'

why it could not be headed by Pinot, who was identified too closely
with the Vichy administration.

One more meeting was needed before Mitterrand's dispositions
were complete. On February 13, he returned to Montmaur for a fourth
time for discussions with Mauduit and other members of 'the Chain'.
Jacques de Montjoye and Etienne Gagnaire, of the Prisoners' Action
Centre in Lyon, were also present, as was de Gaulle's nephew, Michel
Cailliau. A battle was brewing. Cailliau was courageous, naïve, excit-
able – 'de Gaulle in caricature', as his colleague, Edgar Morin, put
it – deeply hostile to the Left and suspicious of Jews and Freemasons.[24]
He regarded Mitterrand and his associates as 'milk and Vichy water'.

Cailliau urged immediate armed struggle and an intelligence operation to help the Free French and the Allies. Mitterrand agreed that
they should prepare for direct resistance against the enemy but insisted,
'this is not the moment'. Cailliau afterwards quoted him as saying:
'So you kill a German, and provoke the shooting of fifty hostages in
reprisal. Is that what you want?' – which was Maurice Pinot's position.
Sabotage was legitimate and should be encouraged,[25] Mitterrand said,
but the new movement's main task should be to prevent the returned
PoWs, now numbering more than half a million, from being herded
into Vichy-led movements which supported Pierre Laval. In the end,
Mitterrand's arguments won the day. Cailliau was appointed, together
with Mauduit, Mitterrand, Jean-Albert Roussel from the Mutual Aid
Centre for the Allier and, later, Jacques de Montjoye, to a 'National
Committee for Prisoners' Struggle', which was to head the new movement. But the episode caused bad blood. From the start Cailliau had
found Mitterrand antipathetic. Now he hated him.

For Mitterrand, things could hardly have gone better. He was exactly
where he wanted to be, at the centre of a web of influence which
encompassed the ORA, Maurice Pinot and his followers, the Chantiers,
the Compagnons, and the Mutual Aid Centres. Pinot, Mauduit and
de Montjoye – all a decade or more his senior – remained the dominant figures. But he was well placed for whatever might follow. And
his winning streak continued. In March the ORA agreed to subsidise
the future Pinot–Mitterrand movement – Pin'–Mitt', as Cailliau deri-
sively called it – providing funds for Mitterrand himself and for a
secretary, sixteen-year-old Ginette Caillard, who had worked previously
at the Commissariat.

That month Mitterrand called Jacques Bénet and another friend from his student days, a discreet young Breton named Pol Pilven, to come and help him. Two others, Jacques Marot, who was working with the Compagnons in Lyon, and André Bettencourt, agreed to undertake special missions. Bénet proved a gifted organiser and spent the spring and early summer laying the foundations of a Resistance network among members of the Mutual Aid Centres who wanted to do more than social work and were ready to confront the Germans directly.

Meanwhile the relationship between the nascent prisoners' movement and the ORA was fleshed out. One consisted of ex-PoWs, all former soldiers; the other of army officers: there was a natural synergy between them. By April 1943, Mitterrand was in regular contact not only with General Revers, but directly with General Aubert Frère, the overall chief of the ORA who had once been de Gaulle's commanding officer. More funds were made available and he was able to take on Jean Munier, who had been repatriated from Ziegenhain during the winter, for 3,000 francs (£16 or US $65) a month, as his first full-time agent.

By this time Michel Cailliau's relations with the other members of the 'National Committee' set up in February had reached breaking point. He was in disagreement not only with Mitterrand but with Mauduit and Montjoye over money, facilities and policy. At the end of April, he announced that he was leaving and would not return until the Committee was ready to undertake 'real resistance'.

Such rivalries were not unusual. The Resistance was not always a selfless, chivalrous fraternity. It was not that kind of war. Its leaders were strong characters, under enormous pressure, at the mercy of informers, risking torture and death if caught. Working together did not come easily.

But in this case the fracture went deeper. In 1943, de Gaulle was not yet the unchallenged symbol of French resistance that he would later become. He had a rival: General Henri Giraud, ten years his senior and with a war record as impressive as his own. Giraud had been captured in May 1940 and incarcerated in the fortress of Koenigstein, near Dresden. After nearly two years of preparation, he staged a spectacular escape on April 17 1942 and made his way to Vichy. The US President, Franklin Roosevelt, who loathed de Gaulle, regarding him, correctly, as troublesome, haughty and impervious to

American control, saw in Giraud the possibility of a 'third way' between Vichy and the man of whom Churchill said that the heaviest cross he had ever had to bear was the Cross of Lorraine.

When the Allies invaded North Africa as a first step towards the reconquest of Europe, the Americans turned to Giraud to win over Vichy's troops in the region to their cause. In December, he was named head of the Civil and Military Command in Algiers. The following month, at Casablanca, he and de Gaulle shook hands in the presence of their respective mentors, Roosevelt and Churchill. For most of the next year, they engaged in a stubborn struggle for power.

Cailliau, naturally, supported his uncle. Mitterrand was in Giraud's camp.

Not only was the ORA, which financed the prisoners' movement, a Giraudist organisation, but Colonel de Linares, one of the founders of Mauduit's group, 'the Chain', was Giraud's aide-de-camp. Mitterrand also had ties to Giraud of a more personal kind. The general's son, Henri, whom he had met before the war, had served in the cavalry with his sister Colette's husband, Pierre Landry, and the two had become close friends. His brother Robert's father-in-law, Colonel (now General) Cahier, was a Giraudist, as was Jacques le Corbeiller, who had helped find him his first job in Vichy and was now on Giraud's staff.

Equally important, Giraud, unlike de Gaulle, had not broken with Pétain. He condemned the Vichy government's policies, but not the Marshal himself. It was possible in the spring of 1943 to be both *maréchaliste* and Giraudist. That was Mitterrand's position. He believed that Pétain had behaved honourably. But the 86-year-old Marshal had shown himself to be powerless to protect France. The shield having sundered, only the sword remained.

Whether it should be wielded by de Gaulle or Giraud, or perhaps an alliance of the two, was still an open question. Throughout the spring and early summer, the two generals struggled to assert control over the burgeoning internal Resistance in order to reinforce their own power. Jacques de Montjoye was approached by an emissary of the Armée Secrète (Secret Army), which had been created by de Gaulle's plenipotentiary in France, Jean Moulin, out of the paramilitary units of the three main resistance movements in the South: Combat, Libération and Franc-Tireur. The prisoners' movement was invited to join them. Mitterrand turned down the proposal. 'The Secret

Army is Gaullist and takes its orders from London,' he told de Montjoye. '[We] should remain independent and [in any case], we are more on the Giraudist side.'

Overtures from the Gaullists continued. In April 1943, Mitterrand went to a meeting in Lyon with a man named Lahire, who turned out to be none other than his childhood friend, Pierre de Bénouville, now a trusted aide to Henri Frenay of Combat, who headed the Mouvement Unifié de la Résistance (Unified Resistance Movement), set up not long before to coordinate the three main movements in the South. They drove to a village near Mâcon, where Mitterrand found Frenay waiting for him in the back room of a bistro. The first contact went well. Frenay thought Mitterrand 'intelligent and cultivated . . . with a lively appearance and a smile which worried me a little because it reminded me of d'Astier [the dynamic but uncontrollable leader of Libération]'. Mitterrand returned the compliment: Frenay was 'solid as a rock and a visionary at the same time'.

Frenay wanted to know what the prisoners' movement represented and how Mitterrand intended to cooperate with other resistance organisations. Pinot, through Bernard de Chalvron, had already been in contact with Frenay's colleague, Claude Bourdet, as well as with d'Astier and Pascal Copeau of Libération and Eugène Claudius-Petit of Franc-Tireur. At first none of them had been able to understand why the ex-PoWs wanted to form their own group rather than joining an existing movement. But Pinot had explained that the shared experience of the camps had created 'mutual trust and unity of views' among the returnees which meant they would be more effective if they worked together. That was accepted. The problem was that Frenay and his friends wanted to deal with one prisoners' movement, not two. Cailliau, since his break with Montmaur, had redoubled his efforts to launch his own network, which he called the Mouvement de résistance de prisonniers de guerre et déportés (MRPGD). It was numerically weaker than the Pinot–Mitterrand group, but he was de Gaulle's nephew and that meant he could not be ignored. Frenay was not concerned about Mitterrand's *maréchaliste* past – he had himself at one time sympathised with Pétain – and immediately saw the interest of a movement which could exploit the prisoner infrastructure which Vichy had created. The difficulty was how to bring the two groups together.

The next move, apparently at the urging of de Gaulle's staff in London, came from Cailliau's side. His deputy, Philippe Dechartre, who had recently been repatriated from Germany, was delegated to meet Mitterrand in Lyon at the end of May.[26] He was not enthusiastic. Like Cailliau he thought Mitterrand's kind of resistance was phoney: too political, too compromised with Pétain and Vichy. Resistance meant 'blowing up trains, carrying out intelligence work', not sending off food parcels. 'I did not like Vichy,' he said later, 'and I did not like Mitterrand. I did not like him at all . . . I knew I would have nothing to say to him and he would have nothing to say to me.' But it turned out otherwise:

The rendezvous was for five o'clock in the morning on the platform of the railway station at Lyon-Perrache . . . It wasn't a station like today: there were engines belching steam, trains whistling . . . it was cold and foggy, the railway tracks were ghostly . . . and there was that sneaking fear in the pit of your stomach. You kept looking round to see if between the wagons there wasn't one of those standard-issue raincoats. So there I was on the platform, pacing up and down, when I saw [a figure] emerging from the mist, like a phantom . . . This individual was wearing an overcoat that was rather long, knickerbockers – like golfing trousers tied at the knee – which he wore without stockings; heavy mountain shoes, short socks so that his calves were bare, a long red scarf, a small moustache and his hair slicked down with brillantine.[27] It was all a bit over the top: he looked like a South American sub-lieutenant . . . There were just the two of us on the platform, so it had to be him . . . And I said to him: 'Look, [Mitterrand], I am here only from a sense of duty . . . What you are doing isn't resistance. I didn't want to meet you, I'm not in favour of us joining together, but that's what the General wants so I have to go along with it. But I don't like it.' And Mitterrand said to me: 'I see. So you're a Bolshevik. All right . . .' It really started badly. But we were there and we had to do something. So we talked about organisational problems . . . And I have to say, as we kept talking in that fog . . . I began to discover a man that I was not expecting at all. A man who was extremely charming, subtle . . . and prodigiously intelligent. Everything he said to me seemed right – they were things I would have liked to say myself but which he said far better than I could ever have said them . . . Something

happened. A friendship was born. A real, deep friendship . . . That day
he truly astonished me.[28]

The same month, the balance of influence between de Gaulle and
Giraud underwent a decisive shift when the leaders of the pre-war
political parties and of all the main resistance movements, communist
and non-communist, in the North as well as the South, with the sole
exception of the Giraudist ORA, agreed to take part in a National
Resistance Council, headed by Jean Moulin. On May 27, the day before
Mitterrand and Dechartre talked in Lyon, they met in Paris and formally
pledged allegiance to de Gaulle. Three days later the General flew
secretly to Algiers where he and Giraud agreed on June 4 to head jointly
the French National Liberation Committee which would become the
supreme French military and civilian body in the war against Germany.

To Roosevelt's dismay, de Gaulle, his position strengthened by the
Resistance Council's backing, now held most of the cards. On instructions from the White House, General Eisenhower, the Supreme Allied
Commander in North Africa, threatened to cut off arms supplies to
French forces unless de Gaulle toed Washington's line. He disdainfully
refused. A month later the Americans backed off and in August reluctantly joined the other Allies in recognising the new joint leadership.

Meanwhile Frenay made one last effort to reconcile Mitterrand and
Cailliau. Towards the end of June, he called both men to Lyon for a
meeting with key Resistance leaders. Mitterrand, as was his habit, was
late, and Cailliau took the opportunity for a tirade against his rival's
relations with Vichy. It was clear, Frenay wrote afterwards, that they
'cordially detested each other'. In fact Frenay and his colleagues had
already made up their minds. Mitterrand's movement was the more
interesting. Nonetheless, Frenay arranged for the two men to dine
together that evening and extracted an agreement that representatives
of the two groups would liaise once a month.

Cailliau was not fooled. Frenay supported Mitterrand. His one
trump card was that de Gaulle might intervene in his favour. In July
he left for Algiers to seek his uncle's support.

In the summer of 1943, Mitterrand was leading a double life.

He remained a member of the 'National Committee' set up at
Montmaur in February, which was now enlarged to include Bénet,

Pilven and Pinot, giving him and his allies a majority. At the same time he had created the nucleus of a separate prisoners' organisation, which he called the RNPG (le Rassemblement national de prisonniers de guerre, or National Rally of Prisoners of War), into which the 'Committee' would eventually be subsumed.[29]

To help him run the new movement, he drew on three distinct circles of friends and former associates: veterans of Ziegenhain like Jean Munier, joined later by Bernard Finifter and Patrice Pelat, whose escapes had followed his own; a second circle, consisting of former comrades from the Marian hostel – Bénet and Pilven, but also Bettencourt, Marot and Alfred Ferréol de Ferry, who was working in Vichy as a translator; and a third one, made up of colleagues from the Commissariat – Maurice Pinot; Jean Védrine, a recent arrival from the camps to whom Mitterrand gave responsibility for work in the Mutual Aid Centres; Marcel Barrois, his partner at the Centre for the Allier, which still served as their unofficial headquarters, and Jean Bertin, a lawyer from Nancy, both of whom now joined Munier as paid full-time agents.

He also had dual identities. One was François Mitterrand, who had worked for the Commissariat and lived in an apartment in the rue Nationale, in the centre of Vichy. The other was a man who used some thirty different aliases, many of them taken from Dieppe, where the civil registry had been destroyed by a bombing raid, making them impossible to verify, and who most frequently called himself Morland, after the Paris metro station, Sully-Morland, on the opposite bank of the Seine from the Boulevard St Germain in his beloved Latin Quarter, a *nom de guerre* which had the merit of containing the first and last letters of his own name.

This double, or multiple, existence pleased him.

His new life was 'absorbing, and I like it, [even though it is] difficult and perhaps dangerous, in any case complicated', he wrote. 'I have a premonition of what it will lead to and I'm not afraid of that.' He was confident, he added, that by the time he finished he would have accomplished a great deal of what he had set out to achieve. Another letter that summer radiated the same faith in himself and his uncommon destiny:

I am full of ideas and insights, and I have the feeling that, each time, when it comes to the interplay of events, I am right [in my judgements].

I can love my fellow beings and exert influence on them [not as individuals, each with their own faults,] but only as a mass . . . If a crowd, or a people, be within my grasp, I know I can figure out their truth, their story, what makes them tick . . . It's a dangerous game, and incomplete, for the greatest men must have loved each individual and drawn from that love the virtues of example and leadership. [I am not in that league] . . . but still, what strength is in me! If I am only given the chance, I feel [my] strength is fit to rule.[30]

Coming back down to earth, he had the grace to add that, like everyone else, he was a mass of contradictions.

Chief among them was the contradiction between Morland and Mitterrand.

As Morland, he had created a paramilitary group, led by Jean Munier to undertake sabotage and, when the occasion required, to 'neutralise' pro-Nazi elements. In the autumn of 1943, Munier and Patrice Pelat prospected sites for parachuting arms, working with the special services of the Giraudist ORA, directed from London by Captain Pierre Lejeune, and with Alain de Beaufort, a Gaullist agent, who was based in Clermont-Ferrand and was later awarded the Military Cross for his work with the British SOE. Morland was listed as a member of the ORA paramilitary network and kept in regular contact with the movement's chiefs in the South – Colonel Henri Zeller and his deputy, Lieutenant-Colonel Pfister – through whom he received most of his funds. Drops were signalled by a codeword broadcast by the French service of the BBC and some of the arms received were reserved for Morland's movement.[31] He developed the tradecraft of clandestinity and donned multiple disguises. In one, he remembered, he looked like 'an Argentine tango dancer'; in another he was an art gallery owner, carrying a portfolio of paintings. The signal for recognition was to have half of a five-franc note in one's hand.

As Mitterrand, he remained Marcel Barrois's deputy at the Allier Centre. He continued to write for Vichy publications and maintained close ties with Paul Racine, a young official in Pétain's private office. As a cover, a friend appointed him to the Students' National Service, a fictitious employment which gave him a government identity card. He attended press conferences given by the new Commissioner, André Masson, and forged what would prove a lasting friendship with

Jean-Paul Martin, a young civil servant whom he had known in Paris as a law student and who now worked for Henri Cado, the right-hand man of René Bousquet at the Interior Ministry. Almost certainly with Bousquet's approval, Martin became the movement's 'mole', providing official seals, 'genuine' false papers and warnings of impending raids by the Gestapo and the Milice.[32]

That spring Mitterrand was awarded the *francisque*, the Marshal's personal decoration, given for services to the 'National Revolution'.[33] He was not the only Resistance figure to receive it. Bernard de Chalvron of Super-NAP, afterwards a Gaullist ambassador, and Raymond Marcellin, who joined Marie-Madeleine Fourcade's Alliance network and later became de Gaulle's Interior Minister, were both decorated by Pétain. So was Maurice Couve de Murville, who that year became a member of the National Liberation Committee in Algiers and subsequently served as Prime Minister. All acted under instructions from de Gaulle's staff in London. To Mitterrand, as to the others, the *francisque* was an ideal cover.[34] Flaunting Pétain's private emblem while fighting against Vichy indulged his taste for provocation.

The question may be asked (in France it has been asked incessantly for the last sixty years): at what point did Mitterrand break irrevocably with Vichy and commit himself to the Resistance with no possibility of going back?

He himself gave many different answers, some so improbable that they merely cast doubt on the others. A case can be made for November 1942, when the Germans occupied the South. More plausibly the moment of truth may be situated in February 1943, when his movement first contacted the ORA.[35] By then Mitterrand had been engaging in Resistance-related activities for the best part of a year. So why did it take him so long to decide? Was he hedging his bets? Or drawing the maximum advantage from an ambiguous situation?

To turn the question on its head, why did he stick out his neck at all when more than 99 per cent of his fellow citizens were unwilling to lift a finger if it might expose them to the slightest risk?

He probably did not know himself. All that can be said for certain is that by the summer of 1943 his mind was made up.

On July 10, in Paris, some 3,500 ex-prisoners gathered in the Salle Wagram, close to the Arc de Triomphe, for a pro-Vichy PoW congress in the presence of André Masson and several other ministers. Halfway through Masson's speech, as he was defending Laval's policy of sending French labourers to Germany in return for selective POW releases, a young man got up on a chair and shouted: 'Monsieur, you have been lying! . . . We have no lessons in patriotism to receive from you!'[36] François Mitterrand, for it was he, accused Masson of 'a shameful deal . . . using our comrades in [the camps] as a means of blackmail to justify the deportation of French workers'.[37] The Commissioner, shaking with rage, threatened to have him brought before Laval and Pétain. Paul Racine, who was present, thought he would be arrested. But the hall was on Mitterrand's side. He was asked to show his identity papers; then, surrounded by supporters, he left.[38]

The protest was courageous to the point of foolhardiness, although not out of character for a man who had repeatedly told those close to him that he would prefer to die taking risks than 'watch [life] pass by from my window'. Whatever his prior hesitations, the Rubicon had now been crossed.[39]

From then on, Mitterrand and his colleagues were suspect. In the autumn, a roguish aristocrat named Georges Dobrowolsky, who had been with him at Ziegenhain and subsequently joined the prisoners' movement in Vichy, was arrested at the Spanish border. Interrogated by the Gestapo about the RNPG's activities, 'Dobro' remained silent. He was shot.[40] Some weeks later, Mitterrand's former flatmate, Serge Miller, was arrested in Paris. He, too, refused to talk and was sent to a concentration camp.[41] It was clear to all of them that it was only a matter of time before the net closed around the movement's leaders.

Meanwhile in Algiers, the struggle between de Gaulle and Giraud was coming to a head. The Gaullists began systematically absorbing and, where that was not possible, marginalising the forces the Giraudists had controlled. It was time for Mitterrand's movement to broaden its ties beyond the ORA and build bridges to de Gaulle's representatives. In Paris, Maurice Pinot met d'Astier, the head of Libération, who was about to leave for Algiers.[42] Mitterrand contacted de Chalvron at Super-NAP and Frenay's associates, Claude Bourdet and Pascal Copeau.

During this time his old adversary, Michel Cailliau, had not been idle. He had spent part of the summer in London, where he had met Colonel

Passy, the head of the Gaullist intelligence service, the BCRA (Bureau Central de Renseignements et d'Action), and registered the MRPGD as a prisoners' resistance organisation under the name the 'Charette Network', which ensured that, after the war, its members would have the status and benefits accorded to the Free French armed forces. Then he went to Algiers, where he stayed as de Gaulle's guest. By the time he returned to France in October 1943, he felt certain he had convinced the General that his own movement, the 'Charette Network', was the only one worth dealing with, and that Pin'–Mitt', as he called it, was anti-Gaullist, devoted to Pétain and 'waiting to see which way the wind blew'. Mitterrand, he told his uncle, was a collaborationist, wedded to the extreme Right. He was clever and untrustworthy.

Two weeks after Cailliau's return, Mitterrand joined Maurice Pinot and Védrine at the farm near Bellegarde-en-Marche where they had met to discuss strategy in February. It was the weekend of Halloween.

They agreed to reinforce the clandestine network which Bénet and Védrine had been setting up among the Mutual Aid Centres and to start an underground newspaper, *l'Homme libre* ('The Free Man'), named after the nationalist journal which Georges Clemenceau had founded before the First World War. But the main business at hand was the despatch of an envoy to de Gaulle. Pinot wanted to send Marcel Haedrich. But Mitterrand insisted that he had a better chance of winning the General's ear and Barrois and Bénet agreed. Nominally the movement's leadership remained collegial, but Pinot, the oldest and most influential among them, preferred to remain in the background. Insensibly, the others began to accept Mitterrand as their chief.

'I am lying in wait for the future,' he exulted in a letter to Marie-Claire Sarrazin. 'I am getting ready, body and soul, to make my entrance into the century . . . There are men who believe in me, and I am afraid for them. I believe in no one, and that makes me afraid for myself. But the path is inspiring.' To André Bettencourt, whom he met shortly afterwards in Paris, he spoke of the need to 'get oneself credentials' so as to be able to 'do something once the war is over'.[43] It was one of a series of remarks that summer and autumn which suggested that his political ambitions were becoming keener. He evidently saw the journey to meet de Gaulle as a step in that direction.

At that moment, however, other more urgent concerns intervened.

That weekend the Gestapo raided the workshop producing false papers which had been set up in Vichy eighteen months earlier by Barrois and Roussel. Neither was present, but four other members of the group were arrested and sent to Germany, where two died in concentration camps. A week later, on November 11, the Gestapo made a second raid, this time on the house in the rue Nationale where Mitterrand had been living. The landlord, Jean Renaud, and Pol Pilven, who was occupying Mitterrand's room while he was away, were both arrested and deported. Renaud died in a camp; Pilven survived. Jean Munier, who was also there when the Germans arrived, climbed out of a second-floor window, slid down a drainpipe and fled through a neighbour's courtyard. Ginette, the secretary, hid in a cupboard which no one bothered to search. Munier warned his colleagues in the ORA, and Colonel Pfister's wife, Fanny, hurried to the station where Mitterrand was arriving from Paris that afternoon. On the platform, the Gestapo, too, were waiting. 'I was just getting out of my carriage when I recognised [her],' Mitterrand remembered. 'She pretended to bump into me and pushed me back inside. "Don't get out, don't get out!", she whispered. "The Gestapo are here."'[44]

On the night of Monday, November 15 1943, accompanied by Colonel Pierre du Passage, the head of ORA liaison between the Southern and Northern Zones, Mitterrand took off in a single-engined Lysander from a pick-up point, which the RAF had code-named 'Indigestion', in a field in the commune of Soucelles, near Angers, 200 miles west of Paris. Before leaving he had had two meetings with General Revers, now the ORA supremo following the arrest of General Frère. For both of them, the overriding question was how the Giraudists and their allies would fit into the new scheme of things, now that de Gaulle was in sole charge.

When they landed at Tangmere in Kent, Mitterrand and du Passage were met by Captain Lejeune of the ORA, with whom they stayed at his residence-cum-office in Devonshire Close, a quiet mews between Regent's Park and Broadcasting House, the headquarters of the BBC.[45] After initial debriefings, they were received on November 23 by Colonel Maurice Buckmaster, the legendary head of the French section of the SOE, who noted on his report that they were both from 'a Giraudist organisation in France'. Mitterrand was described as being 'concerned with the military aspect of the organisation and also with . . . prisoners of war'. According to the minutes,

> He did not say much during the interrogation, as [du Passage] answered most of the questions . . . However, he travelled a great deal both in the [Northern] Zone and in the [Southern] Zone, living intermittently at Vichy. He changed his address frequently, staying at one place only a day and never longer than a week [so that] . . . the Germans would never catch up with him. A week ago, the Gestapo visited the address he had just left . . . He . . . cannot give any specific reason why . . . The Gestapo know his real name, but he hopes they have not got his description. He states that all regular officers and NCOs [among the PoWs] are at the disposal of the clandestine army and may be sent to whichever group requires them at any moment.[46]

Part of the interrogation was taken up with discussion of the relations between Giraudists and Gaullists. Du Passage, speaking for both of them, assured Buckmaster that their movement was loyal to Giraud not in person but as the French army's commander-in-chief, and 'if de Gaulle were to become C-in-C tomorrow, it would be to him that they would give their allegiance'.

Mitterrand was more forthcoming at a meeting at the end of that week with Jean Warisse, the London representative of Henri Frenay, whom de Gaulle had recently appointed as Commissioner for Prisoners of War and Deportees.

He told Warisse that he was in London on behalf of 'a movement directed solely at escaped and repatriated prisoners of war'. It was led by a 'Committee of Five', comprising himself; his deputy, Marcel Barrois; Maurice Pinot, who 'having broken off all contact with Vichy is now living in hiding in Paris'; Jacques Bénet, in charge of propaganda in the Northern Zone; and Jean Munier, who dealt with arms and parachute drops.[47] They had groups in fifty-two *départements* – including 300 men in Nice, 350 in Clermont-Ferrand, 75 in the Ardèche – and were in contact with twenty PoW camps in Germany. Besides opposing attempts by Vichy to take control of the prisoners' movement, he said, all its members were 'at the disposal of the Resistance'.

As in his account to Buckmaster, Mitterrand gilded the truth. But de Gaulle's staff in London was accustomed to Resistance envoys embellishing their activities when they came to seek recognition and support. Michel Cailliau had done the same three months earlier and had trashed Mitterrand personally for good measure. Mitterrand did not respond ad hominem, but told Warisse that Cailliau's movement 'was based only on an overactive imagination', which was unfair – Cailliau's movement, despite the eccentricities of its leader, was a serious organisation with networks in several parts of France – but less unfair than the invective which Cailliau had levelled at 'Pin' Mitt'. Mitterrand said he wanted to go to Algiers to allow Frenay to verify his claims and to 'resolve the question of the Charette Network' because 'there is no room in France for two prisoners' movements, the more so since there is only one which exists in reality'.[48] He added that his own movement had no wish to become politicised. It had decided to join the Resistance 'without asking whether that Resistance depended on de Gaulle, on Giraud or whichever other leader'.

On Saturday, November 27, the same day that Mitterrand met Warisse, de Gaulle issued a decree in Algiers ordering the Giraudist and Gaullist special services to merge. Colonel Passy remained head of the BCRA, now renamed the BRAL, the London Bureau for Intelligence and Action, which henceforth incorporated Lejeune's operation. Mitterrand, who had held the Giraudist rank of commandant, found himself promoted, through no effort of his own, as a Gaullist *chargé de mission*, 1st class (equivalent to captain).[49] Two days later, at Frenay's request, Passy gave instructions for him to proceed to Algiers, where he arrived on December 3. Shortly afterwards – neither he nor Frenay could remember the exact date – the new Commissioner for Prisoners of War escorted him into the presence of de Gaulle. Mitterrand left divergent accounts of the meeting. But the one he wished to be remembered was given a few months before his death:

I can see him now, seated in his chair, his big hands hanging down as though he did not know what to do with them. He stood up, greeted me without formality, rather relaxed, even affable. His first remark took me aback a little: 'So you came aboard an English plane' . . . We talked about the prisoners of war. De Gaulle attached great importance to propaganda in the PoW camps and to the action of those who escaped once they returned to France. The return of one and a half million prisoners [when the war ended] would pose problems which needed to be studied without delay. The priority, in his view, was to unify the three rival [prisoners'] movements: my movement, the RNPG . . . Cailliau's movement, the MRPGD . . . and the [communist] CNPG, the National Committee for Prisoners of War . . . It was he who first revealed to me the existence of a communist organisation . . . I pointed out to him that a movement like the one I was leading, made up entirely of escaped prisoners, knew the Germans better than others and was the only one which was properly structured . . . I told him that in my view, Michel Cailliau was not able to take charge of something of this importance . . . He wouldn't listen to my arguments and told me in conclusion: 'You have to accept. Our parachute drops, financial aid, military aid, everything depends on that.' [I said that] I accepted unity, but not the designation of [Cailliau] as leader.[50]

In retrospect it is clear that de Gaulle was testing him. At one point, like d'Astier and Bourdet earlier, he asked Mitterrand, 'Why a resistance movement for prisoners? Why not for hairdressers or cooks?' But he already knew the answer, and in any case his main concern was that there be not three prisoners' movements but one. Frenay, who had been won over by Mitterrand's intelligence, had paved the way. Now the General, too, recognised that this young man was leadership material – tricky, no doubt; difficult to control; and no more subservient than he was himself, but leadership material all the same. The fact that Mitterrand was a Giraudist was not the disadvantage it might seem, for the Giraudists were precisely the people that the General wanted to win to his side. Nor was he blind to the defects of his nephew, Michel Cailliau, for a man who hated his rivals so fiercely would never be able to unite them. Cailliau in the end was hoist by his own petard: he had so vilified Mitterrand that he put himself out of the race.

The issue of Mitterrand's attitude to Vichy, which Cailliau had made his main angle of attack, turned out not to be a problem. De Gaulle had already accepted into his ranks other men who had been far more deeply involved in the Pétainist regime than Mitterrand ever was. At the end of 1943 he was starting to look ahead to the time, once the war was over, when national reconciliation and healing would be the order of the day. Frenay would write later that winter:

[As regards Mitterrand's] sentiments towards the policies of Vichy . . . he himself saw General de Gaulle and . . . had a long and extremely frank discussion with him. The latter . . . was perfectly informed about Mitterrand's conduct . . . I will sum up [Mitterrand's] position, which is also my own. The whole drama of France has been that, for a time, honest men, with no ulterior motive, believed in Marshal Pétain and placed their confidence in him. No doubt they were deceived, but they were deceived sincerely, and if they were mistaken, one cannot hold that against them as a crime . . . As [we all] know, the immense majority of French people put their confidence in Pétain at one time or another. Systematically rejecting them will lead only in the final analysis to [our own] isolation.[51]

Nonetheless, it was a bruising encounter. De Gaulle was twice Mitterrand's age. When he had flown to London from France three and a half years before, he had had nothing but the clothes he stood up in and his own indomitable will. From that he had created a movement which would ensure that France had a place among the victorious allies and the status, after the war ended, of one of the world's five great powers. It was an astonishing achievement, which had required standing up to the combined pressures of Churchill, Roosevelt and Stalin. Small wonder that Mitterrand said afterwards that he had found de Gaulle's demeanour chilling.

The upshot was that the General, with Frenay's encouragement, came down on Mitterrand's side. Cailliau was informed in January 1944 that he had been named, together with Mitterrand and Bénet, to a three-man collegial leadership which would bring the prisoners' movements into a single unified organisation. Since Mitterrand, with Bénet's backing, had the majority, he would hold power. The same month, as an imprimatur of de Gaulle's approval, his spokesman, Maurice Schumann, broadcast on the BBC a glowing account of Mitterrand's intervention against Masson at the Salle Wagram the previous summer, which, without naming him, described him as a 'valiant patriot' who had exemplified the 'prisoner spirit' against 'the minister of Anti-France'.[52]

This first meeting between Mitterrand and de Gaulle left traces on both sides.

If de Gaulle was already thinking of post-war France and what would need to be done there, so was Mitterrand. 'There is a country to be remade,' he enthused to his friend, Georges Dayan, whom he had met again in Algiers that winter.[53] The General was too good a judge of men not to recognise the younger man's ambition.

Mitterrand, for his part, had mixed feelings about the leader of the Free French. Later he would acknowledge having felt deep admiration for de Gaulle's courage at that time: 'His tenacity in resisting the domination of Churchill and Roosevelt and preserving the rights of France has remained for me the model of political firmness. This was the moment at which he was greatest.'

However, he resented bitterly the way de Gaulle had seized control of the Resistance, and claimed to have told him at their meeting that those fighting inside France had their own rules and did not 'simply carry out orders from outside'. One may wonder whether he actually said that to the General's face but he certainly thought it. Like Frenay, he felt that the major part of de Gaulle's influence outside France came from the Resistance, which the General had played no part in initiating and from which he was now trying to appropriate credit and prestige.* Frenay had given up trying to maintain his movement's independence and rallied to the General's side, as had Emmanuel d'Astier de la Vigerie. In November, the two most turbulent, and politically threatening, non-communist Resistance chiefs had both

* Beginning in the summer of 1940, small resistance groups formed spontaneously in different parts of France. A year later, after Germany attacked Russia, communist networks developed. The British SOE provided the only outside support at first and remained the main source of finance and arms until France was liberated. De Gaulle's Free French in London had little contact with the Resistance until the winter of 1941, when Jean Moulin was sent to France with a mandate to unify the movements under Gaullist leadership. Moulin faced considerable hostility. Most resistance fighters accepted de Gaulle as a symbol, even as a commander, but not as a political leader. The General's aides made matters worse by trying to micromanage resistance activities from London. The first chief of the Armée Secrète, General Delestraint, was an orthodox soldier who, like de Gaulle himself, had little understanding of what running a resistance movement entailed. Moulin, in his efforts to impose London's control, threatened to withhold weapons shipments and finance from recalcitrant organisations. Ill feeling was at a peak in the summer of 1943, when, in June, shortly after successfully establishing the National Resistance Council, Moulin was arrested by the Gestapo. He died two weeks later, having remained silent despite severe torture. It was never established whether he was betrayed by one of his opponents within the Resistance and, if so, by whom; by an informer with other motives; or whether his capture was the result of a successful German intelligence operation.

been given posts as Commissioners, which meant they were safely in Algiers under de Gaulle's watchful eye – 'neutralised', as Mitterrand put it. He did not wish to be in that position himself.[54] For decades afterwards, he grumbled about the way de Gaulle had hijacked the Resistance for his own ends.[55]

> Our resistance, on French territory, in ceaseless contact with torture and death, was of a different order to the resistance from outside. I did not accept the pre-eminence that the latter arrogated to itself. I did not agree that the term, Resistance, should be applied to the battle waged from London and Algiers, which was an episode of traditional warfare . . . I was proud of a combat whose glory . . . has been confiscated from the people of whom I was one.

In 1981, when he finally came to power, he said he wanted to make it a priority to set the record straight. Others demurred, pointing out that there were more pressing tasks, and he did not insist. But it continued to rankle with him until the end of his life.

De Gaulle had decided that Mitterrand was the most capable leader for a new, united prisoners' movement. Frenay had made clear his personal support, telling colleagues that 'without [Mitterrand] the tasks given me by the National Liberation Committee risk not being fulfilled'. But when it came to getting him back to France, none of that seemed to help.

Whether because of the residual paranoia between Gaullists and Giraudists, or the venom distilled by Michel Cailliau, who continued to believe that he could sabotage Mitterrand's ascendancy, or, more likely, a combination of both, he found it impossible to obtain a place on a plane out of Algiers. Subverting government directives is not uniquely a French pastime, but, even in times of war, French officials take a delight in it which puts other nations to shame. Cailliau had urged his uncle to find Mitterrand a post in the army, so as to keep him away from France. Cailliau's friends on the General's staff imagined sending him to the Italian front. But no instruction came from de Gaulle and the plan was abandoned.[56] Mitterrand told a British journalist, Alastair Forbes of the *Daily Mail*, with whom he struck up an acquaintance, that he was 'disgusted by the idiotic witch-hunts and sectarianism' which he found in North Africa and could not wait to get home because there, at least, the word 'Gaullist' simply meant a good Frenchman, not 'an *appellation contrôlée*' with all kinds of purity tests.

In desperation, a few days after Christmas, Mitterrand sought help from a family friend, Commandant Ernoul de la Chénelière, who was a member of Giraud's staff. As he was explaining his predicament, Giraud himself walked in.

> He had a justified reputation as a magnificent warrior [Mitterrand wrote] . . . but once you took away the heroic images of . . . his escape from Koenigstein, suspended from a 12-metre rope,. . . his falsetto voice and tapering moustache, which seemed to be stuck on with glue, gave him the quaint, almost unreal, look of a soldier out of an illustrated magazine from before 1914.[57]

On learning of his visitor's difficulties, Giraud exclaimed: 'I'm not surprised. The only thing those people from London understand is playing politics.' Mitterrand thanked him. But if he had had any lingering doubts, he knew now that 'this cavalry officer, whose horse thought more clearly than he did' would never be a match for de Gaulle.

Next day, with Giraud's help, he was on a flight to Marrakesh. There he stayed with the music hall star, Josephine Baker, who had been attached since the outbreak of the war to the Giraudist special services under Colonel Paillole. She lived in a fairy-tale palace, furnished in Moorish style with richly decorated cedar-wood ceilings, which belonged to Sidi Mohamed ben Mennebi, the son of the former Grand Vizier. Paillole's people had good relations with the SOE, and on New Year's Day Mitterrand found himself aboard an RAF plane taking General Montgomery back to Britain, where, after his victory over Rommel at El Alamein, he was to take command of Allied ground forces for the invasion of Normandy the following summer.[58]

In London Mitterrand stayed once more with Captain Lejeune at the old Giraudist headquarters in Devonshire Close, before moving in February to the Mount Royal Hotel, a palatial art deco building in Bryanston Street near Marble Arch, where Frenay usually put up. He was provided with a 7.65mm automatic and trained in its use at an SOE firing range in Baker Street. He also took lessons in parachute jumping in case the British should send him back that way. But nothing seemed to help: his return was blocked. In the middle of the month, Frenay flew from Algiers to join him. While Mitterrand spent his evenings playing bridge with Colonel Passy and other Gaullist luminaries, Frenay fretted that his protégé had been kicking his heels for six weeks when he should have been at work in France. 'I ask you to do everything possible,' he told d'Astier's representative in London, 'so that [Mitterrand's] departure be given priority.' Still nothing happened. Cailliau was fighting to stave off the inevitable and his friends in London were doing what they could to help.

In the end it was the British who came to Mitterrand's aid. On the night of Saturday, February 26, he embarked at Dartmouth on Coastal Forces Motor Gunboat 502, which was assigned to SOE missions ferrying Resistance operatives to and from France.[59] They passed the German convoy route without incident and hove to about a mile off Bonaparte Beach near the Breton village of Beg an Fry, 50 miles west of St Malo. The beach was defended by a German 75mm gun emplacement and a heavy machine-gun nest. Mitterrand and two others took their places in a 14-foot rubber dinghy and, with two British sailors rowing, set out in the darkness for the shore.[60] He remembered afterwards 'what a lot of noise oars can make, splashing in the dark'. But no one heard. They were met by a local fisherman, who made them supper and then drove them in his van along the coast to Morlaix, where Mitterrand took a train to Paris.

On arrival at Montparnasse station, in the southern part of the city, he was walking along the platform when, as he later recounted, he was stopped by a French police control. 'Open your bag,' he was ordered. Wondering which would be the best way to run, he slowly did as he was told. As well as personal effects, the suitcase contained letters from Frenay, a cyanide pill, and on top of his pyjamas, the 7.65mm automatic. The policeman took one look and snapped: 'This is a check for black-market food. Now get the hell out of here!'[61]

In the three and a half months that Mitterrand had been away, much had changed in France. As resistance activity had increased, the Gestapo had stepped up reprisals against the civilian population. The Milice, under Joseph Darnand, who replaced René Bousquet as secretary-general of the police, had become a law unto itself, carrying out arbitrary executions and massacres. In January 1944, Darnand was given ministerial rank and entered the government, together with Philippe Henriot and, later, Marcel Déat, whose Nazi sympathies made even a man like Laval seem patriotic by comparison. Hitler turned up the heat on Vichy, demanding that it participate directly in the fight against the Allies. Pétain and Laval refused, but feared that France, after the example of Norway, would be placed under a Quisling-like figure heading a Nazi puppet government. The Compulsory Work Service (STO, or Service de Travail Obligatoire), introduced a year before at the Germans' insistence to requisition young Frenchmen to compensate for the labour shortage in Germany, had caused some 200,000 young men to go into hiding, of whom about a quarter had made their way to the *maquis*.

The prospect of German defeat intensified the spiral of hatred and fear.

The Resistance was galvanised by the thought of victory and revenge. The Germans and their French sympathisers responded by sowing terror.

During Mitterrand's absence Munier had worked to develop the movement's paramilitary capacities. Through the *maquis* in Burgundy, he had acquired a stock of arms which he succeeded in transporting to a cache in the suburbs of Paris.[62] In December, after the raids on the RNPG in Vichy, he had shot dead the chief of the local Milice. Munier's colleague, Jacques Pâris, who had been sent the previous year for training in resistance techniques with the ORA in North Africa, had blown up a railway depot in the Ardèche, south of Lyon, and was reconnoitring new parachute drop zones and training *maquis-ards* to man them.

Not all the news was positive. Towards the end of January, Antoine Mauduit, the founder of 'the Chain', was betrayed by an informer and arrested. One of Mitterrand's first acts after his return was to send Munier to Marseille, where Mauduit was imprisoned, to see if a rescue was possible. It was not. Soon afterwards Mauduit was transferred to Buchenwald, together with Guy Fric, the RNPG leader in Clermont-Ferrand, who had been detained in February. Fric survived the war. Mauduit died on May 9 1945, the day after the Allied victory.[63]

Mitterrand's priority, however, remained the fusion of the three prisoners' organisations that had been decided in Algiers.

Michel Cailliau, he discovered, had again been manoeuvring behind the scenes. In his absence, Cailliau had tried to persuade Bénet and Marcel Barrois to agree to a merger under his own leadership in the hope of presenting Mitterrand (and also the General) with a fait accompli. When that failed, he sought to use the communist group, the CNPG, whose formation, it later transpired, he had himself encouraged the previous summer, to dilute his rival's influence.[64]

But Cailliau had reckoned without Henri Frenay.[65] In a series of increasingly exasperated telegrams the Commissioner insisted that what had been decided in Algiers 'cannot be modified'. Mitterrand was to be in charge of the prisoners' movement in France; Bénet of propaganda, Mutual Aid Centres and returnees' welfare; and Cailliau, everything connected with the PoW camps in Germany, notably intelligence, sabotage, and measures to maintain prisoners' morale.

By the time Mitterrand returned at the end of February, Cailliau had run out of arguments.

On March 12 1944, a Sunday, delegates from the three movements met in an artist's studio near Port Royal, in the Latin Quarter,[66] under the chairmanship of Antoine Avinin, one of the founders of Franc-Tireur, representing the National Resistance Council. Mitterrand and Bénet represented the RNPG, and Robert Paumier, the communists. Cailliau did not attend. Mortified by his rival's success, he sent in his place Philippe Dechartre, accompanied by Jacques Bourgeois, the head of the MRPGD in the Northern Zone. Mitterrand, who spoke first, questioned Paumier's right to be there, arguing that his group, the CNPG, was 'unknown in London and Algiers', and that de Gaulle had asked him to merge his movement with Cailliau's, 'not with [the Communists]' (which was bending the truth but a good line of attack). Dechartre, supported by Avinin, backed Paumier's candidacy, and Mitterrand – as he had no doubt expected – was forced to give way.

The Executive Committee of the new unified movement, to be known as the MNPGD, the National Movement of Prisoners of War and Deportees, comprised Mitterrand, Bénet, Dechartre and Paumier, which deprived Mitterrand's group of its built-in majority. To that extent Cailliau's rearguard action had succeeded. But it was a hollow victory. Mitterrand remained first among equals and could usually count on Dechartre's support. The following day Cailliau announced his withdrawal from the movement and left for North Africa. To the end of his life he never understood why his uncle had preferred Mitterrand and died, in 2000, a still-embittered man.

The MNPGD came under the authority of the National Resistance Council,[67] which meant that financially it was secure. It had a modest amount of weaponry. It was more united on paper than on the ground, but the struggles of the past year were over and its mission was now clearly defined: to mobilise the 600,000 returned prisoners behind de Gaulle's leadership for the insurrection that would accompany the coming battle for France. A tract that summer set out the movement's goals:

> Disorganise the enemy's communications. Sabotage the railways. Derail trains and cut the tracks. Hunt down the killers from Darnand's Milice who are massacring Frenchmen for the Boches. Disorganise the enemy's [economic] production and use force to stop the deportation of French workers to Germany.
>
> Step up the armed struggle in all its forms against German army units . . .
>
> Civil servants, sabotage the orders of Vichy. Policemen, soldiers and gendarmes, come over to the patriots and bring with you your arms . . .
>
> Let there be no quarter for the murderers! . . . In all your meetings, everywhere . . . let the great voice of vengeance and justice ring out against the barbarous foreigner who wanted to enslave our land . . . Remember all the martyrs that the Boches have shot down, those patriots who died singing the Marseillaise and proclaiming their love for our France.
>
> Let nothing stop you in your thirst for vengeance and freedom![68]

Over the next three months, Mitterrand consolidated his authority. Although the movement's leadership remained officially collegial, Dechartre left for Algiers to seek additional funds and arms, which meant he was replaced by a less senior figure; Bénet accompanied him; and Paumier was also replaced, leaving Mitterrand the only one of the original four still in place.[69] Shortly afterwards he took direct control of the Northern Zone, with Munier and Pelat in charge of

military operations and a communist, Georges Thevenin, in Paris
(where the communists were so well organised that it made no sense
to name anyone else); while the South – the former Free Zone – was
entrusted to Etienne Gagnaire and Jacques Pâris.

Conditions, however, were becoming more and more dangerous.
'The beast that is being beaten to death is multiplying its terror,'
Paumier wrote.

Those who knew Mitterrand that spring were struck by his cold-
blooded recklessness. He wore a light-blue English suit, purchased in
London, at a time when anything English raised a red flag of suspicion.
He smoked English cigarettes, which had a distinctive, instantly recog-
nisable odour compared with the dark tobacco of Gauloises and
Gitanes. The writer, Marguerite Duras, found him 'carefree to the
point of folly'. 'Your courage was reasonable, careful and quite mad,'
she told him years later. 'It was as if . . . behaving almost suicidally
had become the true passion of your life.' François Terrasse, Marie-
Louise's brother, encountered him on the metro and felt his behaviour
was so provocative that he might be arrested any day. Philippe
Dechartre recalled: 'He had no nerves . . . He was at home in the
Resistance. He was in the place where he should be.'

Was he following the contrarian adage that the best way not to be
noticed is to stand out in a crowd? Or was it just his usual delight in
pushing his luck to the limit – the small boy at Touvent who would
put his finger within a millimetre of a forbidden object and claim he
was doing nothing wrong?

In his own way, Mitterrand was prudent. He frequently changed
his appearance and constantly changed his address, staying sometimes
with friends from his Jarnac days – with Jean Bouvyer, the one-time
follower of the Cagoule, who was living with Mitterrand's sister,
Marie-Josèphe; or with Jean's mother, Antoinette – at others with
Marguerite Duras and the *ménage à trois* which she maintained with
her husband, the writer, Robert Antelme, and her lover, Dionys
Mascolo, at their apartment in the rue Dupin. Mitterrand had met
Antelme and his friend, Georges Beauchamp, shortly before his journey
to London, when Jacques Bénet had brought him to Paris to meet
Resistance contacts. Beauchamp quickly became a trusted member
of his inner circle. Other hideouts were provided by Patrice Pelat's
girlfriend, Christine Gouze, whose family in Burgundy, unbeknown

to Mitterrand at the time, had been sheltering Henri Frenay when they had first met near Mâcon, what seemed like a century ago.

But no matter what he did, the Gestapo was closing in.

In April 1944, Marcel Barrois, Mitterrand's colleague from the Aid Centre in Vichy, who had deputised for him during his absence, was arrested and deported to Dachau. Three months later, along with more than 500 others, he died of suffocation and thirst, when SS guards refused to open the shuttered wagons of a train which was immobilised in temperatures of 40 degrees.

The Germans did not always have the upper hand.

Munier had a rendezvous in the Place St Michel with Michel Grilickès, a *maquisard* whose family had perished at the hands of the Nazis. Three Germans in civilian clothes got out of a police car and walked towards them. Without blinking, Grilickès shot all three dead and vanished into the crowd. Munier was awestruck. 'That was a boy,' he wrote later, 'possessed of a truly astonishing promptitude of attack.'

Not long afterwards, he and Mitterrand were at lunch with several others at a restaurant in Montparnasse when a German police patrol entered. Instead of asking for identity papers, as they usually did, they asked people at each table to identify each other. 'We [always] called each other by code names,' Mitterrand explained. 'They had realised that we never knew the "real" names figuring on each other's identity cards – a necessary precaution in the event of arrest and torture.' The group was about to be exposed when Munier produced a document which stopped the police in their tracks. It was an *ausweis*, a military pass, in the name of Jean Munier, signed by Adolf Hitler in person. They saluted and left.

Munier explained afterwards how it had come into his possession. In August 1942, he had been working in a *kommando* in Kassel when the city was bombed by the Allies, leaving many hundreds injured. He and another prisoner had seized the opportunity to escape. As they were making their way out of the city, they heard a woman's moans coming from the debris of a ruined building. They stopped and dug her out of the rubble, together with her baby. By then it was too late to flee. However, when German soldiers arrived to recapture them, the local townspeople said they were heroes and demanded that they be released. For some weeks, nothing happened. Then, one day, Munier was summoned by the head of his *kommando* and presented to 'a highly decorated officer', who told him that the woman they had rescued was the wife of one of Hitler's staff officers. They were to be repatriated immediately, 'by order of the Führer'.

It was, Mitterrand said, 'literally a magic paper'.[70]

But miracles could not happen every time. On June 1, the Executive Committee of the MNPGD convened at Jean Bertin's apartment in the Avenue Charles Floquet, not far from the Eiffel Tower. During the meeting, the doorbell rang. When Bertin came out, the visitor put a revolver to his chest and told him he was being taken for questioning. The others escaped through a ground-floor window. During his interrogation, it became clear that the Germans had mistaken him for Mitterrand, whom they knew only under the *nom de guerre*, Morland. He was deported to Buchenwald.

That same evening, another meeting was to be held at Marguerite Duras's flat in the rue Dupin. She was absent, but Robert Antelme, his sister Marie-Louise, and two other volunteers were there. Munier arrived early and chatted to them for a while. But he was uneasy. 'I felt something was wrong,' he said later, 'and I decided to leave.' On the street outside, a man in gold-rimmed spectacles demanded to see his papers. Munier punched him in the face and ran. The street was blocked by two police cars, with a German officer standing between them. 'Before he had time to react, I hurled myself on top of him, thrust him violently aside, and left my pursuers behind.' Munier found Pelat and together they telephoned Duras's apartment to warn them that the Gestapo was outside. An unfamiliar voice answered. Mitterrand, meanwhile, had been waiting for Robert Antelme at the Brasserie Lipp, ten minutes' walk away on the Boulevard St Germain. When he did not appear, he, too, telephoned the apartment and got the same unfamiliar voice. Antelme and his three companions were arrested and sent to concentration camps.

Next day, Munier and Grilickès recovered one of the movement's arms caches and a stock of false papers from another supposedly safe house nearby, minutes before the Gestapo arrived. Dionys Mascolo returned to the rue Dupin and while the writer, Albert Camus, kept watch outside, took the movement's archives from their hiding place, which the Germans had failed to discover, and concealed them among piles of authors' manuscripts at the office of Camus's publisher, Gallimard. A week later, Munier and Pierre Steverlynck, who ran the underground printing shop which produced the movement's tracts, walked into a Gestapo ambush. Steverlynck was wounded and died in hospital four days later. Munier got away.

After the Normandy landings on June 4 1944, the pressure intensified further.

Pierre Coursol, who had succeeded Marcel Barrois at the Aid Centre in Vichy, was interrogated about Mitterrand's whereabouts and severely tortured. At the beginning of July it was the turn of Henry Guerin, a close friend of Bernard de Chalvron of Super-NAP, who had been arrested some weeks before. Guerin had been Maurice Pinot's representative in the Occupied Zone and had resigned with him in January 1943. He, too, was asked about Mitterrand's activities. His Gestapo interrogators were brutes, he remembered, and after beating his backside raw, subjected him to what would later be called 'water-boarding'. 'The bath was full of excrement and other kinds of filth,' he wrote later. 'One of them had a stethoscope to check your heart, and when he thought you couldn't take any more they got you out.'* In August he was deported to Dora, a sub-camp of Buchenwald.

The succession of raids and arrests convinced Mitterrand that there were traitors in the movement. His suspicions fell on Jacques Bourgeois, the former head of Cailliau's network in the Northern Zone, and his deputy, Albert Médina. They both had artistic backgrounds, not a typical profile for members of the Resistance – Bourgeois had been a music critic; Médina was an actor – and shared a flat near the vast white basilica of Sacré Coeur which dominates Montmartre. The evidence against them was circumstantial and came in part from Marguerite Duras, then engaged in an ambiguous relationship with a French Gestapo agent named Charles Delval, who had told her that he would free her husband if she would lead him to Mitterrand. Delval had taken part in the raids on June 1 and appeared well informed about the movement. Duras had deflected his overtures but, on Mitterrand's instructions, continued to see him in the hope that he

---

* Guerin nevertheless noted a detail suggesting a difference in attitude between Nazi interrogators and Americans in the same line of work sixty years later. When the ordeal was over, one of his torturers, 'a fat fellow with a round face, said to me in German, "Well done. You didn't talk.", and gave me a glass of brandy and a packet of French cigarettes.'

would reveal his sources.[71] By the end of July, Mitterrand had concluded that Bourgeois and Médina would have to be liquidated on the grounds that even if they were not traitors, they had neglected elementary security and, by their imprudence, were putting lives at risk.

At that point, the military situation abruptly changed. For six weeks after the Normandy landings, the Allied armies had made slow progress against determined German defences. In the last week of July, they broke through. Hitler refused to authorise a retreat, and by the weekend of August 12, the German Seventh Army was bottled up near the town of Malaise. Three days later, French, American and British troops began landing in Provence.

In Paris that was the signal for a wave of strikes: over the next 72 hours, the staff of the metro, railwaymen, postmen, gendarmes and police stopped work. Newspapers ceased to appear. The German-controlled state radio fell silent.

The city's population sensed that after four years of occupation, freedom – and vengeance – were at hand. The atmosphere became electric. Alexandre Parodi, de Gaulle's chief representative in France, who had come secretly to Paris from Algiers in April, worried that a premature insurrection would end in a bloodbath if the outnumbered but better-armed Germans used massive force against it – a Stalingrad in reverse, leaving the city in ruins before the Allied armies arrived. Although he did not know it, those were indeed Hitler's orders, and an SS division had been despatched to ensure that they were carried out. On August 17, a Thursday, Parodi met the National Resistance Council to see whether they could hold off the uprising which was threatening to erupt on all sides. They realised that it was impossible. Paris was about to explode.

The previous spring de Gaulle had decreed the formation of a provisional government to take charge until the members of the National Liberation Committee could arrive from Algiers. At Frenay's suggestion he had named Mitterrand secretary-general for Prisoners of War and Deportees. On Friday afternoon, the fifteen members of this new body were summoned to receive Parodi's instructions.[72] But events were already running ahead of them. That morning a general strike had been proclaimed. Without waiting for instructions, Colonel Henri Rol-Tanguy, the regional chief of Franc-Tireurs et Partisans, whom Parodi had appointed to lead the insurrection, plastered the city with posters calling for general mobilisation.

Mitterrand and the others were told not to take control of their ministries, still staffed by Vichy officials, until the uprising began.

But on Saturday morning they heard machine-gun fire coming from the Place de la Concorde. Without waiting for the signal, a group of partisans had occupied the Préfecture de Police. Men in shirtsleeves wielding axes cut the trees lining the boulevards to erect barricades against German tanks.

In the afternoon, the Germans counter-attacked. Mitterrand and Jean Munier were caught in crossfire in the Latin Quarter when a German troop transport tried to force a roadblock on the Boulevard St Michel. Soon afterwards, four of Munier's men were captured by the Germans in a firefight and taken to the Gare du Nord to be shot. Three managed to escape; the fourth was executed. That evening an MNPGD detachment occupied the Prisoners' Bureau in the Place de Clichy in the north-west of Paris, which Mitterrand made his temporary headquarters.

The following day, Sunday, they took over half a dozen other buildings which had been used as offices by the Vichy Commissariat of Prisoners of War and therefore fell under Mitterrand's responsibility, including the Commissariat itself, in the rue Meyerbeer, a side street next to the Opera. André Pernin, a print worker who accompanied Mitterrand to the Commissioner's first-floor office, remembered him entering with a drawn pistol. The incumbent, Robert Moreau, a civil servant of the old school who had reluctantly accepted the job after Masson's resignation, stood up politely and asked how he could help. "You can go," Mitterrand replied. The Commissioner, very calmly, tried to open a negotiation. "Sir, there is nothing to talk about," Mitterrand told him. "This is the revolution! You will have to give up your place."'

The Commissariat was a hundred yards from the *Kommandantur*, the German Military Command headquarters, which was protected by rolls of barbed wire, spiked wooden barriers and several tanks stationed outside. Munier posted six well-armed men outside and Mitterrand started work as a minister with two boxes of Molotov cocktails on the floor beside his desk in case the building should be attacked.

For several days, the situation remained on a knife-edge. Unknown to the insurrection's leaders, Eisenhower and General Omar Bradley had decided to bypass Paris in order not to slow down their advance. The recapture of the city was not planned until October. Parodi sent couriers to Mitterrand and the other secretaries-general, telling them to do nothing which might draw the Germans' attention to the buildings they were occupying. When the insurrectional government met at the Prime Minister's office, the Hôtel Matignon, he issued a formal instruction that they should lie low until the security situation clarified.

Mitterrand went to the ministry on his bicycle each day. Even as the skirmishes continued, normality returned:

> You saw the Germans in the streets. Tanks went by. From time to time shots rang out. It didn't stop people doing their shopping, there were queues for milk and bread. Then suddenly someone would open fire . . . People threw themselves on the ground. After a while life went on as before. In other quarters of Paris, not far away, you were not even aware there was fighting.[73]

Help came from an unlikely quarter. The Swedish consul, Raoul Nordling, persuaded the new German Military Governor, General von Choltitz, to agree to a truce. It was honoured only sporadically but allowed the Resistance to regroup and rearm. Von Choltitz knew that the war was lost, and when Hitler renewed his orders to blow the bridges across the Seine and unleash the maximum of destruction on the city, he ignored them. Even so, by the time the insurrection ended, some 2,800 Frenchmen and more than 3,000 Germans had been killed.

Meanwhile, on Tuesday morning, August 22, Colonel Rol-Tanguy sent emissaries to the Allies at Argentan, south of Caen, to say that more than half of Paris had been liberated, but without help the uprising might collapse.

While Eisenhower and Bradley hesitated, General Henri Leclerc, the French Commander of the 2nd Armoured Division, decided to force their hand. Eisenhower had promised de Gaulle that French troops would be the first to enter Paris. Without seeking authorisation from his American superior, General Gerow, Leclerc despatched a reconnaissance unit which covered the 150 miles to the capital in 48 hours, linking up with the Resistance and, on Thursday evening, occupying a position in front of the City Hall, where the National Resistance Council had established its base. Next morning, Leclerc's main force arrived to an ecstatic welcome from the beleaguered population, and in the afternoon von Choltitz signed the surrender at Montparnasse railway station.

In other ways, too, normal life was resuming. Patrice Pelat, at the head of a battalion of irregulars, commandeered the offices of a collaborationist journal and printing press. On Tuesday they had put out the first openly published issue of the MNPGD's clandestine newspaper, *l'Homme libre*. In a front-page editorial, Mitterrand set out his conception of the role which the prisoners had played:

> For three days, Paris has been fighting. For three days an army raised from each quarter, each street, has been hunting the invader and winning back the right to live . . . Victory . . . belongs to all those who pay for it, and pay dearly with their pain and their blood . . . In Germany, as in France, the PoWs have waged a struggle without mercy . . . They have made illustrious the word 'prisoner', which from this time on will never again mean giving up the fight. We must proclaim that from the rooftops . . . All over France, the prisoners of war, united in the same movement, have given meaning to the coming triumph. Captive sons of a captive country, dogs that people believed were being taken for a whipping, they are proving that when freedom is fiercely guarded as an inalienable right in the very depths of one's being, it contains in itself all victories.[74]

This was not mere rhetoric. Mitterrand understood, as did de Gaulle, who had been a prisoner in the First War, that the 1.5 million PoWs would assume national importance once the war was over. To most French people they were an embarrassment, a living reminder of a defeat which the country desperately wished to forget. To empower them, Mitterrand realised, it was necessary to change their image from that of agents of defeat to agents of victory.

Philippe Dechartre wrote admiringly later: 'He saw it straight off . . . If the mass of PoWs were absolved of their captivity by their [actions in the] Resistance, they would represent a [huge] political stake. To the rest of us, that never even crossed our minds . . . A handful of men who fought for the Resistance gave value to [the prisoners] as a whole. It gave [them] moral value.' By the end of the war, according to figures compiled by the Free French, the MNPGD armed detachments numbered 22,000 men, operating from command centres in Paris, Rouen in Normandy, Neussargues in the Massif Central and Nancy in the north-east. These men, Mitterrand wrote later, won citations for valour 'for slowing the Germans' withdrawal into Normandy; . . . for freeing a large part of the Aveyron [in the south of the Massif Central]; for fighting on the Plateau de Glières [in Savoy]; for conquering several valleys [above Nice] and in the Hautes Alpes [around Montmaur]'. The prisoners, he insisted, had been condemned for a military debacle that was not of their making. In August 1944, he was certain that his future would be bound up with theirs.

General de Gaulle had arrived in Normandy the previous weekend. He reached Paris on the afternoon of Friday, August 25, shortly after von Choltitz had signed the German surrender. That night, in a speech broadcast throughout France, he addressed the crowds gathered in front of the City Hall:

> Why should we hide the emotion that is catching at our throats, men and women, here in our own home, in Paris which today stands tall ? . . .
>
> Paris! Paris abused! Paris broken! Paris martyred! But Paris freed! Freed by its own efforts, freed by its people working together with the armies of France, with the support and assistance of the whole of France, of the France which fights, the only France, the true France, the eternal France . . .
>
> The enemy is tottering but not yet beaten . . . It will not be enough for us to have . . . chased him off our land . . . We want to enter his territory as we should, as victors . . . It is for that revenge, that vengeance and that justice that we will continue to fight until . . . complete and final victory.[75]

Mitterrand and two colleagues, together with other ministers and members of the National Resistance Council, led by Moulin's successor, Georges Bidault, stood behind him as he spoke. At one point, the crush in the room was such that de Gaulle, saluting the crowd from a balcony, was about to lose his balance. 'Stop pushing, stop pushing, for God's sake,' he cried. Mitterrand and Pierre de Chevigné, who later became Defence Minister, grabbed hold of the great man's legs and pulled him back inside.[76]

The General's speech that night offered a blueprint for the country's future. Between the lines, he was making two essential points: France would fight alongside its allies in order to have a place at the table when the victors divided the spoils; and the 'France that fights, the only France, the true France' would be the country's image once the war was over.

In this Gaullist reading of history, Vichy had been just a bad dream. The new priorities were reconciliation and national unity. When Georges Bidault suggested that he proclaim the restoration of the Republic, de Gaulle replied: 'The Republic never ceased to exist . . . Vichy was and remains null and void.' That was also Mitterrand's view. For the rest of his life, like de Gaulle, he rejected any suggestion that France should be held responsible for the misdeeds of the Vichy regime. It was a fiction, but a convenient one, and it enabled the country to move on, not being seriously questioned until those who had lived through those years had given place to a younger generation of leaders.

The following afternoon, de Gaulle went to the Arc de Triomphe to light the flame at the Tomb of the Unknown Soldier. Then, accompanied by the leaders of the Resistance and members of the provisional government, he walked down the Champs-Elysées, acclaimed by delirious crowds.

On Sunday morning, August 27, the General chaired the one and only Cabinet meeting held before the arrival of the titular government from Algiers. Alexandre Parodi presented the fifteen acting ministers lined up to greet him – Mitterrand, as the youngest, coming last. 'You again!' said de Gaulle, which, given that he was the one who had named him, was either a backhanded compliment or an ironic recognition that this minister was not like the others. That, at least, was how Mitterrand took it.[77] Years later, he recalled his feelings when de Gaulle began to speak:

I still have in my ears his monologue that day. I was listening, watching, admiring . . . Now that I have lived through other historic days, I have learnt to economise emotions of that kind. But then I was 27 years old, I had depths of enthusiasm and a propensity to magnify events. And I had reason to be wide-eyed: it was the beginning of an epoch, and it was General de Gaulle . . . Nobody spoke as he did the language of the State . . . De Gaulle didn't put matters in terms [of right or wrong]. He existed. His deeds created him . . . [To him] the motherland was a mystical soil, drawn by the hand of God and inhabited by a worker-soldier people. In its hours of peril, this land, made for that people, would naturally give forth the hero that it needed. This time, the hero was him.[78]

Henri Frenay and his colleagues arrived in Paris a week later.[79] It was a moment to which Mitterrand had not been looking forward. 'He had been hoping,' Frenay wrote later, 'that I would be appointed to other government functions and that he could become Minister for Prisoners, Deportees and Refugees . . . Obviously that hope was disappointed.' His first experience as a member of the government had lasted all of fifteen days. Frenay offered him the post of secretary-general at the ministry, which would have made him the top permanent official, but he declined. François Mitterrand, Frenay grumbled afterwards, harboured grander ambitions.[80]

4

Loose Ends, New Beginnings

In September 1944, Mitterrand, then in his late twenties, was still a bachelor. That was in large part due to his mortification at the hands of Marie-Louise Terrasse, which would influence his relationships with women for the remainder of his life. His colleagues at Vichy remembered her photograph, prominently displayed in his room, and in the winter of 1943, when he went to Algiers, his brother Jacques was astonished to find that he still kept her engagement ring, which he had pretended to throw into the River Seine, in his breast pocket.

That did not mean he had been celibate. At Vichy he had a long-running affair with his cousin, Marie-Claire Sarrazin, which helped him through his loss. 'I am not suffering,' he wrote to a friend, 'I am now able to love someone else.' In Algiers he found consolation in the arms of a young nurse, Louquette, the daughter of a senior Gaullist officer. But as Jacques put it, 'he wasn't yet cured'. For that, he needed to fall in love, or at least – here a nuance is necessary – to find a girl he could love and marry.

In wartime, when each day may be the last, emotions become more intense. Jean Munier and Mitterrand's secretary, Ginette, had married in February 1944 and Bernard Finifter soon after. Patrice Pelat was having a rapturous affair with Christine Gouze, whose apartment served as a meeting place for Mitterrand and members of his movement. It was there, in March, not long after his return from London, that he noticed on the piano a framed photograph of a young woman, Christine's sister, Danielle, then nineteen years old. Family legend has it that he declared forthwith, 'I shall marry her'.[1] Like most legends, it need not be taken literally, but it reflected an underlying truth: François was captivated by 'this girl with cat's eyes', as he called her, and, for the first time since breaking up with Marie-Louise, felt seriously attracted.

Danielle was quite different from his ex-fiancée. She was prettier, less sophisticated and, above all, wide-eyed and ingenuous. Perhaps that was what he had wanted all along.

Christine, ten years older than her sister, saw at once what was in the wind. 'I have a fiancé for you,' she told Danielle and arranged for her to come to Paris in April, during the Easter holidays, to meet this dashing young man who appeared so smitten with her.

As had happened with Marie-Louise, the first meeting did not go well. Danielle was a gauche adolescent whose idea of fun was bicycle rides in the country and romps with her dog, a golden-haired Briard named Mario. Men were not something she understood. Refusing her sister's entreaties to dress up and put on nylons for this first, supposedly romantic encounter, she wore her usual schoolgirl socks and, when François teased her, stammered, blushed, and, as she wrote later, 'ended up like an offended hedgehog'. He was definitely 'not the kind of boy to melt a teenage girl's heart'.

However, that night, after she and Christine got back home, François phoned to say he was coming over. There was a crisis: a safe house had been raided. As she watched him, working through the night with Pelat, Finifter and Jean Munier, she started to see him in a different light: 'totally in control of himself, a leader . . . All of them were amazingly calm, lucid, and efficient . . .' She was impressed and, at the same time, apprehensive.

In June, when the Gestapo raided Robert Antelme's apartment, among the documents they seized was Danielle's photograph. Mitterrand sent a messenger who waited for her outside the high school in Lyon where she was taking her baccalaureate and took her to a place of safety. She never did pass her exams. Shortly afterwards, he visited her at Cluny, in Burgundy, where her parents lived, and in July they became engaged. 'It was all at a hundred miles an hour,' she wrote many years later. 'During the lunch [to celebrate our engagement], I felt it was all beyond me . . . I was a young girl, emerging from a protected childhood, and already this man wanted to marry me . . . He was there, talking about our future family . . . and I knew hardly anything about him.' Perceptively, she wondered whether he had been disappointed in love. Did he love her for herself or for her spontaneity and innocence?

That summer, after the Normandy landings, the local *maquis* had occupied Cluny. Danielle volunteered as a nurse at a field hospital for the wounded. Arms were parachuted in by the Allies and a German counter-attack beaten off with heavy loss of life on August 11. The Gouze family, along with many others, fled to the surrounding hills. When they returned, to find the area around the church flattened by German bombing, a familiar face was waiting for her. Jean Munier and his young wife, Ginette, had come 60 miles by bicycle from Dijon, the county seat, to take her back with them to his parents' home, where François thought she would be safer until the fighting was over. A month later, when General de Lattre de Tassigny's troops entered Dijon on their northward march from Provence, she watched from her window as an open car, with two young men inside, threaded its way among the tanks. François and Jean Munier had driven from Paris, criss-crossing enemy lines as the Germans retreated and the front moved slowly east.

The two couples returned together. Danielle and François moved into an apartment in an upper-class district at Auteuil, on the edge of the Bois de Boulogne, in the same building where her sister, Christine, had set up house with Patrice Pelat. Five weeks later, on Saturday, October 28, they were married, with Christine, Pelat, Jean Munier and Henri Frenay as witnesses, at the Church of St Séverin, in the Latin Quarter, across the river from Notre Dame. The bride wore a couture wedding gown of white silk faille and a fine silk veil – obtained from heaven knows what privileged storehouse in those times of wartime penury – and carried a bouquet of edelweiss, which Christine had turned Paris upside down to find. When they came out after the ceremony, 'Colonel' Patrice's men from the MNPGD irregulars were waiting, in their best uniforms, on either side of the red carpet, with drawn swords forming an arch.

François had turned 28 two days earlier. Danielle was one day short of her 20th birthday. They formed a radiant young couple. Only François's brother, Jacques, wondered afterwards whether he had married on the rebound. That was too harsh. Danielle kept love letters from their courtship smudged with François's tears. But, on his side, it would be a love based on complicity, shared memories and the familiarity and understanding that develops over time, rather than an exclusive, overwhelming passion. The François Mitterrand who married Danielle Gouze was a very different person from the lovelorn young man who had been putty in the hands of his 'Beatrice', Marie-Louise Terrasse, four years before, and he made that brutally clear from the start.

At the wedding reception, even before the cake had been cut, he began to look anxiously about him and asked a guest for the time. 'I shall have to go,' he whispered to her. "There's a meeting of the MNPGD and they're waiting for me.' The scales fell from Danielle's eyes. 'Today! The day of our . . .' But she was not easily fazed. 'I'm coming too,' she told him. So it was that François joined his colleagues in white tie and tails, accompanied by his wife in her wedding dress, for a rather boring, routine meeting.

That was how it would be all their lives. He would do as he pleased; she would find a way to deal with it. Somehow they kept enough common ground to be able to smile at the absurdity of it all. That night she made him promise that in future he would keep free the last week of October – the week of their two birthdays and their wedding – for just the two of them. It was one more promise he would break. The following week he vanished 'on MNPGD business', reappearing several days later, as though it were nothing unusual, after she had spent days frantically telephoning their friends to find out where he could be. She learnt to live with that and with much else besides.

Mitterrand was more than difficult as a husband: he was often impossible. He demanded absolute freedom and found the slightest constraint intolerable. Not long after the wedding, she asked him brightly, when he came home one evening, 'How did your day go, darling?' The reply drew blood: 'I did not marry you under the regime of the Inquisition.'

She tried to explain his behaviour by telling herself that his obsessive need for personal liberty was the result of the months he had spent in captivity in Germany, his penchant for secrecy a holdover from working underground in the Resistance. In fact it was his character. He refused to wear a wristwatch, supposedly because every watch he tried stopped after a couple of days, but actually because he hated having to be on time. Ever since childhood he had been refractory to all discipline unless self-imposed, and now it had been made far worse by his experience with Marie-Louise Terrasse. The one occasion in his life when he had voluntarily surrendered his liberty, offering it up as a sacrifice to the woman he loved, it had been thrown back in his face. He would never put himself in such a position of dependency again.

Before long, Danielle realised that she had married a 'husband [who] excels in the practice of seduction directed at young women'. François was a Don Juan.[2] The same instinct for conquest that had made him pursue so doggedly Marie-Louise, and later Danielle herself, and which would afterwards serve him so well in his political career, had found a new field for action. It was as though he had decided that since an exclusive, overwhelming commitment would not work for him, he would make his future relations with women as wide-ranging, uncommitted and pleasurable as possible. Even Marie-Louise, her marriage to the Polish count in ruins, eventually invited him into her bed.[3] But their relationship had changed. François was now the one in control. The old demons had been exorcised and they became simply good friends.

Danielle learnt to live with that, too. 'As the years passed, I wasn't affected so much. [I was] his wife . . . faithful at my post. He would see what I was made of.' It was not the close, intimate relationship she had dreamed of, and there were times when she wondered whether she would have been happier married to one of the young students who had paid court to her as a schoolgirl. But she had chosen François Mitterrand, she wrote later, 'for better *and* for worse'.[4]

Wars rarely have tidy endings. Paris had been liberated, but it would take four more months before the whole of France was free. During that time, those who had flocked to the Resistance in the final days, when it was certain who would win, sought to expiate their cowardice by wreaking vengeance on anyone they could accuse of having been baser than themselves. The easiest targets were women who had slept with Germans. Danielle remembered how, at Dijon, she and François had watched 'women being stripped naked, having their heads shaved, being slapped about . . . It was bestial, unworthy.' Even Mitterrand, as the leader of a resistance movement, was powerless to intervene. 'If you'd tried, before you could prove you were from the Resistance, they would have killed you.' Many of those paraded through the streets had swastikas painted on their bodies and placards hung round their necks, naming their supposed offence. For the overwhelming majority, the charge was what was termed 'horizontal collaboration'. They included Frenchwomen married to Germans, or with German boyfriends; women who had worked in German households in order to support their families; and thousands of prostitutes, whose profession in France was legal. 'My cunt is international, but my heart is French!' one of them tearfully explained. The mob beat her anyway.

Some 20,000 women were treated in this way, and another 12,000 people were executed, fewer than two thousand of them after judicial process.[5]

Mitterrand approved one such killing, though whether he ordered it or assumed responsibility afterwards is not clear. An Italian accused of working for the Gestapo was executed in a garden behind the MNPGD headquarters. Afterwards it was said that the man was innocent and had been denounced by a jealous neighbour.

The movement's armed detachments, under Patrice Pelat and Jean Munier, established a makeshift prison in a hotel near the central market, Les Halles, where alleged 'collaborators and traitors' were interrogated. Other Resistance groups did the same. At the beginning of September, Jacques Bourgeois, who had been suspected of betraying Jean Bertin and Robert Antelme to the Gestapo, was detained. Edgar Morin, who had earlier persuaded Mitterrand that Bourgeois and his colleague, Médina, would have to be liquidated, went to question him with Dionys Mascolo. Both were nauseated by 'the bedrooms, turned into cells, prisoners who had been horribly beaten' and the guards, who inflicted tortures because 'when we were arrested, that's what they did to us'. Morin recommended that the charges against the two men be dropped. 'I said, "It's over now . . . Let's leave it. I don't care any more . . ." In my moral code, you kill in wartime, but when the danger has passed, you spare.' His colleague, Philippe Dechartre, on his return from North Africa, decided that Bourgeois was innocent and ordered his release. Soon afterwards the place was closed.

Mitterrand set out his views on the purge, or 'cleansing' as it was called, which swept across France in the wake of the German retreat, in an editorial in the movement's newspaper, *l'Homme libre*, at the beginning of September:

The people of France are waiting for [Justice] to lift its sword and cut. That requires that the cleansing be efficient. There are heads to be cut off. Let them be cut off! But let us choose those who committed treason knowing full well what they were about. The others should be freed from [the strain of living under] a vague threat.[6]

The distinction was important. Those who had actively helped the Germans should be punished without mercy. Those who had merely gone along with the system, whether at Vichy or elsewhere, were in a different category. Here, in miniature, was the whole debate over Vichy and its role which would traumatise France through the 1940s and for decades beyond. With very few exceptions, the whole of France had 'gone along with the system'. Mitterrand argued, like de Gaulle, that in the interests of national reconciliation, the unresisting majority had to be accepted back into the fold.

In the autumn of 1944, the General's first priority was to re-establish control over the country he had won back.

Roosevelt had wanted to impose on France an American administration, the AMGOT, or Allied Military Government for Occupied Territories. French-speaking Americans had been recruited to run it and French currency notes printed, modelled on the dollar. That idea had bitten the dust when Leclerc's troops had been the first to reach Paris. Even so, Roosevelt's successor, Harry Truman, withheld recognition of de Gaulle's government until mid-October.

Once the Americans had been seen off, the next problem was the Communist Party. In the provinces, communist-led Liberation Committees refused to surrender authority to the administrators de Gaulle sent from Paris. For several weeks the country teetered on the brink of civil war. The stand-off ended only when the General brought Communist ministers into the government and proclaimed an amnesty for the Communist Party leader, Maurice Thorez, who then told his followers that their first priority was victory over Germany.

That left the non-communist Resistance, which wanted to fight on against the Germans while retaining its existing military formations. De Gaulle would have none of it. For him, the Resistance had done its job and must now disband. Starting in September, the irregulars were either demobilised or incorporated into Leclerc's First French Army. Among them went several hundred men of the MNPGD battalion, which had been commanded by Patrice Pelat.

In the space of a few days, Mitterrand had lost both his troops and his government responsibilities. He was still de facto head of the MNPGD. But to play a role in the future, that would not be enough. He needed to bring together not merely the few thousand activists of the prisoners' movement, nor even the few hundred thousand in the Aid Centres, but all those who would flood back from the camps once the war was over. Then he would be at the head of a formidable political force.

From the MNPGD's new headquarters, in an aristocratic building near the Arc de Triomphe, at the top of the Champs-Elysées, Mitterrand set about creating a new organisation, the National Federation of Prisoners of War, or FNPG. It took him eight months. He learnt to play off the extremes, assuring the conservatives in the Aid Centres that they would hold the middle ground while promising the Communists that a merger would give them increased influence among the prisoners as a whole. Travelling constantly, he built up a network of friendships in the regional organisations which, Jean Védrine wrote later, 'proved more solid and effective, when there were important decisions to be taken, than orthodox party channels'.

Not everyone was won over. 'He was too self-assured, too humorous . . . too "political" not to attract criticism,' Védrine noted. 'To some he seemed individualistic and cold.' His chronic lateness for appointments and meetings exasperated friends and enemies alike. Subsequently he would insist that politics was not an art but a trade, to be learnt from the bottom up. The bargaining that winter and spring, and the debates at the founding congress that followed, were his apprenticeship.

The Federation, when it was established in April 1945, had more than a million members, making it the second-largest organisation in the country, outnumbered only by the communist trades union confederation, the CGT. Its President, Louis Devaux, was managing director of Cartier, the jewellers. He had headed the Aid Centres' National Committee and had also worked for the Gaullist intelligence service, channelling part of Cartier's profits to the Resistance during the war.[7] Mitterrand was one of three Vice-Presidents and Jean Védrine, the Secretary. Among the original MNPGD leaders, Michel Cailliau's group had been eliminated. The sole communist member of the board had to be co-opted because the congress refused to elect him. The

others were all from Pin'–Mitt' (the RNPG) or from the Aid Centres.
The Federation soon became the government's prime interlocutor on
PoW issues. By the end of 1945, its membership reached almost two
million.

Once the euphoria over Liberation and its new freedoms had died
down, the French found themselves materially even worse off than
during the Occupation. The winter of 1944 had been grim. Over the
previous four years, three million buildings had been destroyed and
600,000 people killed, more than all the war dead of the United
States and Britain combined. Two and a half million able-bodied
men, prisoners and workers, were away in Germany. France had
been bled white by war reparations to Berlin totalling 1.5 trillion
francs (£4.5 billion or US $18 billion at the exchange rates of the
time). Much of the country's basic infrastructure, port facilities,
more than 9,000 bridges and hundreds of miles of railways had been
bombed; 80 per cent of its locomotives and 90 per cent of its road
transport was out of action. As a result, despite a good harvest,
there were acute food shortages in the towns. Industrial production
was at 20 per cent of its pre-war level. The government printed
money, fuelling inflation.

Thus it was to a country on the verge of collapse that the prisoners
began to return. Henri Frenay had hoped for an orderly repatriation,
spread over several months. But the Allies had no way to feed those
released from the camps and sent them back as fast as they could. At
the peak, 40,000 a day were arriving in France, a million by the end
of May. The FNPG, through the Aid Centres, played a key role and
the migration took place more smoothly than anyone had dared hope.
But the penury with which the prisoners were confronted, after five
years in the Stalags, meant feelings were running high. Matters were
made worse by the Communists, who, with victory assured, saw no
reason for restraint. Frenay, a notorious anti-communist, became their
scapegoat for everything the government was doing wrong.

Mitterrand initially defended him.[8] But his margin for manoeuvre
was limited. The two men were known to be close. To take the
Minister's side against his own members, whose grievances were real,
would have been suicidal. At the end of May, Mitterrand penned a
blistering attack on the government for its failure to act decisively,

focussing on the issue which angered the returnees more than any other:

> The government is not known . . . for the sin of excessive weakness . . . But it is disturbing to see that [its members], who were fierce and implacable against the enemy without, are so timid when it comes to confronting that adversary within, which goes by the name of black market. Journalists have been shot; yesterday a general, 75 years old, was sentenced to death. But it seems we have to believe that the skins of these traffickers and spivs are too precious to go before a firing squad. You should remember this advice: if you execute 15 of them in public – and they are not hard to find – you will have solved in large part a problem which is exercising too many experts and too few honest men.[9]

The violence of Mitterrand's broadside was designed to show his prisoner constituency that he was leading the charge on their behalf, and that he was doing so against the government as a whole rather than Frenay alone.

The Communists saw through it and denounced the article as a fraud. They wished to concentrate on Frenay. He was the man the prisoners blamed for their troubles, and the more the Communists attacked him, the more support they would get. Defamatory posters, accusing the Minister of wasting resources, delaying the prisoners' return and discriminating against Jews and Leftists, were plastered all over Paris. On Sunday, June 2, the Communists called for mass demonstrations. Mitterrand and the rest of the FNPG Committee decided they had no choice but to go along lest they be disavowed by their base. That afternoon, 50,000 people marched up the Champs-Elysées to the Arc de Triomphe, where Mitterrand and two others laid a wreath. The procession continued to Frenay's Ministry, on the nearby Avenue Foch, where a group of rowdies, shouting, 'Frenay to the gallows!', tried to break through police lines.

It was then announced that de Gaulle would receive a delegation and the demonstrators dispersed.

Two days later, Mitterrand and another FNPG leader, Jean Cornuau, accompanied by Georges Thevenin, representing the Communists, were ushered into de Gaulle's presence. The General was in a foul mood. He accused Mitterrand of 'pissing vinegar' on Frenay, who deserved better, and refused to listen when Mitterrand explained that he and his companions had 'done no more than express the returnees' feelings, which it was in the government's interests to know and to take into account'. When Cornuau expressed astonishment that de Gaulle, who had been a prisoner himself in the First War, showed so little understanding of the PoWs' difficulties, he provoked another tirade. De Gaulle, Cornuau said afterwards, had been 'irate and arrogant' and the 30-minute meeting, 'painful and difficult'. It did, though, have some beneficial effects. Money was found to provide the prisoners with emergency aid, and the Ministry discovered supplies of cloth, of which it had previously claimed ignorance, which were used to make them clothes.

The Communists wound down their campaign. Mitterrand and Frenay patched up their relationship. By July, the repatriations were complete. Three months later, Frenay stepped down. The Ministry's task was over and when the next government was formed, he was not replaced.

Danielle had resigned herself to living on her own. Her husband's behaviour on their wedding day turned out to be the shape of things to come. She said later that 'he had learned bad habits', meaning that he was never there. She hated Auteuil, a 'soulless place, no street life, no animation', where she had no friends. The Muniers had returned to Dijon and the Finifters had moved to Toulouse. Patrice Pelat had also left. Three days before they were to marry, Christine learnt that he was having an affair with a ballerina and broke off the engagement. François worked frantically all that winter, nursing the FNPG into existence and writing for *Libres* ('Free'), as the movement's newspaper was now called, having become its managing editor after communist print workers had forced the resignation of his colleagues, Charles Moulin and Marcel Haedrich, for allegedly being too soft on Vichy.

The following spring, Danielle travelled to Jarnac for the first time to visit François's father, then in the last stages of a long battle with prostate cancer. The town, like the family, made her claustrophobic. 'It's very pretty, Jarnac,' she said later, 'but . . . the walls are all ten feet high, you can't see in anywhere . . . It's totally opposed to my temperament.' The shutters, latched against the sun so that only a single ray of light could enter, reflected a culture of 'discretion, even secrecy, modesty and inwardness'.

François felt at home there. She did not. But his father liked her and told her shortly before he died: 'I feared your entry into our family; now I am happy for it.' It was Joseph's testament to her. In normal times, the Mitterrands concealed their feelings behind walls as impenetrable as those of the town. Danielle had not been brought up that way.

She realised later, she wrote, that their backgrounds were different in every possible way. Her parents were openly affectionate with each other, agnostic, left-wing, and deeply committed to the principles of secular education; François's were prudish, devoutly Roman Catholic, right-wing, and committed to church schooling. She had been brought up as an only child, both her siblings being much older; François's childhood had been spent among a tribe of brothers and sisters and cousins. Her father was a high-school principal whom the Vichy administration had dismissed for refusing to divulge the names of his Jewish pupils, a man who had worked with the local *maquis* and had given shelter to leaders like Frenay; François's owned a vinegar works and, under the Occupation, had accepted the status quo. Her family was radical; his, conservative.

The differences were manageable. François dazzled her. She enchanted and amused him. But his overwhelming ambition meant they were rarely together. He had confiscated her youth, she complained, and now he was always away. He knew in his heart that was true. 'I am cutting back,' he wrote to Georges Dayan. 'What is the point of working if you have no time for your private life?' But saying it was one thing, doing it, another. By the summer of 1945, Danielle was deeply unhappy:

> Little by little, I learnt to stop asking questions . . . I learnt to bite my tongue every time I was going to ask, 'what have you been doing?' If you keep biting your tongue for fear of asking questions, you stop asking altogether and you finish . . . you finish by living in another way. It obliged me to become another person, to become someone else. I used to be an extrovert. I learnt to be introverted.[10]

The one great joy in her life was that she was expecting a child. The baby, Pascal, was born in June. His mother took him to Cluny to spend August with her parents. Then tragedy struck. He died suddenly at the age of three months from infantile cholera,[11] probably from unpasteurised milk, a common problem at a time when one infant in ten in Paris died before the age of one.

For both of them, it was a horrible time. But Mitterrand had his work. Danielle had only emptiness. 'It was a drama for him,' she said later, 'but not in the same way as it was for me. I was utterly distraught . . . He was caught up almost at once in his professional activities again. I was twenty years old. I had carried [the baby] for nine months, and everything I had built up in my adolescent's mind – because I was still an adolescent . . . it took away my reason to live.' Pascal's death left a scar which lasted the rest of her life. Friends remembered how, fifty years later, she would suddenly start talking about him and how old he would have been had he survived.

She was desperate to get away from Auteuil. They moved briefly to the nearby suburb of Neuilly, another haunt of the upper middle classes which Danielle found equally repellent, before eventually François found a bourgeois apartment, with high stucco ceilings and spacious reception rooms, in the rue Guynemer, in the Latin Quarter, overlooking the Luxembourg Gardens.[12] There she tried to rebuild her life. Thinking that she might get closer to him if she became his secretary, she registered for a shorthand-typing course. 'Bad idea,' she wrote later. Having her control his agenda would have cramped his style. 'You can never be my secretary,' he told her, 'let's not mix family and work.'

Life continued. She discovered a talent for bookbinding. In December 1946, a second son, Jean-Christophe, was born, followed two years later by Gilbert. But she was not at ease in her role as a mother. 'My mind was often elsewhere,' she wrote, 'with others of my age, still students, whose company I enjoyed.' She was a girl, not yet a woman, not because of her years – others, including François's sisters, had married at a younger age – but because she resented the sacrifice of that 'mad youthfulness' which had attracted him in the first place and of which she was now deprived.

Death wears the same habits whether it comes to a single child or to an entire people. But what France, and the rest of the world, discovered when the Nazi concentration camps were opened was an industrialisation of death unlike anything seen before or since. At the end of April 1945, de Gaulle, who made it a point of honour that France be associated with every Allied operation, despatched a delegation, comprising Mitterrand, Jacques Bénet and their communist colleague, Pierre Bugeaud, to join General John Lewis, the US Head of Mission for the European theatre, who had been charged with administering what were now known to have been death camps. They went first to Landsberg, which the Germans had claimed was a 'place of convalescence' for the sick. Bugeaud recounted what they found:

> On the parade ground, under piles of cut branches, were hundreds of bodies, burnt with flame-throwers. There was a cooking area which had never been used. Everyone there had starved to death. Further on was a sight which will stay forever in my memory: a common grave where corpses, discoloured by putrefaction, were washed by a powdery snow falling gently, stark against the red soil . . .[13]

Mitterrand remembered the emptiness. 'It was inconceivable, hallucinating . . . There was not a single survivor.' Mass graves contained thousands of bodies, 'tied together, three by three'.

Next came Dachau. The railway line to the camp went straight through the town. 'Bodies could be seen in the freight wagons and strewn beside the road,' Bugeaud wrote. 'I questioned a woman with her little girl. She said she knew nothing about any of that. It was less than a hundred yards from the entrance to the camp.' Inside it was still worse. Mitterrand remembered:

> Death was everywhere. The gas ovens, people who had been hanged and shot. A typhus epidemic added to the torments of the survivors. I was present at the execution of German soldiers after the Americans' arrival. At each volley, the inmates threw their hats in the air and shouted for joy. I watched two young Germans who had been shot being thrown into holes in the ground. I went closer. They were still breathing, whimpering. At that moment, somewhere in Germany, someone who loved them was praying for them. That person's grief was surely nothing compared to the suffering of the inmates. But I couldn't stop myself thinking about it.[14]

Did he really think that at the time? One may be permitted to doubt it. Those words were written long after the event. There may have been a genuine confusion between what he thought then and what he thought afterwards. But much of his account was deliberate invention . . . or at least embellishment.

De Gaulle did not, as Mitterrand claimed, choose him personally to represent France on the mission to the camps. The FNPG had been asked to provide a three-man delegation and he had been chosen as a member. The French group had not 'taken possession with the Americans' of Landsberg and Dachau, as he wrote later. It had arrived two days after their liberation by US troops.[15] Mitterrand may have seen the bodies of dead SS guards – which perhaps inspired his reflections – but the executions had ended well before he reached Dachau.[16] Even the one episode of the visit which was truly miraculous – their chance encounter with Robert Antelme, Marguerite Duras's husband, who had been deported after the raid on the flat in the rue Dupin the previous June – was not quite as he said.

As Mitterrand recounted it, they had been walking through a field of corpses when he heard a voice calling faintly, 'François!' It was Antelme, who had arrived four days earlier from Buchenwald after a thirteen-day journey without food, which only 800 out of 4,800 prisoners had survived, in the same train, gorged with corpses, that they had seen outside the camp. Bugeaud's account was quite different. After leaving Mitterrand talking to the Americans, he had wandered off on his own. A prisoner had told him that Antelme was in the sanitary block and he had rushed back to tell Mitterrand and Bénet. They found Antelme, unrecognisable, trembling with fever, waiting with other prisoners to be deloused. He weighed barely five stone (70 lb), having survived the previous two weeks by drinking melted snow.

Despite Mitterrand's entreaties that they be allowed to take Antelme back with them, the Americans refused, citing the typhoid epidemic raging in the camp. On his return, he gave Dionys Mascolo and Georges Beauchamp petrol coupons, uniforms and false papers showing them to be French officers, and sent them on a rescue mission. When they found Antelme, they dressed him in an officer's uniform and smuggled him past a sentry post with the connivance of a communist guard, holding him up between them, pretending he was drunk. Beauchamp drove all day, and much of the night and next morning, until they reached Verdun. There they stopped for lunch at a restaurant.

As they carried him inside, the room fell silent. It was the day after

VE Day. At the sight of this dying, skeletal wraith – a vision of what might have been, had the Nazis won – everyone stood up and bowed.

Mitterrand was waiting at the apartment with Marguerite when they arrived. When she saw Antelme, she screamed and fled. The doctors said he was so weak he could not last the night. But he did. Marguerite nursed him. Mitterrand and Mascolo visited him every day. A month later he was pronounced to be out of danger.

In July 1945, Pétain was put on trial for treason. Mitterrand covered the case for *Libres*. He used the occasion for a vitriolic attack on Daladier, Neville Chamberlain's partner in the policy of appeasement, and all the others who were now 'beating their *mea culpas* on other people's breasts'. It was, he said, 'a treason trial in which so many small treasons are laid out that the heart grows weary', with politicians condemning as criminals the military leaders they themselves had appointed. They should all be put 'in the same basket, accusers and accused together, accomplices in the same cowardice or betrayal, accomplices in our misfortune'.

Of Pétain himself, he said little, suggesting between the lines that the elderly Marshal was being used as a scapegoat for the actions of those who had made him a figurehead. De Gaulle thought much the same. 'Old age,' the General wrote, 'is a shipwreck . . . and the old age of Marshal Pétain became identified with the shipwreck of France.' Yet a scapegoat was what the country needed. De Gaulle commuted his death sentence to life imprisonment, but in later years refused the pleas of his supporters for his remains to be transferred to Verdun, the battlefield where his armies had triumphed.

For the next four years the Special Court continued its work, pronouncing eighteen death sentences, of which three, including those against Laval and Darnand, were carried out, while a host of lower-level Special Courts judged less prominent defendants. Like other Resistance leaders, Mitterrand was frequently solicited for testimonials on behalf of those accused of collaborating. Some, like Jean-Paul Martin, Bousquet's aide at the police department at Vichy, had rendered sterling service to the Resistance and should never have been in court at all. Others were personal or family friends whose 'missteps' he thought merited indulgence: Gabriel Jeantet, who had edited the Pétainist magazine, *France: revue de l'État nouveau*, to which he had been a contributor; François Meténier, another ex-Cagoulard, who had saved the life of his sister, Colette; François Moreau, a childhood friend from Jarnac, who had headed a youth centre at Vichy; Yves Dautun, a cousin several times removed, who had worked with the French fascist leader, Jacques Doriot; and many others.

For the most part, Mitterrand's interventions could be justified. Meténier was an adventurer and a rogue, Jeantet a misguided intellectual, Moreau a nonentity.

But the case of Jean Bouvyer, the ex-felon of the Cagoule, was fundamentally different. Bouvyer was spineless and amoral, and had spent three years working for the Commissariat for Jewish Questions, where his tasks included liaison with the Gestapo and assisting in the spoliation of Jewish-owned businesses. Mitterrand claimed afterwards that he had been unaware of Bouvyer's anti-Jewish activities. That is hard to credit. His gesture on Bouvyer's behalf seems rather to have been an example of a principle which throughout his life he erected into an article of faith: friendship, once given, should never be taken away. In this case the friendship was with Jean's mother, Antoinette, who became godmother to his son, Jean-Christophe, and to whom both he and Danielle were extremely close.

It was a principle for which he would later pay dearly when allies and adversaries alike anathematised him for relationships which they held to be inexcusable – all the more incongruous in a man who normally held that principles, like ideology, were a straitjacket, a short cut to ready-made answers which rarely fitted the issues at hand. Like the philosopher, Gabriel Marcel, whom Mitterrand had read as a student in the 1930s, he viewed principles as an excuse for not thinking through the rights and wrongs of each particular situation.[17] But in the case of friendship, such reasoning fell by the wayside. Where a friend was concerned, Mitterrand's reputation for ambivalence, for devious manoeuvring, for intellectual finesse, no longer applied. He was not merely straightforward and loyal but pigheaded to the point of unreason.

In the summer of 1945, Mitterrand had a wife, a baby and little visible means of support. Being Vice-President of the FNPG brought responsibilities and a great deal of work but no money. At *Libres*, where he received a small salary as managing editor, he faced a running battle with the communists. Marcel Haedrich's departure had solved nothing.

Mitterrand wanted to turn it into an evening newspaper with wide, popular appeal. At the end of the year, he and Georges Beauchamp relaunched the paper under a new title, *Soir-Express* ('Evening Express'). It folded after six months.

Mitterrand had always assumed that he had plenty of options. During the war he had talked of becoming a diplomat. Now he spoke of a career as a writer, or as an academic, teaching history and law.[18] But nothing materialised. In the end, his friends from the Marian hostel, François Dalle and André Bettencourt, who both worked for the cosmetics company, l'Oréal, came to the rescue. Before the war, to promote its cosmetics sales, the company had published a women's magazine, *Votre Beauté* ('Your Beauty'), which it had been forced to close because of wartime paper shortages. Now it was to be revived and Mitterrand could have the job of Editor. It gave him a comfortable salary, an office and a secretary, enough time to write for *Libres* and, later, *Soir-Express*, and five months to prepare the first issue, which appeared in December 1945 under the title, 'Your Beauty Notebooks'. His idea was to give a literary slant to women's fashion concerns. It was a tall order. Three issues later, after heated discussions with the owners, *Votre Beauté* reverted to its traditional, pre-war, glossy format. Mitterrand's days as a fashion editor were numbered.

The only other possibility was politics.

In the winter of 1944, immediately after France had been liberated, many non-communist Resistance leaders had dreamed of a political movement, different from the pre-war parties, which would carry forward the 'Resistance spirit' of self-sacrifice and social justice. Frenay wanted 'a synthesis of socialism and freedom' through a left-wing party, modelled on the Labour Party in Britain, which would challenge the Communists on their home ground. He asked de Gaulle to lead it, but the General, too proud at that stage to soil his hands with politics, haughtily refused. Mitterrand had hoped to build a party based on the prisoners' movement. He extolled the spirit of unity and solidarity that the PoWs had shown in the camps and denounced 'partisan spirit' as the prime cause of France's ills. But it quickly became clear that a prisoners' party would not work.

The PoWs are united by shared memories. They are not united by a doctrine. Could they be? No! . . . In one sense that's a good thing.

Uniformity of thought is the sign of human degradation . . . But if
it is impossible to bind them to a doctrine, it is impossible to gather
them into a single party.[19]

Such a party was 'a sentimental illusion which was bound to fail . . .
Opposing interests arise, life resumes its course.'

But if party politics was the only way forward, which party should
he join?

On October 21 1945, 20 million French men – and women, who
were enfranchised for the first time – voted into office a new parliament in the first legislative elections for nearly ten years. The same
day they decided by referendum to charge its members with elabo-
rating a new constitution to replace the defunct Third Republic. De
Gaulle was named Prime Minister at the head of a tripartite government comprising Socialists, Communists and Christian Democrats,
each of which had obtained about a quarter of the popular vote, the
remainder having gone to a sprinkling of small centrist parties.

Mitterrand, like many others, found the outcome disheartening. It
seemed that the war had changed nothing. French politics was still
being made by men who would sell out their principles for a share
of power.

He had been tempted to stand for election as part of a list of
moderate left-wing candidates in the Vosges, in eastern France. But
voting was on the basis of proportional representation and he abandoned the idea when it became clear that he had no chance of winning
a seat.[20]

That Mitterrand should have leaned towards the Left was hardly a
surprise. From the social Catholicism of his student days to his experiences as a PoW, when class was an irrelevance – from his months
as an army NCO dealing with incompetent officers, to life in the
Resistance, where everyone was equal – everything he had lived
through since the late 1930s was calculated to turn him away from
the traditional values with which he had grown up. All his closest
friends were on the Left: Georges Dayan, Beauchamp, Finifter, Munier
and Pelat, not to mention Antelme and Marguerite Duras and others
further removed. Men like Maurice Pinot and Antoine Mauduit, at
Montmaur, who had been his early mentors, had been strongly
committed to social justice. His wife, Danielle, far from a negligible

influence, was from a dyed-in-the-wool socialist family and had strong socialist convictions herself. Her father, Antoine, had impressed him as a man of rare probity and courage.

In *Libres* his editorials rolled out a drumbeat of left-wing rhetoric, denouncing the moneyed classes, the bourgeoisie and exploiters of the working man. The bourgeoisie, he had written, had appeased Hitler at Munich in a vain attempt to halt the advance of communism. The result? '[In 1939] the Russians and Germans joined forces . . . and there was war as well.' Five years later, during the liberation of Paris, while the bourgeoisie was still waiting to see which way the wind would blow, the prisoners' armed detachments – all from working-class suburbs – were 'poorly clothed, ill-equipped, dirty, and possessed astonishing nobility'. Money, he maintained, was at the root of all France's ills, the object of a soulless pilgrimage to 'a place of blasphemy'.

> The slave [is] not always who one thinks . . . Our great ancestors [the leaders of the French Revolution] dethroned kings . . . but did not understand that the most powerful king of all was still there taunting [them]. Money, the money-king! . . . No, we have not won our freedom! We may talk about democracy and tolerance, solidarity and brotherhood, but that will all crumble into dust if we fail to discern the enemy, which, under cover of those fine words, watches our every move. Facing the international of money stands our international [of prisoners]. In the camps I too was a slave. I am not so sure that I am not one still. Facing the international of money is the international of men, myself among them, which unites millions of human beings in chains.[21]

In his first book, *Les Prisonniers de guerre devant la politique* (Prisoners of War Confronting Politics), published in November 1945, he returned to this theme: Social justice, he wrote, was threatened by 'financial oligarchies' and to impose it in France would require 'revolutionary will'. Each former PoW would have to choose his own path, but for himself, he had already chosen: '[We are] enemies of a social structure where what is called "order" serves as a pretext for the exploitation of the labouring masses, [and] we . . . want a Revolution which conforms to the eternal aspirations of our people . . . [in] the revolutionary tradition . . . of freedom and justice.'

Marx and Lenin could hardly have put it better.

Yet Mitterrand was still very far from making up his mind where his loyalties would ultimately lie. Did that mean that his leftist rhetoric was no more than an opportunistic ploy, designed to curry favour with his PoW followers? Not entirely. Mitterrand's loathing of the power of money and his belief in social justice were constants throughout his long career. But the language in which he chose to express them would vary dramatically, depending on his audience and the circumstances of the time.

In July 1945, he had written to Georges Dayan: 'Politically, I'm really hesitating . . . I'd be quite willing to join the Socialists, but they are such old clots. The Communists are a pain and the others are all varlets and knaves.'

Six months later, he had got no further. 'To join the Socialist Party would be a bore. Internal ructions; old and deficient cadres; anarchy in the [provincial] federations. If I went, I'd quickly be eaten and lost, and I've no intention of going into a party the way one enters into religion.' Not 'entering into religion' was one of François Mitterrand's favourite phrases at that time. In the winter of 1945, he was not about to commit himself blindly to anything. Neither to the Socialists nor to the Right.[22]

With the Right, Mitterrand's links were more tenuous. After the war ended, he had again been exposed to the influence of his family and right-wing friends. Notwithstanding his confrontation with de Gaulle over the prisoners' demonstration in the summer of 1945 – the General, he said later, appreciated 'those who stood up to him' – he continued to admire him, comparing his 'words of greatness' with the mediocrity of France's pre-war leaders and dismissing as improbable the fears then being expressed on the Left that de Gaulle would seize power and become a dictator. But the one moderate right-wing party which might have attracted him, the Christian Democrats, he found as antipathetic as the Socialists. 'Joining the Christian Democrats would be a bore too,' he told Dayan. 'Their clientele is for the most part conservative, their leaders are rather nonentities, and their Catholic allegiance is embarrassing even to a Catholic like me.'

The one thing he was certain of was his repudiation of communism. The battles he had fought with the Communists for control of the prisoners' movement had left him respecting them as individuals but utterly repelled by their methods. 'They are impossible,' he told Dayan,

'Their obedience is so rigid that they have no latitude for friendship or human [contact]. What does one do? Let them take you over, or fight them? I prefer the second.' But even that was complicated. They had treated the prisoners' movement as 'a colony to be taken over and exploited'. But to reject them would have been 'harmful, to the extent that we would have lost useful men . . . who represented a particularly living part of the Nation.'[23]

Between the lines, here was a question which would be central to Mitterrand's political strategy for the next forty years: how could the Communists be integrated into a larger left-wing grouping, which could not function effectively without them but which they would seek to dominate or, if that failed, to disrupt?

On January 20 1946, de Gaulle announced his resignation, disgusted by the constant carping that parliamentary life entailed and increasingly at odds with the National Assembly over the shape of the future constitution. He was replaced by Félix Gouin, a Socialist who had been among the few pre-war MPs to have voted against Pétain.

'When de Gaulle withdrew,' Mitterrand wrote later, 'I felt that part of France's greatness had gone too.' The General had been confident that the country would quickly call for his return. But the call did not come. Four months afterwards, the constitutional proposals were submitted to another referendum and narrowly rejected. Fresh elections were scheduled for June.

Mitterrand reviewed his options yet again. He could not bring himself either to join the Socialists ('sclerotic') or the pre-war Radical Party ('from another age'). There was a middle-of-the-road alternative, the UDSR, or Democratic Socialist Union of the Resistance, which Frenay and a group of colleagues had founded in June 1945.[24] But it was a dog's breakfast of a party, whose membership, as one writer put it, ranged 'from the left of the Right to the right of the Left'. With some reluctance Mitterrand concluded that, notwithstanding his left-wing preferences, the easiest and probably the only way to win a parliamentary seat was to seek the support of the Right.

With the help of Patrice Pelat, who had married the daughter of a wealthy Gaullist and was making a career in business, he obtained the backing of a group of right-wing parties in Neuilly,[25] the affluent Parisian suburb which Danielle had detested almost as much as Auteuil.

The group was led nationally by the former Prime Minister, Édouard Daladier, whom Mitterrand loathed. But if that was the price he had to pay in order to get elected, that was what he would do.

In the event, the Right served him little better than the Left. His list came fifth, which meant he did not obtain a seat, although he won enough votes to give his main right-wing rival, Edmond Barrachin, a serious fright. Afterwards he wrote to Dayan that his loss was 'only to have been expected' and he would try again in the autumn, when a further constitutional referendum would trigger yet another round of elections, the third in just over a year.[26]

Mitterrand calculated that he had acquired sufficient nuisance value to make it worthwhile for Barrachin to find him a place elsewhere – and that proved to be correct. When they met to discuss their respective positions, the older man suggested that he campaign in the Nièvre, an isolated, rural department in the Massif Central, 150 miles south-east of Paris. Mitterrand objected that he knew no one in that part of France. Barrachin smiled and told him that that was an advantage in politics: at least he had no enemies there. The strong point of the Nièvre, he explained, was that there was a Communist candidate who could be beaten and no obvious right-wing challenger since the Christian Democrats were tarnished by their association with the Communists in the tripartite government. He would therefore be well placed to win the support of anti-communists across the board.

The Radical Party leader, Henri Queuille, who had concluded an electoral pact with Barrachin's party, gave him similar advice.[27]

Much of rural France in the 1930s and '40s still lived under the shadow of the *ancien régime*. The great lords might no longer control the lives of the peasantry as they had before 1789. But when election time came round, they were still able to get out the vote.

Barrachin contacted the marquis de Roualle, a wealthy devotee of stag-hunting and a staunch opponent of the Left, who agreed to finance Mitterrand's campaign. Jacques de Montjoye, who, with Mitterrand and Antoine Mauduit at Montmaur, had been the third of the 'three Ms' who had founded the prisoners' movement, also promised to help through a friend, the marquis Denys de Champeaux, a leading figure in the *maquis* in the Nièvre and a relative of the duc de la Palisse, one of the peers of France.

Having been parachuted in at the last moment – over the objections of the *préfet* (the government commissioner), who tried to have his candidature annulled – Mitterrand started campaigning two weeks before Election Day. Danielle, then seven and a half months pregnant with Jean-Christophe, remembered driving from village to village on country roads which went nowhere, getting so lost that one night they had to sleep in the car. 'It wasn't the Morvan [the eastern part of the Nièvre] like it is today,' she recalled. 'After seven o'clock at night in the villages all the shutters were closed as though there were brigands in the forest.' The area was deeply conservative and steeped in tradition. Mitterrand had just turned 30. Danielle was 22 and looked younger, with a fringe and a floppy beret which gave her the appearance of an urchin. At one campaign stop, the local mayor took one look at her and told him: 'You'll never be elected here with a wife like that!'

But the image of two innocents abroad was undercut by the rhetoric of the campaign.

Mitterrand was backed by a coalition of five centrist and right-wing parties,[28] on whose behalf he pledged to struggle against 'bolshevisation'. He declared his opposition to 'rules and regulations' for farming and commerce, to bureaucracy, to the corporate State, to 'muddle and failure', and to nationalisation – one of the battle cries of the tripartite government, which had taken into state ownership the major banks and insurance companies, as well as air transport, electricity, gas, mines, and the automobile manufacturer, Renault, seized for collaborating during the war. In his campaign statement, he urged that private property be respected (which pleased the landlords), and that educational freedoms and religious harmony be guaranteed (which delighted the clergy), and he called on the people of the Nièvre 'to stand firm before the communist danger which the weakness of the Socialists and the disclaimers of the Christian Democrats have put comfortably in power. [The] three ruling parties, even if they fight among themselves for the brief space of an election campaign, have always been in agreement to install a political and economic directorate which is the forerunner of dictatorship.'

In the context of the time, this was by no means extreme.

The three partners in the tripartite government – the Christian Democrats, the Communists and the Socialists – had concluded an unnatural marriage of convenience whose sole purpose was to enable them to hold power. It was not necessary to be right-wing to view that as abhorrent. Nonetheless, Mitterrand's opposition to nationalisation, his defence of private property and church schools, and his focus on the 'communist danger', made him a candidate the Right was happy to support. On November 10 1946, he was elected MP for the Nièvre by a wide margin.[29] As he later acknowledged, it was the fruit of 'a cocktail of votes ranging from diehard anti-Gaullists to Gaullists who were barking mad and dreaming already of a *coup d'état*'.

What had happened to the man who had assured Georges Dayan a year earlier, 'My ideal is the unity of the workers and [I] shall remain faithful to their taking power'? Compromise is the essence of politics. He was now a politician.

5

The Staircase of Power

The new Fourth Republic, whose constitution had been approved in a referendum in October 1946, a month before Mitterrand's election, had a bicameral parliament, a President who was largely, but not entirely, a figurehead, and a Prime Minister whose powers, or so it was hoped, would counterbalance those of parliament, ensuring governments which would last. Mitterrand had voted against it, arguing that it was a prescription for all the same weaknesses that had made the Third Republic unworkable.

Until then, the system of tripartite government had survived because the three main parties – the Christian Democrats, the Communists and the Socialists – all wanted a say in the drafting. Once the constitution was in place, that was no longer the case. The legacy of the war and their shared opposition to German reconstruction, which had helped to bring them together, also became less important. Instead a new conflict emerged: the Cold War, which intensified the antagonism between the Communists and their partners at a time when the French were losing patience with the government's inability to stamp out the black market, hold down prices and provide a decent standard of living. Within a few months, the Communists would be forced out of government, opening the way to a new configuration, which would determine the shape of Fourth Republic politics for the next five years. 'Third Force' governments, as subsequent administrations would be called, drew support from all the parties occupying the middle ground of French politics while the two extremes, the Communists on the Left and the Gaullists on the Right, were both excluded from power.

The outcome might have been different had de Gaulle been more willing to compromise. Many, including Mitterrand, had hoped for a strong, authoritarian State with a single national party. But the General ruled that out. It carried too many echoes of fascism and, in any case, as he spelt out in a landmark speech in Bayeux in June 1946, he wished to remain 'above parties', heading a presidential system in which he would represent the whole nation. Others had urged a Westminster-style democracy. But the pre-war parties, which had regained legitimacy since the General had brought them into the National Resistance Council in 1943, were steadfastly opposed and he himself did not support it. For de Gaulle it was a presidential system or nothing. By the time he realised that he would have to be more flexible, creating the RPF ('Rally of the French People') early in 1947 to provide political support, it was too late. The window of opportunity had closed and would not reopen for another eleven years.

That left a remodelled version of the Third Republic as the only choice. No one was enthusiastic and when, eventually, after nearly two years of discussion, the constitution was passed, a record number chose not to participate. Barely a third of the electorate voted in favour.

On December 16, the new National Assembly met for the first time to vote on the investiture of the veteran Socialist, Léon Blum, as head of an interim government pending the election of a Head of State.[1] Mitterrand, like all freshman MPs, was appointed to a parliamentary commission, or in his case, to two, Communications and Press.[2] He registered as an independent but affiliated to the UDSR parliamentary group, that being the party which seemed best to represent his somewhat fluctuating political allegiance.

The nomination of a leading figure from the Third Republic as interim Premier augured ill for the choices that would follow. A month later, the two houses of parliament, meeting in joint session at Versailles, chose Vincent Auriol, also a Socialist and a Third Republic luminary, as President. The heads of the National Assembly and the Senate were likewise prominent Third Republic figures. When Auriol designated the new Prime Minister, his choice fell on yet another Third Republic stalwart, Paul Ramadier, who had been a member of Blum's Popular Front government in 1936.

It may be argued that there was no other option. The former leaders of the Third Republic were all that was available. But the effect was to restore the tawdry, time-worn practices which had been the undoing of the French State a decade earlier. France was back in the bad old days of which Neville Chamberlain had written before the war: 'As a friend she has two faults which destroy half her value: she can never keep a secret for more than half an hour or a government for more than nine months.'[3]

Ramadier, a large, expansive figure with a warm southern accent, a goatee beard and a reputation for good living, delivered the *coup de grâce*. Convinced that, in a parliamentary democracy, parliament should be supreme, he sought parliamentary approval of his government not once but twice: firstly of himself as Prime Minister and then of the members of his Cabinet. It set a fatal precedent, which all subsequent prime ministers felt obliged to follow. This double investiture, which was not required by the constitution, meant that the choice of ministers was determined not by the head of government but by horse-trading among the party leaders. Accordingly the twenty-seven ministers Ramadier appointed were drawn from six different parties, their numbers calibrated to reflect their parliamentary strengths: the Socialists had ten portfolios; the Christian Democrats and the Communists five each; the Radicals three; the UDSR and a small party representing the traditional right wing, two each.

Eugène Claudius-Petit, the President of the UDSR parliamentary group, had been offered the post of Minister for War Veterans but had refused, saying he 'did not want to spend his time inaugurating war memorials'. Instead he proposed François Mitterrand.

At first sight it was a surprising gesture. Claudius-Petit had met Mitterrand in 1943 when Frenay was trying vainly to make peace between him and de Gaulle's nephew, Michel Cailliau. The encounter had not gone well. Claudius, as he was known in the Resistance, had started as a cabinet-maker's apprentice at the age of sixteen, becoming a trade union organiser and later an art teacher. As a leader of Franc-Tireur, and later a founding member of the National Resistance Council, he regarded Vichy as little better than the Nazis. Mitterrand – always ready to see both sides of a question – had tried to persuade him that not everything in Pétain's 'National Revolution' was bad. With experience he would learn that it was sometimes better to keep such ideas to himself.

Nonetheless, Claudius-Petit recognised the younger man's strengths, and he was a sufficiently astute politician to understand that if

Mitterrand were a success as minister, he would bring to the UDSR the support of the prisoners' movement which he used to lead. 'He's a young man who has shaken things up a lot among the PoWs,' he told Ramadier. 'If you want peace and quiet, take him.'[4]

Mitterrand was 'radiant with joy' at his good fortune, a colleague remembered. Not only was he a minister after barely six weeks in parliament,[5] but at the age of 30 he was the youngest member of the Cabinet since the French Revolution, 150 years earlier.[6]

His new career got off to a bumpy start. The Ministry of War Veterans and Victims of War, which had been set up after de Gaulle's resignation, had been headed for almost a year by a member of the Communist Party Central Committee named Laurent Casanova, who had transformed it into a communist stronghold. Not content with dismissing several hundred career civil servants for alleged incompetence and recruiting communist militants to replace them, he had requisitioned more than 300 lorries, formerly used to repatriate PoWs from Germany, to transport the party faithful to Communist Party rallies. When Léon Blum became Prime Minister, Casanova was replaced by a Socialist, who tried to undo the damage, returning the lorries to the Defence Ministry and, on the pretext of an austerity programme, issuing dismissal notices to more than a hundred of the new communist recruits. The response had been a ministry-wide strike.

When Mitterrand arrived to take possession, he found the gates blocked by a picket line, leading one newspaper to surmise that he would begin his ministerial duties in the neighbourhood bistro. After all-night negotiations, the strikers agreed to let him enter in return for a pledge to suspend the dismissals pending a decision by a mediation committee. Once inside, he announced that all the department heads, who had joined the strike in violation of civil service rules, would be replaced by officials of the prisoners' movement, the FNPG.

The strike leader, a communist trade unionist named Zimmermann, was a strong character. 'He exerted such authority,' one of Mitterrand's aides remembered, 'that when he entered a room full of civil servants, everyone stood up as though he were the Minister.' Zimmermann demanded talks.

Mitterrand's brother, Robert, whom he had appointed his Chief of

Staff,* described what followed. After the communist delegation, more than a dozen strong, with Zimmermann at its head, had filed into the Minister's office, Mitterrand invited them to state their case. 'We have temporarily called off the strike,' Zimmermann began, 'but we won't allow the Ministry to use that to terminate the benefits we have obtained. As for the dismissals, we demand . . .'

At that point, Robert reported, the Minister interrupted: 'Mr Zimmermann, as you know this is the first time I have been a minister, and perhaps I have too high an idea of what the function entails, but it is not at all in these terms that I conceive a dialogue between a minister and his staff. If you wish to finish your statement, I would ask you to change your language.'

Nothing daunted, his interlocutor ploughed on. 'I will indeed finish,' he said, 'but I want to make clear that we find your decisions unacceptable and we demand . . .' Mitterrand stood up and said, in the tone which officials employ when they have just concluded a satisfactory agreement: 'Very good, I see that you persist in your vocabulary. I consider our meeting to be over. I will not receive you again. If you have any further problems . . . you will deal with my Chief of Staff.' Whereupon he turned and left.

In the end the two sides reached a discreet understanding. There was no more talk of strikes and, in return, some of the department heads who had been suspended were allowed to stay on. But over the next nine months, Mitterrand removed, one by one, the most intransigent among them.

The anecdote is revealing not so much for the issues at stake, although one may wonder how many other 30-year-olds, finding themselves suddenly members of a government, would have been able to finesse such an unpromising situation, but rather for the light that it casts on Mitterrand's approach. First he found a device – a mediation committee – to defuse the primary conflict. Next he seized the initiative

* In France the *Directeur de Cabinet* is a political appointee comparable to Chief of Staff in the US system. The nearest equivalent in Britain is Principal Private Secretary, but the *Directeur* also has many of the powers of a Permanent Secretary. There is also a *Chef de Cabinet*, which is rendered here as Private Secretary. At the French President's and Prime Minister's offices, this hierarchy is headed by a Secretary-General, also a political appointee. Confusingly, the same post exists in the French Foreign Ministry, but there describes the top permanent official.

by threatening the strike leaders with dismissal on the unassailable ground that they had violated government regulations. Finally, having moved the battle on to his own turf, he used the power of his office to outface his opponents.

To Mitterrand, the reality of power was indissociable from its appearance. A minister who did not make himself respected could not influence those around him. 'He exercised his responsibilities with authority, never deviating from the rigour which the duties of State imposed,' Robert wrote later. 'In consequence, many people found him cold and difficult to approach.' It was not the first time others had remarked on his coldness. His comrades at Ziegenhain and his colleagues in the prisoners' movement had often made the same observation. Robert thought it was 'his way of protecting himself against the various interests which sought to influence his position'. In fact, it was his character. Mitterrand kept his distance. Robert's successor, Pierre Nicolay, who worked with him for decades, found him 'cold and correct, unsociable'. His friend, Charles Moulin, wrote of him at this time:

He was very thin, lively and impassioned, bursting with energy, some-times peremptory, sometimes impulsive, and skilful at charming others with words or the twinkle in his eye, authoritarian or affectionate. In general people like him, though some find him a bit distant, abrupt and disdainful . . . Too sure of himself, an ambitious rising star. The man is multiple and varied. He readily puckers his eyes but doesn't succeed in hiding the sparkle of his inquisitive, restless gaze. He knows how to put on . . . the cold mask of a politician using language that is often dry and caustic. No doubt that is his reality, but it is also the façade of a man who has not yet lost the timidity of adolescence, a man who wants to make others forget that he is still very young . . . He knows what he wants and what he is worth . . . He weighs things up, reflects, fixes his line of conduct, and then against everyone and everything, follows it through to the end.[7]

It was an attitude which won respect and which he respected in others. When the Cabinet met the following Wednesday, the veteran Communist Party leader, Maurice Thorez, then deputy Prime Minister, whom he had kept informed of his discussions with the strikers, came up to him and said: 'I understand, there are things you have to do when you're a minister. You did well!'[8]

The basis of Mitterrand's political strength as Minister for War Veterans was, as Claudius-Petit had anticipated, his influence in the prisoners' movement. The main problems for the returned PoWs in 1947 were economic. Threatened by hyperinflation like that in Germany after the First War, the government had imposed a price and wage freeze. Industrial production was still barely 40 per cent of the pre-war level. Farmers had reverted to subsistence agriculture. One in five of the working population was making a living through the black market. A report to President Truman that spring warned bluntly that without help, Britain and France would be bankrupt by the end of the year. 'Europe is steadily deteriorating . . . Millions of people in the cities are slowly starving . . . The modern system of division of labour has almost broken down . . . [The present situation] represents the absolute minimum . . . If it should be lowered, there will be revolution.'

In this climate, finding money for former PoWs, tarred with the stigma of a defeat which their fellow citizens were trying hard to forget, required considerable ingenuity. Mitterrand was able to get increased pensions for war widows and orphans by threatening in parliament to block subsidies to other groups whose electoral weight was more important. But not all his efforts were as successful. Under the Geneva Conventions, the Germans had been required to pay officers and those who had worked in the *kommandos*. However on their return to France, they had had to surrender this money, which was in German marks. Pressed by Mitterrand to disburse the sums owed, the Finance Ministry argued that, since the currency had become worthless, no payment was due. When he protested, the Ministry replied that it was the same situation as for tourists who went on holiday abroad and brought back worthless banknotes: they had to take the loss themselves – an analogy which did not go down well with men who had just spent five years in prison camps because they had fought to defend their country.

The other key demand was for a pension like that provided to veterans of the First War. In January 1948, after months of argument, Mitterrand was able to authorise the issuing to former PoWs of a war veterans card, conferring pension rights. The decision was hailed by the FNPG as a triumph. But it would take another two years and a violent demonstration by more than 100,000 prisoners, who invaded the Champs-Elysées, skirmishing with the police, before the measure was finally implemented.

The political landscape changed dramatically during the year and a half that Mitterrand was in office. The departure of the Communists, whom Ramadier dismissed in May 1947 after they voted against the government's policy in Indochina, set the stage for a massive house-cleaning. It was discovered that the Minister for Reconstruction, Charles Tillon, one of the founders of the communist resistance movement, Franc-Tireurs et Partisans, had put more than 1,500 communist militants on his ministry's payroll, including, according to a government audit, 'three cooks, seven head cooks, a kitchen manager, two laboratory assistants, a building worker, the headmistress of a girls' school, the head of a sponsorship organisation, a museum director, three *maîtres d'hôtel*, four film projectionists, a darkroom assistant, telephone operators, accountants, unskilled workers, night watchmen . . . 150 chauffeurs and a number of contract workers serving as "bodyguards" for the minister.' Other Communist ministers had done the same. The interlopers were fired and measures taken to curb the influence of 'legitimate' communist officials.

No longer constrained by the presence of Communist ministers in the government, the CGT, the Party-controlled trades' union confed-eration, vowed to bring the regime to its knees. It marked the begin-ning of a long autumn of discontent. In October 1947, Paris was without public transport. The mines went on strike, then the steel-works, then the railways. There was widespread rioting. At one point three million workers were on the streets. Food shortages appeared: Paris received less than a tenth of its normal supply of flour and a quarter of its milk. Trains were derailed and arms caches found, raising fears of an insurrection.

The confidential memorandum submitted to President Truman six months earlier, that France was in danger of tipping over into revolu-tion, no longer seemed far-fetched. Troops were posted to guard parliament, and the government sought emergency powers to call up 80,000 reservists.

Mitterrand supported the Christian Democrat Prime Minister, Robert Schuman, who by now had replaced Ramadier, in taking a tough line.

He had kept his post as War Veterans Minister in the new administration and argued forcefully before the Cabinet that the government must stand firm. The Communists were exploiting the workers' misery, he said, and 'it was a matter of not letting them get away with it.' For several weeks, the country teetered on the brink. Earlier that year, the US Under-Secretary of State, Dean Acheson, had warned the White House: 'With communists infiltrating the administration, the factories and the army, and its economic problems getting constantly worse, France is ripe to fall into Moscow's lap.' Wild rumours circulated that the Russians would parachute in arms, as the Allies had to the Resistance during the war.

Through four days and nights, from November 29 to December 3, 1947, the National Assembly sat continuously in a session whose verbal violence has not been equalled before or since. The Communists accused the government and its supporters, most of whom had fought in the Resistance, of being, among other things, 'dogs, bastards, Hitlerites, bloodsuckers, followers of Goebbels, fascists and murderers'. Infuriated by the attacks on Schuman, Mitterrand accused the principal Communist orator, Jacques Duclos, of igniting a new Reichstag fire, to which a Communist MP retorted that the government to which he belonged was composed of 'crooks and counterfeiters'.

But support for the strike was waning, and a week after the parliamentary debate, the CGT abruptly announced that it would end. Four months later, amid recriminations about excessive politicisation, the confederation split, losing part of its membership to a newly formed socialist-led union federation, Force Ouvrière ('Working Force').

That year marked the high point of Communist influence in France. Never again would the Party be able to imperil the fabric of the State. But the conflict had left the country bankrupt. Truman advanced $280 million in emergency aid, on condition that the Communists were kept out of government, and, in April 1948, the Marshall Plan, which provided American finance for the reconstruction of Europe, began to take effect. Another wave of strikes started that autumn, again in the mining regions. Forty-five thousand troops were brought back from Germany and given orders to fire on the strikers if attacked. After a month of violent clashes, the movement faltered.

Twice the CGT had called the miners on to the streets and twice the government had stood firm. They would not come out again.

The international situation had changed too. The Soviet Union, a wartime ally, was now increasingly perceived as a threat. Anticommunism became the glue that held the 'Third Force' together. Communist Party membership, which had reached a million at the war's end, fell by four-fifths. The surge of enthusiasm which had followed Liberation, as people hoped for political renewal, was over. Other parties also saw their membership decline: the Socialists lost half their activists, the Christian Democrats, three-quarters. Even the Gaullist RPF, which had won 40 per cent of the vote in municipal elections in 1947, was beginning to run out of steam. The fervour was gone. After ten years of war, Occupation and political turmoil, France was returning to normal.

Robert Schuman was the antithesis of Ramadier. An unflappable, slim, slightly stooped northerner, who 'seemed to have been born old', as one of his friends put it, he had grown up on the border of Luxembourg in an area which repeatedly changed hands between France and Germany. He would later become one of the founders of the European Coal and Steel Community, the forerunner of the European Union. In September 1948, after just six weeks out of power, he was asked to form a new government and proposed François Mitterrand, then aged 31, for the post of Interior Minister, one of the two or three most important jobs in the Cabinet. For so young a man, it would have been a highly unusual promotion. That Schuman, a good judge of character, should have considered him was a notable tribute to his competence. Vincent Auriol wrote in his diary:

> I told [Schuman] he was an excellent choice. He is serious and intelligent . . . Mitterrand accepted, but when the UDSR learnt of it, they refused. [That is] the tyranny of the parties ! . . . They fear social unrest, so they want to leave the post to the Socialists . . . Mitterrand . . . was keen to take it, but they threatened to exclude him [from the parliamentary group].[9]

In the event, Schuman's government lasted only three days, so it was no great loss. His successor, the Radical leader, Henri Queuille, thought of Mitterrand as a possible Finance Minister. Léon Blum had pointed out that Raymond Poincaré, who became Finance Minister in 1894 at the age of 33 and went on to become French President and five times Prime Minister, 'was scarcely older than [Mitterrand] is now', a comparison which any French politician would find flattering. Fortunately for Mitterrand, Queuille decided to keep the post for himself. France's finances were in a ruinous state, and if there was one area of government for which the young minister showed no aptitude, it was economics.

Under Queuille, an affable, courteous man, with the air of a country doctor, who employed his considerable political acumen to conciliate rather than constrain, Mitterrand served for a year as Secretary of State for Information.[10]

Television was in its infancy. When regular broadcasts started in 1949, only one household in a thousand, mainly in Paris, owned a TV set. But radio, which had been nationalised at the end of the war, and newspapers, which were privately owned, had enormous influence. Both were under constant pressure to toe the government line. Freedom of the press was a fine concept, espoused by all political parties, but, as Mitterrand soon discovered, whenever the government was criticised, it did not take long for the interphone from the Prime Minister's office at Matignon to ring with an irate demand that he do a better job of keeping his troops in order. Each morning, Georges Dayan, whom he had called back from a profitable law career in Algeria to become his *Chef de Cabinet*, met the Head of Radio News to issue guidelines for the day's coverage.

He soon realised that it was impossible to keep everyone happy.

When the Communists accused him in parliament of exercising an 'absolutely abominable' tyranny over the media, Mitterrand replied: 'I do indeed try as much as I can to prevent the Communist Party's propaganda being broadcast. I admit that it is not always easy, but I try.' The Christian Democrats then insisted that, as minister responsible for film censorship, he order cuts in sequences deemed offensive to Catholics in Pierre Chenal's new comedy, *Clochemerle*, which recounted the burlesque conflict between a mayor and the local gentry over the installation of a urinal opposite the village church. On a less contentious note, in 1949 he revived the Cannes Film Festival, where *The Third Man*, with Orson Welles, received that year's Palme d'Or.

The French media have a more consciously symbiotic relationship with government than is acceptable in Anglo-Saxon countries, and

Mitterrand was not above a little bribery to keep his erstwhile colleagues in line. Marcel Haedrich, his predecessor at *Libres*, who now edited *Samedi Soir*, remembered being summoned to his office to be asked whether there was anything the Minister could do for him. When he demurred, Mitterrand wondered whether a new car might help. 'Citroën had just started up again, and [he] gave me a voucher for a new model. It was superb, metallic grey, at the price fixed by the government, half what I had paid for my old clunker which I was able to sell at a profit. Such were the benefits of penury and politics.'

The Minister also used his influence in more personal ways. Jean d'Arcy, his Chief of Staff at the Secretariat, went on to a senior post at French television. A year later, he contacted d'Arcy to arrange an audition for a young woman who he thought might make a good television presenter, a certain Marie-Louise Terrasse. She went on to build a career as one of the country's best-loved television personalities.

Mitterrand enjoyed ministerial office. There was a formality about it which resonated with the rituals of his childhood. The noncon-formist, who refused discipline, needed the reassurance of rules. He dressed invariably in a white shirt, black tie and navy blue suit. When a photographer, commissioned to prepare a feature article, asked him to wear something more casual, the ministerial wardrobe was found to contain only a row of dark blue suits.

At the Secretariat, he was as punctilious about protocol as he had been at the War Veterans Ministry. When a wealthy landowner with newspaper interests in the Nièvre came to seek government backing and was rash enough to suggest that it might help the Minister's career if he signed the relevant papers quickly, he was immediately shown the door. Years later, the episode still grated. 'I was exasperated to the highest degree,' Mitterrand fumed. 'Seriously! How could anyone permit themselves to use that kind of language to a representative of the State?'[11]

He appreciated Ramadier, who had given him fatherly advice during his first months as a minister; Queuille, 'straightforward and subtle, though not cut out for difficult times'; and Schuman, meditative and solitary, with whom he used to exchange flippant notes during Cabinet meetings. He approved of Vincent Auriol, who after his inauguration had told the Cabinet that he expected them to wear formal dress, to speak only when invited to do so and to address each other in a digni-fied manner. Thirty-four years later, as President himself, he laid down the same rules at his own first Cabinet meeting.[12]

In the summer of 1950, François Mitterrand moved a step higher in the government hierarchy. Queuille's government had fallen the previous October after a dispute with the Socialists over wage restraint. Eight months later, after his successor, Georges Bidault, had been voted out of office over the same issue, Auriol had invited René Pleven, the President of the UDSR, to form a government. Pleven, a Breton, born with the century, was a discreet conciliator and a noted Anglophile whose diplomatic skills had made him de Gaulle's closest collaborator in London. He appointed Mitterrand Minister of Overseas Territories with responsibility for the French colonies in sub-Saharan Africa.*

Mitterrand wrote later that the post was 'the major experience of my political life, which determined the way I would evolve'. In Africa he had found a cause that was not merely interesting but inspiring.

His experience of the continent had begun as a child, when he and his brother, Robert, had brought home African school-friends from college in Angoulême. As a student he had demonstrated in support of Italy's right to colonise Ethiopia, but he had also written that a man's worth did not depend on the colour of his skin. In 1940 the German invasion had given him occasion to reflect on that further. Many of the troops in the colonial infantry regiments which bore the brunt of the German assault were from French West Africa. When Mitterrand awoke in hospital at Bruyères after being operated on for shrapnel wounds, the soldier in the bed next to him was Senegalese. Altogether 17,000 African soldiers died fighting for France during the war. Yet when Paris was liberated, in August 1944, Leclerc's 2nd Armoured Division was laundered all-White. The Americans, whose troops were still segregated, had insisted, with the acquiescence of

---

* Mitterrand's portfolio encompassed French West and Equatorial Africa; the Oceanic territories (New Caledonia, Tahiti, Wallis and Futuna, the Marquesas); St Pierre et Miquelon; Pondicherry and four other French trading posts in India. Tunisia and Morocco were the responsibility of the Foreign Ministry. Algeria, which was divided into three *départements* and considered to be part of France, came under the Interior Ministry, as did the French West Indies, French Guiana, and the Indian Ocean island of Réunion. Indochina was handled by a newly established Ministry for Associated States.

the British, that Black soldiers be replaced by White men, with the result that more than a quarter of Leclerc's 'French' were actually Spanish, Syrian or North African.

The Second World War was a catalyst for nationalism everywhere, loosening colonial bonds. But whereas the British recognised that independence, already granted to the White dominions, Australia, Canada and New Zealand, would inevitably follow elsewhere, the French remained locked into the policies laid down by the Brazzaville Conference, called by de Gaulle in 1944, which explicitly excluded 'any idea of autonomy, all possibility of evolution outside the French bloc of the Empire, [or] the eventual constitution, even in the future, of self-government in the colonies'. To France, the Empire was crucial both to national pride and to its status as a major post-war power. By the time Mitterrand became Minister of Overseas Territories, the country was bogged down in a full-scale war in Indochina and had suppressed with great brutality uprisings in Algeria in 1945, which left 20,000 dead, and in Madagascar in 1947, where more than 80,000 – 2 per cent of the population – had died. Britain, by contrast, had already granted independence to Burma, Ceylon (Sri Lanka) and India and Pakistan; and the Gold Coast (Ghana) was advancing along the same road.

Mitterrand had visited French North Africa for a holiday with the Dayans in 1947. He had been dazzled by the beauty of the landscapes and the archaeological sites and shocked by the poverty. He never forgot the chief of an Algerian village telling him, 'You can't meet all the children because we don't have enough clothes for all of them.' Two years later, in the winter of 1949, he made a long tour through West Africa, visiting Bénin, Mali, Niger and Senegal as well as Liberia and Ghana.[13] He was overwhelmed by the timelessness, the immensity, the immutability of Africa. 'Africa sleeps and is motionless,' he wrote in his diary. 'Her limbs are spread out over so many latitudes that she feels neither voyages, nor passages, nor messages. She knows nothing of foreigners, researchers or wanderers. She does not stir.'

In a book published three years later, he laid out the vision that his journey had conjured up:

> If the African world limits itself to its geographical frontiers, it will
> have no centre of gravity . . . Bound to France in a political, economic
> and spiritual entity, it will clear four centuries in a single leap and fulfil

its modern role . . . From the Congo to the Rhine, the third continent will be in balance around France as its centre . . . If we consider that colossal bloc spreading out from Lille to Brazzaville and from [Chad] to [Senegal], 7000 kilometres long and 3000 kilometres wide, cut only by the western part of the Mediterranean, [our] first duty should be to defend this one indisputable historical reality: Eurafrican France, which currently contains or controls 85 million people . . . For the French, who wring their hands, suffocating within the narrow borders of their old country, what an exalting prospect! On them may depend the future of a continent.[14]

'Eurafrican France' was an alluring mirage, which would persist until the late 1950s, derived from the principles of the Union Française (French Union), an association of all French territories, created after the Second World War, which held that men were equal – French Africans would some day evolve into African Frenchmen – but countries were not.

The French Union was the French Empire in new clothes, with Paris at its centre. The correct policy was to 'reform and preserve' the system as it was, in order to maintain a huge swathe of pink on the map from which France would draw prestige and power. But French Africa was not an island: political tensions were rising there as everywhere else on the continent. In the Ivory Coast in the winter of 1949, when the Governor ordered the disbandment of indigenous agricultural cooperatives rioting broke out.

The principal nationalist leader in the colony, Félix Houphouet-Boigny, then in his forties, owned one of the country's biggest coffee plantations. The son of a traditional chief, he had qualified as a doctor and afterwards founded a political party, the African Democratic Rally or RDA. By 1950, it had half a dozen MPs in the National Assembly in Paris, including Houphouet himself. They had affiliated to the Communist parliamentary group because the Communists were at that time the only French party to oppose colonialism. When the Cold War set in, this connection became an embarrassment. To the French settlers and their right-wing allies, Houphouet was a Black Stalinist. Mitterrand's predecessor, a Christian Democrat with pronounced right-wing views, issued a warrant for his arrest and ordered the party banned.

After taking office in July, Pleven arranged for Houphouet to come out of hiding and make a discreet visit to Paris. There a deal was struck: if the RDA disaffiliated from the Communists and promised not to campaign for independence, the ban on the party would be lifted and the government would listen sympathetically to the Africans' grievances.

At that point, Mitterrand was called in to flesh out the details. 'Don't wait,' Pleven is supposed to have told an aide. 'Call him at once. He takes umbrage like a prima donna.'

It turned out that the RDA's demands were modest. Houphouet wanted Africans to be permitted to stand for election to the all-White local councils; the introduction of a Labour Code to regulate wages and working hours; and the standardisation of commodity prices. African growers, Houphouet explained, were paid only a fraction of the price obtained by White farmers for the same weight and quality of crop. Mitterrand promised the government's support for these and other reforms, including an end to petty apartheid in hotels and restaurants.

In October 1950, Houphouet kept his side of the bargain. The RDA formally disaffiliated from the Communist parliamentary group.

Four months later, Mitterrand travelled to Abidjan to inaugurate a new port complex. At a reception at the Cercle Français, to which, on his insistence, the RDA members of parliament had been invited, a group of prominent settlers, with the Governor beside them, began venting their discontent. 'You are handing Africa to the Blacks and, what is worse, Black communists,' they told him. 'Your policy is anti-French. You are sacrificing us.'

Mitterrand cut them off. 'I advise you that from now on, if you continue to make such statements, I will issue orders for you to be prosecuted.' The following day, he overheard a senior French official telling one of the African MPs, Gabriel Lisette, later Prime Minister of Chad, 'As soon as that minister of yours is out of here, you'll get a good kick up the arse.'

Both the Governor and the functionary in question were on the next plane back to Paris.

The settlers' protests continued. A telegram was sent to President Auriol, accusing Mitterrand of 'delivering the Ivory Coast to international communism in the person of the Stalinist Houphouet-Boigny'.

A Gaullist MP declared that Houphouet had put his country 'to fire and the sword'.

Auriol summoned Mitterrand and told him, 'I know you are in the right, but we have to take all these protests into account.'

René Pleven had been shrewd. It had been he who had decided the new policy. But no one held him responsible. Mitterrand took all the heat. Later, when Pleven's strategy had been vindicated and the Ivory Coast under Houphouet was held up as a model of enlightened policy, Mitterrand turned that to his advantage, insisting that it had been his initiative from the start. He was stretching the truth. Pleven had received Houphouet first and agreed the basis for the accord. But the Prime Minister could hardly complain if, having deflected the blame, he also missed the credit. The initiative marked a turning point in France's relations with sub-Saharan Africa. Even if Mitterrand had not originated it, he had brought it to fulfilment. For the first time he discovered that politics was not just a matter of managing the demands of interest groups. It was possible, in a small way, to change history.

By the time Pleven became Prime Minister, the UDSR had come to be known as the 'hinge party' of parliament, a small group of MPs, rarely numbering more than twenty in an assembly of over 600, who straddled the middle ground and helped to hold governing coalitions together. With two exceptions, of four weeks in 1946 and six months in 1958, every government in the Fourth Republic included at least one UDSR minister.

Over time, however, its political complexion changed. In January 1947, when Mitterrand had become a member, Pleven, who admired the Westminster system, hoped to make it a French version of the British Liberal Party. But soon three factions formed: 'dedicated Gaullists', who, while remaining members of the UDSR, joined the RPF when it was set up in April of that year; 'sentimental Gaullists', as Claudius-Petit called them, who revered the person of the General but not all his policies;[15] and Mitterrand, who had entered the movement by a different route, through parliament rather than the party, and politically, though not sentimentally, was hostile to de Gaulle.

He did not remain isolated for long. In May 1947, at the UDSR's first congress, a fault line developed between the 'dedicated Gaullists', who supported the General's call for a change to a presidential regime, and everyone else, who wanted to keep, but improve, the existing parliamentary system. At the second congress, in 1948, Mitterrand clashed with the Gaullist standard-bearer, René Capitant. 'I am going to speak as a heretic,' he said, 'and I realise that doesn't please. But . . . [even de Gaulle] can make mistakes and we have the right to say so.' He was supported by Pleven and by Claudius-Petit, who interjected: 'De Gaulle is not God the Father!'

A fracture was beginning to develop.

In November, Mitterrand for the first time compared de Gaulle to Napoleon III, who had seized power in a *coup d'état* in December 1851, overthrowing the Second Republic. A month later, the 'dedicated Gaullists' formed a separate parliamentary group. At the third congress, in May 1949, Capitant accused Mitterrand of struggling 'against the RPF and de Gaulle himself' and warned that he would finish up by taking over the party. Mitterrand responded that a split was becoming inevitable and would have the merit of clarity, ending a situation 'in which we no longer know who are friends and who are enemies'. The Gaullists stormed out.

Five months later Mitterrand was named President of the UDSR parliamentary group. In little more than two years, he had transformed his role in the party from that of an outsider to principal spokesman for the anti-RPF majority. Pleven, as party President, remained above the fray. But his efforts at conciliation had failed and his position had been weakened. From then on, Mitterrand began packing the party's regional federations with supporters drawn from the prisoners' movement.[16] Over the next two years, thirty members of the FNPG were elected to the seventy-strong UDSR executive committee.

Years afterwards Pleven reflected bitterly: '[He] had a consummate art, and a pronounced taste, for intra-party manoeuvre. He enjoyed it and spent as much time on it as was needed.'

By then the five-year parliamentary term was drawing to a close. In June 1951, elections were held. In the Nièvre, Mitterrand was again supported by a coalition including the UDSR, the Radicals and two small right-wing parties.[17] Despite his ministerial duties, he had not neglected his constituency. In 1947, he had been elected to the town council at Nevers and two years later to the Conseil Général, the provincial council of the *département*. Danielle grumbled that he spent all his time there. Partly to keep her quiet and partly to establish himself more firmly in the area, he rented an old cottage from the parish priest in the hamlet of Champagne, near Clamecy. It had low ceilings, stone floors and a big garden with fruit trees. The only heat was from an open log fire and in winter the place froze. But it enabled him to escape what he called 'the phoniness of Paris, with its conventions that kill the real rhythm of life' and in the warmer months the family joined him for weekends. The campaign was difficult because of the presence of a candidate from the Gaullist RPF, which had not existed five years earlier. He was re-elected, but with a reduced margin.

In the ensuing negotiations to form a new government,[18] the Christian Democrats warned Pleven that if Mitterrand remained a minister, they would withdraw their support.

The pretext was a bizarre incident the previous spring in which the Governor-General of Senegal, a socialist named Paul Béchard, had sued a local newspaper for defamation. Béchard was known to be anti-clerical. A missionary journal, seeking to embarrass him, published, in violation of the law, a transcript of the court proceedings. The two priests responsible, both White Fathers, were convicted and each fined a nominal 50 francs (5 pence or 15 cents). The trial provoked an outcry which soon assumed hysterical proportions. Mitterrand, as the minister responsible, was accused in parliament of having put 'two White Fathers on the bench where normally sit thieves, crooks and prostitutes'. One of his opponents in the Nièvre told an election meeting that he had 'had two White Fathers shot'. To the Christian Democrats, the Catholic party par excellence, whose supporters in the colonies blamed Mitterrand for 'selling out Africa to the Blacks', it was too good an opportunity to miss. More than 400 MPs approved a motion reducing his ministry's budget by a symbolic 1,000 francs.

Pleven may well have welcomed the opportunity to clip the wings of his young colleague, who was beginning to develop a following in the party which threatened his own position.[19] For whatever combination of reasons, Mitterrand's name was missing when the new government was announced.

It turned out not to be a good idea.

As a minister, Mitterrand had been restrained by loyalty to the man who had appointed him. Out of office and, what was more, removed for implementing policies which Pleven himself had laid down, there was no longer any reason for him not to put his own career first. As head of the UDSR parliamentary group, Mitterrand continued to support Pleven's government. But within the party, the gloves were off.

At the UDSR's 5th congress, in Marseille in October 1951, Mitterrand's supporters obtained a majority on the Executive Committee. There were rumours of fraud. The Secretary-General, Joseph Lanet, noted in his report that some of the new Committee members had joined the party only a few days before. Pleven was re-elected President, and would remain so for two more years. But Lanet was replaced by a Mitterrand loyalist, Joseph Perrin, who was also President of the FNPG, and the party's Executive Committee and Political Bureau were packed with Mitterrand's allies.

The same networks of trusted associates that had helped him rise in the Resistance and the prisoners' movement had gone into action for him again. Georges Dayan became Assistant Secretary-General. Georges Beauchamp, Jacques Bénet, Jean Bertin and Pierre Merli all assumed leading posts.

When, in November 1953, Pleven finally threw in the towel and Mitterrand was elected to succeed him, one of the former President's supporters wrote disgustedly: 'The UDSR has become a branch of the FNPG.' Pleven himself was stoical, observing laconically, 'Mitterrand is not a man with whom to go alone on a tiger hunt.'

Pleven's ousting was not only, or even mainly, a result of political intrigue. The 1951 elections had been disappointing. The UDSR and its allies had won nine fewer seats than in 1946 and could barely form a parliamentary group.[20] Pleven's age was also a factor: Mitterrand was fifteen years younger and hungrier. But above all it reflected the fact that the political boundaries were shifting. The RPF had splintered and de Gaulle, turning his back on politics, had gone home to Normandy to write his memoirs. The time for 'Third Force' governments was past. The Socialists went into opposition, leaving the field free for the Christian Democrats to lead a series of unstable Centre-Right coalitions. Mitterrand had urged an alliance with the Socialists to end a situation where, as one writer put it, the UDSR was condemned to be forever 'the left wing of a right-wing majority of which it is a willing hostage'. But Pleven and the dwindling band of 'sentimental Gaullists' had refused to change tack. As they drifted towards the Right, Mitterrand was moving slowly to the Left and taking the core of the party with him.

It was as much by force of circumstances as by a conscious deci-sion. Mitterrand was pulled that way by his companions, his friends, his wife, his concern for social justice, and his instinctive dislike of the moneyed classes. But increasingly he also saw the political logic of many of the Left's positions. On watershed issues like colonial reform and an end to state aid for church schools, he found himself on the Socialists' side. Like them he blamed de Gaulle for his role in starting the Indochina war,[21] and he was beginning to share their fear that the General's presidential ambitions would one day become a threat to democracy. His conversion was incomplete and ambiguous. 'Notions of Right and Left,' he told the UDSR congress in 1954, the first he addressed as President, 'have lost much of their meaning. This old division has been swept away.' But imperceptibly, almost despite himself, the bourgeois values of his youth were being left behind.

The UDSR, under Mitterrand as well as Pleven, espoused two great contradictory causes: the French Union, meaning, above all, France's African possessions; and European unity. Like the British, convinced for decades that they could have all the advantages of being both within and without the European Union, the French in the 1950s were determined to see no conflict between their European and African ambitions.

To Mitterrand, as to most European leaders in the aftermath of the war, unifying Europe was the key to peace. *Plus jamais ça!* – Never again! – had not kept the peace after the First War. If Europe were ever to break the ruinous cycle of battles and destruction in which it had been locked for centuries, it would be by creating an institutional framework which would so bind its peoples together as to make armed conflict impossible. In May 1948, as Minister for War Veterans, Mitterrand had attended the Congress of Europe at The Hague, where Winston Churchill had spoken prophetically of the Union that was to come:

We shall only save ourselves from the perils which draw near by forget-ting the hatreds of the past, by letting national rancours and revenges die, by progressively effacing frontiers and barriers which aggravate and congeal our divisions, and by rejoicing together in that glorious treasure of literature, of romance, of ethics, of thought and toleration belonging to all, which . . . by our quarrels, our follies, by our fearful wars and the cruel and awful deeds that spring from war and tyrants, we have almost cast away . . . Mutual aid in the economic field and joint military defence must inevitably be accompanied step by step with a parallel policy of closer political unity. It is said with truth that this involves some sacrifice or merger of national sovereignty. But it is also possible and not less agreeable to regard it as the gradual assumption by all the nations concerned of that larger sovereignty which can alone protect their diverse and distinctive customs and characteristics and their national traditions.[22]

Danielle, who accompanied him, was still dazzled, 60 years later. 'That was the moment it all started,' she remembered. 'Churchill's speech was like a clap of thunder.' Among the audience were Konrad Adenauer, the future West German Chancellor; Harold Macmillan, who would become Britain's Prime Minister; Altiero Spinelli of Italy; three former French premiers; and Maurice Schumann, representing de Gaulle.

The Congress led to the creation of the Council of Europe as a political and parliamentary forum for European integration. In 1950, other measures followed: the European Court of Human Rights was established, and Robert Schuman proposed the European Coal and Steel Community between France, Germany, Italy and the Benelux countries, in order, as he put it, to make a new war 'not only unthinkable but materially impossible'.

Mitterrand was enthusiastic. 'There is no possibility of modernisation if we remain within our own frontiers,' he declared the following year. But he added a proviso: 'France [must be] the prime mover of Europe.' Churchill's premonitory words about renouncing sovereignty were coming home to roost.

The first serious test of the Europeans' will to unite – and the first major setback to Churchill's vision – was already looming on the horizon. The cause lay 8,000 miles away in Korea, where in June 1950 the communist North, supported by China and the Soviet Union, had invaded the American-backed South. The world suddenly discovered that the Cold War could turn hot. In London, Paris and Washington, the possibility of a Soviet invasion of Western Europe was on everybody's lips. In the French elections the following summer, UDSR candidates asked voters: 'Do you, or do you not, want France to become a Soviet state?' Mitterrand spoke against the Communists' 'fanatical, military one-party rule'. Others warned that 'if the Red Army invades', it would mean 'the destruction of civilisation [and] the most barbarous . . . of tyrannies'.

To meet the Soviet threat, the Americans demanded the immediate rearmament of West Germany. France, having fought three wars against the Germans in the previous eighty years, was violently opposed. A compromise was eventually reached to set up a European Defence Community, analogous to the Coal and Steel Community, in which German soldiers would be integrated with French and British troops in a European army answering to a European Defence Minister under the control of a European parliament. A treaty to that effect was signed. But it was light years ahead of its time. The idea of French and German soldiers fighting alongside each other so soon after the war was too much for many Frenchmen. The entire country was divided. When finally, in August 1954, parliament was asked to ratify the accord, the government refused to say whether it supported the treaty or not. In the end MPs decided not to hold a vote, which meant that it was rejected.

The predictable result was that Germany rearmed, as the Americans had wanted all along, becoming a full member of NATO; the European Army was aborted; and a curious organisation, the Western European Union, a kind of talking shop for defence matters, was set up to serve as a pretext for doing nothing further about European military co-operation until its dissolution more than half a century later.[23]

Mitterrand drew from the debate a lesson which would prove important for his later career: to win support for European integration, rational considerations were not enough. It was possible to move ahead with practical cooperation, which did not impinge directly on sovereignty, like the Treaty of Rome which created the European Economic Community in 1957. But to break down deeply ingrained, atavistic barriers of culture and identity required an emotional as well as a political dynamic. Besides protecting people's pocketbooks, it was necessary to weave a dream powerful enough to overcome their fears.

As Mitterrand continued his rise through the political hierarchy, two time bombs were ticking: Indochina and North Africa.

Against the advice of General Leclerc, the commander whose 2nd Armoured Division had participated in the liberation of Paris, the

French government had decided on a military, rather than a political, response to Ho Chi Minh's campaign for Vietnamese independence. In the autumn of 1950, after the first major disaster of the war, when the Viet Minh destroyed a French column withdrawing from the town of Cao Bang, opinion in the Cabinet was divided. Mitterrand wanted more troops to strengthen the French Expeditionary Corps. Pleven wanted more help from America. The Socialist, Gaston Defferre, suggested an international conference to find a political solution.

Only Pierre Mendès France, who led the left wing of the Radical Party and was not a member of the government, was willing to call a spade a spade. 'Without a military solution,' he told parliament, 'the only possibility is negotiation.' That was not what the government wanted to hear. It was willing to offer an ersatz independence – increased autonomy for the three Indochinese territories under continuing French suzerainty – but not the real thing, fearing that if Vietnam obtained its freedom it would set off a chain reaction in other French overseas possessions. By the time parliament accepted the logic of Mendes's position, France had no cards left. On May 7 1954, the French garrison at Dien Bien Phu capitulated. To all intents and purposes, the Viet Minh had won. What was there left to negotiate?

In the week that followed, the French Defence Council met three times to discuss the possibility of using nuclear weapons. The Deputy Prime Minister, Paul Reynaud, said France 'should envisage with the Americans the use of the H-bomb against China, to face the communist bloc with the risk of world war'. The proposal was put to President Eisenhower, who instantly rejected it.

On June 12 the government resigned. Five days later Mendès France told parliament that if he were invested as Prime Minister, he would end the war within a month or step down.

Mendès was then 47 years old. He was Jewish, which was no longer quite the handicap it had been in the 1930s but still attracted anti-Semitic abuse from those on the far Right. Idealistic, inflexible, rational, rigorous and direct, detesting ambiguity and compromise, he was often referred to as 'the conscience of the Left'. During the war, when he joined de Gaulle in London, he had turned down an office job and enrolled in the air force, flying sorties over Occupied France. Under the Fourth Republic, he had refused government posts, saying that he would not serve unless he was sure he would be able to act. Consistent in all he did, he now announced that he would not accept the prime ministership unless he had a majority without Communist support. The Communists voted for him anyway.

The following day Mendès began drawing up a list of Cabinet members. It was not something he was good at. After almost twenty years as an MP, he had learnt little and cared less about the arcana of political patronage. But he knew someone who did.[24]

That night he sent word to Mitterrand to join him at his apartment near the Ranelagh Gardens, adjoining the Bois de Boulogne. They had first met in Algiers in 1944. Mendès respected Mitterrand and had written a preface to his book on colonial policy in which he had praised his 'lucidity . . . and intellectual and political courage'. Mitterrand, in turn, looked on Mendès with feelings akin to reverence, regarding him as the answer to the country's 'need for renewal'. Mitterrand, as René Pleven had discovered, could weigh the strengths and weaknesses of his colleagues with a jeweller's finesse. That was what Mendès now needed.

After Mitterrand had spent some time considering the draft list which the Prime Minister handed him, Mendès asked him which post he envisaged for himself. 'The Interior,' he replied. The older man hesitated. 'It's that or nothing,' Mitterrand told him. Mendès acquiesced. The rest of the Cabinet was settled within the hour. Three other UDSR members received portfolios, including Eugène Claudius-Petit, who eight years earlier had recommended Mitterrand for the War Veterans post, and Joseph Lanet, who was recompensed for having eased his path to the party presidency. His friend, André Bettencourt, representing a right-wing party, the National Centre for Independents and Peasants, the CNIP, was made Secretary for Information. But the majority of those named were Radicals or Gaullists.[25]

Mendès was as good as his word. During the night of July 20, a peace agreement was signed in Geneva, bringing to an end eight years of fighting in which 20,000 French soldiers, 30,000 colonial troops and hundreds of thousands of Vietnamese had died. Vietnam was partitioned. The Americans, obsessed by what was termed 'the war against communism', refused to recognise that nationalism was at the root of the Indochinese conflict and supported the government in the South in its refusal to hold promised elections, so paving the way to the Vietnam

War. But that lay ten years in the future. In 1954, the Western powers were unanimous in saluting Mendès France's achievement, a victory of the vanquished obtained by an honesty so transparent that all his opponents recognised there was nothing more he could give. Even the US Secretary of State, John Foster Dulles, the apostle of anti-communism, enthused: 'This guy is terrific!' He returned to Paris a national hero.

The Interior Ministry was Mitterrand's first top-level Cabinet post. Logically it should have marked the last stage before he could aspire to be Prime Minister.[26] Instead it provided an apprenticeship in the pitfalls of high office.

Two weeks after his appointment, the Paris police chief, Jean Baylot, a prominent Freemason linked to the right wing of the Radical Party, told him that fliers had been discovered, apparently printed by the Communist Party, calling for violent demonstrations on Bastille Day, July 14. Baylot, like J. Edgar Hoover in America, had a fearsome reputation, having allegedly compiled compromising dossiers on all the country's leading politicians. He urged Mitterrand to forbid the demonstration, as his right-wing predecessors had done, pointing out that the previous year, 'communist elements' had defied the ban, provoking clashes with the police in which seven people had died and more than a hundred had been injured.[27]

The mid-1950s were a time of anti-communist hysteria all over the West. In America, McCarthyism was at its height. In Germany and France, ex-members of the Gestapo and the Vichy police were being secretly rehabilitated to work for the security services which wished to make use of their anti-communist 'expertise'. No minister could afford to show weakness towards the Soviet threat.

A few days later Mitterrand learnt that the fliers had been fabricated by Baylot's underlings. Another report from the police chief – that a group of veterans had stockpiled arms and was likewise planning to make trouble – proved equally unfounded. The arms, the Special Branch told Mitterrand, were a few First World War rifles. They, too, had been planted by Baylot's men.[28]

With Mendès France's agreement, Mitterrand decided that Baylot should go.

On July 8, a Thursday, he placed the issue on the agenda for the following week's Cabinet meeting. 'From then on,' he said later, 'I was kept awake at night. On every side, influential people kept telephoning to advise me to go back on my decision.'[29] Two days later he was summoned by René Coty, an elderly right-wing politician who had succeeded Vincent Auriol as President six months before. 'Coty was in a foul mood and told me straight off that he would not accept Baylot's departure. I replied that he did not have the right [and that, if he insisted,]. . . I would resign and address parliament from the back benches that very afternoon to demand his impeachment for exceeding his constitutional prerogatives.' Mendès supported him and Coty backed down. But not without one final *passe d'armes*:

COTY: Mr Mitterrand, I am warning you, if you authorise the demonstration on July 14 and there are deaths, you will be held personally responsible.

MITTERRAND: I hope, Mr President, that you will not hold me responsible for any deaths until the eighth, because last year . . . on July 14, seven people died in a demonstration which had been forbidden.[30]

Baylot was fired.[31] The demonstration passed off without incident.

There the matter should have ended. But both Mendès and Coty knew something which Mitterrand did not. A week earlier one of Baylot's aides, Commissioner Jean Dides, had approached Christian Fouchet, the Gaullist Minister for Moroccan and Tunisian Affairs, with a sensational revelation.

The previous day, Dides said, the Communist Party Politburo had heard a detailed account of the deliberations of the Defence Council, the supreme French military planning body, which had met at the end of June to discuss the government's strategy in Indochina if the Geneva talks should fail. As proof, he gave Fouchet a typed copy of what purported to be the minutes of the Politburo meeting, which he said he had obtained from a highly placed informant in the party apparatus. They indicated that the source of the leak was an unnamed minister. When Fouchet asked why Dides did not report the matter to Mitterrand, who as Interior Minister was responsible for security, he said he suspected Mitterrand of being the minister in question. By another channel, Dides sent the same information to Coty. Fouchet went straight to Mendès, who immediately initiated an inquiry but neglected to inform Mitterrand or anyone else in the government about what was under way.

Baylot and Dides were an odd pair. Baylot had fought in the Resistance; Dides had collaborated with the Germans, was notoriously anti-Semitic and had strong links to the extreme Right. They had been brought together by a hatred of communism. With Baylot's blessing, Dides had set up a secret network within the police to fight against communist subversion. That was how he claimed to have discovered Mitterrand's alleged treason.

Within 48 hours, Mendès learnt that the previous, right-wing government had been told of similar leaks from a Defence Council meeting in May, but had not bothered to pass on the information. That ruled out Mitterrand, who was not then a minister. Yet Mendès continued to keep him in the dark. Baylot, Dides, the Director of Criminal Investigations, Robert Hirsch, and the head of the counter-espionage service, the DST, Roger Wybot, all of whom reported to Mitterrand, had knowledge of the leaks, but were instructed to tell no one, including their own minister, what was going on.

On the face of it, the Prime Minister's behaviour was incomprehensible.

It is true that his mind was elsewhere.[32] The Geneva negotiations, on which his future depended, were at a crucial stage. Crises were brewing in North Africa and over the European Defence Community. Nonetheless, it was an extraordinary misjudgement.

Had Mendès launched an official investigation at once, instead of keeping the affair under wraps, it would have been nipped in the bud. Instead, he let it fester, giving the impression that he harboured doubts about his young colleague's trustworthiness even though he now knew he could not have been involved. That, at least, was the construction Mitterrand put on it, when, on September 8, two days before the Defence Council was next due to meet, Mendès finally took him into his confidence.

Those close to him remember he was shattered. That night he stayed in his office, unable to sleep. 'I was the only one to know that I was completely innocent,' he told a friend later, 'and I was also the only one to be certain that I could never prove it.' The following day, he did what Mendès should have done in July and ordered a full-scale police inquiry. It did not take long to bear fruit. On September 18, Dides sought another meeting with Fouchet, this time to claim that the minutes of the September Defence Council had been leaked. DST agents arrested him and searched the apartment of his informant, a self-described communist named André Baranès. It emerged that Baranès, posing as a journalist, had obtained the minutes from two pacifists employed at the Defence Ministry. Either Dides or Baranès, or a third person, had then inserted them into fictitious transcripts of Politburo meetings, in order to make it appear that a minister was betraying State secrets.

Baranès's motives were venal. A confidence trickster of unusual charm and persuasiveness, who seemed to have sprung from the pages of a bad spy novel, he had adroitly exploited the paranoia of the time, providing succulent (and largely fabricated) morsels of 'intelligence' to Western secret services in return for lavish retainers, which he invested in a lingerie shop run by his wife not far from the red-light district in Pigalle.[33]

But what was Dides's role?

The government was convinced that he, and perhaps Baylot as well, were part of a high-level conspiracy.[34] Dides and his backers, it was argued, wanted to show that neither Mendès France's administration, nor that of his conservative predecessors, could be trusted with the country's future. By allowing rumours of the scandal to spread in the press and among right-wing circles in parliament, they hoped to desta-bilise the regime, opening the way for a more muscular, authoritarian government which, even if it were too late for Indochina, would keep an iron grip on France's remaining overseas possessions, notably in North Africa.[35]

It was not implausible. Jean-Paul Martin, who had known Mitterrand since they had been students together and had then acted as his informant in the Police Department at Vichy, was now his deputy Chief of Staff. He drew a parallel with the Affair of the Queen's Necklace, which so discredited the monarchy at the end of the eight-eenth century that it paved the way for the French Revolution that led Louis XVI to the scaffold. Roger Wybot, the DST chief, had a different explanation. He was convinced it was a communist, rather than a right-wing, plot, engineered by Baranès with Politburo backing, perhaps on the direct orders of Moscow, to undermine the French State, discrediting the democratic system and paving the way for a communist *coup de force*. But whatever the interpretation, everyone felt certain that it was part of a political plot.

Subsequent events lent credence to that view.

Once the source of the leaks had been established and the machination exposed, it should have come to an end. Instead it resumed with redoubled vigour.

The main right-wing newspapers – *L'Aurore*, *Le Figaro* and *La Croix* – denounced Mitterrand and Mendès France as Soviet agents. Mendès, it was claimed, had made a deal in Geneva with the Soviet Foreign Minister, Vyacheslav Molotov, whereby in return for peace in Indochina, France would sabotage the European Defence Community. The *Washington Post* and the *New York Times* piled in with reports that France was 'turning Red'. In November, further documents, allegedly from communist sources, brought fresh accusations of Mitterrand's 'treason', leading to calls for his impeachment.

Some of the charges were so grotesque that even mainstream right-wing politicians felt obliged to take his side. A leading Gaullist, Jacques Chaban-Delmas told Coty that the affair was 'odious' and he personally guaranteed Mitterrand's innocence. But the atmosphere had become so highly charged that the President rebuffed him. 'How can you guarantee it?' he bristled.

At the beginning of December, when the furore was at its height, an independent right-wing MP, Jean Legendre, claimed in parliament that Mitterrand had caused the French army's defeat at Dien Bien Phu by passing information to the Viet Minh about French military planning. The fact that he was not then a member of the government was beside the point, Legendre argued. His guilt was proved by his failure to launch a timely investigation into the Defence Council leaks. Thus Mitterrand found himself in the invidious position of having publicly to defend an error which was not his own but his Prime Minister's and of which he was the principal victim:

For several weeks, the government of Mr Mendès France, like its predecessor, was abused. It believed that the documents in its possession were authentic. [In fact] they were . . . falsified . . . Why didn't the government's inquiries make progress in July and August? It is easy for those who have never had to lead such an investigation . . . to think that it can be concluded rapidly . . . [especially] when it is based on documents that have been deliberately falsified in such a way as . . . to direct suspicion at politicians whom one opposes, one detests, one loathes, and in the first place at the Prime Minister and the Minister of the Interior . . . The falsification [of these documents] took place either at the level of Baranès . . . or at the level of Dides . . . It was Commissioner Dides's arrest that . . . opened the way for us to discover the truth . . .

[Mr Legendre] has wished to show that . . . every time there have been leaks, it was due to the complicity or treason of a member of the government . . . That is what I find infamous – yes, infamous! – on the part of the person making those claims . . .

I beg you to excuse me if I seem a little irritated, but . . . embedded in the most secret machinery of the State, [we have found] rottenness, lies and treason . . . We must put an end, once and for all, to these parallel police networks, grafted on to the forces of the law . . .

From the public gallery: What about those who died at Dien Bien Phu? [*Applause*]

[I see that] the opponents of the regime, who are not absent from this parliament, would like to use this debate to let it be thought that Dien Bien Phu was the result of treason. That is intolerable. I have given you the facts we have found . . . All the rest is invention . . .

How do you explain that [Dides], the man receiving these documents through [Baranès], never wondered where they were coming from? . . . All this time wasted, whose fault was it? . . . The moment an official inquiry was entrusted to the DST . . . [it] led to the discovery of the guilty parties . . . In [Dides's] so-called anti-communist network, there was a huge part of bluff. Nothing is more dangerous than the replacement of legally constituted organs . . . by shady backroom organisations and gangs affiliated to clans each working for its own ends . . . And in the end, who benefits? . . . Whose ends has all this served?[36]

It was a robust reply to a classic parliamentary campaign of innuendo and denigration. But between the lines, visible only to the man to whom it was addressed – 'All this time wasted, whose fault was it? The moment an official inquiry was entrusted to the DST . . .' – was a stinging rebuke to Mendès France.

Christmas came and the agitation died down, supplanted by other concerns. Two years later, under a different government, Baranès's accomplices in the Defence Ministry were given prison terms; Baranès himself was acquitted; Dides and Baylot were not charged.

But the 'Leaks Affair', as it became known, had lasting consequences.

Between Mitterrand and Mendès France, it left a wound which
never healed. Mendès maintained that he had acted from a sense of
duty that required him to treat every member of the Defence Council
as a potential suspect. His wife said later, 'if [it had been] his own
son, he would have acted the same way'. One may be permitted to
doubt that. Even after his son's innocence had become obvious? The
argument did not hold up. The truth was that Mendès had been blind.
To Mitterrand, for whom fidelity was the greatest of virtues, it was
an unconscionable betrayal.[37] Outwardly they remained close,
expressing admiration for each other and, at critical moments,
providing mutual support.[38] But inside, something was broken.[39]

Mud sticks. Dides, in the eyes of the far Right, was an anti-communist patriot, which made up for everything else. Mitterrand was hated
for his efforts at colonial reform, for his sympathies for 'the Stalinist,
Houphouet-Boigny' and, perhaps above all, because this 'brilliant
political animal', as Jean Lacouture described him, was too clever by
half. Where Mendès was transparent, Mitterrand was perceived as
duplicitous. Claude Bourdet, Frenay's associate in the Resistance movement, Combat, who had strong left-wing views, was struck by the
fact that Mitterrand 'always had two or three policies up his sleeve,
rather than just one. It explains why he was not trusted.'

But that was part of who Mitterrand was and there was not much
he could do about it, any more than he could change his coldness or
the distance he maintained toward his subordinates.

That, too, had made matters worse during the 'Leaks Affair'. On
July 14, at the very beginning of the crisis, he had summoned Robert
Hirsch, the Criminal Investigation chief. Hirsch recounted later that
he had been intending to inform Mitterrand about the leaks, but the
Minister would not let him speak. 'He told me: "I don't wish to waste
my time in pointless discussions. I am informing you that [Jean] Mairey
will replace you. You will go to Rouen [as prefect of the province of
the Seine Maritime] . . ." Naturally, having been told that he did not
want to talk to me, I said nothing . . . about the leaks.'

Mitterrand's haughtiness was not quite what it seemed. He had
nothing against Hirsch, he explained later, he simply wanted his own
men in key posts. His coldness was intended to protect himself in an

awkward situation – in this case a transfer which he thought Hirsch would see as a demotion. In fact the police chief was delighted. His wife's family was from Rouen and she had been badgering him for months to try to get a transfer there.

Like the perception of trickiness, the icy veneer behind which Mitterrand took refuge often did him a disservice.

Mitterrand's question, *cui bono?* – 'Who stands to gain?' – was never answered. Some suspected the plot was nurtured by right-wing Gaullist leaders or settler groups in North Africa. Mitterrand himself noted that the extreme right-wing MP and lawyer, Jean-Louis Tixier-Vignancour, had taken an interest in the case. 'All I want,' Tixier had proclaimed, 'is a tribune to hammer Mendès France and Mitterrand.'[40]

But it was all supposition.[41] Nothing was ever proved.

In that respect, as in many others, the 'Leaks Affair' was an eerie precursor, in some senses a progenitor, of events at the Observatory five years later. The suspicions that it generated among the Right never entirely abated. From then on, Mitterrand was the man to bring down. François Mauriac, who had recently been awarded the Nobel Prize for Literature, wrote perceptively in *l'Express* the following spring: 'The inexpiable hatred of his opponents designates François Mitterrand as one of the leaders . . . of that Left which one day will have to be rebuilt.' Nolens volens, events were conspiring to push him in that direction.

6

Requiem for Empire

As peace returned to Indochina, a new conflict was unfolding which would also last eight years and would have much more far-reaching consequences. The conflagration in Algeria would bring France to the brink of civil war. By the time it ended, more than a million French men, women and children would have been uprooted from their homes; the French Union, fig leaf for an Empire which had outlived its time, would be swept away; and the Fourth Republic, another survival from a bygone age, would founder.

The opening skirmishes were played out at the margins, in Tunisia and Morocco. In both countries, French protectorates rather than colonies, pressure for internal self-government had been building since the war. In 1952, the Tunisian nationalist leader, Habib Bourguiba, had been detained, triggering widespread unrest. That winter, after French settlers murdered Bourguiba's deputy, the violence spread to neighbouring Morocco. In Casablanca, the army used tanks to quell rioters. Moroccan nationalists were lynched by European mobs. Dozens died and there were hundreds of arrests.

The Sultan of Morocco, Mohammed V, had a rival, the Pasha of Marrakesh, whom the Right regarded as more malleable. The conservative government of Joseph Laniel, which took power six months later, decided the Sultan should go. At a Cabinet meeting on August 19, Mitterrand protested that removing him would solve nothing. The government, he said, was abdicating its responsibilities to the settlers and the local French officials they controlled. 'After a few months the same problems will arise all over again . . . The former Sultan, in his exile, will [become] the symbol of revolution and the hero of national independence.' Several other ministers supported him. But to no effect. The following day the Sultan was deposed and exiled to Corsica.

Mitterrand threatened to resign but allowed himself to be persuaded not to.

Next it was the turn of Tunisia. Mitterrand had argued that summer that, if Tunisian nationalism was on the rise, it was because France had failed to give the Tunisians a more attractive alternative:

> Nationalism is a solution of despair resulting from the failure of our policies . . . There are 400 million Muslims in the world, and in the course of the last fifteen years, 370 million of them have acquired . . . their national independence. Just think, only 30 million Muslims remain within a state framework which is . . . not autonomous, and these Muslims are ours, they are French . . . The first duty of France is to do everything to ensure that [our] links with them are not broken . . . that our African brothers remain one with our destiny . . . We will not do that if . . . we remain silent and offer them no future . . . That is what bothers me [about] Tunisia . . . Do you think a State is viable when, to keep order, we have to enforce a state of emergency for fourteen years? Do you really think that is a success story? I say no . . . What matters is to find, for Tunisia and for Morocco . . . the best way [for us] to remain there . . . Once order is restored, [we need] bold and skilful reforms.[1]

The analysis was not wrong but the conclusion was addled. If 90 per cent of the world's Muslims were independent, it should have been blindingly obvious that the other 10 per cent would wish to follow. But neither Mitterrand nor anyone else in the French government was ready to accept that. In 1953, independence for North Africa was unthinkable. Two weeks after the row over Morocco, the Christian Democrat Foreign Minister, Georges Bidault, who, in the words of an aide, 'understood absolutely nothing about nationalism in North Africa', appointed a hard-line administrator as Tunisia's new Governor. Mitterrand protested that such a decision should have been discussed by the Cabinet. Bidault retorted acidly: 'The Cabinet does not discuss what happens in all the villages of France. Tunis is just a village.' This time Mitterrand did resign.

Nine months later, Tunisia was in a state of insurrection.

After Pierre Mendès France took office, no sooner was the ink dry on the Geneva Accords than he set out for Tunis and announced full internal self-government. At the time, he envisaged a transition period of ten years before independence. In the event, Tunisia became independent, with Bourguiba as Prime Minister, in March 1956.

Morocco was more complicated. Mendès France ruled out any possibility of the Sultan's return. But Edgar Faure, who succeeded him, soon realised that that would not work. Nationalist agitation grew exponentially: by the spring of 1955, four or five terrorist attacks were taking place each day. Extremist organisations were formed among the 300,000 French settlers, denouncing 'the rot that has set in due to the incompetence of the useless people who pretend to govern us'. But the 'White Hand', as one such group called itself, was no more successful in stemming the tide than its counterpart, the 'Red Hand', had been in Tunisia. Faure's government approved the Sultan's return in November that year. Over the objections of the Gaullists and Bidault's Christian Democrats, Morocco became independent two weeks before Tunisia.

That was the curtain-raiser. Parliament had approved the independence of Tunisia and Morocco on the understanding that there would be a quid pro quo. The protectorates would be allowed to evolve, but Algeria would remain French.

The main drama was about to begin.

With hindsight it defies understanding that anyone could have thought that the nine million Arabs of Algeria, where the settler population was one million, would continue to accept colonial rule when their neighbours, Morocco and Tunisia, whose combined Arab population was 11 million, with half a million settlers, had achieved full independence. Nonetheless, that is what the French government firmly believed.

Since the uprising in Sétif in May 1945, which the army had repressed with terrible bloodshed, Algeria had been quiet. Mitterrand visited Algiers as War Veterans Minister in September 1947, the same week that the French parliament passed legislation allowing Algerians to vote for a regional assembly. The new law provided for two electoral colleges, one for Algerians, the other for French citizens, each electing sixty deputies. The Governor-General, Yves Chataigneau, told the young minister that since Algeria was French, Algerians of all races should have the same rights. But Chataigneau was an exception. His successors aligned themselves with the settlers, closing their eyes when election results were falsified to exclude nationalist representatives.

A Radical Party senator, Henri Borgeaud, who had extensive land-holdings in the country, explained jovially: 'Algerian political cooking is done in an Algerian pot by Algerian chefs, by which, of course, I mean Europeans in Algeria.'

In the late spring of 1954, Mitterrand, then in opposition, tried to organise a conference in Algiers to discuss how the territory should be associated in the future with metropolitan France. The local author-ities banned it.[2] No one in Algiers wanted to admit that there might be political problems. Everyone was 'living under the illusion that the only issues were economic and social'.

As minister, Mitterrand was as blinkered as most of his colleagues about the long-term future of France's overseas territories. He opposed granting independence to Tunisia and Morocco, arguing that internal autonomy was enough. But he did understand that Algeria could not fail to be affected by the upheavals taking place everywhere else in the Arab world. Tunisia and Morocco were in ferment, Libya was already independent, the Sudan was about to become so, and in Egypt, King Farouk had been deposed and a radical army colonel, Gamal Abdel Nasser, had seized power.

Mendès France acknowledged later that Mitterrand warned him repeatedly in the summer of 1954 that trouble was brewing in Algeria, but 'at that time, I did not think it was burning, that it was going to explode. Mitterrand felt it. He sensed early on that there was a risk things would go badly.'

Shortly after his appointment as Interior Minister, Mitterrand received a report that a former French army sergeant named Ahmed Ben Bella had been sent from Cairo to Libya, where military training camps for young Algerians were believed to have been set up. Ben Bella, the report said, was the leader of a newly formed Liberation Army and was preparing for 'direct action'. The report was accurate. Ben Bella would later be identified as one of the nine founding members of the revolutionary committee behind the FLN, the Algerian National Liberation Front, which had decided, at a meeting in Cairo that spring, to launch an armed rebellion against French rule.[3]

In October, Mitterrand visited Algiers. Publicly he declared himself 'full of optimism' that the territory was 'calm and prosperous'.

Privately he told Mendès France on his return that 'things are getting worse and worse. We are going to have to act very quickly.' But neither of them yet realised how critical the situation had become.*⁴

Ten days later, on the eve of All Saints, October 31 1954, the FLN launched more than sixty attacks in different parts of Algeria. Police stations were fire-bombed, railway lines sabotaged, telephone lines cut and French settlers attacked. Seven people died. For 24 hours there was pandemonium. The Governor-General requested extra troops. There were no planes to fly them out. The General Staff insisted that, even if planes could be found, there were no troops to be had. The French commander in Algeria panicked, proposing to evacuate isolated areas that were too difficult to defend.

Then the pendulum swung the other way. Mitterrand reassured the Cabinet: 'Only about a hundred individuals were involved and at no time did the population follow.' Mendès maintained that, 'contrary to what has been said, Algeria is calm'. Later Mitterrand would speak of 'a few terrorist attacks whose consequences, in my opinion, have been greatly exaggerated'. For a while that seemed to be so. Scattered violence continued, but the army, reinforced by units from Indochina, appeared to have the situation under control.⁵

In parliament, the government proclaimed a policy of firmness. 'There will be neither hesitation nor time-wasting nor half-measures,' Mendès France declared on November 12. 'There will be no kid gloves for sedition, no compromise with it, and everyone here and [in Algeria] should know that.' Mitterrand spoke the same language:

> Algeria is part of France . . . the [three] provinces which make up Algeria are provinces of the French Republic . . . The law applies everywhere [in France], and that law is French law. All those who try, in one way

* Not for lack of warning. The veteran nationalist, Ferhat Abbas, had written some weeks earlier that Algerians had lost patience with France. '[Their] anger is at its peak and [their] silence reflects contempt and revolt. Algeria is not calm, and the divorce could very soon become irrevocable.' On October 23, the day Mitterrand returned to Paris, the Chief of Security in Algiers, Jean Vaujour, sent him word that 'we may be on the eve of terrorist attacks in Algeria. It is impossible to be absolutely certain, but in my judgement it is to be feared.' Mitterrand replied that he 'would think about it'. A week later, the insurrection began. After two years of open rebellion in Tunisia and Morocco, which appeared to have left Algeria untouched, the government had fallen victim to its own propaganda that Algeria, being 'French', was different.

or another, to create disorder and attempt to secede, will be struck down by every means the law puts at our disposal.[6]

The previous week Mitterrand had banned a moderate nationalist group, led by Messali Hadj, and ordered the arrests of thousands of its members. It was an error. Messali's movement had played no part in the attacks. Its dissolution drove its members into the arms of the FLN and deprived the government of an Arab interlocutor. Not that the government had any intention of negotiating. Mitterrand told a parliamentary commission that month that the rebellion made discussion impossible, unless 'in its terminal form, that of war'.

The expression reflected his predilection for striking phrases but was ill-chosen, for in subbed-down form in the newspapers it became, 'in Algeria the only form of negotiation is war', which was not quite what he had said. Yet it conveyed well enough his attitude. Neither he nor Mendès France understood the depth of the Arab revolt. Both believed that 'merciless repression' was necessary to put down the rebellion and that moderate reforms would suffice to eliminate its causes. The 'temptations', as Mitterrand called them, of independence and secession had to be ruled out because they would remove 'the only chance France still has to remain a world power: a Franco-African ensemble stretching from the North Sea to the Congo'.

None of them realised that they were witnessing the beginning of a war which would mark France for generations to come.*

In November 1954, Mitterrand drafted a programme of economic and social reforms designed to give 'equal chances for all who are born on Algerian soil, regardless of their origin', accompanied by increased investment in the territory's infrastructure, a rise in the minimum wage and measures to redistribute arable land to Arab villagers. The settlers were not pleased. The word 'reform', one of their leaders commented, is 'inelegant and inopportune. It gives the impression of a promise, when the task today is to restore law and order.'

* During the French presidential elections in 2002, 2007 and 2012, where immigration, especially from North Africa, was a major campaign issue, it was widely acknowledged that France's difficulties in integrating its Arab population, even those born in France of the second or third generation, were rooted in the hatreds and incomprehension sown fifty years earlier during the Algerian war.

Six weeks later, on January 5 1955, the Cabinet discussed measures to extend Arab voting rights, and a new proposal to merge the metropolitan and territorial police forces, in order, as Mitterrand put it, to prevent the 'independence of the latter being compromised'; in other words, to stop the police being used as an instrument to maintain the settlers' monopoly of power.[7]

No decision was taken on voting rights. But the proposal to amalgamate the police was approved. Henri Borgeaud warned Mendès that if it went ahead, he and his allies would bring down the government. In parliament, Mitterrand was accused of sowing the seeds of division. Algerians, he was told, were 'not bothered about political rights', their only interest was 'bread and housing'.

Borgeaud was as good as his word and, the following month, the government fell. Even without the *ultras'* opposition, there was no majority in parliament for change. Mitterrand himself was reluctant to go beyond the prevailing consensus. He told the UDSR that summer that he was personally 'very conservative and very hostile' towards those who wished to sever the links between France and its overseas possessions. Some degree of autonomy would be needed, he acknowledged, because 'you cannot stop these children we are training, who aspire to take charge . . . from having this responsibility. [Otherwise] you will set them against you, the more so because now they . . . read the papers, they come to Paris, they know how the world works.' But those who advocated full self-government were 'partisans of abandonment'. A paternalistic nineteenth-century empire-builder would not have put it differently.

The best answer, Mitterrand believed, was for Algeria to be integrated with metropolitan France. If that proved impossible, France and its overseas possessions should be brought together in a federal state.

Mitterrand's orthodoxy mirrored the immobilism of the Fourth Republic. Only in the most exceptional circumstances, such as those which brought Mendès France to power with a mandate to end the war in Indochina, was a government able to break the mould and act decisively. The rest of the time was spent in a game of musical chairs, where the same establishment figures changed ministries and, in different combinations, formed governments whose policies were virtually indistinguishable because they were all tributary to the same parliamentary base. To be accepted in this system, a politician should not make waves. Mitterrand's goal was to head the government.[8] He had bragged to friends some years earlier: 'any fool can be Prime Minister at 50. I will do it at 40!' As Interior Minister, the third-ranking post in the Cabinet, within striking distance of the top job, he would take great care to do nothing which might rock the boat, even if that meant keeping silent about policies which in other circumstances he would have denounced as barbarous.

The use of torture was a case in point.

Mitterrand knew that torture was routinely practised by the police not only in Algeria but in all the French North African territories. Four years earlier, the former Resistance leader, Claude Bourdet, had asked in the left-wing weekly, *France Observateur*, 'Is there a Gestapo in Algeria?' After the FLN launched the insurrection in November, Mitterrand issued a directive, reminding the police in Algeria that there must be no repetition of 'the errors that have occurred in the past' towards 'Muslim French citizens'. It was hardly robust, and became still less so when buried out of sight in a confidential circular.

Speaking publicly in parliament a few days later, a Christian Democrat MP, Jacques Fonlupt-Esperaber, also a former member of the Resistance, was more courageous. 'To affront the dignity of the human person, even the smallest among us, no matter what his origin or religion,' he said, 'is an outrage against all and, in truth, the most dreadful of threats to France's future in Algeria as elsewhere.' He was heard out in silence and, at the next elections, was not selected as a candidate.* But the problem did not go away. On January 13 1955, *France Observateur* published another article by Bourdet, all the more

* The silence of US congressmen, Democrats and Republicans alike, when confronted with 'enhanced interrogation techniques' during the administration of George W. Bush, is a reminder that French politicians in the 1950s were not alone in thinking torture an appropriate response to Arab terrorism. French historians have since tried to explain their leaders' acquiescence in barbaric practices by the context of the Cold War, the universal belief in France at that time that Algeria was part of the 'homeland', and the lack of priority, half a century ago, accorded to human rights. The American experience suggests rather that in both cases, the primary cause was the reluctance of politicians, when the lives of soldiers were at stake, to take a moral stance at the risk of being branded unpatriotic.

poignant because the practices he described were those he had experienced himself at the hands of the Nazis:

> The torture known as *la baignoire* [a form of water-boarding], the pumping of water into the anus, the use of electric shocks to the mucous membranes, the armpits or the spine, are the preferred methods because if they are 'carried out well' they leave no visible trace. This explains why the torturers do not present their prisoners before a judge until five to ten days after their arrest . . . Once these Gestapists have dictated to their half-dead victim the 'confession' they are pleased to make him sign, the rest of his stay with the police is spent getting him back into a fit state, even, if necessary, giving him [medical] treatment – Yes! They do that – so that he will be presentable when brought before the judge.[9]

Two days later François Mauriac added his voice with a stinging denunciation of police methods published in *l'Express*. Mendès promised an inquiry. A confidential report, submitted to the government six weeks later, listed in ghastly detail the methods the police were using, but concluded they were unavoidable and that, in difficult circumstances, the police were doing a good job. Mitterrand's opinion seems to have been little different. When a lawyer in Algiers protested that the clients she was defending had been tortured, he told her politely she must be mistaken.

In the last days of Mendès's government, an Algerian Muslim MP, after detailing the tortures to which his compatriots were subjected, told parliament, 'I can tell you that my co-religionists in the villages who do not speak a word of French now know what electricity is. Do you believe that sowing all this hatred is going to help any of us?' Mitterrand interjected that the only way to end these 'unfortunate habits' was to change the make-up of the police force, which the government was doing. The MP was not convinced. 'Without urgent reforms,' he told the assembly, 'you are opening the way to blood and tears.'

In December 1955, Edgar Faure, who had succeeded Mendès France, called a snap parliamentary election. The campaign turned out to be agitated. France had become prosperous in the ten years since the end of the war. But people viewed that as the fruit of their own efforts, achieved not thanks to the government but despite it. The political class as a whole was the object of growing contempt, blamed for instability at home and declining prestige abroad.

A new political force had sprung up to exploit this disaffection: the far right-wing Poujadist party, which had been founded to give voice to small shopkeepers and self-employed artisans. It quickly became a magnet for malcontents of all stripes – of which France, in the mid-1950s, was not in short supply – especially among the young. Its leader, Pierre Poujade, the proprietor of a stationery shop in a small town in south-western France, had begun his political career by organising a tax revolt. He was flamboyant, charismatic and within two years found himself at the head of a vociferous national movement. The Poujadists' slogans were 'Unite or croak!' and *'Sortez les sortants!'*, which meant 'Kick the bums out!'

The Poujadists practised systematic disruption, which made good political sense at a time when two out of three French citizens told pollsters that parliament disgusted them.

Favourite Poujadist tactics included 'bombarding with projectiles (tomatoes, fruit, trays of vegetables, empty bottles, etc.); cutting off electricity at meetings; taking candidates hostage; locking the doors of meeting halls; vandalism; and thuggery'. In the Charente, the harassment became so bad that a leading Radical, Félix Gaillard, was forced to cancel all his meetings for the last week of the campaign. In the Nièvre, Mitterrand was honoured by a visit from Poujade himself, whose wife, Yvette, screamed at him: 'MPs like you should be hanged . . . Your sort should be crushed like slugs.' Almost all his meetings were disrupted by fist fights, provoked by Poujadist supporters, and at the small town of Lucenay, in the Morvan, on December 14, he was hit on the head by a flying bottle.

Backed by the same Centre-Right coalition which had brought him victory in 1946 and 1951, Mitterrand himself was assured of re-election. But the UDSR was struggling. Its chief ally, the Radical Party, had refused to agree a list of constituencies where each party would give way to the other to avoid splitting the vote. This was standard practice in the Fourth Republic, but Mendès, moralistic as ever, had rejected it as horse-trading.

Fearing a mediocre result in his first election as party leader, Mitterrand had campaigned round the clock. On Christmas Day, the last Sunday before the vote, he collapsed in the middle of his speech. He had been hoping that if the UDSR did well, he might be invited to form the next government. He said later that it had not been due to any physical ailment, but sheer frustration at seeing that prize slip from his grasp.[10]

When the votes were counted, the outcome was as bad as Mitterrand had feared. The UDSR obtained six seats, half as many as in the outgoing parliament, and was able to form a parliamentary group only with the affiliation of the thirteen African MPs in Houphouet-Boigny's RDA. The Communists, with 25 per cent of the vote and 150 seats, emerged as the strongest party. The Poujadists, at the other end of the political spectrum, won 51 seats (of which 11 were later invalidated). In the mainstream the Socialists, the Christian Democrats and the traditional Right were level-pegging with roughly 90 seats each.

As Mitterrand had anticipated, Mendès's refusal to cut a deal had left the Radicals with substantially fewer seats than before. First Edgar Faure, then Mendès, declined Coty's invitation to try to form a government.

On February 1 1956, after a four-week hiatus, Guy Mollet was sworn in as the first Socialist Prime Minister for eight years. The previous week Mitterrand had presided over a meeting of the UDSR Executive Committee at which Mendès had been roundly condemned for causing the party's electoral losses. They had voted to back Mollet. Mitterrand endorsed the decision, not from pique at Mendès's refusal to play the parliamentary game, nor even from resentment at his conduct in the 'Leaks Affair', eighteen months earlier, which he did not and would not forget, but from calculations of his own interest. He was convinced that a Socialist-led administration would not last for more than a few months and that, when it fell, President Coty would be obliged to ask him to form the next government.

With parliament so finely divided, the Socialists needed all the support they could get. In return for the UDSR's backing, Mollet offered Mitterrand the post of Justice Minister, or 'Guardian of the Seals', second only to the Prime Minister in the government hierarchy.[11]

Mollet took office determined to bring peace to Algeria. During the campaign he had written that voters faced a choice 'between recon- ciliation . . . and an imbecile war with no end'. He had laid out his programme shortly before his investiture: neither withdrawal nor blind repression, but the maintenance of French rule; the introduction of a single electoral college for Europeans and Arabs; and social and economic reforms to reduce inequalities between the two communities.

To launch the new policy with a striking gesture, he planned a surprise visit to Algiers, like that which Mendès France had made to Tunis, eighteen months earlier. But news of the trip leaked out and the police sent back ominous reports that the settlers were mobilising for massive anti-government protests.

The *ultras* were up in arms because Mollet had decided to replace Jacques Soustelle, a dissident Gaullist whom Mendès had appointed as Governor-General of Algeria, with a veteran army officer, General Georges Catroux, who would hold Cabinet rank. Soustelle had initially been deeply unpopular. But gradually his insistence that Algeria must remain an integral part of France, his reluctant acceptance of 'enhanced interrogations' and his decision to authorise collective reprisals against Arab villages which supported the FLN – a chilling echo of Nazi practices during the Occupation – won the Europeans' support. When, on February 2, Soustelle was recalled to Paris, tens of thousands of settlers organised emotional demonstrations in Algiers and other cities, demanding that he remain.

It would have been difficult to find a worse moment for a newly elected Prime Minister to venture into the Algerian minefield. Mitterrand and Mendès, who had been named Minister of State, both urged him to postpone the visit. He refused.

As soon as Mollet landed in Algiers on the afternoon of February 6, he realised his mistake. The entire 12-mile length of the drive from the airport into the centre of the city was lined on both sides with soldiers and police at 10-yard intervals. The schools, the shops and the factories were shuttered and deserted, many of them draped in black. In the central square, before the Governor-General's Office, 50,000 people had gathered. When the Prime Minister and his delegation arrived to lay a wreath at the war memorial, the crowd erupted. They hurled clods of earth, paving stones, pebbles, metal bolts, fruit, vegetables and even tear-gas grenades, distributed by sympathetic police officers. His police escort managed to get him away to the Summer Palace, the Governor-General's official residence. The crowd followed and tried to storm the building. Jean Mairey, who, after working with

Mitterrand at the Interior Ministry, had been transferred to become Chief of Security in Algiers, ordered machine-guns with live ammunition to be set up, aimed at the rioters. 'I couldn't let the Prime Minister . . . be killed,' he explained later. 'I wasn't happy about it, but that was the point we had reached.'

In the event, salvation came from General Catroux, who had remained in Paris. With Mollet besieged inside the Palace, he decided that the only course open to him was to step down. It was the news the crowd had been hoping for. Their objective attained, the demonstrators dispersed.

The effects of the rioting, and of Mollet's humiliation, became clear over the next few months. The settlers had proved to themselves that if they were sufficiently determined, they could force the government in Paris to back off. By failing to use force against European rioters, when Arab protests were always put down with bloodshed, the government had acquiesced in a double standard: for all the talk of equality, there was one set of rules for Whites, another for Muslims. Guy Mollet might insist that the only model for Algeria was 'a cease-fire, followed by [new] elections, followed by negotiations', and that force was not an answer unless accompanied by reforms, but in practice the restoration of order became the government's sole priority.

With hindsight it is clear that Algeria had passed the point of no return many months before. But at the time, as Mollet's predecessor, Edgar Faure, acknowledged, with notable understatement, even 'the most lucid [of us] lacked clear-sightedness'.

While Faure was Prime Minister, in August 1955, seventy-one European men, women, children and infants had been slaughtered by the FLN at the port of Philippeville (now Skikda), on the north-eastern coast, in response to Soustelle's policy of collective reprisals. In the days that followed, the army executed more than a thousand Arabs, most of them ordinary townsfolk who were rounded up, taken to the town stadium and shot.[12] Extremists among the settlers, some of them former members of the Resistance, others supporters of Vichy, created terrorist groups on the model of the 'Red Hand' in Tunisia and the 'White Hand' in Morocco.

The Interior Minister, Maurice Bourgès-Maunoury, told parliament:

'How can one avoid – I do not excuse; I am just trying to explain – men who have seen their whole family with their throats cut losing their reason for a few minutes?'

By the time Mollet took office, twenty French citizens, both Arab and European, were being murdered every day. Officially sixteen rebels were killed daily, but the true figure was many times higher. Captured rebels were often tortured for information and then executed, which meant they did not figure in the government statistics.

In a secret report to the government, Jean Mairey compared the French army to the SS and his own police force to the Gestapo.

On February 15 1956, the Cabinet agreed in principle that the government should take 'exceptional, "dictatorial" powers' to resolve the Algerian problem. The minutes of the discussion show Mitterrand among the ministers favouring a hard line. The following month parliament approved legislation allowing the army to undertake police duties and substituting military tribunals for the civilian courts, even in cases entailing the death penalty. As Interior Minister, eighteen months earlier, Mitterrand had rejected a similar proposal. Now he signed off on it, together with Mollet; the new Algerian Governor-General, Robert Lacoste; and Bourgès-Maunoury, who had been appointed Defence Minister.[13]

Soon afterwards Mendès-France resigned. By 'ignoring the feelings and the misery of the indigenous population', he said, Mollet risked the loss not only of Algeria but of the whole of French Africa. Late in life, Mitterrand acknowledged that at that point he should have resigned too.

In June, the Cabinet discussed expediting the execution of Algerian prisoners who had been sentenced to death. Once again Mitterrand was in favour.

Over the next twelve months, forty-four Arabs and one European, a nationalist sympathiser, were sent to the guillotine. Each case was reviewed by the Supreme Council of the Magistracy, which made recommendations to President Coty, who then chose whether or not to commute the sentence. In at least thirty-two cases – some of the records are missing – Mitterrand, who, as Justice Minister, was Vice-President of the Council, recommended that the sentences be carried out. Jean-Claude Périer, a lawyer who also sat on the Council, remembered:

He already had a well-established reputation for authoritarianism when he took up his post and he made that felt. He was feared . . . [He] did not hide the fact that we were at war in Algeria and that, in his view, Justice was the means through which the State made its authority clear . . . Anything opposed to the authority of France must be pursued and punished. In war, you give no quarter . . . [His approach] was really very repressive. One can't deny that. But that was his vision of Algeria. He thought it was the best solution . . . There were two men in Mitterrand, the Justice Minister: first, a man who was open to all the questions of individual freedoms, and at the same time – which is quite paradoxical – a fighter, almost a man of war, in everything concerning government action. Open to liberties, but in favour of tough public action. That may seem contradictory, but with him every-thing was contradictory, and at the same time in harmony.[14]

Mitterrand adopted a similar attitude to the use of torture, which, as the situation deteriorated, was becoming more and more widespread. The government, at the highest levels, was well aware of what was being done. Périer remembered photographs, in the dossiers submitted to the Supreme Council, 'showing the corpses of victims on which tortures had been carried out that were beyond anything you could even imagine. It was unbearable.' The newspaper, *Le Monde*, wrote of the existence of 'veritable laboratories of torture' throughout Algeria, concluding ominously: 'One cannot defend a noble cause by foul means.'

The situation grew worse with every passing month.

The FLN ordered indiscriminate killing of European adults in Algiers and other cities. Foreign Legionnaires sent to relieve a company of their comrades in the Aurès Mountains found instead sixty mutilated corpses with their genitals stuffed into their mouths. Parts of the French army descended into barbarism, killing every Arab in their path. The conflict plumbed depths of savagery unknown in colonial wars elsewhere.

All this Mitterrand knew. He had his own informants in Algiers, among them the Prosecutor-General, Jean Reliquet, who sent him regular briefings.

Others, emulating Mendès France, resigned in protest. In October 1956, when the military forced down a plane with Ben Bella and three other FLN leaders aboard, the minister responsible for Moroccan and Tunisian Affairs, Alain Savary, a Socialist, quit the government. Not only had the army acted without Cabinet authorisation and in violation of international law, but the operation upended secret talks that were taking place with the rebels to try to achieve a ceasefire. Realistically the talks had no chance of success; but the action made continued contacts impossible. Asked by a journalist why he had not followed Savary's lead, Mitterrand replied weakly: 'One can't keep resigning all the time.'

That he believed that Algeria must remain French; that tough measures, no matter how regrettable, were necessary to achieve that; that the war, no matter how terrible, was a stage which the two countries had to pass through before peace could be achieved within some kind of Federation – all that was plausible. But it did not explain the limpet-like tenacity with which he clung to his post.

It did not explain, either, why he kept silent in April when Claude Bourdet was arrested for an article which the Defence Minister, Bourgès-Maunoury, claimed had 'damaged army morale'. It was the first time since the Nazi Occupation that a French journalist had been imprisoned for what he had written. Mendès France, then still a minister, immediately protested. Mollet, who saw at once the stupidity of what had been done, ordered his immediate release. But Mitterrand, who, as Justice Minister, was most directly involved, said nothing.[15]

Nor did it explain why he went out of his way to reassure an influential group of right-wing politicians – including Jacques Soustelle; the Gaullist senator, Michel Debré; and an up-and-coming young MP named Valéry Giscard d'Estaing – that they had nothing to fear from investigations into a bazooka attack on the office of the army commander in Algiers, General Raoul Salan, undertaken on the orders of a mysterious 'Committee of Six' of which they were alleged to be members.

The only explanation which covered everything he did that year – including his acquiescence in torture and his approval of military courts which he had rejected less than two years before – was that he had decided to subordinate all his actions to the overriding goal of becoming the next Prime Minister.

Opposing Bourgès, an influential colleague, was not a good idea if you were seeking to become head of government. On the other hand, having right-wingers in your debt, as well as allies in the Centre and on the Left, might be extremely helpful.

Only Mitterrand himself could have said exactly what was going on in his head during those twelve months. But the obstinacy with which he stuck to his strategy, even after it had become clear that Mollet's policies would fail and the whole concept of French Algeria was misconceived, was in character. Once he had decided something – in this case to hang on in government in the belief that it would pave the way for him to reach the highest post – he refused to let go even after it had become obvious that the gamble was lost. By the winter of 1956, he began to see that himself. His Chief of Staff, Pierre Nicolay, remembered that he became 'taciturn and irascible . . . You couldn't approach him any more . . . He became distant, totally silent.'[16] In Mollet's government, even hardliners like Bourgès and Robert Lacoste came out looking better. At least they knew what they believed in and were straightforward about it. Mitterrand seemed to believe in nothing except his own advancement.

'Mitterrand is both angel and demon,' Jacques Duhamel, later a Gaullist minister, told a journalist. 'Since a tender age, [he] has played two roles at once.' When, in the last months of his life, Mitterrand told Georges-Marc Benamou that he had felt 'ill at ease' in the Fourth Republic, it was this period that he had in mind.

That autumn an event occurred which would have profound implications for Algeria, for the Middle East and for the whole of the Western world.

On October 29 1956, Israel invaded the Sinai peninsula. A week later, British and French paratroops took Port Said. After another week they were within hours of winning control of the whole of the Suez Canal Zone. At which point, under intense pressure from President Eisenhower and the Soviet Head of State, Nikolai Bulganin, the British and French governments were forced to call a ceasefire.

The Suez fiasco, as it became known, had immense consequences. Britain and France lost for ever their dominant role in the Middle East. The US took the first steps towards a special security relationship with Israel, which until then it had kept at arm's length. Guy Mollet launched the French nuclear weapons programme, convinced that it was the only way for France to remain a major power; and, while he was at it, to thank Israel for its support in the ill-fated expedition, he agreed to help the Jewish State acquire nuclear weapons. The French army, already smarting from the abandonment of Indochina and now finding itself pulled up short on the verge of military victory in Egypt, lost confidence in the political authorities.

A putsch was smouldering. In December, General Jacques Faure, the deputy commandant in Algiers, who had close ties to the extreme Right, began gathering support for a military coup. The plot was discovered and those involved received a slap on the wrist. But it would only be a matter of time before it would happen again.

For Guy Mollet, the Suez disaster was a second Munich, a capitulation not to Hitler but to the hegemony of America and Russia. For the rest of his term in office, he ignored the war in Algeria, concentrating instead on Europe, where the following spring the six founding members of the European Economic Community – France, Germany, Italy and the Benelux countries – signed the Treaty of Rome.

The result was that, after Suez, the French army in Algeria had free rein.

That winter Jean Mairey submitted another devastating report on military violence against the Arab population. Bourgès-Maunoury fired him and gave instructions that he be forbidden to enter Algeria again. The following month, January 1957, after the assassination by the FLN of one of the leaders of the *ultras*, Lacoste placed Algiers under military rule.

General Jacques Massu's paratroops were charged with restoring order, which they did with their customary vigour. Twenty thousand Arabs were rounded up and placed in internment camps. Interrogation centres, no longer 'laboratories', practised torture on an industrial scale. Thousands who succumbed during questioning, or were 'too damaged, . . . no longer in a state where they could be shown', were thrown into the sea, weighted down with concrete. The Bay of Algiers became a marine cemetery. Bodies washed ashore were known as 'Bigeard's shrimps', after the French colonel whose paratroop unit distinguished itself in such operations. The repression brought a brief respite, but drove most of the capital's Arab population into the arms of the rebels.

For Mitterrand, Suez was a sign that the government's days were numbered.

In a speech to the UDSR, he accepted for the first time that Algeria might be granted internal self-government, but only if, unlike in Tunisia and Morocco, 'we are sure it will go no further' and the territory would remain part of France.[17] In private he no longer ruled out independence as a long-term possibility. Within the Cabinet, he joined Gaston Defferre, the Socialist Minister of Overseas Territories, and his old ally, Jacques Chaban-Delmas, the Minister of State, in calling for a fundamental change of policy. The government, he said, should proclaim an unconditional ceasefire and resume negotiations.

Mollet was unmoved. 'We are all in the same boat,' the Prime Minister told them. The policy would not be changed.

Two months later, in March, Mitterrand wrote to Mollet to protest that 'out of 900 persons arrested by the paratroops, only 39 have been presented in court. [The judiciary] is in total ignorance of the fate of the others.' Lacoste was furious. 'Your prosecutor-general knows nothing!' he raged back. 'It's not 900 who have disappeared but 3,000!' That proves, Mitterrand retorted, 'that Mr Reliquet is not given to exaggeration.' The following week, he blocked a proposal to extend the power of the military tribunals. On that occasion, for the first time in an official letter from one minister to another, the word 'torture' was employed. 'You are not unaware,' he wrote to Bourgès-Maunoury, 'of the cases of torture of which certain military units have been guilty and for which they should be brought to account before a judge.' The Defence Minister was livid. To say that he was 'aware' of such things, and was doing nothing about them, amounted to accusing him of complicity.[18]

But it was all far too little, too late. Mitterrand had known for years that the law was being trampled underfoot in Algeria. To start putting down markers in the spring of 1957, and even then only within the government, was totally unconvincing.[19] In parliament, before the Justice Commission, in April, he finally acknowledged for the first time in public that there had been 'cases of physical abuse . . . and an increase in arbitrary detentions'. But, given the scale of the abuse, it was a very feeble admission. These 'regrettable facts', he assured his listeners, were far less frequent than the newspapers claimed, 'although more than there should be'.

Mitterrand's refusal to take a moral stand proved not only weak but misguided. When, at long last, in May 1957, after sixteen months in power – a record of longevity in the Fourth Republic – Mollet's government fell, Coty called on his rival, Bourgès-Maunoury, to form the new government.[20] Despite their political differences, Bourgès asked Mitterrand to stay on as Justice Minister. He declined. If Mollet had been unable to bring peace to Algeria, his successor was unlikely to do better.[21]

In the next four months, France had three governments. Bourgès-Maunoury lasted until the end of September. He was succeeded by Antoine Pinay, whose administration survived one day, followed by Guy Mollet, who remained in office for less than a week.

At that point, Mitterrand felt once again that he had a real chance of being nominated as Prime Minister. Instead, in November 1957, Coty named Félix Gaillard, a brilliant young economist in the Radical Party who, the day after his 38th birthday, became the youngest head of the French government since Napoleon. Mitterrand knew and appreciated Gaillard. 'I often had the impression,' he said (many years later, after Gaillard had been killed in a yachting accident), 'that he was more intelligent than I was, that he thought faster than I did, that he was more seductive to women. In some ways, he gave me a complex. But he lacked perseverance.' Mitterrand proved as much, one blazing hot summer's day, when he and Gaillard played tennis at the home of a relative of a young left-wing lawyer named Robert Badinter. 'Félix Gaillard was much better, more talented, stronger, more skilful,' Badinter remembered. 'Yet to everyone's surprise, Mitterrand was the winner. He was much more determined. He wore him down, in three and a half hours.' Mitterrand confessed later to Badinter that, after 'that stupid tennis match', it took him two months to recover. But that was not the point. What mattered was that he had won.

Gaillard's government survived five months and, like Bourgès-Maunoury's before it, was brought down by events in Algeria. His fall, on April 16, finally opened the way for Mitterrand's nomination.

René Coty first summoned the Christian Democrat, Georges Bidault, who failed to obtain the backing even of his own party. Then he called Mitterrand. 'He asked me: "Will you accept the votes of the Communists?"', Mitterrand recounted. 'I replied: "Of course. And if that's not enough, I will ask for them." Coty responded: "In that case it's impossible.'"[22] The story was plainly untrue. With one exception – that of Pierre Mendès France – every government in the Fourth Republic had accepted the votes of Communist MPs. It was no more a problem for Coty than for anyone else. That Mitterrand should make such a claim many years later, at a time when he wished to pretend that he had always favoured an alliance with the Communist Party, was understandable. But that was not what had caused Coty to refuse him his chance. For some reason, Mitterrand acknowledged in a letter next day to his friend, Henri Friol, who was Coty's Chief of Staff, the President did not trust him.[23] He never worked out why. It might have stemmed from the 'Leaks Affair', when Coty had sided with his accusers. It might even have been – irony of ironies! – that his performance as Justice Minister had aroused the old man's contempt. Whatever the root cause, after sounding out Pleven, who, like Bidault, was unable to muster sufficient support, the President finally named a Christian Democrat, Pierre Pflimlin, who was sworn in on May 14.

Coty claimed afterwards that he had expected Pflimlin's government to fall quickly. Had that happened, he told a colleague, 'I would have called on François Mitterrand, whose statesmanlike qualities I have often appreciated.'[24] That was also untrue. Two weeks later, when Mitterrand met the President again at the head of a UDSR delegation, Coty's remarks were surreal:[25]

> The President [said to me] in a paternal tone: 'I would very well have called you, Mr Mitterrand. I recognise your abilities and I appreciate your courage. But if I had given you the mission to form a government, given your reputation down there, it would have risked causing troubles in Algiers . . .' Troubles in Algiers! The least one could say at the end of May 1958 was that the troubles were already there. The problem wasn't making them, but bringing them to an end.

If Mitterrand's reputation in Algeria ruled him out as a potential Prime Minister, why had Coty said that if Pflimlin fell, he would have named him? Behind the polite dissimulation, Coty was plainly determined that, on his watch, Mitterrand's name would not go forward.[26] The UDSR leader had held almost a dozen ministerial posts, including two of the top three in the Cabinet. Coty had designated others who were younger and far less experienced.[27] To Mitterrand, however, he never offered that chance. His dream of becoming Prime Minister was not only unfulfilled. With Coty it had been vain from the outset.[28]

Edgar Faure, with his usual verve, summed up the challenge the government faced. 'The Algerian problem,' he said, 'is a problem in the fourth dimension, and there is only one man in France who can move about up there.' Shortly after meeting Mitterrand, the President invited the man of the fourth dimension to come to the Elysée. After twelve years in the wilderness, General de Gaulle was back. The following day he was sworn in as the 25th and last Prime Minister of the Fourth Republic.

Since early spring, the possibility of the General's return had been on everybody's lips.[29] In March, tens of thousands of posters had appeared in towns all over France, urging: 'Let us call de Gaulle!' At the beginning of May, René Coty despatched an emissary to the General's home at Colombey-les-Deux-Églises, asking what his attitude would be if the country asked him to return. Four days later, de Gaulle sent a noncommittal reply. But in private he made clear that he would 'face up to his responsibilities and take over the reins of the nation' if the situation required it.

On May 13, a Tuesday, a demonstration was called in Algiers to mourn three French soldiers who had been taken prisoner and executed by the FLN. The government was confident that it had the situation in hand. When a colleague arrived from Algiers to warn Pflimlin that the army was on the brink of revolt, the Prime Minister replied: 'All that's police fiction, my dear friend . . . You've been too long in the sun.'

But under the sun, the earth was moving.

That afternoon, the demonstration spun out of control. While the police stood by, tens of thousands of settlers rampaged through the Governor-General's Office, smashing furniture, tearing doors from their hinges and throwing equipment and files out of the windows. To restore calm, the paratroop commander, General Massu, agreed, at the rioters' demand, to lead a Committee of Public Safety to uphold French rule, with Léon Delbecque as his deputy. Delbecque, a leading *ultra*, had just arrived from Paris, where he had been working secretly with sympathisers on the army's General Staff to prepare to place the French capital under military rule to await de Gaulle's return. Algiers was in a state of insurrection and there was every reason to think that, if it continued, the troubles would spread to France itself.

Mitterrand was at the National Assembly for the debate on Pflimlin's investiture when news of these events reached Paris.

The government was paralysed. That night there were calls, each more improbable than the last, for troops to be ordered to open fire on the rioters; for de Gaulle and his staff to be arrested; for the General to be drugged and compelled to issue a statement condemning the revolt. In the early hours of the morning, Pflimlin was sworn in. Fifteen minutes later, speaking from the balcony of the Governor-General's Office, Massu appealed to de Gaulle 'to set up a Government of National Salvation which alone can save Algeria'. A Cabinet meeting at 4.30 a.m. broke up without taking any decision.

Two days later the army commander, General Salan, threw his weight behind the rebels, declaring, at the end of an emotional speech to the people of Algiers: 'Long live General de Gaulle!' That night, in a brief statement, de Gaulle reacted publicly for the first time:

> Formerly the country, in its deepest being, put its confidence in me to lead it, in its entirety, to salvation. Today, facing the trials which confront it once again, may it know that I hold myself ready to assume the powers of the Republic.[30]

In Algiers, there were scenes of wild enthusiasm. In Paris, the Left and Centre – Communists, Radicals, Socialists and UDSR – protested that de Gaulle had not condemned the generals' sedition.

In fact 'the Great Charles' was in an invidious position. To convince the politicians, and the country as a whole, that he alone was capable of mastering the situation and restoring calm, it was necessary that the military flout the legitimate authority of the State. If he wished to regain power, he had no choice but to remain silent while sedition triumphed.[31] But by doing so he opened himself to the charge that he was returning to power by a putsch. He might argue that the authority of the State had crumbled to such a degree that it no longer merited the army's support.[32] But rebellion is rebellion, no matter what it is called. In May 1958, as in June 1940, Charles de Gaulle was on the side of those who had rebelled against the lawful government.*

At a press conference on Monday, May 19, the first he had held for three years, the General made clear that he intended to be 'the master of the hour'. Among those packed in to hear him at the Hôtel d'Orsay, in the cavernous nineteenth-century railway station of that name on the Left Bank of the Seine, were Graham Greene and François Mauriac's younger brother, Jean, who was mesmerised by his performance.

'He was triumphant,' Jean wrote afterwards, 'utterly certain of his return to power. Ironic, mocking, sardonic, witty. He made everyone laugh. [For two hours] he was by turns light-hearted and serious, optimistic and dramatic, with a youthfulness and verve that were riveting.'

Pflimlin and Guy Mollet listened on the radio as de Gaulle majestically dismissed the notion that he might curtail political freedoms. 'Have I ever done so?' he asked. 'On the contrary, I have re-established them when they had disappeared. Do you think that at the age of 67, I am about to launch a career as a dictator?'

The contentious, and unanswerable, question of his support for the insurrection he eluded with a pirouette: the leaders in Algeria, he noted, 'have not been the object of any disciplinary measure by the government, which has even delegated to them its authority. Why, then, do you want me – who holds no public office – to condemn them for sedition?'

For the next week, de Gaulle stood aside as the government's unity fractured. First Mollet, then Pflimlin himself, put out feelers to the General's staff. Preparations for direct military intervention, which Léon Delbecque had initiated ten days earlier, gathered pace. 'Operation Resurrection' as it had been named, would involve the sending of paratroops to seize strategic points around Paris and install the General in power. Officially de Gaulle disapproved. But he was well informed about its planning, and the signals he sent out privately were sufficiently ambiguous to keep the threat alive. The weekend following his press

* In June 1940, when de Gaulle appealed to the French from London to resist the German Occupation, Pétain was at the head of a lawful government established under the constitution of the Third Republic, which continued in existence until July 10. Although in May 1958 he went to great lengths to insist that he had returned to power legally, and not, as he put it, 'in a tumult of generals', speaking much later he acknowledged three acts of military rebellion in his life: in 1940, against Pétain; in August 1944, against the government of Pierre Laval, during the Occupation; and during the Algerian crisis which returned him to power in 1958.

conference, supporters of the insurrectionists, led by a far-Right MP, Pascal Arrighi, seized control in Corsica. It was a sideshow of no importance, but psychologically it raised the stakes. Next day, General Ely, who had resigned a few days earlier as Chief of the General Staff, noted in his diary: 'The risk of civil war is growing.' From then on, the Prime Minister slept in a different place each night. Only de Gaulle was unperturbed, instructing Georges Pompidou, who had worked with him since the 1940s, to start preparing the speech he would make on his accession to power.

Was 'Resurrection' a real possibility? The military and the political authorities thought so. To de Gaulle, it was a means of exerting pressure on the government to transfer power peacefully. Would he have let it go ahead if all else had failed? The balance of evidence suggests that he would. Certainly he kept the option open until the last possible moment. If it did not happen, it was because, in the end, he found he did not need it.[33]

At 4 a.m. on May 29, Pflimlin resigned. President Coty appealed to 'the most illustrious of Frenchmen' to form a Government of National Salvation to bring the country back from 'the brink of civil war', a proposition which the General graciously accepted.

Throughout these days of high drama, Mitterrand, like his colleagues, had been an impotent bystander. In principle, he had not been hostile to the General's return. Despite their political differences, and his run-ins with de Gaulle's supporters in the battle for leadership of the UDSR, the General remained for him a reference, a symbol of the greatness of France, who merited respect. At dinner at his apartment one evening with a group of colleagues, when one of them made a disobliging remark about the General, Mitterrand cut him off: 'I will not permit anyone to speak of General de Gaulle in that tone at my table.' In March 1958, at a time when debate about his possible comeback was already in full spate, he wrote in Le Monde that 'no Frenchman alive is more worthy of a permanent place in History than the leader of Free France' and expressed the hope that, through him, some 'as yet unknown agreement' would be found to lead the country towards harmony and peace.

A few days earlier, Maurice Duverger, a respected political commentator, had written in the same newspaper that the only question about de Gaulle's return was: 'When?' For Mitterrand, it was not 'When?' but

'How?', and as the events of May played out, he liked less and less what he saw.

He knew nothing yet about 'Resurrection' and still less about de Gaulle's part in it. But the General's refusal to condemn the rebellion and his evident determination to use it as a lever for his return to power raised disturbing questions. On May 25, when Arrighi and the paratroopers seized power in Corsica, Mitterrand spoke in parliament for the first time of a *pronunciamento* – a military putsch – in the making. Four days later, after Coty's appeal to de Gaulle to form a government, he spent the afternoon walking along the Left Bank of the Seine, pondering his future:

> It was a day of clear, pale sun. The watery surface of the river glinted under the changing light of the sky. I wondered to myself . . . Should I defend a political system which was incapable of giving France its proper rank? Or should I lend a helping hand to the conspiracy which was about to destroy it? . . . Everything invited me to agree to the liquidation of the Fourth Republic, with its warring ceremonial kings, its stewards who ruled in their stead, this dinginess of a dying breath. But everything separated me too from this dictatorship, which under a mask of meekness could be seen by the naked eye . . .[34]

It was perhaps the most difficult decision he would have to take in the whole of his political career. Should he throw in his lot with the General? Or strike out on his own? 'He was debating within himself', his friend André Rousselet remembered. In the days that followed, most of Mitterrand's colleagues in the UDSR and in the other centrist parties would rally to de Gaulle's standard. Guy Mollet and even the 'Stalinist', Félix Houphouet-Boigny, accepted posts in the new government. But Mitterrand was not prepared to serve in the General's shadow. He refused to play second fiddle – to de Gaulle or anyone else.

By the time he returned to the National Assembly, he had made up his mind. He would vote against de Gaulle. 'We are going to have him for twenty years,' he told his friend, Jean Pinel, '[and] I am the only one who is capable of opposing him.'[35] It was an astonishing prediction. Twenty-three years would elapse before the elections of May 1981 brought Mitterrand to power.[36]

On Saturday afternoon, de Gaulle received the parliamentary

leadership (except the Communists, who were not invited) at the Hôtel La Pérouse, where he stayed when he was in Paris, not far from the Arc de Triomphe. Roger Duveau, who accompanied Mitterrand, representing the UDSR, remembered being struck by the General's enormous feet, shod in light yellow leather. He was courteous, affable, soliciting each one's opinions, assuring them that he was 'in agreement with most of your views'. Those present, including Mendès France, Mollet, Ramadier and several other former prime ministers, Mitterrand wrote later, 'bowed and scraped' before him. When his own turn came to speak, he remembered feeling nervous. He began in an elliptical manner by noting 'the impermanence of things'. De Gaulle interrupted to ask what he was trying to say. 'You will understand, *mon général*,' he replied, 'if you will kindly let me speak':

> I will not vote for you until you disavow publicly the Public Safety Committee in Algiers and the military insurrection. A republican regime cannot be born out of the constraints of a putsch . . . During these last days we have embarked on the perilous and unwonted path of the *pronunciamento*, which until now has been the preserve of South American republics . . . After the generals, next it will be the turn of the colonels . . . You tell us that, to face these kinds of tragedies which risk bringing the ruin of France, there is only one recourse: yourself, *mon général*. But you are mortal![37]

It was, as the French like to say, 'a fart in church'. For once de Gaulle could not find the right words. 'I can see where you are leading,' he snapped, before getting up and walking out. 'You want my death. Well I am ready.'

Next day, June 1, parliament met exceptionally on a Sunday to debate his investiture. Mitterrand used the occasion for a memorable philippic, in which he explained his reasons for opposing de Gaulle's being sworn in:

> When, on September 10 1944, General de Gaulle presented himself before the Consultative Assembly . . . he had with him two companions called honour and patriotism. His companions today, which he no doubt did not choose but which have followed him, are named coup and sedition.
> General de Gaulle's presence [here] means that, even though he

may not wish it, from now on violent minorities will be able to launch with impunity victorious assaults against democracy . . .

The dilemma parliament faces is as follows: Either we accept a Prime Minister – whose merits are immense and whose role is supposed to permit national reconciliation, but who has already been elected by the Committee in Algiers – or we . . . will be chased away . . . We do not accept that ultimatum . . .

General de Gaulle . . . was called back in the first place by an undisciplined army. In law, the powers that will be conferred on him tonight will have been bestowed by the representatives of the nation. In fact he holds them already as the result of a *coup d'état*.[38]

His attack extended beyond de Gaulle to those responsible for the Fourth Republic's demise. 'While there was still time to resist [the insurrection] and uphold the law . . . the government disappeared,' he said. 'It died, as it had lived, with a whimper.' The General, he recalled, 'eloquent as always, precise as always, severe as always', had condemned the old system. Yet his new government included that system's 'most representative figures', Mollet on the Left, Pinay on the Right, and the Christian Democrat, Pflimlin – all former prime ministers. Where was the coherence in that?

When he finished, only the Communists and a handful of Socialists applauded.

With this speech, Mitterrand burnt his boats, not only with de Gaulle but with a wide swathe of parliamentary opinion, stretching from the Centre to the far Right.

It was typical of him. He always hung on to a position far longer than was reasonable and then made a sudden, bold, reckless, leap into the unknown. In his private life, he had gone on hoping that Marie-Louise Terrasse would respond to his love long after it was clear to all around him that the relationship was doomed; then he made a snap decision to marry Danielle, whose background and family values were totally different from his own. At Vichy, he had hesitated, equivocated and agonised for more than a year before committing himself to the Resistance with an excessive, defiant act of bravado at the Salle Wagram in Paris. In the Fourth Republic, he had held on as Justice Minister in the hope that, by manipulating slippery parliamentary combinations, he would eventually become Prime Minister. When de Gaulle's return finally convinced him that that was impossible, he leapt away once more, this time into opposition.[39]

Only two political groupings in France consistently opposed de Gaulle: the extreme Right and (parts of) the Left. Whatever interest Mitterrand might once have felt in the far Right, as a student in the 1930s, was long since forgotten. In the new circumstances provoked by de Gaulle's return, his future – as the applause which greeted his speech made clear – lay with the Left. There was a nice symmetry about it. Now that the General was back, occupying the Centre and Right of the political spectrum, Mitterrand, his self-proclaimed challenger, was displaced towards the terrain held by the Communists and the left wing of the Socialist Party.[40] All other considerations aside, there was nowhere else he could go.

De Gaulle was invested as Prime Minister that night by a large majority. In the UDSR group, ten MPs voted for him, only Mitterrand and three others against. The following day, he was entrusted with 'full powers', as Pétain had been, eighteen years earlier, though in this case for a duration limited to six months while a new constitution was drawn up.

Two days later, he set out for Algiers, where he was given a tick-ertape welcome, worthy of Fifth Avenue in New York, reassuring the Arab population and encouraging the *ultras* with his promise, *'Je vous ai compris!'*, to believe, at least for a time, that he was on their side. He himself had no such illusions. Back in Paris, he told his Chief of Staff, Pierre Lefranc:

> They are dreaming . . . They forget that there are nine million Muslims for a million Europeans . . . What is the army down there? A few colonels who think that they are Giap [the Viet Minh commander who defeated the French at Dien Bien Phu]. And the French? The big settlers cling to their rights; the little ones panic . . . We cannot keep Algeria. Believe me, I am the first to regret it, but the proportion of Europeans is too small . . . We will have to find a form of cooperation where the rights of France will be protected.[41]

Algeria's fate was sealed. The only question was what could be saved from the wreckage and how the process would play out before the curtain was rung down.

In August it was the turn of Black Africa to feel the General's implacable logic. Two years earlier, Gaston Defferre had persuaded parliament to pass a law giving the French territories in sub-Saharan Africa internal self-government. The measure had provided a safety valve for nationalist aspirations. But by the time de Gaulle took office, pressure was building for the next step. He responded by proposing a Franco-African Community in which each country would enjoy enhanced autonomy and also have the right to secede.

Mitterrand and the rest of the non-communist Left were wrong-footed. Here was de Gaulle, doing in a matter of weeks for Black Africa what successive parliamentary governments had failed to do for years.

Mitterrand's thinking had evolved since his condescending reference to the subject peoples as 'children' in 1955. He had approved Defferre's formula for 'self-government within the French Union'. He had accepted that integration would not work: if applied consistently, it would make France, for demographic reasons, the colony of its own colonies. He understood that in a Federal Republic, the rules would need to be the same for all, France, Algeria and Black Africa, and that neither the settlers nor the FLN would accept that. But he was still unwilling to recognise that the 'disaster' of independence – as he had called it five years earlier – might be the only answer. In this, as in much else, de Gaulle was streets ahead of him.

By September 1958, the new constitution was ready.

It followed closely the blueprint the General had laid out at Bayeux in 1946. The stranglehold exerted by the parties on the political process was lifted. For the first time since the Second Empire – when Louis-Napoleon Bonaparte, afterwards Napoleon III, had also been brought to power by a coup – France would have a strong executive president, elected by indirect suffrage for a seven-year term and endowed with greater powers than any of his Western counterparts. He named the Prime Minister and members of the Cabinet and could revoke their appointments at any time. If France faced 'a grave and immediate danger', he was authorised to take 'whatever measures the circum-stances require' without reference to parliament or any other consti-tutional body, a far looser formulation than in the United States or Britain. Parliament could bring down the government by refusing a vote of confidence, but the Head of State could dissolve parliament at will, equivalent to a US President being able to call fresh congressional elections whenever he saw fit. And as though that were not enough, in practice – if not in law – the President had what was called a 'reserved domain', which gave him, rather than the government, the last word on policy in foreign affairs and defence.[42]

The constitutional referendum, held on September 28, in the overseas territories as well as metropolitan France, was a triumph. Nearly 80 per cent of those who took part (and 96 per cent in Algeria, where Arabs voted en masse for the first time) were in favour. It was hardly a surprise. The propaganda apparatus of the State had been mobilised as never before to ensure that only the General's side of the argument was heard. To most voters, it was a plebiscite for or against de Gaulle. Those who voted against him did so to protest at the manner in which he had returned to power; from doubts about the wisdom of concentrating such sovereign authority in one pair of hands; and from fears that parliament, having for so long been too powerful, would now be stripped of its proper role – or, as in the case of Mitterrand and Mendès France, for a combination of all those reasons.

A small minority on the far Right worried that it would give the General carte blanche to offer independence to French Africa and eventually to Algeria as well.

That proved to be the case. When the people of Guinea voted against the constitution and rejected membership of the proposed Franco-African Community, de Gaulle retaliated with a pettiness which, at various times in his career, marred his authentic grandeur. Guinea became independent and, overnight, all economic and political relations with the former colony were cut. Eighteen months later, the rest of the Community followed suit.

Mitterrand's dream of a Eurafrican France, extending 'from Lille to the Congo, from Chad to Senegal', was over, buried by a man who had seen more quickly and more clearly than he that France's colonial empire was a relic of the past. Not until much later would he bring himself to admit: 'I was wrong to try to reconcile what was unreconcilable . . . Colonial emancipation can only be global and complete.'

Mitterrand's career, in the closing months of 1958, was in danger of becoming a relic of the past too.

Parliamentary elections were called on Sunday, November 23, with a second round a week later. Unlike the previous elections in which

Mitterrand had taken part, where proportional representation was applied at the level of each *département*, de Gaulle, for the first time since 1936, had reintroduced a first-past-the-post system with single-seat constituencies. The area around Nevers, where Mitterrand had been a municipal councillor, had a moderate right-wing electorate. In the past they had supported him, but they were 'as unstable as the sands of the River Loire' and this time he thought they would vote for a Gaullist. Instead he chose to stand in the sprawling constituency in the east of the Nièvre, the Morvan, whose hardscrabble farming communities were more sympathetic to the Left.

In the first round, he finished third, behind a Gaullist and a Socialist, Dr Daniel Benoist. Normally he would have been expected to stand down in favour of the better-placed left-wing candidate. But Mitterrand's relations with Benoist were execrable and he decided to remain in the race. The good doctor was enraged, and distributed pamphlets depicting Mitterrand with a hammer and sickle and the Pétainist *francisque* to suggest that he was in league both with the Communists and the extreme Right. In fact the Communists did support him – the first time they had done so – though less because of a convergence of views than because he had voted against the new constitution, whereas Benoist, like Guy Mollet, had campaigned in its favour.

The following Sunday, when the votes were counted, the Gaullist was elected with 40.3 per cent, Mitterrand came second with 32.1 per cent, and Benoist, third with 27 per cent. In the tidal wave of support for the General which washed over France that month, many others – including Mendès France, Edgar Faure and Édouard Daladier, all former prime ministers – were also swept away. The Socialists hung on to only 40 seats out of nearly a hundred in the previous parliament. Communist strength declined from 150 to 10.

But that was scant consolation. After twelve years as an MP, during which he had been a minister eleven times, Mitterrand was out of a job.

7

Crossing the Desert

In the war, when Mitterrand had been wounded, captured, sent to a prison camp and forced to acknowledge that his fiancée, the great passion of his life, was slipping from his grasp, he had shown that he was at his best when he had his back to the wall. The trials he faced after de Gaulle's return were less dramatic but scarcely less difficult.

On January 8 1959, the Fourth Republic expired peacefully in its sleep.

Its record was much less bad than its reputation suggested. In its twelve years of existence, it had healed – or at least papered over – the wounds left by the Occupation; affirmed France's role as a global power; helped establish the European Common Market; and laid the foundations of the *'trente glorieuses'*, the three decades of prosperity which would continue until the Oil Shocks of the 1970s. But the Fourth Republic was unloved and all those associated with it were discredited.

Almost overnight, Mitterrand became yesterday's man.

The UDSR, to which he had devoted so much time and effort, had ceased to exist as a parliamentary force and barely survived as a political party. A new left-wing movement, the Union of Democratic Forces or UFD, was established by Pierre Mendès France as a refuge for survivors of the Gaullist shipwreck. But it quickly became clear that it was going nowhere. Another left-wing group, the Parti Socialiste Autonome (Autonomous Socialist Party) or PSA, split off from the Socialist Party and, together with three or four other left-wing fragments, formed the core of what would be termed the 'New Left', so-called to differentiate it from the Molletists, whose archaic official title was 'The French Section of the Workers International' (SFIO). The PSA appeared to have better prospects. But it wanted nothing to do with Mollet's former Justice Minister. Mitterrand was too marked by his failure to speak out against torture, too tarnished by his Fourth Republic image, too retrograde and reactionary in his attitude to decolonisation. Alain Savary, who had resigned from Mollet's government in protest against its Algerian policies, delivered the *coup de grâce*, declaring, 'We have enough Franciscans in the PSA already.' Savary, who had joined de Gaulle in London in 1940, was not referring to Mitterrand's Catholic upbringing but to the *francisque* which he had been awarded by Pétain.

The time Mitterrand had spent at Vichy and his earlier, supposed links with the extreme Right, while a student in the 1930s, were never long forgotten. Usually it was the Gaullists who attacked him as a Pétainist or an ex-member of the Cagoule. This time the bullet came from the other side. Mitterrand made light of it at the time, but his rejection by the 'New Left' scarred him. Years later Savary and a high-flying young intellectual named Michel Rocard, whom Mitterrand suspected – wrongly – of being among those who had blackballed him, would have cause to regret what had happened that spring.

The only political post he then held, outside the moribund UDSR, was as a modest provincial councillor for the *département* of the Nièvre. But the support networks he had built up there over the previous twelve years stood him in good stead. In March he was elected Mayor of Château-Chinon, the chief town of the Morvan, and on April 26 1959, after less than half a year out of office – during which, for the first time in his life, he had had to earn his living as a lawyer, acting as defence counsel in a series of civil and criminal cases – he returned to parliament as senator for the Nièvre.

It was just as well. His forays into the world of jurisprudence were not a great success. Georges Dayan, for whose law office he worked, remembered: 'If you gave him a case where a lot of money could be made, he would always win, but in such a way that we never made a penny out of it.'

Back in the mainstream of national politics, Mitterrand settled into his new role as the bête noire of the Gaullists. 'Was [de Gaulle] part of the plot [in Algiers]?' he asked, a few weeks after the General assumed the presidency. 'No! He was no more part of the plot than God was part of the Creation!' The elections of 1958, he said, had signalled the start of 'a totalitarian process . . . [marked by] brainwashing and intoxication by radio, television and the press'. Even more than the General, he targeted the *ultras*. As Interior Minister, five years earlier, he had earned their lasting enmity by proposing to amalgamate Algeria's police force with that of metropolitan France. Now he taunted them as the tail which wanted to wag the dog:

> Forty-three million French citizens have the right to speak, not just the [one] million in Algeria . . . To allow a minority [European] commu-nity to maintain a false equilibrium against the [Muslim] majority by institutional devices which will not withstand the tide of history will lead in the end either to that community being crushed or to its carrying out the same kind of absolutely unacceptable operation as the Whites in South Africa, who have founded their domination on unjust laws. We should not let them choose. It's not their private affair. Since they insist they are French, it is for France to choose in their name . . . In all circumstances, [we must demonstrate] an implacable will to prevent the minority dominating . . . and imposing, in the name of the integ-rity of France, out-of-date worn-out concepts which in reality represent only [its own] seditious interests . . . We should say to those French citizens [in Algeria] who are of [European] origin: . . . 'Each of you represents only one 43-millionth . . . part of the nation . . .' One small part cannot lay down the law to the whole country.[1]

In the Senate, his favourite quarry was Michel Debré, whom de Gaulle had appointed Prime Minister. Before May 1958, Debré had published a weekly newspaper, *Le Courrier de la colère* ('The Anger Post'), which had been one of the *ultras'* principal propaganda sheets and had campaigned for de Gaulle's return. The Prime Minister, Mitterrand told the senators, equated reform in Algeria with treason, 'because he is truly, deeply, unshakeably convinced, and nothing can alter that conviction, that the moment that he stops using force, everything will be lost'. His sincerity was undeniable, he declared, but 'if we wait until the guns are silent, the only ones left to hear France's voice will be a mute people amid ruins'.

De Gaulle saw that danger. In an interview with a settler newspaper in Oran in April 1959, he warned that 'the Algeria of papa is dead, and those who don't understand that will die with her'. Change was coming, and those, like Debré, who were wedded to the settlers' cause, had either to submit or rebel. The Prime Minister swallowed his pride and submitted.

In September, the General made an announcement which increased tension sharply on both sides of the Mediterranean. Once law and order had been restored, he said, Algerians would be allowed to decide their own future. They had three choices: independence, which, he asserted, would bring 'appalling misery, frightful political chaos, gener-alised throat-cutting and before long a bellicose dictatorship of communists'; 'Frenchification', whereby all Algerians, regardless of their origin, would become 'an integral part of the French people'; or self-government as an associated state.[2]

The *ultras*, and parts of the army, viewed that as a betrayal. Mitterrand's sniping at 'French Algeria' and its supporters, at a time when de Gaulle's intentions appeared increasingly uncertain, set the stage for the machination that became the Observatory Affair.

If the mechanisms of the plot which caused Mitterrand to act as he did in the autumn of 1959 – allowing himself to be enticed by Robert Pesquet, a former extreme right-wing MP, into acquiescing in a faked assassination attempt – are no longer in doubt, the identities of those behind the conspiracy, in which Pesquet was a cat's-paw, a 'lamplighter' as the French put it, remain elusive.

Whoever masterminded the scheme was a man of perverse intel-ligence and remarkable intuition about human vulnerabilities. Pesquet was nimble and cunning. But he was not in that league.

Mitterrand believed that Michel Debré was responsible.

The theory was plausible. Maurice Bourgès-Maunoury, whom Pesquet had initially approached, was the one man, apart from himself, who, when they were both ministers in the government of Guy Mollet, had had access to the secret files on the Bazooka Affair in which Debré had been implicated.[3] The prosecutor in Algiers, Jean Reliquet, had thought the evidence sufficiently solid to request the lifting of Debré's parliamentary immunity. Mitterrand and Bourgès had decided, for political reasons, not to let the case proceed. But both were in a position to know embarrassing details of Debré's role and perhaps to have kept in a safe place copies of incriminating documents. Now Debré was seeking the lifting of Mitterrand's immunity on the grounds that he had omitted to inform the police of his conversations with

Pesquet until the latter's role had been made public, which, the government argued, was tantamount to contempt of court.

The charge was bizarre. An 'omission', under French law, does not constitute judicial contempt. But that was not Debré's problem. He was determined to use every means at his disposal to prolong his opponent's agony.[4] Mitterrand had savaged Debré over Algeria. Now the Prime Minister was taking his revenge.

When the Senate met in November, Mitterrand hit back, recalling how 'in February 1957, [when I was Justice Minister] a man was waiting to see me at the Chancellery . . . I received him. He protested his innocence in an affair which had just broken . . . Doubtless in the dossier there were accusations and troubling confessions, but he would explain all that later. He just needed time, which he would not have . . . if I asked for the lifting of [his] parliamentary immunity.' After an interminable pause, while Mitterrand looked slowly around the packed benches, he drove home his advantage: 'The man walking nervously around my office . . . was the Prime Minister, Michel Debré!'[5]

The attack won him a reprieve. But a week later, the Senate lifted his immunity anyway, by 175 votes to 27, and in December the investigating magistrate preferred charges.

At that point, however, a complication arose. Roland Dumas, who represented Mitterrand, discovered that the magistrate and the prosecutor, both of whom had been named to the case by the Justice Ministry, were personal friends of Pesquet, which not only provided grounds for annulling the procedure but raised intriguing questions about how and on whose instructions the pair had been appointed.[6]

By then Debré was having second thoughts. A trial in open court risked opening a can of worms. He had nothing to gain, and much to lose, by allowing the case to continue.

In fact there are good reasons for thinking that the Prime Minister was not among the authors of Mitterrand's misfortunes. He exploited them to the hilt once they became known, but he almost certainly did not originate them, nor would it have been in his interest to do so.[7] The Bazooka Affair was a red herring. Far from explaining Pesquet's choice of Mitterrand and Bourgès as targets, it gave Debré a strong incentive *not* to do anything which might cause the secret files to be reopened. The Prime Minister was intelligent enough to realise that pushing Mitterrand into a corner, far from silencing him, would goad him to counter-attack, which was exactly what happened. The reference in Mitterrand's speech to 'accusations and troubling confessions' was a clear enough warning to Debré that if he did not back off, those 'troubling confessions' would be made public.

By then it was too late to terminate the proceedings. But nor did they advance. Mitterrand never had his day in court. He was never acquitted of contempt and the charge was never withdrawn. The case was simply allowed to die.[8]

Pesquet, in exile in Switzerland, at a time when his political friends had deserted him, would later accuse Jean-Louis Tixier-Vignancour, the standard-bearer of the extreme Right in the 1950s and '60s, of having concocted the plot.[9] Tixier had been in touch with Pesquet in the weeks before the attack, and afterwards defended him. An orator of rare eloquence, with a booming voice and barnstorming emotional range, Tixier was – in the words of Roland Dumas, who had pleaded in court against him – 'more strange and twisted than you could possibly imagine'. Dumas, too, believed that Tixier was responsible. He had 'half-admitted it', Dumas said, and had predicted: 'There will be a great trial. It will give us a tribune to defend French Algeria.'[10]

Did the conspiracy reach higher? André Rousselet thought it had been fomented by the entourage of Georges Bidault, the former Christian Democrat leader, who was at odds with de Gaulle over Algeria and later joined the *ultras* in rebellion against him. Bidault had given false evidence against Mitterrand during the 'Leaks Affair'. Testimony also emerged that two other leading supporters of 'French Algeria', Léon Delbecque and Jacques Soustelle, had discussed ways to 'eliminate' Mitterrand. But both denied it and the investigation was abandoned. In the end, it was all conjecture.

For Mitterrand, the first two weeks after the Observatory Affair were critical. That was when, in Rousselet's words, 'nothing was ruled out'. Once Debré started attacking him, the worst was over. He had someone to fight.

Long-time supporters, like François Mauriac and Jean-Jacques Servan-Schreiber, rallied to his side. Patrice Pelat, his mentor in captivity and colleague in the Resistance, now a successful businessman, who had become estranged after breaking off his engagement to Danielle's sister, Christine, returned to tell him: 'François, I am first and foremost your friend.' Mendès France spoke out on his behalf. One of the Young Turks of the Radical Party, Charles Hernu, whose political career would from then on be linked to Mitterrand's, volunteered his support, telling him that he did not believe a word of Pesquet's allegations.[11]

Danielle and others in Mitterrand's inner circle used to say that, during this period, he could count his friends on the fingers of one hand.

It was not quite that bad. In early November 1959, when the campaign against him was at its height, Rousselet and a few others organised a seminar at Poigny-la-Forêt, in the countryside near Rambouillet, 30 miles west of Paris, to try to lift his spirits. About twenty-five people, mainly from the UDSR and the prisoners' move-ment, turned up to show support.[12] But for a man who had spent more than a decade at the top of the political tree, it was a terrible comedown. Danielle did the rounds of her friends, trying to drum up sympathy. 'François told me, "Don't! You're heading for a huge disappointment" . . . They were all friends from the Resistance. Someone you had been with in the Resistance could not betray you. Well . . . they did betray us.'

She went to see the Lazareffs, the owners of *France Soir*, then the newspaper with the biggest circulation in France, who had cultivated the Mitterrands, inviting her regularly to their property at Louveciennes where the artistic, intellectual and political elite of Paris congregated every weekend. 'It was the worst slap in the face, the worst snub, of my life,' she recalled. 'Everyone just stared at me. No one moved . . . [Eventually] I found Pierre [Lazareff], and Pierre said to me: "Of course we believe François, but . . ." I never saw them again.'

It was the same with Jacques Chaban-Delmas and his wife, with Henri Frenay and many others. For Danielle, 'there was no "but"'. Many friendships were found wanting that winter.

Her courage was all the more striking because it followed a long period in which their marriage had been slowly coming apart.

It had started with François's absences. He was constantly away on business for the UDSR or absorbed by his work as a minister or campaigning to help a colleague. 'He wasn't there, he wasn't there,' Danielle remembered. 'He wasn't there with the children. He wasn't there when I was changing them as babies. Every weekend, I was alone with them. I taught them to say: "Papa is in the Nièvre".'

In Paris, too, he would disappear without explanation. It might be a government crisis, an all-night meeting of the UDSR bureau, a stay-over at the Dayans or at the home of another close friend. Or a love affair.

Aided by that redoubtable aphrodisiac that comes with political power, Mitterrand, the shy young student who had languished under the spell of Marie-Louise Terrasse, had become a formidable King of Hearts. 'When you are 34 years old, a good looking young man, a champion tennis player, a hunter of elephants in Africa and of whales in the Gulf of Gabon,' gushed a celebrity magazine, 'the female voter is a sweet prey, willingly consenting.' Even Françoise Giroud, an able chronicler of French mores, as tough-minded as any of her male colleagues, wrote that Mitterrand's overpowering charm, which had frightened women away in his youth, became mesmerising as he matured:

> When he unwound, he was irresistible . . . Like Casanova, he had a golden tongue, the gift of pleasing with words, of bewitching with a phrase, of dazzling with a remark . . . When, at a gathering, a woman . . . attracted him, . . . he would single her out with a look, fix her with his gaze and she would melt. No one knows how many passions he inspired in young women who never got over him and remained faithful to him in their hearts. If he had wanted to, he could have seduced a stone – economical in his gestures, his eyes shining with mischief, his voice velvety, his words enveloping you like a shawl. And he wanted to often . . . Women, with politics, were the great passion of his life.[13]

Such a man, whatever his qualities and however scintillating he might be, was not easy as a marriage partner. Danielle had come to terms with his infidelities early on and there were times when she was able to laugh at them. When François took up his post as Justice Minister, she accompanied him to the Chancellery to find, in the Minister's apartments, an enormous bunch of red roses with a note from a female admirer. She took it upon herself to reply: 'The consideration you have shown for us as a couple is equalled only by your generosity. I am so very touched. Danielle.'

But there was an emptiness in her life which neither her bookbinding, at which she excelled,[14] nor her children could fill. 'Not having anyone to talk to, I lost the taste for conversation and discussion. I lived as a recluse. Isolation and withdrawal led me down into a terrifying gulf of anti-social behaviour, from which I could find no escape.'

The shared nightmare of the Observatory Affair brought her and François back together. The relationship stabilised. But not as it had been before.

In 1958, Danielle had taken a lover.

Jean Balenci was a gym teacher at a nearby secondary school. They had met three years earlier, when he was 19 and she was 31. He was strongly built, muscular and athletic: contemporary photographs show him performing somersaults in diving competitions. Danielle was pretty and slim with an ingenuous charm which made all Mitterrand's male colleagues want to flirt. Jean had fallen in love with her. 'It happened little by little, imperceptibly,' he remembered. 'I couldn't even say at what moment it started. It just happened, as these things do.' On her side, she was lonely and, as she said later, 'where there is loneliness, something will come to fill it. If it isn't filled in one way, it will search for another.'

François accepted the relationship. Jean was easy-going and Gilbert and Jean-Christophe adored him. He taught them tennis and took them on skiing holidays, helping to make up for their absent father. 'We did not set out to have separate lives,' Danielle explained. 'Things happened, day by day, which meant that it worked out that way. But it was not something we had organised.' Neither she nor François ever spoke of divorce.[15] One day, she remembered, 'I said to him: "You know, we are an odd couple," and he took my hand in his, and said: "But you are my wife".' Much later, she rationalised the relationship, saying, 'If you are fundamentally attached to each other, and you really want to stay together, to live separate loves is not inconceivable.' He told friends: 'I do not see how I can forbid to my wife what I allow to myself.'

François observed the conventions. They were a married couple; they might have separate bedrooms and no conjugal relations. But they were united by a complicity which would continue until his death nearly forty years later. After the winter of 1959, they appeared in public more frequently together, at restaurants and the theatre.

As an opposition member of the Senate, a somnolent institution where the good and the great of French politics are kicked gently upstairs, there were few calls on his time. He started work on a book about Lorenzo de Medici, the fifteenth-century ruler of Florence, patron of Leonardo da Vinci, Michelangelo and Machiavelli. It was never completed but gave him an excuse to pay frequent visits to Florence and Venice, which he adored. He travelled to India and to China, where he tried to persuade Mao Zedong that Algeria was unlike other colonies and France needed guarantees that the European minority would be protected. The Chairman was unconvinced. The month-long journey produced a book, *La Chine au défi* ('The Chinese Challenge'), which was principally notable for the fact that, like other Western visitors, Mitterrand saw no sign of the famine, then at its height, which, by the time it ended a year later, would claim 38 million Chinese lives.[16]

In the Nièvre, where the Observatory Affair might as well have been on another planet, and at Hossegor, on the Atlantic coast in the *département* of the Landes, near Biarritz, where the family had a holiday home, he could escape from national politics and find solace in literature.

Mitterrand delighted in rare editions. One of his favourite pastimes, whether in or out of office, was browsing among the *bouquinistes'* stalls on the banks of the Seine and spending lazy afternoons exploring the shelves of antiquarian booksellers. At Hossegor he could immerse himself in Chateaubriand, Saint-Simon and Pascal, after whom he had named his first son. He read Lamartine and Stendhal, Jean Giono and Bernanos, and the poems of Aragon and Saint-John Perse, many of which he could recite by heart.

Hossegor had been Danielle's idea. After they married, they had argued over whether to spend the holidays with his family or hers. François had suggested neutral territory, the Île de Ré, off the coast of Brittany, where he had vacationed as a teenager. Danielle hated it. She found herself marooned on an island where it rained all the time, and on the rare occasions when François could get away from his ministerial duties to join her, their young nanny flirted with him.

The following year, when he suggested that she reserve the same place again, she temporised until she could tell him with a straight face that 'everything is fully booked'. So they joined Georges Beauchamp and his wife, who had taken a house at Hossegor for the summer.

The resort was, and still is, an oasis of middle-class propriety. A notice on the outskirts sets the tone: 'In town, we dress properly.' Neat, bijou villas, with whitewashed walls and small gardens that cry out for plaster gnomes, nestle in the lee of immense, grass-covered sand dunes, swept by a wind which, even in August, brings breakers rolling in from the Atlantic. Further back, overlooking a lake, lie the genteel homes of notabilities. Everything is as it should be, comfortable and well ordered.

To Danielle, Hossegor was a nod towards what she knew she could never be – 'a little bourgeois wife with a husband who was always there at mealtimes'. To François it resonated with the middle-class upbringing that had made him choose to live at Auteuil and in the rue Guynemer. He played golf and struck up friendships with other well-to-do visitors. Danielle's sister, Christine, who had just married the actor, Roger Hanin, often joined them for the summer. In 1955 they decided to buy a piece of land, on which they built a simple, not very attractive villa with a patio and a pine tree in front, where they could relax and there was room for the children to play. With some reluctance, François gave up the cottage in the Nièvre: he could not afford both. Instead he rented a bare, sparsely furnished hotel room in an old hostelry near Château-Chinon, Le Vieux Morvan, which served as his base when visiting his constituency. Holidays from now on would be spent in the Landes.

At the golf club at Hossegor, Mitterrand met Pierre Pingeot, a well-connected industrialist related to the Michelin tyre family, who headed a company making automobile parts in Clermont-Ferrand. They were the same age, from similar backgrounds, and soon became friends. The Pingeots' second daughter, Anne, then fourteen, remembered the first time her father brought Mitterrand and André Rousselet home from the golf course for a drink. 'It was fascinating . . . unforgettable.' They opened a window on to a different world.

The Pingeots were an old-school upper-middle-class Catholic family from the provinces, who, on her mother's side, were, in Anne's words, 'a generation behind the times'. Her maternal grandfather, a retired general, had strong nineteenth-century views about a woman's place being in the home. 'Women should not work, nor should they study – the worst thing a woman could do was to wear glasses and pass the baccalaureate; in any case, they were inferior beings . . .

Yvonne and Joseph Mitterrand at the time of their marriage in 1906.

The siblings: François (fourth from left), between his younger brother, Jacques, and Robert, a year older, *c.*1923.

At St Paul's College, Angoulême, *c.*1932.

Goalkeeper (front row, centre) in the school soccer team.

Protesting against 'the Wog invasion', February 1935. Mitterrand is in the front row on the left.

At Stalag IXA in Germany, 1941 (back row, right).

With his brother, Robert, during the 'phoney war' in 1939.

With Marshal Pétain at Vichy, October 1942. Marcel Barrois (centre) helped found the prisoners' resistance movement, the RNPG.

'Morland' on his return to France after meeting de Gaulle in Algiers, March 1944.

Marie-Louise Terrasse, aged 20.

François and Danielle on their wedding day, October 28 1944.

Addressing
a meeting
of the PoWs'
federation,
the FNPG.

With Henri Frenay (left) at the
War Veterans Ministry, 1945.

Interior Minister in
the government of
Pierre Mendès France
(right), 1954.

Big game hunting in West Africa in the 1950s.

At the Cannes Film Festival in 1956 with Danielle (right) and Brigitte Bardot (back to camera), whose film *And God Created Woman* was the success – and the scandal – of the year.

le choix est clair...

CANDIDAT DES REPUBLICAINS

FRANÇAISES, FRANÇAIS,
prenez en mains votre avenir

A contemporary newspaper cutting showing a
campaign poster for the 1965 presidential election,
urging French voters to 'take their future in hand'.

Anne Pingeot, photographed
by François Mitterrand on a
beach near Hossegor.

Jean-Christophe Mitterrand (left), with his younger brother, Gilbert, and their parents on his
nineteenth birthday, which coincided with the second round of the election.

Danielle overseeing the rebuilding at Latche, 1967.

Anne and François at Charles Salzmann's home in the Lozère, 1973.

That's what I was brought up with, all through my childhood,' she recalled. 'There was no question of getting a job. I was expected to do something decorative and then get married. That was the programme laid out for me.'

But by the late 1950s, even in the French countryside, those timeless certainties were beginning to erode. Anne got her baccalaureate and in September 1961, shortly after she turned eighteen, went to Paris to study at the École des Métiers d'Art (College of Arts and Crafts). Her mother, Thérèse, installed her in a former convent which had been converted into a Catholic hostel for young women of good family from the provinces. 'I discovered Paris. What happiness – it was freedom!' Anne recalled. After three years she obtained her diploma as a master craftsman in stained glass. But by then her parents' carefully laid plans to pair her off with a suitable young man from their own milieu were in ruins.

The two families – the Mitterrands and the Pingeots – had grown close. Every summer they spent the holidays at Hossegor. Anne was three years older than Mitterrand's son, Jean-Christophe, and the first year she was in Paris, François acted as her guardian. But the time they had shared at Hossegor had sown the seeds of what would follow. Anne was quick, intelligent, passionate about art, a slim, lively brunette with green eyes, a ready laugh and an enchanting smile. She captivated him. He charmed her. 'He was so interesting,' she remembered. 'People like that, who are on a higher level, multiply life for you by their knowledge.' Six years after they had first met, they fell in love.

'It wasn't at all what was supposed to happen,' Anne would say later. 'I had been overwhelmed.'

Don Juan had met his match. He was 47; she was 20. There was no question of his leaving Danielle. Since the Observatory, if not before, they had known that they would stay together. But Anne gave him that surge of energy – a 'regeneration', she would call it – that comes to a man, still in the full vigour of life, on the threshold of middle age, who suddenly finds his existence transformed by a consuming and reciprocated passion for a girl less than half his age.

Danielle had taken Jean Balenci not out of passion but loneliness. François found in Anne the other great love of his life. She was the Beatrice that he had sought, and not found, in Marie-Louise Terrasse.

His friends used to wonder why he did not seek a divorce. Some thought he feared a separation would damage his career; others that he remained with Danielle because of the Catholic values which he had absorbed as a child and a traditional, almost feudalistic attitude that held family, singular or plural, to be sacred. Anne had a different explanation. 'Once he had made a choice, he stuck to it. Danielle was a choice he had made and he would not leave her.' There was another consideration, too, she thought: the death of the Mitterrands' first-born son, Pascal. 'Losing a child creates a bond between a man and a woman which is indestructible.'[17]

That may indeed have played a part. But the real reason was simpler. He loved them both. All political leaders run on egoism. Private and public life are different sides of the same coin. Mitterrand's behaviour was supremely egoistic. But the two women who shared his life were strong, original characters with minds of their own, as they would show, in different ways, throughout the time they were with him. If they accepted their situation, it was because they chose to and because Mitterrand managed the two relationships, and the families that resulted, in ways that enabled them, if not to cohabit, at least to coexist.

The 1960s was a decade of emancipation and prosperity in Europe. In Britain, 'Supermac', as the newspapers called Harold Macmillan, had coined the slogan, 'We've never had it so good'. In America a wealthy young Bostonian named John Fitzgerald Kennedy was elected to a White House which the press would dub Camelot.

Only in France did nothing go right. There were strikes for higher wages; the biggest farmers' protests in living memory; and, overshadowing everything else, like a shroud for a country locked into its past, the never-ending war in Algeria.

Since de Gaulle's announcement of self-determination, the *ultras* had been restive. In January 1960, matters came to a head. European extremists barricaded themselves into the University of Algiers, provoking a firefight with police in which twenty-two people died and more than 200 were wounded. The goal was to force the army to take power and despatch paratroops to Paris to seize control of the capital and the rest of metropolitan France. For a week, the fate of the Fifth Republic hung in the balance. The government drew up contingency plans to move to Belgium if Paris were attacked. But insurrections, like bicycles, topple unless they move forward. De

Gaulle, in military uniform, delivered one of those imperious, soaring speeches, of which, alone among twentieth-century statesmen, he and Winston Churchill had the secret. The army hesitated. The barricades collapsed.

The revolt had several consequences. De Gaulle removed the settlers' sympathisers, including Massu and Jacques Soustelle, from military and government posts. He launched a muscular charm offensive to win back the support of the army, whose loyalty, he now realised, could no longer be taken for granted. And he started talks with the FLN.

The *ultras* did not give up. A year later a small group of extremists, led by Soustelle and Raoul Salan, created the OAS, the Secret Army Organisation, whose mission was to use all available means, including terror and assassination, to prevent Algerian independence. In April 1961, Salan and three other generals staged a putsch. De Gaulle, once more in uniform, appeared on television to warn that, unless the putschists surrendered, there would be civil war. Jean Lacouture, then a young journalist with *Le Monde*, was among the millions of French people glued to their sets that night:

> We saw appearing on our screens the old Jacobin inquisitor, whose redoubtable physiognomy had, with a few imperious growls, fifteen months before, brought the barricades crashing down . . . The look was piercing, the mask twisted with anger, the clenched fists resting on the table either side of the microphone like two pistols of the hero of a cowboy film.[18]

The General was in blistering form. After denouncing the *pronunciamento* undertaken by 'a quart-pot of retired generals' whose actions were 'leading the nation straight to disaster', he proclaimed solemnly: 'In the name of France, I order that all means – I say clearly, all means – shall be used to stop these men . . . I forbid any Frenchman, and firstly, any soldier, to carry out their orders . . . The future of usurpers must be that which is reserved for them by the rigour of the law.' The melodrama was deliberate. It forced the military, above all the rank-and-file, gathered around transistor radios in bases all over Algeria, to measure the extent of the mess that its officers were leading them into.

The putsch collapsed. But the 'dirty war' of the OAS was just beginning.

Americans have never experienced systematic urban terrorism. Historically it has been limited to Europe, the Maghreb, the Middle East and parts of West Asia. The OAS campaign was a textbook example of the use of terror to try to force a government to reverse its policies by provoking a spiral of violence which exceeds the limits a democracy can sustain.

The summer of 1961 saw a constant drumbeat of murders of officials and army and police officers, both in Algeria and in metropolitan France. In September, de Gaulle's car was ambushed as he was being driven back to Colombey for the weekend. The attack failed because, inexplicably, the main charge of plastic explosive did not detonate. The following month, 30,000 Algerian immigrants demonstrated in Paris in favour of independence. The police, infiltrated by OAS provocateurs, reacted with a level of violence not seen in the French capital since the destruction of the Commune almost a century before. Twelve thousand of the protesters were rounded up and detained at a football stadium. Many were tortured. More than a hundred were acknowledged officially to have died and hundreds more were injured. For days after, bodies were found floating in the Seine.

After seven years of warfare, the situation had polarised. 'All the Muslims are with the FLN,' de Gaulle told the Cabinet, 'and practically all the Europeans are with the OAS.'

In March 1962, after the FLN agreed to a ceasefire, leading to independence, the OAS vowed to block the accords. For the next two months, all over the country, more than a hundred bombs exploded every day. In Paris, members of the Cabinet went in constant fear of assassination. In Algiers French soldiers opened fire on OAS supporters, killing forty-six Europeans and injuring more than a hundred. Initially the FLN retaliated against known OAS activists and spared the European population at large. But after Algerian independence on July 5 1962, the Arabs' long-repressed anger boiled over. As in France, after the German retreat, those who had been the last to join the struggle were at the forefront of the reprisals that followed. In Oran, as many as five thousand Europeans may have been massacred; no accurate figure was ever established. Far worse was the fate of the *harkis*, the Arabs who had sided with the French. At least 30,000 – and possibly several times that number – were slaughtered, often with appalling cruelty. Men were boiled alive, buried alive, emasculated.

Over the next two years, all but a tiny minority of the settlers, many from families which had lived in Algeria for generations, returned to France. Each person was allowed to take only two suitcases of personal possessions. They brought with them accumulated hatreds which would poison race relations in France for decades to come.

The settlers in Algeria, Mitterrand wrote later, had 'wanted to keep everything . . . They lost everything.'

The OAS and its supporters made one last effort to settle scores with the author of their misfortunes. On the evening of August 22, the General and his wife left the Elysée to drive to the military airport near Versailles from which they would fly to Colombey. At Petit Clamart, about three miles beyond the city limits, their car was ambushed. The subsequent investigation showed that almost 200 bullets had been fired, of which several passed within inches of the presidential couple. None of the occupants had even a scratch. When they reached the airport, de Gaulle, his suit still covered with fragments of glass, inspected the honour guard. His wife reminded an aide 'not to forget the chickens' which had been packed for the following day's lunch. The only casualty that night was the police commandant at Colombey, who died of a heart attack after learning what had happened.

It was the final spasm of yet another war, the third in twenty years, after Indochina and the debacle of 1940, which France had lost.

The violence in Algeria obliterated all other considerations. Apart from two rather superficial speeches in the Senate in 1961, in which he was reduced to accusing de Gaulle of 'making war just enough not to win it and peace just enough not to conclude it', Mitterrand remained silent. Like the rest of the non-communist Left he had nothing to propose. In any case he was still shackled by the Observatory Affair. All he could do was keep quiet and hope that, as time passed, that 'enormous, fantastic piece of stupidity', as François Dalle had called it, would eventually be forgotten.

In the autumn, the General announced a referendum on introducing direct suffrage for future presidential elections. Until then the Head of State had been elected indirectly, by a college of some 80,000 mayors, provincial councillors, MPs and senators. Now, using as a pretext the failed attempt to assassinate him at Petit Clamart, de Gaulle proposed that 'at the end of my term in office, or if death or illness should interrupt it', the next President should be chosen by the people.

Shortly afterwards he called legislative elections. It was a favourite political trick: the referendum served as a plebiscite and the voters' enthusiasm then spilled over into their choice of MPs. It did not work quite as well as he had hoped. But 62 per cent voted yes in the referendum and the Gaullists consolidated their position in parliament.

'If we don't do anything silly, we shall be there for thirty years,' the Information Minister, Alain Peyrefitte, gloated. The General's followers won 233 seats, which, with the support of right-wing allies, gave them a two-thirds majority. The Christian Democrat vote collapsed and de Gaulle's most vocal opponents – Mendès France in the Eure; the pre-war Prime Minister, Paul Reynaud, in Dunkerque; and Pascal Arrighi and the champions of 'French Algeria' – were all eliminated.

All except one. Like Asterix's mythical village of Armorique, which held out against imperial Rome, the Morvan, the gritty farming constituency in the eastern part of the Nièvre, where Mitterrand had been defeated four years earlier, stood firm against the Gaullist onslaught.

During his years in the wilderness, Mitterrand had patched up relations with his Socialist rival, Dr Benoist, who in the second round stood down in his favour. The right-wing vote was divided, and on November 25, he was elected with 67 per cent of the vote. His rehabilitation was far from complete. But at least now he was back in the saddle, able to resume the career which, three years earlier, had so nearly been brought to a premature end.

8

De Gaulle Again

In the winter of 1958, shortly after de Gaulle's return, when the fortunes of the left-wing parties and of Mitterrand himself were at their lowest ebb, he had explained to Roland Dumas, then in hospital with a bone fracture from a skiing accident, his ideas for winning power. Mitterrand, who exalted friendship – 'to have a friend, you have to be a friend' – used to visit him a couple of times a week. One day, Dumas remembered, he took out a notebook and drew a circle. With one small group, he explained, they could create a political structure. Mitterrand then drew a second, larger circle around it: the first group would enter a bigger group and gain control of it from within. Finally he drew a third circle, taking up the entire page. In this way, by stages, he told Dumas, they could colonise the whole of the Left.

It was the same tactic that he had used to win mastery of Pin'–Mitt' in the Resistance, of the prisoners' movement in the spring of 1945, and of the UDSR in the early 1950s, working not through orthodox, vertical, organisational channels but through networks of lateral contacts and circles of friends so attached to him that they were to all intents and purposes disciples.

Mitterrand's ostracism by the young men of the Autonomous Socialist Party, the PSA, coupled with the fallout from the Observatory Affair, seemed to deal a body blow to this elegant construction. In 1960, when he attended meetings of the 'New Left', always arriving late and sitting a little apart, the Chairman, Gilles Martinet, remembered being passed notes, warning: 'If you let him speak, we shall leave.'

Mitterrand persisted. 'Each sarcasm, each invective, was a whiplash pushing him to meet the challenge,' his brother, Robert, wrote. 'These trials just made him more determined.'

In fact being barred from the PSA was the best thing that could have happened to him. Had he been accepted he would have been surrounded by idealistic, ambitious youngsters, squabbling over political theory and utterly devoted to his mentor-cum-rival, Pierre Mendès France.

Instead, in June 1960, Mitterrand founded a political club, the League for Republican Combat, or LCR, which took its inspiration from the Fabian Society, a socialist think-tank affiliated to the British Labour Party.[1]

Unlike Britain, where 'the club', strategically located in Mayfair, redolent of leather armchairs, deep carpets, chandeliers and high ceilings, good whisky, fine claret and indifferent food, has been traditionally a social institution, France, ever since the Revolution in 1789, has had clubs whose *raison d'être* was political. In the waning days of the Fourth Republic, they had taken on a new lease of life. One of the oldest, the Club des Jacobins, whose original members had included Mirabeau, Robespierre and Saint-Just, had been resuscitated in 1951 by Charles Hernu, the young Radical who had rallied to Mitterrand after the Observatory Affair. By the early 1960s, more than a hundred clubs were active, occupying the void created by the failure of the traditional parties to offer an alternative to the Gaullist juggernaut.

Most were small. Mitterrand's League for Republican Combat had only forty members, most of them close friends, like Beauchamp, Dayan and Joseph Perrin, who had been with him since the war or earlier, and younger men like Dumas and Louis Mermaz, the future Speaker of the National Assembly, who had joined him in the 1950s. It was the first of the circles which he had drawn in his notebook at Dumas's bedside, eighteen months earlier.

The end of the Algerian war had brought hopes of a return to normality. But de Gaulle's decision to introduce direct suffrage for the election of the Head of State convinced Mitterrand and many others that they were witnessing a dangerous extension of presidential power. In 1958, he said, the General had 'cooked up a constitutional pie, [using as ingredients] a lark and a horse, the lark being democracy and the horse, personal power'. Since then,

the modest part reserved for democracy has been shrinking to the point where it disappears, while the large part reserved for personal power has been growing to take up the whole space . . . What the Head of State is after is absolute power to do whatever he pleases . . . It is not even . . . a presidential regime. [It] is in fact the regime which all through time has been known only by one name and that name is dictatorship. It matters little to me whether this dictatorship is paternalistic or cruel . . . Dictatorships are paternalistic or cruel depending on their need, and they know only one need: permanence . . .'[2]

The tone had changed since the aftermath of the Observatory Affair. Whatever Mitterrand's admiration for de Gaulle as a statesman, as the man to measure himself against, even, in some senses, as an anti-model, the General was now his declared enemy and was to be treated as such.

Polemics aside, Mitterrand's criticism of de Gaulle's use of power could not easily be dismissed. The General had pushed through the referendum on direct suffrage despite a ruling by the country's highest administrative court, the Council of State, that he was exceeding his powers. He had then browbeaten the Constitutional Council, the equivalent of the US Supreme Court, into declaring itself incompetent in the matter. The mild-mannered, well-respected President of the Senate, Gaston Monnerville, a Radical, was so incensed that he accused him of 'warping the normal interplay of the institutions, openly violating the constitution . . . and abusing the people'.

Half a century later, the questionable legality of the General's methods has been forgotten. The constitution of the Fifth Republic remains the cornerstone of French political life and, apart from occasional tinkering at the margins, no one wishes to change it.[3]

But in 1962 de Gaulle's actions were viewed as a disguised *coup d'état*. He acknowledged himself that the introduction of direct suffrage had been a declaration of war against the political parties. 'I wanted to break [them],' he told the Cabinet shortly after the referendum. 'I was the only one able to do it . . . and I was right when all the others were wrong . . . The parties are beyond redemption.'

In this climate, Mitterrand's tirades fell on receptive ears.

De Gaulle was not a dictator, but nor was he a very good democrat. France, in the 1960s, was not a very good democracy either.

In 1961, a High Military Tribunal had been set up to deal with terrorists, an understandable necessity during the Algerian war. But when it pronounced a sentence with which de Gaulle disagreed (imprisonment, rather than the death sentence, on General Salan in May 1962), he ordered that it be disbanded and replaced by a Military Court of Justice. After the Council of State ruled that the new body was illegal, he replaced it with a State Security Court which, as its name implied, bore an unfortunate resemblance to similar institutions in the People's Democracies in the East. Even the right-wing newspaper, *Le Figaro*, asked why the struggle against subversion could not be carried out 'without offending gravely against the essential principles of the law'. When the judiciary and the executive branch came into conflict, the government expected the judiciary to give way and woe betide the judge who failed to do so.[4]

The General's attitude to radio and television was much the same: they were there to obey. The government had a monopoly – no private broadcasting station was permitted in France – and used it exclusively for its own propaganda.

Not all of this should be laid at de Gaulle's door. The tradition of a strong centralised state was deeply rooted. But the General's personality, his military background and his army officer's conviction that subordinates should follow orders, did not improve matters.

Heir to Colbert and Richelieu, the Jacobins and Napoleon, he was now in his early seventies, his sight was deteriorating, he was developing a prostate condition and increasingly feeling his age.[5] At each new setback, he would ruminate morbidly about the imminence of death before pulling himself together and bludgeoning his opponents.[6] With the impatience not of youth but of old age came an outsize idea of his own role – he spoke of being 'the incarnation of the legitimacy of the nation' and mused that, when he died, 'there will be nothing to replace me . . . I have re-established the monarchy in my favour, but after me, no one will be able to impose himself on the country.'

When the Algerian war no longer provided an alibi for the General's methods, the terrain for the opposition became more favourable.

Like Saint-Just, the 25-year-old revolutionary who had called for Louis XVI to be executed not for his crimes but for his tyranny, Mitterrand attacked not de Gaulle's policies but the Sovereign himself. 'One does not reign innocently,' Saint-Just had famously declared.[7] Mitterrand made that the centrepiece of an incendiary, book-length polemic, *Le Coup d'état permanent*, published in May 1964:

Times of misfortune secrete a singular race of men who flourish only in storms and torments. [For] de Gaulle, [in 1940 when] disaster overtook France, it was a deliverance . . . War and defeat allowed de Gaulle to demonstrate his stature . . .

[But] once France was liberated . . . there was no longer any misfortune which would allow [him] to sink his teeth into the weft of French politics . . . With nothing to do, he languished . . . It is a Gaullist truth: there can be no France to save unless France first is lost! Oh, what a temptation to give things a helping hand so as to bring that moment closer! . . . At Colombey, impatience was setting in. Would misfortune arrive in time for the man who was living in the secret hope of one last rendezvous to measure himself against it?

For de Gaulle, the absolute evil was not the war, the abandonment of Indochina and Algeria . . . It was the Fourth Republic . . . He knew that decolonisation was . . . inexorable. But [he gave] the impression that everything could still be saved if only he returned to power. [To that end] he fed the rancours of nationalism, transfixed the army with the impossible hope that the situation could be reversed, and won the favours of the colonialists.

That is how Gaullism worked.

Gaullism? What Gaullism? . . . Does it still deserve the name, this Gaullism that . . . concluded an astonishing alliance . . . with both divisions of French nationalism, passing over the schism of 1940? . . . Former members of the [Gaullist] networks and the Free French intelligence service in London; of the fascist party of Jacques Doriot; of the Milice; not to mention the captains of the world of business; the old guard of Action Française; the extreme Right of Pierre Poujade; the failures who were nostalgic for fascism – all of them supported him![8]

Mitterrand considered the *Coup d'état permanent* to be the best book he ever wrote. It was certainly the most ferocious, the most coherent and original – a venomous caricature, in the pure style of a nineteenth-century pamphleteer, of a colossus whose feet, if not made of clay, had surreptitiously crossed the border of illegality to bring their owner back to power. For that was the core of Mitterrand's argument. De Gaulle, he wrote, had been 'a lucid and courageous soldier' who, in 1940, had come to France's aid, but 'I deplore his attempt to benefit illicitly from that glory, the incomparable historical achievement that was his.' He had taken office through 'the kind of break-in which precedes a burglary', founding his regime with 'an astonishing mixture of duplicity and boldness' on a *coup d'état* which gave him personal power at the expense of the personal freedoms of the nation.

Ridicule being the most powerful weapon in a polemicist's armoury, Mitterrand illustrated his thesis with the case of a humble citizen named Vicari:

Vicari? Why Vicari? Who is Vicari? Fair questions, for the official gazettes have neglected to inform the French people . . . of the act of which Vicari was the author. That act is recounted in a judgment by the 17th Magistrates' Division of the Higher Court of the *Département* of the Seine, pronounced at a public hearing on April 1 1963 under the rubric, 'Offences against the President of the Republic', which stated:

'Given that Vicari has admitted . . . that he shouted "Hou hou!" and whistled as the presidential motorcade passed by, taking the Head of State to the Arc de Triomphe; [Given that] the accused claims he did so to attract the attention of a friend in the crowd on the other side of the road, [but] that this explanation cannot be accepted because Mr Vicari was unable to name the friend concerned; [and given that] the shouts of Mr Vicari . . . were of a nature to cause offence to the President of the Republic, [the Court] declares Vicari guilty and sentences him to a fine of 1000 francs [£100 or US $280] plus costs.'

So Vicari cried 'Hou hou!' at General de Gaulle on the Champs-Elysées and his 'Hou hou!' shook the foundations of the State . . . No doubt some ill-intentioned spirits [will try to defend him], but every honest person knows that a country capable of punishing 'Hou hou!' with a 1,000 franc fine is a country defended against anarchy, against terrorism, against regicide, in short against anti-Gaullism and above all against that spontaneous, shameless, exclamatory anti-Gaullism which dares to stage intolerable excesses right in the middle of the public thoroughfare . . . Nothing could be more damaging than to let these 'Hou hous!' spread and take all the space reserved for vivats and bravos.

[What is more], the same day that Vicari proffered his 'Hou hou!', and at the very same spot, another citizen of the same sort [named Castaing], of equal incivility and vulgarity, went so far – without it being possible to establish from his conduct that he was conspiring with the first-named, which, had it been so, would undoubtedly have revealed the existence of a plot – as to shout three words, which, when combined in a phrase, also constituted a deliberate offence to the Head of State: 'Go and retire!' Fortunately, as in the first case, the 17th Division was watching. By means of a 500 franc fine, order and morality were safeguarded . . .

It is noteworthy . . . that in the scales of justice, to invite General de Gaulle to return to Colombey-les-Deux-Églises to enjoy a well-merited rest costs only half as much as . . . that enigmatic 'Hou hou!', which might be a password or a call for insurrection . . . a crime of *lèse-majesté*, a challenge to History, an affront to a legend, a cry of sedition.[9]

Mitterrand's task was made easier by the tendency of the law to be an ass but he was making a serious point. In de Gaulle's France, the law was not only an ass but a subservient one. And when that was not enough, the Service d'Action Civique (Civic Action Service) or SAC, a Gaullist militia controlled by Jacques Foccart, the General's *éminence grise*, which had been set up to counter the OAS and was notorious for its strong-arm tactics and its ties with the underworld, was available for more unsavoury tasks.

The separation of powers was systematically undermined. The General himself, in a much-quoted passage, had explained at a news conference in January 1964 his view of how the presidency should function:

> The indivisible authority of the State is delegated in its entirety to the President by the people who have elected him. There is no authority either ministerial, civil, military or judicial which can be conferred or maintained other than by him. It is for him to find the balance between the supreme domain, which is his alone, and those [domains] in which he delegates his powers to others.[10]

De Gaulle's biographer, Jean Lacouture, who was among the journalists present, wrote years afterwards that 'no one could hear . . . those incandescent words without feeling they were witnessing a vast restoration of centuries of monarchical power'. Mitterrand seized on them as the ultimate proof of the General's decadence:

What is the Fifth Republic if not the possession of power by one man? And who is he, this one man, de Gaulle? Duce, Führer, Caudillo, Conducator, Guide?* . . . I call the Gaullist regime a dictatorship because, when all is said and done, that is what it most resembles . . . 'There is no authority [*dixit* the General], other than that conferred or maintained by him'. No need for a 101-gun salute to herald the accession of a sovereign. A few words, spoken in a neutral tone of voice, sufficed.[11]

The *Coup d'état permanent* established Mitterrand as the Saint-Just of the opposition. For the first time a left-wing leader had attacked the Right with the same virulence, if not the same tone or methods, that the extremist journals of the 1930s, *Gringoire* and *Le Crapouillot*, had once employed to savage the Left. Four and a half years after the Observatory Affair, he was again a contender for power. But he was 'a' leader, not yet 'the' leader of the anti-Gaullist opposition.

In 1963, the political clubs, which until then had been little more than talking shops, began to organise. That September, at Mitterrand's instigation, Georges Beauchamp and Charles Hernu established a co-ordinating committee, called the Centre for Institutional Action, which brought together the 'Jacobins' and Mitterrand's League for Republican Combat. It foreshadowed a much larger movement with an equally cumbersome name, the Convention of Republican Institutions, whose founding congress, the following year, was attended by 600 delegates representing the clubs, the Socialist and Radical parties, the Christian Democrats, the 'Unified Socialist Party', or PSU, which had by then replaced the PSA in the alphabet soup from which French parties draw their names, as well as delegates from Masonic lodges, Catholic movements, trades unions and student federations. The Convention became the vehicle to unify the Left. A Standing Committee was elected, dominated by Mitterrand's allies and supporters.

The second circle was now in place.

The name he had chosen was not innocent. The Convention of 1792 had voted to send Louis XVI to the guillotine. Fast-forward 170 years and the Convention of 1964 aimed to bring down the republican monarch, Charles de Gaulle.

* Respectively Mussolini, Hitler, Franco, the Romanian dictator, Nicolae Ceauşescu, and Muammar Gaddafi of Libya.

But who should be chosen as challenger?

Hernu's 'Jacobins' favoured Mitterrand. The 'New Left' disagreed. The weekly magazine, *l'Express*, edited by Jean-Jacques Servan-Schreiber, launched a campaign to find the ideal candidate, whom it called 'Mr X'. A consensus developed that the man who would fit the bill best was the Mayor of Marseille, Gaston Defferre. And since the suspense could not be maintained indefinitely, in the spring of 1964, more than a year and a half before the election was due, Defferre confirmed that he was willing to stand.

The Mayor of Marseille was calm, methodical and patient, a man with his feet on the ground who radiated reassurance. It was thought that his reputation as a conciliator would enable him to unite the opposition. The downside was that he was uncharismatic, ill at ease with crowds and, as a speaker, in the judgement of the French historian, Pierre Viansson-Ponté, 'able in a matter of minutes to discourage his most ardent supporters, transform[ing] a warm, lively audience into a cold, silent assembly which puts up with, rather than listens to, his dry, distant words'.

At first, everything seemed to be going Defferre's way. In April 1964, Mitterrand had a run-in with Georges Pompidou, in which, for once, he came off badly. The Prime Minister, whom he had savaged as de Gaulle's poodle, hit back:

> The truth is, Mr Mitterrand, that you are faithful to the Fourth Republic, [in other words] to a path sown with disasters and sometimes with dishonour . . . The future is not on your side. It is not with ghosts . . . The French people don't always know what they want, but they do know what they don't want. And what they don't want is to fall again into your dreadful hands. Were they tempted to forget that, you would always be there, thank God, to remind them.[12]

To Defferre's backers, here was the proof that they had made a wise choice. Mitterrand was too vulnerable to the charge that he was yesterday's man.

But as the campaign developed, problems emerged. Both Mitterrand and Pierre Mendès France promised Defferre their support, and Mitterrand worked actively on his behalf. The third of the left-wing heavyweights, Guy Mollet, the Socialist Party leader, was reticent.

Apart from personal animosities – he and Defferre loathed each other – they disagreed profoundly over strategy.

Mollet wanted a campaign founded on the values of the Left.

Defferre wanted a grand alliance, embracing everyone from the Centre-Right to the non-communist Left, modelled on the Democratic Party in America which had brought John F. Kennedy to power. It sounded progressive and modern. But beneath the new clothes, it was the same old 'Third Force' approach that had been used in the late 1940s, based on the exclusion of the two extremes, the Communists and the Gaullists.

The original Third Force had bitten the dust in September 1951, when Mollet's Socialists walked out after a dispute with the Christian Democrats over state financing for church schools. *Plus ça change, plus c'est la même chose.* In the early hours of the morning on June 18 1965, after more than a year of negotiations, Defferre's candidacy collapsed for the same reasons. Officially the cause was the schools issue – the eternal stumbling block between Left and Right in France – but the root of the problem was deeper. The Christian Democrats were a right-wing party. As Mitterrand had realised from the start – although he had been careful not to say so – agreement between them and the Socialists would always be a mirage.

A week later Defferre confirmed his withdrawal. 'Mr X' had imploded. Less than six months before the elections, the Left was without a candidate.

In Mitterrand's view, Defferre's candidacy failed because it had been misconceived. Right and Left could be temporary allies, but only in exceptional circumstances and for a very limited time. What was needed to confront de Gaulle was not a dog's breakfast of parties spanning the whole of the centre ground, but unity on the Left, which meant coming to terms with the Communists.

The question was, how could he bring that about?

Mitterrand's experiences with the Communist Party during and after the war, first in the Resistance, then with the prisoners' federation, the FNPG, and its newspaper, *Libres*, had left him in two minds. On the one hand, as he had told Georges Dayan, the Communists were 'a pain' – so rigid that dialogue was impossible and bent on taking control of every organisation they joined. On the other, they were a force in the Resistance, and afterwards in post-war politics, which it would be foolish to ignore. 'We can't do anything,' he had told Philippe Dechartre, 'unless we take into account communist arithmetic.' As individuals, Mitterrand found, they often merited respect. He had got on well with Maurice Thorez when they had both been ministers, and knew and liked Thorez's successor as Communist Party leader, Waldeck Rochet, whom he had first met in London as the Party's representative with the Free French in 1944. Waldeck was from a poor farming family and had started work as a cowherd at the age of eight. Mitterrand had appreciated his company and had carried back to France a letter for his wife.

Politically, in the late '40s and early '50s, he and the Communists had been poles apart. The Right, for its own purposes, had tried to paint him as a communist sympathiser. But in three successive elections from 1946 to 1956, he had been returned to parliament by conservative voters in the Nièvre on a staunchly anti-communist platform.

Mitterrand's aim at that time had been to weaken the Communists by stealing their clothes. Since the late 1940s, he had argued that the goal must be to reduce Communist support to below 10 per cent, because then 'they can no longer do harm'. In 1955 he told the UDSR, 'The more Communist MPs are elected, the more . . . it bites into the representation of the socialist or liberal Left, and makes the constitution of a Centre-Left majority difficult if not impossible.' The solution was for the non-communist Left 'to realise a certain number of perfectly acceptable working-class social ideals which the Communists have confiscated'. As long as the left-wing parties were perceived as being in the pocket of the ruling class, paying no more than lip service to the goals of the workers they were supposed to represent, the latter would inevitably conclude that the Communists were the only party which could be relied on to support them.

After de Gaulle's reappearance upended the political chessboard, Mitterrand and the Communists started to develop a tentative rapport based on their shared opposition to the General's return to power.[13] On May 28 1958, Mitterrand took part in a demonstration of 200,000 people in Paris, organised jointly by the left-wing parties, including the Communists, to defend the Fourth Republic. Afterwards, Communist MPs applauded his speech attacking de Gaulle in parliament.

Since the Soviet leader, Nikita Khrushchev, had launched de-Stalinisation two years earlier, the French Communist Party had been searching for ways to end its isolation. Mitterrand, for his part, was beginning to understand that as long as communist voters were locked in an electoral ghetto the victory of the Left was impossible. But to sup with Thorez and his friends it was necessary to use a long spoon. In the 1950s, any non-communist politician seen dealing with the 'Party of Moscow' would be treated as a pariah. 'The Communists are not on the Left,' Guy Mollet liked to say, 'They are in the East.' For a time Mitterrand maintained a prudent distance. 'The working class,' he declared, 'knows perfectly well that the Communist Party is playing games.' When the Party's Central Committee next met, his old friend, Waldeck, retorted: 'François Mitterrand is not unaware that anti-communism plays the game of fascism.'

It marked the beginning of a very long hesitation waltz.

In the November 1958 elections, the Communist Party candidate in the Morvan stood down in Mitterrand's favour. The following spring, in an interview with the Radical journal, La Nef ('The Nave'), he said the future of the Left depended on uniting all 'those who so wish' against de Gaulle and his allies. The formulation was deliberately vague but it could be interpreted as meaning that the Communists were included. Six months later, after the Observatory Affair, the Communists were the only group in the Senate to vote unanimously against the lifting of Mitterrand's parliamentary immunity.

For the next three years, while he remained in the political wilderness, nothing moved. But the decision to introduce direct suffrage for the presidential election and the prospect of the Gaullists indefinitely consolidating their hold on power persuaded the Socialists, for the first time, to conclude an electoral pact with the Communists for the second round of the 1962 parliamentary elections. Both parties did better than expected. The following year Mitterrand drew the lesson, urging 'all republicans' – in other words, the whole of the Left – to unite in 1965 behind a single presidential candidate:

My attitude toward the Communists is simple: everything which contributes to the struggle and to victory over a regime which shows a tendency to the dictatorship of one man and the establishment of a one-party system is good. Four to five million voters, who are from the people, vote communist. To neglect their support and their votes would be culpable or just plain stupid.[14]

Mitterrand's strategy was to create a common front of four groups: the nascent Convention of Republican Institutions; the Socialists and the Radical Party; the 'New Left', led by the Unified Socialist Party, the PSU, of which Mendès France was the guru; and the Communists.

To the Socialists he proclaimed his left-wing credentials. 'I personally believe,' he told a party colloquium, 'that the choice of socialism is the only response to the Gaullist experience,' adding, in a backhanded reference to his problems with the PSU: 'That is a statement of principle and I am not going to take an exam [to prove it] every six months!'

The Radicals, whose new leader, Maurice Faure, six years Mitterrand's junior, had been among the few to offer him a helping hand after the Observatory Affair, were a broad church whose members ranged from the Centre-Left to the Centre-Right. They included right-wing notables to whom the Socialists, not to speak of the Communists, were anathema, and vice versa. But Mitterrand made a point of attending their congresses and affiliated himself to their parliamentary group.

He could do little to influence the 'New Left'. But he calculated that if the others joined together, the PSU would have no choice but to follow.

The Communists, at a time when the Kremlin was supporting the 'parliamentary road to socialism', were open to an arrangement.

It was a delicate balancing act.

Straddling contradictions was the kind of exercise at which Mitterrand excelled. As long as Defferre was standing he could do nothing. But he was able to keep the pieces in place throughout the eighteen months that it took for 'Mr X's' candidacy to unravel.

On June 25 1965, when the Mayor of Marseille withdrew, the way was finally open. Mitterrand had been expecting it since the beginning of the year.[15] But now that the moment had arrived, the ground still needed to be prepared. For another two and a half months, he waited, testing the extent of his support and trying to flush out potential opponents.

The first to rally to his cause was Pierre Mendès France. Mendès's decision, once it became known, did not please the 'New Left'. The leaders of the PSU besieged his apartment near the Bois de Boulogne, pleading with him to stand himself, because otherwise 'it will be that villain, Mitterrand'. But Mendès was adamant. He considered the Fifth Republic to be fundamentally undemocratic and the direct election of the President a vulgar Americanism which reduced the primary act of the country's political life to the level of a horse race on which the electorate was invited to place bets. He refused to have any part in it. Moreover, he added – serving up the argument of last resort he always used at such moments – France was not yet ready to elect a Jewish President. He told Mitterrand that he could not approve an alliance with the Communists, but Mitterrand said he would go ahead anyway. They agreed to disagree.

Maurice Faure promised his support and Waldeck Rochet sent word that the Communist Party viewed Mitterrand's candidature favourably.[16]

That left Guy Mollet. The Socialist Party leader worried that if Mitterrand succeeded, his own position would be threatened. But, like Mendès, he had no desire to stand himself. *Faute de mieux*, the Socialists acquiesced, but not without setting conditions.

'The Socialists . . . let me run,' Mitterrand wrote later, 'but at the end of a tether on which they kept a firm hold. All contact with the Communists was forbidden to me under pain of their support being withdrawn. I realised a little late that they wanted a candidate who [would not] reach out too far either to the Left or the Right and who would disappear without trace as soon as the election was over.'

In fact all Mitterrand's rivals had reached the same conclusion. No one could beat de Gaulle. There was a good chance that whoever tried would make such a dismal performance that his career would never recover. Better to let Mitterrand try his luck as an independent than risk the reputation of a mainstream party leader.

On September 5, he returned to Paris from Hossegor, where he had spent part of the summer with Danielle and the children.

Three days later, de Gaulle gave a press conference at the Elysée about the European Community, which France was then boycotting under the so-called 'policy of the empty chair' in protest against attempts to replace the principle of unanimity by majority decision-making, seen by the General as an infringement of sovereignty. As he was completing his diatribe against 'the areopagus of stateless, irresponsible technocrats' in Brussels, the French news agency flashed: 'Mitterrand candidate'.

He had timed the declaration deliberately to steal the General's thunder. It fell horribly flat. Press coverage was minimal and largely negative.

Mitterrand's problem was that he was seen, on the Left even more than on the Right, as unprincipled and devious, a 'ghost' from the Fourth Republic, as Pompidou had called him, prepared to accept any compromise so long as it would bring him to power. *Le Canard enchaîné* wrote that he was 'so labyrinthine that he gets lost in his own diversions and ends up trapped in . . . an undergrowth of intrigues which might be taken from a novel'. Jean-Jacques Servan-Schreiber, who had been for so long his loyal supporter, predicted in *l'Express* that he would take the Left to its worst defeat for a hundred years. Jean-Paul Sartre, in *Les temps modernes*, wrote that if Mitterrand was the Left's candidate, it was 'because he expresses its deliquescence'. Pierre Viansson-Ponté called him 'the worst candidate possible'.

But it was the venom of an article in *Le Monde* by a left-wing lawyer, Pierre Stibbe, that stung Mitterrand most. The writer, speaking for the PSU, described the perfect candidate: 'a man of absolute moral rigour, [immune from] personal attack, [never guilty of] opportunism, naked ambition, a taste for intrigue or for mounting "affairs", or compromises with the regime of Vichy' – in short everything, or so he implied, that Mitterrand was not.

'[That] article alone,' he wrote later, 'would have removed my last hesitations, had I had any.'

In private the back-stabbing was still worse. A PSU leader, Marc Heurgon, asked: 'The Right is not putting forward Pesquet. Why are we presenting Mitterrand?'

All through the autumn, attempts continued to find an alternative. Servan-Schreiber urged Maurice Faure to stand. He refused. The PSU tried to draft Daniel Mayer, Mollet's predecessor as Socialist Party chief. He refused too.[17] Then, at the beginning of October, Mollet himself, supposedly one of Mitterrand's main backers, suggested that Antoine Pinay, who had begun his career under the Third Republic, might be tempted out of retirement. That the head of the Socialist Party should publicly favour an elderly right-winger as the best chance to oppose de Gaulle was so outlandish that even Mitterrand was taken aback. Pinay had indeed been tempted, but after looking at the arithmetic and realising that he would be trounced, had decided to leave well alone.[18]

Mendès France tried to set things straight, declaring in an interview at the end of October:

> It seems that some on the Left have scruples [about François Mitterrand]. Let me say here something which for me is decisive. On every serious matter for the last 25 years, I have always found him on the right side of the barricades . . . Mitterrand is the man best placed to unite the whole range of socialist and democratic votes. I do not see how anyone can still hesitate. I am voting for him, and I ask those who have confidence in me to vote for him too.[19]

But even Mendès was reluctant to campaign for him, leading some to wonder whether he was not hoping secretly that the younger man would break his teeth against the Gaullist fortress. It was not so, but his attitude offended Mitterrand and revived the bad blood between them.[20]

The PSU eventually decided, as Mitterrand had anticipated, that it had no choice but to support him, but it did so with bad grace. Michel Rocard came up with the formula, 'critical support', which enabled the party to save face and gave Mitterrand another reason to bear him a lasting grudge. Even then, Gilles Martinet and other diehards engaged in a guerrilla campaign. Claude Estier, a long-time ally, discovered one evening that Martinet's journal, *Le Nouvel Observateur*, had set up that week's cover story with the headline, 'Mitterrand, Never!' He was able, *in extremis*, to persuade the typesetters to amend it to 'Mitterrand, Why?'

Even for a man who thrived on adversity, it was a daunting challenge. He wrote later:

> I was alone. I had neither the support of a party, nor of a Church, nor of a counter-Church, nor of a newspaper, nor of a current of opinion. I had no money and no expectation of [getting] any . . . So many reasons not to be a candidate or so many reasons to be one.[21]

That was overdrawn. He had the backing of the Communists and the Federation of the Democratic Socialist Left, the FGDS, yet another ephemeral organisation with a name that stuck to the tongue, which had been created by Hernu and a sympathetic industrialist, François de Grossouvre, as an umbrella movement for the Convention, the Socialists, the Radicals, what remained of the UDSR and two smaller left-wing parties. But keeping them all together required extraordinary contortions of political ingenuity.

He had little money – by his own account, less than a million francs (£100,000 or US $240,000)* – and his campaign staff consisted of a dozen volunteers, crammed into four small rooms at the former offices of the UDSR in the rue du Louvre in central Paris. Paulette Decraene, who later became his secretary, remembered: 'The equipment was rundown, we had three phone lines, four typewriters and a duplicating machine out of the ark, which if you weren't careful spilled greasy black ink over everything.'[22] Her husband, Philippe, a journalist with

---

* André Rousselet, who was Mitterrand's campaign treasurer, maintained almost half a century later an exemplary discretion about the source of the candidate's funds. In addition to the 970,000 francs declared officially by his campaign committee, headed by the President of the Paris Bar Association, René-William Thorp, others contributed *sub rosa*. A key figure was René Bousquet, then Deputy Director-General of the Banque d'Indochine and, in that capacity, the point man at election time for the Conseil National du Patronat Français, which represented French industry. The former Vichy police chief had been cleared of charges of collaboration by the Special Court in 1949, early in the Cold War, at a time when communists rather than collaborators were the French government's main concern. Mitterrand had met him shortly afterwards through Jean-Paul Martin. In 1965, the Patronat no longer distributed envelopes stuffed with cash to MPs at election time, as its President, Georges Villiers, had during the Fourth Republic, but it continued to 'support' non-communist candidates of all political persuasions if it appeared that they had a promising future. Bousquet had persuaded Villiers and his colleagues that Mitterrand should be taken seriously. André Bettencourt, who had married the heiress to the Oréal fortune, Liliane Schueller, and François de Grossouvre, who had an exclusive contract to bottle Coca-Cola in France, were also generous. Some money came directly from big companies. Laurence Soudet, then on Mitterrand's campaign staff, recalled going to see the Secretary-General of the French oil company, ELF, who, like her husband, was a member of the Council of State, to be given 'an envelope full of cash. He said to me, "Look, here's another envelope. It's twice as big. It's for de Gaulle."' One of the principal donors to Mitterrand's campaign, she said, was the Communist Party. Some funds also came from the Socialists. How much Mitterrand raised altogether is uncertain. Franz-Olivier Giesbert estimated not more than two million francs, ten times less than de Gaulle, who in addition to contributions from industry had the whole apparatus of the State at the service of his re-election campaign. Bousquet was also the Administrator of *La Dépêche du midi*, the leading newspaper in south-western France, with whose owner, Evelyne Baylet, he had a long-running affair. The *Dépêche*, which supported the Radical Party, backed Mitterrand in 1965.

the French news agency, lugged sacks of fliers after work each evening
to the Central Post Office, for mailing to the provinces. Even Danielle's
partner, Jean Balenci, was roped in to accompany the candidate on
campaign trips in a four-seater light aircraft, which was all they could
afford. One day they flew through gale-force winds to Corsica to
discover that Mitterrand's rally had been cancelled because the storm
was still so violent that tiles were being blown off roofs. Another
journey, to the Massif Central, almost came to grief when the pilot
found a herd of cows grazing on the grass runway and had to make
low-level passes to frighten them off before the plane could land.

But what they lacked in means they made up for in enthusiasm.
Their slogan was: 'A young President for a modern France!'

In October, Jean Lecanuet, the new Christian Democrat leader,
declared his candidacy. He was 45 years old, handsome, energetic and
quick-thinking. The press dubbed him 'the French Kennedy'. Against
de Gaulle, thirty years his senior, he was the future challenging the
past.

On the extreme-Right, Mitterrand's old adversary, Jean-Louis Tixier-
Vignancour, tilted quixotically at the Gaullist windmill, winning
amused attention but not necessarily votes.

Finally, on November 4, a week before the deadline for candidates
to declare themselves, General de Gaulle announced on television
that, as expected, he would seek a second term because otherwise,
he warned balefully, 'the Republic will immediately collapse and France
will have to undergo, this time with no possible recourse, a confounding
of the State even more disastrous than those it has known before.' In
other words, 'après moi le déluge'.

The opinion polls predicted that de Gaulle would triumph with 66
per cent of the vote. Mitterrand was credited with 16 per cent.

De Gaulle's announcement opened the way to three weeks of
campaigning which, as one journalist wrote, were 'literally stupefying'.
For the first time the government was compelled to allow its political
opponents to speak freely on television.[23] The nation was mesmerised.

Lecanuet came across well, looking breezy and modern, totally at
ease in the 'high-tech world' of the 1960s. De Gaulle, who, as his lead
began to erode, eventually decided that he would have to campaign
after all, looked his age, visibly ill at ease at having to compete publicly
with upstarts.

Mitterrand was still worse.

Television is a caustic medium, exposing and amplifying traits which normally remain hidden. In Mitterrand's case, what came across was a constant battle to control his own nervousness. Georges Dayan told him, 'when you speak, your eyes keep blinking as if you were flashing the headlights of your car.' But it was stronger than he was. Mitterrand was an introvert. Television did not come naturally. In 1965 each appearance was an ordeal. He grumbled that the technicians made his voice sound like Donald Duck. The truth, as he admitted later, was that he was simply not very good at it.

Nevertheless it was television that made the campaign catch fire. By late November, de Gaulle's projected score had fallen to 51 per cent.

On the Left, the sniping at Mitterrand's candidature ceased. He criss-crossed the country, working 20 hours a day, speaking at rallies where each crowd was bigger and more enthusiastic than the one before: 5,000 in Paris on November 22; nearly 10,000 in Lille the next day; twice as many at Grenoble.

As the campaign drew to a close, he was buoyed up by the certainty that at last he had found the right path. 'In politics,' he told Pierre Mauroy, a young Socialist Party leader, 'there are ideas, and there are men. If we can gather together a hundred men who are determined and who agree on the main elements of policy . . . one day we will rule France.'

On December 5, at 8 p.m., the results exceeded both the opinion polls and his own expectations: de Gaulle, 44.6 per cent; Mitterrand, 31.7; Lecanuet, 15.6 and Tixier-Vignancour, 5.2. He had forced the General into a run-off. 'Blasphemy!' wrote Pierre Viansson-Ponté in *Le Monde*.

Mitterrand had understood what no one else had seen. A presidential election by direct suffrage was fundamentally different from anything France had experienced before. It was not, as Mendès France would have liked, a choice between two programmes. It was not, as de Gaulle believed, a referendum on his policies.[24] It was a choice between personalities. The General? Or someone else? The only programme Mitterrand offered was to 'oppose the arbitrariness of personal power, chauvinistic nationalism and social conservatism', which, as the right-wing *Figaro* commented, was vague enough for almost everyone to support. And that, of course, was the point. In 1965, the General's outsize ego so dominated the political landscape that the identity of his opponent was secondary. So long as the challenger offered a credible alternative, the only thing that counted, in Mendès's dismissive metaphor, was which horse would win.

De Gaulle groused and threatened to give up before pulling himself together and throwing himself back into the fray. But in the campaign for the second round, the dynamic had changed. It was no longer de Gaulle towering over a few midgets. The General was face to face with a single adversary, whom he now had to take seriously and whose stature was accordingly transformed.

Pompidou urged him to attack Mitterrand for colluding with the Communists. 'Absolutely not!' the General told him. 'No question of a campaign of Left against Right. That's what Mitterrand is dreaming of. We won't make him that gift.' De Gaulle, quicker on the uptake than his Prime Minister, had grasped the new rules. Mitterrand's strength was the support of a large part of the Left. To oppose him, de Gaulle needed to appeal to both Left and Right.

On the principle that an enemy's enemy is a friend, Tixier-Vignancour called on his followers to give Mitterrand their backing, as did some former leaders of the OAS. To those who urged him to refuse support from such unsavoury quarters, Mitterrand retorted that it was not up to him to select those who wished to vote for him.[25] But he rejected the idea of a compromise with the Christian Democrats, even if that meant only a lukewarm endorsement from Lecanuet. The first round had convinced him that his future lay with the Left.

In this single combat, both sides told their partisans to lie low.

When the Interior Minister, Roger Frey, informed de Gaulle that he had discovered a photograph of Mitterrand at Vichy with Marshal Pétain, the General forbade him to use it. 'We must think of the future,' de Gaulle told him. 'One never knows what it will bring. This man may one day, perhaps, be President of France. Let us not sully him.' Ministers were instructed not to raise the Observatory Affair. Mitterrand abandoned the incendiary language of the *Coup d'état permanent*. They duelled on a basis if not of equality at least of wary respect. Mitterrand knew he could not win. There were moments when de Gaulle was not so sure.

On December 19, when all the votes had been counted, de Gaulle was re-elected with 55.2 per cent. Mitterrand obtained 44.8. It was an honourable result. Yet for the General, the winner, it carried a whiff of failure. He had been forced to come down from his pedestal and, for the first time since his return to power, to acknowledge a serious rival. The Statue had revealed a weakness which, less than four years later, would bring his rule to an end.

In contrast, Mitterrand, the loser, had proved himself a president-in-waiting. The Observatory and his long years as a minister under the Fourth Republic had been relegated to the background. If not yet the Left's undisputed leader, he had become its dominant figure. Mendès France and Mollet retained influence, but they, rather than Mitterrand, now appeared as yesterday's men. In the country at large, the election had given him a status which, six months earlier, was unimaginable.

François Mitterrand's transformation in the winter of 1965 was due above all to a system which he had strenuously opposed.

Had the President still been chosen by a college of 80,000 conservative dignitaries, drawn from every village and small town in France, no left-wing candidate could ever have succeeded. De Gaulle had embraced direct suffrage as establishing a mystic bond between President and people, legitimising the regalian role of the Head of State as elected monarch. Mitterrand had condemned it as incompatible with parliamentary democracy and a dangerous extension of the President's already vast powers. But every coin has two sides. By elevating the presidency to new heights, de Gaulle had also made it dependent on the people. It would prove to be the crucial step in France's evolution towards modern democracy.

If the General's reform opened the way for Mitterrand's ascension, other factors also played their part.

Moscow, for foreign policy reasons, had wanted de Gaulle to stay in power. Loyal to the Western Alliance but recalcitrant to Washington's hegemony, he had established diplomatic relations with China (breaking the US-led diplomatic embargo); loosened French links with NATO; and obstructed progress towards European unity. That was more than enough to make him the Kremlin's candidate. It was Mitterrand's good fortune that Waldeck Rochet, who had taken over from Maurice Thorez only four months earlier, had decided to put the French Communist Party's interests first. Supporting Mitterrand's campaign, Waldeck decided, was its best hope of breaking out of isolation and regaining a meaningful role in French politics. The fact that he and Mitterrand had known and appreciated each other in London during the war had helped. Had the Party been in different hands, Mitterrand might well have been unable to maintain the delicate balancing act which kept both the Socialists and the Communists on board.

There was also a psychological component.

Mitterrand's brother, Robert, wrote that his pugnacity was fuelled by a desire for revenge. The 'Leaks Affair' and, above all, the events at the Observatory had been exploited by the Right to try to destroy his political career. François Mitterrand was not a man to forgive and forget. The cold anger that found expression in the vitriol of the *Coup d'état permanent* redoubled his determination to prove his enemies wrong.

So did his relationship with Anne Pingeot, which had begun in the summer of 1963.

Laurence Soudet, who became their close friend, had been introduced to Mitterrand in the early 1960s by her fiancé, Pierre, who had worked for him when he had been Justice Minister. The Soudets had a cottage at Gordes, a pretty hill-village in Provence. François and Anne often stayed with them. 'We made a foursome,' she remembered. 'We went out all the time together. Ah, youth!'

As Laurence told it, François became a different person after he fell in love with Anne. 'I can tell you exactly when he changed. It was the month before Kennedy was killed . . . It was extraordinary. His private, personal and intellectual life suddenly all came together.' He changed both in small ways, giving up smoking, developing a passion for architecture, in which he had shown little interest before, and in larger ones, becoming fascinated by 'the way great historical figures had built their societies, rather than just the cultivation of power'. But above all, she said, the relationship provided 'an affective continuity which gave him solidity as a human being . . . which ultimately had an effect on his political life. Obviously, that's very difficult to evaluate, but I'm convinced it played a part.'

The interplay of private life and public career is always opaque, indirect and invisible to outsiders. In August 1965, two years after their relationship had begun and a month before he declared his candidature, he and Anne became lovers. It was the final proof – after periods of doubt and hesitation, including a trial separation which had only confirmed the strength of their feelings – that for both of them a new world was opening. One may legitimately wonder whether there was not a connection between that private fulfilment and the energy and confidence which Mitterrand brought to the presidential campaign that followed. What is certain is that the relationship gave him a stability he had not known before. Anne said later she felt the basis of the understanding which developed between them was that they shared 'the same values . . . which were patriarchal and corresponded to his childhood . . . He was a man who kept everything in different compartments, and in that particular compartment – the compartment of his childhood, which was very deep – he and I were completely on the same wavelength.'

Danielle was then living her own life with Jean Balenci. Before he had become committed to Anne, Mitterrand had been 'a free spirit', as Laurence Soudet put it, 'with adventures left and right'. Afterwards he settled down.

Mitterrand emerged from the election not only with enhanced stature but with a new faith in socialism. Georges Dayan dated his conversion to a meeting in Toulouse, on the eve of the second round. Coal miners, wearing white helmets, formed a guard of honour. Every Radical and Socialist leader in the south-west, led by Gaston Monnerville, the President of the Senate, was there to show support. The crowd acclaimed him in triumph. Thirty years later, he remembered: 'The bigger the auditorium, the happier I was. Ah, that meeting in Toulouse! . . . Those 30,000 faces, looking up at me!' To Dayan, it was the moment of illumination. 'After that, he was no longer the same. There was a fervour in him.'

Was his conversion sincere? Many thought so. Perhaps it was. But Mitterrand's oft-repeated claim that those who knew him best knew only 30 per cent of his thinking left room for doubt. And even then . . . '30 per cent?' asked Louis Mermaz, '10 per cent, I would say'. Mermaz's colleague, Louis Mexandeau, remembered his speeches in the presidential campaign as being 'more like Gambetta [a moderate nineteenth-century republican] than Lenin'.[26] But sincere or not, the die had been cast. From the winter of 1965, socialism was François Mitterrand's lodestar.

France, he now argued, was sociologically on the Left – more than half the population consisted of workers, low-paid public servants, artisans and farm labourers – yet politically the majority was on the Right. The challenge was to make the two coincide. It could only be done by creating a union of all the left-wing parties so that instead of fighting against each other they joined forces against the Right. The electoral alliance for the presidential election, under the umbrella of the Federation of the Left, the FGDS, was a start. But a detailed analysis of the figures showed that in his contest with de Gaulle, a significant proportion of working-class voters had either stayed at home or supported his opponent.[27] To be able one day to win power, the Federation would need to be strengthened and enlarged.

Between the two rounds of the election, on December 9, Mitterrand had been elected FGDS President. In that capacity, he would spend the next fifteen months trying to create the broad unified movement he was convinced the Left required.

His first plan – to build the Federation into 'a vast movement on the lines of the [British] Labour Party', the same ambition that had animated Henri Frenay in 1945[28] – failed miserably. The Socialists and the Radicals were both determined to defend their own turf. Mitterrand's next goal, to enlarge the Federation's appeal, also proved a chimera. The Centre-Right was willing to flirt but not to be seduced. 'Like Defferre, Mitterrand is making eyes at the "good" Christian Democrats,' Waldeck Rochet told his colleagues, 'but there is no reason to think that in a few months he will find any of the Christian Democrats good.'

He was right. Mitterrand gave up.

Only in his third objective was the FGDS President successful: the creation of a common front with the Communists.

Mollet once more dragged his feet. 'When we go 10 kilometres,' Mitterrand complained, 'Mollet spends nine kilometres putting up an anti-communist façade . . . and then, in the last 500 metres, he is obliged . . . to come round to my point of view.' Nonetheless, on December 20 1966, Mitterrand and Waldeck Rochet, on behalf of the FGDS and the Communists, signed an electoral pact for the parliamentary elections the following spring.

There was still no common programme other than a vague commitment to oppose 'personal power'. Nonetheless, it was only the second time since the French Communists and Socialists had parted company in 1920, three years after the Bolshevik Revolution, that they had agreed to cooperate even that much.[29]

The elections, in March 1967, proved beyond the shadow of a doubt that Mitterrand's strategy was well founded.

The Gaullist vote collapsed. Even with the support of a moderate right-wing party led by Valéry Giscard d'Estaing, a technocrat in his early forties who had been the General's Finance Minister but had left after differences with Georges Pompidou, the government's parliamentary majority was reduced to a single seat.

The Communists and the Federation both increased their vote and several of Mitterrand's inner circle, including André Rousselet and his confidant, Georges Dayan, neither of whom was by nature inclined to public political performance, were elected as MPs. The Convention passed from one MP – himself – to sixteen. His brother, Robert, who stood in the Corrèze, was defeated by a young man named Jacques Chirac, then an aide to Pompidou.

But just as defeat can contain the seeds of victory, the reverse is also true.

Four days after the second round, the FGDS Executive Committee met at Socialist Party headquarters. There Guy Mollet made clear that there could be no question of transforming the Federation into a broad-church movement, as Mitterrand and some of Mollet's colleagues, including Defferre and Pierre Mauroy, had wished.[30] The Socialists would continue as before, under his stewardship. The Federation staggered on for another eighteen months. But with no further elections in the offing to force them to stay together, the Socialists, the Radicals and the Convention increasingly went their separate ways.

In the summer of 1967, for the second time in his career, Mitterrand put politics to one side. He continued to speak in parliament, to nurse his constituency in the Nièvre and to chair meetings of the Convention. But most of his energy went elsewhere.

Two years earlier, on holiday at Hossegor, during a hike through the pine forests which march southward in a stately arc along the Atlantic coast to Biarritz, he had stumbled on a clearing with a wooden house in ruins and a sheepcote nearby. The place, which the locals called Latche, enchanted him. He brought Anne to see it. 'Look at this!' he told her, 'we can make a home for ourselves here.' She was enthusiastic.

'It was our trysting place,' she said later. 'It wasn't far from Hossegor, it was marvellous.' The owner, an elderly aristocrat, Baron Etchegoin, agreed to sell and Mitterrand signed for the purchase in August. Three hectares of the surrounding forest belonged in part to two nephews who were on a visit to America and it was agreed that they would sign later. But then came the presidential election. When Mitterrand returned the following year, the baron had changed his mind. 'He's furious,' the notary told him. 'He says, "that rascal Mitterrand, who forced the General into a run-off, he'll never have my pines."'

By then Mitterrand, too, had had to change his plans. Latche would be home . . . not to Anne but to Danielle. He had assumed that, given Danielle's relationship with Jean Balenci, she would have no objection. He was wrong. She put her foot down.

'When you are young, you think you are so strong,' Anne would say later. 'I thought I was. [For Latche] I'd done some designs for the sheepcote. I thought it was for us. What an idiot I was!' Forty years afterwards she could smile at her own innocence, but at the time she was devastated. 'When something like that happens,' she said, 'you know you're not the one he prefers. That's the hardest thing to accept.'

There were other difficulties. François might have settled down, but he was still, as she put it, 'free'. She wondered whether it was partly the 'abandoned child complex', making him seek solace in the arms of others. But whatever the reason, his 'lapses' continued. Moreover her own behaviour flew in the face not only of social convention – still a force to be reckoned with in the provinces – but of everything that her traditional, staunchly Catholic family believed in. 'It was a sin,' she said later, 'and I tried to make up for it by living an exemplary life.' François was the only partner she would ever have. 'On my side,' she said, 'I knew I would never be with anyone else':

To admire someone so much, never to be bored for a moment, to have the same interests . . . [For us] everything was in a state of perpetual renewal . . . It was thirty-two years of happiness. And unhappiness! Because it was hard too . . . I was not the preferred one. [But] François had a saying which I think goes to the heart of things. 'No love is eternal unless it is thwarted'. Beware of a love which is easy and where everything goes well! When love is difficult not just sometimes but all the time, it lives for ever.[31]

The baronial decision sparked one of those judicial imbroglios, drawn from the pages of Marcel Pagnol, in which southern France rejoices. Etchegoin refused to give the Mitterrands access across his land, making it legally impossible for them to start building. They went ahead anyway. Then he threatened to erect barriers, so that trucks could not get through, but was dissuaded by a neighbour, who pointed out that in a region where land was always unfenced, he would make himself ridiculous. So he planted a barrier of pines instead. 'Those poor pines,' Danielle remembered, 'they kept getting sick. Whenever we came on holiday, they died.'

The stand-off, pitting Don Camillo against Peppone, continued for more than twenty years. At last, shortly before his death, the baron relented. By then de Gaulle had been succeeded by Pompidou and Valéry Giscard d'Estaing, both on the Right, and by Mitterrand himself. 'You can sign with him,' the baron told his nephews. 'After all, what Giscard did was even worse.'

The ruined house at Latche had been built by a family of *gemmeurs*, a now all but forgotten profession of men who tap pine resin in the forests in the same way that rubber is tapped from heveas. It stood on a grassy knoll in a glade, a long, low one-storey dwelling of half-timbered brick, amid green oaks and acacias, with the original carved woodwork of a gallery just barely holding up inside.[32] By the beginning of 1968, restoration was complete. The house was simplicity itself: three minuscule bedrooms for Danielle and the two boys, a living area, a terrace at the back, and, forty yards away, the sheepcote, a square building with a pyramidal, tiled roof and a stone pillar at its centre, which François made his lair – bedroom, library and study rolled into one.

Latche was different from anywhere they had lived before.[33] Because it represented a victory over Anne, Danielle was at pains to assert her rights.[34] It would remain, for the rest of her life, the family home, '[a place] for my children and grand-children,. . . a house with a story to tell, a house whose walls bounced back memories of the lives of others, [guarding] secrets of love, of disputes, of children's cries and adolescent pleasures, which, unconsciously, we would absorb'. For François, too, it became the *sanctum sanctorum* of his 'official family'.

At a time when he was finally breaking free of the bourgeois attitudes instilled by his Catholic upbringing and the well-heeled, cosseted, Parisian circles in which his siblings moved, Latche was a declaration of independence. To Danielle it brought memories of her youth at Cluny; to François, a reminder of childhood at his grandparents' farm at Touvent among the copses and meadows of the Charente.

There remained his other life to think of. Anne had realised early on that since she was determined to spend her life with François and they could not marry, she would have to be independent. A diploma in the techniques of medieval stained glass, however much the subject fascinated her, would not pay the rent. On François's advice, she decided to become a museum curator, which would allow her to work in a field she loved – the arts – and would give her, as a government servant, the security that he could not. But for that it was necessary to have a university degree, so, for the next four years, she studied at the Law Faculty where François had been a student thirty years earlier. He had suggested it because he would be able to help her – and he was as good as his word. She remembered how, between the two rounds of the presidential election in 1965, he had sat up helping her with an essay. 'When I think of it now, I'm ashamed,' she said. 'A candidate for the presidency of the Republic had better things to do than assist me with my homework about communal law . . . But he made time. Which proves he must have been in love because you had to be a complete lunatic to do something like that.'

That was another quality for which Anne admired him. 'He was able to detach himself from the things around him in a way which was astounding . . . His self-control was simply extraordinary.' In later life, amid his official duties, he had the same ability to shut out everything around him and bury himself in a book as he had had when a small boy amid the hubbub of his brothers and sisters at Jarnac. 'It allowed him to maintain a distance,' she said. 'Distance was his talent.'

Whenever they were able to, they travelled. He took her to Italy, where they stayed with the English writer and socialite, Violet Trefusis, a long-standing friend, at l'Ombrellino, her medieval villa, once the home of Galileo, in the hills overlooking Florence.[35] At Christmas, every other year, they went to Israel with the Soudets, and in 1967 after the Six Day War were able for the first time to visit Mount Sinai.

Israel fascinated him. He had what Laurence Soudet called 'a life-long obsession' with the Holy Land and its past. The Bible, he wrote later, was 'a terrifying book, full of massacres and ruthlessness . . . But what force and what poetry!'

By the time they returned, François had decided that he and Anne still needed a place of their own. The following spring he bought two small pieces of land in Gordes, on the other side of the village from the Soudets, set back from the highway with a view southward over the massif of the Luberon. They did not build at once. But it was another step towards accepting that he now had two families to support.

For France, as for most of Western Europe, the middle years of the 1960s were a jubilant time. They were the peak of the 'trente glorieuses', the new era of post-war prosperity. For the first time since the eighteenth century, French GDP overtook Britain's. De Gaulle rode a wave of nationalism. He told the United States that it would be defeated in Vietnam, a truth which earned him few friends in Washington, and infuriated Canada by proclaiming, 'Long live Free Quebec!' France quit the military structure of NATO, developed an independent nuclear arsenal and became in 1965 the third nation after the Soviet Union and the US to put a satellite into space.

The first motorways opened; girls sunbathed bare-breasted on the beach at St Tropez; and André Courrèges and Mary Quant competed for authorship of the miniskirt. It was a period of optimism and hope.

But even the best of times pall. By the spring of 1968, the country seemed to be stuck in a rut. De Gaulle grumbled to his aide-de-camp, François Flohic: 'This is no longer fun. There is nothing difficult, nothing heroic, to do any more.'

'France is bored', headlined Le Monde in an editorial complaining that young people all over the world were demonstrating for freedom, but in France the only thing students seemed to care about was 'whether girls would be allowed into the boys' dormitories, which . . . is a rather limited conception of human rights'. While that may have been true in the early stages, the mood rapidly changed. At Nanterre, in the west of Paris, students occupied teaching blocks to protest against the Vietnam War. When the authorities ordered the faculty closed, they moved to the Sorbonne.

Thus was lit the touchpaper of a social explosion which would remain embedded in the nation's consciousness ever afterwards as 'May 68'.

The root cause of the upheavals which shook not only Europe but the United States and much of Asia in the late 1960s was the extraordinary burst of energy which accompanied the coming of age of the baby boomers, the generation born twenty years earlier which had never experienced wartime deprivation and now found itself confronted by outdated social or political structures which refused to move with the times. In China Mao used this energy to fuel the Cultural Revolution. In Eastern Europe it was channelled by reformist intellectuals who hoped to democratise the Soviet system. In America it was directed against racism and the misdeeds of the military-industrial complex, symbolised by the drafting of young men to what de Gaulle called Washington's 'odious war' in Vietnam. In France and most of the rest of Western Europe,* it was anarchistic and hostile both towards political parties and the official trades unions.

From his balcony on the rue Guynemer, overlooking the Luxembourg Gardens, Mitterrand had a grandstand view of the growing agitation. Like de Gaulle and the rest of the French political establishment, he felt, as Danielle said later, 'out of sync with events'.

At the beginning of April, he had told an interviewer that he thought France was finally ready to elect a left-wing Head of State. Now ten years of patient effort were being put at risk by groups of nihilistic young people who knew what they disliked but had no idea what they wanted in its place. 'I can't make sense of this movement,' he complained. 'Yes, imagination is on the streets, but the leaders have nothing to say.' He grouched about 'a revolution with long hair but short on ideas'. When students invaded the offices of the Convention, in the rue du Louvre, he told them peevishly: 'Being young doesn't last very long. You spend a lot more time being old.'

On the afternoon of May 3, a Friday, the government decided to evacuate the Sorbonne by force, violating a centuries-old compact that universities, like churches, were a sanctuary for dissenters. The students erected barricades and dug up cobblestones to hurl at the police. The response was immediate and brutal. That night twenty students were

---

* Britain was a partial exception. Whether because the parliamentary system was more flexible, because there was less of a sense of social blockage or because there was greater tolerance of the sexual revolution than in a Catholic country like France, where even the sale of condoms had been forbidden until 1967 – Mitterrand, during the presidential election of 1965, was one of the first French politicians to call publicly for the legalisation of family planning – the 'Swinging Sixties' in Britain were a time of cultural and social change but of significantly less overt political conflict than elsewhere.

injured and several hundred detained for questioning, of whom thirty were charged with public order offences. 'May 68' had begun.

On Sunday, ten students were given suspended sentences and four others two months in prison. Within hours, fresh barricades were thrown up in the Latin Quarter. That night 400 students and 200 policemen were injured. By the end of the week, the 6th and 7th *arrondissements* of Paris resembled a war zone. Clouds of tear gas hung in the air, eerily illuminated by the explosions of Molotov cocktails. The streets were littered with the burnt-out wrecks of cars.

De Gaulle, who had insisted on repression, was beginning to have second thoughts. His Defence Minister, Pierre Messmer, proposed bringing in the paratroops and declaring martial law. Louis Joxe, the Justice Minister, said soberly: 'You cannot treat children as rebels.'

When Pompidou returned on the evening of Saturday, May 11, from a ten-day visit to the Near East, the General was still in two minds. The Prime Minister convinced him to give negotiation a chance. That night he announced on television that the Sorbonne would reopen after the weekend, courses would resume and the four imprisoned activists would be able to appeal their sentences.

His overture succeeded to the extent that the tension eased and, for the next two weeks, there was no more rioting. But the government was perceived to have capitulated and the agitation continued and spread.

On Monday, May 13, the 10th anniversary of the insurrection in Algiers which had brought de Gaulle to power, the trades unions declared a one-day general strike. More than half a million people, students and workers together,[36] marched from the Gare de l'Est, in the north of Paris, past the Place de la République and the Bastille, across the Seine to skirt the Latin Quarter before dispersing at Denfert Rochereau in the south. In the vanguard were Daniel Cohn-Bendit, Alain Geismar and other student leaders, followed by the unions, headed by the Secretary-General of the CGT, Georges Séguy, and then, much further back, the politicians, Mitterrand, Mendès France, Mollet and Waldeck Rochet, lost among the crowd like so many pointless hangers-on.

The mood was good humoured. The marchers' banners carried slogans which were already plastered on all the walls of Paris, some political – '10 years is enough!', 'De Gaulle to the gallows!', and 'We are all German Jews!', a reference to an ill-considered article in the

Communist newspaper, *l'Humanité*, denouncing Cohn-Bendit as 'a German anarchist' – others proclaiming 'To forbid is forbidden'; 'Be realistic, ask for the impossible!', 'Under the cobblestones is the beach' and 'Marx is dead, God also, and I'm not feeling too well myself'.

It was one of those extraordinary periods, like that which followed the fall of the Berlin Wall in 1989 or the Democracy Wall movement in China, which come only once in a generation, when timeless barriers collapse and overnight the unthinkable becomes not only possible but banal. For a full month, France was caught up in a frenzy of debate – part student rag, part movement for change – in which Maoists, Trotskyists, Situationists and adepts of Althusser and Marcuse sought to mobilise the masses in the universities and factories to build a luminous new world.

For Mitterrand, it should have brought back memories of his own student days in the Latin Quarter in the service of the ineffable Ferdinand Lop. Not so. The generations were too far apart. The parallel escaped him. Instead he went ahead with a long-planned trip to the provinces, where he spoke on subjects largely unconnected with the crisis which was then transfixing France.[37] Once back in Paris, he denounced the brutality of the police and the hypocrisy of the Gaullists for condemning student insurgents when they themselves had taken power thanks to an insurrection. In parliament, defending a censorship motion which came within a handful of votes of succeeding, he told Georges Pompidou: 'You have lost everything. You must go.' But it meant nothing. In the incandescent climate of May 1968, parliament was irrelevant. The students' slogan said it all: 'Power is in the streets'.

Mitterrand did make one approach to the students. Georges Dayan arranged a meeting at his home in the rue de Rivoli, close to the City Hall, with Alain Geismar, the President of the University Teachers' Union. Geismar had been a member of Mitterrand's campaign committee in 1965 and was one of the few insurgent leaders interested in building bridges to left-wing politicians.[38] But when he reported back to his colleagues afterwards, Geismar said, they made him 'feel like a zombie'. Most of them saw in Mitterrand a Justice Minister who had done nothing to stop torture in Algeria; an ally of the 'Stalinist villains', as Cohn-Bendit called the Communists; an unprincipled opportunist. He was jeered and whistled at. The students' watchword became: 'Neither de Gaulle nor Mitterrand!'

A year later Mitterrand attempted an explanation: 'The very fact of . . . having confronted General de Gaulle in the presidential election . . . had paradoxically . . . identified me with the dignitaries of the regime against which I had never stopped fighting. The regime and I belonged to the same slice of history . . . Those who wanted a future without de Gaulle also wanted a future without me.'

By the weekend of Sunday May 19, France was paralysed. All over the country, workers occupied factories and installed self-management committees.

In Paris there was no public transport and no petrol for private cars. The students occupied the Odeon theatre opposite the Senate and held impassioned debates, where anyone was free to join in – workers, housewives, celebrities, writers, company directors, even the occasional politician – while in the wings, and in the Luxembourg Gardens across the road, under the Mitterrand family's windows, young people abandoned their clothes and inhibitions and put into practice the slogan, earthier than the 'Make love, not war' of their American counterparts: 'Have orgasms without limit'.

The General's spokesman quoted him as saying: 'Reforms, yes. Shit-in-the-bed, no!'*

At the end of that week, with nine million workers, more than half the workforce, on strike, the President announced a referendum on 'renovation' and 'participation', the first to be applied to the universities and the second to the role of workers in their enterprises. If the referendum proposal were defeated, he added, he would step down.

The speech was not a success. The one part that stuck in everyone's minds was the hint that he might resign. The students coined a new slogan: 'The shit-in-the-bed is him!'

That night the rioting resumed. Once again, the police clamped

---

*'La réforme, oui; la chienlit, non!' The word, chienlit, earlier spelt chie-en-lit ('shit-in-the-bed') and pronounced accordingly, was first used in print in the sixteenth century by Rabelais who included it in a long list of what he called 'diffamatory epithets'. It originally denoted a character in street carnivals who appeared in a nightshirt with a brown smudge (sometimes of mustard) on his backside, and by extension, in the plural, street-players generally. In modern usage it has come to mean disorder. The General presumably intended it in both senses: the carnival on the streets and the chaos it was creating.

down hard. De Gaulle did not sleep. 'It's me, now, that they are going for,' he told his aides. 'It's my departure that they want.' For several days he kept silent. There was a growing sense, not only among the opposition but also among his own supporters, that he would have to go. His brother-in-law, Jacques Vendroux, wrote in his diary: 'the wind of defeatism is blowing more and more strongly'.

The person most often cited to replace de Gaulle was not Mitterrand but Pierre Mendès France. Mitterrand was too close to the Communists, too stained by the Fourth Republic. Mendès was esteemed as a symbol of probity, respected by the students and acceptable to a wide swathe of opinion on both Left and Right.

The realisation that, if he did not move quickly, the initiative would pass to a rival convinced Mitterrand that it was time to act. On Sunday May 26, he told a mass meeting in Château-Chinon: 'We are facing a regime which is tottering, supplicating, a regime which has capitulated before the rising force of an angry people . . . The Republic awaits us!'

It was an error of judgement which would cost him dear.

Mitterrand's fear of being outflanked by Mendès France had blinded him to the fact that the wind was beginning to change. De Gaulle had not seen it either. Pompidou was more clear-sighted. At dawn on Monday, May 27, the Prime Minister completed a marathon 72-hour negotiation resulting in major concessions to the trades unions on wages and working conditions. When the agreement was put to a vote, the workforce rejected it and demanded better terms. Pompidou was unfazed, telling de Gaulle that in time they would come round. He was right. Not only were the unions and the political establishment – Communists, Socialists, Centre and Right – united in wanting the agitation to end, but public opinion was at last starting to tire of the chaos and disruption that the students and the strikes were creating.

The following morning Mitterrand gave a press conference in the somewhat improbable velvet-and-gilt setting of the Continental Hotel, between the Place Vendôme and the Tuileries Gardens, at which he called for the formation of a government-in-waiting.

The Gaullist regime, he declared, 'no longer has even the appearance of power'. To avoid a political vacuum if the General's referendum were defeated and he were obliged to step down, it was wise to plan ahead. He proposed Mendès France as Prime Minister.[39] Asked who should become President, he replied that that would be for the electorate to decide but he would certainly stand as a candidate. It was a carefully weighed, circumspect statement, which had been approved earlier that morning by the FGDS Executive Committee, including Guy Mollet and the new Radical Party leader, René Billères, and at first it was well received The logic behind it, Mitterrand explained afterwards, was to prevent de Gaulle portraying the referendum as 'either me or chaos' by showing that there was a credible alternative ready to take his place.

He had reckoned without Georges Pompidou. Despite (or perhaps because of) his background as a banker with Rothschilds, his never having held elected office, his years working quietly behind the scenes in the General's shadow, the Prime Minister was a formidable tactician, nick-named by his colleagues Raminagrobis – the large, well-rounded, purring cat of La Fontaine's fable with deceptively sharp claws. Although French television never normally covered the opposition, a camera crew myst-eriously appeared to record Mitterrand's announcement. That night the main item in the evening news was a montage of his press conference.

'It was cleverly done,' Mitterrand admitted later. 'I looked like an apprentice dictator, ill-shaven, fanatical, chin stuck out and arm outstretched as though in [a Nazi salute]'. The effect was catastrophic. Georges Dayan returned from the provinces horrified by the comments he had heard. 'Who does he think he is, your friend?' one local activist had asked, 'A Führer, that's what he is.'

But neither Pompidou nor Mitterrand nor anyone else in the polit-ical establishment could have anticipated what came next.

Shortly after eleven o'clock the following morning, de Gaulle left the Elysée with his wife for the heliport at Issy-les-Moulineaux, just outside Paris. From there, they headed east. At Saint-Dizier, 120 miles from Paris, they refuelled at the end of a runway, out of sight of the control tower. The police helicopter escorting them was ordered to leave. Only then did the General tell the pilot his destination. The rest of the way they flew at low altitude to avoid radar and maintained radio silence. No one in France, not even the Prime Minister, knew that de Gaulle had left the country to meet General Jacques Massu at French Military Headquarters at Baden Baden, just across the border in Germany.

Massu himself was as surprised as everyone else. When de Gaulle's aide-de-camp, François Flohic, telephoned from the landing strip to tell him that the General had arrived, he answered, 'Who? . . . Give me five minutes. I've got no clothes on, I'm having a siesta.' It emerged later that he had been up much of the previous night, drinking with Marshal Koshevoi, the Soviet Commander in East Germany.

De Gaulle's first words when Massu presented himself were, 'It's all fucked.' For half an hour, Massu gave him a pep talk. Then the General lunched alone. By the time he had finished, his doubts were laid to rest.[40]

Afterwards it would be claimed that de Gaulle's flight to Germany was a clever ploy to create panic by his absence in order that he might return to a triumphal welcome from a grateful nation, or alternatively that he had sought out Massu in order to assure himself of the army's support. It was nothing of the sort.

Once the crisis was over, the General was an astute enough politician to let the rumours have free rein.[41] But the truth was that he had been on the point of giving up. Before taking a decision he had had the good sense to go and see an old fellow soldier who would call a spade a spade. He acknowledged as much some months later, telling Madame Massu: 'it was Providence that put your husband in my path'.

While he had been at Baden Baden, the Communists had organised a show of force, a march of several hundred thousand people from the City Hall to the Gare St Lazare, half a mile from the Elysée. *Le Monde* devoted its front page next day to 'the tandem of tomorrow', Mitterrand and Mendès France.

Before it reached the news-stands it was already out of date.

The following afternoon, after the Cabinet had met, de Gaulle spoke on the radio. The choice of medium was deliberate, recalling his wartime speeches. One of his staff commented: 'He's put on his 1940 boots again'. For the first time since the crisis began, the General found the words he needed. 'I shall not withdraw. I have a mandate from the people. I shall fulfil it.' At Pompidou's urging, he announced that, instead of the planned referendum, he would dissolve parliament and call fresh elections. Also at Pompidou's urging, he accused the Communists of threatening France with 'a totalitarian . . . dictatorship [built on] the ambition and hatred of politicians who belong on the scrap heap'. It was dishonest and unfair, but politically it made perfect sense. The Communist Party was the scarecrow the Gaullists needed to send the people of France running for safety – back into the General's arms.

Soon after he finished speaking, crowds began gathering at the Place de la Concorde. It was not the spontaneous manifestation of support which the Gaullists later claimed: André Malraux and others had been at work in the shadows for a week, organising a counter-demonstration. But the result far exceeded their expectations. Nearly a million people marched up the Champs-Elysées to the Arc de Triomphe in a sea of red-white-and-blue French flags with the Gaullist 'barons' – Debré, Chaban-Delmas, Joxe, Maurice Schumann and Pierre Messmer – at their head. 'De Gaulle is not alone,' they chanted, 'Mitterrand, charlatan!', 'Mitterrand to the gallows' and 'Mitterrand, you failed.'

The crowd included many who were simply exasperated by the *chienlit*, the 'shit-in-the-bed', which was making everyone's life impossible. But the doctoring of the television coverage of Mitterrand's news conference, which Pompidou had arranged, also played a part. Mitterrand wrote later that the French, having encouraged him to fight against de Gaulle, had recoiled in horror when they realised that the deity was about to be dethroned. They were not yet ready for a parricide.

Timing is everything in politics. In 1968, the timing was not right. Once de Gaulle had found his feet again, there was nothing Mitterrand could do.

After the demonstration that night, the agitation faded, the students returned to their exams, the factories reopened and the country got back to work. In June, the General's followers rode a tidal wave of support back into the National Assembly. Gaullists won 360 out of 485 seats, a triumph on a scale not seen since the time of Louis XVIII after the fall of Napoleon in 1815. It was achieved in part through massive State-sponsored intimidation. In the Nièvre, where Mitterrand campaigned, members of Foccart's Service d'Action Civique, wearing helmets and wielding iron bars, descended on the villages, warning the inhabitants that left-wing terrorists were trying to seize power. Mitterrand's opponent depicted him as an agent of communism and, to show what awaited the population if he were re-elected, a red flag with the hammer and sickle was flown from the top of a church tower. All over France, as de Gaulle himself acknowledged, the elections were driven by fear. Mitterrand held on to his seat by a narrow margin after a run-off. But all the other MPs from the Convention who had been elected fifteen months earlier were soundly defeated. The Socialists and the Communists each lost more than half their parliamentary strength.

For Mitterrand there was an ugly symmetry about it. In May 1958, de Gaulle had returned to power, ending his hopes of becoming Prime Minister under the Fourth Republic. Ten years later, almost to the day,[42] a herd of feckless students, barely out of their teens, had trampled into the ground the prospect of a Union of the Left on which he had placed his hopes for becoming President.

Mitterrand insisted later that he had sympathised all along with the students' cause.[43] One may be forgiven for disbelieving him. In his more candid moments, he fumed at what he called the 'thoughtlessness' of 'the gibberish Left', these 'ninnies [and] little frauds . . . who have given 400 seats to the Right' by 'stacking up ideologies glued on top of each other'. The one lesson he drew was that the traditional parties had to change if they were to win the support of the voters of tomorrow.

But that seemed further away than ever.

After the June 1968 elections, Mitterrand became so isolated that he sat in parliament as an independent. The Socialists and the Radicals blamed him for destroying their electoral chances with his press conference (which, at the time, they had warmly applauded) that Pompidou-Raminagrobis had so cleverly used against them. In July, Gaston Defferre suggested that the moment had come for him to step down as President of the Federation of the Left. In November, when he eventually did so, his farewell speech was heard out in silence. Only Pierre Mauroy and the left-wing Radical, Robert Fabre, deigned to thank him and shake his hand. Afterwards he quoted Chateaubriand: 'There are times when one has to dispense one's contempt economically because there are so many who need it.'

Mitterrand's departure spelled the end of the Federation. It had died, he wrote, because 'it was unable to overcome the resistance of the parties which had delegated to it only the appearance of power'. In three short years, the credit that he had built up as de Gaulle's challenger in 1965 had run into the sand.

The Communists had not helped. When Mitterrand had proposed his government-in-waiting, Waldeck Rochet had been reticent. He objected to Mendès France as Prime Minister because of his anti-communist views and, more importantly, he worried that if de Gaulle were to resign it might provoke a military coup. A month later, when the General called snap elections, the Communists, for the first time since 1962, failed to conclude a second-round pact with the Socialists, increasing both parties' losses. The final straw came in August, when the Soviet Union invaded Czechoslovakia and they were forced back into their ghetto, condemned once more by public opinion as tools of a hostile and aggressive foreign power.

Thus by the autumn of 1968, both pillars of Mitterrand's political strategy had come crashing to the ground. The Communists were beyond the pale. The non-communist Left was more disunited than ever.

He withdrew to Latche to work on a new book, *Ma part de vérité* ('My Portion of Truth'), which, after three years of a semi-truce with de Gaulle, would show flashes of the same virulence as the *Coup d'état permanent*.[44] But it was no longer quite the same de Gaulle. Pompidou, not the General, had organised the Gaullist resistance and reconquest in May 1968. Pompidou, not the General, had stage-managed the June elections. The elderly President knew it and was mortified. Part of his authority had been usurped by another. In July, he replaced Pompidou by Maurice Couve de Murville, who had been his Foreign Minister. But the former dauphin did not leave the scene quietly. That winter he made clear that, when de Gaulle stepped down, he would be a candidate to succeed him, provoking the General to warn that he intended to serve out his full term, ending in December 1972, when he would be 82 years old.

That was not to be.

De Gaulle had not given up the idea of the referendum on 'renovation' and 'participation' which he had originally planned the previous spring. The subject had been modified: now it would be a proposal to increase the powers of the regions at the expense of the Senate, whose role would become essentially consultative. Couve de Murville tried hard to dissuade him. So did the rest of the Cabinet. But the General had the bit between his teeth and the more others argued against it, the more determined he was to press ahead.

In February, he realised that the vote would probably go against him. But by then it was too late for him to draw back. On the night of April 27 1969, a Sunday, when the verdict was announced, 52.4 per cent had voted 'no' and 47.6 per cent 'yes'. Shortly after midnight a laconic communiqué declared: 'I am ceasing to exercise my functions of President of the Republic. This decision takes effect at midday today.' He left neither with a bang nor a whimper but with majestic indifference. 'Deep down,' he told François Flohic the following afternoon, 'I am not sorry it ended like this. [If I had stayed] what would have awaited me? Difficulties which could only . . . have worn me out with no benefit to France.'

Towards the end of his life, Mitterrand would concede that de Gaulle had ended his long career 'on the side of democracy'. Nothing obliged him to step down when the referendum went against him. He had not hesitated.

An election to choose his successor was scheduled five weeks later.

The President of the Senate, Alain Poher, a Christian Democrat, who, under the constitution, became interim President, announced that he would stand. So did Georges Pompidou.

On the Left confusion reigned. The Communists proposed that Mitterrand stand again as he had in 1965. The Socialists vetoed the idea. Mitterrand was sidelined not only, as he charged later, because 'a small group of men who formed a cabal of intrigue took it on themselves to destroy the hopes of the people' – a reference to Guy Mollet and his allies – but because the opinion polls, which, a year earlier, had predicted that he would defeat Pompidou by 53 to 47 per cent, now gave him only 18 per cent. In his absence Gaston Defferre announced that he was going to try again and if elected would appoint Mendès France as Prime Minister. That ended any chance of a common front with the Communists.

On Election Day, Sunday, June 1, the Left put forward four candidates: Jacques Duclos for the Communist Party, Defferre for the Socialists, Michel Rocard for the PSU and a young man named Alain Krivine representing a small Trotskyist faction.

Mitterrand was out in the cold. As things turned out, it was exactly the right place to be.

When the results of the first round were announced, Pompidou had a comfortable lead over his Centre-Right challenger, Alain Poher.

Jacques Duclos, for the Communists, won 22.5 per cent, proving that, despite the crushing of the Prague Spring, the party faithful were still able to get out the vote. Rocard received 3 per cent, a creditable score for a representative of a fringe party. But the Socialists, who had been hoping to outdo Duclos or at least to give him a good run for his money, were annihilated. Defferre, despite Mendès France's backing, obtained only 5.1 per cent. Servan-Schreiber's prediction of the 'worst defeat since the Second Empire' had come true, one election late.

The outcome was so bad that no one found anything to say.

In 1965, Mitterrand had proved that a united front of the Left could put up a good fight even against de Gaulle. Four years later, when the different parties went their separate ways, the results were beyond awful. In that summer of 1969, his rivals self-destructed. It would take time to sink in but the message was clear. There was now only one possible way forward.

9

Union of the Left

When Georges Pompidou took office in June 1969, the French Right was in a stronger position than at any time in the previous half-century. In the presidential election, the Left had failed to get a candidate through to the second round. In parliament, the government had an overwhelming majority until the next elections, still four years away. The opposition was in disarray. Guy Mollet, who had ruled the Socialists in autocratic fashion since 1946, clung to his post if for no other reason than to prevent Mitterrand uniting the Left without him. The Radicals were split between leftists and rightists, most of their energy absorbed by the effort to stay together. The Communists were in internal exile and Waldeck Rochet had been diagnosed with the early stages of Parkinson's disease.

In this discouraging situation, Mitterrand was strangely serene.

'I am the most hated man in France,' he told Michèle Cotta, a young journalist to whom he had taken a fancy some years earlier. 'Doesn't that mean that one day I have the chance of being the best loved?' By then he had been in politics long enough to have learnt that when the pendulum swings far enough one way, it is only a matter of time before it will swing back.

He set himself three tasks. To establish publicly his socialist beliefs beyond any possibility of dispute in order to be in a position to assume the leadership of the new left-wing movement which he was convinced would eventually arise. Secondly, to continue the strategy that he had explained to Roland Dumas ten years earlier, to colonise and bring under control, one circle at a time, the whole of the non-communist Left. He had failed with the FGDS because the defences of the traditional parties had been too strong, but, now that the Socialists and the Radicals had suffered a series of crushing defeats, their resistance would be weaker. Thirdly, once the first two stages were complete, to establish not just an electoral cartel but a common programme with the Communists, so that when the next elections arrived, the Left would go into battle united.

The first part was the easiest. *Ma part de vérité*, published a few days after Pompidou's election, provided for the first time a coherent explanation of the long, erratic journey he had made from a Catholic upbringing in the provinces, his association with the far Right, life in a PoW camp, Vichy and the Resistance, through the political confusion of the Fourth Republic, to the return of de Gaulle and, finally, his transfiguration, whether real or imagined, during the 1965 presidential campaign. His account elided some of the trickiest episodes but he recognised that, to be credible, he needed to acknowledge both his own contradictions and his continuing doubts. The book was a success, largely because of its honesty:

> I was not born on the Left and, still less, socialist . . . I will make things worse by confessing that subsequently I manifested no early enthusiasm.
>
> I could have become a socialist under the impact of ideas or events, at university for instance, or during the war. No. Effective grace took its time about making its way to my side . . . I did not become [a socialist] by doing a job which would have instilled in me class reflexes [or] by joining a political movement which . . . would have trained me in its ideological disciplines.
>
> In fact, I have no pretensions. I made my commitment simply for the sake of justice . . . I obeyed, I suppose, an innate feeling [rooted in] my family background . . . which held that hierarchies founded on privilege and money were the worst offence against nature. To those around me, the idea that money might be more important than the values which underpinned their lives – motherland, religion, freedom, dignity – was revolting. [Money] was the enemy, the agent of corruption, with which one had no dealings. Their Christian faith strengthened this belief [but] at the same time deflected it . . . They felt a bit contemptuous of a revolution attached to material objectives. [They were light years away from] adhering intellectually to socialist theories . . .
>
> What I learnt in captivity [as a PoW] reduced that distance for me. [But] I did not suddenly encounter the god of socialism on some street

corner . . . I did not throw myself on my knees and weep with joy . . . Socialism . . . has many revealed truths and in each chapel it has priests who watch, decide and punish . . . Rare are those who prefer counsel to precepts, study to dogma . . . That put me off at first . . . I thought it was possible for capitalist society to be brought to reform itself . . . But as I looked more and more with eyes that did not see, in the end I recognised a certain truth. It happened, as it were, by a succession of brush-strokes . . . It wasn't a matter of choosing between the Fourth and the Fifth Republics, but between capitalism and socialism. That is the conclusion I reached. You ask me, what is the Left? The Left [for me] now is socialism.[1]

The reservations were important. Unlike Mollet and unlike the Communists, Mitterrand did not embrace socialism as an ideological straitjacket.

But no less important was his declaration of faith. The core of his political creed, a belief in social justice, went back to his youth. There had been, he admitted, moments when 'I rebelled against it, when I did not want to commit myself, when I turned my back' – a reference to his reliance on a right-wing constituency as an MP in the Nièvre and his failure as Minister of Justice to speak out against torture in Algeria. But wanting social justice was one thing. Being a socialist was another. That had come about gradually in the decade after de Gaulle's return. His views took on a new consistency, a new 'density' as one French writer put it, until in the summer of 1969 he resigned himself to the conclusion that socialism was the only means by which he could achieve his goals.[2] There was a parallel with his decision to join the Resistance at Vichy nearly thirty years before. It was less from conviction than from a process of elimination which ruled out any other choice.

From then on his political vocabulary changed.

For the first time in his life, Mitterrand studied the socialist classics. In *Ma part de vérité*, he quoted passages from Marx and Lenin, writing about class conflict and capitalism, the domination of the bourgeoisie and workers' alienation, terms from the socialist playbook which had never figured in his earlier essays. It was made easier by May 1968, which had given a new, revolutionary edge to left-wing political discourse. But it did not come naturally to him and he could not resist a sideways swipe at 'the disputes and excommunications' of Marxist theoreticians. Socialism, he declared, was not a 'vitrified mummy preserved in the shop window of the guardians of the Faith . . . It is also and above all enthusiasm, collective action, the communion of men in search of justice!' But the new vocabulary and the concepts that went with it were part of the arsenal he needed in order to prevail over his rivals. Deliberately he staked out a position more radical than that of Mollet or Michel Rocard. 'The liberal Left,' he said, 'is too close to capitalism.' The Socialists could not be both 'on the side of the exploiters and of the exploited'.

The message was that, recent convert though he might be, he was the man best equipped to win back for the Socialists the support they had lost to the Communists by their failure to offer anything better.

Next came the difficult part.

Throughout the brief lifespan of the FGDS, the main obstacle to change had been Guy Mollet. Eleven years Mitterrand's senior, he ruled the Socialist Party with an iron hand, installing loyalists in key positions and systematically blocking any initiative by others. With trademark horn-rimmed spectacles, he looked more like an accountant than the schoolteacher he actually was, while a cigarette perpetually hanging from his upper lip suggested long nights of negotiation in nicotine-filled rooms. Mollet freely acknowledged his errors, notably over Algeria and Suez, but minimised their import, asserting: 'the priest who fails in no way mars the religion in whose name he speaks'. He lived in the northern French town of Arras in an apartment so small that when, as Prime Minister, he allowed himself the luxury of having a bathroom installed, the only place they could find to put it was in the entrance hall. Yet alongside a simplicity as mule-headed as it was genuine, Mollet had a knack for intrigue which rivalled Mitterrand's own. He was not a man to yield without a struggle.

In February 1969, as yet another round of discussions was beginning about the formation of a new movement to unite the non-communist Left, Mitterrand told Mollet bluntly over dinner one night that he thought the time had come for him to step down and make way for someone younger. From a man who usually took pains not to show his hand, the confidence was surprising. But Mitterrand had concluded that the only way to shift the immovable Socialist Secretary-General would be to confront him head on.

Three months later, Mollet gave his response.

On Sunday, May 4, citing de Gaulle's resignation the previous weekend, he called an urgent meeting of the Socialist Party, the Convention and two other small left-wing groups to approve a charter for the projected new movement, which he suggested should be named the New Socialist Party. Sensing a trap, Mitterrand refused to attend. He had already warned some months earlier that 'if it is going to be just a matter of putting paint on worm-eaten benches, we will not be the paint'. A second group, led by Jean Poperen, an ex-Communist who had broken with the Party in 1956, also stayed away. But Mollet and the remaining group, led by Alain Savary, the man who had blackballed Mitterrand when he had sought to join the 'New Left' nine years earlier, went ahead anyway.

'It's salami tactics, comrade,' one of Mollet's aides explained afterwards. 'We've already got Savary . . . Next we will take in Poperen. And we are working to absorb the members of the Convention despite Mitterrand.'

The strategy looked like succeeding. At a second meeting in the Paris suburb of Issy-les-Moulineaux that summer, Poperen and his supporters, as Mollet had anticipated, rallied to the New Socialist Party, which now formally committed itself to the long-desired Union of the Left. For Mitterrand, this was the worst possible outcome. Not only was the Convention isolated but the new movement was advocating the very policies that Mitterrand himself had long championed. What possible justification could there be for continuing to hold aloof? Slowly the Convention's members began haemorrhaging towards the new body that Mollet's forceps had ingeniously brought into being.

But at that point the Socialist leader made a fatal error.

Instead of confirming his dauphin, Pierre Mauroy, to succeed him, he engineered the election of Alain Savary, who he thought would be more malleable and easier to control. As a condition of his appointment, Mollet had insisted that several of his close aides retain key positions. The result was what Louis Mexandeau called a 'cloister government', in which Savary enjoyed the appearance of power but Mollet continued to pull the strings from his supposed 'retirement'.

Mauroy, who controlled the Party's powerful northern region federation, was furious. For the moment there was nothing he could do. But in time his anger would make itself felt. Meanwhile Mitterrand redoubled his efforts to maintain the Convention's independence, travelling widely, addressing meetings in small provincial towns, a thousand people here, 1,500 there, constantly preaching the need for left-wing unity. The town meeting was then one of the few ways for an opposition leader to make his voice heard. Radio and television were still in the hands of the State. It was as though Mitterrand had returned to the beginning of his career, building a following a few members at a time. The Convention bore up better than he had feared. From 12,000 activists in the autumn of 1968, it stabilised at 8,000 two years later. And the enthusiasm with which he was received reassured him that the support he had acquired during the 1965 campaign against de Gaulle was not entirely lost.

By the summer of 1970, Savary's leadership was increasingly under challenge. He was respected and well liked, but he was a mild-mannered professor, without charisma and all too obviously under Mollet's thumb. Defferre, whose federation in Marseille was the second largest after Mauroy's, had been urging him for months to strike out on his own and fire the henchmen Mollet had left to watch over him. To no avail. That was not Savary's style.

Defferre and Mauroy did not have a majority even if they joined forces. But a third group, on the far Left of the Party, led by an idiosyncratic young technocrat named Jean-Pierre Chevènement, was also disenchanted. If the three were to unite, Savary's leadership – and Mollet's control – would be threatened.

Mitterrand did not instigate their disaffection. But he nursed it.

In November 1970 he decided the time had come to act. 'I had only one gun, which could fire one shot, and one cartridge,' he said later. At Château-Chinon that month he issued an appeal to 'all political organisations favourable [to] organic socialist unity' to set up without delay a 'National Delegation' to work for 'the resurrection of a big and powerful Socialist Party' which would attract the young. In December the Convention, at its annual assembly, approved the initiative after a debate sufficiently stormy to convince Mollet that the appeal was genuine. The 'Delegation' was established, one third of its members from the Convention, two thirds Socialists and their allies. It was agreed that a Congress of Unity would be held the following summer in the dormitory suburb of Épinay on the northern outskirts of Paris. For voting purposes the Convention would be treated as having 10,000 members, the Socialists 70,000.

Mollet and Savary had every reason to be pleased with themselves. The last slice of the salami was waiting to be eaten. After two years of splendid, but rather lonely, isolation, Mitterrand and his Convention had been forced to come in from the cold. Their surrender was to be unconditional. Mitterrand gave Savary to believe that when the merger was completed he would not even seek a place on the new Executive Committee.

In the weeks leading up to the Congress, Mollet felt uneasy. He had a nose for such things. But he could not put his finger on what was wrong.

Mitterrand, Mauroy and Defferre had been meeting secretly since January.

All three wanted an end to Mollet's influence. Mitterrand had little difficulty convincing the others that the only way to do that was to get rid of Savary too. Within the Party, everyone was growing impatient with the slow pace of change. One of Mollet's loyalists told Mitterrand that spring: 'the Party is going nowhere without you. Alain Savary has failed . . . Too cautious, too hesitant, too many scruples.'

The timing was finally right. Shortly before the Congress, Chevènement was brought into the plot. Then Mitterrand fine-tuned the machination which was to confound his opponents. Louis Mermaz, for the Convention, and Mauroy and Defferre, on behalf of their two federations, were to present rival motions for debate as alternatives to the 'official' motion which would be tabled by Savary. Mitterrand himself rewrote both texts, giving one a radical left-wing tonality, emphasising unity, and the other a more liberal, social-democratic slant, in order to make them sufficiently different for no one to suspect that their supporters were planning to collude, but sufficiently close on essentials that, when the moment came, a synthesis would be credible, enabling the two groups to come together.

But first he set an ambush.

The morning of Saturday, June 12 1971, was taken up with routine business. Savary presented a proposal for a change in the voting system to strengthen the Executive Committee by making it more difficult for those who supported dissident motions to obtain representation. To everyone's surprise, Chevènement proposed an amendment: proportional representation on the Committee for all whose motions obtained more than 5 per cent of the vote. To Mollet's fury, the ammendment – supported by the Convention, Mauroy and Defferre as well as Chevènement's group – carried the day.

The blow was totally unexpected. It was not fatal – all else being equal, Savary could still expect a majority on the new Executive Committee – but dissidents would be more strongly represented than had been the case hitherto. During the lunch break, a young member of the Convention, Gilles Catoire, pushing open the door of a small conference room, stumbled on a conclave of Mollet, Savary and Jean Poperen. Mollet, beside himself with rage, was fuming at the other two: 'How could you let it happen, to lose the Party like this?'

The following day, Sunday, the leaders presented their groups' motions. Mitterrand gave a rousing speech, proclaiming his confidence in the Party's future, which he compared with the passivity of the recent past. 'Now that we have a new party,' he told the 900 delegates packed into the hall,

> I want its first mission to be to conquer . . . I want this party to take power! I know, I know, I'm starting badly. Already the sin of electoralism! Yes, I too would like . . . the transformation of our society . . . to commence with a change in our own consciousness and the consciousness of the masses. But we must also win power! To remain a splinter group is not my vocation, nor that of those who vote this motion with me.[3]

It was a language of hope in the tradition of Léon Blum and Jean Jaurès, the emblematic figures of French socialism. Unity, Mitterrand declared, could not be held hostage to a prior ideological accord with the Communists, as Mollet and Savary wished, because in that case it would never happen. Unity must be built on a practical basis, to win back the support the Socialists had lost to the Communist Party, to attract liberal democrats who wanted change even if they disagreed with socialist methods, to convince the 'leftists' and the youth whose demands had exploded on to the streets in May 1968. What policies should be followed once that unity was achieved? It was up to the Congress to decide:

> Reform or revolution? I want to say . . . yes, revolution! . . . Whether it is violent or peaceful, revolution is first and foremost a rupture. Whoever does not accept a rupture . . . with the established order,

[with] capitalist society, that person, I say, cannot be a member of the Socialist Party . . . There is not and will never be a socialist society without collective ownership of the main means of production, exchange and research . . . The real enemy, . . . the only enemy, because it includes everything else . . . is the monopoly! The term is broad, it covers the power of money in all its forms: money which corrupts, money which buys, money which crushes, money which kills, money which ruins, money which rots men's consciences! Those who govern us politically are merely the executives of this monopoly. As for our base, . . . our base is the class front . . . the Union of the Left.[4]

Fighting words, which contrasted all the more strongly with the warmed-up platitudes of Guy Mollet, who spoke next. Mollet could be a skilful orator on his own turf, but this time he floundered, unable to find the words to retrieve the situation. When the ballots were counted, Mitterrand's motion, supported by Mauroy, Defferre, Chevènement and the Convention, received 43,926 votes, just over 2,000 more than the motion of Savary's team. That Sunday afternoon, he became de facto First Secretary – a position formally confirmed three days later – of a party of which the previous Friday he had not even been a member.

Luck had been on Mitterrand's side.

The veteran co-leader of the northern federation, Augustin Laurent, an ally of Mollet who could have prevented Mauroy from switching his votes to Mitterrand, was persuaded to go home early. Other delegations from distant provinces also left ahead of time, in some cases handing their mandates to Mitterrand's sympathisers to use as they thought best. With 4,000 abstentions and blank votes, the margin of victory was so narrow that the slightest misstep could have reversed it. Or it could all have come unstuck at a much earlier stage. Had Michel Rocard decided that spring to join the Socialists, bringing with him his followers in the PSU, not only would Mitterrand's takeover have been blocked but Rocard himself might have been chosen as Savary's successor. He acknowledged years later that he had been so involved in the PSU's internecine doctrinal squabbling that he had failed to see that the opportunity of a lifetime was passing him by.

Mitterrand's gamble had paid off. He had fired his one shot from his one gun and he had won.

*

As leader of the Socialist Party – the adjective 'New' had been dropped – Mitterrand was again the acknowledged standard-bearer of the Left, as he had been after the 1965 election against de Gaulle. The General, the colossus who for a quarter of a century had dominated France, had died suddenly from a ruptured artery eight months before Georges Pompidou, announcing his death to the French people, said simply: 'France is a widow.'

But whereas, in 1965 and the years that followed, Mitterrand had constantly to fend off potential rivals, after Épinay his pre-eminence was unchallenged. Mendès France withdrew from active politics. Mollet also left the scene. Michel Rocard retained a following but the PSU was marginalised.

In March 1972, the Socialists approved a 'programme of government', setting out for the first time the policies Mitterrand would implement if the Left obtained a majority in the parliamentary elections due the following year. With a title – 'To Change Life' – inspired by May 1968, it listed ninety-one propositions, some of which, including a minimum wage of 1,000 francs (then £100 or US $240) a month, higher old age pensions, cheaper health and free hospital care, were to take effect 'within hours' of a socialist government taking office.

Much of the rest was standard left-wing boilerplate of the kind attempted, with varying degrees of success, throughout Western Europe: equal wages for women; a 40-hour working week (against an average in France of 45 hours, the longest in the European Community); the reduction of the retirement age to 60 for those 'carrying out arduous work'; the granting of an extra week of paid holiday in winter (making a total of five weeks a year, compared with two weeks on average in the USA and, at that time, three weeks in Britain); and nationalisation of banks, insurance companies and key industries.

There were occasional verbal flourishes. 'The banks,' it declared, 'are the new Lords of Creation.' The 'privileged classes, the exploiters and profiteers' were 'enemies of the people'. The final goal was to replace the 'unjust and decadent society' built on capitalism with 'a classless society' which would operate by self-management. But the method was to be reform, not revolution. Mitterrand had already covered himself in his speech at Épinay, declaring that 'without playing with words, the everyday struggle for deep structural reform can also be revolutionary in nature'. To drive home the point, the programme insisted on 'gradual processes and sustained effort', noting that France, as part of Western Europe, trading in a world dominated by the US dollar, could survive 'only if it wins the gamble of industrial expansion'. Socialism would fail unless it took that into account.

The constitution of the Fifth Republic was to be kept largely intact. The presidential mandate would be reduced from seven years to five; special courts and capital punishment abolished; radio and television freed from government control; abortion legalised; and France's overseas territories granted self-determination.

In short, the programme conformed to the Party's new emblem, a clenched fist (signifying strength) holding a rose (the symbol of dreams). No one had done an accurate costing, but inevitably the dreams were to be paid for by higher taxes, including a wealth tax, increased estate duties and a tax on capital gains. The goal was to reduce income differentials so as to create an egalitarian society in which 'the privileges of fortune will be extinguished' and 'the needs of all will count for more than the profit of the few'.

All that now remained was to bring the Communists on board.

Ever since 1963, Thorez and his successors had been on record urging the Socialists to negotiate a Common Programme. Mitterrand had taken a step in that direction when, five years later, he and Waldeck Rochet had signed a Common Platform committing them to work together.[5] But a 'Programme', setting out agreed policies, was a very different proposition.

To the Communists it would bring democratic respectability – notwithstanding Duclos's impressive showing in the 1969 elections, French public opinion was still up in arms over the Soviet invasion of Czechoslovakia – and reassure the Party's main constituency, the industrial workforce, that a Communist–Socialist coalition had a real chance of coming to power, thereby encouraging it to resist the blandishments of the pleiad of Maoist and Trotskyist groups which had surfaced after May 1968 and were now competing for its favour.

To Mitterrand it was a way to sap Communist strength. In *Ma part de vérité* he had spelt out his objective: to reverse in favour of the Socialists, at the Communists' expense, 'the internal balance of forces on the Left, which has been to [our] detriment for the last thirty years'. A Common Programme was the best way to achieve that.

But Mitterrand's opposite number was no longer the affable Waldeck Rochet. There was a new acting Secretary-General, Georges Marchais, who had started his career as an aircraft factory worker and had risen through the trades union movement. Marchais had reservations. But the logic of the Socialists' proposal proved too strong: an alliance with the non-communist Left was the only way for the Party to return to the mainstream of French political life. In April 1972 Marchais agreed to talks.

The Common Programme they negotiated closely resembled the 'programme of government' which the Socialists had published a month earlier. Over Marchais's objections, Mitterrand insisted on maintaining a clause giving the President the right to name a new Prime Minister if parliament voted a censure motion, rather than being obliged to call new elections: the provision was crucial, because otherwise the Communists could threaten to bring down the government and go to the country whenever they thought it to their advantage. Marchais also had to accept the Socialists' position on French membership of NATO and on the 'primordial' importance of the European Community, about to be enlarged by the admission of Britain, Denmark and Ireland. To Mitterrand, European unity was the key to overcoming the division of the world into the rival blocs agreed by Stalin and Roosevelt at Yalta and thus to the eventual dissolution of the two great military alliances. Even the French nuclear deterrent, the *force de frappe* ('strike force'), which Charles Hernu, now the Socialists' defence spokesman, had persuaded Mitterrand to retain, received the Communists' reluctant approval.

The one area on which Marchais and his colleagues were not prepared to budge was economic policy, which interested Mitterrand least. The Communist leader insisted that the role of the State be expanded through enhanced central planning and increased government control of the financial sector and demanded the nationalisation of nine major industrial groups, instead of five as the Socialists' programme proposed. But Mitterrand dug in his heels against including the steel industry. During the final all-night negotiating session on June 26, Gaston Defferre, whose distrust of the Communists was undiminished, accused Marchais of trying to impose 'hackneyed recipes for state-ownership' which were thirty years out of date. A few minutes later, the meeting was close to breakdown:

MITTERRAND: There is no way that nationalising steel is justified . . .

MARCHAIS: But you are going back on what you said! You're calling into question what we discussed before. My word, you want the shirt off our backs!

MITTERRAND: Listen – as regards nationalisations, you can increase the stakes
afterwards if that's what you want. We Socialists are serious: we want a
linkage between nationalisations, self-management and economic policy.
You people are always tempted to go overboard . . .

MARCHAIS: For us it's a key issue.

MITTERRAND: Too bad. We have reached our limit.[6]

After a 20-minute break to allow tempers to cool, Marchais backed
down.

Only on one point did he refuse to compromise. The Socialists
favoured 'worker self-management' in state-owned industries to
prevent the emergence of a command economy. The Communists
insisted on 'democratic management', the system in use in the Soviet
bloc. For Marchais, it was a face-saver. When the two leaders signed
at 5 a.m., it was the one area in 90 pages of text where, failing to find
common ground, they offered alternative proposals.

The agreement was – to use a much-overworked word – historic.
For the first time since they had split at the Congress of Tours in 1920,
Socialists and Communists had agreed to govern together. No less
important, between the lines, the Communists had accepted the rules
of parliamentary democracy: if the government was voted down, they
would leave power. Only once before had Communist ministers
entered the government in France and that was at the end of the war,
under de Gaulle, when Moscow was still an ally. Even in 1936, during
the Popular Front, the Communists had supported Léon Blum's administration but had not participated. To proclaim a Socialist–Communist
coalition in the early 1970s, in the midst of the Cold War, when Soviet
power was at its height and the Kremlin both financed and managed
the communist movement worldwide, strained credulity. Nowhere
else in the West was the appointment of communist ministers envisaged. Foreign socialists looked askance at Mitterrand's heresy.

Next morning he flew to Vienna, where the Socialist International
was holding its triennial congress. There he explained to the assembled
dignitaries, including the Austrian Chancellor, Bruno Kreisky, the
Israeli Prime Minister, Golda Meir, and Harold Wilson, soon to become

Britain's Prime Minister, what the French Socialists were up to. 'Our fundamental objective,' he said, 'is to remake a powerful Socialist Party on the terrain which the Communist Party itself is occupying, in order to show that out of five million communist voters, three million can vote socialist.' No one could disagree with that. But it was a gamble. Who could say whether it would pay off? Two days later the Communist newspaper, *l'Humanité*, proclaiming its confidence that the balance of forces would remain in the Party's favour, dismissed the Vienna speech as wishful thinking. And that of course was the point. *Кто кого* ('Who whom?'), as the Russians succinctly say. In this fatal embrace, which one would strangle the other?

Mitterrand was not cut out to be the head of a large party organisation. After Épinay he had asked Pierre Mauroy to take the job of First Secretary but Mauroy had declined. So he made the best of what he could not help. But the constraints of the job exasperated him. He hated having to be on time for meetings. It was hardly new. His lateness was legendary. Françoise Giroud remembered:

> You always had to wait two or three hours before he came. And when eventually he did turn up, he would launch into such a complicated and improbable explanation that it was obvious he was making it up. The more he became entangled in his story, the more irritated he became that no one believed him . . . And if, by chance, he was on time, to go to a lunch for example, the idea of being punctual would so disconcert him that he would immediately invent something that he had to do, a file to consult or an article to read, in order to be sure to arrive an hour after everyone else.[7]

In the 1950s, as Interior Minister, he had once received the Algerian nationalist leader, Ferhat Abbas. After Abbas had been waiting in an anteroom for an hour and a half, an aide went in to find the cause of the delay. Mitterrand was reading the cartoons in *France Soir*. It was not that he had intended a political snub. Nor was it just rudeness or thoughtlessness or even egoism – though it was certainly all those things too. The explanation was less rational. He had a visceral reaction against any kind of restriction – whether in politics, private life or the realm of ideas. Punctuality was a straitjacket he refused to accept.

It did not make him an ideal candidate for the daily grind of running
the Socialist Party apparatus, with its chores and protocol and weari-
some routine.

The UDSR and the Convention, both with limited memberships
and an easy-going tolerance of internal dissent, had been simple to
manage. The Socialist Party, with a membership of more than 100,000,
its federations and factions perpetually jockeying for advantage, was a
very different sort of beast.[8] Throughout his career, Mitterrand had
operated through overlapping networks of friends and followers. Now
he found himself having to direct a vertical chain of command. He
knew it had to be done. Socialism 'has not the slightest chance of
succeeding', he told an interviewer, 'without . . . big parties. Having
understood that, I have drawn the necessary conclusion: it's finished
with splinter groups!' He was as good as his word. But he did not find
it particularly congenial.

Complicating his task was the fact that he was a recent convert,
surrounded by men (and the occasional woman, in what was then
still a male-dominated party) who had paid their dues to Marx for
years or decades. He had mastered the jargon and was able to make
the appropriate responses but it often sounded strained. 'Mitterrand
did not become socialist,' Guy Mollet mocked, 'he learnt to speak
socialist'.[9] Gilles Martinet, a long-time critic who was among the first
to defect from the PSU after Épinay, was more perceptive. 'When
[Mitterrand] talked about "the exploitation of man by man"', he wrote,
'I used to look at my feet. [But] he is the best strategist that, up to
now, the Left has ever had . . . He was the first to analyse [how to
reach our goal] with the cold, lucid eyes of a wartime Commander-
in-chief.' Mitterrand was well aware that his socialist rhetoric rang
hollow and some years later, when there was no longer a need to act
the part, references to capitalism and class struggle disappeared from
his vocabulary. Ideology was another constraint that he preferred to
do without. In an interview with the magazine, *l'Expansion*, shortly
after the Common Programme was signed, he explained:

A lot of Marxists are not really Marxist, in the sense that Marx's thinking
was spontaneous and rich, while they spend their time making it
sterile . . . The dogmatism of all the Communists and of certain Socialists
is very irritating. I find none of that freedom of the spirit which is the

first of freedoms, from which all the others follow. You should know that I will die a liberal in every sense and especially in intellectual matters. I do not believe that there is a revealed truth in the life of human beings.[10]

Mitterrand's problem was how to weld a party with such disparate origins into a single organisation, capable of winning power. To enforce ideological unity, as Mollet had done, was not his style and in any case, as even Mollet had admitted, it was often impossible: the Socialists were simply too divided.

Poperen and Savary had spent years at the head of separate small parties, or *groupuscules*, as the French describe them. Within the main-stream, Chevènement and his colleagues, who called themselves the 'Centre for Socialist Study and Research' or CERES, were crypto-communist; Mauroy and Defferre, heading semi-independent fief-doms, were moderate social democrats; while another group, including Max Lejeune, the erstwhile champion of the French army in Algeria, was so far to the Right it was hardly socialist at all.

The answer, he decided, was to do what he had always done: to forge unity not around a programme but around his own person.

In France this was much less unusual than it would be in an Anglo-Saxon country. Whereas in America or Britain you are first and fore-most a Democrat or a Republican, Conservative or Labour, and only afterwards a supporter of a particular leader, in France a new party comes into being when a new leader appears, and then disappears or changes its name or merges with another movement when that leader leaves the scene. Hence the bewildering proliferation of ephemeral groups which flower and fade along with the fortunes of the political personalities whose ambitions they are created to serve.*

---

* It would be tedious even to begin to list the now-vanished and, for the most part, forgotten parties created to further the aspirations of French presidential and prime ministerial contenders: the RPF and later the UNR to support de Gaulle; the UDSR, a vehicle for Pleven and Mitterrand; the RPR for Jacques Chirac; the UDF for Valéry Giscard d'Estaing, and so on ad infinitum. Of the dozen or so parties active in French politics in the second decade of the twenty-first century, only two, the Communists and Radicals, existed under their present names before 1970. The latter, originally a left-wing movement which drifted to the Centre and finally to the Right, is the oldest French party, established in 1901. By comparison the British Conservative Party originated in the seventeenth century, the US Democratic Party was founded in the 1830s and the Republican Party in 1854.

The first months were difficult.

After Épinay, where Mitterrand had won control by the narrowest of margins, the defeated factions denounced a 'hold-up' by an unnatural alliance of Chevènement and Mauroy–Defferre, the far Left and the Right. 'The Party has been hijacked,' headlined the *Nouvel Observateur*. When the Common Programme was signed, a few inveterate anti-communists from the early days, including the unreconstructible Max Lejeune, packed their bags and left. But their departure was more than made up for a few weeks later when dissidents in the Radical Party, calling themselves the MRG or Mouvement des Radicaux de Gauche (Left-Radical Movement), led by Maurice Faure, René Billères and Robert Fabre, joined the new alliance.

Gradually even the most sceptical acknowledged that Mitterrand had been the only possible choice.

In February 1973, three months before the legal deadline, the government called parliamentary elections. It was Mitterrand's first test as Socialist Party leader. He campaigned round the clock, addressing four or five meetings a day, often hundreds of miles apart, in a France where there were still few motorways and mobile phones had yet to be invented. Louis Mexandeau, standing as a candidate in Normandy, remembered one evening when Mitterrand finished speaking in Limoges at 5 p.m. with a meeting due in Caen, 300 miles to the north, two hours later, only to discover that his flight had been cancelled because of an air controllers' strike. A local activist volunteered to drive him. 'He drove at 100 miles an hour, which made me worry a bit,' Mitterrand recounted. 'Then he said, "You've got to look on the bright side. I've had two heart attacks in the last few months."' They arrived at 10.30 p.m. and Mitterrand began addressing a crowd of 3,000 who had been waiting for four hours. At around midnight there was a phone call from Lisieux, a town 20 miles away, where another 700 people had gathered at 6.30 p.m., gone home to dinner and then reassembled. Mitterrand's message to cancel because of the strike had not got through and they were still waiting. The day ended at 3 a.m.

The elections vindicated Mitterrand's strategy. The Socialists and their allies won 21.7 per cent of the vote and 102 seats, the Communists 21.3 per cent and 73 seats, in both cases roughly double their representation in the outgoing parliament. It was almost as good a showing as in 1967.

Three months later, at the party congress in Grenoble, the last notable holdouts against Mitterrand's leadership, Jean Poperen and his followers, laid down their arms. After the votes were counted, the First Secretary had the support of 92 per cent of the membership. Only a handful of Guy Mollet's supporters still contested the new line. In terms of doctrine, unity was still as elusive as ever. But at least the Party was functioning as a single entity and François Mitterrand had consolidated his position as its leader.

On the evening of April 2 1974, a Tuesday, Mitterrand was dining alone at the Brasserie Lipp, working on a speech he was to give in parliament that week, when the owner, Roger Cazes, came up and whispered to him: 'They say the President has died.'

The country had been aware for more than a year that Georges Pompidou was ill. At a meeting with Richard Nixon in Reykjavik the previous summer, his face had been swollen from cortisone treatment, he walked hesitantly and at times slurred his words. He had been diagnosed with a rare and painful form of leukaemia which affects the bone marrow. As his illness progressed, the press and the political elite could talk of little else. Mitterrand refused to join in. Asked by a journalist in March about the President's health, he had responded sharply: 'Pompidou cancels his appointments? So what! Anyone can have a nasty flu. Me too . . .' The dying President, who had no love for the Socialist leader, appreciated his decorum, telling colleagues: 'One of the few who has acted correctly in this matter is Mitterrand.' But even though it had been widely expected, Pompidou's death, when it came, was a shock. Roger Cazes remembered an expression of 'almost unbearable anguish' on Mitterrand's face when he heard the news. It meant another presidential election, another trial of strength. The Socialist Party, which he had conquered less than three years earlier, could have done with more time to prepare.

When he reached home that night, he drafted a political obituary, insidious in its catalogue of Pompidou's failures – 'What will he have left as a memory of his time? Nothing or so little. That is the cruelty of his fate, not the fact that his life was cut short' – which was published the following weekend in the party newspaper, l'Unité.

For the next few days Mitterrand lay low, leaving Pierre Mauroy to fend off his partners' attempts to contact him. The Communists were miffed. 'Marchais writes to Mitterrand and it's Mauroy who replies?' the Secretary-General complained. 'Something's not right.'

There were reasons for his silence. If he stood, he wanted carte blanche, the freedom to campaign not as the candidate of a party – neither his own nor, still less, the Communists – but as an independent able to appeal to the electorate as a whole. It was a huge responsibility. 'It's as though I'm on the edge of a precipice and I have to jump,' he told Maurice Faure. This time he had a real chance of winning. If he failed he would dash the hopes that not only the Socialist Party but the whole of the Left was placing on his shoulders.

On Monday, April 8, when the official mourning was over, Mitterrand announced that he would be a candidate. So did the Finance Minister, Valéry Giscard d'Estaing. Jacques Chaban-Delmas, the Gaullist Mayor of Bordeaux, jumped in even sooner, attracting accusations of indecent haste when the President's body was not yet cold. Chaban had little choice. It was Mitterrand's good fortune to be the sole candidate of the Left. The Socialists, the Communists and even, for the first time, the PSU, had all lined up behind him. The Right was fielding a plethora of more or less Gaullist candidates. Edgar Faure; Pierre Messmer, who had succeeded Chaban as Prime Minister; and Christian Fouchet, Mitterrand's colleague at the time of the 'Leaks Affair', all briefly entered the race only to withdraw later. Another Gaullist, Jean Royer, stood as the champion of small shopkeepers, urging a revival of traditional morality and castigating the new fashion for erotic films, which earned him fifteen days of fame as the cynosure of French cartoonists. Jean-Marie le Pen, participating for the first time in a presidential election, succeeded Tixier-Vignancour as the standard-bearer of the extreme Right.

Mitterrand had begun planning for the election a year earlier when it had become clear that Pompidou's health was deteriorating. Claude Perdriel, the managing director of the *Nouvel Observateur*, had been sent to America in the summer of 1973 to study the campaign of George McGovern against Richard Nixon and had returned full of new ideas for marketing techniques, direct mailings and niche-targeting to mobilise the vote. He told Mitterrand in December that he would need a year to fine-tune a strategy. The President had died four months later.

Unlike in 1965, when Mitterrand's campaign had been run by a handful of volunteers out of four cramped offices in the rue du Louvre, in 1974 he rented the whole of the third floor of the Tour Montparnasse, a 59-storey skyscraper, then the tallest in Europe, which had been Georges Pompidou's parting, and diversely appreciated, gift to the elegant city laid out by Baron Haussmann a century before.*

Three candidates were in with a serious chance: Chaban-Delmas for the Gaullists; Giscard for the Centre-Right; and Mitterrand for the Left.

However Chaban's campaign disintegrated almost at once, mainly because his own party stabbed him in the back. Jacques Chirac, who was then emerging as the dominant force in the Gaullist party – Georges Pompidou had nicknamed him 'my bulldozer' – had decided that his interests lay with Giscard and organised things in such a way that the party's election manifesto did not even mention Chaban's name. As though that were not enough, anonymous tracts were distributed accusing Chaban of being a homosexual, a Jew and, for good measure, of having murdered his wife.

It was never established who was responsible, but suspicion fell on Michel Poniatowski, a descendant of Polish princes who had served as Health Minister under Pompidou and was the architect of Giscard's campaign. Ponia, as he was called, was not noted for subtlety. As soon as the campaign began, he arranged for the income tax authorities to carry out a surprise audit of Mitterrand's tax returns. It was so crude that even Mitterrand had to smile. Needless to say, nothing was found.

Chaban's eclipse was a blow. A tight contest on the Right would have enhanced the image of unity on the Left. Now it was down to a two-man race.

Valéry Giscard d'Estaing was ferociously intelligent, quick-thinking and cultivated, a polymath with aristocratic pretensions all the more marked because they were of recent date. He was slim, tall, good-looking, attractive to women and above all, at 48, ten years junior to

---

* This time André Rousselet, who was again in charge of fund-raising, was able to gather some tens of millions of francs (upwards of £3 million or US $7 million). Substantial sums were provided by Socialist-led municipalities, but nothing by the Communist Party. Additional contributions came, as before, from wealthy individuals who counted themselves as Mitterrand's friends – among them André Bettencourt, René Bousquet and François de Grossouvre – and from the Patronat, the French industrialists' confederation.

Mitterrand, who for the first time was no longer the youngest, brightest boy in the class. In short, he was a formidable opponent.

Their first debate, broadcast on the radio on April 25, set the tone for those that followed. Mitterrand attacked Giscard on his economic record, potentially a winning argument at a time when the US and Western Europe were undergoing the worst downturn since the Great Depression, exacerbated by a quadrupling of oil prices. The French stock market had lost 50 per cent of its value, unemployment was rising and inflation was running at nearly 14 per cent, three times the level of the 1960s. 'You have been Finance Minister for eleven years,' Mitterrand told him. 'And you have been a minister eleven times,' Giscard retorted, implying that a man of the Fourth Republic was incapable of dealing with a modern economy.

Giscard had another arrow in his quiver: the threat of communism. De Gaulle had used it to great effect in June 1968. Now, when Mitterrand accused him of representing 'the law of the jungle . . . and the power of money', the Finance Minister rejoined that his opponent was planning to overthrow the established order and introduce a 'collectivist organisation' of society. 'In order to make men free,' he declared, 'we do not need to herd them into a tunnel.'

In the run-up to the first round, neither side made a serious gaffe. The Communists avoided anything which might give Giscard the chance to run a scare campaign. Mitterrand concentrated on the recession and Giscard's handling of the economy. By the time Election Day arrived, he had spoken at more than thirty meetings before half a million people, appeared dozens of times on radio and television and given hundreds of interviews.

But would that be enough?

On the evening of Sunday, May 5, when the results came in, Mitterrand had 43.2 per cent of the vote, Giscard 32.6 and Chaban 15.1. It was a vastly better showing than in 1965. But to Mitterrand it was a disappointment. He had been hoping for another 1 or 1.5 per cent.[11] The pollsters said the second round would be too close to call. Mitterrand would need at least one in five of those who had supported Giscard's right-wing rivals to switch their votes to the Left. Not quite impossible. But difficult.

At that point Mitterrand made a tactical error. For the next four days he concentrated on preparing for the one formal television debate of the campaign, which Giscard was widely expected to win. While he did so, part of the momentum that had been built up over the previous weeks was lost.

The debate, which took place the following Friday, produced a memorable phrase. Mitterrand had been vaunting the Left's superiority in matters of social justice when Giscard shot back: 'Mr Mitterrand, you do not have a monopoly on the heart.' At least one person watching – the writer, Jean Lacouture, who was rooting for the Left – felt at that moment the battle was lost. However, that was an intellectual's reaction, not necessarily that of the ordinary viewer. Giscard came across better on the small screen – more photogenic, more relaxed – and repeatedly he got under Mitterrand's guard. But his arrogance and his habit of talking down to his opponent as though to an obtuse student antagonised as much of the audience as his brilliance seduced.

Pierre Viansson-Ponté, writing in *Le Monde*, compared him to 'the boy at the top of the class who can't resist giving others lessons', while Mitterrand came across as a solid peasant, 'leaning firmly on the handle of his plough as he traces a deep furrow'. Opinion surveys shortly after the debate showed no significant change in either man's support.

The following week Mitterrand began regaining ground. Already, on the eve of the first round, he had told a colleague that he felt he was 'level pegging, but with a slight advantage'. Now, he said, 'the tide is rising'.

Giscard's camp began to panic.

Poniatowski launched a campaign to portray Mitterrand as the agent of a Soviet fifth column, warning: 'All the European countries which have communist governments are occupied at this moment by Russian troops.' Two days before the second round, anonymous tracts, similar to those which had vilified Chaban, were distributed throughout France, asserting that Mitterrand was being blackmailed by the Communists who were said to have discovered that he had deposited a large amount of embezzled funds in a Jewish-owned Swiss bank.

That afternoon Alain Poher, the President of the Senate who was acting Head of State, told Mitterrand that all the information at his disposal, notably the reports of the *préfèts* in each *département*, gave him as the winner in the second round. Every other indicator was pointing in the same direction. For the first time, Mitterrand began to believe that his hour had come. He asked Gaston Defferre, whom he planned to name as Prime Minister, to draw up a list of possible Cabinet members. Pierre Mendès France was to be Foreign Minister, Mauroy would take the Interior, while the rest of the government would be made up of Socialists with two Left-Radicals and two or three Communists.[12]

When the verdict was announced on Sunday night, May 19, Giscard squeaked through by a margin of 425,000 votes. He received 50.81 per cent, Mitterrand 49.19.

It was the best result the Left had had since the war: 12.7 million votes compared with 10.6 million in 1965. But Mitterrand had not quite obtained the 20 per cent of crossover votes that he needed from the Centre, and the Right had done a better job than the Left of mobilising those who had abstained in the first round. In working-class areas where Mollet's supporters were dominant, Socialist Party organisations had dragged their feet in getting out the vote and the Communists had in some cases been less supportive than they might have been.

But the root cause lay elsewhere.

In the final days, France had hesitated, holding its breath. When the moment came to vote, fear proved more powerful than the desire for change. Giscard represented continuity. Mitterrand, in alliance with the Communists, in the middle of the Cold War, meant a leap into the unknown. The country was still not ready. The corollary, given the closeness of the result, was that next time round, the Left could expect to win. Mitterrand said the following week: 'It came too early . . . The situation needed to ripen a bit more. If the presidential election had been held at the normal time, in 1976, I believe I would have been elected without too much difficulty.'

The defeat was all the more painful because Mitterrand had been convinced that victory was within his grasp. 'I felt myself ready,' he said. 'I felt at one with the movement of history.' On election night, he thanked those who had voted for him, whose sorrow, he said, was 'on the same scale as their hopes' but urged them 'to remain united and share my resolution'. Afterwards he told his colleagues: 'Our fight continues. Because you represent the world of youth and labour, your victory is ineluctable.'

Your victory? Had he decided to pack it in? In the weeks that followed, he was sorely tempted. He told Jean Daniel of the *Nouvel Observateur*:

> Let's be clear. I will never find circumstances like that again. I was in a position to govern. Physically I had all the faculties to do so: now they may start declining. And honestly, it doesn't excite me that much any more . . . Do you think I dream all the time about being President of the Republic? Of course . . . I would have enjoyed being Head of State, but it's not fundamental, not at all. [Do I want to keep battling away at the head of the Socialist Party?] No, I'd rather be doing something else . . . I have a duty . . . to those who voted for me. But there are many things which would please me better than having to debate with Giscard d'Estaing and his men. He certainly has qualities, but he interests me less than three oak trees in a field or a good novel. I sometimes wonder why I should want to stay shut up to the end in that closed universe. I don't say that from weariness, but seventeen years of struggle – it's beginning to feel long.[13]

A month later, he was still debating what to do. One evening during a visit to Normandy, he told Louis Mexandeau bluntly: 'I am wondering if it wouldn't be better to stop.' When Mexandeau protested that he could not do that, he answered, 'Yes, but you know better than anyone what this means as a way of life. To go on means the daily sacrifice of every single day I have, Sundays included.'

It was the same *cri de coeur* that he had addressed to Georges Dayan, shortly after the birth of his first son, Pascal: 'What is the point . . . if you have no time for your private life?' Now, twenty-nine years later, another new and compelling reason was about to come into his life to prompt that question again.

Her name was Mazarine Marie and she was born on December 18 1974 at a private nursing home in Avignon. Eighteen months earlier, Anne Pingeot had given Mitterrand an ultimatum. She was thirty years old, she told him. She had her own career – in 1970 she had passed the examination to become a curator and had started work at the Louvre inventorying nineteenth-century sculpture, a field in which she would become an authority. She knew that she could never become his wife. But she wanted their child. François at first demurred. At 57, was it right to bring into the world a child whose father, in the nature of things, might not live long enough to see him through to adulthood? Anne was adamant. If he refused, she said, it raised questions about whether they should continue their relationship. He capitulated. During the election campaign, she told him she was pregnant.

It was a courageous choice. Single motherhood in the 1970s, even in tolerant France, was not as socially acceptable as it is today. That autumn François, with Danielle in tow, travelled to Cuba at the head of a Socialist Party delegation. 'I was in despair,' Anne remembered. 'There I was, [seven months] pregnant, and he was off with his wife in Cuba!' To keep busy, she went to London to improve her English, and found herself one day in Highgate cemetery, meditating before the tomb of Karl Marx, without whose baleful influence François might never have gone to Cuba at all. In the event, the trip left a bad taste in his mouth too. While there, Danielle met Fidel Castro, the first step in an enduring love affair with left-wing movements in Latin America which her husband would later have cause to regret.

Mazarine, André Rousselet liked to say, 'is a gift that they gave to each other'. Anne used to joke that 'she was the one real gift he ever gave me'. Since they could not marry, it was their way of plighting their troth. François Mitterrand might not be sentimental, but he was romantic. All his life he wrote poems, with which he was never satisfied, which were never published and which were often not very good, but which betrayed a spiritual longing. One of the better ones, in praise of ancient Greece, written before he met Anne, was a metaphor for a love which was forever out of reach:

> Your face,
> For centuries
> I have set out on its quest . . .
> Is it a veil or the forest,
> Which, on your forehead, flames and falls back,
> Like a black tress with a golden fold? . . .
> Your face, for centuries
> I touch with my hand.
> What strange absence is there of myself in you,
> That, like water in the desert at a time of great heat,

He who leans above it sees no reflection of his face.
The sand which runs between my fingers
Has the softness of a river that never ends . . .
For centuries I have searched.
Who is the prey?
You, her or me?[14]

Mitterrand had wanted a daughter. For the next twenty years, Mazarine would be the light of his life. He and Anne named her after Cardinal Mazarin, the great seventeenth-century statesman whose *Breviary for Politicians* was among his pillow books. Marie was for the Catholic faith they both honoured in the breach.

Danielle was informed of Mazarine's birth almost at once by the inevitable 'well-meaning friend'. She absorbed the blow. It did not really change anything. Over the years, her relationship with François had stabilised. She busied herself with the family home at Latche, gardening and looking after the dogs and the two donkeys, Noisette and Marron (Hazelnut and Chestnut), which François had acquired after a friend had convinced him that an effort was needed to preserve the race.

In Paris, they decided to leave the rue Guynemer: rents were rising and Danielle felt that when François retired they would no longer be able to afford it.

She was attracted to an area just behind the Boulevard St Germain, close to the banks of the Seine and Notre Dame. But it was due for redevelopment. Then in 1971 a preservation order was issued. Shortly afterwards a sixteenth-century house in the rue de Bièvre came up for sale. It had an impressive gateway, big enough for a carriage to pass through, leading into a pocket handkerchief of a courtyard. The house itself was a ruin, with squatters occupying the first floor. The building next door had collapsed altogether – a small garden now occupies the place where it once stood – and the outside wall leaned alarmingly into the void. But Danielle had made up her mind. She said afterwards that she had found her vocation: breathing new life into dying homes – first at Latche, now in Paris – so that they could welcome a family again. With the money from the sale of the villa at Hossegor and a mortgage, they bought the property in partnership with Roland Dumas, who was then a successful lawyer, representing among others Picasso and Giacometti. One of François's Resistance colleagues who needed an apartment for his daughter also contributed. After two years of restoration work, at Easter 1973, they were able to move in.[15]

The house, like its occupants, was eccentric: a warren of small rooms at improbable angles with not one wall perpendicular, not a single floor level, as if taken from the Victorian nursery rhyme about the man 'who bought a crooked cat which caught a crooked mouse, and they all lived together in a little crooked house'.

The beams were of oak from trading ships, hardened by the sea. The central stone staircase, which had twisted on its axis but still served as the pivot holding the rest of the house together, was retained, but they added a minuscule elevator, 'for our old age', Danielle explained. François planted a magnolia tree in the courtyard, with rose bushes and a rhododendron. Ivy covered the inner wall.

The change of residence did not go entirely as planned.

Le Canard enchaîné, which also acquired new premises that year, discovered that 'plumbers' from the French counter-intelligence agency, the DST, had installed microphones in the walls during the renovation, with wires leading across the roof towards a nearby police station. Almost a dozen DST officers were identified as having taken part in the operation. Subsequent investigations revealed that the Mitterrands' new home had also been equipped with listening devices. When workmen were called in to investigate, they found bugs embedded in the plaster. As in the case of the Canard, wires led towards the local police post.

Responsibility was traced back to the then Interior Minister, Raymond Marcellin. The government and the courts hushed up the affair, arguing that the information was classified.

For Mitterrand, the move to the rue de Bièvre, like that from Hossegor to Latche, six years earlier, mirrored the changes in his life. He was back in the Latin Quarter of his youth, redolent of Moroccan couscous restaurants and echoing with the cries of barrow boys and the memory of the artisans and labourers, the carters and wine-sellers, who had populated it a century before. Over the next few decades, gentrification would sap the area of its vitality. But in the early 1970s it fitted the character of the man that Mitterrand had become, a left-wing political leader who refused to be categorised, a conformist whose sense of social propriety was equalled only by the casualness with which he broke the establishment's rules.

Danielle had her bedroom, which she designed with an open-plan bathroom, on the first floor. Not far away was the room of her partner, Jean Balenci, 'no bigger than a ship's cabin', as a later occupant complained. François's bedroom, lined with books, was on the second floor. The top floor, the pigeon-loft as the family called it, reached by a steep oak staircase, was his office, guarded by a redoubtable secretary ensconced in a cubby hole by the entrance, Marie-Claire Papegay, who had been with him since the 1950s.

The Mitterrands' younger son, Gilbert, who was studying law in Paris, also had a room there. Jean-Christophe, the older boy, was in Africa, working for the French news agency, AFP. They had not had an easy childhood. Danielle was often on edge, François was rarely there. Gilbert coped. Jean-Christophe found it harder. He felt, he wrote later, that he had always been 'the boy from next door'. Now, finally, it seemed, they had both settled down.

Jean Balenci had become a member of the family. Usually he was the one who went out to buy croissants in the morning and fetch the newspapers. He and François breakfasted together. They all spent the holidays at Hossegor and, later, at Latche. To outsiders he was introduced as a distant cousin.

The 1974 election campaign required Danielle to play a more prominent public role. Giscard had made a point of showcasing his wife, Anne-Aymone, and their four children, as a model French family. Mitterrand felt obliged to do the same. Danielle joined him at a press conference at which he addressed feminist issues, and accompanied him on his travels. Jean kept in the background. So did Anne. Occasionally she attended his political meetings, sitting discreetly two or three rows back. To his entourage, she was just one of the many attractive young women the candidate trailed in his wake.

Giscard was well aware of his rival's delicate situation but, given his own extra-conjugal adventures, was hardly in a position to throw the first stone. The furthest he dared go was to make a series of heavy-handed references to Anne's home town, Clermont-Ferrand – 'a town which knows you well, Mr Mitterrand' – during their televised campaign debate. It was a transparent attempt to put his opponent off balance. Mitterrand did not flinch.

After Mazarine's birth, the 'second family' took on added importance. They finished building the cottage at Gordes. A year earlier, Anne had bought a small apartment for herself, using money which her parents had originally set aside for her dowry, in the rue Jacob, ten minutes' walk from the rue de Bièvre.[16] A few trusted friends were in the couple's confidence: Madeleine Séchan, who had arranged Anne's confinement at Avignon; Laurence Soudet; the lawyer, Robert Badinter and his wife, Elizabeth; and François de Grossouvre, who frequently carried out sensitive missions on Mitterrand's behalf and became Mazarine's godfather.[17] But outside this inner circle, in theory, no one knew.[18]

By the autumn of 1974, Mitterrand's doubts were behind him.[19] No matter how important Anne and Danielle might be, he was not ready to give up his political career.

After the unification of the Socialist Party at Épinay, the only significant non-communist left-wing party to have maintained its independence had been the PSU. Some of its leading lights, like Gilles Martinet and his followers, had moved quickly to join Mitterrand, while others had been absorbed by Trotskyist groups on the far Left. For a long time Michel Rocard had remained convinced that the PSU had a future. But some months before Pompidou's death he realised that 'trying to transform this chaotic, leftist magma into a real political force' was a waste of effort. That spring he had held discreet conversations with Pierre Mauroy about a possible merger.

The presidential election offered an opportunity to go further. On April 11, three days after Mitterrand declared his candidacy, Rocard offered his services to the campaign. For the next month, he worked with Jacques Attali, a gifted young man whose multiple talents included, in Franz-Olivier Giesbert's cruel but perceptive description, 'retailing other people's ideas, droning praises and delivering flattery'. Together they got the candidate up to speed on economic matters so that Giscard could not trip him up. While Rocard was about it, he floated the idea of a conference once the elections were over to discuss amalgamating the Socialists, the PSU and several other small left-wing Christian groups with which it was loosely associated.

The 'Socialist Assizes', as they were called, were held in Paris in October. To Mitterrand they were a continuation of the process begun at Épinay to unite the whole of the non-communist Left. But Rocard had made his move too late. The PSU split. About a quarter of its membership came over to the Socialists. The remainder decided to continue as before, on the fringes of the far Left, advocating utopian socialism based on worker-management.

With Rocard came Jacques Delors, an economist with the Bank of France who had worked with Chaban-Delmas when he was Pompidou's Prime Minister; Edgard Pisani, a left-wing Gaullist who had also been a minister under Pompidou; and Edmond Maire, the leader of the non-communist trades union federation, the CFDT. The newcomers represented only 2 to 3 per cent of the Socialist Party's membership, which that year reached 140,000. But they brought new blood to revivify a party still composed largely of survivors from Mollet's era and their arrival brought the possibility of rebalancing its different factions.

This problem of factions – or 'currents' as the Socialists preferred to call them – drove Mitterrand to distraction. Every socialist, he grumbled at the opening session of the Assizes, is convinced that 'he alone knows the truth of the Law and the Prophets'. In private, he was harsher. The Party was a mess of 'socialist bric-a-brac', worse than the UDSR twenty years earlier. 'Each one has his prayer stool, his chapel, his religion.'

Chevènement's faction, CERES, which had been instrumental in his victory at Épinay, was a particular bane of his existence. It was 'a fake communist party made up of real petty bourgeois', he snapped. At the beginning of 1975, after Chevènement and his followers had criticised Mitterrand's leadership as not being sufficiently 'revolutionary', they were excluded from the party's leading bodies. How can we govern France, Mitterrand asked, if we can't govern ourselves? The Socialists were incorrigible, Mitterrand complained. In party branches all over France, 'dogmatic mediocrities' exercised 'a petty reign of terror'. He told a meeting at Châtellerault in September 1976: 'We aren't much, are we, we Socialists? Our party is just an amalgam of individuals . . . Permit me to think that I am still a factor bringing you together. Do you want me to go? Frankly, without being coy about it, I'd like to do just that.'

The fractiousness of the Socialists was a time bomb which would one day explode. But a more immediate challenge was looming. The Union of the Left, the key to Mitterrand's strategy for winning power, was under threat.

★

For the first two years after the signing of the Common Programme, the Socialists professed to take the Communists at their word. 'It is not my problem to know whether the Communists are sincere,' Mitterrand told an interviewer in the winter of 1972. 'I simply have to make sure that everything takes place as if they are.'

Three months later, the success of both parties in the parliamentary elections comforted the Communists' decision to form an alliance. That autumn, the 1973 Middle East war and the Oil Shock that followed deepened the ideological divide between them, the Communists arguing that the collapse of the capitalist system was at hand, the Socialists that capitalism was merely changing its tactics. But in practice they worked together as before.

In the 1974 presidential election, Moscow signalled its preference for Valéry Giscard d'Estaing, just as it had for de Gaulle in 1965. This time the signal was more provocative. The Soviet Ambassador, Stepan Chervonenko, paid a well-publicised visit to Giscard between the two rounds of voting. To those of Georges Marchais's colleagues in the Communist Party who had reservations about the alliance, it was a welcome reminder that they were not alone.

During the presidential campaign, Marchais's statements raised questions about his intentions. If Mitterrand won, he said, and 'the government has twenty or twenty-one ministers, [only] six or seven will be Communists'. *Six or seven?* Any mention of Communist ministers, no matter how it was phrased, risked frightening away part of the electorate. To state publicly that a third of the government might be Communist smacked of deliberate sabotage. Or was it simply that Marchais had misread the situation? Many years later, Mitterrand would accuse the Communist leadership of 'obvious ill-will'. At the time he was not so sure.[20] His failure to win the full quota of communist votes, which had helped to produce Giscard's razor-thin victory, may have been partly a result of dissonant signals from Marchais and his colleagues, but it also reflected doubts among the rank and file.[21] Not every communist was ready to support a candidate who wanted to keep the alliance with America and work for European unity.

The turning-point came four months later. A string of by-elections at the end of September, which returned five new Socialist MPs, proved beyond doubt that the alliance was eroding Communist support. To hardliners in the Politburo, led by Roland Leroy, it was time to call a halt. The Socialists' attitude, he charged, 'aims at weakening the position of the French Communist Party'. Mitterrand had never made any secret of that. But only now, it seemed, had the penny finally dropped.

Georges Marchais denounced the Socialists as class traitors bent on undermining the Union of the Left and ready to do a deal with the Right at the first available opportunity.

At Mitterrand's insistence, the Party turned a deaf ear. To engage in polemics, he said, would play into Marchais's hands. At a meeting of the Secretariat that winter, he recounted an acid fable about the dangers of creating 'a dialectic of disunion':

> One day . . . *l'Humanité* accuses Pierre Mauroy of having raped a little girl in a street in Lille. Pierre Mauroy shrugs his shoulders. He finds the story absurd. Next day *l'Humanité* splashes it across three columns . . . with the little girl's name and the time and date of the crime . . . Pierre Mauroy shakes his head. [On that date] he had been in Poland addressing a meeting of 3,000 people . . . The following day, *l'Humanité* does it again with an enormous headline right across the front page: 'The Rape of Lille: Mauroy is hiding . . .' This time Mauroy is angry. He calls a press conference . . . Next day . . . a journalist writes: 'Pierre Mauroy re-launches the debate.'[22]

The Communist leaders, he said, were 'obliged to have us as allies. History leaves them no choice. But they don't like . . . the Union of the Left . . . It is up to us . . . to stop them breaking it.' Socialism and communism were not the same thing. 'All our efforts are aimed at eliminating the difference, but we will not achieve that by ceasing to be ourselves.'

By the end of 1974, the Communists were exactly where Mitterrand wanted them: locked into the trap he had sprung two years earlier when the Politburo had approved the Common Programme.

They could not say he had not warned them. In a dozen or more speeches over the previous decade, he had spelled out precisely what he intended to do. Not to destroy the Communist Party – it was still useful for mobilising those parts of the Left which the Socialists could not reach – but to reduce it to a supporting role.

Now they realised that he had meant what he said.

But it was too late. If the Communists were seen to be responsible for breaking the Union of the Left, their electorate would not forgive them. All they could do was try to force the Socialists to take more account of their concerns and, if that failed, to destabilise them so that, when a split occurred, Mitterrand's party would get most of the blame. That was what he wanted to prevent. Three years after the champagne corks had popped to mark the signing of the Socialist–Communist alliance, the question, 'Who whom?', had been answered, not to the Communists' advantage. Small wonder that the party leadership was writhing like a nest of snakes, trying to find a way out of the pit in which the Socialists had confined them.

In April 1975, Mitterrand was to lead a Socialist delegation to Moscow. Two weeks before they were to set out, the Russians cancelled. No reason was given. However, he had been outspoken about the plight of Soviet Jews, whose right to emigrate was restricted. He had also criticised the banishment of Alexander Solzhenitsyn and the exile of the cellist, Mstislav Rostropovich. And he had condemned the Portuguese Communists, the last Stalinists in Western Europe, for sending party thugs to wreck the newspaper offices of their rival, Mario Soares's Socialist Party, in Lisbon. The Italian and Spanish Communists had condemned their Portuguese comrades. Marchais had remained silent. 'Farewell, free press!' Mitterrand had written, 'The French Communists are embarrassed.'

The clumsiness of the Russians' cancellation made even Marchais wince. After an outcry in the French press, the Soviet leaders changed their minds. On April 24 Mitterrand arrived in Moscow and two days later was ushered into the Kremlin office of the General Secretary, Leonid Brezhnev, of whom afterwards he left a curiously sympathetic portrait. Brezhnev, he wrote, was 'a pope of transition', determined to keep the Soviet Union moving forward because he feared that otherwise he would fall from power. In fairness to Mitterrand, Brezhnev in 1975 still came across as an energetic, bombastic figure, very different from the decrepit old man he became two years later. But he was already ill. Charles Salzmann, who accompanied Mitterrand and, unknown to their hosts, was a Russian-speaker, told him afterwards that at one point Brezhnev had asked an aide: 'How do I sound?

I sometimes find it difficult to articulate properly.' In his account of the meeting, Mitterrand did not mention that, perhaps from the same delicacy that had made him keep silent about Georges Pompidou's long illness.

Not all his judgements were off-beam. He was right about Brezhnev being a transitional figure. He was right, too, in detecting the first flickerings of self-doubt in the system, marked by an unwillingness to use prison camps with the same ruthlessness as in the past. Brezhnev and his colleagues had rolled back some of the liberalising reforms brought in by Khrushchev but not all.

In Eastern Europe and in the West, national communist parties were growing restive. The Italian and Spanish Party leaders, Enrico Berlinguer and Santiago Carillo, were developing a pluralistic, democratic approach to communist government which would come to be known as Eurocommunism. The Politburo's guardian of the Tables of the Law, the austere Mikhail Suslov, whom Mitterrand also met, wanted none of that. The contradictions of capitalism, he insisted, were so impoverishing the West that revolution was inevitable. To prove his point, one of Suslov's acolytes assured Mitterrand that the average British worker was able to eat meat only twice a month.

The talks in Moscow made Mitterrand realise that the Common Programme was unique. No other communist party, whether in Italy, Spain, or anywhere else, had concluded an alliance with a Socialist Party with a view to eventual participation in a coalition government. The Russians were torn. On the one hand they wanted good relations with whoever would next rule France. On the other they were terrified that a new model of socialist society would arise in Europe which would be different, if not antagonistic, to their own. Philippe Robrieux, the foremost historian of the French Communist Party, himself an ex-Communist, spelt out for Mitterrand the Kremlin's dilemma: 'You belong to the Socialist International, which Moscow considers its most stubborn adversary. The possibility of a left-wing government headed by a Socialist with popular backing dismays them . . . For Brezhnev, you represent every possible disadvantage.'[23]

For Mitterrand that was no problem. In the spring of 1975, it seemed that everything was going his way.

In private he was contemptuous of Marchais's leadership. 'My historic good fortune,' he said in an off-the-record conversation, 'is the unbelievable intellectual mediocrity of the Communist leaders. Look at them! . . . You can manipulate them as you like. Each one is stupider than the others. All their reactions are predictable . . . If I had been facing people of the level of the Italian Communist Party leaders, it would have been much harder for me.'

But pride comes before a fall: Georges Marchais was more cunning than Mitterrand gave him credit for.

In July 1975, the Party published a previously confidential report which Marchais had given to the Central Committee three years earlier, immediately after Mitterrand's speech in Vienna. In it he warned his colleagues that the signature of the Common Programme did not mean that the Socialists had changed their colours. 'Their permanent characteristics . . . are fear that the working class and the masses will start moving, hesitancy towards class combat against big capital, a tendency to compromise . . . and class collaboration.'

It marked the beginning of a year-long attempt by the Communists to regain the initiative.

By reminding his own party that, far from being Mitterrand's dupe, he had measured from the outset the perils of dealing with the Socialists, Marchais silenced those who wanted to accuse him of adventurism. By reminding his partners that they had a history of class treachery – which for most of the past twenty years had been no more than the truth – he put them on the defensive. Mitterrand might dismiss his remarks as 'grotesque', but they gave him pause. Two months later he told a Socialist Party seminar that the Common Programme was not sacrosanct. 'We need a back-up plan,' he said. 'We can't keep being dependent on a partner which wants to get back its freedom.'

But Marchais was just getting into his stride.

The following January he announced that the French Communist Party was following its Italian and Spanish counterparts in abandoning the 'dictatorship of the proletariat', until then a core concept of Leninism. A month later, at the Party's 22nd congress, he promised that the Communists would build 'socialism in the colours of France'. In March 1976, he joined Carillo and Berlinguer in approving the fundamental principles of Eurocommunism. It was logical enough. If the French Communists loosened the umbilical cord with Moscow and rid themselves of Leninist jargon, Marchais argued, they would win back those parts of the electorate which the Socialists had wooed away.

The problem was that Eurocommunism was essentially socialism under another name. If that was what you wanted, why not vote for the real thing?

A succession of election results over the following year suggested that significant numbers of communist voters had drawn precisely that conclusion. But the *coup de grâce* came in the spring of 1977. In the municipal elections – vital for all parties because control of town halls provided access to financial resources – the Left won 50.8 per cent of the vote against 41.9 per cent for the Right. For the Socialists, it was a triumph, a 'tidal wave', as *Le Monde* put it. 'France has given herself,' Mitterrand exulted. But for the Communists, it was a disaster. The Socialists had won twice as many of the biggest towns as they had.

Had it been up to Marchais, the French Communists might have persisted. The results were not actually as bad as the headline figures implied. But it was no longer his call. That winter the Kremlin had belatedly reacted to the Eurocommunist heresy. Soviet ideologists denounced 'parliamentary cretinism' and accused Western Communists who allied themselves with socialist parties of revisionism. That could only apply to the French. It was time for the Union of the Left to be broken.

Ten days after the elections, Marchais told Mitterrand that the Common Programme, now five years old, needed to be revised. Somewhat reluctantly, the Socialists agreed. The following month Mitterrand was to appear in a television debate with Raymond Barre, the rotund and orotund economist who had succeeded Chirac as Giscard's Prime Minister.[24] On the eve of the broadcast, *l'Humanité* published a costing of the Common Programme purporting to show that it would double government spending. Mitterrand, never at his best on economic topics, was crucified by the portly professor.

When the three partners – Communists, Socialists and Left-Radicals – met on May 17, the knives were out. 'The Communist Party is trying to free itself from the constraints of the alliance [which] has made us the leading political force in the country,' Mitterrand said afterwards, 'but it cannot admit to this crime without attracting people's anger.'

Four months later the talks foundered in a manner that neither of the principals had foreseen. Robert Fabre, the normally mild-mannered head of the Left-Radicals, incensed by the Communists' intransigence, stormed out to announce before the television cameras that his party was breaking off negotiations. Fabre's outburst – his 'fifteen minutes of fame', as one observer unkindly put it – gave Marchais the opening he was looking for. For another week the Socialists and the Communists argued about the extent of the nationalisation programme, the issue that had come close to killing the Common Programme at birth five years earlier. At 1.20 a.m. on September 23, the delegations separated without agreement. This time the rift was final.

Mitterrand had been expecting it since the summer. 'The primary enemy of the Communist Party is the Socialist Party,' he had told Georges Dayan over dinner one night. 'Their primary enemy within the Socialist Party is me.'

With hindsight it is obvious that whatever strategy the French Communists adopted in the 1970s was doomed to fail. The communist movement was already entering a period of global historical decline. But no one saw that at the time. The buzzword among the European Left was 'convergence', based on the now forgotten notion that the Western and Soviet systems would gradually come together as a by-product of détente. No Western leader – not Mitterrand, not Giscard, not Jimmy Carter or Ronald Reagan, not Margaret Thatcher – imagined in their wildest dreams that, little more than a decade later, the Soviet Empire would collapse and most of the rest of the communist world with it.

In 1977, Marchais's strategy seemed reasonable. Since embracing the Socialists had not worked, the Communist Party would hunker down in its corner, pose as the champion of the 'authentic Left' and wait for the Socialists to fall apart under the weight of their internal contradictions.

Mitterrand's strategy was the mirror image of Marchais's. Sooner or later, he felt certain, the Communists would have no choice but to return to the fold. 'They can't continue as they are,' he told an interviewer in February 1978, two weeks before the first round of parliamentary elections. 'Thanks to their policy, [we] can claim to be both the party of the Union of the Left and the party which resists the Communists. I come out on top on every count. It's too good to be true.'

That spring it seemed that he would be proved right. Giscard warned that if the Left won a parliamentary majority, as the opinion polls were indicating, he would not resign, but nor would he be able to prevent the new government carrying out the Left's policies. If the French failed to make 'the right choice', they would have to live with the consequences. Mitterrand, who by then was thinking along the same lines, decided he would name Pierre Mauroy Prime Minister so as to be able to concentrate on the presidential election which would follow in 1981.

It turned out to be a fine example of counting chickens before they hatched.

He realised too late that Marchais was determined to take the strategy of rupture to its logical conclusion. The last thing the Communists wanted was a victory of the Left. Surreptitiously they made common cause with the Right to prevent a Socialist victory. Mitterrand's efforts to reassure communist voters – Socialist candidates would stand down, he promised, whenever the Communists were better placed, even if the Communists refused to do the same – alienated moderate voters without significantly increasing communist support.

On the evening of March 12, when the results from the first round came in, the Socialists had far fewer than the seven million votes that Mitterrand had hoped for. They had made a good showing, garnering, for the first time, more support than any other party. But it was not what they needed.

The Communists were cock-a-hoop. 'Everything is set for a beautiful defeat!' one Politburo member crowed.

And so it was.

The ill feeling generated by the collapse of the Common Programme meant that in the second round many Socialists refused to vote for Communist candidates, and vice versa. Mitterrand might insist, 'Our hopes rest on one word: Union!', but the electorate refused to follow. The Union of the Left was definitively broken. In terms of the percentage of votes cast, the Socialists still achieved their best result ever. But in the new assembly, the Left had 199 seats (113 Socialists and Left-Radicals; 86 Communists), while the Right had 277. Giscard would remain in power for the rest of his seven-year term.

10

Politics is War

For the second time in four years, Mitterrand had failed to deliver. In 1974, when the Left had been united, he had missed the presidency by a whisker. Now the Left's disunity had snatched away a parliamentary victory which had been within its grasp. The stage was set for a challenge to his leadership.

Chevènement's group, CERES, which represented about a quarter of the party membership, had been up in arms since the previous summer over Mitterrand's refusal to seek a compromise with the Communists to preserve the Common Programme. A second, more serious, threat came from Michel Rocard and his supporters on the right wing of the Party. Since the previous summer they had been staking out a position based on the values of the 'Second Left', the reformist tradition in France, as against the 'First Left', the Jacobin revolutionary heritage which Mitterrand claimed to represent. Now, on the night of the second round, Rocard declared: 'The Left has once again missed its appointment with History. Is that our fate? Is it completely impossible for the Left to govern this country? I say: No.'

This time the gauntlet had been thrown down. Rocard was putting himself forward as the face of a modern, new, reformist Socialist Party, capable of defeating the Right where the older generation had failed. Mitterrand had no illusions. 'This fellow wants power,' he told Georges Dayan. 'Well, he will get a war. It's just starting and I can tell you it will be without mercy.'

Had it been anyone else, he might have reacted differently. But Rocard was a red rag to a bull. Their incompatibility was legendary. One was Protestant, the other, Catholic; one read Galbraith and Keynes, the other, Lamartine and Tolstoy; one was a social democrat, the other a Left republican; one was mercurial, the other reflective.

None of that precluded their working together. But they constantly rubbed each other up the wrong way. Rocard, fourteen years Mitterrand's junior, had immense qualities of intellect and charisma, arguably greater than any of the other young leaders around him. But even when he set out to win Mitterrand's esteem, he managed to do so in a way that the First Secretary found exasperating. The chemistry was wrong. They simply loathed each other.

A few weeks before his death, questioned about those with whom he had crossed swords during his long career, Mitterrand was generous to all except one: only about Michel Rocard could he not find a good word to say.

Ever since the 1960s, he had had an intuition that Rocard's ambition might one day threaten his own. But now that it had happened, he found himself with a problem. Together CERES and the 'Second Left' made up 40 per cent of the Party. To make matters worse, Mauroy, who controlled another 20 per cent, was also disaffected. For that, Mitterrand had only himself to blame. The Mayor of Lille had been instrumental in bringing him to power at Épinay. But he had never belonged to the inner circle of those who had been with Mitterrand in the UDSR and the Convention, like Dumas and Mermaz. Mauroy was a bluff, gregarious northerner for whom camaraderie was second nature. He had come to feel, not without reason, that no matter what he did he would remain a country cousin.

The last straw had been Mitterrand's decision, shortly after the elections, to take personal control of the Party's finances. Mauroy had devised a system of fictitious 'consultancy bureaux', which worked for Socialist town councils and retroceded the major part of their fees to the Party for political use. Over time he had built it into a nation-wide network generating sufficient funds to ensure the Party's financial health. That Mitterrand should have the gall to demand that he surrender that role, without even bothering to discuss it with him, Mauroy found outrageous. He had another reason to be concerned. 'Frankly, if he gets his hands on the finances,' he confided, 'I don't know where the money will go.' It was one of Mitterrand's weaknesses. Money as such held no interest for him, provided that it was available when he needed it. Where it came from was not his concern. It was for convenience, not personal enrichment: the ability to buy a rare edition of a book which caught his eye; to reward a favourite; or to pay court to a young woman who had bestowed her favours on him.

Mauroy refused to step aside.

For Mitterrand it was a rude awakening. Since the elections, his popularity, as measured by the opinion polls, had been in free fall. Before the year was out, Rocard would be credited with the support of 40 per cent of the electorate as a potential presidential candidate, Mitterrand with only 27 per cent. The serious press predicted that his career was drawing to a close. He wondered whether Mauroy was positioning himself for a bid for the party leadership, but dismissed the thought as absurd. 'Mauroy is weak,' he told friends. 'He lacks the means of his ambition and he knows it.'

Nevertheless, Mitterrand was aware that in order to take on Rocard he needed, at the very least, Mauroy to remain neutral. The Mayor of Lille was on good terms with the leader of the 'Second Left', having facilitated his admission to the Party four years earlier. It was fence-mending time. Over dinner with Mauroy in June 1978, at Gaston Defferre's country house near Marseille, the First Secretary deployed all his charm. The Party, he agreed, should be run more democrati-cally. Mauroy's role was crucial and his responsibilities, including control of the Party's finances, would be respected. By the end of the evening, amity had been restored.

But then, five days later, Mitterrand's allies issued a manifesto, warning that the 'modernistic, technical' approach championed by Rocard (who was not named) was 'a mortal danger' to the Party and must be resolutely opposed.

Mauroy was furious. Mitterrand had made a double misjudgement. He had misunderstood Mauroy's motives: the Mayor of Lille was neither weak nor ambitious, he merely wanted the Party to be prop-erly run. He had also totally misjudged Mauroy's reaction. By trying to be too clever, laying a trap to force Mauroy's hand and make him take sides against Rocard, Mitterrand produced a result exactly oppo-site to that which he had intended.

All the pent-up anger which Mauroy had accumulated over the previous seven years boiled over. 'Who do they take me for?' he raged. 'They want to get rid of Rocard because he overshadows someone and they expect me to be their accomplice?'

At a series of meetings, while Mitterrand sat glowering beside him, a furious Mauroy unleashed a litany of complaints. The signatories of the manifesto, he said, were guilty of 'factional activities'. Those who had been members of the Convention were not 'the party nobility [beside] the common herd which the rest of us represent. For myself, I don't need your lessons in socialism.' Addressing Mitterrand directly, he went on: 'The climate here is of the end of a reign. To want to remove certain elements of the Party [leadership] is intolerable.' Later, at a meeting which Mitterrand did not attend, he was still more explicit. The First Secretary, he said, violated the principles of collective leadership; took decisions without consultation; and 'tried to make people believe that some in the Party are loyal supporters of the Union of the Left and others are not. This is a false distinction that's been trumped up to disguise what is actually a clash of personalities.'[1]

Mauroy was right; Mitterrand was wrong. But politics is not about right and wrong. It is about power.

Throughout the winter of 1978 and the following spring, Mitterrand's supporters kept up a steady drumbeat of criticism against the Rocard–Mauroy alliance. Rocard was accused of revisionism; Mauroy of parricide – having 'killed' Guy Mollet he wanted to do the same to Mitterrand.

Rocard retorted that Mitterrand and his brand of socialism were 'archaic'. At the next party congress at Metz, in April, he sneered, the First Secretary would only get the 'old-age pensioners' vote'.

But now it was Rocard's turn to make an error of judgement. He let slip that he expected Pierre Mauroy to be Mitterrand's successor.

'What an imbecile!', Mauroy exploded. 'He's nice, intelligent, competent and all the rest. But he's the kind of person who throws banana skins under your feet without even meaning to. He understands nothing of politics.' What Rocard had failed to realise was that Chevènement's CERES, which now held the balance of power between Mitterrand and his critics, was happy to call the First Secretary to order but had no intention of making him step down. Any suggestion that Mitterrand might go and Rocard and his allies take over could only push Chevènement and his followers into Mitterrand's arms.

More than a mistake, it was recipe for certain defeat.

When the Socialists convened at Metz in April 1979, Mitterrand's motion received 47 per cent of the votes; Rocard, 21 per cent; Mauroy, 17 per cent; and the CERES, 15 per cent. Mitterrand, supported by

Chevènement and his followers, formed the new leadership. The rebels were punished. Mauroy and Rocard were cast out into opposition.

As though to give the lie to Rocard's charge of archaism, the First Secretary packed the new Executive Committee with young men who had joined him after Épinay, known as the 'sabras' because they had never been members of any other party.[2] Lionel Jospin, 41, a former Trotskyist, sometime diplomat and university professor, succeeded Mauroy as Mitterrand's deputy. Paul Quilès, 37, an engineer, was put in charge of the Party federations. The youngest, Laurent Fabius, the son of a French art dealer, became Party spokesman at the age of 31. All were civil service high-flyers who had had blisteringly successful academic careers. All were ambitious, determined and ruthless. The leadership was ring-fenced.

The congress of Metz marked a turning point. For the first time since Épinay, Mitterrand had had to fight to keep his post. To ensure Chevènement's support, which he needed to fend off Rocard's challenge, he had moved sharply to the Left. Having embraced a platform calling for 'a break with the economic structures of the past', he was stuck with it. Accordingly the Socialist programme for the 1981 presidential election, the '110 Propositions', which laid out the policies he would follow once he had been elected, was no less radical, and in some respects more extravagant, than the Common Programme with the Communists which had lapsed two years before.

The '110 Propositions' accused the United States of manipulating the world economic order and brainwashing Western Europe by a 'cultural war which aims not kill but to paralyse' – Marx's 'opium of the people' purveyed by Hollywood. The Soviet Union was portrayed as the hapless target of the Western powers which were using the existence of dissent among Soviet intellectuals as the basis for 'a gigantic enterprise of destabilisation of the Left and ideological remobilisation of capitalism'. In terms of domestic policy, the 'propositions' were equally far-fetched. 'They were the root of all the problems, all the lyricism and the ever-increasing social demands,' Pierre Mauroy said later. Another commentator wrote simply: 'The Socialists . . . lost all contact with reality'.

Mitterrand disagreed. The '110 Propositions' would make the Left dream. Dreams, not realities, won elections.

The question, however, was would the electorate vote for him?

Mitterrand might have secured control of the Socialist Party but in the country his image was dismal. Asked for the first words that came to mind when Mitterrand's name was mentioned, 55 per cent replied 'a man of the past', 41 per cent, 'ambitious' and 29 per cent 'fickle'. Rocard was more popular than ever. Forty-six per cent wanted him as a candidate compared to 25 per cent for Mitterrand.

At Metz, Rocard had given an undertaking not to stand if Mitterrand did so.

That did not suit the First Secretary's plans. He wanted Rocard to self-destruct before he entered the stage himself. For months he tried to cajole the younger man to break cover and declare himself. But Rocard was wary. The longer he held back, the more the electorate liked him. Mitterrand appeared to hesitate, asking members of his inner circle – now without Georges Dayan, who had died the previous summer – what they thought of his chances. It was pure pretence. Why crush Rocard at Metz if it were only to stand aside eighteen months later?

Finally, on October 18 1980, Rocard decided he could wait no longer. He called Mitterrand to inform him that he would announce his candidacy the next day. 'As you like. It's up to you,' the First Secretary replied. 'I too will speak soon.' When Rocard put down the phone, his face was pale. He told his companions: 'Mitterrand is going to stand.' But he had gone too far to turn back.

The following evening, as Rocard prepared to make his announcement live into the television news from the town hall of Conflans-Sainte-Honorine, on the River Seine just north of Paris, where he was mayor, Mitterrand twisted the knife in the wound. An aide passed Rocard a news agency despatch. That afternoon the First Secretary had warned: 'Any candidate who declares himself before his federation has given its approval is not a candidate . . . No one can carry our colours . . . unless he can unite the Socialists and defend our programme.'

When Rocard went on the air, a few minutes later, his face was haggard and his hands trembled. He looked like a man going to his own execution. His candidature had imploded before it had even begun.

Mitterrand, who had told the Executive Committee a few months earlier, 'under no circumstances will I be party to a fight where the knives are already out and the daggers are seeking backs to stab', had won his battle, but by using the same methods that he had so haughtily denounced.

Three weeks later, on Saturday, November 8, the First Secretary told the Executive Committee that he had decided to stand. The same day he published a volume of conversations, *Ici et maintenant* ('Here and Now'), offering an overview of the '110 Propositions', leavened with anecdotes and insights into his thinking.

Rocard announced his withdrawal.

But what chance did Mitterrand have against Giscard, to whom all the opinion polls gave an unbeatable lead?

That winter he was uncharacteristically quiet. Instead of launching his campaign, he went to the United States for a conference on 'Eurosocialism' – a subject which interested Americans about as much as Latin hexameters – and then travelled on to Tel Aviv in December to attend a congress of the Israeli Labour Party. He stayed in Israel for Christmas with Anne and Mazarine, who was now six years old. Then in February 1981, less than three months before Election Day, he spent a fortnight travelling in China and North Korea, where he met Deng Xiaoping and Kim Il Sung. The prevailing view in the French press was that he was giving himself a pre-retirement present. Mitterrand knew that he had no hope of victory, it was said, so he was going through the motions, intending to step down as party leader in the summer, after his third and final attempt at the presidency had failed.[3]

By March 1981, the four principals were all in the starting blocks. Marchais had announced that he would stand the previous October. Mitterrand's candidacy and his programme, the '110 Propositions', were approved at the end of January by a special party congress which named Lionel Jospin First Secretary in his place. Jacques Chirac, representing the Gaullists, entered the race in February. Giscard waited until Monday, March 2, to confirm that he would seek re-election.

As in 1978, Giscard and Marchais were objective allies. For both, the first priority was to keep Mitterrand out of power: Giscard in order to win a second term; Marchais because he was convinced that a Socialist government would be against the Communists' interests. 'Under the Right,' he assured the Politburo, 'we can regain our health.'

The third candidate, Jacques Chirac, was the joker in the pack.

He was young – in 1981 still only 48 years old – bursting with nervous energy, a man who bounded rather than walked, a chain-smoker with a prodigious appetite, endless curiosity and a passion for primitive art. In 1974, Giscard had appointed him Prime Minister. But the President had insisted on occupying the whole of the political stage and after two years in office Chirac quit, the only French Prime Minister ever to resign against the wishes of the President who had appointed him. Afterwards he became Mayor of Paris, leading the Gaullist party, now renamed the 'Rally for the Republic' or RPR, in trench warfare against Giscard's 'Union for French Democracy', the UDF, which he denounced as 'the party of the foreigner', a reference to Giscard's alleged failure to defend French interests against the European bureaucracy in Brussels.

At the time, few realised how deeply this new fault line on the Right would transform the country's electoral geography. One who did was Charles Salzmann, Mitterrand's election strategist, who argued in a note in August 1980 – at a time when every newspaper in France was giving Giscard a 20 to 40 per cent lead over his Socialist challenger – that if Chirac decided to stand, Mitterrand could expect to win the second round with 52 per cent of the vote to Giscard's 48.

Chirac would be Mitterrand's secret weapon.

They met discreetly over dinner at the home of Édith Cresson, a lively redhead who was at that time the only woman in the Socialists' fifteen-member Secretariat. 'If I'm not elected,' Mitterrand told him, 'it will be annoying but in the end not so serious . . . I already have my place in History . . . But for you, if Giscard wins again, it will be hard . . . He won't do you any favours.' Chirac listened. He could see a common interest.

Tactical considerations aside, the 'fundamentals', as they are called in the world of finance, were also stacking up against the incumbent.

During his seven years in power, Giscard had lowered the voting age to eighteen; raised the minimum wage; legalised abortion; launched a vast infrastructure programme – more motorways were built; the TGV high speed train service was developed; and the country's antiquated telephone service was revamped – and he had created the G6, predecessor of the G7, G8 and G20, which brought together for the first time at Rambouillet in 1975 the leaders of the world's main industrialised nations. But the second Oil Shock in 1979 had stunted economic growth. Inflation was eroding household income. Unemployment had doubled to exceed one million.

As if that were not enough, the President had exasperated a size-able part of the electorate by his personal eccentricities. His punc-tiliousness over protocol – at State banquets he insisted on being served first, and would allow no one to sit opposite him so that he could gaze regally over the assembled gathering – made him appear ridiculous. His efforts to be close to 'ordinary French people', paying carefully stage-managed visits to their homes with cameras in attend-ance, and inviting refuse collectors to visit him at the Elysée, came across as crass. Like many highly intelligent people, he found it diffi-cult to be natural with others less gifted than himself and the awkward-ness showed.

Already at the time of the parliamentary elections in 1978, the French had hesitated over whether to keep him in power.

Then came the affair of Bokassa's diamonds. Jean-Bedel Bokassa, the Idi Amin of French-speaking Africa, had risen through the ranks of the French army before seizing power in his country, the Central African Republic, in 1965. Seven years later he proclaimed himself President for life and in 1976 was consecrated Emperor. He was consid-ered pro-French, which was felt to compensate for the violence of his regime, and in the early 1970s, at Bokassa's invitation, Giscard had gone big game hunting there. After his enthronement, amid sump-tuous Napoleonic pageantry which cost an estimated £10 million (US $20 million) in one of the world's poorest states, Giscard tried to back away. But it was too late. Soon after the Emperor fell, in 1979, *Le Canard enchaîné* revealed that he had made the French President gifts of diamonds which, under French law, Giscard should have turned over to the State. The President's supporters protested that the gems had little value, but the harm was done. Henceforward he was impli-cated in an unsavoury tale of corruption involving a murderous buffoon whom his government had foolishly patronised. It was not an ideal situation in which to embark on a re-election bid. Giscard proceeded to make it worse by trying to dismiss the affair as being of no importance.

Georges Marchais had his troubles too. In 1981, being tagged as 'the Party of Moscow' did not give the French Communists widespread

appeal. The Soviet leadership was geriatric; the Soviet army was occupying Afghanistan; Cuban troops were acting as Soviet proxies in
Angola. To add to Marchais's troubles, his war record was under attack.
It had been discovered that he had worked in Germany under the Nazis
for much longer than he had admitted and that for at least part of that
time he had been a volunteer, not a forced labourer as he had claimed.
Marchais had been unable to offer a convincing rebuttal.

Jacques Chirac had no skeletons in the cupboard. But nor did he
have any illusions that he would make it through to the second round.
He was there to assert himself against Giscard and to position himself
for the next election, in 1988, by which time, he devoutly hoped, the
President would have left the scene.

That left Mitterrand.

His problem was his image: tricky, unreliable, too-clever-by-half, a
has-been who could not be trusted further than you could throw him.
Changing that, Charles Salzmann wrote, was 'the number one
priority'. Salzmann recommended that he emphasise his provincial
roots, depicting himself as a man with his feet on the ground, close
to nature, whose dominant traits were contemplation, tranquillity,
inner strength and willpower. 'Three escapes from PoW camps – third
time lucky,' Salzmann assured him. 'It will be the same with the
presidential election.'

As though to test that proposition, Mitterrand spent the beginning
of March with the West German Social Democrat, Willy Brandt,
retracing the itinerary of his first escape attempt, from Kassel to the
Swiss border, forty years earlier.

Mitterrand's stroke of genius, however, was in his choice of the
man to orchestrate Salzmann's proposals.

Jacques Seguela was a flamboyant publicist who headed a leading
French advertising agency, drove around Paris in a pink Rolls-Royce
and had recently published a best-selling memoir entitled *Don't Tell
My Mother I'm in Advertising: She Thinks I'm Working as a Pianist in a
Brothel*. He had offered his services the previous year to Mitterrand,
Chirac and Giscard. Only Mitterrand had accepted. The result was
the first truly modern election campaign in French history. Seguela
did what Claude Perdriel had hoped to do in 1974 but had been unable
to put into practice because Pompidou had died too soon.

Mitterrand underwent what today would be called a makeover.

Seguela made him change his wardrobe. 'No one will listen to what you say about solidarity if you dress like a banker,' he said. 'Dress to the "Left" – gradations of colour, and unstructured materials like wool.' A dental surgeon reshaped his eye teeth, which had a slightly vampirish look. When Mitterrand had objected, Seguela told him: 'If you don't [fix them], you'll always excite mistrust . . . You'll never be elected President of the Republic with teeth like that.' He was instructed to 'hold your back straight, with your chin out'; to move his hands naturally when speaking on television; to get into training for interviews and, above all, 'never to learn a line by heart because you can't be spontaneous twice'.

For once in his life he did as he was told.

Seguela came up with a slogan – *La Force Tranquille* ('Calm Strength'), a term which had first appeared in Victor Hugo's novel, *Les Misérables*, more than a century before, and had subsequently been taken up by Blum and Jaurès – and a campaign poster showing a close-up of a statesmanlike Mitterrand with a country village and its church tower in the background. Mitterrand jibbed at the church tower. 'I don't want to look like the village priest,' he complained. It was made less prominent, shading into the haze. But the message of reassurance was intact. Mitterrand was 'part of the landscape of France', as he had written in *Ici et maintenant* the previous autumn. He could be trusted with the country's future.

In interviews and speeches he made that his theme. The Communists would not be part of the government if he won, he said . . . at least, not initially. Society would be changed 'by contract, rather than by decree'. The working week would be reduced to 35 hours and hundreds of thousands of civil servants would be recruited to reduce unemployment; government spending would increase by 5 per cent a year; and, as he had promised before, everyone would get an extra week of paid holiday. How it was to be financed was not stated but, after five years of austerity under Giscard and Barre, a lot of middle- and working-class French people thought it sounded rather good.

The only issue on which Mitterrand took a risk was the abolition of the death penalty. Although it figured among the '110 Propositions', nearly two out of three French people were against it. In March, he told an interviewer that if elected he would do it anyway. Whether by calculation or good luck, it worked to his advantage. Mitterrand, voters discovered, was willing to take a stand on an issue he believed in, even if it was unpopular.

On Sunday, April 26, when the results of the first round came in, Giscard was in the lead, as expected, with 28.3 per cent, Mitterrand came second with 25.8 and Chirac third with 18 per cent. The surprise was the collapse of the Communist vote. Georges Marchais obtained 15.3 per cent, a million and a half votes fewer than in the parliamentary elections three years earlier and the first time since the war that Communist support had fallen below 20 per cent.

To the uninitiated, Giscard looked to be a shoo-in.

Right-wing candidates had won nearly 50 per cent of the vote. Mitterrand had only 26 per cent and could count on perhaps another 5 or 6 per cent from those who had voted for the ecologists and for three minor left-wing candidates. But that made at best 32 per cent. Georges Marchais did the arithmetic. 'The Left does not have a majority in this country,' he told the Politburo after the first round. 'The Right will mobilise and pull ahead.'

But on both sides, treason was in the air.

Publicly Marchais appealed to communist voters to support Mitterrand. But through the Party's internal channels, Communist officials were urged 'to act with true revolutionary courage and get out the vote for Giscard'.

Chirac announced that 'personally' he would vote for Giscard but refused to call on his supporters to do the same. Philippe Dechartre, Mitterrand's old partner in the Resistance who had later become a Gaullist minister, took care of the rest. At the beginning of May, he issued a public appeal to the RPR rank and file and the right-wing electorate generally to vote against Giscard, who he said was a traitor to the Gaullist cause:

> What choice do we have? . . . [Mr Giscard d'Estaing] based his political career on General de Gaulle's departure, which he [himself] provoked . . . The result of his seven years in power can be summed up in three phrases: record unemployment, galloping inflation, and the weakening of French influence in the world. Are we going to continue for seven more years to drain our country of its substance, to drive our youth to despair, to paralyse our democracy, . . . to dilapidate the heritage of General de Gaulle and Georges Pompidou, . . . to tie a

rope around our own necks? . . . I appeal to you without hesitation to vote for François Mitterrand. [His] election does not carry the risk of a change of social system or a threat to our freedoms . . . It is the condition for the renewal of our country.[4]

Giscard was relying on the same argument that had helped him to victory in 1974 and had produced a landslide for de Gaulle and Pompidou in the parliamentary elections of 1968: if the Left won, the Communists would take power.

The problem was that it did not work any more. As Dechartre noted, with only 15 per cent of the vote the Communists were no longer a danger. He might have added that if they were in decline, it was largely Mitterrand's doing.

In the ritual television debate, the 'communist danger' failed to give Giscard traction. The previous summer, the President had broken ranks with the rest of the West and travelled to Poland to meet Brezhnev, then the subject of a diplomatic boycott in retaliation against the invasion of Afghanistan. Mitterrand had lampooned him as 'the little messenger boy of Warsaw'. On economic issues, too, the Socialist candidate had done his homework. When Giscard began to lecture him on exchange rates, he let him continue for a while before rattling off the relevant figures as though they were something a child would have known.[5] Systematically, he quoted Chirac's attacks on Giscard's administration. It was the incumbent's greatest vulnerability and Mitterrand exploited it for all it was worth.

As the campaign drew to a close, it became clear that the result would hinge on a paradox. Which would be greater: the number of right-wing voters supporting the left-wing candidate, Mitterrand? Or the number of Communists voting for the right-wing candidate, Giscard?

At 8 p.m. on Sunday, May 10 1981, France discovered that it had a Socialist President.

Mitterrand had been certain of the outcome for several days. When the first exit polls came through early that evening, he telephoned Anne in Paris to tell her. At Château-Chinon, where he had voted and waited for the results, Danielle was with him. For both women, it was a moment in which joy, fear and anguish were equally mixed. Their lives were about to change in ways over which they had no control.

'Do you understand what this means, a President of the Republic from the Left, today, in France?' Mitterrand had asked Paul Quilès as they had flown back from the final campaign meeting in Nantes two days earlier. 'Do you realise what this means for History?' It was a question he would keep repeating on Sunday night as the results started to come in. In the end he had 51.76 per cent of the vote, Giscard 48.24 per cent – within a quarter of a percentage point of Charles Salzmann's prediction nine months earlier. Although he had known it was going to happen, it was as though, after thirty-five years of political struggle, he had not dared to let himself believe. Not to tempt fate, he had drafted a statement to read if he lost, but not if he won. Now he jotted down a brief declaration thanking those who had voted for him and calling on the people of France 'to find the path to needed reconciliation'. To Danielle, as they stood together at the town hall, looking out at the ecstatic crowd, he said: 'Oh, my Danou, what is happening to us?'

She wrote later that it only really dawned on her that François had won when, heading back to Paris through the pouring rain, an escort of police motorcyclists materialised from nowhere and the toll gates of the motorway opened before them. She went home to the rue de Bièvre. The President-elect stopped briefly to join the festivities at the Socialist Party's new headquarters in the rue de Solferino, on the Left Bank of the Seine, just across the road from de Gaulle's old offices. Then he, too, turned in for the night. At the Bastille, the symbol of the Left's victories since the French Revolution, where the Socialists had organised a mass celebration, 100,000 people caroused in the rain. Anne's brother tried to persuade her to accompany him there. She shook her head. Mazarine had to be up for school next morning.

II

The Novitiate

On Monday morning, May 11 1981, half of France – the half that had been up till 5 a.m. dancing in the Place de la Bastille, the Champs-Elysées and their equivalents in the provinces – went to work with a hangover.

The other half was panic-stricken.

More than thirty years later, it is hard to conceive the degree of alarm and disarray among the Right and its supporters which Mitterrand's victory provoked. Much of it was completely irrational but that did not make it any less real. 'There was real terror,' Anne remembered. 'People thought it would be the French Revolution all over again and they'd bring out the guillotine. You can't imagine how frightened they were.' Businessmen cancelled plans for new investment. Wealthy families were caught driving to Switzerland with the boots of their cars stuffed with jewellery and gold bars. The franc was in free fall. Mitterrand had sent emissaries secretly to West Germany before the election to discuss measures to stabilise the currency in the event of a left-wing victory, as he had done seven years earlier in 1974. But the fire sale was beyond the power of central bankers to stop. In the ten days between his election and investiture, the Bank of France spent $5 billion, a third of the country's reserves, in a fruitless effort to stop the haemorrhaging of capital. Newspapers like *Minute*, reflecting the views of the extreme Right, warned that the country would be sovietised: the Communists would pull the strings behind the scenes; private property would be confiscated; and a punitive wealth tax would expropriate the rich.

In the United States, the administration swallowed hard. The US Ambassador, Arthur Hartman, had been assuring the White House that Giscard would win. Ronald Reagan, who was about to label the

Soviet Union 'an evil empire', did not take kindly to the idea of a key Western ally being ruled by a man who had come to power with communist support. Jacques Attali asked Samuel Pisar, a highly regarded Polish-American lawyer and Auschwitz survivor who had worked for President Kennedy, to intervene on Mitterrand's behalf. Pisar flew to Washington between the two rounds and saw Reagan on the evening the results were announced. He told the President that he was authorised to give him a formal assurance that, whatever role the Communists might play, the policy of France, as a member of the alliance, would remain unchanged. Reagan heard him out but waited 48 hours before sending Mitterrand a congratulatory telegram.[1]

The 1981 election reopened a social fracture in France of which Alexis de Tocqueville had written when King Louis-Philippe had been forced to abdicate in February 1848: 'society was cut in two: those who had nothing united in common greed, and those who had something united in common terror'.

Since the last authentic left-wing government under the Popular Front in 1936, the fissure had been papered over. Vichy had been right-wing. During the Fourth Republic, France had been governed by self-interested coalitions. Since 1958 the Right had been continuously in power. That the Left, in the person of François Mitterrand, should suddenly snatch away what the bourgeoisie and the economic elite had come to regard as their birthright was felt to be obscene.

De Gaulle's son-in-law, General Alain de Boissieu, Grand Chancellor of the Légion d'honneur, declared that he would resign rather than bestow on Mitterrand the grand sash of the Order, a prerogative of the Head of State, accusing him of collaboration during his time at Vichy. In the brouhaha that followed, two members of the Council of the Order, outraged by his statement, stepped down in protest; hundreds of people threatened to turn in their decorations; Admiral Sanguinetti and nearly forty of the General's closest companions during the war demanded de Boissieu's dismissal; and Colonel Passy, the wartime intelligence chief in London, issued a statement pointing out that de Gaulle himself had named Mitterrand head of the prisoners' resistance movement. De Boissieu rowed back, claiming that he had acted 'from conscience' because Mitterrand had called his father-in-law a dictator in his book, the *Coup d'état permanent*. But it was a sign of things to come. Throughout his presidency, Mitterrand would be the butt of vindictiveness and vilification on the basis of his war record, principally from the Right but also, at times, from those who claimed to be his supporters.

As he set about organising the new government, he recalled being torn between 'exaltation on the one hand, and anguish on the other [at] the magnitude of the task ahead'.

It was all the more difficult because the Socialists had been out of power for so long that only three leaders had previous ministerial experience: Mitterrand himself, Gaston Defferre and Alain Savary.[2] He decided to put aside his differences with Pierre Mauroy and name him Prime Minister, as he had intended in 1978. Defferre would be Minister of the Interior, and Jacques Delors in charge of Finance. Among the twenty-five full Cabinet members were two Left-Radicals, including Mitterrand's old accomplice, Maurice Faure, who became Justice Minister, and a solitary left-wing Gaullist, Michel Jobert, who had worked with Mendès France and then served as Foreign Minister under Pompidou. Jobert was responsible for Foreign Trade. The rest were Socialists, including Chevènement, Rocard, Mermaz and Pierre Joxe, representing the various 'currents' in the Party, as well as the youngest of the 'sabras', Laurent Fabius, who became Delors's deputy.

On May 19, two days before the transfer of power, Giscard delivered his farewell speech on television. It was a strangely inept performance for such an intelligent man, who in private was erudite, witty and thoughtful. Blaming his defeat on 'an economic, social and moral crisis without precedent for fifty years' (as though France's devastation during the war were a minor problem by comparison), Giscard portrayed himself as the victim of misunderstanding and injustice. His record, he implied, was blameless: one day the French would regret what they had done and ask him to return. Ending his address with the words *au revoir*, he stood up theatrically and walked slowly away, leaving the camera focussed for almost a minute on an empty chair to the strains of the Marseillaise. Mitterrand said afterwards that he had been surprised by such 'insolence towards the people'.

The President-elect observed the rites, too, but in his own fashion.

On the morning after the election, Mitterrand went to the cemetery at Montparnasse where Georges Dayan was buried. Normally he prided himself on mastering his emotions, always finding the right words to comfort the distress of others. But two years earlier, at

Dayan's funeral, he had been so overcome that he could not speak. Georges had often teased him: 'What a shame to think that François Mitterrand will never be President. What a gap in his biography! Mind you, in a few years' time he'll be so old that we'll be able to tell him he used to be President and he'll believe it.' Now at last it had happened and Georges was not there to see it.

Mitterrand wanted the ceremonies for his inauguration to give a sense of the Socialist programme, 'To Change Life'. After the formal handover at the Elysée, which Giscard, ill-advised to the end, chose to leave on foot, exposing himself to boos and catcalls from the crowd gathered outside, the new President was driven across the Seine and through the Latin Quarter to the rue Soufflot, opposite the Luxembourg Gardens. There, accompanied by the luminaries of the Left, he walked up the hill to the Panthéon, the abbey church which had been converted into a mausoleum during the Revolution to honour France's great men and women. Arm in arm, gathered in a joyous confusion behind him, were not only French socialists but the former West German Chancellor, Willy Brandt; the widow of the assassinated Chilean President, Salvador Allende; past and present heads of government from all over Europe, among them Olof Palme of Sweden, Felipe González of Spain, Mário Soares from Portugal and the Italian, Bettino Craxi; as well as a clutch of Nobel prize-winners, writers and artists, including Gabriel García Márquez, Arthur Miller, William Styron and the Greek actress, Melina Mercouri. As the crowd chanted Mitterrand's name, the orchestra and massed choirs of Paris, directed by Daniel Barenboim, played the 'Ode to Joy' from Beethoven's Ninth Symphony. People climbed lamp-posts, photographers jumped barriers, policemen struggled to hold back the crowd. When the President reached the square before the mausoleum, the procession halted and he entered alone, carrying a single red rose. Inside, as millions watched on television, he laid roses on the tombs of Jean Jaurès, his socialist forerunner; Jean Moulin, symbol of the Resistance; and the nineteenth-century humanist, Victor Schoelcher, who had fought for the abolition of slavery in the French colonies.

By then the timing had gone badly awry. The motorcycle escort, finding its agreed exit route blocked by the crowds, had passed directly in front of the orchestra. A furious Barenboim threw down his baton and stopped conducting. The crowd was making so much noise that no one noticed. But when, with much difficulty, the maestro was persuaded to resume, he insisted on starting again from the beginning.

As a result, when Mitterrand emerged from the crypt to stand on the steps of the mausoleum, still holding a red rose, instead of approaching the end of the piece the orchestra was only halfway through. Defferre, the Interior Minister-designate, panicked. The President, immobile, framed against the vast stone portico, made a perfect target for a sniper on the roofs. An urgent message was sent to Barenboim asking him to stop. But having been interrupted once already, he was in no mood to be messed about again. The orchestra played on. Imperturbable, Mitterrand stood in the drizzle for nine interminable minutes, savouring his triumph. Then the great Spanish tenor, Placido Domingo, sang the Marseillaise. As the closing notes resounded across the square, the heavens opened in a downpour, the barriers collapsed, the police lost control and the President was engulfed in a frenzy of popular exultation. It took 20 minutes before they could get him to his car and the cortège was able to leave.

It was not an inauguration. It was an apotheosis.

Earlier, at the Elysée, Mitterrand had spelt out his goals. 'I wish to convince, not to conquer,' he told the assembled dignitaries. 'There was only one victor on May 10 1981: Hope! May it become the most shared quality in France! . . . My aim is to bring the French people together, as the President of all, for the great causes which await us, creating . . . a true national community' based on 'a new alliance of socialism and freedom'.

Alongside reconciliation he sketched out other priorities: social justice – '[amid] injustice [and] intolerance there can be no order and security', he said; and overseas development – to end a situation where 'two thirds of the planet . . . provide men and goods and receive in return hunger and contempt'.

But the main lesson of the election was that the 'political majority of the French people have identified with the social majority', giving a voice to those 'millions and millions of men and women, the ferment of our people, who, for two centuries, in peace and in war, by their labour and by the shedding of their blood, have fashioned the History of France, without having access to it except through brief but glorious fractures of our society'.

Jacques Chirac, the Mayor of Paris, to whom he paid a formal call that afternoon, urged him to temper his actions with realism. Mitterrand replied that he would keep the promises he had made. National reconciliation was one thing. The 'glorious fracture' of the established order was another. That was what he had been elected for and that is what he would do.

Unlike the United States, where a transition team works for two and a half months to ensure that the incoming President is up to speed, or Britain where the Prime Minister's Office is run by career civil servants who serve impartially both Left and Right, France adopts a scorched earth policy when a new President arrives. At the Elysée and the Prime Minister's residence, the Hôtel Matignon, every filing cabinet is emptied, every desk cleared, every computer drive wiped clean and every senior official replaced. At the summit of the State, the new administration has to be built from scratch. The support staff – the ushers, the gardeners, the drivers, the chefs, the typists and the switchboard operators – stay on. In other ministries, so do the administrative personnel. But anyone who has anything to do with policy-making leaves. With rare exceptions, such posts are considered too political for one regime to inherit the expertise of another.

In Mitterrand's case the break was even more pronounced. No one on the permanent staff at the Elysée could remember the last left-wing incumbent, Vincent Auriol, who had retired thirty years earlier and in any case had been a constitutional not an executive Head of State.

The President's secretary, Marie-Claire Papegay, remembered that at the luncheon which followed Mitterrand's investiture, a grandiose affair with *foie gras aux truffes* and *blanquette de veau*, washed down with a 1966 Château Yquem and a 1970 Château Talbot, followed by raspberry sorbet and Dom Perignon, the phalanx of liveried butlers, accustomed to the fastidiousness of the previous regime, looked askance at these 'country bumpkins who did not know how to use a knife and fork'. Mitterrand's brother-in-law, the actor, Roger Hanin, wrote afterwards that they had all felt like 'squatters'.

During the handover ceremony, Giscard had told Mitterrand that the United States and Egypt were working with French intelligence on a plan to destabilise the Libyan leader, Colonel Gaddafi, and that Brezhnev would probably be succeeded by his Chief of Staff, Konstantin Chernenko. He gave Mitterrand the secret codes which enable the French President to order a nuclear attack and then they both watched as a similar exchange took place between the outgoing and incoming military advisers.* Apart from a ritual request, made during all such transitions, that Mitterrand find appropriate positions for a few of Giscard's close aides, that was it. In the evening, after the palace emptied, a young lawyer named Michel Vauzelle, whom Mitterrand later appointed government spokesman, found himself in the office where de Gaulle had once presided, alone but for a staff officer manning the telephones and telexes, with the fate of one of the world's five nuclear powers in his hands until the President and the rest of his staff returned the following morning.

Then, within days, far faster than any of them had thought possible, it all became routine.

Mitterrand toyed with the idea of moving the presidency from the Elysée to the Invalides, the great nineteenth-century hospital for war-wounded on the Left Bank of the Seine where Napoleon lies entombed, just as de Gaulle, before him, had thought of moving to the fourteenth-century castle at Vincennes, east of Paris, where Louis XIV resided before the construction of his palace at Versailles. The Elysée, originally an elegant country retreat built amid parkland on the outskirts of the city, once home to the King's mistress, the marquise de Pompadour, has an impressive courtyard, suited to formal occasions, and probably the most beautiful gardens in Paris, but it is too small and ill-adapted to house all the services required to run a modern State. In the end, however, he decided to stay put. To move would be too costly and disruptive.

On his first full day as President, Friday, May 22, Mitterrand laid down the ground rules. There would be no meetings of advisers on his watch – no kitchen cabinet, no ad hoc committees to hammer out agreed positions for his approval. Each of the 170 or so political advisers who staffed the different services – African Affairs, Agriculture, the Diplomatic Unit, Economy and Finance, Education and Research, Environment, Housing and Solidarity, Industry, Internal Affairs, Media

---

* Mitterrand confessed years later that he put the codes in his jacket pocket and promptly forgot about them, remembering their existence only the next day when the suit was already on its way to the cleaners. Jimmy Carter had a similar misadventure, although in his case the codes were recovered more easily as his suit had been sent for cleaning within the White House.

and Public Opinion – would be expected to produce policy recommendations, either on his or her own initiative or at the President's
request. These would transit vertically, filtered by the Secretary-
General, Pierre Bérégovoy, a former trade unionist and one of the
few senior socialist leaders of working-class origin, for Mitterrand to
study in the solitude of his office and return by the same channel.

A favourite technique was to set two or three advisers to work on
the same problem, each in ignorance of the other, to see what they
would come up with. Sometimes the President would append a terse
comment, written in blue ink with a fountain pen. The novelist, Érik
Orsenna, who spent three years as one of Mitterrand's speech-writers,
a thankless task if ever there was one since he systematically rewrote
everything that was drafted for him, remembered his first grandilo-
quent effort being sent back with the caustic annotation: 'Who do
you take me for? Who do you take *yourself* for?'

More often notes would be returned with a single word, *Vu*
('Viewed'). It was then up to the writer to judge whether that meant
'I will think about it', or 'Go ahead', or 'Wait and see'.

After thirty years in party politics, Mitterrand was allergic to the
culture of conclaves and smoke-filled rooms. As head of the UDSR
and then the Socialist Party, he had had no choice. Interminable
committee meetings were part of the way of life. But not as Head
of State. Just as he organised his circles of friendship in disparate
layers to which he alone possessed the keys, so at the Elysée Mitterrand
sat at the centre of a vast spider's web in which every filament led in
only one direction: inward to the seat of power.

De Gaulle had also worked like that. But Mitterrand went further.
Disguising his intentions was a means of retaining the initiative. Roger
Hanin recalled a conversation with Joseph Franceschi, who became
Mitterrand's Security Minister. 'François mistrusts everything and
everyone,' Franceschi said. '[It is] fundamental. He trusts no one. No
one at all.' It put Hanin in mind of a passage from the Bible which
Mitterrand often quoted, where Jesus made clear that he had known
all along that 'he whom I trust' would one day betray him. The
conclusion Mitterrand drew was that everyone was capable of betrayal.
'Why such mistrust?' Hanin asked himself. 'No one is born like that.'

Part of the answer surely lay in the experiences of his own past:
the risk of betrayal in the war; his betrayal by Marie-Louise Terrasse;

his own betrayal of Danielle; his betrayal by Pierre Mendès France, whom he embraced emotionally on the day of his investiture, declaring, 'Without you, none of this would have been possible', but whom he never forgave for having suspected him in the 'Leaks Affair'; his betrayal at the Observatory by Pesquet and then by so many of his friends; Mauroy's betrayal at Metz when he joined forces with Michel Rocard . . . The list went on and on. Yet one may wonder whether his constant watchfulness did not stem as much from his character as from the cursus of his life. A man who examines each side of every question, who never takes a decision without instinctively assessing the advantages and disadvantages of making a contrary choice, is not a man to accept unquestioningly the professions of loyalty of friends or to take at face value the proposals of his aides.

At the Elysée, formal meetings were kept to a minimum. On Wednesday mornings, when the ministers gathered in the Salon Murat, the proceedings were as stylised as the gilded pillars and coffered ceilings, chandeliers and silken wall-hangings of the Cabinet room. As in Auriol's day, no one was permitted to speak unless the President asked him to do so. Mitterrand informed the government of his views. Ministers introduced forthcoming legislation, and were often rapped over the knuckles when their presentations were long-winded. Discussion was usually limited. Cabinet meetings approved decisions; they did not make them. In the first year they were followed by a lunch with the Socialist Party leadership, but it was discontinued when Mitterrand found leaks appearing in the press.[3]

Wednesdays apart, he preferred to meet his advisers one-on-one. Twice a week he had a tête-à-tête with the Prime Minister. He saw Bérégovoy each evening and others as the situation required. The only exception was a breakfast each Tuesday with Mauroy and the Socialist Party leader, Lionel Jospin, to coordinate the government's parliamentary support.

In informal settings the President was more accessible. Jacques Attali, who had been given the position of Special Adviser and occupied the office next to Mitterrand's, often joined him on Monday mornings for a round of golf with André Rousselet, his Chief of Staff, or for a stroll through the Latin Quarter to visit antiquarian bookshops, followed at a discreet distance by a cohort of plain-clothes police. The one piece of advice Giscard had offered him during the handover was not to let himself become a prisoner of his function. The new President took it to heart, spending more nights at the rue de Bièvre with Danielle, at Anne's flat nearby or with other female companions who had caught his eye, than in the presidential apartments. He continued to frequent his favourite restaurants, Le Divellec on the Left Bank, La Marée on the Right, Fouquet's on the Champs-Elysées, dining with an eclectic circle of friends and acquaintances, among them Jean Riboud, the Chairman of Schlumberger, the world's largest oil services company with its head-quarters in Houston, Texas; Pierre Bergé, the head of Yves Saint Laurent; and the comedian, Coluche, an icon of left-wing disrespect who founded a network of free restaurants, now a French institution, which every winter provides millions of meals to the homeless and indigent.

Where the Elysée was organised along monastic lines – each adviser isolated in his cell, working on a masterpiece for the greater glory of God, relieved only by unauthorised get-togethers over lunch or a drink in the evening to which God (in this case Mitterrand) chose to turn a blind eye – so, in the wider world outside, the President embraced a range of influences so diverse that nothing, unless he chose to make it so, was taboo. In this way he acquired an astrologer, Elizabeth Teissier, whose clients included the King of Spain, not because he believed in her predictions – though he was far too polite to tell her so – but because it intrigued him to 'think outside the box'.

The two strands were complementary. On the one hand, the rigidity and discipline of the presidential machine; on the other, the freedom to consider problems unconventionally, without ideological prejudice or preconceived constraints. For a man who had concentrated in his hands greater power than any of his predecessors, arguably including even de Gaulle, it was a necessary balance. While there would be abuses during the fourteen years Mitterrand spent in office, they were fewer than might have been expected given the extraordinary latitude which the institutions of the Fifth Republic allow a French President. But ambiguity, mistrust and solitude remained the foundations of the new incumbent's system of rule. The choice of the Panthéon for his inauguration had not been innocent. From the start, François Mitterrand was set to become a republican monarch.

His first action on taking office was to dissolve the National Assembly and call parliamentary elections. To those who advised him to wait, he replied: 'There's no question . . . The momentum of May 10 gives us our best chance of winning.' Four weeks later, that judgement was vindicated. On Sunday, June 21, the Left won 329 seats – 44 for the Communists, the remainder for the Socialists and Left-Radicals – and the Right, 151 seats with 11 independents. It was not quite the tidal wave of 1968, when the Right had won 360 seats, but it was close. 'Take a good look,' Mitterrand told those gathered in his office that night. 'You will not see the like of this again.'[4]

That Communist ministers would join the government was a given. It was not, as was officially claimed, out of 'fairness' (a concept as elusive in politics as the Higgs boson in physics). While it was true that the Communists were wedded, against their will, to Mitterrand's cause, the Socialists had an overwhelming majority on their own and could manage perfectly well without them. Rather the decision was a continuation of the policy Mitterrand had laid out in Vienna in 1972. The longer he could hold Georges Marchais's party in a poisoned embrace, the more the strength would be sucked out of it; the more he forced it to compromise with Socialist policies of which it disapproved, the more disaffected he would make its core supporters. And this time there was a bonus. As de Gaulle and his successors had discovered in 1946, having the Communists in government meant that the CGT, which the Party controlled, was hamstrung, unable to foment strikes against government policies without appearing to disavow its own party leadership. As long as Mitterrand could keep the Communists with him and the Right in disarray, he would have a free hand to promote whatever reforms he wished.

After much haggling, the Politburo approved a 'programme of government' with the Socialists and accepted four portfolios, one fewer than the Party had hoped for, all essentially technical and all potentially in the front line in the event of labour unrest: Transport, Health, Employment and the Civil Service.

That afternoon, Tuesday, June 23, three hours before the composition of the new government was made public, the Foreign Minister, Claude Cheysson, a veteran diplomat who had worked as a European Commissioner in Brussels, telephoned Reagan's Secretary of State, Al Haig, to give him the news. Vice-President George Bush was due in Paris to meet Mitterrand next morning. Haig, an administration 'hawk', enquired whether the visit was still on, apparently hoping that the French would cancel. 'Of course,' Cheysson answered. 'It was you who chose the date.' Mitterrand, meanwhile, sent a personal message to Reagan on the 'blue line', the secure telex between the Elysée and the White House, assuring the US President that France would assume 'all its commitments, [which] in the field of security are clear and precise, within the framework of the Atlantic Alliance [and] following the principles of an open economy'.

Bush arrived at the Elysée next day at noon, making a discreet entrance through the southern gate, the 'Grille du Coq', while the new ministers, Communists included, left through the main courtyard after a Cabinet meeting at which they pledged to put their government responsibilities before party loyalty.

The Vice-President, whose intelligence the French respected, had been briefed on the Communist–Socialist 'programme' and chose to make that the focus of his attack, rather than complaining about the presence of Communist ministers. The US, he said, was concerned that the wording of the accord between the two parties appeared to weaken France's rejection of Soviet medium-range nuclear missiles in Europe; that it failed to make a forceful enough condemnation of the Soviet invasion of Afghanistan; that it denounced US intervention to prop up a right-wing dictatorship in El Salvador but not Vietnam's intervention in Cambodia; and that its commitment to NATO was lukewarm.

It was the cue for Mitterrand to give him a magisterial dressing-down. On Soviet missiles, Afghanistan and Vietnam, the President assured him, France's position was unchanged. The two-party agreement had been limited deliberately 'to points which cause the Communists special difficulty' and marked 'an enormous climb-down' on their part:

In France foreign policy is determined by the President of the Republic . . . In some respects you may think . . . that the President has too much power. But that is how it is and I intend to use that power. [The Communists] have agreed to humiliate themselves in exchange for four government posts . . . If they don't do their jobs properly, I can fire them . . . There have been Communists in France for sixty years. This is the first time that a leader has been able to reduce their influence. That suggests that my method may not be so bad. You must distinguish between strategy and tactics. Tactically . . . with four Communists in government, in unimportant ministries, they find themselves associated with my economic policies and it's impossible for them to foment social troubles . . . In a broader, long-term strategic perspective, the goal is [to weaken them and strengthen the Socialists]. In French politics there are no greater enemies than the Communists and the Socialists, [but] they are linked, because they represent the same social strata. The approach I have adopted is the only way to bring that about.[5]

He went on to speak of his own experience. He had joined the Socialist Party, he told Bush, not from love of Marxism but because it was a means for the Left to win power. The Communists had had disproportionate strength in France partly because of their heroism during the war and partly for cultural reasons:

You have to understand what communism represents in a Catholic country. Have you never been struck by the fact that communists are more numerous in Catholic than in Protestant countries? It is because the Roman Church instilled discipline among Catholics with the result that when they joined a different 'church' they did not question its orders. Protestants have to find their own salvation. There is no hierarchy to tell them what to think.[6]

He understood America's difficulties, he said. 'I realise that . . . you are worried about contagion in Italy* . . . But my first task here is to resolve the problems of France.'

Bush returned the compliment. The presence of Communist ministers, he said – using that term for the first time during the meeting – had indeed alarmed America, but 'thanks to your explanations we now see things more clearly'.

Back in Washington, Secretary of State Haig did not.

---

* Such fears have been a constant of American foreign policy under both Democratic and Republican administrations. In the 1960s the Vietnam War gave rise to the domino theory in Asia; in the 1980s Washington worried that Communist participation in government would spread from France to Italy, Spain and Portugal; thirty years later, after the Arab Spring, there was anxiety that anti-Western Islamic regimes would replace the Arab dictatorships ousted by popular revolts. Only once in the last century have these predictions of 'contagion' been borne out, and that was in the case of decolonisation after the Second World War which, for ideological reasons, the United States supported, not always to its own advantage.

That night the State Department, with the approval of the White House, warned that 'the tone and content of our relationship' would be affected by the arrival of Communists in the French government 'or in any government of our western European allies'. Unnamed officials were quoted expressing doubts as to whether France could be trusted with NATO secrets.

Bush, who received the text at the end of a banquet at the US Embassy, took Mauroy aside. 'I'll get this corrected,' he said. 'Don't worry about it.' He was as good as his word. But by then the damage was done. From the far Left to the far Right, the French were outraged. 'Ronald Reagan is mistaken if he thinks France is El Salvador,' thundered the right-wing *Figaro*, while the Communist newspaper, *l'Humanité*, declared, 'France is . . . allied to the US. It is not an American protectorate.' In a rare show of unity, the former Gaullist Prime Minister, Pierre Messmer, joined Cheysson in describing the American comments as 'unacceptable'.

Only Mitterrand saw the lighter side. 'They say: Mr Reagan is cross! So? Mr Reagan sneezes. So? . . . I didn't ask myself whether my decision would be to the liking of this country or that . . . The American reaction is their business. My decision is my business.'

The President's meeting with Bush and the tiff that followed were a first step towards changing the Reagan administration's attitude to the new French regime. The next came in July when Mitterrand attended the G7 summit in Ottawa.

The summit itself was signally unproductive. 'Is that what an international gathering is about?' Attali wrote on his return. 'A meeting where nothing is decided, where the discussions are empty, the communiqués so meaningless that everyone can agree to them, and where whoever is cleverest at manipulating the news media appears as the winner?' But on the sidelines, in the gardens of the Montebello Hotel, Mitterrand had his first tête-à-tête with Reagan.

It started in classic Californian style: the US President was droll, charming and convivial, radiating his usual rose-coloured view of America in the midst of a hostile world. The US economy, he promised Mitterrand, would begin to recover the following spring and Europe would reap the fruits. As for the Russians, their days were numbered: their economy was seizing up and their oil industry going south.

At that point 'François' took the opportunity to tell 'Ron', as they were now calling each other, that he had learnt something which might be of interest. He had been briefed the previous week by Marcel Chalet, the head of the DST, the French counter-espionage service, about a sensational intelligence coup. In April, Chalet had told him, a senior official in the Soviet State Security Committee, the KGB, had made contact with a French businessman who was among the service's correspondents in Moscow. The Russian, who had been given the code name, Farewell, had brought with him a sheaf of documents which the businessman had photocopied and sent back to Paris. They had been analysed by specialists. The verdict was unequivocal: they were genuine and unlike anything seen in the West before. France, Mitterrand told Reagan, was willing to share with the Americans the entire intelligence trove – already about a thousand top secret Soviet documents, which were continuing to come in at the rate of several hundred a month. They included operational directives signed by the KGB head, Yuri Andropov; 'Eyes Only' reports, marked with a code that indicated they were destined for the General Secretary in person; and annotations in Brezhnev's handwriting.

Reagan would note soberly later that it was by far the biggest intelligence coup since the Second World War.

What Mitterrand did not know, because Chalet had neglected to mention it, was that the DST, whose remit was normally limited to France and which had no operational network in Moscow, had approached the CIA for help soon after Farewell had made his initial approach. The two services had been working together for several months and Reagan was already well aware of the value of what the French had found. Hollywood pro that he was, the US President did not let on, instead expressing admiration and amazement.[7]

If it was a test of France's commitment to the alliance, Mitterrand had passed with flying colours. Three years later, when he learnt of the role the CIA had played, he reflected ruefully that 'we must have looked very clever "revealing" the affair . . . in Ottawa'. But he was not the only one to have been wrong-footed. Al Haig's decision a month earlier to have the State Department cast doubt on France's ability to keep NATO secrets did not look very clever either.

By the time Farewell fell silent in February 1982, he had given his French handlers nearly 3,000 pages of documentation, most of it dealing with industrial espionage, including a list of 222 Soviet spies from 'Line X' of the KGB's Directorate T, charged with gathering scientific and technological secrets, attached to embassies and trade missions in the US and nine other Western countries, and 170 officers from other KGB directorates. Armed with that knowledge, the CIA fed the Russians fake data, which derailed a number of important Soviet industrial programmes, and stalled others, contributing indirectly to the Soviet Union's collapse and dismemberment eight years later.

Mitterrand spoke afterwards of having had 'serious doubts' whether 'Farewell' had ever existed. Might not the documents that the DST acquired, while genuine, have been planted by the CIA to verify his loyalty?

It was not as paranoid a theory as it might sound. Every high-profile double agent in history, from Mata Hari to Penkovsky, attracted suspicions of manipulation or ulterior motives, and the information Farewell had provided was so extraordinary that it invited disbelief. But when the full story became known, it was confirmed that he was indeed a genuine source. His name was Vladimir Vetrov, an electronics engineer who had been recruited by the KGB as a student and attached to the Soviet Embassy in Paris in the late 1960s to collect technical intelligence. On his return to Moscow he had been promoted to the rank of colonel but had gradually lost faith in the Soviet system. In December 1980 he had started putting out feelers to the French, leading to a meeting the following April with the businessman, a representative of the electronics firm, Thomson, whom he had known during his posting in Paris. He was what was called in the trade a 'walk-in', probably the most important in a century. It turned out that his sudden silence ten months later had had nothing to do with his espionage activities: he had been arrested after a fight with his mistress, whom he had tried to stab to death in a park, afterwards killing a policeman who came to separate them. His KGB superiors had initially treated it as manslaughter and he had been sentenced to twelve years' imprisonment. But at some point, a year or so later, the case was re-examined.

According to one version, he had mentioned in a letter to his wife a 'big affair' in which he had been engaged and this had caught the attention of the prison censors. In another version, he was inadvertently betrayed by a blunder on the part of the DST.

In January 1983, it was discovered that the Russians had planted bugs in the fax machines at the French Embassy in Moscow, which had enabled them to read all the diplomatic traffic to Paris for the previous seven years.[8] Mitterrand then decided to expel forty-seven

Soviet diplomats, trade officials and journalists whose names were on the list of KGB agents which Farewell had provided.[9] 'We have to make [the USSR] understand that [espionage] is a game, and if you are caught, too bad,' he told the Cabinet. 'The Russians must get used to the idea that . . . France is not for sale. [They] must realise they are not dealing with a country that is lily-livered. Once they take that on board, things will go better.'

When the Soviet deputy head of mission, Nikolai Afanassevsky, called at the Foreign Ministry to make the ritual protest customary on such occasions, Cheysson's Chief of Staff, François Scheer, in order to demonstrate that France had serious grounds for its action, showed him the cover-sheet of a voluminous dossier from the Farewell file dealing with the KGB's programme of scientific and technical espionage activities against the West. Afanassevsky saw it for only a few seconds, but it was long enough for him to read the Cyrillic code stamped on it which the DST had neglected to mask. Not only was it a Politburo document but it was a xerox of Brezhnev's copy.

Whether because of Afanassevsky's report or because of his own indiscretions, 'Farewell' was tried for high treason in December 1984, sentenced to death and shot a month later.[10]

The Farewell dossier laid to rest whatever lingering doubts the Reagan administration had about the French government's loyalty, Communist ministers notwithstanding. But one more element was needed before the relationship with Washington would assume its final form. It would overturn yet another of the preconceptions that the Americans had entertained when Mitterrand came to power and in a manner which no one in Washington had anticipated.

On Sunday, May 24 1981, three days after Mitterrand's inauguration, the West German Chancellor, Helmut Schmidt, became the first foreign leader to visit France under the new regime. Schmidt, a Social Democrat, had been close to Giscard. Although he had known since the previous summer that Mitterrand stood a good chance of winning, he had not hesitated to speak out on his friend's behalf, declaring that Mitterrand's victory would be 'a misfortune'.

In diplomacy, however, interests trump emotions. The Franco-German tandem had been the driving force in Europe ever since de Gaulle and Adenauer had signed a Friendship Treaty in 1963, sealing the two countries' reconciliation and committing them to mutual consultations on major political and economic issues.

Britain might have joined them to form a triumvirate, as Macmillan and Churchill had both hoped. But de Gaulle had opposed British entry into the EEC on the grounds that London was an American submarine and would torpedo efforts for unity. Ten years later, after Georges Pompidou lifted the French veto, that might have changed. It did not. Britain's identity is rooted in its difference. Even a strong leader like Margaret Thatcher, who, sometimes despite herself, did more to strengthen Britain's position in the European Union than any other Prime Minister before or since, did not change the mindset of a nation which always gave the impression of being dragged kicking and screaming into a political grouping where its every instinct proclaimed it did not wish to be. Britain was in but not *of* Europe. The French and the Germans were the locomotive.

The British would get on board, reluctantly if at all, Mitterrand said, only when they realised that the train was already leaving the station.

The talks that Sunday were not about the European Community, however. The subject was the balance of nuclear arms in Europe.

More than thirty years later, it is humbling to look back at the ignorance of the general public, and of the news media which informed it, about what was then the world's cardinal issue. Ever since the 1950s, the nightmare in European capitals had been a decoupling of the US nuclear deterrent from the continent's defence. Everything that happened over the next twenty years – first the NATO doctrine of 'flexible response' in 1967, which held that a conventional attack should be met by graduated 'appropriate means' covering the whole gamut of conventional and nuclear weaponry; then the SALT (Strategic Arms Limitation Treaty) accords in 1971 and 1973, which guaranteed strategic parity and Mutual Assured Destruction – made Europeans feel safer, yet in fact made the continent more dangerous.

'Flexible response', Mitterrand wrote later, 'is antinomic to the very idea of dissuasion . . . What kind of terror is it if it is used in moderation?' It made the use of US strategic nuclear arms to defend Europe no longer automatic but hypothetical, which as President Carter acknowledged, really meant 'improbable'. Given Mutual Assured Destruction, it was unthinkable for either superpower to employ the strategic weaponry it possessed. If war broke out, it was likely to remain confined to the European battlefield where the Russians had decisive conventional superiority.

At that point, however, the Kremlin overreached. Early in 1977, Moscow began to deploy mobile SS-20 intermediate-range nuclear missiles capable of hitting targets anywhere in Western Europe.

Helmut Schmidt was the first European statesman to react. In a carefully worded speech in London that October, he had called for urgent steps to 'maintain the balance of . . . deterrence'. Two years later, President Carter approved what became known as the 'dual track strategy': either the Soviet Union must dismantle its 225 SS-20s – each carrying three independently targetable warheads with almost forty times the destructive power of the bomb dropped at Hiroshima – or in December 1983 NATO would deploy a matching force of 108 Pershing mobile intermediate-range nuclear missiles, based in West Germany, and 464 nuclear-armed cruise missiles, based in Belgium, Britain, West Germany, Holland and Italy.

Schmidt had come to Paris to ask whether the new French government supported this decision.

Mitterrand was categorical. As Schmidt had anticipated, he favoured deployment. That was not a surprise. The new President had been a late convert to nuclear deterrence, but he had publicly reproached Giscard for having hesitated to commit to the 'dual track strategy' lest it antagonise Moscow, a criticism with which Schmidt privately agreed. What the Chancellor had not expected was the robustness of Mitterrand's stance. For decades French presidents had tried to singularise France's relationship with Russia as a sort of 'special relationship', not at the same level as Britain's with America but nonetheless marked by an affinity which other European nations did not have. De Gaulle, echoing Napoleon, had dreamed of a Europe reaching 'from the Atlantic to the Urals', and insisted that French nuclear weapons were aimed not at Moscow but at any power which might threaten France (in theory including even the US). Giscard had called for a multi-polar world, free of superpower hegemony, and had tried to build a personal rapport with Brezhnev. Mitterrand was made of different stuff. His understanding of Russia came mainly from his long struggle with the French Communists and his reading of Russian literature. But that had been enough to convince him that the Kremlin responded best to the language of force.

France would not participate in the negotiations on Pershing and cruise missile deployments, he told Schmidt, because it was not a member of NATO's military command and in any case it would do nothing which might compromise the independence of its own nuclear deterrent. But the deployments were vital, both to restore the balance of terror and, more importantly, to re-couple the United States to Europe. NATO's 'flexible strategy', Mitterrand told his visitor, was nonsensical. If there were nuclear war – an eventuality which he thought unlikely – it would be total war. There would be no time for graduated escalation. The Soviet Union must understand that if it used its SS-20s, the United States would respond with Pershings. If Pershings were launched against targets on Russian soil, the Soviet Union would retaliate with submarine-launched nuclear missiles off the US coast, which would take the same time to reach US cities – about six to eight minutes – as the Pershings would take to hit Russian cities. The result would be mutual annihilation. It followed that once the Pershings were deployed, both sides would be forced to recognise that the use not only of strategic missiles but also of intermediate forces was ruled out and at that point meaningful disarmament could begin.

Schmidt was won over. Here was a left-wing French President, with Communists in his government, being far more clear-headed than any of his predecessors, even his good friend, Valéry Giscard d'Estaing.

The understanding between France and West Germany which was sealed that afternoon would prove crucial for East–West relations and for Europe throughout the decade that followed. But before it could start to bear fruit, the Americans put a wrench in the works.

In November 1981, Ronald Reagan proposed that both the US and Russia should renounce all intermediate-range nuclear forces in the European theatre – not only SS-20s, but American Pershings and cruise missiles too. Mitterrand and Schmidt were blind-sided. 'Option Zero', as Reagan called it, would ensure that Europe and the US remained decoupled. Reagan's nuclear planners were well aware of that. A nuclear war confined to the European theatre which the United States might survive unscathed had its attractions for Washington. But the Kremlin, then headed by the ailing Leonid Brezhnev and later, after his death in November 1982, by Yuri Andropov, former head of the KGB, failed to see that for a transitory gain – temporary superiority in medium-range nuclear weapons – it was passing up an opportunity to remove the entire European theatre from US nuclear protection.

The stand-off lasted a year before Reagan was forced to acknowledge that 'Option Zero' was not going to work and the 'dual track strategy' resumed.

By then the Russians had become convinced that the growing strength of the pacifist movement in the West, with its slogan, 'Better Red than Dead', would make the deployment of Pershings impossible. Opposition to 'Euromissiles', as they were called, was strongest in West Germany, where that autumn Schmidt's Social Democrats had been replaced by a Christian-Democrat-led coalition headed by Helmut Kohl. It was becoming urgent for Mitterrand to lay out the French position and, if possible, to do so in such a way as to change the terms of the European debate.

The occasion came the following January, when he travelled to Bonn to address the West German parliament on the 20th anniversary of the Franco-German Friendship Treaty.

As was often the case when Mitterrand was planning a major speech, he left the drafting to the last possible minute. On January 19 1983, a Wednesday, the day before he was due to speak, he summoned the Defence and Foreign Ministers and a group of close aides to tell them that the text they had prepared was 'tragically useless' and they had better try again. The next version was little better. At 11 p.m. he summoned them for a third time and, after several hours of discussion, left them to work through the night on a new version. The following morning Mitterrand rewrote it himself for a fourth time in the plane. While he held talks with Kohl, his secretary prepared a clean copy on a typewriter with a German keyboard, which gave rise to some original spellings. But still he was not satisfied. Ten minutes before he was to appear, he closeted himself in an office to make further revisions.

West German officials, who had expected a text for translation hours if not days before, were tearing their hair out. How was it possible for the French to be so disorganised?

The speech turned out to be worth waiting for.

A simple idea governs French thinking: war must remain impossible and those who are tempted by it must be deterred. [It is] our conviction that nuclear weapons, as the instrument of deterrence, are,

whether one likes it or not, the guarantee of peace from the moment
that there is a balance of forces . . . The maintenance of this balance
requires that no region of Europe be left defenceless against nuclear
weapons directed specifically against it. Anyone who gambles on
'decoupling' the European and American continents would, in our
view, be calling into question . . . the maintenance of peace. I think –
and I say – that this 'decoupling' is a danger in itself,. . . a danger
which weighs particularly on those European countries which do not
possess nuclear arms.[11]

Decades later, it is difficult to appreciate the impact of those few
sentences. Mitterrand's argument was that the pacifists, by seeking to
leave Europe defenceless, were inviting a new war in which non-
nuclear powers like West Germany would find themselves in the front
line. Later that year he would encapsulate the thought in an aphorism:
'Pacifism . . . is in the West; the missiles are in the East'.[12]

The speech was a game-changer.

The Russians were furious. Kohl was delighted – as well he might
be: Mitterrand's backing comforted the Christian Democrats in their
support of deployment and helped Kohl to victory in the parliamentary elections which were held two months later. The Americans, after
drawing a deep breath, applauded.[13] Henry Kissinger telephoned to
say he had found the speech 'quite remarkable'. Reagan, declaring
that Mitterrand's remarks were 'of inestimable value', thanked him
for 'strengthening the Alliance at a time when the European countries
have to admit their . . . anxiety before the pressure of public opinion'.
After the Farewell episode, it was the final proof of French loyalty.
Mitterrand had already made unpublicised decisions to grant French
port facilities to US nuclear submarines and to ease overflight restrictions for NATO aircraft. Now his support for the deployment of
Pershings in West Germany left even the most hawkish members of
the administration with no reason to question the French leader's
foreign policy stance. Kissinger would later describe him as 'a very
good ally, the best of all the French presidents', while Reagan was on
record as having said, in an aside which would not have gone down
well had it come to the ears of Margaret Thatcher, 'You know, François,
there's probably more common ground in foreign policy between the
US and France than between the US and any other country.' That

might be true of nuclear arms, but in other areas it would be sorely tested in the first years of Mitterrand's time in office.

Partly from ideological considerations, partly for reasons of national pride, France and the USA were often at loggerheads. Latin America was a prime example. Washington supported right-wing oligarchies in countries like El Salvador, arguing that they were the best defence against the inroads of communism; France supported the oligarchies' opponents, arguing that US backing for Latin American dictatorships was giving communism its chance. It was a dialogue of the deaf. 'Reagan will end up proving to the American public that he was right,' Mitterrand grumbled. 'His policies reinforce hard-line revolutionaries [who] have no choice but to take the Soviet side. It's a vicious circle, and one for which the USA bears a great responsibility.'

Mitterrand set out his position at the North–South Conference at Cancun, in Mexico, in October 1981, pleading for increased aid, better terms of trade and debt relief for the poorest countries.

> Non-assistance to a people in danger is not yet an offence under inter-national law, but it is a moral and political fault that has already cost too many deaths and too much suffering . . . for us to continue to commit it . . . France says no to the despair which pushes towards violence those deprived of any other way to make themselves heard. It says no to the attitude which tramples underfoot public freedoms only to outlaw afterwards those who take up arms to defend those freedoms.
>
> To all freedom fighters, France extends a message of hope . . . Homage to the humiliated, to the émigrés, to those exiled from their own land, who wish to live and to live free! Homage to those who are gagged, who are persecuted, who are tortured, who wish to live and to live free! Homage to those who have been detained, who have disappeared, who have been assassinated, who wished to live and to live free! Homage to the priests who have been ill-treated, the trades unionists who have been imprisoned, the unemployed who sell their blood to survive, the Indians hunted down in their forests, the workers without rights, the peasants without land, those who resist without arms and who want to live and to live free! To all these, France says: Courage! Freedom will triumph.[14]

It was a fine left-wing diatribe in favour of social justice, but not calculated to endear him to a right-wing Republican administration, least of all in America's backyard where many of the regimes he denounced were on life-support from the CIA. To no one's surprise, the Cancun conference achieved nothing.

Economic policy was another apple of discord.

The Americans eventually learnt not to keep asking French officials to explain 'the difference between your economic policy and that of a communist country', as Reagan's sherpa, Richard Allen (soon to become US National Security Adviser) and the President's economic adviser, Ed Meese, had at the Ottawa G7 summit in July. But the Republicans' 'supply side economics' had no place for Mitterrand's ideas about state ownership of the means of production, reducing social inequalities and promoting consumer-led growth. Nor did Washington wish to understand that Europe's economic interests might be different from those of the United States. The Europeans were willing to stand firm against Soviet nuclear threats but they were not willing to forgo Soviet bloc trade.

At Ottawa there had been preliminary skirmishes. Reagan called for a strengthening of COCOM, the Western coordinating committee charged with restricting exports of sensitive technology to Soviet bloc countries and China. Mitterrand retorted: 'We are not going to start a blockade, as Napoleon did [against nineteenth-century Russia]. It never works. Why create food shortages in countries which are already starving?' That was a jibe at the hypocrisy of the American position. America's main export to the USSR was grain, which was unaffected by COCOM restrictions. Europe exported machinery. At a time when global growth was being strangled by high US interest rates, which Washington insisted were needed to fight inflation, the Europeans were not about to make additional sacrifices for a policy which, even if justified, would ratchet up to unacceptable levels the economic and social strains to which their own countries were subjected.

The result was a stalemate. Reagan refused to lower interest rates. The Europeans refused to restrict East–West trade.

In December 1981, after the Polish leader, General Jaruzelski, declared martial law and placed under house arrest the leaders of the free trade union, Solidarność, who had demanded political reforms, the US President tried again. Washington imposed stiff economic

sanctions and asked the Europeans to cancel plans to help build a huge
new pipeline from Siberia to provide natural gas for European industry.
To back up this 'request', a senior US official was despatched to Europe
to warn the three countries concerned – France, West Germany and
Italy – that if the pipeline project went ahead, the US Navy might not
continue to assure protection of their oil supplies from the Gulf.

It was exactly the wrong approach. Mitterrand was still fuming
over his first encounter with America's economic 'hegemonism' at
Ottawa – its 'crude way', as he put it, 'of summoning its allies with
a whistle when in fact it is serving its own national interests'. Now
Washington was threatening France directly if it did not toe the
American line. The French response was not long in coming. A month
later, Paris and Moscow signed an agreement whereby not only would
French companies participate in the pipeline's construction but France
would buy 8 billion cubic metres of Russian gas annually for twenty-
five years. West Germany and Italy followed suit.

Reagan wrote twice to 'François' expressing 'deep concern'.

At the next G7 summit in Versailles, in June 1982, France and West
Germany fended off a fresh US offensive to try to restrict export
credits to the Soviet bloc. Two weeks later Reagan announced an
embargo on the export of machinery for the gas pipeline by European
subsidiaries of American firms.

This time Mitterrand made it known that if the embargo were
enforced, France would boycott future G7 meetings. 'I have no intention,' he told the Cabinet, 'of becoming the Americans' buffoon.' It
was left to George Shultz, who succeeded Haig as Secretary of State,
to find a way out of the mess. But the face-saving solution that he
came up with, after months of negotiation, opened another can of
worms. On the morning of November 13, the Elysée received a draft
of a radio address which Reagan was to make that afternoon,
announcing that the embargo would be replaced by a binding system
of consultation under which the Allies pledged 'not to engage in trade
arrangements which contribute to the . . . strategic advantage of the
USSR or serve to preferentially aid [its] economy'.

Mitterrand exploded. 'It's intolerable and unacceptable,' he said. 'If
we go down this road it means accepting that France is no longer
independent.'

In a statement, which the President himself drafted, the French

Foreign Ministry announced that, contrary to what Reagan had said in his broadcast, France was not party to such an agreement and did not consider itself bound by it. Mitterrand told the Cabinet afterwards: 'By taking France out of the NATO military command, [de Gaulle] refused military integration [under US leadership]. I refuse economic integration.'

The following weekend he wrote to Reagan: '[Our Alliance] should draw its strength from our diversity. It is in respecting the national character of each State . . . that we will promote the growth in each of our countries of a common will for defence.'

It was not about East–West trade. It was about national independence. In the French view – not just that of Mitterrand, but of all shades of French political opinion – the United States was seeking to transform the G7 into a political directorate under American leadership to order the affairs of the non-communist world. In the process, the interests of its allies were trampled underfoot. Mitterrand's diplomatic adviser, Hubert Védrine, who would later become French Foreign Minister, summed it up. When the Americans want something, he said, 'they're terrifying, they behave like door-to-door vacuum cleaner salesmen', and when they decide to act, 'they care as little about the effects their actions have on us as we would care about the fallout our policies might have on Luxembourg'.

The nub of the problem was power.

That had been brought home to Mitterrand at a meeting with Reagan earlier that year. The Americans were up in arms because France had accorded recognition to the Farabundo Marti resistance movement in El Salvador – then a prey to death squads organised by the US-backed military dictatorship – and had supplied modest quantities of arms to the left-wing government in Nicaragua. 'We cannot tolerate the slightest presence of Marxism south of the Rio Grande,' Reagan had told him. 'We are afraid that it will be contagious and Mexico will be infected by communism.' Mitterrand was struck by the symmetry. The Monroe Doctrine was the mirror image of the Brezhnev doctrine: no communism south of the Rio Grande, no capitalism east of the Elbe.

France might no longer have the substance of power but it insisted on the semblance. By the spring of 1983, after Mitterrand's speech in Bonn and the expulsion of Soviet diplomats in April, the Americans were starting to take that on board.

There was a last, ugly spasm of rancour at Williamsburg, in Virginia, when the G7 met in May. Once again, Reagan was determined to twist his allies' arms to present a common front against the Soviet Union, proposing that NATO be expanded by some form of association with Japan and that the G7 give public backing to his now moribund 'Option Zero' proposal. Mitterrand rejected both. He was completely isolated. None of the others wanted to go to war in order to defend Japan – which was the implication of the US position – but neither Margaret Thatcher, who faced elections a week later, nor Helmut Kohl, engaged in a battle of wills with Moscow over Euromissile deployment, was ready to risk a rupture with Washington over what, in the end, were merely words on paper. During the closing session on security, Reagan lost his temper at Mitterrand's intransigence, at one point slamming down his fist with such force that his dossiers flew to the other end of the table. Eventually a compromise was reached. The final declaration made no mention either of NATO expansion or of 'Option Zero', but Mitterrand was forced to accept a clause asserting that the security of the group's members was 'indivisible and must be approached on a global basis'. It was anodyne enough, but Mitterrand thought it brought the G7 an unacceptable step closer to becoming a global alliance.

Williamsburg left a bad taste on both sides. But nations' interests outweigh the exasperation of their leaders. A month later, in a conciliatory gesture, Mitterrand received the NATO Foreign Ministers in Paris for the first meeting of the Alliance Council in the French capital since de Gaulle's decision to leave the military command in 1966.

In November, the West German parliament approved, by 286 votes to 226 – the Greens and Social Democrats voting against – the installation of Pershings and cruise missiles. 'Option Zero' was dead. It remained only for the US formally to withdraw it. By then, Reagan's mind was on his re-election campaign. Europe – and France – receded into oblivion. But the administration had drawn the lesson. Vernon Walters, the francophone former Deputy Director of the CIA who became Reagan's Ambassador to the UN, explained: 'France is a difficult ally, but it's easy to reach agreement so long as you treat her as an equal and don't speak condescendingly.' A simple enough principle, but apparently too difficult for a superpower to apply.

*

In foreign policy, the first thirty months of Mitterrand's tenure were a success. After a period of mutual testing, France's relationships with both the US and the Soviet Union had settled into a pattern of wary respect. True, no progress had been made to resolve the problems of the European Community, hamstrung by Britain's demands for a budget rebate. But in Mitterrand's view, no agreement with the British would be possible until Mrs Thatcher had exhausted both her arguments and her partners and had her back to the wall. In the meantime, the only thing to do was to wait.

The one part of the world where things were not going well for him was the Middle East, the 'complicated Orient', as de Gaulle had called it, where tensions were not only boiling over – an all too frequent state of affairs – but, much more serious, spilling on to the streets of Paris.

Mitterrand had come to office with a long record of supporting Israel. In August 1947, he was one of only two French Cabinet ministers to urge the government to give asylum to the Jewish refugee ship, the *Exodus*. Two years later he visited Jerusalem. From the 1950s onwards, he travelled there frequently, drawn year after year to the biblical landscapes which fascinated and inspired him, forging in the process a firm friendship with the Labour Party leader, Shimon Peres. His elder son, Jean-Christophe, spent five months as a student on a kibbutz in Galilee. Neither his experiences in the 1930s in Paris, when anti-Semitism was rampant, nor in Vichy, where he had written for anti-Semitic magazines, had prepared him for such an affinity with the Jewish State. But views, like circumstances, change. For Mitterrand, as for many others, the revelation of the Holocaust had shown the Jews, and Palestine, in a new light.

Where de Gaulle had characterised the Israeli people as 'an elite people, sure of itself and domineering'[15] – a judgement which had shocked Israelis but reflected France's sense of its own interests in the region – Mitterrand called them 'noble and proud'.

His sympathies for Israel had their limits. Supporting the Jewish people's right to a peaceful, secure existence did not mean automatically supporting Israeli policies. Visiting Gaza in the late 1970s he had been appalled by the misery of the Palestinian refugee camps and had urged mutual recognition between Israel and the PLO (Palestine Liberation Organisation), whose leader, Yasser Arafat, he had met in

Cairo in 1974. But he had never been particularly drawn to the Arab world and he resented what he saw as a pro-Arab bias in French policy under Pompidou and Giscard. One of his first acts as President was to revoke a circular issued by Raymond Barre in 1977, authorising French companies to comply with the Arab boycott of Israel, a decision which he was warned, wrongly as it turned out, would earn him the lasting enmity of Arab governments. He told his staff he intended to make Israel the destination for his first State visit abroad.

However Israel under the leadership of Menachem Begin, the steely, nationalistic chief of the right-wing Likud Party, was not as Mitterrand had hoped.

In June, less than three weeks after his inauguration, Israeli jets bombed a French-built nuclear power plant in Iraq, killing a French technician. Begin had authorised the raid to galvanise his supporters during his re-election campaign. Mitterrand took it as a personal affront. It soured his relations with the Israeli Prime Minister, whom he came to regard as one of the main obstacles to peace in the region, and marked the beginning of an interminable apprenticeship in the politics of a part of the world torn by racial, religious, sectarian and ethnic hatreds more vicious and opaque than he had believed possible.

Instead of Israel, Mitterrand's first State visit was to Saudi Arabia. Compared to the rest of the Middle Eastern minefield, it was almost neutral territory. The Saudis provided half of France's oil and had 30 billion francs (£3 billion, or US $7 billion) on deposit in French banks, the withdrawal of which would have been disastrous at a time when the franc was under constant attack. He assured Crown Prince Fahd that France would continue to back Iraq in its war against Iran, which had broken out the previous autumn, that the staunchly anti-communist kingdom had nothing to fear from a left-wing government in Paris and that French policy in the region would remain 'balanced'.

What Mitterrand meant by 'balanced' was made clear six months later, when, on March 3 1982, after having delayed his journey to Israel a second time in protest against Begin's announcement of the annexation of the Golan Heights, he finally arrived in Tel Aviv.

He was the first French Head of State to travel to the Holy Land since the crusader king, Louis IX, seven centuries earlier, and, apart from the Pope, the first leader of any European country to visit Israel since its foundation. That day Mitterrand went out of his way to be

conciliatory. When Begin angrily ruled out any possibility of a
Palestinian State and denounced the PLO as 'a gang of killers', the
French President gently reminded him that Arabs and Jews were 'by
definition descended from the same father'. He reserved his main
statement, however, for the Israeli parliament, the Knesset, the
following afternoon. He sat up much of the night, writing and
rewriting it in his suite at the King David Hotel. It was the speech of
a man walking on eggshells, determined to convey, politely but clearly,
ideas his hosts did not wish to hear:

> The most [fundamental right], it seems to me, is that each of us has the
> irreducible right to live. That right is yours . . . It is also that of the peoples
> who surround you. In saying this, I am thinking, naturally, of the
> Palestinians of Gaza and the West Bank . . . France recognises no forbidden
> topics. Its duty is to speak one and the same language, everywhere and at
> all times . . . Why do I wish the Arabs of Gaza and the West Bank to
> possess a homeland? Because one cannot ask anybody to give up his
> identity. It is for the Palestinians, as for others, no matter where they come
> from . . . to decide for themselves their own fate. Dialogue supposes prior
> mutual recognition of the other's right to exist. [It also] supposes that each
> party can take that right to its logical conclusion, which, for the Palestinians
> as for others, can mean, when the time comes, a State.[16]

The fatal words, 'Palestinian' and 'State', had been uttered and, what
was more, in Jerusalem itself. No matter what oratorical precautions
Mitterrand used – noting that the PLO, which 'speaks in the name of
the [Palestinian] fighters', could not expect to take part in peace talks
so long as it denied Israel's right to exist; and warning both sides
against 'any unilateral act which might delay the coming of peace', a
reference to Israel's evident desire to invade southern Lebanon – the
speech was explosive.

Begin, speaking from a wheelchair, to which he was confined with
a broken leg, reacted furiously, comparing the PLO to the Nazis. The
Arab States complained that Mitterrand had not gone far enough.
Washington kept silent. The Europeans applauded.

Three months later, on June 4, while the G7 leaders were meeting
at Versailles, the Israeli Air Force bombarded PLO refugee camps in
southern Lebanon and West Beirut, ostensibly in retaliation for the

attempted assassination of the Israeli Ambassador in London, Shlomo Argov, the previous day. Argov's shooting, as the Israelis well knew, had nothing to do with the PLO. It was the work of Abu Nidal, the most feared and ruthless of the leaders of the so-called 'Rejectionist Front' which called for total war against the Jewish State and opposed any form of contact between Palestinians and Israelis. Abu Nidal and Menachem Begin were on opposite sides but, in certain respects, had similar objectives. Both rejected the peace process and both wanted to destroy the PLO, the only Palestinian organisation capable of accomplishing it. That the PLO should be blamed for Abu Nidal's work suited each of them very well.

On June 6, 20,000 Israeli troops crossed into southern Lebanon. Begin told Mitterrand that it was a limited operation and that his soldiers would not advance more than 25 miles into Lebanese territory. A week later it was clear that, far from being limited, Israel, with Reagan's backing, was bent on the PLO's destruction. The US vetoed a French resolution in the Security Council calling for the neutralisation of Beirut. By the beginning of July, 10,000 people had been killed during the Israeli advance. At that point, Reagan began to waver. But it took another five weeks before he agreed to put pressure on Begin to agree to a multinational peacekeeping force of Americans, French and Italians, which would separate the two sides and protect the departure of Arafat and 15,000 of his fighters to a new base in Tunisia.

By then relations between Mitterrand and Begin were execrable. Responding to a journalist's question, Mitterrand had acknowledged a parallel between the Israeli army's actions in Beirut and events at Oradour-sur-Glane, a village in central France destroyed in 1944 by a Nazi SS division which had massacred all 642 inhabitants. Begin accused Mitterrand of anti-Semitism. Two days later Israeli artillery bombarded the French Embassy in Beirut. The Lebanese capital is not 25 but 60 miles north of the Israeli border. Mitterrand told his entourage: 'Begin lied to me.'

The reference to Oradour proved tragically prophetic. Despite warnings from Arafat and Claude Cheysson that more bloodshed was inevitable if the peacekeepers left, the US Secretary of State, George Shultz, insisted that the Marines should withdraw, ahead of plan, on September 10. The Italians followed. Mitterrand, realising that French troops would be in an impossible position if they stayed on alone, responsible for whatever might happen and lacking the force to prevent it, ordered them to leave too.

Next day, the newly elected Christian President of Lebanon, Bachir Gemayel, was assassinated. With the authorisation of Begin and his Defence Minister, Ariel Sharon, the Israeli Army occupied West Beirut on the pretext of preventing inter-communal violence. That night, Christian militiamen entered the Palestinian ghettos of Sabra, Chatila and Borj el-Brajneh, all of which were under Israeli army control. While Israeli troops stood by, they slaughtered at least 800, probably more than two thousand, Palestinian civilians, many of them women and children, who were hastily buried in mass graves.

The Americans, aghast at their misjudgement, insisted that the multinational force return at once.[17] The Israelis withdrew from the city and for the first time accepted the presence of UN observers. Mitterrand concluded that Israel's responsibility in the massacres was 'both direct and indirect'. A UN investigation said more gingerly 'direct or indirect'. In Israel itself, Shimon Peres accused Begin and Ariel Sharon of personal responsibility for the killings, a charge endorsed in Sharon's case by the government-appointed Kahan Commission, which recommended that he be dismissed and never again permitted to hold public office. Begin ignored the report and Sharon went on to become Israeli Prime Minister.

For Mitterrand, the Lebanese imbroglio had three immediate effects.

His relationship with the Israelis became extremely strained. That did not make him pro-Palestinian, but he was increasingly convinced that Arafat and the PLO held the key to an eventual peace settlement.

Secondly, he concluded that as long as Begin and the Likud remained in office, meaningful negotiations would be impossible.[18] The United States had the power but not the will to overcome Israeli obduracy. Mitterrand saw a striking example of that a few months after Sabra and Chatila. Shultz had told Cheysson that the US might be ready to recognise the PLO if Arafat would accept Israel's right to exist. The Palestinian leader agreed, on condition that France guaranteed that the Americans would keep their word. Two weeks later Shultz wrote to Cheysson to say that Washington could not commit itself unless Israel gave its prior accord to the arrangement.

The French Ambassador to Washington, Bernard Vernier-Palliez, a leading industrialist with no particular political affiliation (under

Giscard, he had headed the French car-maker, Renault), explained in a lengthy telegram to Mitterrand the root of the American problem:

> American actions . . . in everything related to the Middle East are incomprehensible unless one takes into account the extraordinary power of the Israeli Lobby. Its ability to mobilise the Jewish electorate, the extent of its financial resources, the effectiveness of its organisation which blindly serves the interests of Jerusalem, allow it to exert pressure on the Administration and to control Congress better than the Administration itself can. [It acts] not only to deter the Administration from adopting . . . positions unfavourable to the Israeli government, and to block in Congress actions by the Executive which displease it, but also to promote policies openly opposed to that of the White House . . . When Israel's interests are at stake, Congress, which very often [in other contexts] acts as a brake on adventurism, is likely, on the contrary, to urge on the Executive, encouraging it to take heavy risks.[19]

His conclusion was that progress towards a Middle East settlement would require not only a new government in Israel but also an American president prepared, if not to confront the Israeli lobby, at least to keep it at arm's length.

The third effect of the Israeli invasion was for Mitterrand the most troubling. It had reinforced a spiral of terrorist violence which, while hardly new to the region – terrorism had been endemic for decades, first by Jewish groups against the British, then by Palestinians against the Israelis – was about to change its nature, creating a dynamic of hatred against which Western governments in general and France in particular would find themselves powerless.[20]

Far from being eradicated, as Begin had hoped, terrorism spread exponentially, acquiring an Islamic as well as a Palestinian dimension.[21] Yitzhak Rabin, who succeeded Sharon as Defence Minister, said later: 'Of all the surprises of the war in Lebanon, of which most were bad, the most dangerous was to see the Shiites let out of their bottle.'[22]

Throughout the 1970s, France had been largely spared from Middle Eastern terrorism.[23] Giscard's intelligence services had sealed a Faustian pact with the principal groups concerned: the authorities would turn a blind eye, allowing them to use French territory for logistics and communications, so long as they abstained from attacks against French targets or on French soil. In October 1980 this unspoken truce had been briefly shattered when a bomb exploded outside a synagogue in the rue Copernic, near the Arc de Triomphe, at the top of the Champs-Elysées, killing four people and injuring forty-six. But no further incident occurred and it was treated as a one-off, an unexplained anomaly that did not call into question the basic understanding that France was a sanctuary.

Then, in September 1981, the French Ambassador in Beirut, Louis Delamare, was driving home for lunch when two gunmen forced his car to stop not far from a Syrian army checkpoint and shot him dead at point-blank range through the car window.

Mitterrand was convinced that Syria was responsible. President Hafez al-Assad, who regarded Lebanon as a Syrian protectorate, had taken umbrage at France supplying arms to the Christian-led Lebanese government. In retaliation, Mitterrand ordered the DGSE, the French external intelligence service, to track down and kill the men who had carried out the attack and, as a warning, to detonate a car bomb in front of the ruling Baath Party headquarters in Damascus. According to Gilles Ménage, his security adviser, both missions were 'in large measure accomplished'.

The following spring, in April 1982, a bomb exploded in Paris outside the offices of *Al watan al arabi*, an Arabic-language weekly hostile to Assad's regime, killing a passer-by and injuring sixty-three others. Two Syrian diplomats were immediately expelled and the French Ambassador recalled from Damascus.

It marked the beginning of a long and terrible summer.

In the six months from March to September 1982, seventeen people were killed and 160 injured in nearly twenty separate terrorist attacks in France. Thirteen more died and twenty-two were injured in attacks on French interests in Lebanon.

The actors and motives varied. The Venezuelan terrorist, Ilich Ramirez Sanchez, better known as Carlos, orchestrated several attacks to try to secure the release of two members of his network who had been arrested in Paris the previous winter.[24] The Secret Army for the Liberation of Armenia, ASALA, a Lebanese-based movement with links both to Carlos and to the Palestinian Rejectionist Front, which targeted Turkish diplomats because of Ankara's denial of the Armenian genocide, carried out four more attacks. Another group, the Armed

Revolutionary Lebanese Fractions, FARL, about which little was known, assassinated an Israeli and an American diplomat.[25] In July, Abu Nidal's organisation, Fatah–Revolutionary Council, shot to death the deputy head of the PLO bureau in Paris. A month later, as Mitterrand was preparing to send back to the Lebanon the French contingent of the multinational force, four masked assailants machine-gunned a kosher restaurant in the rue des Rosiers (Rosetree Street), in a predominantly Jewish quarter of Paris, killing six people and injuring twenty-three.

In France, as elsewhere in Europe, people grew accustomed to security guards searching their bags as they entered department stores; to municipal dustbins welded shut lest they be used to conceal explosives; buildings emptied and streets sealed off for bomb alerts which were almost always hoaxes but just occasionally were not; soldiers with automatic weapons patrolling in groups of three in airports and stations; and the pervasive fear, on buses and underground trains, that a fellow passenger might be waiting for the moment to leave an innocent-looking bag or rucksack filled with penthrite in a corner or under a seat.[26]

But whereas in the rest of Europe much of the terrorism was home-grown – the IRA and the Irish National Liberation Army in Britain, the Basque ETA in Spain and anarcho-Maoist groups like the Red Army Faction in Germany and the Red Brigades in Italy – in France, almost every attack proved to have a Middle Eastern connection.*

Gradually the DST began to find common threads. Both the attack

---

* There were other sources of terrorism in France in the 1980s, but none came close to attaining the intensity of those originating in the Middle East (or with Middle Eastern connections, like Action Directe, an extreme left-wing French group, some of whose members had attended training camps in Lebanon, which had links to the Rejectionist Front as well as to the Red Brigades and the Red Army Faction). Corsican separatists, after a brief truce when Mitterrand took office, resumed their attacks, but they were either directed against property – empty holiday homes belonging to families from the French mainland – or were symbolic actions against French police stations. There was also some spillover into the French Basque country from the ETA conflict in Spain. During Franco's rule, France had turned a blind eye to ETA activities on its soil. After the Dictator's death attitudes changed slowly. It was not until 1982, when the Spanish Socialist, Felipe González, took office, that the French and Spanish police forces began to cooperate and the first ETA members were extradited. With rare exceptions, Corsican and Basque terrorism in France were no more than irritants, as were the occasional actions of Breton nationalists.

on the synagogue in the rue Copernic, and that in the rue des Rosiers, two years earlier, were now recognised as the work of Abu Nidal.[27] But what was the message behind them? The first had occurred shortly after an EEC summit in Venice had affirmed the Palestinians' right to self-determination and recognised the PLO as their legitimate representative. The second came as Mitterrand was trying to save Arafat's movement from annihilation in Beirut. Those accustomed to the coded language of violence in Beirut thought that the French would be able to figure out that they were a warning that support for the PLO would carry a heavy price. But who in the West, or even in Israel, in the early 1980s, was capable of understanding that attacks on a synagogue and a Jewish restaurant were actually aimed not at Jews or at Israel, but stemmed from the mutual hatred of two Palestinian organisations?[28]

Mitterand's journey to Israel in March and his support of the PLO had proved a lethal combination.

If the French government was unable to decipher the message which Abu Nidal was seeking to convey, it had a shrewd idea of who might be behind him. Syria, Iraq and Libya were the Rejectionist Front's main financial backers. In September 1982, François de Grossouvre arranged a meeting near Bordeaux between the head of the DGSE, Pierre Marion, and Rifaat al-Assad, the President's brother and head of the Syrian intelligence service, who had come to France for eye treatment. In return for the promise of improved relations between Paris and Damascus, Assad promised that Syria would end its operations on French soil and restrain the activities of Abu Nidal and other rejectionist movements. Iraq, by then heavily dependent on France for military supplies in the war against Iran, also agreed to help.

As though a giant switch had been thrown, the attacks abruptly ceased. For the remainder of that autumn and winter and through the following spring, France was calm again. But another, much more powerful force, whose role was even less understood in Paris than that of the Rejectionist Front, was lurking in the shadows: the regime of Ayatollah Khomeini in Teheran.

If the United States was the 'Great Satan' in the eyes of the Islamic Republic, France was the 'Little Satan'. Although Khomeini had been given asylum in France in the months before the Shah's fall, the

Iranians were not pleased when Giscard accorded the same right to the Shah's last Prime Minister, Shapour Bakhtiar, a French-educated academic who had fought with the International Brigades in Spain. In July 1980, Anis Naccache, a balding, mustachioed Lebanese in his thirties who had recently converted to Shiism, was sent from Teheran to assassinate Bakhtiar at his home in Paris. The attack was bungled. Bakhtiar was unharmed, but a policeman and a passer-by were killed and a second policeman paralysed for life. Naccache and four accomplices were arrested.

A year later, the former Iranian President, Abulhassan Banisadr, who had been impeached after falling out with Khomeini, defected to France with Massoud Radjavi, the leader of the People's Mujahideen, an Islamic revolutionary party of Marxist inspiration which had helped Khomeini to power but afterwards, suspected of disloyalty, had been ruthlessly persecuted. In the weeks between Banisadr's fall and his defection, Radjavi's followers had blown up the Islamic Republic Party headquarters, killing seventy people, including Ayatollah Beheshti, the most powerful leader after Khomeini. When it became known that they were in Paris, the Iranian authorities reacted with fury. The French Embassy in Teheran was encircled by Revolutionary Guards and the stage seemed set for a repeat of the American hostage-taking which had poisoned the last year of Jimmy Carter's presidency. In the end the Iranians backed off and the French community, comprising some 200 businessmen, diplomats and residents, was allowed to leave on August 12. Two and a half weeks later, another Mujahideen bomb attack killed Banisadr's newly elected successor, President Mohammed-Ali Rajai, and his Prime Minister, and came close to killing Khomeini himself.

For a 'small Satan', that was already a great deal of provocation.

France had given asylum to Bakhtiar and Banisadr. If only by default, it was allowing the Mujahideen, who had made their headquarters at Auvers-sur-Oise, north of Paris, a virtually free hand to organise terrorist attacks in Iran. Mitterrand had urged rather half-heartedly that the Mujahideen's activities 'at least when visible, should be forbidden' but he did nothing to ensure the order was carried out.[29] Moreover that spring, the President had agreed, albeit with some reluctance, to provide Iraq with five Super-Etendard attack aircraft equipped with air-to-sea Exocet missiles. It was a new contract and marked a significant escalation of French support for Baghdad.

Mitterrand found Saddam Hussein antipathetic. His wife, Danielle, a militant supporter of Third World causes, was outraged by the repression of the Kurds. 'I said to him: "François, why are you doing this? Why are you selling him arms?"', she remembered. 'He said to me: "If France doesn't do it, it will be someone else and France won't have the benefit". I said: "But it's a matter of honour". He replied: "Yes, and that doesn't put food on the table."'

There was another, more important reason. Mitterrand was convinced that unless Teheran was stopped, Islamic fundamentalism risked spreading throughout the Middle East. He wanted to maintain the existing balance between the Persian and Arab worlds, which meant supporting Iraq enough to prevent Saddam's defeat but not enough to allow him to win. It did not endear him to the Mullahs.

For Teheran the last straw came in May 1982 when Anis Naccache and his accomplices were sentenced to long terms of imprisonment. No one in France paid much attention. It seemed a straightforward case. Only much later would it be understood that, for the Iranian theocracy, this was the biggest problem of all.[30]

The Mullahs' response was not long in coming.

On July 15, a powerful suitcase bomb exploded at the Turkish Airlines counter at Orly, south of Paris, killing eight people and injuring fifty-two. At first sight it was simply another Armenian attack against Turkey, albeit on a larger scale than in the past. However the Armenian group, ASALA, which claimed to have been responsible, had close ties to Teheran. Could the explosion at Orly have an Iranian connection?[31] At the Elysée, as Gilles Ménage later admitted, that thought never crossed anyone's mind.

A second warning followed in August, when an Air France plane was hijacked from Vienna to Teheran by a group of five Lebanese who said they had done so to protest against 'the French government's crimes in Iraq' and specifically the sale of the French warplanes. Shortly afterwards, Iran stated that it 'would not sit by with folded arms' if the delivery of the Super-Etendards went ahead. It accused Mitterrand of 'setting Lebanon on fire, pouring bombs on the Muslim population with the aid of Israel,' and raised the spectre of an oil blockade.

But Mitterrand had committed himself. Whatever the risks, there was no way France could back out without forfeiting its credibility in the Arab world.

On October 8 1983, the five aircraft arrived in Iraq.

Fifteen days later, in the early morning of Sunday, October 23, two enormous explosions reverberated across Beirut. At the US Marines' base at Beirut Airport, a suicide bomber in a lorry packed with 900 kilograms of explosives killed 241 American soldiers and injured 105 others. It was the deadliest attack on US forces since the Vietnam War. A few miles away, on the seafront, a similarly loaded truck crashed through the concrete barriers protecting the HQ of the French para-troop detachment, killing fifty-eight soldiers and leaving fifteen more buried in the rubble. In Paris it was 4.20 a.m. Mitterrand was awakened and immediately despatched the Defence Minister, Charles Hernu, to the scene. That night he flew to Lebanon too, arriving at dawn on Monday morning. He told the Lebanese President, Bachir Gemayel's older brother, Amin: 'France is staying in Lebanon, and will remain true to . . . its commitments'. It was not the words that mattered. Mitterrand's presence signified that France would not be scared off.

The question, as ever, was who was behind it all. Who had carried out the attacks and who had pulled the strings?

The group which claimed responsibility, Islamic Jihad (Holy War), was at that time so little understood that the CIA thought the term was just a generic label used by multiple organisations carrying out terrorist activities.[32] But there was a clue in the communiqué it issued: 'We are Lebanese Muslims who follow the precepts of the Koran . . . We want no [foreign force] in Lebanon, neither Israelis nor Syrians. We want an Islamic Republic.'

That was the signature of Iran. Only Teheran wanted an Islamic Republic in Lebanon. The American Defence Secretary, Caspar Weinberger, cottoned on faster than anyone else. Israel, as usual, blamed the PLO. Mitterrand admitted he was confused. On his return he told the Cabinet:

> Beirut is a city that is completely mad: everyone shoots at everyone else. What was the origin of the attack against [our troops]? People talk about the Iranians, linking their intervention to the problem of the Super-Etendards which we delivered to Iraq. But Khomeini did not wait for the Super-Etendards to step up his influence over the Shiite groups in Lebanon. Khomeini and the Iranian revolution exert an extraordinary attraction on these groups . . . [much] greater than that

of Gaddafi . . . There is also the influence of Hafez al-Assad, who is trying to pose as Nasser's successor. These three influences [Iranian, Libyan and Syrian] are both in collusion and rivals. They try to outbid each other . . . Mr Reagan envisages reprisals. On my side, if I knew who I were dealing with, I would not hesitate – but I refuse to hit back blindly . . . The Americans at the present time are artificially focussing their suspicions on Iran. I do not think the attack was ordered by Iran because if that had been the case they would not have destroyed the American base. Indeed, I wonder if it's not to avoid overly antagonising the Syrians that the Americans are pointing the finger at Iran.[33]

His statement, made in the secrecy of the Cabinet room, showed a government floundering about in the dark. No one in France understood what was happening in Lebanon.[34] Mitterrand discounted Iranian involve-ment in the attacks because he knew that the Americans were already secretly supplying Teheran with arms – eighteen months *before* the official US investigation into what became the Iran-Contra Affair claimed that they had begun – and would not therefore have been a target. He repeated in an interview later the same day: 'We are not at all Iran's enemies . . . We have no reason to consider Iran . . . as an enemy.'

No reason? A week later he knew better. The attack was traced back to Hussein Moussawi, the pro-Iranian Shiite leader whose head-quarters were in the Bekaa Valley, east of Beirut. Yitzhak Rabin concluded sombrely: 'We have let the Devil out of his box'.

At the beginning of November, Mitterrand approved a riposte.

It was a fiasco. When the DGSE tried to set off a car bomb outside the Iranian Embassy in southern Beirut, not only did the detonators fail but the attack had been mounted so clumsily that it had France's fingerprints all over it.

Ten days later the President tried again. French aircraft bombed a barracks at Baalbek used by Moussawi's followers. Technically the attack succeeded: fourteen Iranian revolutionary guards and a dozen Shiite militiamen were killed. But the barracks turned out to have been half empty, and Reagan, who had urged Mitterrand to coordinate the attack with an American raid on the same day, backed out at the last moment, apparently to protect the emerging relationship with Teheran which he was nurturing with US arms supplies. What was supposed to be a graphic demonstration of Western resolve to punish pro-Iranian terrorism ended as a damp squib. Relations between Paris and Teheran were further envenomed. The Shiites' hatred of France grew.

Meanwhile another crisis was simmering. Yasser Arafat, who had imprudently returned to Lebanon that summer, was holed up with 4,000 armed followers in the northern Lebanese port of Tripoli, under attack from the sea by Israeli naval forces and from the land by dissident Palestinian militias backed by Syria, which was threatening to raze the city with artillery. The Israeli government of Yitzhak Shamir, who had succeeded Begin, was committed to Arafat's destruction. Assad was opposed to the creation of a Palestinian State on the grounds that it would imply recognition of Israel and therefore wanted Arafat crushed on the grounds that he was the leader most likely to bring such a state into being.

Mitterrand argued that removing the PLO chief would leave the field open to the Rejectionist Front and would unleash against Israel and its allies a terrorist onslaught far more violent than anything experienced before.

In December 1982, after two months of negotiations, the Security Council passed a resolution allowing PLO units to leave Tripoli under the protection of the UN flag.[35] *In extremis*, for the second time in eighteen months, Mitterrand had saved Arafat and his forces from annihilation. A few days before Christmas, five Greek merchant ships, escorted by ten French warships, including an aircraft carrier, set out for Tunis, carrying the Palestinian leader and his followers. Mitterrand had warned both Israel and Syria that any attack on the convoy would be repelled by force.

It proved to be France's swansong in Lebanon.

A few weeks later, the civil war resumed. Beirut was once again divided between Christian East and Muslim West. The Multinational Force had reached the end of the road. First the Americans and British, then the Italians and finally the French returned home, licking their wounds, leaving Christians and Muslims to resume, under the watchful eyes of the regional power-brokers, Israel and Syria, a conflict which had begun many centuries before.

For Mitterrand, this first exposure to the politics of the Middle East was a dolorous revelation. More than most Western leaders, he was at ease in complicated situations. The region fascinated him as the

cradle of Western civilisation. But the impenetrable complexity of
the tensions he found there left him bemused.

The one clear lesson he drew was that the French intelligence
services were not up to the job. Both the DST and the DGSE were
products of the Cold War, enjoying close links to the French Right
and to the Americans and locked into a logic of East–West rivalry
which meant they were ill equipped to meet the challenges of the
1980s. His distrust was reinforced by a wariness of the police and the
security services which went back to his experience as Interior
Minister at the time of the 'Leaks Affair', thirty years earlier. To
Mitterrand intuition and analysis were almost always more helpful
in assessing the course of events than espionage and intelligence-
gathering.

In the autumn of 1982, shortly after the attack by Abu Nidal's group
in the rue des Rosiers, he decided to replace the heads of all the
services responsible for the anti-terrorist struggle.[36] Some, he felt, were
incompetent. All showed 'an absence of determination and preparation in a situation which completely overwhelmed them'. Moreover
there was constant rivalry between the different forces involved – the
police (answering to the Interior Ministry), the gendarmes (controlled
by the Ministry of Defence), the DST, the Criminal Investigation
Department, the DGSE and the Special Branch – which refused to
share information and at times sabotaged each other's operations.[37]

To try to overcome these failings, Mitterrand announced the creation of an 'anti-terrorist cell' at the Elysée to coordinate intelligence
from all the various services and undertake punctual operations of
its own. It was placed under the authority of Commander Christian
Prouteau, who headed the Gendarmerie's highly regarded Special
Intervention Force, the GIGN, equivalent to Britain's SAS or America's
Delta Force.

Prouteau had been recruited by André Rousselet a few months earlier
to reorganise the President's security detail. The unit he created, the
GSPR (Special Group for the Protection of the President), consisted
initially of thirty-six officers, operating in shifts to ensure round-the-
clock security wherever Mitterrand might be. Given the President's
complicated private life, Prouteau and his men had to watch over both
his 'official' family at the rue de Bièvre, where Danielle – now no longer
with Jean Balenci, who had decided that the time had come to

establish a family of his own* – held court, and the 'unofficial' one, Anne and Mazarine, who, shortly after Mitterrand's election, moved from their home in the rue Jacob in the Latin Quarter to a grace-and-favour apartment on the quai Branly, close to the Seine in a well-heeled area by the Invalides. Prouteau was told the move was for security reasons, but that was only part of the explanation. With the presidential election behind him and Mazarine growing up, Mitterrand had decided he should give priority to his second family rather than Danielle. In his eighteen years with Anne, it was the first time – apart from brief holidays at Gordes – that they had been able to share a home. 'In the evenings he came back [from the Elysée],' she remembered, 'and we had a normal life. That means so much. We were together [not just occasionally] but every day . . . It was good.' Looking back, years later, it was the simple things that stuck in her mind: shopping in the market for dinner for the three of them and, above all, the breakfasts they had together. 'We did everything the other way round from normal people's lives,' she said. 'Usually you start by living together and finish differently. For us it was the reverse.'

The officers of the GSPR knew how to be discreet. During Mitterrand's presidency, there was never a leak from that quarter about his private affairs. Gradually he became reconciled to what at first had seemed an intolerable intrusion. The 'guardian angels' were part of his life.

At Souzy-la-Briche, a small, very private château, 25 miles south of Paris, belonging to the State, where Mitterrand and Anne liked to spend weekends, the young officers played with Mazarine and took her horse-riding. In the pine forests at Latche and the olive groves at Gordes, and at his other favourite weekend retreats – François de Grossouvre's manor house in the Bourbonnais, north of Clermont-Ferrand; the home

---

* There are conflicting versions of why the relationship ended. Jean was still living at the rue de Bièvre at the time of Mitterrand's election but, as he explained later, found Danielle increasingly taken up with Third World causes and his own role reduced to that of a factotum, 'looking after the dogs and the garden at Latche . . . By then I was forty-five and I felt that I needed to think about the future.' Danielle may also have thought that, with her husband now President, the time had come to break off the arrangement. Others, including Pierre Tourlier, have written that she was deeply unhappy at Jean's departure. Wherever the truth lies, Mitterrand stayed on good terms with Jean throughout his years in office, giving him the use of the presidential estates to indulge his passion for hunting.

of Robert and Elizabeth Badinter in Picardy; and a hunting estate in the Sologne owned by Patrice Pelat, his mentor at the PoW camp at Ziegenhain – they formed an invisible presence, 'a protection so water-tight,' Gilles Ménage wrote, 'that even the Interior Minister, [officially] responsible for his security, [often] did not know where he was'. They guarded not only the President but all those within what had become his extended family cocoon.

While the GSPR quickly won acceptance as part of the presidential establishment, the 'anti-terrorist cell' did not.

When first mooted it had seemed a sensible enough idea. A means of coordinating the anti-terrorist struggle and the intelligence that resulted was sorely needed. But the 'cell' existed outside the established hierarchies, which provoked ill feeling and rivalry, and, after a series of well-publicised blunders by one of Prouteau's more uncontrollable associates, it came close to being shut down.[38]

Mitterrand maintained it for reasons which had little to do with its original functions. In August 1983, the extreme right-wing weekly, *Minute*, began publishing a series of articles touching on his private life, culminating in December with a story entitled, 'The President's Swedish Lady Friend', about Christina Forsne, an attractive young journalist working in Paris whom Mitterrand had met through Prime Minister Olof Palme a few years earlier and with whom he had been having a long-running affair. *Minute* respected the conventions. There was no explicit suggestion of illicit amours. Nonetheless the President was alarmed.

Much worse was to come. In December that year, Jean-Edern Hallier, a gifted but wildly eccentric writer whose hopes for an impor-tant cultural post had been disappointed after Mitterrand's election, announced that he was working on a new book to be called *Tonton and Mazarine*.*

It was to be a fictionalised exposé of Mitterrand's depravity – 'polit-ical porno', as Hallier put it – in which the story of the 'bastard child', Mazarine, was mixed with anti-Semitism, a homosexual love affair

---

* The name, 'Tonton', a children's term for 'Uncle', was first applied to Mitterrand by his chauffeur, Pierre Tourlier, as a code word for use in communicating with Socialist Party headquarters on CB (Citizens Band) radio in the 1970s, when portable telephones barely existed. It was picked up by the satirical weekly, *Le Canard enchaîné*, and after Mitterrand's election became a familiar nickname in the press.

between the President and one of his ministers and graphic descriptions of orgies in which Mitterrand and the author had supposedly taken part.

Minute was manageable: it represented a part of the political spectrum which was deeply hostile to the Left but which behaved rationally. Jean-Edern Hallier did not.

In 1982, he had staged his own kidnapping, claiming to have been taken hostage by terrorists. Soon afterwards he arranged for a powerful bomb to explode in a flat vacated shortly beforehand by Régis Debray, a left-wing writer who advised Mitterrand on Third World affairs. From the balcony of his sumptuous apartment in the Place des Vosges – the French equivalent of Berkeley Square or Central Park West – Hallier used to shoot at the pigeons in the square below with a heavy-calibre pistol. On one occasion he had arrived at the Elysée, demanding to see Mitterrand, in a monk's habit and handcuffs; on another, claiming that he had come to seek the President's pardon, he wore a white robe with a rope round his neck, like one of the Burghers of Calais surrendering to King Edward III in 1347. He refused to pay his taxes or parking tickets and, when summonsed, presented the government with a bill of three-quarters of a million francs for services as 'an ideological mercenary'. In other times he might have been a court jester, but in 1983 he was a jester whose antics no longer amused.

France is traditionally tolerant of eccentric intellectuals, but Hallier had gone too far. Mitterrand told his police chief, Pierre Verbrugge, that he was not concerned if *Minute* published 'a photo [of me] with a pretty woman'; he was not even particularly exercised by what Hallier might write about him. Roland Dumas remembered his first comment, after skimming through the manuscript: 'It's quite something. What an ordeal! [Reading] it will be like undergoing psychoanalysis.' But the idea that anyone should take aim at his nine-year-old daughter revolted him.

The 'anti-terrorist cell' was ordered to make Hallier their priority. One of its members, Daniel Gamba, wrote later:

We couldn't threaten him [physically], but we needed him to think we could. [So] we filled his life with anomalies. You can't imagine, unless you've been through it, the pressure of that kind of harassment. You leave home and find two tyres on your car have been slashed. You get calls at all hours with no one ever at the other end. You see the same unknown individual several times in the same day [in totally unrelated places]. Those around you find odd things happening too . . . Unless you have been trained to resist that, you become terrified. [Such] pressure was illegal . . . Jean-Edern Hallier developed a persecution complex which was in fact well-founded. [And because of his reputation as a megalomaniac,] the unanimous reaction was that it was just a new publicity stunt.[39]

Thousands of hours were spent by the 'cell' and by other branches of the security services on a massive campaign of intimidation. On Mitterrand's instructions, Hallier's telephone and the lines of everyone with whom he and his family were in contact were tapped round the clock. Dumas recalled the President saying, 'I know where he is and what he is doing at every moment of the day and night'.

In the end Hallier gave up. No French publisher was willing to take the risk of issuing what was in any case a libellous book. *Minute*, as Mitterrand had anticipated, toned down its attacks too.

The Hallier affair was revealing for the light it cast not only on Mitterrand's attitude but on the conduct of those around him. To his advisers at the Elysée, to the security services and to the government, it was normal for the State to mobilise its resources to protect the President's private life. Fifteen years later, Gilles Ménage, who played a key role in organising Hallier's surveillance, would write with a straight face, at the same time as the Monica Lewinsky scandal was raging in the United States: 'I do not think that [the authorities] in any other Western democracy, confronted with a situation of this kind, would have acted differently.'

In such matters a gulf existed between France and most of its partners.

Even in Greece or Italy, where marital infidelity is viewed more tolerantly than in the Anglo-Saxon world, the existence of the President's second family would have been splashed across every front page. In France the news media kept silent. One may argue that this was a good thing – politicians are entitled to privacy as much as anyone else – or one may insist, as Anglo-Saxon countries do, on the public's 'right to know'. Either way, French rules were different. No one remonstrated with Mitterrand that, by authorising the police to eavesdrop on Hallier and launch a campaign of harassment against him, he was breaking the law. On the contrary his aides maintained that it was necessary to ensure the President's security – 'in the broad sense', as Ménage delicately put it – and was therefore justified.*

It was part of a larger problem. In the *Coup d'état permanent*, Mitterrand had exposed the regalian temptations of the system de Gaulle had created – only, twenty years later, to slip into the General's clothes as though they had been made to measure. Every President of the Fifth Republic has artfully blurred the distinction between private means and State funds, personal and State power. The Hallier affair led Mitterrand to rely increasingly on Prouteau's 'cell' and on the GSPR as a personal police force. They protected him both as President and as a private individual.

The 'second family' was not the only or even the most important personal secret that Mitterrand wished to keep.

During the election campaign in 1981, he had announced that, while he was in office, he would have a medical check-up and publish the results every six months as a guarantee that there would be no repetition of the last years of Pompidou's presidency, when it had been an open secret that the President was dying of leukaemia but officially no one would say so.[40] In July, two months after his election, the first check-up showed him to be in perfect health. He played tennis and golf; he did not smoke and drank little; and he was not overweight.

The trouble started that autumn, shortly before Mitterrand left for Cancun. He complained of backache and developed a limp. To his entourage he said he had hurt his back playing tennis. But the pain persisted.

On his return from Mexico he was taken secretly to the Val-de-Grâce military hospital in Paris. Tests suggested prostate cancer, the disease which had killed his father.

Ten days later, on Monday evening, November 16, Mitterrand's

---

* After Mitterrand's death, the courts took a different view. In November 2005, the 16th Chamber of the Paris Criminal Court sentenced Ménage and Prouteau to suspended prison terms of six and eight months respectively, which were immediately amnestied, and to fines of 5,000 euros (£3,300 or US $6,000), for invasion of privacy. The court upheld claims for compensation on behalf of Hallier and his family, Edwy Plenel of *Le Monde* and four others. Mitterrand was held responsible for the order to place them under surveillance.

doctor, Claude Gubler, brought one of France's leading urologists, Professor Adolphe Steg, to the private apartments at the Elysée. The verdict was unequivocal. As the President sat slumped in a chair in the bathroom, Steg told him: 'It's my duty not to hide the truth. You have a cancer of the prostate which has spread into the bone and the metastasis is significant.' Gubler remembered Mitterrand's reaction: '"I'm done for," he muttered to himself. Steg began again: "You can't say that. You can never say you're done for . . ." Mitterrand interrupted. "Stop your fairy tales. I'm done for". . . It was extremely hard, painful to see. The President's face turned grey. He bowed his head and said no more.'

He was actually in a far worse state than Steg had told him. Prostate cancer usually metastasises to the bone only when it is already well advanced. Unless they could stop it spreading, Steg told Gubler afterwards, Mitterrand would die in a matter of months. Even if the metastasis could be halted, the average life expectancy for people with his condition was three years. Only in very rare cases did they live longer.

That night Mitterrand told Anne. But Danielle was kept in the dark and, like the rest of the country, would not learn of his cancer for another ten years.

The treatment began next morning. He received a perfusion every day for two weeks, then every two days for the next three months. After that it was a course of pills of which he was not allowed to know the content. 'Medicine is my business,' Gubler told him. 'Politics is yours. To each his field.' He accepted the treatment, the doctor wrote later, because he could feel that it was working. Within a month, the pain was gone. But the medicines he was taking increased the risk of haemophilia, bone fractures and embolism. In Hamburg for a summit meeting with Schmidt in May 1982, he developed phlebitis. Gubler was summoned to his room in the early hours of the morning to find him complaining of chest pains, which he treated with a massive dose of anti-coagulant to prevent blood clots, praying that it would not trigger internal bleeding. It did not and Mitterrand convinced himself that it had been nothing more than a chest cold.

In December 1981, when the next medical bulletin was due, Gubler was ordered to lie. 'Whatever happens, we cannot reveal it,' Mitterrand told him. 'It's a State secret. You are bound by this secret.' That bulletin, like those which followed, affirmed that the President was in good health.

It was dishonest. But what was the alternative?

To admit that the President had cancer, six months after his election, would make him a lame duck, not only at home but abroad, where the knowledge that he might be dying would deprive France of much of its clout in international negotiations. Typically in such circumstances foreign governments hold back until they know that they have a stable partner capable of following through on agreements, even to the point of deliberately delaying decisions until the successor takes office, as Iran did in January 1980 by not announcing the release of the US Embassy hostages until a few hours after Carter had handed over to Reagan. In the public arena, the illness of a leader can have insidious effects. How much weight would the West German parliament and public opinion have given to Mitterrand's appeal to install Euromissiles if it had been thought that he was at death's door?

In theory Mitterrand had other options. He could have resigned. But that would have been a betrayal of a different kind, dashing the hopes, without reason if it turned out that he recovered, of all those who had put their trust in him and given him their votes. Or he could have announced that he had cancer and sought a fresh mandate from the people. In December 1981, Mitterrand was still at the height of his popularity with a 60 per cent approval rate (a situation which would continue until mid-1982). If he had revealed his illness and campaigned on a platform of truth-telling and probity, arguing that he was willing and able to continue in office to implement the programme for which he had been elected and was seeking the nation's endorsement to do so, he would probably have been returned to office, possibly by a triumphal margin.

Given Mitterrand's habit of exploring every alternative before taking any important decision, it is hard to believe that he did not at least consider those courses. But if so, he quickly rejected them.

A snap election would make sense only if he could wage a vigorous campaign. His next medical bulletin was due to be issued only five weeks after the cancer had been confirmed. That meant the election would be held in January when he was still under intensive treatment and it was far too early to tell whether it would succeed. At that stage, when the cancer was still spreading, an exhausting campaign might have killed him. Yet he could hardly ask the French to return him to office if he gave the impression that he was too ill to govern. In theory a new election was a possibility but in practice it was ruled out.

Once the first untruthful bulletin had been published, it was too late to turn back. Mitterrand was locked into a cycle of deceit. A year later, against all expectations, the cancer was in remission. But by then the economy was deteriorating, the opposition was regaining its spirits and public opinion was turning against him. The moment for honesty had passed.

In the first year after his election, the 'glorious fracture' Mitterrand had promised was enshrined in the laws of the land. French workers were given a fifth week of paid holidays; the retirement age was lowered from 65 to 60; the working week was cut from 40 to 39 hours with no reduction in pay; workers were given increased protection against arbitrary dismissal; the minimum wage and social security payments to the most disadvantaged families were substantially augmented; hundreds of thousands of civil servants were recruited; banks, insurance companies and key industrial corporations were nationalised; 130,000 illegal immigrants who were able to prove that they had jobs were given residence permits; and emergency laws against rioting, dating from the 1960s and '70s, were repealed.

It was not painless. For months, parliament was locked in violent debate, reminding some elderly backbenchers of the heroic battles between Gaullists and Communists under the Fourth Republic, twenty-five years earlier. One young right-wing MP announced that he was emigrating to Austria, another compared the Left to the Nazis, bent on making factory owners 'wear a yellow star', while a third promised it would all end 'with punches in the face'.

The opposition delayed the enactment of the new measures, which, verbal excesses aside, was no more than its constitutional role. But it was unable to prevent them.

'We've started the true rupture with capitalism,' Mitterrand exulted. 'Class struggle is not dead. It is going to have a second youth!'

For a few brief euphoric months, France became a twentieth-century Land of Cockaigne, where, in the description of a medieval troubadour, 'the houses were made of barley sugar and cakes, the streets were paved with pastry and the shops supplied goods for nothing'. There was even an ephemeral Ministry of Free Time, responsible for tourism, sport and 'social leisure, mass education and open-air activities'.[41]

There were just two problems with this beguiling if slightly Orwellian vision of organised happiness.

The first was that when Mitterrand came to power in May 1981, the whole of the Western world was already in recession. In the US, interest rates neared 20 per cent, forcing other countries to follow suit to maintain the value of their currencies against the dollar, and unemployment reached the highest level since the Great Depression. In Britain, where three million were jobless and inflation peaked at 22 per cent, that summer saw the worst inner-city riots since 1919.

France was less hard hit: unemployment at the end of 1981 stood at 1.8 million and inflation remained in line with the peak US figure of 13.5 per cent. Nonetheless, pursuing expansion at a time when the rest of the industrialised world was committed to deflation, as Mitterrand did in 1981 and the first half of 1982, was economic madness. Pierre Mauroy admitted as much years later: 'We had all our canvas up, sailing alone with a following wind, while our competitors had their mainsails down and were reefing the rest.' At Ottawa and Versailles, Mitterrand tried to persuade his G7 colleagues that their insistence on deflation was doing more harm than good. 'High interest rates are not the only answer,' he told Reagan. 'There is a level of unemployment beyond which the risk of a social explosion exceeds the risks posed by inflation. [The United States] must understand that [its policies] are weakening us and in so doing it is creating political and military dangers'. Reagan turned a deaf ear. He was right. Mitterrand was wrong. Mastering inflation was the indispensable precondition for recovery.

The new French President was not blind to the difficulties. He had told Jacques Attali soon after his election: 'There will be three stages: implementing the programme of reforms; then a long and difficult period of managing the crisis; and finally, we will emerge successfully from the tunnel.'

But his strategy was predicated on having two years of consumer-fuelled growth 'to change life', as the Socialist Party programme put it, before recovery would kick in and the government could put on the brakes to stop the economy overheating. It was wishful thinking. The upturn in the US did not come until the winter of 1982 and most of Europe remained mired in recession for several years longer.

Had Mitterrand been an economist, he would have seen the danger signs sooner. Instead, in a long tradition of left-wing utopianism, not limited to France, he insisted that 'by creating confidence, [political will] can modify the behaviour of economic actors'.[42] 'You can do what you like with the economy,' he maintained. 'Statesmen don't need to be economists. They just have to know how to carry the people with them.' It was un-Marxist and unreasoning, but in the halcyon months of 1981, most of the French Socialist Party thought the same way.

Reagan was no economist either, but at least he had the good sense to do what his advisers told him. Mitterrand did not. His Prime Minister, Pierre Mauroy, was no more an economist than he was, but he was a solid northerner and had his feet on the ground. Although he never opposed the President publicly, he made no secret of his reservations in private. 'We've got off to a very bad start,' he said two months after Mitterrand's election. 'If it goes on like this, we'll end up with them throwing rotten tomatoes at us as we leave.'

The few who understood clearly the gravity of the crisis were either, like Jacques Delors and Michel Rocard, not in the President's camp – which meant that he preferred not to listen to them – or, like Delors's deputy, Laurent Fabius, so determined to keep Mitterrand's favour that they backed his policies regardless. In November that year, when Delors called for a 'pause' in the reforms, Mitterrand was furious and insisted that he retract. Rocard blamed himself later for not having spoken out more strongly. 'Mitterrand,' he wrote, was 'purely political, allergic to economic and financial arguments. [He] believed that everything depended on pulling strings and political will. [It was] lunacy!'

The recession, deeper and more enduring than had been predicted by the optimistic forecasts both of French government analysts and of the OECD (Organisation for Economic Cooperation and Development), was the main cause of the failure of Mitterrand's economic programme.

But there was also a second problem.

The French Socialists were living in a time warp.

The Left had not held power in France since 1936. Elsewhere in Western Europe – in Belgium, Britain, West Germany, Italy and the Scandinavian countries – left-wing governments had spent decades experimenting with social policy, discovering what worked and what did not. Nationalisation had been a socialist buzzword from 1945 until the 1960s. But since then its attractions had palled. Governments had proved on the whole to be less efficient managers than their private-sector counterparts.

The seemingly naïve questions of White House officials like Richard Allen and Ed Meese, who likened Mitterrand's nationalisations to those in a communist system, were not quite as dumb as they sounded. Not only was France's economic strategy in 1981 taken almost word for word from the Common Programme, which the Socialists had worked out with the Communists nine years earlier, with no allowance for the two Oil Shocks and all the other economic changes that had occurred in between, but one of its guiding principles – state ownership of the means of production – was a holdover from the nineteenth century which was irrelevant to the conditions of Western Europe a hundred years later.

The same was true of lowering the retirement age and shortening the working week as a means of job creation. This assumed that there was a limited amount of work to go round and that dividing it up into smaller portions would mean that more workers could be employed. It was a seductive theory, but wherever it had been attempted on a large scale – mainly in the communist bloc – it had led to massive inefficiencies.

Mitterrand's programme was not merely archaic, as Michel Rocard had complained. It was an anachronism.

Even those parts which did work had a downside. The recruitment of more civil servants certainly helped to slow the rise of unemployment. But paying for them widened the budget deficit and dragged down the rest of the economy. The same applied to the decision to grant residence to illegal immigrants. It was compassionate and generous. But it encouraged a flood of new arrivals hoping that they, too, might benefit from the government's largesse.

The core policy of the new programme – raising incomes to spark a consumer-led boom – also failed. French manufacturers, wary of the Left's policies, were reluctant to increase production.[43] Accordingly more than half the extra money that the government put in people's pockets was spent on imports, mainly automobiles, household goods and electronics, from West Germany, Italy and Japan, thereby doubling France's trade deficit.

Since the Left was convinced that its policies could not be wrong, the problems had to be the result of deliberate sabotage by its opponents.

Mitterrand set the tone, grumbling that the government was too slow to remove right-wing officials who 'keep throwing up roadblocks'. Paul Quilès, one of his 'sabras', declared, paraphrasing Robespierre, that it was 'not a matter of saying that heads should fall, but of saying which ones, and quickly'. Another party stalwart, André Laignel, declared that the Right was 'juridically wrong because politically [they are] in a minority'.

Mauroy was furious. 'These people are doing everything in their power to make the public panic,' he raged. 'If they were trying to make us fail, they wouldn't behave differently.'

But countries, like people, learn from their own mistakes, not from those of others. The French Socialists had to absorb in months knowledge which their neighbours had accumulated over decades. Moreover, as even Delors later admitted, Mitterrand had little choice but to pursue the policies for which he had been elected.[44] Amid the elation which followed his victory, it would have been politically suicidal for the first authentically left-wing government to hold power in France for forty-five years to launch its term in office by embracing the principles of the Right. It was more than just a case of making the best of what could not be helped. Mitterrand really did believe – or wanted to believe – that, given sufficient political will, France could triumph over economic reality. The learning curve was painful and steep. It was a very bruising first twelve months.

By the summer of 1982, every economic indicator was flashing red.

Mitterrand postponed a policy decision lest it detract from that year's G7 summit, which he hosted in the opulent surroundings of Louis XIV's palace at Versailles, a setting that conveyed the image, and the memory, of the greatness of France and flattered his sense of history. But once his fellow leaders had departed, the day of reckoning could no longer be put off. On Wednesday June 9, Mitterrand gave a news conference at the Elysée, the second of his presidency, at which he revealed, in terms so elliptical that few of those present realised the significance of what he was saying, that change was in the air. The word 'unemployment' did not pass his lips, an implicit admission that for the moment that battle had been lost. He spoke instead of the deteriorating global economy, acknowledging that it had 'taken [the government] time to coordinate, to grasp the

objectives, to harmonise [its policies] and to attack the most urgent
tasks'. Using the analogy of a cycle race, he declared that the first
phase was now over and the second was about to begin.

> [In] the Tour de France, when [the teams] start the second stage, they
> are still heading for the same goal as in the first stage, that is, towards
> victory . . . even if, to get there, there is a change in the nature of the
> stages as they go from one to another. At one point, they are in the
> plains . . . At another, in the mountains. But it doesn't alter the fact
> that the goal remains the same.[45]

To those able to decode the metaphor, it meant that the months of
plenty were over. France was heading into difficult times which would
require much greater efforts from all segments of society. The illusion
of a consumer-led boom was abandoned. In its place would come a
new emphasis on balancing the budget, fighting inflation, restructuring
and modernising industry, investing and innovating.

That weekend the franc was devalued by 9.75 per cent against the
Deutschmark, which, in the wake of an earlier devaluation of 8.5 per
cent the previous October, meant that it had lost almost a fifth of its
value against the West German currency in nine months. On Sunday,
Mitterrand chaired a Cabinet committee at the Elysée which approved
the accompanying austerity programme: a four-month price and wage
freeze; a cap on the budget deficit at 3 per cent of GNP; and a commitment to bring inflation below 8 per cent in 1983. Two years after the
United States, newly socialist France had joined the rest of the industrialised world in a forced deflationary spiral to get its economy back
into balance.

The government did not admit that there had been a change in
direction. The word 'austerity' was taboo. The Left insisted that its
role was to redistribute wealth more equitably even if the national
cake was meagre – redistributing penury, as Mauroy wistfully put it.[46]
Officially the strategy was unaltered; only the tactics were different.

In private, however, the Cabinet was divided.

The left wing of the Socialist Party, represented by Jean-Pierre
Chevènement, supported by the Communists, wanted France to go
it alone, abandoning the exchange-rate limits of the European
Monetary System (EMS), which allowed European currencies to

fluctuate narrowly against each other while jointly floating against the US dollar but in return required governments to act together when the system came under strain. Released from the constraints of the EMS, Chevènement argued, the franc could float freely – as sterling did, Britain at that time having declined to join the exchange rate mechanism – and the government, no longer obliged to keep looking over its shoulder at the reactions of its European partners, would be able to continue the expansionist economic policies and accompanying social reforms for which Mitterrand had been elected.

Mauroy and Delors were adamantly opposed, arguing that if France left the EMS, the franc would go through the floor and the government would be forced to go, cap in hand, to the IMF for a bail-out, as the Labour government had in Britain six years earlier.

Mitterrand equivocated. When the Cabinet met the following week, he gave both sides reason to hope. He accused America of behaving with its usual 'holier-than-thou egoism' and ganging up with the other 'big capitalist countries' to try to prove that France could not do without them. That was music to the ears of Chevènement and his Communist allies. On the other hand, he said, the French Left had accepted the principle of a free-market economy and it had to live with the consequences, which pleased Mauroy and Delors. Only if the price-and-wage freeze failed, he concluded, might it be necessary to contemplate 'a third phase, which could lead us to leave the EMS'.

This last remark was a way to put pressure on Mauroy to ensure that the freeze succeeded. It was also designed to show that the policy was not set in concrete. If it did not work, there was an alternative.

Mitterrand had two irons in the fire and for the next few months he intended to keep it that way. Apart from economic considerations, he had a political reason to delay: town council elections, the first national test of opinion since 1981, were due the following March. A major change of economic policy – whether by tightening the screws of the austerity programme or leaving the EMS – would be risky before that hurdle had been cleared.

Hurrying slowly suited him in other ways. On topics that he understood well – foreign affairs, defence, cultural and social policy – he could weigh up the advice he was given, discard what he disliked and integrate the essentials. On economic matters it was different. He understood the choices being offered to him but he lacked the intimate command of financial and economic grammar that would enable him to arbitrate instinctively as he did in other fields. The result was that he faced a critical choice – whether to stay in the EMS or to leave it; whether to confirm France's leading role in Europe or to strike out alone – in a domain in which he was reliant on the judgements of others.[47]

Mitterrand hated being dependent. His inclination was to hold back until, through sheer weariness, a solution imposed itself.

In any case the experts disagreed among themselves. Jacques Attali organised a lunch for France's leading economists in Mitterrand's private apartments at the Elysée. 'It was bedlam,' he said later. 'Everyone had a different opinion. No two of them said the same thing.'

The captains of French industry were no better. François Dalle, now head of l'Oréal, pleaded with Mitterrand to stay in the EMS. Jean Riboud, of Schlumberger, another friend of thirty years' standing, championed the opposing view. The 'evening visitors', as Mauroy baptised Riboud's group, argued that if the franc were allowed to float, the French economy would recover its dynamism, productivity would increase and the country would 'produce more and produce better', in Chevènement's phrase, creating a virtuous circle in which inflation and unemployment would both fall. Mitterrand was intrigued. Riboud was a larger-than-life character, one of the world's most highly paid capitalists, on good terms with the Communists (whose network had helped him survive the horrors of Buchenwald) and a noted patron of contemporary art. He was the inspiration for a speech Mitterrand gave in September 1982 at Figeac, in south-west France, attacking 'the growth of the tax burden, high interest rates and over-indebtedness' for French companies, the first time that anyone on the Left had spoken publicly in such terms.

While the 'visitors' pulled one way, Mauroy pulled the other. Mitterrand hesitated.

The government massaged the unemployment figures to try to keep them below the symbolic figure of two million.[48] The indexing of wages to price rises, introduced under Giscard, was rescinded, and by the beginning of 1983, inflation had been brought below 10 per cent. Mauroy was able to claim success. But it was clear it could not last. The trade deficit continued to widen. New measures were inevitable. Mitterrand's dilemma was unchanged. To stay in the EMS and in Europe? Or to head into uncharted waters?

*

On Sunday, March 6 1983, Helmut Kohl's Christian Democrats and their allies won a resounding victory in the West German parliamentary elections. A week later, in the French municipal elections, the Socialists lost thirty-one towns of more than 30,000 inhabitants and gained only one, Châtellerault, midway between Paris and Bordeaux, where Édith Cresson became mayor. Mitterrand had feared worse. Left-wing voters were disenchanted with the wage freeze and rising unemployment. It was a shot across the government's bows – 'a narrow escape', as he told the Cabinet – but nothing comparable to the debacle that the Right had suffered in 1977, when it had lost control of fifty-five large towns. Back on political terrain, Mitterrand steeled himself to act.

The next ten days were the most critical and among the most criticised of his fourteen years in power.

He knew that the franc would have to be devalued against the Deutschmark yet again – for the third time in eighteen months. But should it be done within the EMS? Or outside?

The stakes were huge.

It is always difficult, and usually pointless, to speculate on where History might have led had it taken another course. But if a different choice had prevailed in Paris in March 1983, the Maastricht Treaty, engineered by Kohl and Mitterrand, would almost certainly not have been signed. The common currency, the euro, willed as an instrument of convergence between European states, would probably never have been launched.[49]

Mitterrand's actions that week were more coherent than his adversaries gave him credit for, but with a larger part of improvisation than he would afterwards admit. Since he had no way to assess independently the validity of the conflicting economic theses, he approached it the way he knew best: by ramping up the political pressure on the different protagonists.[50]

On the morning of Monday, March 14, Mitterrand told Pierre Mauroy he had decided that France should leave the EMS. He asked him 'to stay on at Matignon at least to get the new policy started'. Mauroy refused. 'I don't agree,' he told the President. 'Leaving the EMS would be a catastrophe.' Mitterrand asked him to think it over. That evening, when Mauroy returned with a letter of resignation in his pocket, he told Mitterrand that he was sticking to his position.

'Your policies are courageous and you are courageous,' the President replied. 'But it is costing us dear politically. I will see. Do your job as Prime Minister. Let us not talk of resignation.'

The following afternoon, Mitterrand sounded out Delors. Would the Finance Minister accept the post of Prime Minister if France left the EMS? Delors, like Mauroy, declined.

On Wednesday, Mitterrand asked Fabius, who had been urging him to leave the EMS, to think through what he would do if he replaced Delors. At Attali's suggestion, Fabius called in the Permanent Secretary to the Treasury, Michel Camdessus, who, as Attali had anticipated, spelt out for him the effects of leaving the exchange rate mechanism: the franc would lose at least 20 per cent of its value against other currencies, and since the country's reserves were exhausted, the only way to defend it would be to raise interest rates to unheard-of levels, which would starve industry of credit and asphyxiate investment.

'I saw Fabius suddenly change colour,' Camdessus wrote later. 'He had not realised all the consequences of abruptly uncoupling the franc.' The young minister went back to Mitterrand and told him he had changed his mind. Leaving the EMS would mean more austerity, not less, and would make the modernisation of French industry impossible.

Within the Cabinet that left only one holdout. Pierre Bérégovoy, who had left the Elysée the previous autumn to become Minister of Social Affairs, continued to believe that France would do better outside the EMS.*

On Thursday, Mitterrand asked him to 'form a government' on the basis of France remaining in the EMS. In French, the expression is ambiguous: it could mean either, 'draw up a list of ministers' or 'prepare to lead a new government'. Bérégovoy set to work.

The conclusion cried out. Those who opposed leaving the EMS – Mauroy and Delors – were willing to put their jobs on the line; those who had been in favour – Bérégovoy and Fabius – were not.

Yet still Mitterrand refused to commit himself.

This was his 'de Gaulle moment'. Where the General had been called back to power in 1958 with a mandate to keep Algeria French, only to

---

* The Industry Minister, Jean-Pierre Chevènement, who had been the strongest advocate within the government of leaving the EMS, had resigned some weeks earlier in a fit of pique after Mitterrand had rapped him over the knuckles for taking too Stalinist a view of his ministerial functions.

be forced to bow before the wind of decolonisation and grant Algeria independence, so Mitterrand, having been elected to reject the liberal economic model, found himself forced to do the opposite because of the economic blizzard blowing in the rest of the industrialised world.

He hated it. French sovereignty was being flouted and his own freedom of action reduced to nothing. He knew now that remaining within the EMS was the only reasonable choice. But he was not ready to lock himself into a policy on such a crucial issue until he was convinced that every alternative was ruled out.

This was the time when Jean Riboud said of him: 'He is so afraid that someone may read in his face what he has decided that he hesitates to admit even to himself what he is really thinking.'

However actions speak louder than words, and words are louder than thoughts.

In Brussels that weekend, the EEC finance ministers met in emergency session to deal with yet another crisis over the exchange rate of the franc. For France's partners, the game had gone on long enough. The consensus was that Mitterrand was bluffing. If France was really set on leaving the EMS, why negotiate at all? The best Delors could get was an 8 per cent devaluation, with the West Germans doing most of the heavy lifting by revaluing the mark, but on condition that France undertook not to erect trade barriers against other EEC members and that the austerity programme was intensified. Mitterrand raged at being dictated to. But that was the choice he had made. If France wanted to stay in the EMS, it had to align itself with the policies of its EEC partners.

It was a political more than an economic decision. To Mitterrand, France's fate lay with Europe. Whatever else was at stake, he would do nothing which might dilute French influence on the continent's political future.

One piece of unfinished business remained, trivial by comparison with the strategic drama of the previous week, but important nonetheless. Who would be Prime Minister? Four days earlier, Mitterrand had offered the post to Delors. Then he had allowed Bérégovoy to believe that he had been offered it too, while sending multiple signals to Mauroy that he would be asked to stay on.

Throughout Monday, March 21, and most of the following day, the

President pondered. Finally, after lunch on Tuesday, he asked Delors to head the new government. But on one condition: he would have to accept Fabius as Finance Minister. Delors jibbed. If he were at Matignon, he explained, he would need a completely free hand in economic policy. It was 'a crime of *lèse-constitution*,' Delors acknowledged afterwards. 'In the Fifth Republic, you don't dictate conditions to the President.' Mitterrand 'was very angry [but] he controlled himself and we left it at that. I quit the Elysée feeling that I hadn't handled it very well.' Some thought Mitterrand had been miffed at Delors's hostility to Fabius, whom the President regarded as a protégé and in whom he had great hopes for the future. But it was more complicated than that. To the Socialist Party and, still more, to the Communists, Delors was an outsider. With Fabius and Bérégovoy to keep him in check, his nomination would be grudgingly accepted. If he did not want to act as a team player, the appointment did not make sense.

Bérégovoy had never been a serious candidate and Mitterrand let him down gently: he would stay on as Social Affairs Minister, ranking third in the government.

Mauroy, who by then was so convinced that he would be replaced that he had already called in movers to start packing up his files, arrived at the Elysée shortly before 7 p.m., resignation letter again in hand, to be told that he would continue as Prime Minister. Delors was left at Finance. He preceded Bérégovoy in the hierarchy and, by way of consolation, Mitterrand got Fabius off his back by appointing the younger man Minister of Industry. The new government, whose make-up was announced just before midnight, was half the size of the old with 15 Cabinet members instead of 34. Michel Jobert, the regime's solitary Gaullist, was replaced by Édith Cresson, rewarded for her victory at Châtellerault.

Three days later, on Friday, March 25, Mitterrand chaired an emergency Cabinet meeting to approve the austerity programme that Delors and his colleagues had drawn up.

The plan was unprecedented. In 1981, the Left had pumped into the economy the equivalent of 1 per cent of GNP. Now, less than two years later, it would claw back twice that much. Altogether 65 billion francs (£6.5 billion, or US $10 billion) of government and household spending was to be amputated in 1983. Exchange controls were brought in; income tax raised; new taxes imposed on alcohol and tobacco;

hospital charges increased; savings not only encouraged but for most taxpayers made obligatory through government loans to which they were compelled to subscribe; and the budget deficit sharply reduced. Still worse was to come. In 1984, taxes increased by a further 8 per cent, government spending by 2 per cent less, the harshest dose of deflation the French had had to endure for almost forty years.

The change of policy initiated in June 1982 and confirmed nine months later was a disavowal of everything Mitterrand had stood for since he had become First Secretary of the Socialist Party more than a decade earlier. His wife, Danielle, spoke for the Party's core when she said long after: 'He was happy, those first two years. Because he could do what he wanted to do. But afterwards? Afterwards he had to act like all the rest.' There was some truth in that. He confided to a friend:

> You remember what they called 'the honeymoon period' in 1981. That was an extraordinary moment. I could do anything . . . I am not saying I was tempted, but still, I sometimes thought of it, a utopia like that. I saw myself shaking up the country . . . Robespierre . . . Lenin . . . Towards a kind of collectivism . . . I would have left my mark on history, I would have got France moving for four years . . . I would have nationalised everything. Why not! [But] I know why I did not do it. You can guess . . .[51]

He did not do it because he was not Robespierre or Lenin. In a country with a defiantly revolutionary tradition, he had known that it was essential to act fast, to wage 'a frontal combat against capitalism', as Louis Mermaz put it, 'to make the world of money submit to our will'. But Mitterrand was not a revolutionary. Intellectually the idea attracted him but he had never been ready to tear down the existing order and replace it with something new. His goal was more modest: to improve society as it was.

From the summer of 1983 Mitterrand's overriding aim was to get France back on its feet so that it could compete on equal terms with its European partners. It saddened him that his initial strategy had failed, not just because of the political consequences but because he felt that it had been morally right. However, he was willing to reinvent himself and meet a new set of challenges.

The transition was painful. In the autumn of 1982, after one of Mauroy's aides had called for the austerity plan to be reinforced, he had told the Prime Minister icily: 'I did not appoint you to carry out the policies of Mrs Thatcher. And if, for some extraordinary reason, I intended to follow in her footsteps, I would not choose you to do so.'

Yet that was exactly what he had done. Not only was he following Thatcherite prescriptions for returning the economy to health but he had maintained Mauroy in his post to enforce them.

The decision to keep the same Prime Minister turned out to be a boon. Had he appointed Delors, it would have signalled much more strongly that the government was changing course. Mauroy's presence emphasised continuity and made it easier for the Socialists, not to mention the Communists, to swallow what for most of them was a very bitter pill.

For the second austerity plan, in March 1983, as for the first, nine months earlier, the Socialist Party maintained that the direction of policy was unaltered, even if, to use Mitterrand's Tour de France analogy, the stage through the mountains was now full of hairpin bends. It was a hard sell and provoked some noteworthy verbal contortions. Mermaz spoke in terms of 'a respite', Mauroy of 'a period of management', Jospin of 'a parenthesis'. It was not very honest but it helped the Left through a seriously bad patch. 'For us,' Jospin explained, 'it was a way to accept what had happened, albeit with great difficulty, without denying it outright and without criticising the government.'

At public meetings, Mitterrand reminded his supporters that the key reforms of the first year – the 39-hour week; retirement at 60; the fifth week of paid holiday; the rise in the minimum wage – had all been left untouched. In private he insisted that, even if France had been forced to capitulate to the free-market norms of its partners, the government would continue to promote social justice and to protect those who were most vulnerable. When Delors wanted an across-the-board increase in Social Security charges, Mitterrand instructed Mauroy instead to impose a surtax on the incomes of the rich.

Margaret Thatcher was scandalised. Danielle remembered her husband returning from an Anglo-French summit chuckling over her latest advice. 'But what are you thinking of, François, doing something like that?' she had asked him. 'There aren't enough rich people to be worth it. Tax the poor instead! At least there are plenty of them.'

The story may have been embellished in the telling. But it summed up well enough the distance Mitterrand sought to maintain between his image – if not the reality of his policies – and that of the Iron Lady across the Channel. 'If we follow Britain, the US and Germany,' he warned the Cabinet, 'we may have an effect on the indices, but we will lose our majority.'

That was a real concern. Already Alain Krivine and others on the far Left were accusing the government of 'making those who are the victims of the crisis pay for it'. Parliamentary elections were still three years away. But Mitterrand's popularity had been hard hit by what was perceived as his indecisiveness, not just during the crucial ten days when France's future in the EMS and, with it, the future of the government, had been hanging in the balance, but over the whole of the previous year, when the country seemed to be rudderless and people were asking themselves, 'Is there a pilot in the plane?'

Only after it became clear in June 1983 that Delors's strategy would succeed did he finally throw his weight behind it. 'Suddenly nothing could stop him,' wrote Serge July, the influential editor of the left-wing daily, Libération. 'The word [austerity] used to burn his lips. [Now] he shouts it from the rooftops, like an adoptive father proudly brandishing his new progeny.'

Strikes broke out as the trades unions found themselves torn between the need for political solidarity with the Left and the growing anger of their members. But, as even some on the Right acknowledged, there was less unrest than there might have been given the brutality of the 180-degree turn the government had undertaken.[52] That summer, for the first time, Mitterrand conceded publicly that he had made mistakes in his handling of the economy. When he took office, he said, he should have devalued at once (as Delors and Rocard had urged). 'But I was carried away by victory. It went to our heads. We underestimated the length of the international crisis [and] overestimated the goodwill of the Americans', a reference to Reagan's refusal to lower US interest rates.

Mitterrand had been converted. He spoke with the zeal of a born-again Christian about the need for modernisation, the conversion of the rust-belt industries, the necessity for profit and – echoing Deng Xiaoping in China, whom he had visited in Beijing in May and who had recently presided over a similar sea change in left-wing ideology –

the right to become rich, 'provided it is by personal effort, [not] by speculation'. There was no more talk of 'a rupture with capitalism' and still less of 'class struggle having a second youth'. Now he insisted that class struggle was not the Socialist Party's objective: the reason he wanted more social justice was in order that it should cease.

Speaking on television that autumn he declared that the tax burden, which had increased by almost 1 per cent a year since Giscard's arrival in power in 1974, had become intolerable. In the next budget, it would be reduced by 80 billion francs (£8 billion, or US $10 billion). In the event, the reduction was not fully achieved. But at least it stopped increasing.[53]

The decision to put a cap on taxation, although it made good economic sense, was as much political as economic. Mitterrand needed to win back the middle-class electorate which had helped him to victory in 1981. He revealed the key to his thinking at a Cabinet meeting six weeks after the second austerity plan was approved. 'The economic measures we have taken,' he said, 'are neither right-wing nor left-wing. They are an attempt to spare – not as much as we should – the categories that are most disadvantaged . . . There's no reason to feel guilty. If we had not started out by [trying to give] more [social] justice, who would be our audience today?'

Social justice, not socialism, was once more the guiding star. After seventeen years, from the winter of 1965 to mid-1983, spent riding a wave of left-wing rhetoric, Mitterrand had returned to his roots. The ideological garb he had assumed to win power had at last been sloughed off. It had never been a good fit. Part of him regretted the lost illusions. Part of him was glad to be rid of them.

12

The Sphinx

By the winter of 1983, Mitterrand had taken the two strategic decisions – supporting the deployment of Euromissiles and remaining in the EMS – which together would determine the course of the next stage of his presidency.

Relations with the two superpowers, the United States and the Soviet Union, had stabilised. In the Middle East, the 'complicated Orient', France had been forced to recognise the limits of its power. At home, the wave of terrorism appeared to have subsided. The country was entering the second frame of the triptych which Mitterrand had imagined when he came to power, the 'long and difficult period of managing the crisis' that was to end, or so he hoped, with the Left emerging successfully from austerity to triumph in the parliamentary elections due in 1986. It was the midpoint of the legislature elected in a left-wing landslide two and a half years before – a time for taking stock and reflecting on what remained to be done.

The first task, dictated by the political calendar, was to try to break the logjam in Europe, where a dispute over Britain's budget contribution was blocking progress on everything else. On January 1 1984, France took over for six months the rotating EEC presidency.

Mitterrand, like Pompidou before him, had initially hoped to engineer a balance between Britain and West Germany which would allow France to advance its European agenda by playing off one against the other. To that end he had gone out of his way to cultivate Margaret Thatcher. In the first months he was in office, to the dismay of most of the French Left, he had remained silent, in public at least, about the deaths of ten Irish Republican hunger strikers near Belfast. The following year France was the first Western country to declare unconditional support for Britain in the Falklands conflict, a position all the more striking in view of Mitterrand's recent championing of the rights of developing nations at Cancun.

In the latter case it was not just a matter of showing that the French, in times of trouble, were Britain's most reliable allies, in contrast to the embarrassed hesitations of the Reagan administration, which, mindful of its ties with the military dictatorships of Latin America, tried unsuccessfully to broker a compromise with Argentina before reluctantly agreeing to back the British position. It was a way to put down a marker. France, too, had a confetti of empire scattered around the globe. What Argentina was attempting in the Falklands, others might do to French possessions like Mayotte or Réunion, in the Indian Ocean, or Clipperton Island in the Pacific off the coast of Mexico. Would-be predators needed to know that, were that to happen, France would react as Britain had done.

The morning after the invasion, Mitterrand telephoned Thatcher to assure her of his support. His call was totally unexpected. 'I shall never forget,' she said later, 'that quick, timely and energetic gesture.' Like other EEC nations, France refused to break diplomatic relations with Buenos Aires or to take a position on the islands' sovereignty. But short of that the French President did everything in his power to help. At Thatcher's request, he delayed a shipment of Exocet air-to-sea missiles to Peru lest they find their way to the Argentinians and, after an Exocet had disabled a British destroyer, HMS *Sheffield*, he ordered that the British be given details of the missiles' radar guidance codes. A French squadron of Super Etendards, an aircraft then in service with the Argentine air force, was flown to RAF Wyton near Cambridge to enable British pilots to familiarise themselves with the plane's characteristics.

At a personal level Mitterrand and Thatcher were an odd couple. She was single-minded and obdurate, with no place in her vocabulary for ambiguity, nuance or compromise. He was in every way the opposite. Yet they managed to strike up a rapport. Attali thought it was because Mitterrand was intrigued by her as a woman, not just as a fellow leader. Anne Lauvergeon, who was later his deputy Chief of Staff, offered a different perspective: 'He was one of the few in Europe who treated her as an equal. She appreciated that.'

Thatcher spoke passable French, but with a strong accent which made Mitterrand say: 'If you close your eyes, you could think she's

Jane Birkin.'* Not to be outdone, he would trot out his few words of English, which had not noticeably progressed since his homestays as a thirteen-year-old in Kent.

He respected her. She liked him. 'She has the eyes of Caligula,' he mused on the way back from one visit to London, 'and the mouth of Marilyn Monroe.'[1]

From the outset Thatcher made clear that there were two major problems she wanted resolved. The first was to put a cap on the Common Agricultural Policy, which guaranteed farmers minimum prices for their produce and absorbed 75 per cent of the EEC budget. It mainly benefited France and, to a lesser extent, Italy and West Germany, while Britain got little back because it had too few farmers to profit from it. Moreover the guarantees were leading to massive overproduction. 'It's a matter of common sense,' she told Mitterrand the first time they met. 'It's not rational to spend a growing part of the community budget on surpluses that cost more and more.'

The second problem, she argued, was that Britain, as a net contributor, was paying more than its fair share. To correct that, she wanted a permanent rebate. The issue was not new. But nor was it as simple as she liked to make out. One of the reasons Britain regarded its contribution as excessive was that, for historical reasons, much of its trade was with countries outside Europe. Accordingly the customs duties it levied on non-EEC goods, which it forwarded to Brussels, were larger than those of its partners. Thatcher insisted that these payments were part of Britain's contribution. None of the other member states counted them that way. In 1980, the year after her election, she had obtained a provisional two-year rebate, which was subsequently extended, amounting to almost two-thirds of the British payment.[2] But a permanent settlement had eluded her.

In January 1984, Mitterrand received Thatcher in Paris.

To his dismay she insisted on reopening the negotiation from scratch, rather than building on the provisional accord reached three and a half years earlier. The reason soon became clear. In 1983, she had accepted a much lower payment, only 750 million euros, compared

---

* The British singer and actress who, with Serge Gainsbourg, was responsible for one of the iconic love songs of the 1960s, 'Je t'aime, moi non plus,' whose lyrics were thought to be so suggestive that it was banned by the BBC and radio stations in Spain, Switzerland and other European countries.

to 1.175 billion in 1980.[3] But the difference, some 400 million, had been more than made up for by overpayments from Brussels, made in the previous three years, which she now refused to return.

At the next EEC summit, held under Mitterrand's chairmanship in March 1984, Britain was offered a rebate of one billion euros a year, guaranteed for five years. Thatcher refused. Would she accept, she was asked, if the figure was raised to 1.1 billion? Again she refused. The minimum she would accept was 1.3 billion.

It was one refusal too many. Britain's partners lost patience. Mitterrand wondered aloud whether the British should have a place in the Community at all.[4] He was not alone. Kohl had asked Thatcher: 'Margaret, how do you think Churchill and Adenauer would behave if they were in our place?' She was unmoved. This was the period, one official recalled, when 'the only time she said "yes" was when she was asked, "Are you against it?"'

Two months later, Mitterrand and Kohl met in Paris to plot their strategy. Mitterrand wanted to limit the rebate to one billion. Kohl thought they would have to offer 1.1 billion:

KOHL: [Thatcher] understands that she will have to give way, but she doesn't want to admit it. She has talked too much about it in parliament . . . She's terribly afraid that if she does [accept a lower figure] it will be seen as an admission that she got it wrong.

MITTERRAND: Maybe . . . We'll have to find a way to dress it up, to create an appearance [of success for her]. [But] 1.1 billion is too much. The problem with her is that she always takes a compromise proposal as a new starting point . . . She thinks she's at Trafalgar. In [March] she behaved like a child who wanted two spoonfuls of jam on her bread and was told she couldn't have them.

KOHL: What a waste of energy on this British problem! Together we have to find a way to prevent it continuing.[5]

At the end of May, the 'Ten' reconvened in the former royal palace at Fontainebleau, where in 1814 Napoleon had been forced to abdicate by a coalition of his European opponents, a year before his final defeat by Britain and Prussia at Waterloo.

This time, Mitterrand felt, the shoe was on the other foot. In great secrecy, Roland Dumas, whom Mitterrand had appointed Minister of

European Affairs, and his German counterpart, Hans-Dietrich Genscher, had worked out a plan under which, if Thatcher continued to refuse a settlement, the other nine would continue to operate the Common Agricultural Policy and other key EEC programmes without her.[6] The idea was to sideline the Community institutions in Brussels by creating a web of intergovernmental agreements from which Britain would be excluded. It would then find itself a member of an EEC which had been reduced to an empty shell. Whether countries like Denmark, Ireland and the Netherlands would in practice have gone along with such a radical solution is uncertain. But it offered a theoretical alternative if she dug in her heels.

Thatcher had stated publicly that she wanted a rebate of 1.2 billion euros that year, 1.25 billion in 1985, and 90 per cent of what she called the 'excess' in Britain's payments thereafter. Over dinner, on the opening day, Mitterrand offered one billion for the first two years and 60 per cent thereafter.

Foreign Secretary Geoffrey Howe described their respective negotiating tactics: 'my approach is rather like a police line – it's flexible, when the crowd pushes in one place the line gives way a bit, elsewhere it moves forward, but it never breaks. The Prime Minister builds a brick wall. It resists. The disadvantage is that if her position becomes untenable, she ends up having to knock it down.'[7]

That was what happened. Next morning Mitterrand made his final offer: one billion euros for two years, then 65 per cent. After lunch, she had a private meeting with Kohl, who confirmed West Germany's support for the French position. Then Mitterrand, also privately, told her the offer was 'to take or to leave'. Attali wrote afterwards that she 'cracked like glass, on the verge of tears. She just wanted to get it over with . . . An astonishing sight!' At the plenary session that afternoon, Britain's partners agreed to make it 66 per cent, rather than 65. It was significantly less than she had turned down in March but it enabled her to claim that she had achieved a two-thirds reduction.

Mitterrand kept his word. The deal was dressed up as a British success and the Iron Lady was able to return to London in triumph.[8] But a few days later he told Henry Kissinger: 'She only speaks in figures. She has a strong personality, but not much in the way of long-term views [and] she's not used to meeting resistance . . . She won't always find herself facing the Argentinians or the Labour Party.'

The importance of Fontainebleau, however, lay elsewhere.

After almost a decade in which the European Community had marked time, haggling over milk quotas, the wine lake, the butter mountain and fishing rights, the resolution of the dispute over the British rebate opened the way to progress on a host of other issues.

The summit agreed to increase the Community's budget by raising the levy on Value Added Tax from one to 1.4 per cent. It approved the entry of Spain and Portugal, which had been hanging fire since 1977. The first serious measures were taken to rationalise spending on agriculture. More important for the long term, two working groups were created, one of which laid the foundations for the Single European Act, signed in February 1986, paving the way for European Union, while the other produced proposals to make Europe more relevant to its citizens. Between them they would lead, within two years, to improvements in the single market; the lifting of internal border controls under the Schengen Agreement; enhanced political cooperation; the Erasmus programme for exchanges among European universities; a larger role for the European Parliament; and a uniform European passport.

The floodgates had opened. Despite difficult economic conditions in almost all the member states, they had come to a collective recognition that they would do better together than each one by itself. It was the start of a period of political and economic change on a scale not seen in Europe since the end of the Second World War.

The Fontainebleau summit succeeded because of the entente between Mitterrand and Helmut Kohl. It was their decision over breakfast in the Hôtel de l'Aigle Noir, an eighteenth-century hostelry opposite the palace grounds, to rebuff Margaret Thatcher's efforts to obtain a rebate in excess of 65 per cent that had made agreement possible. Mitterrand had established his bona fides in the eyes of the West German Chancellor with his speech to the Bundestag, eighteen months before, backing Kohl's decision to install Euromissiles on German soil. But their understanding had begun earlier. Three days after Kohl's election, in October 1982, he had flown to Paris to assure Mitterrand of the importance he attached to the Franco-German relationship. Part of their conversation had been about the war. Kohl had been 15 in 1945, Mitterrand, 28. Both were from a generation whose commitment to Europe was founded on memories of carnage. At one point, Kohl had told him:

> I would like to talk to you very openly, as a younger man to someone older whom he trusts. You are a man steeped in history and literature. I am too . . . I want to tell you something. My grandfather had a son who died in the War of '14 . . . My father named his elder son after [him]. That son died in turn in the war in '45. My own son has the same name as my [dead] brother. He's now starting his military service. He knows very well the meaning of freedom. We want to meet the challenge which consists of having both freedom and peace.[9]

It was a language Mitterrand understood. But until Fontainebleau he had worried that Kohl might switch his support to Britain, with which he had a common interest because West Germany was also a net contributor to the Community budget. That had not happened.

Helmut Kohl was a massive bear of a man, a *bon vivant*, bluff, hearty and expansive, with unusual political acumen. He would become the longest-serving German Chancellor since Bismarck and perhaps the most underrated Western statesman of the twentieth century. Mitterrand, introverted and ambivalent, was not an obvious soulmate. Yet they found unexpected common interests, including the philosophy of religion. Jean-Louis Bianco, who had taken over from Bérégovoy as Elysée Secretary-General, remembered listening to them for hours 'discussing the relationship between pietism and quietism'. For the next decade they formed a political partnership closer and more enduring than that of Thatcher and Reagan. Only once in their time together would Kohl strike out on his own, leaving Mitterrand off balance, and that in circumstances so particular that the Frenchman acknowledged privately he might have done the same. Both felt passionately about the future of Europe. Kohl saw himself playing the same role with Mitterrand as Adenauer, his political mentor, had earlier played with de Gaulle.

Three months after Fontainebleau, in September 1984 at Verdun, where 700,000 French and German soldiers had died in 1916, they created a poignant symbol of that shared desire for peace. Standing bareheaded at the ossuary at Douaumont, in the battlefield where Kohl's uncle had died in the First War and Mitterrand had been taken prisoner in the Second, they linked hands in the driving rain while a military band played the German and French anthems.[10] In both countries, the image remained embedded in people's minds. It signified a final turning of the page, consigning to the history books the last echoes of the fratricidal conflicts which had ravaged the heartland of Europe three times in seventy years. Other steps followed, including the creation in 1987 of a Franco-German army brigade, first bruited at the time of the ill-fated European Defence Community Treaty, thirty years earlier. But nothing would match the emotional impact of the image of the two leaders, standing silently, hand in hand, before a coffin draped with the French and German flags.

While in Europe French policy accumulated successes, at home Mitterrand was struggling. On top of the austerity programme, which was grimly continuing, he had been confronted by what in America would be called 'culture wars'.

Among the '110 Propositions' were three dealing with socio-cultural issues. The first two went through without difficulty. The administration of justice was brought into line with the rest of Europe through the abolition of special courts and the death penalty; and a vast programme of devolution was initiated to reduce the centralised power of the State, which had been both a strength and a weakness of the French system since the seventeenth century.

When Mitterrand had been Mayor of Château-Chinon and President of the Conseil Général (Provincial Council) of the Nièvre, he had experienced at first hand the meddling of the *préfets*, the government commissioners, who always insisted on having the last word. As President he considered at one point doing away with them altogether but in the end contented himself with a massive transfer of power and resources from Paris to the local and provincial authorities, the first such shift since the Revolution, two centuries before.[11] It turned out to be a mixed blessing. The dead hand of the State gave way to the cronyism and corruption of local politics. But it brought new energy and flexibility to what had been a sclerotic system. In the same vein the state monopoly in broadcasting was relaxed. In 1982, well after the rest of Western Europe, the government authorised private radio stations, followed two years later by commercial television.*

But Mitterrand's third campaign promise was an altogether different matter.

Proposition 90 envisaged the creation of 'a grand, unified, secular, public service of national education', a seemingly harmless formulation masking an issue which was political dynamite. The proposition had been worded with great care: the change, it said, would be negotiated 'without [imposing] a monopoly' and existing contracts for private schools would be respected. It was more conciliatory than the Common Programme drawn up by the Socialists and Communists nine years earlier, which had declared bluntly: 'private schools . . . will, as a general rule, be nationalised'. Nonetheless, the juxtaposition of the three words, 'unified', 'secular' and 'public' was enough to reopen one of the oldest and deepest wounds in French politics.

Mitterrand had been aware of the danger. As a young MP in 1951, he had seen the quarrel over public subsidies for private education so poison relations between the Socialists and the Christian Democrats that it not only brought down the government but made any future coalition between them impossible. But there was no way to avoid it. Bringing the mainly Roman Catholic private schools into a unified State education system was the key demand of the French teachers' unions, and since the 800,000 or so public school teachers were a core component of the Socialist Party's support, they could not be ignored.

Like the argument over gun laws in America, the 'schools quarrel'

---

* The treatment of the private radio stations offered a salutary tale of the perils of political correctness. Mauroy, with Mitterrand's support, refused to allow them to take advertising lest they fall into the hands of big business. 'Advertising is the enemy!' a group of left-wing producers declared, 'Halt the domination of money!' The predictable, and predicted, result was the opposite to that intended: community and cultural radio stations, which the Socialists wished to encourage, were starved of funds and forced to close, while stations backing the opposition, financed by big business, prospered. In 1984 Mitterrand acknowledged his error. Similarly muddled thinking prompted a bill to prevent excessive concentration of the press, an attempt to limit the power of the right-wing press baron, Robert Hersant, who controlled *Le Figaro* and *France Soir*. The bill, which was widely condemned, on the Left as well as the Right, as inimical to press freedom, was ruled unconstitutional. It was a good lesson in the futility of trying to achieve pluralism by dictate, whether in the media or anywhere else.

in France is incomprehensible to foreigners. Both are rooted in history.
Both are inherently irrational.

Until 1789, all education in France was in the hands of the Church.
That ended with the Revolution, which proclaimed an inalienable
right to free public education for all. Twenty years later Napoleon
published a law stating that no school might be established in France
unless authorised by the State. Gradually, however, the Church clawed
back its prerogatives. A fissure developed in French society between
those who supported Church schools, offering a religious education,
and those who backed the Revolution and a secular state school system.
In the 1950s and '60s right-wing governments passed a series of laws
reaffirming the Church's educational role. By 1981, when Mitterrand
came to power, the left-wing parties, which saw themselves as the
Revolution's heirs, were looking for revenge.

The President found himself in an uncomfortable position.

Although formally agnostic, he had had a Catholic upbringing. As
he told Kohl, also a Catholic, 'I was brought up in that environment,
and I have remained faithful to what is most profound in it.' Yet he
had come to power as head of a party which believed the Church's
role in education, like that of any other public organisation, must be
under state control.

Between the two rounds of the election, Mitterrand had reassured
moderate voters that 'no [private] school will be forced to integrate . . .
I intend to convince, not to coerce.' From an electoral standpoint, that
may have been wise. But it meant the government's hands were tied
when it came to introducing new legislation. Alain Savary, whom
Mitterrand had appointed Education Minister, was obliged to honour
the candidate's promise that the new system would be 'the result of a
negotiation, not a unilateral decision'.

Over the next three years, this would have profound consequences.

Savary and Mitterrand were not close. Some suspected that, in
giving him the education portfolio, Mitterrand was handing him a
poisoned chalice.[12] That seems not to have been the case. Whatever
their differences in the past, Mitterrand respected Savary as a man of
principle – in 1956 he had resigned from Mollet's government in protest
against Ben Bella's arrest – and he was one of only a handful of
Socialist leaders with previous ministerial experience. He was well
qualified to handle what was clearly going to be a delicate task.

After five months of discussions with Church leaders, representatives of the private schools parents' associations and the state school teachers' unions, Savary concluded that there were three main obstacles to agreement. The Church rejected the idea of making private school teachers public functionaries like their state counterparts. Cardinal Lustiger, the archbishop of Paris, said such a step would 'imperil the identity of the Catholic school' because headmasters and headmistresses would no longer control their staff. Secondly, the parents' associations wanted families to have the freedom to choose which schools their children would attend. Under the government's plan, private schools, like state schools, would be allowed to enrol children only from their own districts, a measure intended to promote social mixing. Thirdly, the teachers' unions wanted an end to public subsidies for private education.

With small changes, these would remain the principal stumbling blocks for the next two and a half years.

What began as an educational dispute soon became politicised. When, in April 1982, more than 100,000 people – mainly middle-class parents, many accompanied by their children – held a protest meeting at Pantin, on the outskirts of Paris, the leaders of the right-wing parties turned it into a platform to accuse the Socialists of destroying educational freedoms. Two weeks later, twice as many left-wing demonstrators gathered for a riposte. Attitudes were hardening. Speakers who urged tolerance were booed.

That autumn the government offered a significant concession. The terms 'public', 'secular' and 'unified' were abandoned. Sensing weakness, hardliners in the Catholic hierarchy insisted that that did not go far enough. In reprisal, Socialist town councils in many parts of France unilaterally halted subsidies to Church schools, provoking a rash of lawsuits. A year later, in December 1983, with the situation still deadlocked, Savary decided that, even without agreement, they should delay no longer. Mitterrand, who until then had kept his distance from the negotiations, told the Cabinet that he agreed:

We are in the presence of a major problem in the nation's life, the very image of a problem which is insoluble . . . The negotiations have failed because it could not be otherwise. It was not possible to make either of the two parties, whose stances were irreconcilable, accept a solution

which would have undermined its position . . . Any attempt to reconcile them is doomed to failure. We should not try, it just destroys our
credit. The government was excessively optimistic. It thought a compromise was possible and it isn't. From now on, it's a matter of taking a
decision. To think that the two sides will ever agree is an illusion.[13]

The *government* had been excessively optimistic? The government? It
was Mitterrand who had insisted on negotiations which he now said
had been misconceived. He was not being honest, least of all to Pierre
Mauroy and Alain Savary, who had had to try to carry out what he
now acknowledged to have been from the outset an impossible assign-
ment. Such is the duplicity of princes.

In fact Mitterrand had already decided to abandon the whole
venture.[14] But he was not yet willing to say so. In a best case, the
government might be able to pass a limited reform, allowing Mauroy
and Savary to save face. In a worst case the issue would have to be
buried.

The next six months were a calvary. While Mitterrand tried to focus
on the problems of the European Community, the National Union
of Parents' Associations organised mass meetings to demonstrate the
country's opposition: 80,000 people gathered in Bordeaux in January;
150,000 in Lyon; 300,000 in Lille; 400,000 in Rennes; and more than
600,000 at Versailles in March. Two out of three French people – and,
what was more, one in two left-wing voters – viewed the proposed
measures as an attack on their freedom of choice.

The Left's argument that a two-speed education system was inherently unjust came across as intolerant and archaic. All France's main
partners, including the US, Britain and Germany, allowed private and
public schools to coexist. Education was education. In the end, what
did it matter, when the curriculum was the same for all, whether
teachers were public servants or belonged to the private sector?

That the teachers' unions were blinkered was not a surprise. That
Mitterrand, knowing full well the risks of such an approach, should
have allowed them to take the government hostage was harder to
explain.

Much later the President offered a curious and self-serving explanation. The proponents of a unified, lay school system, he said, were so
fixated on the issue that it was necessary to attempt a reform in order

for them to get it out of their system. 'It was . . . a psychoanalytical catharsis . . . If it worked, I would be able to congratulate myself on putting an end to such a long-standing quarrel. If it didn't . . . the country would be inoculated against it for a long time to come.' Even as post hoc justification, it was singularly unconvincing. The truth was that Mitterrand had decided from the start that whatever he did would rebound against him so it was better not to get involved.

On Thursday, May 24 1984, a bill – of sorts – was approved by parliament.

Parts of the text read as though they were straight out of *Animal Farm*. One clause, imposed by the Party's left wing, laid down that 'a private kindergarten may not be opened in a commune which does not already have a public kindergarten.' The rationale was that a town council should not be forced to subsidise a private crèche if it lacked the means to finance a public one. The result would be to deprive families of any kindergarten at all. Politically it was indefensible. The ideological tail was wagging the government dog.

A month later, on June 24, a Sunday, well over a million people marched through Paris in protest. It was the biggest demonstration in France since 1945, exceeding even the huge marches of May 1968.

No cars were set on fire, no barricades erected, no policemen hurt. Right-wing politicians, including Jacques Chirac and Valéry Giscard d'Estaing, marched with the representatives of their communes. At the Place de la Bastille, the traditional rallying point for the Left, Church leaders made unyielding speeches before the crowd dispersed as peacefully as it had come.

The message was polite, but clear. Enough was enough.

The following week all Mitterrand's time was taken up with the Fontainebleau summit. But an idea was beginning to take shape. In February, Michel Charasse, a senator from the Auvergne, in central France, who had been with him since the 1960s and handled consti-tutional matters at the Elysée, had raised the possibility of a refer-endum to resolve the schools issue. Charasse was an original, a small, round, cigar-smoking ball of energy so unpredictable and hard to control that his colleagues compared him to itching powder, but with a legal mind as sharp as Mitterrand's was politically acute. At the beginning of July, Mitterrand decided that his idea was worth trying but with a significant twist. There would be not one, but two referendums: the first to change the constitution so as to permit the government to consult the nation directly on social issues; the second to seek a verdict on the educational reform.

To hold a referendum, both houses of parliament had to agree. The Senate, controlled by the Right, was in favour of a referendum on Savary's proposals, which it was confident the President would lose. Indeed, the Senate majority leader, Charles Pasqua, had suggested it himself only ten days earlier. But a referendum on a referendum, offering people greater freedom to express their opinions about the country's affairs, which the President would win by a large margin, was a very different matter.

It was the kind of pirouette at which Mitterrand excelled.

The aim was not to resolve the schools issue but to kill it. If, as he expected, the Senate rejected the initiative, the referendum would never be held and the problem which had caused all the trouble, the educational reform, would disappear without trace. Moreover the Left, which was gaining an unwelcome reputation for restricting liberties, would be able to point to the referendum as proof of its desire to expand them.

Mitterrand announced his new initiative on the evening of July 12. 'The schools affair is over,' he told party leaders in his office afterwards. 'Perhaps not for ever, but at least for the next ten years.'

As he had anticipated, the Right was caught unawares. Pasqua, having called for a referendum on the schools issue in June, found himself a month later having to argue against it. He accused Mitterrand of turning the procedure into a plebiscite on his rule, the same argument that Mitterrand himself had used twenty years earlier against the referendums organised by General de Gaulle. The Senate duly voted down the government's proposal. The reform was dead. It remained only to tie up the loose ends. A few months later parliament passed a new law giving private schools and their teachers the same rights as before, albeit, to mollify the Socialist Party, with a little less public money.[15] It marked, as one French historian put it, 'the end of a grand republican myth'.

The school war left scars. Savary felt, not without reason, that Mitterrand had thrown him to the dogs. On July 16 he resigned.[16] A day later the rest of the government followed. Mauroy had hesitated but he had been too closely involved in the negotiations to remain in office if Savary left. Mitterrand tried to dissuade him. But they both knew that a new team was needed if the Left were to survive the parliamentary elections, now only twenty months away. Mauroy had been a tower of strength, solid, uncomplaining, always there when needed. As the outgoing Prime Minister left the Elysée, Mitterrand told Attali it was 'the most painful moment of my presidency'.

In his place, Mitterrand named Laurent Fabius, a month short of his thirty-eighth birthday and the youngest ever head of a French government. The appointment was intended to shock. Fabius was not William Pitt the Younger, whose nomination as British Prime Minister in 1783 at the age of 24 was greeted with a piece of doggerel,

> A sight to make all nations stand and stare,
> A kingdom trusted to a schoolboy's care,

but he was of a different generation from the leaders of the opposition: Barre, Chirac and Giscard. Where a more orthodox choice, Bérégovoy, Delors, or even Rocard, would have signalled continuity, Fabius symbolised modernity. He was a young man in tune with a time marked by accelerating financial, industrial, technological, social and cultural mutation, when the world, and France with it, was in the midst of unprecedented change.

The appointment was a gamble. But Mitterrand had an intellectual and political affinity with Fabius that he had with few others, and he wanted to rearrange the chessboard in a way that the opposition would be unable to follow.

To some extent he succeeded. The press caricatured Fabius as a gimmick. A slim, prematurely balding technocrat with elegant, bourgeois manners and a cold, calculating mind, he was portrayed by the cartoonists as a cooler, 'lefty' version of Valéry Giscard d'Estaing. Public opinion was kinder. During the year that followed, he had the confidence of more than half the electorate, while Mitterrand was down to little more than a third, a record of unpopularity unmatched by any of his predecessors.[17]

But it was too little, too late. Fabius himself recognised that he had an impossible task. He was there 'to prepare the elections so that they are lost the least badly possible. I knew that it would be extraordinarily difficult . . . My brief was . . . to avoid so serious a defeat as to [imperil] François Mitterrand's remaining in office.'

How had it come to this? Three years after a landslide victory, Mitterrand faced the near certainty of losing his parliamentary majority and having to coexist, or 'cohabit', as Pompidou's former Chief of Staff, Édouard Balladur, had put it, with a government from the opposition. He could not say he had not seen it coming. Already in 1982, he had told his friend, the industrialist Ambroise Roux: 'What a hiding we are going to get in the elections in 1986!'

He had only himself to blame.

Two of his key initiatives, the drive to reduce unemployment by promoting consumer-led growth and the negotiation to produce a unified schools system, had failed ignominiously, one being transformed into an austerity programme without precedent in post-war France, the other ending in a truce which, after three years of bruising combat, had left the situation essentially unchanged.

In both cases the root cause was Mitterrand's indecisiveness.

Jacques Delors had called for 'a pause' in the Left's economic reforms as early as November 1981: Mitterrand waited fifteen months longer before finally slamming on the brakes. Had he acted in March or even June 1982, instead of March 1983, he would still have been able to enact the symbolic measures which the left-wing electorate had been waiting for – an extra week of paid holiday; retirement at 60; an increase in the minimum wage – and the country would have been a year closer to economic recovery. Had he pushed through the schools reform in the spring of 1982, arguing, as he could have done at that time, that five months of discussion were sufficient proof of the government's willingness to 'convince, not to coerce', the bill would have been put before parliament when the Left was in a position of strength and its opponents still in disarray and would almost certainly have passed.

It is easy to be wise after the event. But the job of a statesman is to take the right decisions at the right time, not a year or two late.

Mitterrand's failures of leadership at home contrasted starkly with his record abroad. On European issues, on the arms race, on relations with the US and the Soviet Union, his judgement was unerring. It was in domestic affairs that he stumbled. The mistakes were not tactical but strategic. Instead of setting out unequivocally a clear policy from the outset, he hesitated, trying to reach impossible compromises between austerity and growth, between the Church and the Socialists, and as a result had the worst of both worlds.

The explanation goes to the core of who Mitterrand was.

He was remote, intimidating and exuded natural leadership. He subjugated those who worked for him by his intellect and culture. But he was an artist, operating by intuition, not a logician sizing up the world with arithmetical precision. Science left him cold. 'Socialism,' he declared, shortly before coming to power, 'is first and foremost a cultural project.' He could not live without novels and poetry. Spiritual questions fascinated him. He read and reread the Bible, not as history or theology but as metaphor. He saw himself as a romantic whose life was a novel in progress.

In the first eighteen months after his election his powers were as close to absolute as exists in a democratic regime. Had he chosen to, he could have laid down any policy he liked and it would have been implemented. That was not how his mind worked. Accused of indecision, he shot back: 'Would you prefer a President who doesn't think before he acts?'

But taken to an extreme, reflection becomes dithering.

His tendency to procrastinate was reinforced by his conception of the presidency. Mitterrand-the-President was not quite the same man as Mitterrand-the-minister or Mitterrand-the-party-leader. The President was there to preside; the government to govern. De Gaulle had organised it that way, with a President above the fray and a Prime Minister who implemented his decisions and courted unpopularity in consequence. The division of roles was not watertight. It was the President, not the Prime Minister, who chaired the Cabinet meetings at which policy was approved. A balance had to be struck, and each President of the Fifth Republic, whether de Gaulle, Pompidou, Giscard or Mitterrand – or later, Chirac, Sarkozy or Hollande – did so in a different way.

Except in the 'reserved domain' of Defence and Foreign Affairs, where, by an unwritten rule, the President alone determined policy and oversaw its execution, Mitterrand was arguably the most 'hands off' of all modern French Heads of State.[18] He liked to quote Cervantes: '*Dar tiempo al tiempo*' ('Give time to time') – but where Don Quixote's comment to Sancho Panza meant merely, 'Do not rush things!', Mitterrand meant they should be allowed to develop to their plenitude before decisive action was taken.[19] That was fine when they developed to his advantage, as had been the case at Fontainebleau, where, after three years of obstreperousness, Margaret Thatcher had been ready to make peace. But over the schools issue, his refusal to intervene caused the situation not to ripen but to rot. From the autumn of 1983, Mitterrand had known that agreement was impossible. He had waited, he explained later, 'to lance the abscess . . . to let the crisis attain its paroxysm to be able then, and only then, to resolve it'. But by that time the damage had been done. Had he acted more forcefully earlier, there might not have been an abscess to lance.

In this unpromising context, Laurent Fabius set about forming his new government. The main question was whether the Communists would continue to take part.

Already in March 1983, when the second austerity plan had been launched, the Politburo had talked about withdrawing, but at that point Marchais had felt it was too soon. 'If we had gone then,' he explained, 'we would have been the ones responsible for the split . . . The women and the men who voted for the Left in 1981 wouldn't have understood.' But the issue was on the table. A month later, Marchais told an interviewer: 'I am not fond of "swallowing grass snakes"', the French expression for humiliation. Mitterrand's insistence that austerity be accompanied by modernisation, notably of heavy industry – coal, steel and ship-building – which government subsidies had kept limping along for years to prevent social unrest – complicated the Communists' position still further. Modernisation meant an additional 100,000 job losses, mainly in left-wing bastions in the north-east, Brittany and on the Mediterranean coast.

Mauroy was also unhappy at such a flagrant reversal of the policies which had brought the Left to power. But Mitterrand was adamant. 'We must purge our industry, get it back into a fit state . . . and stop throwing away money on subsidies,' he told the Cabinet.

It was hard, the President admitted, but it was a matter of national survival. 'It's doing nothing which costs jobs and money and in the end [leads to] despair. The crisis is because [we have] not adapted to international competition.' In April 1984 he returned to this theme at a news conference at the Elysée:

Either France will show itself capable of meeting [this challenge] and, in doing so, will ensure its independence and prosperity, or it will be dragged down and head into decline . . . Nothing, nothing at all, will be achieved in a lasting fashion in any field unless we fulfil two essential conditions: the construction of a modern industrial machine, without which we won't be able to sell what we produce; and the training, without delay, of qualified labour to staff this modern industry.[20]

Even before the modernisation programme, industrial unrest had been growing. That spring much of the North was paralysed. Truck drivers blocked the motorways, preventing the distribution of basic supplies. Tens of thousands of steelworkers marched through Paris, shouting, 'Mitterrand, you're fucked!' Mauroy compared it to 1793, the year of the Terror in the French Revolution.

The Communists tried to keep a foot in both camps. *L'Humanité* claimed in a front-page headline: 'We are both in government and with the workers'. But it rang increasingly hollow. Marchais told his colleagues: 'Communist participation in the government has . . . become the central issue.' Although he would never admit it, Mitterrand had adopted the policies which Michel Rocard had advocated at Metz in 1979. On the anniversary of his election, May 10, the President put in the same basket the Right, which, he said, wanted wealth without redistribution, and 'the Left which wants to redistribute everything without bothering to produce'. It was a far cry from the programme the Communists had committed to when they had entered the government three years earlier.

The proof, if proof were needed, that the alliance with the Socialists was working against them came in the elections to the European Parliament in June. The Communist list, headed by Georges Marchais, won 11.2 per cent of the vote, less than half what he had obtained five years earlier and the Party's worst showing in a national election since 1932.[21]

Mauroy's resignation and the choice of Fabius to succeed him were the last straw. As Minister of Industry, Fabius had implemented the modernisation programme with the enthusiasm of a true believer. A Communist colleague in the Cabinet remembered him as possessed by the 'zeal of a neophyte, newly converted to the virtues of capitalist restructuring'.

In the small hours of the morning of July 19, a Thursday, the new Prime Minister received a letter from the Communist Party Central Committee, making continued participation conditional on the government's reversion to policies of growth and full employment. A statement issued later that day said the Party did not have 'the moral right . . . to deceive our supporters or to deceive ourselves' by pretending that the modernisation programme would solve France's problems. Mitterrand tried rather half-heartedly to persuade them to stay on. If the Communists remained in government, the trades unions, notably the CGT, would be slightly more restrained. Moreover the Left was facing elections which it expected to lose. It would be better able to limit its defeat if it went into battle united. But the Party's mind was made up. Mitterrand had nothing to offer which might change it.

As the French Communists retreated into their shell, so, for quite different reasons, did their sponsors in Moscow. In February 1984, as Yuri Andropov lay dying, he had recommended that his protégé, Mikhail Gorbachev, then the Politburo member in charge of Agriculture, should succeed him as Soviet Communist Party General Secretary. But the elderly clique that had come to power with Leonid Brezhnev preferred one of its own. The Central Committee named Konstantin Chernenko, who had been passed over when Andropov was appointed. Like Brezhnev, he was a transitional figure, an ageing oligarch who took refuge in the wooden rhetoric of his mentor. But beneath the surface there was movement, as Mitterrand would discover when he visited Moscow that summer.

Over the previous three years, both countries had staked out hardline positions. Mitterrand's expulsion of Soviet spies and support of the deployment of Pershing and cruise missiles were a reminder that, even with a Socialist government, France had to be treated with respect. Unlike his predecessor, Valéry Giscard d'Estaing, he had refused high-level meetings with the Russians. But he had also resisted US pressure for a trade boycott of the Soviet bloc and was strongly opposed to Reagan's plans for a space-based anti-missile system, the so-called Strategic Defense Initiative (SDI), popularly known as 'Star Wars', which he regarded as impracticable.

In March, a month after Andropov's death, Mitterrand flew to Washington to meet the US President, whom he found more receptive than in the past to the idea of improving East–West relations. Reagan wondered aloud whether Moscow might need reassurance that the West's intentions were peaceful. Mitterrand replied that the Russians suffered from 'an encirclement complex':

I don't believe that [they] are warmongers. Since Peter the Great, they've rarely been aggressors, even if their foreign diplomacy sometimes might make one think [so]. What is to be feared is that they really believe you might be aggressors [against them]. To explain that, you almost have to resort to psychoanalysis, which teaches us that we can be affected by anything that happens to our mother after the third month of pregnancy. They're like that. They continue to live through [the prism of] their country's first three years, [when British and French forces backed the White Russian armies' efforts to annihilate the new Bolshevik regime]. There is a story about a madman who thinks he is a grain of wheat . . . After a long stay [in hospital] and intensive care, he is cured. Everyone is delighted. He leaves and on the way he meets a hen. The madman is terrified and races back to the hospital. 'Oh, but come on!' the doctor says to him. 'You are cured. You know very well you are not a grain of wheat.' And the madman answers: 'Of course I know that. But does the hen know?'[22]

Reagan was intrigued but not entirely convinced. The Kremlin might not be bent on war, he conceded, but it was certainly expansionist, as witness its activities in Africa, Afghanistan and Central America. That was Mitterrand's cue to remind him that 'although my analysis may be different from yours', the Russians would always try their luck when 'circumstances favour them. Wherever there is rottenness, they will come' – a reference to the corrupt military dictatorships that the United States supported in the western hemisphere.

Verbal fencing aside, the meeting went well. Reagan concluded with a story of his own about a Russian woman who had approached Brezhnev, reminding him that they had once slept together and asking him to help her son to get a place at university. 'Of course I'll help,' Brezhnev replied. 'I don't remember the occasion, but it's possible. Tell me, where did we sleep together?' 'At the last Soviet Party Congress,' she answered. 'We were sitting next to each other during one of the speeches and we both dozed off.'

Such is the stuff of summit meetings. Yet even anecdotes can be illuminating about an adversary's, or a partner's, frame of mind. The stories Reagan had told Mitterrand about Russia in previous years had all been viscerally hostile. He returned home convinced that if Reagan won a second term, US policy towards Moscow would become more accommodating.

In June, Mitterrand set out for the Soviet Union. The visit was controversial. It was the first by a Western Head of State or government since the Soviet invasion of Afghanistan, four and a half years earlier, and, as such, marked a breach in the West's diplomatic boycott. It also coincided with a hunger strike by the dissident physicist, Andrei Sakharov, winner of the Nobel Peace Prize, who had been banished to the city of Gorky in the Urals and was protesting against the authorities' refusal to let his wife travel to the West for medical treatment.

At the first plenary meeting, on Thursday morning, June 21, Chernenko read with difficulty, frequently swallowing his words and stumbling over passages, a lengthy prepared statement attacking the US and Western Europe for their 'unfriendly' attitude to Moscow and specifically for the deployment of Pershing and cruise missiles. In reply, Mitterrand repeated what he had said to Reagan about the USSR not being a warmonger, before continuing:

> No one wants war, but it can happen without anyone wanting it, because each side wishes to strengthen its forces without yielding an inch to the other . . . For me, [your] SS-20 missiles are incomprehensible . . . Why do you have these missiles facing us? Why? Because you think I am going to go crazy and attack you? It's absurd! I would prefer not to have SS-20s or Pershings. But once the SS-20s are in place, there has to be an equilibrium.[23]

He went on to speak of human rights and 'cases like that of Sakharov . . . and certain others' where 'the principle of the free circulation of persons should apply'. Chernenko did not respond and Mitterrand did not take it further.[24] But that night, at a welcoming banquet in the Kremlin, he raised the issue again, this time in public. After noting that the Helsinki Conference on European Security and Cooperation (CSCE), nine years earlier, had set out a modus vivendi for the West and the communist bloc, the President continued:

Any restriction of freedom could call into question the principles [we all] accepted at that conference. That is why we sometimes speak to you about the cases of individuals, some of whom have taken on a symbolic dimension . . . Such is the case of Professor Sakharov and of many whose names are unknown.[25]

When he sat down, there was a deathly hush. A French Communist in the delegation remembered Chernenko 'looking like a corpse'. To break the ice, Mitterrand asked Gorbachev, who had arrived late and was sitting on Chernenko's left, why he had not been part of the Soviet delegation at the plenary session that morning. 'That doesn't depend on me, Mr President,' Gorbachev replied. Chernenko then enquired why he had been late. The younger man explained that he had been attending a meeting on agricultural production. 'Everyone always says [our agriculture] is fine,' he went on, 'but it's not true. It's never worked properly.' Taken aback, Chernenko asked what he meant. 'The peasants couldn't care less, transport is a mess, the officials are lazy and incompetent . . .' Gorbachev began. 'Since when?' Chernenko broke in. 'Since 1917,' came the answer. The Russian interpreter, suddenly realising the enormity of what had been said, stopped in mid-sentence.[26]

It was the first encounter between any Western leader and the man who, by the end of the decade, would ring down the curtain on the once invincible Soviet empire, bringing to an end half a century of Cold War. Gorbachev's remarks were so improbable, so unlike anything any Soviet leader had ever said publicly before, that Mitterrand wondered afterwards whether they might have been some kind of provocation.

Next morning the Communist Party daily, *Pravda*, published the text of Mitterrand's speech but censored the reference to Sakharov. Chernenko's speech appeared with two extra sentences, which he had not uttered: 'Those who try to teach us lessons only provoke from us an ironical smile. We shall allow no one to interfere in our affairs.'

Reagan and Margaret Thatcher both wrote to congratulate Mitterrand on his remarks. His intuition of the US President's changing attitude was soon shown to have been correct. In September Reagan received the Soviet Foreign Minister, Andrei Gromyko, the first such contact for five years. Three months later, Gorbachev, paying his first official visit to the West as Soviet No. 2, travelled to London and met Thatcher, who famously declared that 'we can do business together'.

The following spring, Chernenko, who had been suffering from emphysema and a host of related ailments, died of heart failure after barely a year in office. Roland Dumas, who had taken over from Cheysson as French Foreign Minister, happened to be in Moscow that weekend. Gromyko, a dour, granite-faced man who had entered the Foreign Ministry under Stalin, told him in confidence that Gorbachev would be the new leader, adding: 'He has a nice smile but his teeth are made of steel.' Back at the Embassy, Dumas phoned Mitterrand and urged him to cancel all other business and attend the funeral two days later. With some reluctance the President agreed. Arriving late, as usual, he was escorted to the front row, where he found himself being propelled towards the outstretched arms of Yasser Arafat, to be saved in the nick of time by Thatcher, who, seeing his panic-stricken expression, waved him over to join her.

It turned out to be worth the journey. Mitterrand afterwards quoted Gorbachev as having told him in substance later that day: 'What we lack here is initiative and imagination. In a word, what we lack is democracy. I shall try.'[27] Gorbachev remembered the discussion as 'the starting point of a relationship of mutual understanding that arose instantly between us'. On his return to Paris, the President told the Cabinet: 'It really seems that with Gorbachev we have passed from one epoch to another.'

If Russia was changing, America lagged behind. Reagan had dropped his rhetoric about 'the evil Empire' and appeared genuinely to want better relations with Moscow. But he remained committed to the 'Star Wars' initiative and increasingly viewed France – the most inde-pendent-minded of the Allies and the most sceptical about SDI – as a thorn in America's side.

The feeling was mutual. Not long before, Mitterrand had told the Syrian leader, Hafez al-Assad, referring to his relations with Washington, 'We are members of the Atlantic Alliance . . . We are friends. But we are a bit like cat and dog in the same house.'

Two weeks after Gorbachev's appointment, in the spring of 1985, the CIA launched a disinformation campaign in an attempt to torpedo any improvement in Soviet–French relations.[28] To Washington it was one thing for the two superpowers to hold a privileged dialogue between themselves, but quite another to watch from afar the emer-gence of a Franco-Russian entente which risked becoming a pole of opposition to 'Star Wars'. The opening salvo came on March 29, when the newspaper, *Le Monde*, broke the story of Farewell, which until then had been a closely guarded secret. It turned out that the leak had come from Yves Bonnet, who had succeeded Chalet as DST chief. Summoned to explain himself, Bonnet said that William Casey, his opposite number in Washington, concerned that Moscow was reconstituting its intelligence network in France, had urged him to fire a warning shot across the Soviets' bows. Mitterrand sacked him but the damage had been done.[29] Other leaks calculated to exasperate the Russians, attributable directly to CIA sources, continued to appear in the French media and in the *New York Times*.

Meanwhile the White House stepped up pressure on the Allies to join America in SDI research. A circular letter from Reagan – one of his preferred methods of communication and one which always infuriated Mitterrand, whom it reminded of a headmaster calling his staff to a meeting in the school common room – invited NATO Heads of State and government to make up their minds in the next sixty days whether or not to participate. Shortly afterwards the US Defence Secretary, Caspar Weinberger, arrived in Paris to try to win the French President's agreement.

It was a singularly unproductive meeting.

France, Mitterrand told him, rejected the US approach for three reasons: firstly, it risked decoupling the American and European theatres; secondly, it would encourage the Russians to accelerate their own missile development; and thirdly, it would not work. If 5 per cent of the Soviet missiles reached their targets, almost every major city in America would be obliterated. Yet the best estimate was that the Strategic Defense Initiative, when it became operational in 2020, would stop only 80 per cent of the missiles. Weinberger responded that the programme at that stage was merely for research: America wanted to 'bring together as much expertise as possible and use the talents available from its allies'.

To Mitterrand, that was the problem. SDI was not and would never be a serious anti-missile defence system. It was a clever scheme, dreamed up by the Pentagon, to attract European money and brains to a US-led military research programme which would bring immense technological spin-offs for America and confine the Europeans to the role of subcontractors. To sidestep that challenge, he proposed setting up an independent European research programme called EUREKA (The European Research Coordination Agency). It was launched during the summer, becoming a vital platform for European innovation in fields ranging from nuclear fusion to space research. However US pressure for SDI continued and was soon accompanied by two more high-profile American initiatives to which Mitterrand was equally opposed. Reagan wanted the G7 to issue a joint statement on terrorism, which, after America's experiences in Lebanon, was a major preoccupation in Washington. To France, that was unacceptable. The G7 was not the world's policeman. If terrorism was to be discussed, it should be done through intergovernmental talks or through Interpol. The American President also wanted a new round of the GATT, the General Agreement on Tariffs and Trade, to dismantle trade barriers in Europe and Japan, particularly for farm products, in order to reduce the ballooning US trade deficit. Again, Mitterrand refused. Trade talks, he acknowledged, were needed, but if European agriculture was to be discussed, America must agree to submit transport and services to similar scrutiny.

When the G7 met in Bonn in May 1985, the chairman, Helmut Kohl, found himself torn between his principal European partner, France, and Germany's global protector, the US. Reagan agreed to withdraw the US text on SDI. But no compromise was reached over GATT. After the other five leaders had approved the American position, Mitterrand said tersely: 'Not me'. He then launched into a tirade unlike any to which that august gathering had been subjected before:

It is unhealthy that our allies dictate our policy. Some accept that. Not me . . . I hear it being said that no one here wishes to isolate France. Very good. But the fact is that [France] is isolated in this room. It's not healthy. Just as it's not healthy that Europe's affairs should be judged by countries which are far from Europe. If this goes on, I am ready to start a public debate . . . We have to put an end to all this endless paperwork. If these summits don't return to their original conception, France will no longer take part . . . Some of you reached agreements [secretly] between yourselves on [certain] topics before the summit [even] began . . . I don't accept a fait accompli. More generally, we are not the directorate of the world's affairs . . . Nor are we a tribunal to judge friends and allies. If that were the case, I would take care not to put my country in such a situation. If France were treated like that, I

would put an end to it. I would not come any more. [We had] warned
you since February that on SDI and GATT our answer would be no.
So why have we had to talk about it again here?[30]

In the shocked silence that followed, the Canadian Prime Minister,
Brian Mulroney, came to Mitterrand's defence. Afterwards he took
Reagan into a corner. 'You've got to stop this,' he said. 'What do you
think you're doing? You are treating François Mitterrand as an adversary! [France] is our best ally!'

It was Williamsburg all over again but worse. No sooner were relations between Paris and Washington back on even keel than the US
forgot the lesson that Vernon Walters had drawn: France was a good
ally 'so long as you treat her as an equal'. Two short years later, 'Star
Wars' had brought back the Great Power syndrome with a vengeance.

The French President's stand was approved by all shades of opinion
at home and by many elsewhere in Europe. Even the normally hostile
Quotidien de Paris conceded that 'Mitterrand is not wrong about everything'.

But the Reagan administration still did not get it.

On the eve of Gorbachev's first visit to the West, which brought him
to Paris at the beginning of October, the White House announced –
as usual, without prior consultation – that Reagan was inviting all the
G7 leaders to New York later that month to discuss the West's
position on SDI before his own forthcoming meeting with the Soviet
leader in Geneva in mid-November. Mitterrand was outraged. 'To
announce that publicly, two days before Gorbachev's arrival! . . . It's
crazy.' At the following morning's Cabinet meeting, he explained why
France would reject the invitation:

It's not normal that the Seven pretend to lord it over the planet . . .
The situation which is being created de facto by these [improvised]
summits is dangerous . . . Either [France] submits to [the others']
proposals . . . or she doesn't and is treated as a bad ally. To go to New
York in these circumstances would be to recognise America's *imperium*.[31]

Gorbachev had chosen to come first to Paris precisely because France
was the most independent-minded of the major Western countries.
Mitterrand had told the Japanese Prime Minister, Yasuhiro Nakasone,

that summer: 'Great Britain, no matter what qualities Mrs Thatcher might have, is too linked to the United States. The Soviets might just as well talk to Reagan. West Germany has no autonomous defence policy. France is a loyal ally of the US, but its policy is not that of the US.' To Gorbachev, whose primary concern was to prevent an expensive new arms race which the Soviet Union could not afford, it made sense to seek an understanding with Mitterrand, whose reservations about 'Star Wars' echoed his own.

Mitterrand, on his side, was not oblivious to the charms of the unspoken 'special relationship' with Moscow of which his predecessors had dreamed. He had told Gorbachev in March that France and Russia shared 'permanent interests'. The phrase contained an element of wishful thinking. The ties between Paris and Moscow would always be tributary to the imperatives of superpower accommodation.[32] But it was a starting point for both sides to explore the shape of a future which promised to be very different from the past. Gorbachev's signature programmes of *perestroika* and *glasnost* ('reconstruction' and 'transparency') were still many months away. Already, though, he had dropped hints of a tantalising new departure.*

Their discussions focussed on the disarmament talks in Geneva, which had resumed that spring after a fifteen-month hiatus. The Russians insisted that the negotiations must include SDI. The Americans refused, arguing that they should be limited to strategic and intermediate nuclear forces. Mitterrand opened by stressing that he intended to speak frankly.

MITTERRAND: I'm not looking for tension with the United States, but I have a
   straightforward opinion on each problem which relates to war and peace . . .
   President Reagan's conception of SDI is either . . . daydreaming or propaganda . . . If it's daydreaming, the American Chiefs of Staff will realise
   that. I believe a compromise [at Geneva] remains possible . . . [But] one
   may also conclude that the Americans are seeking a position of dominance,
   and in that case no argument will sway them.

* Gorbachev first used the term *perestroika* at a meeting with Soviet Party officials in the winter of 1984, three months before Chernenko's death. It became official Soviet policy fifteen months later and over the next five years was repeatedly redefined to allow a larger place for the private sector, which was virtually non-existent when Gorbachev came to power, and a reduction of the role of central planning.

GORBACHEV: The United States feel certain that in space . . . they will be
able to outstrip and dominate the USSR . . . But the real question is where
is all this leading? If it continues, productive negotiations will be impossible and in space there will be no safeguards.

MITTERRAND: Actually there are two risks: that the one who is ahead is
tempted to take advantage of it, and that the one who fears the lead of
his opponent is tempted to try to stop him . . .

GORBACHEV: In my opinion, if we don't act together, the Reagan administration won't budge.

MITTERRAND: I don't know what will make them budge. They are not very
malleable . . . The Americans don't have much understanding of
Europe . . . The climate which prevails is one of mistrust.[33]

This turned out to be the case. The Americans refused to budge
until the Chiefs of Staff – and through them, the rest of the administration – were forced to recognise that the technological obstacles to
'Star Wars' were such that it would never be a practical proposition.

More intriguing was a passage in Mitterrand's opening remarks
which Gorbachev did not pick up on. Twice the President noted that
France was *presently* an ally of the United States. He went on:

Given the balance of forces in the world, I think things ought to remain
that way . . . But that is a current political reality rather than a perspective for the future . . . Strengthening Western Europe . . . is a perspective for the future [and] not one that should be seen as detrimental to
the USSR. I don't want a Europe which is the auxiliary of a United
States that is on the offensive . . . If new possibilities for a modus
vivendi with the USSR emerge, it would be a good thing.[34]

The thought was not new in itself. Mitterrand had said several times
since his election in 1981 that the division of Europe agreed between
Stalin and Roosevelt at Yalta could not continue for ever. He did not
expect the division to end in his lifetime. No one in the mid-1980s
foresaw that in the next five years the Soviet empire would implode.
He was thinking rather of a possible convergence between the two
halves of Europe. But the fact that he alluded to it in a conversation
with Gorbachev suggested he was already wondering whether the Soviet
leader could be the man who would make that convergence possible.[35]

After Gorbachev's departure, Mitterrand sent a lengthy account of his impressions to Reagan, Thatcher and Kohl. He found the new master of the Kremlin convincing, he told them, not only about internal reform but also about disarmament and an eventual Soviet disengagement from Afghanistan. However the proof of the pudding would be in the eating. To the Cabinet he said Gorbachev was 'conciliatory but not soft' and could be expected to remain in power for a long time to come.

The French nuclear weapons programme was beyond the reach of the Soviet and American negotiators at Geneva but not of human stupidity.

On July 10 1985, a Wednesday, shortly before midnight, two explosions, three minutes apart, reverberated around the harbour in Auckland, New Zealand. The *Rainbow Warrior*, a 40-metre fisheries inspection vessel which had been bought from the British government and refitted by the environmental organisation, Greenpeace, had been holed by two charges of plastic explosive. It had been about to set out at the head of a small flotilla to protest against the resumption of French nuclear testing on the atoll of Mururoa in French Polynesia, 800 miles south-east of Tahiti. Between the two explosions, a Dutch photographer, 35-year-old Fernando Pereira, had returned to the ship to retrieve his camera equipment. The second blast had killed him.

The first news agency despatch arrived on Mitterrand's desk that same evening, Paris time, seven hours after the attack. The President demanded an immediate report. He was told that France had not been involved.

It was the beginning of a very long charade.

Both Mitterrand and those who reported to him were aware from the outset that it could only have been a French operation. Greenpeace and French military intelligence had been playing a cat-and-mouse game in the South Pacific for years.[36] The propellers of Greenpeace vessels had mysteriously come loose, ships' food supplies had been tampered with and vessels boarded and escorted away from French territorial waters. But the *Rainbow Warrior* posed a different problem. Its size and the fact that it had a reinforced hull meant that it would be difficult for the naval vessels France had at its disposal in the area to intercept it 'peacefully' and, since it was equipped with satellite transmission equipment, any attempt to do so would be broadcast live around the world. In April, the Prime Minister, Laurent Fabius, had been informed by the head of the DGSE, Admiral Lacoste, of plans to 'anticipate' the Greenpeace campaign so as to prevent any of its vessels reaching Mururoa.[37] But nothing had been said about sinking the Greenpeace flagship. The only member of the government who was aware that the DGSE's 'Action Service' was planning such an operation was the Defence Minister, Charles Hernu, who kept the Prime Minister in the dark.[38] Although Lacoste was unenthusiastic, the Minister was in favour of going ahead and the 'Action Service' itself, stung by its failures in Lebanon two years earlier – the botched car bomb attack on the Iranian Embassy and then the poor choice of target for the French bombing raid in the Bekaa Valley – was eager to show its mettle.

On May 15, Lacoste had had a meeting with Mitterrand at which the President had emphasised the importance of keeping Greenpeace away from Mururoa and approved the 'neutralisation' of the *Rainbow Warrior*. What exactly was meant by that term?* Lacoste would only

* The question of how much Mitterrand knew has been hotly debated in France. It has been argued that when he used the term 'neutralisation' he must have – or should have – known that that could be interpreted as including military action. However, the balance of the evidence points the other way. Admiral Lacoste's accounts – both in a handwritten report to André Giraud, who became Defence Minister in 1986, and later in his memoirs – were deliberately ambiguous. The Admiral implied – but refused to confirm explicitly – that Mitterrand was not informed that the DGSE intended to blow up the *Rainbow Warrior* in Auckland harbour. Given that his political sympathies lay with the Right, his reluctance unequivocally to exculpate Mitterrand was understandable. On the other hand, if Mitterrand had given a clear order for the *Rainbow Warrior* to be sunk, Lacoste would no doubt have said so. That he did not appears to confirm that Mitterrand was not privy to the plan. Circumstantial evidence supports that conclusion. The normal procedure for the President was to receive a detailed briefing – and to be required to give explicit approval – only where loss of life was expected to result, as in the Lebanese reprisals and the extralegal killing of terrorists, which were examined case by case. For an operation like the one in New Zealand, where no loss of life was envisaged, he would not have been informed in detail. Moreover Mitterrand was chronically averse to micromanaging subordinates. Once he had laid down a policy, he preferred to give those charged with carrying it out, whether ministers or senior officials, a free hand.

That Hernu approved the operation, and then covered up for his subordinates after it failed, is confirmed by a variety of sources. The fact that the Minister had given the green light – a decision which Lacoste would have assumed had Mitterrand's agreement – was a further reason for him not to have discussed it in detail with the President when they met.

say later, 'I did not go into greater detail . . . because the authorisation was sufficiently explicit'.[39]

Once the operation had been bungled, Mitterrand proceeded to dig himself into a very deep hole.

The problem was that not only he but Lacoste, Hernu and a dozen or more others knew exactly what had happened. Hernu had told him on July 14, four days after the explosion, that the DGSE was responsible. But in public all of them continued, more and more implausibly, to deny that they had any knowledge of it.

The pantomime continued until September.

Information leaked out in dribs and drabs, painting a picture of muddle and incompetence on the part of the French secret service worthy of a 1920s silent comedy. Within 48 hours of the attack, two 'Swiss tourists' were arrested in Auckland and, on being allowed to telephone home, called a number at the French Defence Ministry in Paris. Next it was discovered that a second group of French agents had been seen on a yacht the day before the explosion. Finally, on September 17, *Le Monde* reported that a third team, comprising two DGSE frogmen, had carried out the actual attack.

The pantomime was turning into farce. Hernu, who had been in on the plan from the start, issued a statement that night insisting: 'No service, no organisation, under my Ministry, was ordered to carry out any attack.' Next morning, Mitterrand, who had known the truth for weeks, told the Cabinet: 'They have lied to us enough. I want to know!'

It was the signal for the denouement. Summoned to confirm in writing that he had known nothing about the attack, Admiral Lacoste, realising that the political authorities were about to throw him to the wolves, wrote with considerable dignity – one of the few people in the whole affair who showed any – 'My duty requires me not to respond to these questions . . . I recognise the risks and consequences that my attitude implies, and I am ready to assume them.' The following day he was fired. Hernu resigned, still claiming, improbably, that his subordinates had misled him. Despite intense pressure from Fabius, who needed a credible scapegoat, he refused to acknowledge that he had given what he now called the 'stupid order' to sink the Greenpeace ship. It was left to the Prime Minister, after revealing on television the 'cruel truth' that the DGSE had indeed carried out the attack, to announce that the decision to sink the vessel had been taken 'at the level of' Lacoste and Hernu and that, as minister, Hernu was responsible.

There the matter ended. The 'Swiss couple', identified as French agents, were sentenced in New Zealand to ten years' imprisonment for manslaughter. Soon afterwards they were sent to a military base in French Polynesia to serve out the remainder of their sentences, an arrangement facilitated by French warnings that the renewal of EEC preferential tariffs for New Zealand agricultural produce might otherwise be blocked: Henri Nallet, the Agriculture Minister, told the Cabinet, 'It's our prisoners against their butter and lamb.'[40] France paid compensation to Greenpeace, to the New Zealand government and to the family of the dead photographer. The other French agents involved were never officially identified.

The puzzle of the *Rainbow Warrior* affair is not why it happened. All intelligence services commit blunders.[41] As Mitterrand himself said afterwards, if no one had been killed, there would have been no problem.

The puzzle is why the President let it fester. From the start, many of his advisers, including Ménage and Attali and the Interior Minister, Pierre Joxe, had urged him to come clean. If France admitted responsibility, they argued, public opinion would understand that it was a matter of national security. It would be a two-day wonder, the flow of revelations would be staunched, the opposition would be disarmed and in due course compensation would be negotiated through diplomatic channels, which is what would have to happen in any case. Mitterrand refused. The result was that the truth emerged anyway and he and his government were tarred by having clung to an obvious lie.[42]

None of the reasons that have been advanced for his adopting this attitude is convincing. It was said that he wanted to protect Hernu, who had been loyal to him at a time when his fortunes were at rock bottom after the Observatory Affair in 1959. It was true that he was reluctant to let Hernu go and he went out of his way afterwards to show that their friendship was unaltered. But he had realised early on that if things went badly the Defence Minister might have to resign.[43]

More credible is the view that he thought the government would get away with it. Until the middle of September, the New Zealand authorities had no proof that would convince a court of law that

French agents had sunk the *Rainbow Warrior*. The 'Swiss couple' could and did argue that their mission was limited to surveillance, and the crew of the mysterious French yacht seen shortly before the blast was already safely back in France. But Mitterrand had not reckoned on the endless rivalry between the two hierarchies – Defence and Interior, DGSE and DST, gendarmes and police. The crucial evidence of French involvement in the attack emerged not in New Zealand but in France, when *Le Monde* disclosed the existence of the third team of DGSE frogmen.[44]

Mitterrand had known about the third team for a month but had refused to take action. Once it became public, further denial was impossible.

Were other factors involved? It is legitimate to wonder. All Western leaders at times, in the words of the British Cabinet Secretary, Robert Armstrong, paraphrasing Edmund Burke, are 'economical with the truth': de Gaulle was less than honest about Algeria, Reagan tried to bury the Iran-Contra Affair, George W. Bush lied about 'weapons of mass destruction'. But Mitterrand's dissimulation in the case of the *Rainbow Warrior* is harder to explain. It was a 'big lie' about a small matter. Why did he take the risk?

Paradoxically, the fact that it was a small matter may have been part of the answer. Throughout the crisis, Mitterrand repeatedly compared his position to that of de Gaulle, twenty years earlier, when the Moroccan opposition leader, Mehdi Ben Barka, had been kidnapped in Paris, with the complicity of elements of the DGSE (then known as the SDECE). De Gaulle had described the service's implication in the Ben Barka Affair as 'vulgar and subaltern'. On September 11, Mitterrand told the French Cabinet that, by comparison with France's strategic interests, the sinking of the *Rainbow Warrior* was 'a secondary matter, of no great interest, whose importance has been much exaggerated.' A week later he asked his ministers: 'Do people really think that the President of the Republic has to be informed of what this or that special agent may do anywhere in the world?' New Zealand was a small and distant country. In terms of French domestic politics, what had happened to Greenpeace was not going to sway any votes in the forthcoming elections. If Mitterrand refused to get involved, it was partly because, as President, he thought it beneath the dignity of his office. It was not clever. As de Gaulle had said after the Ben Barka

Affair, 'it's all very fine and good not to want to get your hands dirty. But the result is that the State is dirtied instead.'

Gilles Ménage, who was responsible for following the affair at the Elysée and had bombarded Mitterrand with notes, urging him to force Hernu and the DGSE to acknowledge what they had done and get it over with, later chronicled in great detail the President's day-to-day reactions throughout the period.

Ménage was a Mitterrand loyalist and his purpose was to defend the President against charges that he had organised a deliberate 'strategy of lies'. The picture he painted, despite himself, was of chronic drift and paralysis. He wrote of the President refusing to respond to briefings, of 'a manifest lack of lucidity and authority', of 'a state of vacuity and doubt', of 'political decisions which have too long been put off', and of the President's conduct being 'marked by a strange distance [given] the reality of what he had always known about . . . the real scenario of the operation'.

Mitterrand's predilection for allowing crises to ripen, rather than biting the bullet and dealing with them at once, may have played its part too. It was what he had done both during the schools row and when he had been grappling with the austerity programme.

But in the case of the *Rainbow Warrior* the root of the problem was arrogance.

Mitterrand refused to understand that it was not a small matter but, if only in terms of its effect on his own legacy, a huge political misjudgement. Just as the Ben Barka Affair remained a stain on de Gaulle's presidency, so the sinking of the *Rainbow Warrior* would become indelibly associated with Mitterrand's time in power. Thirty years later, in the popular imagery of his life as a politician, the two egregious errors which stood out were the *Rainbow Warrior* and the Observatory Affair. Although very different in their causes and contexts, both left a reek of malfeasance which he was never able to throw off.

The other consequence of the attack and the cover-up was to widen the already yawning gap of mistrust between Mitterrand and the French intelligence services. In August Yves Bonnet had been fired following the leak about Farewell. Now, barely a month later, Lacoste followed. It could not have happened at a worse moment. After a year of relative calm, Middle Eastern terrorism was once more exploding on to the world stage. Mitterrand was no longer confronted only with bomb attacks. He faced a problem to which no Western leader would ever find an adequate solution: hostage-taking.

Despite the withdrawal of the Multinational Force from Lebanon, the Americans had continued to be a target of the nebulous radical Shiite movement associated with the Hezbollah, the 'Party of God'. In Beirut, three American citizens, including the CIA station chief in Lebanon, William Buckley Jnr., had been kidnapped. In each case, Islamic Jihad claimed responsibility.

The goal, like the method, was new. Hostage-taking was a means to put pressure on foreign governments to make concessions on issues unrelated to Lebanon itself. Before long France and Britain would feel the consequences. But first there was a curtain-raiser.

In July 1984 an Air France passenger jet was hijacked from Frankfurt to Teheran. The hijackers demanded the freeing of Anis Naccache and his accomplices in the attempted assassination of Shapour Bakhtiar. In Paris, Roland Dumas had a lengthy meeting with the Iranian chargé d'affaires. Instead of discussing the hijacking, the diplomat insisted on reviewing other long-standing grievances: France's failure to repay a $1 billion loan agreed in the 1970s by the Shah for a French uranium enrichment facility; and the activities in France of Massoud Radjavi and the Mujahideen, who, he said, were still conducting acts of terrorism against Iran. The last point would be tragically underlined two weeks later when twenty-eight people died and more than 300 were injured in a Mujahideen bomb attack on the Teheran railway station. Without addressing the substance of his remarks, Dumas replied that France might soften its stance if the passengers and crew were released and the aircraft returned. Under those conditions, he added, the government would also be willing to examine the situation of Naccache and his companions if the Iranian authorities so requested.

The exchange opened the way for an end to the hijacking but marked the beginning of a lethal misunderstanding. To the Iranians, Dumas's offer meant that the imprisoned Iranian commandos would soon be freed. To Dumas it meant simply that the government was willing to study the issue within the limits of what was possible under French law, which, in the case of men serving life sentences, was not very much.

By December, the French began to realise that Naccache was no ordinary prisoner. He and his companions had come to kill Shapour Bakhtiar because they had been ordered to do so by a *fatwa*, or religious decree, issued by Ayatollah Khomeini himself. To the Iranians, that made their mission not only lawful but sacred. But no one in Paris understood that the fate of Naccache and his companions was not just one grievance among many: it was Teheran's primary demand, beside which all the rest was secondary. Two cultures, with diametrically opposed views of the same set of events, were set to clash head on. As Gilles Ménage wrote later:

Who in France, at the end of 1984, could understand that refusing to free five assassins, convicted . . . after due process of law, could provide serious grounds for unleashing a terrorist campaign? . . . How could one give credit to these threats of reprisals which seemed beyond all common sense? . . . Acts of terrorism in France against public buildings and department stores, against . . . trains and airlines, . . . the assassination of military and civilian figures, kidnappings and hostage-takings in France and Lebanon? It would need the threats to start to be implemented before our disbelief would yield to the evidence.[45]

To muddy the waters further, another group had France in its sights. In October 1984, the DST had arrested in Lyon an individual using the name Abdu-Qadir Saadi, who was soon identified as Georges Ibrahim Abdallah, the head of the FARL, the Armed Revolutionary Lebanese Fractions, which had been responsible for attacks on Israeli and US diplomats in Paris in 1982 and the deaths of two French policemen. The French were still uncertain what the FARL represented. But they knew that Abdallah's lieutenants would not sit idly by and allow their leader to remain in prison indefinitely. The problem was what to do about it? The government was in two minds. The DST was instructed to contact its usual interlocutors – the Algerian, Syrian and Palestinian special services – to urge Abdallah's friends to be patient while the political authorities tried to find a solution.

Not all the news that year was bad. In July, with Mitterrand's approval, the DST had begun secret talks with Abu Nidal's organisation, resulting in an agreement to continue the truce which had been reached with the help of the Syrians eighteen months previously.* In November, the President visited Damascus and, in six hours of talks with Assad, whose intellectual finesse he appreciated better than the brutality of his regime, laid the basis for a more constructive relationship. Syria was committed to the destruction of Israel, to supporting Iran in the war against Iraq and to maintaining its suzerainty in Lebanon. But closer ties with the Syrians offered the prospect of a back-channel to Teheran, which, given the tension between France and Iran, might prove extremely helpful.

The bigger picture, however, was grim. Tensions in Lebanon peaked after the CIA detonated a car bomb on March 8 1985, just after Friday prayers, outside the home of Sheikh Fadlallah, a revered Shia leader regarded as the spiritual leader of the Hezbollah. The bomb attack, in which Fadlallah was unhurt but 172 people died and more than 250 were injured, many of them women and children, provoked brutal factional conflict. It had been ordered by William Casey in retaliation for Islamic Jihad's attack on the marines.

Over the next two and a half weeks, eight American, British and French nationals were taken hostage in Beirut, more than in the whole of the previous three years. On the morning of March 22, the French Vice-Consul, Marcel Fontaine, was kidnapped, followed a few hours later by another diplomat, Marcel Carton, and his daughter, Danièle, an embassy secretary. The next day, Saturday, the head of the French Cultural Centre in Tripoli, Gilles Peyroles, disappeared. In the next four years, ninety more hostages would follow, mainly Americans, French and British, but also Swiss, West Germans, Italians, Russians and citizens of Arab countries.

The FARL issued a communiqué, claiming responsibility for the kidnapping of Peyroles and offering to free him, but not the other three, in return for the release of Georges Ibrahim Abdallah. With

---

* Abu Nidal's interest was both in using France as neutral territory – through the same sort of Faustian pact as Giscard had reached with the Palestinians in the 1970s – and in obtaining the release of two members of his organisation who had been imprisoned there since 1978 for the murder of a PLO representative. He had started to put out feelers to the French through the intermediary of Austrian intelligence in the summer of 1983. A year later formal contacts with the DST began on the basis that the relationship would be 'purely professional, between "action service" and "action service"', and would be broken off immediately if any attack occurred against a French target.

the help of Algeria, a trade-off was worked out. At that point Abdallah had been charged only with using false papers and membership of an illegal organisation, both relatively minor offences. The deal was that he would be brought to trial swiftly, given a short prison term and, taking account of the time he had already served, expelled a few months later. In return the FARL would release Peyroles.

Ten days later the FARL kept their side of the bargain: Peyroles was freed. But France found itself unable to honour its commitment. A few hours after Peyroles had arrived at the French Embassy in Beirut, the DST raided an apartment in Paris which Abdallah had been renting. Inside they found a veritable arsenal. Among the weapons was a gun, which forensic experts found to have been the firearm used in the murders of two of the diplomats killed in Paris in 1982. To free Abdallah had become impossible. Instead he would have to be charged with murder.

Was the timing of the discovery a coincidence? Or had the DST acted in bad faith, negotiating with the Algerians while already knowing that Abdallah was likely to face much more serious charges?

In the end it made little difference. The fundamental error lay elsewhere. Mitterrand had known from the start that Abdallah headed a movement responsible for terrorist killings in France. But instead of stating clearly that no compromise would be permitted, he had equivocated. While the DST continued investigating, seeking evidence of Abdallah's guilt, the political authorities had been casting around for a way to get him off their hands before a terrorist campaign was launched to free him.*

The mishandling of the FARL leader's case should have taught Mitterrand a lesson. It did not.

Four months later, in the autumn of 1985, he agreed to free Abu Nidal's followers who were serving prison terms in France for murder. The Justice Minister, Robert Badinter, protested:

* This is not to say that Mitterrand could have prevented attacks by Abdallah's associates had he taken a firmer stand. The Italians had sentenced two members of the FARL, arrested at about the same time, to fifteen-year terms of imprisonment without attracting reprisals. But imprisoning Abdallah's followers was one thing, imprisoning the leader himself was another. The core group of the FARL, comprising some thirty individuals, including three of Abdallah's brothers, was drawn from Christian clans in three villages in north Lebanon. Its resources were limited. It would have focussed its energies on its leader's release whatever position Mitterrand had adopted.

These are two terrorists with blood on their hands . . . whom we are
putting back into circulation, in other words, to be active again. Freeing
them now will be contrasted with the attitude of firmness adopted by
[others]. A violent campaign will be launched on the theme: the French
government is always weak towards terrorism; it's negotiating with
Abu Nidal and giving way to him . . . Politically that will be difficult
to answer . . . And above all, morally, I am revolted by the idea that
murderers like this should get away with seven years in prison. So they
can start over again?[46]

Mitterrand went ahead anyway. Abu Nidal kept his word. His group
never attacked France again and, contrary to Badinter's fears, the two
terrorists who were freed did not rejoin the movement. But it set an
appalling precedent. Five weeks after their expulsion, the wife of one
of the French hostages in Lebanon told the President:

France made a deal with Abu Nidal. Isn't that negotiating with terrorists? . . . Abu Nidal blackmailed France and France freed two of his
followers. Why, for my husband [and] the others, has France said no?[47]

What could he possibly answer? Ten days later, at a meeting at the Elysée,
he let his bad conscience show, accusing the DST of having put him in
an 'impossible' position by negotiating an accord with Abu Nidal 'without
informing me at the time'. 'I was very reluctant [to agree],' he said, 'I
wasn't pleased at all, and that's a euphemism'. It was completely untrue.
He had been informed from the outset. But he preferred to deny – or
did not have the courage to admit – that it had been his decision.

Mitterrand's inconsistencies reflected the insoluble dilemma which
all democracies face when confronted with terrorism.

On the one hand he believed that the State had an overriding duty
to succour its citizens in distress. In 1980, when Jimmy Carter had
authorised an airborne raid into Iran in a failed attempt to free the
US Embassy hostages, Mitterrand had been one of the few to support
him. 'For myself,' he said, 'I think when a foreign country seizes our
fellow citizens, our compatriots, for whatever reason it may be – if
they were French, this is how I would react – my duty would be to
use every means at my disposal to free them . . . From instinct I won't
criticise someone who tries to save his brother.'

On the other hand he was adamantly opposed to any action implying a surrender of sovereignty under pressure from a foreign State, and still less a terrorist group.

The position that resulted was both ambiguous and illogical.

France would 'do anything except yield', Mitterrand declared. If it did yield, as in practice it often had to, it must be in a manner and at a time which he alone, as Head of State, would choose. Outside the President's own narrow circle of advisers, who all, with the exception of Robert Badinter, endorsed this contorted logic, even the most charitable observer would find it hard to see anything other than a dubious attempt to save face. It meant that the principle of a trade-off between, on the one hand, the release of convicted terrorists, like Abu Nidal's followers or Naccache, and, on the other, the promise that France would be spared future terrorist attacks or that its hostages would be released, was perfectly acceptable, so long as the forms were observed and the French President, rather than the hostage-takers, determined how it was worked out.

Mitterrand's only consolation was that, in different ways, most other Western leaders were doing the same.

France's reputation for weakness, to which Badinter alluded, dated from 1977, when Giscard had expelled Abu Daoud, who had master-minded the killing of Israeli athletes at the Munich Olympics, ignoring extradition requests from both Israel and West Germany. But that was no different from the Italian government's decision, during the *Achille Lauro* affair, to put the Palestinian terrorist, Abu Abbas, discreetly on a plane to Yugoslavia rather than risk the complications of putting him on trial. Reagan liked to insist that he would never deal with terrorists, but when a Trans World Airlines jet on a flight from Athens to Rome was hijacked in the summer of 1986, he backed down. To secure the release of the 39 American hostages, the White House reached a secret agreement with Israel whereby more than 700 Shiite and Palestinian prisoners would be freed in exchange.

'Terrorism worked, it functioned,' Mitterrand told the French Cabinet afterwards. 'On the American side, there was only an appearance of strength'.

'Irangate' was the same. The Reagan administration purchased the release of three American hostages with arms supplies and a ransom.[48] Even Israel, whose reputation for intransigence is unequalled, exchanged – and continues to exchange – thousands of Palestinian prisoners, including convicted terrorists, for captured Israeli soldiers.

Only Margaret Thatcher, in a country where public opinion was more stoical than elsewhere, could afford the luxury of an iron refusal ever to cave in. British policy was to refuse to negotiate on the grounds that doing so would confirm the hostages' value and encourage the kidnappers to raise the stakes. It was a far tougher stance than that of any of Britain's partners. Did the casuistry of other nations serve their hostages better? The evidence is inconclusive but it seems probably not.

In 1985, Mitterrand paid the price for his weakness.

The Iranians felt he had cheated them by failing to follow through on what they interpreted as a promise to release Naccache and his companions. In Lebanon his refusal to release Georges Ibrahim Abdallah after the freeing of Peyroles was taken as meaning that France could not be trusted to keep its word. The negotiations with Abu Nidal were seen as proof that he would buckle if sufficient pressure were applied.

The group which had abducted Marcel Fontaine and Marcel Carton and his daughter was of a very different calibre from the FARL. Islamic Jihad said they would be released once 'France stops intervening directly and indirectly in the war' between Iran and Iraq. No one in Paris realised that that statement meant exactly what it said. Nor did anyone read correctly the signals coming out of Teheran. The Chief of the Revolutionary Guards, Mohsen Rafiqdoust, told the French chargé d'affaires, Jean Perrin, that 'it was time to bring to an end' the problem of Naccache and his companions who 'had only been carrying out their religious duty'. Arafat passed on a message that Khomeini himself was 'pulling the strings' and that the release of Naccache would unblock the situation. In a conciliatory gesture, Marcel Carton's daughter was released.

The Iranians soon saw that they were wasting their time. No one in France understood what they were trying to say. To Mitterrand, the hostages in Lebanon and the possibility of improved relations with Iran were two different things. It was simply inconceivable that there could be a link between them.[49]

On May 22, Teheran stepped up the pressure. Two more hostages were taken: Jean-Paul Kauffmann, a journalist for a French weekly, and Michel Seurat, an Arabist.

But at the Elysée it was not until September that the truth finally dawned.

Two messages were received in Paris that month: one, unofficial, through a Lebanese journalist in Teheran; the other, official, from Assad, but conveyed orally by an emissary as the Syrian President was unwilling to put it in writing. Their substance was the same. The French hostages would be released when France agreed to free the Iranians who had tried to kill Shapour Bakhtiar.

To the Syrian envoy Mitterrand responded that Naccache and his companions would be freed before his term of office ended in 1988, but at a moment of his choosing and on condition that all four French hostages were freed together and at once.[50]

He now grasped that Teheran must have a significant role in the kidnappings in Beirut. How else could it offer what was, in effect, an exchange? But he still did not understand that Iran was not merely complicit in the hostage-taking and attendant 'noises off' but was orchestrating the whole performance. Hence the government's perplexity when, on December 7 1985, with the Christmas shopping rush in full swing, bombs exploded simultaneously in two leading department stores, Galeries Lafayette and Printemps, leaving forty-three people injured. There was no credible claim of responsibility and, after following a number of false trails, investigators concluded that it was probably the work of the FARL.

In fact it was a warning that Iran's patience was running out. Once again the message was not understood. But the Iranians must have concluded that their tactics were having an effect because, less than three weeks later, for reasons which had nothing to do with Iran and everything to do with French domestic politics – parliamentary elections were looming and the government sorely needed a success – Mitterrand improved his offer. He was ready, he told Assad, to grant a pardon to Anis Naccache 'on medical and humanitarian grounds' and to release him *at the same time* as the four French hostages were freed. His four companions would be liberated, as Mitterrand had promised earlier, before the end of his presidential term.[51]

On New Year's Eve, at the Syrian leader's request, the President put the offer in writing, but in very cautious terms. 'I confirm to you,' he wrote, 'the overtures made by France of which you have been informed.' Mitterrand was no more willing than Assad to set out in a formal letter the details of a hostage transfer which, even if it succeeded, meant caving in to blackmail – as Robert Badinter was once again quick to point out:

> Suppose tomorrow two tourists are taken hostage at the Hotel Bristol in Paris and [those responsible] demand that you release without delay a criminal in prison [here] who has been convicted of two murders. I am sure you would not do so. For that would be the end of the justice system in France. The situation today is morally no different. Except that the hostage-taking occurred in Beirut, not the Faubourg St Honoré [in Paris]. . . Nothing seems to me more fraught with danger for the future in the face of terrorists who will remember this example.[52]

Morally the Justice Minister was right. But Mitterrand had made up his mind. And there was a practical difference between the two situations. In Paris, the GIGN could have intervened and there would have been a chance of rescuing the hostages and perhaps of capturing the kidnappers. In Lebanon, that choice was not available. The only alternatives were to negotiate, as Reagan was doing, or to refuse all contact, as Thatcher had in Britain.

Badinter put aside his scruples and signed a decree of pardon with the date left blank for the President to fill in when the moment came.

On January 2 1986, a Thursday, a first hint of difficulties appeared when an Iranian envoy told the French Foreign Ministry that the Iranian authorities would have preferred Mitterrand to spell out more clearly the 'modalities and dates' for the release of Naccache's four companions. But two days later, Assad wrote that he was 'convinced' that there would be 'a rapid resolution' and that they were finally on the verge of achieving 'definitive results'. The plan was for the hostages to be taken to Damascus that evening pending Naccache's release. In Paris, Roland Dumas waited for a signal from the Syrian Foreign Minister for the Iranian assassin to be flown out to Switzerland en route to Teheran, at which point the hostages would be transferred to the French Ambassador and he himself would leave for Syria to escort them home.

The signal did not come.

Instead, early next morning, Assad telephoned Mitterrand to say there had been a hitch but he hoped it would be resolved. In fact, for reasons the French would slowly piece together in the coming weeks, the window of opportunity had closed. The negotiations had collapsed.

A month later the price of that failure was spelt out in blood.

Over three days, starting on Monday, February 3, four bombs exploded in crowded shopping areas and at the Eiffel Tower. More than thirty people were injured, five seriously. The explosives had been placed to create panic and to wound, not to kill. A previously unknown group, the 'Support Committee for Arab and Middle Eastern Political Prisoners', known by its French initials as the CSPPA, announced that it had carried out the attacks and that they would continue until the government released Anis Naccache and his companions; an Armenian terrorist, Varajian Garbidjan, serving a term of life imprisonment for the 1983 Orly Airport attack; and Georges Ibrahim Abdallah of the FARL. That Abdallah's group and ASALA might have played a role in the attacks was not excluded by French investigators. But the timing suggested they were a follow-up to the stalled negotiations at the turn of the year and that the principal goal remained the Iranians' release.

By this time it was clear that several factors had combined to cause the hostage exchange to abort. At some point in the first days of January, Teheran learnt that Michel Seurat, who had been suffering from hepatitis since the autumn, was dying and could not be moved.[53] The Mullahs' hopes that Mitterrand would reduce French arms sales to Iraq had also been disappointed – a new contract for thirty-two Mirage jet fighters had been signed that autumn – and, unlike Reagan, he continued to refuse to sell weaponry to Iran. Furthermore there was no sign of the financial dispute between France and Iran nearing resolution. Why give up a bargaining chip – the hostages – when there had been no movement in return? Moreover, despite Assad's assurances, the Iranians, from Ayatollah Khomeini down, were not convinced that the French President would keep his word. France had promised to free Georges Ibrahim Abdallah in exchange for Peyroles but had not done so. Who was to say that the same thing would not happen to Naccache's four companions once the French hostages had been freed?

There was another consideration too. If, as seemed almost certain, the Left lost its parliamentary majority in the elections in March, it would open the way for the Right to take power. Might a right-wing government offer a more favourable deal? Emissaries from the Gaullist leader, Jacques Chirac, were in contact with Teheran. Even if, as Chirac later insisted, the talks were purely exploratory, it was a God-given opportunity for the Iranians to sow discord among the French political parties, to ratchet up the pressure on Mitterrand to make additional concessions and, not least, to provide an acceptable explanation for having backed out of an agreement which had actually broken down for quite different reasons. After all, who could blame Iran if the French Right, from electoral calculations, had undercut the Socialists by proposing more attractive terms? The truth about what Chirac's envoys offered, or did not offer, and what the Iranians read into it, will almost certainly never be known.[54] But within days of the negotiations foundering, Iranian intermediaries were telling their contacts in the French government: 'Your opposition has offered to do better.'

Elections are rarely decided on the basis of foreign policy. Even with the overhang of terrorism and hostage-taking, that remained true in France in 1986. The shape of the next parliament would be determined by domestic issues.

There the picture was nuanced. The emblematic measures of Mitterrand's first year were still in place and had not been forgotten. Decentralisation had been widely applauded. The ending of the state monopoly over radio and television was overdue (although still incomplete: the French broadcast media remained more subservient to their political masters than those of Britain or the United States). But the 'glorious fracture' Mitterrand had promised – the creation of a new social model through a 'rupture with capitalism' – was long since dead and buried.

In its place he had installed a regime which anywhere else in Europe would have been described as a social democracy,[55] where a careful mixture of state initiative and private enterprise was expected to pull the country out of the economic slough in which the rest of Europe was floundering.

Instead of a rupture, Mitterrand had brought reconciliation – the reconciliation of the working class with the notions of profit and enterprise – and it had turned out to be what France needed. The nationalisations, misconceived at the origin, had had a silver lining. The Left had been forced to create conditions in which the national-ised industries could succeed and, in so doing, had learnt to live with what it had previously denounced as the misdeeds of the capitalist economy. French workers began for the first time to understand – as the Germans had long before them – that profits were the investments, and therefore the jobs, of tomorrow. No longer did the unions declare, 'It's them or us!', as Gaston Defferre had exclaimed in 1981. Economics had the same rules for all, whether State or private sector. There had been difficult moments. When Creusot-Loire, the only large French machine-tool manufacturer, declared bankruptcy with the loss of 10,000 jobs, Fabius and Bérégovoy refused to bail it out, breaking an unwritten rule that French governments would always come to the rescue of companies considered too big to fail. The car-maker, Renault, was allowed to shed 20,000 workers. It had been painful, but the result was that French industry became competitive again. Inflation had been brought under control. Foreign debt had stabilised at 10 per cent of GDP. In the autumn of 1985, after four successive devaluations, the government had even been able to announce a modest revaluation of the franc.

Class antagonisms did not disappear altogether but they became more manageable. Ideological schisms, which had determined French political life since the Revolution, while still present, were in retreat. Socialism, like Catholicism before it, was no longer a defining, trans-cendent world view, but one option among others. With less resistance than anyone would have thought possible, one of the most conserv-ative countries in Europe, profoundly attached to its own rules and traditions, mired in corporatism and an outlandish, almost insular conformity in its thinking and way of life, was dragged into the modern world.

On the other hand unemployment, far from stabilising, had grown by 38 per cent, to 2.4 million, and household income had barely kept pace with inflation.

Mitterrand had reduced some of the most glaring social inequali-ties, but to give more to the poor – or, as the new political correctness had it, the disadvantaged and underprivileged – at a time when the national cake remained the same because of low economic growth, he had had to take more from the rich and the better off. Members of those groups, who in 1981 had given the Left the benefit of the doubt, were not inclined to make the same mistake a second time. Had the economy turned the corner, opening the prospect of sustained growth, that would have mattered less. But as Mitterrand told Jacques Chaban-Delmas, 'we needed another six months or a year for public opinion to feel the effects of the political change of direction in 1982 and '83'. Had he embraced the austerity programme sooner, those effects might already have come through. But he had hesitated. Now he had to face the consequences.

By the summer the only question was not whether the Left would be defeated but by how big a margin.

The Right saw unemployment, insecurity and immigration, the trinity of grievances which most exercised French voters, as a potentially winning cocktail. But the mainstream parties had a rival in exploiting this rich vein of discontent. Mitterrand's old adversary from the 1950s, the ex-paratrooper, veteran of the wars in Algeria and Indochina, Jean-Marie Le Pen, now headed the National Front, an alliance of far-Right splinter groups formed shortly after de Gaulle's death which had recently won a following by playing on the fears that had resulted from the Socialist–Communist coalition taking power. The Front argued that the mainstream Right was too weak and in too much disarray to provide a credible alternative and that a muscular administration was needed, capable of putting France's interests first.

Le Pen had a sulphurous reputation. He had approved the use of torture in Algeria and would later describe the use of the gas chambers to exterminate the Jews as 'a detail' of the Second World War. A powerful orator, unconcerned by accusations of racism, he maintained that he merely 'said out loud what the French people think deep down'. His equation of immigration with joblessness and insecurity resonated strongly not only in working-class areas with high unemployment rates but among elements of the middle and upper classes.

The National Front's emergence created problems and opportunities for both the Left and the Right. It drove a wedge into the traditional right-wing electorate, draining away votes which would otherwise have gone to Chirac's RPR and the centrist parties in Giscard's UDF. That was a boon for the Socialists. Mitterrand had said years before that when he came to power he would 'hang a "saucepan" on to the Right'. Le Pen's National Front was the best 'saucepan' he could ever hope to find. In 1984, before the European elections, the President had given him a discreet helping hand by making it known to French broadcasters that, 'in the interests of democracy', Le Pen, who until then had been excluded from the airwaves, should be allowed to appear like any other party leader. The National Front had gone on to win nearly 11 per cent of the vote that summer, up from a previous best of less than 1 per cent. But the Right had a consolation prize. The Front's rise had co-incided with the vertiginous decline of the Communists, who, since the war, had never won less than 20 per cent of the vote and now saw their support cut in half. The symmetry was striking: the new National Front strongholds – in the industrial north-east and along the Mediterranean coast – were in what had previously been communist areas.[56]

The upshot was that the Right – National Front and mainstream parties combined – had a clear political majority in the nation as a whole, while the Socialists were condemned by the weakness of their Communist allies. That was not what Mitterrand had had in mind when he had told the Socialist International in 1972 that his goal was 'to show that out of five million communist voters, three million can vote socialist'. His stratagem to weaken the Communist Party had succeeded beyond his expectations. But instead of going to the Socialists, their votes had been scattered elsewhere.

His response was to play the National Front card for all it was worth. No. 47 of the '110 Propositions' had been to introduce propor-tional representation for parliamentary, regional and certain types of local elections. In April 1985, the Cabinet approved a bill to that effect, which was enacted by parliament the following July. The Right, predict-ably, cried foul. Mitterrand, said Chirac, was 'a politician of great talent and great experience. [He] mounted this whole operation to let the National Front develop.' It was both true and untrue. The Front had already taken off, as it had shown by its performance in the European elections a year earlier. But by introducing proportional representation, instead of keeping the first-past-the-post constituency system, Mitterrand ensured the election of several dozen extreme right-wing MPs, amputating by the same margin the mainstream right-wing parties' majority.

The effect was to make the contest more complicated than either side had anticipated. A year earlier, the Right had been confident that it could gain control of parliament without having to rely on the National Front's support. Now it was not so sure.

Raymond Barre, who had been Giscard's Prime Minister in the second half of the 1970s and who saw himself as the natural candidate of the Right in the 1988 presidential election, hoped – though he would never admit it – that the assembly would be ungovernable, which would prevent his rival, Chirac, accepting the prime minister-ship under Mitterrand and using it as a springboard for his own presidential ambitions. Accordingly he denounced the prospect of 'cohabitation' between Left and Right as unconstitutional and remained on the sidelines throughout the right-wing parties' campaign. As Election Day approached, Mitterrand's popularity, which had plumbed the depths, improved. After being stuck for months at 38 per cent, the proportion of those with favourable opinions of him rose in November to 41 per cent and three months later to 46 per cent. The President's goal – though, like Barre, he could not admit it – was also an ungovernable parliament, in which the Socialists would not have a majority but the Right would not have one either.

Mitterrand, like Chirac, faced a problem of disunity in his own camp. Fabius, as Prime Minister, and Jospin, as Socialist Party First Secretary, were no longer speaking to each other. Fabius stressed the need to win back the moderate centrist voters who had helped to assure Mitterrand's victory in 1981; Jospin wanted to ensure that the Left came out in force. The President settled the quarrel of personalities by coming down on Jospin's side. But the dilemma over policy was more difficult. Mitterrand needed the support of both the Centre *and* the Left. Squaring that particular circle was beyond even his considerable powers of doublespeak, but it did not stop him trying.

At his first election meeting, in the suburbs of Rouen in Normandy in mid-January, he set out deliberately to encourage the Left, declaring, 'I do not want a France where the strongest, because they are richest, will be able to crush the weakest, because they are poorest'. That galvanised his traditional supporters but left him open to the charge of behaving like a party chieftain rather than Head of State, with the implication, as Chirac was quick to point out, that if the Left were disavowed at the elections, the President would be disavowed too. Three weeks later, at Lille, on February 7 1986, he changed tack:

> The French have the right to choose the [parliamentary] majority they prefer . . . People say to me when I address a meeting like this . . . , 'How dare you! You shouldn't, it's unworthy of a President', forgetting that my predecessors used and misused [their power to influence election campaigns] far more than I have done.
>
> Some say, 'You are [behaving as] a party leader.' No, I'm not a party leader. I used to be. But it isn't me any more. You may have noticed . . .
>
> [I cannot] imagine for a single second that I could assume the essential responsibilities of the French nation without seeking to bring together, to reunite and reconcile . . . Yes, there is a certain model of society which I personally prefer. Not for nothing have I . . . worked for the advent of socialism in France. [But] there is no socialism without freedom. I may have my preferences but I am the President of all French people. I consider the interests of the others to be [even] more exigent than the interests of our own [supporters]. It would be easy to take preference too far. Deep down, I have no preference. What I love . . . is France and the French![57]

This speech, in which he assumed the role of father figure to the nation, came just after the wave of bomb attacks by the CSPPA in Paris. The emphasis on national unity was not unconnected to the resurgence of Middle Eastern terrorism.

The three principal right-wing leaders, Chirac, Giscard and Barre, closed ranks behind him. But their lieutenants – 'featherbrains and demagogues who think they can make political advantage out of the blood of others,' Mitterrand lashed out – had no such qualms, accusing the Left of 'indifference, irresponsibility and laxness'.

As Election Day neared, the bad news from the Middle East reached a crescendo. On March 5, Islamic Jihad announced the 'execution' of Michel Seurat (who in reality had died in January).[58] Three days later, four members of a French television crew were kidnapped in Lebanon. The following week photographs of Seurat's corpse were provided to a news agency. In Paris the bells of Notre-Dame tolled a death knell and news broadcasts observed a minute of silence. On Friday,

March 14, as the campaign drew to a close, the hostage-takers provided video recordings, broadcast on French television that night, of the three other surviving hostages, Marcel Carton, Marcel Fontaine and Jean-Paul Kauffmann, who spoke of their depression and despair of ever regaining freedom.

Throughout that week French government envoys had been negotiating in Teheran in a last-ditch effort to secure their release before Election Day. But as in January, after a semblance of trying to reach an accord, the Iranians broke off the discussions, claiming once again that the opposition was ready to give better terms.[59] Whether they really believed that the incoming government would be more amenable to a hostage exchange than the Socialists is unclear, but they plainly decided that they had nothing to lose by creating bad blood between Mitterrand and his right-wing opponents.[60]

In the end the bomb attacks and hostage-taking had no more effect on the electorate than the sinking of the *Rainbow Warrior*. They were a blow against France, not against a political party, and may even have helped the Left in the sense that Mitterrand was perceived as a steady hand on the tiller in a turbulent time.

The election was contested on familiar domestic themes.

The Socialist Party's slogan was: 'Help! The Right is coming back!' It was not very uplifting, but the image of a right-wing bogeyman, about to take back all the goodies which 'Tonton' and the Socialists had given the poorest members of society was a good scare tactic to mobilise the Left.

The National Front trumpeted, 'France and the French, First!', which resonated with those who felt their heritage was being despoiled by the technocrats in Brussels and by the detritus of the Third World demanding a share of Europe's wealth.

The Gaullists and the UDF, which campaigned on Chirac's slogan, 'I can't wait for tomorrow', found it harder to articulate a distinctive identity because two of their preferred topics, immigration and insecurity, had been hijacked by the far Right. Instead they tried to mobilise the middle ground.

When the ballots were counted, on Sunday, March 16, the Socialists had done better than most in the Party had expected, winning 31 per cent of the vote – their best result ever, apart from the landslide of 1981 – giving them 217 seats, including affiliated members. The

Communists did even worse than in the European elections eighteen months earlier, obtaining 9.8 per cent and 35 seats, the first time since the 1920s the Party had received less than 10 per cent of the vote. The National Front, with an almost identical score, also won 35 seats, the best showing by the extreme Right since the Poujadist high tide in 1956. The Gaullists and the UDF had 290 seats, including affiliated members, just enough to claim an absolute majority, with Chirac's RPR, as expected, the strongest right-wing party.

As it turned out, both sides had got what they wanted.

The victory of the Right was sufficiently narrow – a majority of only three seats – for Mitterrand to continue as President from a position of strength. But it was enough for the mainstream parties to be able to govern without having to keep looking over their shoulder at the National Front. A few days before the vote, Mitterrand had told Henry Kissinger with a certain relish: 'Don't worry. The game that's starting now will be completely new. The most unexpected things are going to happen.' To Americans, used to a system where the powers of the President and Congress are often in opposition, the notion of 'cohabitation' between Left and Right was par for the course. But in the US the respective attributions and prerogatives of executive and legislative authority have been honed over centuries. For France it meant a leap into the unknown. For the first time in the country's history, a President of the Left and a Prime Minister from the Right would have not merely to cohabit – a term Mitterrand disliked; he preferred to speak of 'coexistence' – but to rule in tandem.

13

The Florentine

François Mitterrand was not a man to lay his cards on the table.

He had decided months earlier that he would name Jacques Chirac Prime Minister if, as he anticipated, the mainstream right-wing parties obtained an overall parliamentary majority. There were three principal reasons. Chirac's party, the RPR, was the strongest, so constitutionally he was the natural choice: from the President's point of view, it would show that he was being above-board and transparent. Secondly, if anyone else were designated, there was a risk that, a few weeks or months later, the RPR would provoke a vote of confidence to bring the government down, at which point the President would have to name Chirac anyway, not from a position of strength but under the pressure of events. Thirdly, he sensed that Chirac, of all the right-wing leaders, was the most dangerous opponent. By letting him share power he would fatally weaken him, just as he had done earlier to the Communist Party through the Union of the Left.

Officially, however, his mind was not yet made up. To make it appear that he had not just one but several possible choices, Mitterrand went through the motions of sounding out Giscard and the Mayor of Bordeaux, Jacques Chaban-Delmas, who were also in theory candidates to head the government.

Chaban knew the President well enough to guess his intentions. He warned Chirac: 'In two years Mitterrand will stand again. If you are Prime Minister, you will be standing against him. You should realise the French . . . won't like that and your chances will be diminished.' Chirac disagreed. His principal adviser, Édouard Balladur, who had pioneered the idea of cohabitation, had convinced him that Matignon would be his springboard to the Elysée, as it had once been for his mentor, Georges Pompidou. But the analogy was strained. Pompidou had not tried to stand against de Gaulle. Chirac risked having to stand against Mitterrand. To make that gamble pay off, he would have to show public opinion that he was able to outwit the President even as they worked together. It was a tall order. But Chirac was determined to try.

The result was that for the next two years, cohabitation would play out as a cloak and dagger drama in which, behind a façade of unity, each of the two protagonists tried constantly to stab the other in the back.

The French loved it.

It was new and different. It had never been attempted before. At a time when the old ideological certainties were losing their appeal, the notion that Left and Right should be compelled to work together was infinitely attractive. Two-thirds of those questioned were enthusiastic about cohabitation.

Mitterrand skilfully assumed the posture of a father-figure, watching over the welfare of the country for the greater good of all. Within twenty-four hours of the result he announced on television: 'You have elected a new majority . . . Numerically the majority is narrow, but it exists. It is therefore from among its ranks that I shall name the person I choose to form a government.' It was what people wanted to hear and his popularity soared.

On Tuesday, March 18, the President received Chirac tête-à-tête for more than two hours to discuss the guidelines they would need to follow. The constitution had been drafted by de Gaulle to be elastic, laying down that the Prime Minister 'directs the actions of the government', while the President 'ensures by his arbitration the proper functioning of the powers and continuity of the State', acts as 'the guarantor of national independence' and 'negotiates and ratifies treaties'. The President was 'the Chief of the Armed Forces', the Prime Minister was 'responsible for national defence' and the government 'has the armed forces . . . at its disposal'. Where the powers of one ended and the other began was far from clear. When all were from the same side, responsibility was shared. But now that they were from opposing camps, the rules would have to be written as they went along.

Neither was particularly forthcoming afterwards about what had been said. Chirac agreed in principle that Mitterrand should conserve his prerogatives in the realm of Foreign Policy and Defence, but without saying what those were. Mitterrand agreed that Chirac should accompany him to European and G7 summits, but without saying what role he would play there. Chirac said that, in order to circumvent parliamentary filibusters, he intended 'in some cases' to legislate by *ordonnances*, a type of decree which enables the Cabinet to rule, in certain circumstances, by administrative fiat. Mitterrand replied cautiously that 'in some cases' he would accept that. Two days later Chirac returned to the charge, asking him to authorise the use of decrees for a wide range of legislation as well as the convening of an extra session of parliament if it proved necessary to enact the government's programme. Mitterrand refused.

They did agree, however, that the two most sensitive external ministries, Foreign Affairs and Defence, should be held by relatively non-political figures: Jean-Bernard Raimond, a career diplomat who was then Ambassador to Moscow; and André Giraud, a civil service mandarin who had served as Industry Minister under Giscard.

That afternoon, Thursday, March 20, the Elysée announced that Chirac had been appointed Prime Minister.

The first meeting of the new Cabinet, held exceptionally on a Saturday, would remain seared into the memories of all who were present. Mitterrand entered, followed by the Prime Minister. Without looking at any of them, without shaking hands as was customary, Mitterrand took his seat in silence. Albin Chalandon, the Justice Minister, who had been a minister under Pompidou and de Gaulle, remembered him being 'impressive, frightening even . . . deathly pale and completely turned in on himself . . . His refusal to go round the table shaking hands was a declaration of war.'

'The atmosphere was glacial,' another minister wrote. 'He imposed his authority so strongly that at the end of the meeting we were all like terrorised schoolboys. In a word, the intruders were us.' Mitterrand said afterwards he felt encircled by a band of men '60 per cent of whom hated me and 80 per cent were fighting against me'. The Cabinet meeting had been 'atrocious', he told Attali. But if that was the case, it was because he had deliberately made it so in order to show that this was not 'his' government.

Cohabitation was a misnomer. Coexistence with Chirac was a battleground.

It was the kind of warfare, with his back to the wall, surrounded by hostile forces, at which Mitterrand excelled. 'He suffered,' Patrice

Pelat remembered. 'It was hard for him to see his opponents arrive as conquerors.' But another side of him revelled in it. It was his chance to turn the tables on them and to do so single-handed.

The following Wednesday, after Chirac had laid out before the Cabinet the main lines of the government's programme, Mitterrand again expressed reservations about legislation by decree. In the slightly weary tones of a paterfamilias reminding his offspring yet again not to transgress the rules, he told them: 'It wouldn't please me to have to refuse to sign decrees after the government has already committed itself. We should not multiply sources of conflict when there are more than enough already.'[1] Two weeks later, he repeated the warning. But Chirac, encouraged by Giscard, who told him that Mitterrand would have no choice but to sign a decree which the Cabinet had approved, decided to press ahead anyway.

Matters came to a head on July 14, a Monday, when, in a television interview after the traditional Bastille Day parade, Mitterrand announced that he would refuse to approve decrees on privatisation. 'My duty,' he told his questioner, 'is to ensure France's independence and the national interest.' The government's proposals, he said, would allow foreign interests to acquire stakes in key sectors of the French economy, including enterprises nationalised by de Gaulle in 1945.[2] He was also uncertain that the method of valuation applied was to the country's advantage. If the government wished to proceed, it could take the issue to parliament, which could vote a law accordingly. But without parliamentary approval he was not prepared to sign measures whose justification seemed to him doubtful.

It was better than any soap opera. Here, live on television, a full-scale political crisis was unfolding before the nation's eyes. Would Mitterrand prevail? Would Chirac resign?

The President acknowledged to his aides that he was 'on a knife-edge'.

That evening, the telephone rang. It was Chirac:

MITTERRAND: For at least two months I have repeatedly made clear to you my serious reservations about the use of decrees [for privatisation]. I do not wish to take responsibility for these measures. Decrees on other matters for the most part I will sign, subject to their content. Why not in this case proceed [through parliament]? . . .

CHIRAC: So you want to bring an end to cohabitation?

MITTERRAND: I do not want that. But I assume the consequences of my actions. I don't blame you. You must do as you think best . . . If you had gone through parliament from the outset this might be over by now. I told you I would not sign . . . I will not give way . . .

CHIRAC: According to the lawyers, the President does not have the right to refuse to sign decrees . . .

MITTERRAND: I will not give way . . . If it puts an end to this experience [of cohabitation], well, I shall regret it. [But] I am a free agent. The only thing I want is to finish my mandate properly. That said, if there has to be a crisis, I've been expecting it ever since [the elections]. And I've known what the election results were going to be for four years . . . If you think a crisis is inevitable, I accept it . . . To tell the truth, it's already a miracle that we've managed [to work together] for four months. Let us try to make this miracle last. I warned you, but you did not believe me.[3]

When he put down the phone, Mitterrand turned to Attali and Bianco. 'We will see what he does,' he said. 'He'll change his mind three times and then he'll back down . . . He's not a bad fellow.'

Chirac was in a dilemma. Mitterrand had chosen his ground carefully. How could Chirac convince public opinion that he was justified in provoking a crisis . . . to do what? To sidestep parliament? If he resigned – having done so once before under Giscard – he would be accused of lacking the steady hand that statesmanship requires. If Mitterrand dissolved parliament, proportional representation still applied. The President's popularity was back over 60 per cent. It was not certain that the right-wing parties would be able to improve, or even retain, their majority.[4]

The Young Turks on the Right urged a showdown.

Balladur, supported by the Interior Minister, Charles Pasqua, argued for caution. Reluctantly, Chirac agreed. He dressed it up as an act of responsible government. When the Cabinet met, two days later, he told Mitterrand that to avoid 'a grave political crisis' the government would ask parliament to pass a bill rather than legislating by decree. That night he spoke on television. Mitterrand, he said, had opposed the 'clearly expressed will of the majority', but he had decided to spare the country a crisis 'which the French people would not understand'.

Parliament enacted the required legislation and Mitterrand signed it into law soon afterwards.

For the President, it was a decisive victory.

The pretext was contrived, even flimsy: what difference did it make in the end whether the privatisations were carried out by decree or by parliamentary vote? But it had enabled him to show the country the limits of the Prime Minister's power. Chirac had been scalded. His spokesman, Denis Baudouin, quoted him as saying afterwards: 'I don't want any more problems, no clashes with Mitterrand.' François Bujon de l'Estang, his diplomatic adviser, said: 'It was the turning point . . . From that day on, Mitterrand's recovery was unstoppable.'

Baudouin and de l'Estang both felt that Chirac had made 'a monumental, fatal error' by staying on. So long as the RPR leader remained Prime Minister, Mitterrand would suffocate him. Had he slammed the door and regained his freedom he might have done no better. But by remaining he helped to perpetuate a state of affairs – cohabitation – for which public opinion gave Mitterrand the credit. Jean-Louis Bianco was not alone in thinking that had the Prime Minister risen to the challenge and tendered his resignation, Mitterrand might have been in difficulty.

The President had taken a gamble. He was much less certain of winning than he had let on. Chirac had exposed himself by choosing a modus operandi vulnerable to a presidential veto and Mitterrand had pounced.

That the President's instincts had proved correct said much about the relationship between them. One was cold and introspective, the other warm and extrovert. The Prime Minister was sixteen years younger. To Mitterrand he was 'energetic, tenacious, intelligent and hard-working . . . but he lacks internal solidity and perhaps, also, real character'. Chirac recalled a warning from Pompidou: 'Never let Mitterrand impress you. No matter what he tells you, never believe a word he says.' But then Chirac added: 'It's true that Mitterrand always has that refined, subtle, intelligent way of enveloping you.' Therein lay the difference. Chirac admired Mitterrand and deep down he wanted the President to like him. 'What an artist!' he would say, after Mitterrand had wrought some particularly subtle piece of political magic, 'I take my hat off to him. I don't know how to do that kind of thing.' Mitterrand appreciated Chirac's qualities and was sometimes moved by his generous impulses. But he did not admire him or even regard him as being on the same level. It was an unequal contest.

If the dispute over the signing of decrees established a pecking order for cohabitation, it did not put an end to turf fights.

In April Reagan decided to mount a raid against Libya, suspected, with good reason, of fomenting terrorist attacks against US interests. Thatcher, against the advice of most of her Cabinet, agreed to let American aircraft fly from British bases. Mitterrand and Chirac, who felt the main effect of the raid would be to rally the Arab world behind Gaddafi, decided jointly to forbid the planes to overfly France. Spain did the same. On April 14, the Americans went ahead, killing some sixty Libyans, most of them civilians, including Gaddafi's adopted daughter.

A week later Chirac claimed on television that he was the one who had taken the decision to ban overflights; Mitterrand had merely acquiesced.

The following month the President had his revenge. Chirac insisted on accompanying him to the G7 summit in Tokyo. At the plenary sessions, where each country was represented by the head of delegation and two ministers, the Japanese agreed that he could occupy one of the two ministerial seats. But they insisted that when the delegation leaders met alone, as would be the case at the opening dinner and the first working session, the French Prime Minister would be excluded. To get round that problem, Chirac arrived 24 hours late, pleading pressure of work at home. At a meeting with his Japanese counterpart, Yasuhiro Nakasone, he tried to explain that things had changed in Paris and Mitterrand had lost much of his power. Next day, Japan's biggest newspaper, the *Asahi Shimbun*, published embarrassing extracts from their conversation, including Nakasone's conclusion: 'So to sum up, you are like newly-weds, you don't yet understand each other very well?'

Throughout the three-day summit, the bickering continued. Mitterrand explained to the Japanese press that France 'should only have one voice abroad'. Chirac's adviser, Bujon de l'Estang, rejoined: 'A single voice can express itself through two different mouths.'

But the knockout blow came at the very end. Mitterrand insisted that at the final press conference he should set out the French position. The Prime Minister was seated apart, like a royal consort, neither beside the President nor with the official delegation. To the television audience at home, the image was devastating: Mitterrand spoke for France while Chirac sat and listened.

'I shouldn't have gone to Tokyo,' he acknowledged afterwards.

It was the same story at the EEC summits at The Hague, in June, and in London, in December. Chirac insisted that France should have three chairs at the negotiating table instead of the usual two. 'Mrs Thatcher agrees,' he told Mitterrand. 'She may do,' the President replied, 'but I do not. It's in her interest to weaken France by showing its divisions. It's not in mine.'

There was one last kerfuffle in Madrid the following spring, when Chirac accused his Socialist predecessors of having bungled Spain's entry into the Community. He was publicly reprimanded for it by Mitterrand next morning and, two years later, acknowledged that it had not been a very clever thing to say.

Apart from hair-splitting over protocol, the importance of which was limited to its effect on the two leaders' images at home, there were few substantive disagreements over foreign policy.

After their initial bewilderment, France's partners grew accustomed to dealing with this odd couple that the Gaullist constitution had thrown up. Thatcher and Reagan welcomed Chirac as one of their own, a fellow right-winger who shared their economic goals. Gorbachev sought a middle path, preserving his relationship with Mitterrand while building ties with Chirac in case he should become President afterwards. Helmut Kohl stuck with the devil he knew and maintained the partnership with 'François' that had functioned so well up to then.

There were moments of (expensive) farce, as when President and Prime Minister arrived in Siberia in separate Concordes, which parked on the apron at Novosibirsk nose to nose. There were false notes – or 'quacks', as the French put it – as in November 1986, when, meeting Thatcher, Mitterrand urged an increase in EEC spending on research while Chirac, sitting beside him, looked meaningfully at the British Prime Minister, shaking his head, and then proceeded a few minutes later to advance the contrary opinion. There were moments of truth, as at Brussels in February 1988, when the comradeship between Chirac and Thatcher frayed to the point where the French Prime Minister exploded, 'Bollocks!', after a particularly long day of British obstruction. 'Whenever you start speaking,' he told her, 'you get angry and lay down the law. How do you expect anyone to ask your opinion after that?' And there was constant low-level sniping. The flood of diplomatic telegrams which were normally copied to the Elysée became a trickle after the new team took office and then dried up altogether. Information is the lifeblood of government. When the Elysée's protests were to no avail, back-channels were set up with the help of sympathetic officials who arranged for photocopies of sensitive messages to find their way to Mitterrand's desk.

The one area of foreign policy in which Mitterrand and Chirac had serious differences was arms control.

There had been a preliminary skirmish shortly after Chirac was appointed. He told Mitterrand that he wanted France to participate in Reagan's 'Star Wars' initiative. 'France will never take part as long as I am here,' the President replied. 'If you like I will call a referendum on it and I shall win.' Chirac did not raise it again.

But a much deeper rift developed over doctrine.

To Mitterrand the fundamental paradox from which all nuclear doctrine derived was that nuclear arms were not weapons because they could not be used to win wars. Their only purpose was deterrence. It was essentially what Reagan and Gorbachev had said at Geneva a year earlier: 'a nuclear war cannot be won and must never be fought'. It followed that battlefield nuclear weapons were a contradiction in terms: all types of nuclear weapon, whatever their purpose and range, were by definition strategic. The 'coupling' of Europe to America by the deployment of Pershings and cruise missiles – necessary though it had been to restore the nuclear balance – was an illusion. No matter what mechanisms were put in place, no one could be certain that the United States would come to Europe's aid if its own survival were threatened. That meant that Reagan's 'Option Zero' proposal, which Mitterrand had initially opposed, needed to be exhumed and re-examined. If even battlefield weapons would unleash an uncontrollable nuclear firestorm, what was the point of keeping them? It was the logical conclusion to his opposition to 'flexible response'. Not only was the doctrine vain, because in practice it could never be applied, but it was pernicious, because if it were ever attempted full-scale nuclear war would follow.

Chirac and André Giraud strongly disagreed.

To the Defence Minister, the 'nuclear umbrella' was the foundation of French defence strategy and the concept of 'flexible response', based on the possibility of graduated escalation stopping short of a strategic exchange, was still the core of nuclear planning. It followed that France should modernise its tactical nuclear weapons – Pluton and Hades – and that it needed to develop a mobile missile, the SX, to complement France's land-based nuclear silos on the plateau d'Albion in north-western Provence, which were vulnerable to attack.

Mitterrand rejected that logic. Vulnerability, he argued, was itself an element of deterrence. Any country which wished to attack France would know that destroying its land-based silos would expose it to an automatic counter-strike by French submarine-launched missiles. To add mobile launchers would increase the risk of a blanket nuclear attack, since the adversary would no longer know where France's nuclear arsenal was located. It would in no way enhance French security because the moment an attack was launched it would mean that deterrence had failed.

Between such radically different philosophies there was no middle path. But Mitterrand held the nuclear codes and presided over the meetings of the Defence Council where French nuclear policy was determined. It was not a battle the government could win.

The President was all the more convinced that 'Option Zero' should be revived because he believed that the new leadership in Moscow was sincere about wanting to disarm. 'Gorbachev is the first Soviet statesman to behave like a man of the modern age,' he told Reagan in July 1986. 'His future depends on [raising] Soviet living standards, not the number of missiles he has . . . He's staking his political life on this. Should we help him to succeed? Or on the contrary, should we . . . push him to fail?' Reagan was sceptical: 'Does he really mean to give up the basis of their foreign policy – expansionism and world communism?' he asked. 'So far he hasn't said so.' Nonetheless, the idea that Gorbachev was 'very different from the others', as Reagan put it, was beginning to take hold. Three months later, at Reykjavik, the United States and the Soviet Union came within a hair's breadth of agreement on an 'Option Zero' covering all types of nuclear weapon, tactical, intermediate and strategic, retaining only 100 missiles each in the Asian theatre to counter Chinese nuclear forces.

The understandings which Reagan and Gorbachev reached in private in Iceland that weekend were visionary, offering for the first (and until now the last) time the possibility of completely dismantling the world's two biggest nuclear arsenals.

They foundered because of disagreement over 'Star Wars', which Reagan refused to give up. The Pentagon, the Soviet military and Reagan's allies in Europe breathed a collective sigh of relief. At a hastily arranged meeting in London four days later, Thatcher told Mitterrand: 'Can you imagine? Reagan almost accepted the disappearance of nuclear arms! In that case everything would have been to the Russians' advantage right across the board.'

She had a point. The Russians had 3.5 million men in uniform and 27,000 tanks, several times NATO's forces in the European theatre. If the US nuclear arsenal were eliminated, the only deterrent to a Soviet invasion would be French and British nuclear forces. Pressure from Washington and Moscow for them to be dismantled as well would quickly become irresistible.

'I'm stunned,' she went on,

It's terrible, what happened . . . Reagan has a dream that SDI will rid the world of nuclear weapons. I don't believe in it. But . . . he thinks it will give him a place in the history books and without SDI he wouldn't have that. He's mesmerised by it. It's harder to deal with someone who has a dream than someone who has a real objective.[5]

Mitterrand was more sanguine. He agreed that Reagan's proposals were 'madness [and] brought us close to catastrophe'.[6] But so long as the reduction in strategic forces did not exceed 50 per cent, they would still provide a counterweight to Soviet conventional superiority and the cuts would not be enough to endanger the British and French nuclear forces. Moreover Gorbachev's proposals for 'Option Zero' for intermediate nuclear forces and for the abolition of chemical weapons represented a considerable advance and were well worth pursuing. The real problem, in his view, lay elsewhere:

Do [the Americans] consider the invasion of Europe a cause for war?
[I have] a simple question to put to [them]: What will you do if the
Russians put a foot across the border into Europe? Will you use your
nuclear weapons – yes or no? If yes, that's well and good. If no, our
Alliance isn't serious.[7]

Eight months later, over dinner at the G7 summit in Venice, the subject
came up again:

THATCHER: If war broke out and the Soviets besieged Bonn, would you
employ French atomic weapons?
MITTERRAND: Certainly not.
THATCHER: Then how can you expect the United States one day to come to
the help of Paris?
MITTERRAND: You are deliberately mixing up two different issues. De Gaulle,
Pompidou, Giscard and I have always had a doubt about the United States'
intentions. There's nothing automatic about their intervention . . . That's
why we have our own autonomous deterrent. But we can't use it for just
anything . . . It's not France's role to protect Germany and Western
Europe. That's the mission of the Atlantic Alliance.[8]

Turning to Reagan, he then recalled the words of the Austrian
Chancellor, Kurt Schuschnigg, a month before the Nazi invasion,
'Thus far but no further!', to which almost fifty years earlier, he had
devoted his first published political commentary:

MITTERRAND: You [also] say. 'Thus far and no further!' . . . It's the great
error of the Alliance, this elastic, 'flexible response'. It's only done that
way so that you Americans have a reason not to intervene in Europe.
REAGAN [bristling]: I can assure you of the United States' solidarity. As we
did in two world wars, we will intervene if your nations are threatened.
MITTERRAND: I don't doubt it. But I have no guarantee . . . Let's all understand each other. If our adversary has the slightest doubt about our
determination and capacity to intervene massively and very quickly against
aggression, war is possible. The Russians won't risk an atomic war if [they
know] there will be a massive response. [To Thatcher:] So Madame Prime
Minister, if you imagine yourself in a situation where the Russians are at
Bonn, it means you have already lost.

Mitterrand's views had come full circle. The debate about decoupling was unreal. When Thatcher insisted that 'the great question for NATO is, as always, the American presence in Europe', he responded: 'I don't agree. It's not whether they stay or not that's important. It's what's in their heads.'[9]

In December 1987, 'Option Zero' became a reality. In New York, Reagan and Gorbachev signed the Intermediate Nuclear Forces Treaty, covering non-strategic missiles with a range of more than 500 kilometres. It was the first significant advance in nuclear arms control since the SALT accords fifteen years earlier. Chirac fretted that it would not only uncouple Europe from the US but would undermine another cherished concept, that of using short-range nuclear weapons to deliver a 'final warning' to an aggressor before strategic Armageddon occurred. Giraud grumbled about a nuclear Munich and warned that the continent would be Finlandised.

'In France,' Mitterrand told Kohl, 'some people still want to believe that nuclear war is like traditional warfare. One can't stop people being stupid. Nuclear weapons aren't made to win wars but to prevent them.'

After five years of championing a hard line towards Moscow and a tough stance on nuclear arms, Mitterrand was once more the voice of reason, a more comfortable position for a left-wing leader and more in tune with the times. With 'Gorbymania' sweeping Europe, Chirac and his right-wing allies seemed out of touch – their reluctance to relinquish the doctrines of the Cold War and their insistence on continuing to modernise battlefield nuclear arms, the only category not covered by the New York accords, appearing more and more as a relic of the past. 'I don't understand this kind of refusal that's imprinted on their brains,' Mitterrand said in December. 'We either disarm or arm . . . My choice is made. We must disarm and we must refuse the proposals of those who tell us no.'

Defence and foreign policy apart, the Prime Minister had a virtually free hand provided he respected the forms. Article 20 of the French Constitution lays down that 'the government determines and conducts policy'. Mitterrand's role in internal affairs was that of a bystander.

The emblematic measure of Chirac's government, the privatisation of the banks, insurance companies and other enterprises taken over by the State, both after the war by de Gaulle and later under Mitterrand, was at first a huge success. The number of small shareholders in France increased from one to six million in little more than a year. The State raised 70 billion francs (£7 billion or $11 billion), a profit of 40 per cent on what the Left had paid.

But then came Black Monday – October 19 1987 – when the world's stock markets crashed and the enthusiasm of shareholders waned.

To align France more closely with the standard-bearers of the liberal economy, Britain and the US, Chirac had cut government spending; reduced income and company taxes; abolished price controls, a hold-over from post-war days; and taken measures to make the labour market more flexible and to encourage investment. Other steps, such as the abolition of the wealth tax and an amnesty for the repatriation of capital smuggled out to Switzerland in the first months of Mitterrand's presidency, which benefited the top 0.1 per cent, were more controversial and the government later admitted that politically they had been a mistake. As the fundamentals of the international economy improved – the price of crude oil fell and exchange rates stabilised – the reforms which Mitterrand had launched in 1983 began to bear fruit. The economy grew by 2.2 per cent in 1986 and 4.5 per cent two years later, and inflation fell below 3 per cent, the lowest figure since the 1960s. Only unemployment stubbornly refused to decline.[10]

To try to regain the territory occupied by the National Front, the Interior Minister, Charles Pasqua, approved a series of spectacular measures to combat illegal immigration, culminating in a charter flight on which 101 Malians were expelled – a figure which stuck in people's minds because of Walt Disney's film about Dalmatians. The far Right applauded; the Left was outraged; middle-of-the-road voters squirmed. Chirac came to see it as an error which compromised the government's position in an area where it should have enjoyed wide-spread support. The Socialists had been lax on immigration, particularly during Mitterrand's first year in power, and public opinion was in favour of tightening the rules. By going too far Pasqua triggered a backlash.

The same problem arose over law enforcement, another potential right-wing vote-winner. Chirac's initial moves – to enlarge police powers to carry out identity checks; to introduce a mandatory thirty-year prison term to replace the death penalty; and to set up a special anti-terrorist court – were welcomed. Subsequent proposals, to privatise large parts of the prison system and to jail drug addicts if they refused treatment, attracted widespread criticism and had to be abandoned.

The French applauded when the government corrected the excesses of the Left. But each time it tried to go further to win back the votes of those who had defected to the extreme Right, it alienated the mainstream who made up the bulk of its support.

Mitterrand was not inert. When the Cabinet met each week, he set out his reservations about government policies, which were duly reported in the press. It was a way to remind the public that he existed at home as well as abroad.

There was trench warfare on secondary issues – principally appointments of officials which required the President's signature – just as the US President and Congress arm-wrestle over the appointments of ambassadors and judges. Much of it was 'sheer childishness', Attali noted in his diary. When André Giraud, as Defence Minister, ignored a letter from Mitterrand proposing that his former Chief of Staff, General Saulnier, be elevated to the dignity of *Grand Officier de la Légion d'honneur*, the President said that in that case he would refuse to decorate anyone Giraud proposed. When Charles Pasqua suggested replacing the presidential security detail, Mitterrand warned him: 'If you do that without my agreement . . . I will have nothing further to do with your [security] services, I will manage on my own and I will explain to the country why.'

The President lost some of these squabbles and won others. But on the main planks of the government's programme, his policy was to stand aside. It was a way to give the Prime Minister enough rope to hang himself.

In the winter of 1986, one of the coldest in France for thirty years, Mitterrand's strategy had begun to pay off. Chirac, in his electoral programme, had promised university reform. On paper the proposal was moderate and reasonable: universities would have more autonomy and a bigger say in selecting their students. But coming on top of the crackdown on immigrants, the increased powers of the police and the proposal to imprison drug addicts, it was the straw that broke the camel's back. The students, or at least some of their leaders, were itching for a fight. The government's watchword, 'selection', became a synonym for inequality.

Out of nowhere an inferno erupted. On Monday, November 17, at the University of Paris at Villetaneuse, a few miles north of the city, the students decided to strike. The following weekend, 200,000 people, including Fabius, Mauroy, Rocard and other Socialist Party luminaries, joined a protest organised by the left-wing teachers union, the FEN. Daniel Cohn-Bendit, forewarned by his own experience twenty years earlier, alerted the student leaders: 'Be careful. This is going to get out of hand.' Four days later half a million young people marched through Paris and dozens of provincial towns in the biggest student demonstrations since 1968. The following Thursday, the same number took to the streets a second time to demand that the reform be withdrawn.

By then the mood was growing uglier. That evening the Education Minister, René Monory, received a student delegation but offered no concessions. Shortly before midnight, clashes broke out with the police. Cars were set on fire and Molotov cocktails thrown. By the time the night was over, forty-one demonstrators and twenty policemen were in hospital. One boy lost an eye, another had a fractured skull and a third young man had a hand torn off. Demonstrations and clashes continued throughout the following day, when an Algerian student who was on his way home was chased into a doorway by riot police and beaten to death.

That weekend the government was in an agony of indecision. Mitterrand advised Chirac privately to withdraw the reform. Others, including Pasqua and Chalandon, argued that he must stand firm to preserve the authority of the State. The UDF ministers threatened to resign en bloc unless the reform was abandoned. On Monday, complaining that he was being forced into an act of cowardice, the Prime Minister gave way.

The President, who had remained silent until then, publicly approved the decision. Politically he had to walk a fine line. He had no desire to help the Prime Minister, whose position had been gravely weakened, but nor could he be seen to be exploiting a tragedy which had left one young man dead and several others severely injured. That afternoon he visited the dead student's family at their modest council flat in the suburbs. Afterwards he refused to comment further. The episode spoke for itself.

Chirac's troubles continued through the winter. A rail strike started just before Christmas, followed by a strike on the Paris underground and sporadic stoppages at power stations.

But the collapse of the educational reform was a body blow. It marked another turning point, reinforcing the advantage Mitterrand had gained by his refusal to sign the privatisation decrees five months earlier. The Prime Minister knew it: 'If I withdraw this plan,' he had told his ministers, 'everything will fall apart.' Mitterrand knew it too. 'I don't want to get ahead of myself and I haven't yet taken any decision,' he said a few weeks later, 'but if the election was today and I were a candidate, I would be re-elected with my eyes shut.'

The interplay of President and Prime Minister became inextricable when external and domestic policy overlapped.

That was the case with New Caledonia, a group of islands the size of Wales or New Jersey, in the south-west Pacific 10,000 miles from Paris, which had been under French rule since the mid-nineteenth century. A third of the population of 150,000 were French settlers, 40 per cent indigenous Melanesian Kanaks and the remainder immigrants from other islands in the region. The settlers owned the nickel mines and cattle ranches which were the mainstay of the economy; the Kanaks were subsistence farmers.

When Chirac took office, the main Kanak party, the FLNKS (Kanak Socialist National Liberation Front), controlled the three rural regions of the territory while the settlers had a majority in the capital, Nouméa. Other South Pacific nations had self-government. But the Kanaks, being in a minority, found the path to independence closed.

The root of the problem was the stranglehold the settlers exerted on the administration. Even more than in Algeria in the 1950s, the advancement of the natives had been blocked. After more than a century of French rule, the territory had one Kanak doctor, one magistrate, one army officer, and at the main high school in Nouméa, Kanaks accounted for only 2 per cent of the teachers and 8 per cent of the pupils. Autonomy under those conditions would merely give power to the Whites, as had happened in Rhodesia under Ian Smith in the 1960s. When the minister responsible, Georges Lemoine, told the Cabinet that the FLNKS had sent a group of young men to be trained in Libya, Mitterrand exploded:

If I were Kanak, I would go to Libya too! [This is] an intolerable situation, . . . an offence to everything France stands for . . . What hope does the local population have for the future of their children? We ask ourselves why [the nationalists] are so intransigent. It's easy enough to understand them when you look at your figures.[11]

After elections which the FLNKS boycotted in 1984, France's distant sliver of empire was in a state of insurrection. Mitterrand sent a former Gaullist minister, Edgard Pisani, as the new High Commissioner for the territory with a mandate to open a dialogue. When he landed at the airport, his predecessor's first words were: 'You won't get away without a bloodbath . . . You've arrived too late.'

In fact Pisani succeeded in restoring order, and, on January 7 1985, with Mitterrand's agreement, he announced a referendum on granting New Caledonia 'sovereignty', which was described as independence in association with France. Four days later, however, renewed violence broke out. The following week Mitterrand flew to the territory to see what might be saved. A state of emergency was declared. The referendum was postponed.

In 1986 New Caledonia remained calm. But the gulf between the settlers and the Kanaks continued to widen. Chirac told the Cabinet that the FLNKS was 'manipulated and financed by Libya and the USSR'. Mitterrand commented to Bianco afterwards: 'How reactionary they are! They've understood nothing. I might as well be hearing people talk about Algeria thirty years ago.'

It was no longer a matter of expressing 'extreme reservations', he told Chirac, but of 'deep disagreement with the policy being applied.' The government was making 'a serious, historical error' which could only lead to more bloodshed. When finally the referendum took place in September 1987, the Kanaks staged a boycott. Ninety-eight per cent of those voting opposed independence. Shortly afterwards an all-White jury acquitted seven settlers accused of a massacre of Kanaks two years earlier. The stage was set for an Algeria in miniature, half a world away.

While New Caledonia seethed, Mitterrand confronted another issue where foreign and domestic policy were even more enmeshed: the imbroglio of the French hostages in Lebanon and their counterparts in French jails: Georges Ibrahim Abdallah of the FARL, Varajian Garbidjan of ASALA, and Anis Naccache and his companions.

On March 20 1986, within an hour of Chirac being named Prime Minister, a bomb exploded in a crowded shopping arcade on the Champs-Elysées. Two people were killed and twenty-eight wounded. The CSPPA claimed responsibility and repeated its demand that the prisoners be released. But who did the CSPPA represent? The attacks at the beginning of February had been seen as linked to the Iranians. Was the purpose of this new attack the same? Neither Mitterrand nor Chirac nor any of their advisers had an answer.

For want of a better idea, the Prime Minister decided on a two-track approach: on the one hand to improve relations with Iran, with a view to securing the hostages' release; on the other to use the good offices of Algeria, Syria and the PLO to spread the word that France would be more inclined to release the prisoners it was holding if the attacks ceased.

For six months the new policy of 'normalisation', as Chirac called it, seemed to be working. Talks on the disputed loan resumed in Teheran. The Mujahideen leader, Massoud Radjavi, left 'voluntarily' for Iraq with 200 of his followers. Two members of the French television crew seized in Beirut in March were freed,[12] followed by a third later in the year.

But in September five more bombs exploded in Paris.[13] They had been left in restaurants; outside a department store; in a post office at the Paris City Hall; even, in one case, in the reception area of the *Préfecture de Police*. Eleven people died and 200 were injured. In Beirut the same week the French military attaché was shot dead outside the main gate of the embassy.

Chirac believed the FARL were responsible. In July Georges Ibrahim Abdallah had been sentenced to four years' imprisonment on charges of using false documents. The CSPPA, the Prime Minister thought, hoped to dissuade the government from putting him on trial on the more serious charge of complicity in the murders of US and Israeli diplomats in Paris four years earlier.

Others disagreed. Abu Iyad, the head of the PLO's intelligence service, sent word that the attacks had nothing to do with Abdallah; the key remained the Iran–Iraq War. The Syrians said the same. So did the Algerians. So did Abdallah himself. A French intelligence specialist told the Elysée that to Teheran, 'speaking by explosions' and negotiating were two sides of the same coin.

By December Mitterrand had reached the same conclusion. That month he told Caspar Weinberger, the US Defence Secretary, that for the bomb attacks, as for the hostage-taking, 'Iran is mainly responsible . . . There is a link between Iranian diplomacy and terrorism.'

As the New Year, 1987, began, there were still four French hostages in Lebanon – Carton, Fontaine, Kauffmann and the television crew's producer, Jean-Louis Normandin. A fifth, a journalist named Roger Auque, was seized soon afterwards.

But the fog of uncertainty was about to clear.

In February Abdallah was sentenced to life imprisonment for complicity in the diplomats' murders. That same month a disenchanted young North African immigrant walked into a provincial police station offering information about a terrorist sleeper network in France. Shortly afterwards the DST arrested Fouad Ali Saleh, a 28-year-old Frenchman of Tunisian origin who had studied at the Islamic Revolutionary University in the Holy City of Qom, in Iran, and three principal accomplices.*

A memorandum sent by the agency to Chirac at the end of April – which the government took care to conceal from Mitterrand – described the mechanism of the attacks.[14] A Lebanese emissary smuggled liquid explosives into France. The sleeper network, 'which [consisted] of North Africans who had lived in France for years, were well integrated into the national community [and led] completely normal lives' received the explosives and hid them. 'Those directing the attacks in Lebanon [then] sent teams of two or three men for a few days to Paris to commit one or several acts of blind terror.'

---

* Gilles Ménage wrote fifteen years later that, in March 1983, he had received a report from the DST, citing an intelligence source in Tunisia, according to which 'the chiefs of the Iranian special services, not wanting to be implicated directly in terrorist attacks or sabotage in France, had allegedly contacted the Tunisian fundamentalist movement to employ carefully selected activists residing in France'. Ménage wrote that he had rejected the information 'in a manner as peremptory as it was mistaken', thinking that the Tunisians were seeking to involve France in their own internal problems. In a comment that could apply as much to the White House in its treatment of information about al-Qaeda or Downing Street about the London Underground bombings, he concluded: 'It is one thing to obtain information and quite another to interpret it correctly.'

Most troubling for Chirac was the final paragraph. 'They belong to the Hezbollah but . . . carry out instructions from Qom approved by certain leaders of the Islamic Republic.'

'Normalisation' with Iran, the centrepiece of Chirac's strategy, had been a delusion.

Moreover the 27-year-old interpreter at the Iranian Embassy in Paris, Wahid Gordji, whose father had been Khomeini's doctor, had been in contact with Saleh's group and was suspected of acting as coordinator.

The government was divided. The Interior Minister Charles Pasqua advised breaking off diplomatic relations and expelling the Iranian mission. His colleague at the Foreign Ministry, Jean-Bernard Raimond, proposed negotiations.

While Chirac hesitated, Gordji took refuge in the Iranian Embassy.

At the end of June, the building was surrounded by French police. Iran responded in kind. Faced with the possibility that French diplomats in Teheran might be taken hostage in reprisal, Chirac blew hot and cold. 'At 9.15 this morning in my office,' Mitterrand complained, 'I found the Prime Minister full of bravado towards Iran, telling me: "We should break off diplomatic relations within 48 hours." At 10.45 he was saying: "We must break relations by the end of the week." Three minutes later, [he wanted] just to declare [the Iranian chargé d'affaires] *persona non grata*. Half an hour afterwards he said, "Maybe we should wait . . ."'

Meanwhile, without informing Mitterrand, Chirac authorised secret talks with an Iranian envoy in Geneva. Agreement in principle was reached to allow Gordji to return to Iran in exchange for the release of two French hostages.

On Monday, July 13, when Chirac told the President what was planned, Mitterrand objected. He would agree reluctantly, he said, to exchange Gordji for *all* the hostages but not for just two. That afternoon, at a second meeting, the President demanded that the Iranians be given an ultimatum: if they did not lift the siege of the French Embassy within 48 hours, their chargé d'affaires would be declared *persona non grata* after which, failing an accord, France would break diplomatic relations. The Prime Minister complied.

A few hours before the deadline, Iran issued a matching demand. Unless Gordji were allowed to leave and the siege of the embassy in

Paris lifted, Teheran would break relations. At Mitterrand's insistence, France acted first, announcing the severance of diplomatic ties with immediate effect. The embassy sieges continued. Forty Iranians were confined to the mission in Paris, eleven French diplomats and staff in Teheran. Iranian gunboats attacked a French cargo ship in the Gulf. France complained to the Security Council and sent an aircraft carrier to the region.[15]

But behind the gesticulation, there were signs of change.

Diplomatic telegrams were intercepted suggesting that the Iranian authorities were concerned about what Gordji might reveal if he were questioned by a French judge and about the international repercussions if France were to publish evidence of Iran's use of terrorism as a diplomatic tool. Years later it would become known that a debate was under way in Teheran. Iran's leaders were about to conclude that hostage-taking and the use of terror were not advancing their cause.[16] But none of that was apparent at the time.

Mitterrand was resigned to a long stand-off.[17] Chirac was not.

The Prime Minister was convinced that if he could obtain the hostages' freedom, his chances in the presidential election, now barely nine months away, which had been badly damaged by the student crisis, the dispute over privatisation and, above all, the government's failure to reduce unemployment, would be greatly improved. Without informing the Elysée, he initiated fresh negotiations, both with Iran and, through unofficial intermediaries, with the hostage-takers in Lebanon. On August 5, at their regular tête-à-tête before the weekly Cabinet meeting, he tried for the second time that summer to prepare Mitterrand for the possibility that Gordji might be freed as part of a hostage exchange:

CHIRAC: You know, in the [Gordji] dossier, for the investigating magistrate there's really not very much . . .

MITTERRAND: Have you any idea of the implications of what you have just said? We've broken off diplomatic relations, there have been threats of terrorism and even of war . . . and all that for nothing? You can't think the government will be let off lightly if that's how things are going to be . . . Remember, at a meeting which I called in this office, Mr Pasqua said the dossier [against Gordji] was very weighty.[18]

In fact it had never been that straightforward. Pasqua had indeed told Mitterrand that Gordji was 'a point of reference for Iranian agents both in France and in Europe' and that there was solid evidence against him in the shape of wire-tapped telephone conversations and intercepted radio communications from the embassy.[19] The problem was that none of that would be admissible in a court of law.

The meeting on August 5 was the last time the Prime Minister and the President discussed the hostage issue. Thereafter Chirac dropped any pretence of cooperating with the Elysée. From then on it was each man for himself.

At the end of November, two hostages – Roger Auque and Jean-Louis Normandin – were freed and flown back to France on a government jet. The Prime Minister was at the airport to meet them. Two days later, with Teheran's agreement, Gordji was brought before an investigating magistrate in Paris, who found there was insufficient evidence to charge him. In a matching procedure in Teheran, a French diplomat, Paul Torri, who had been accused of espionage, was brought before an Iranian judge who found that there were no charges to answer. The following day, a Sunday, they were exchanged on the airport tarmac at Karachi. Later it became known that the French government had paid the hostage-takers a ransom of US $3 million. The other countries with hostages in Lebanon, notably Britain and the United States (though it had secretly done the same thing itself), were furious, accusing the French of betrayal.

Mitterrand, who had been kept in the dark, was not pleased either. The outcome – the return of two hostages in exchange for the release of Gordji – was exactly what he had forbidden Chirac in July. But the approaching election had overwhelmed all other considerations. It was not the time or the topic for a confrontation with the government. The Prime Minister insisted that the release of Auque and Normandin was part of a larger deal and that the remaining three hostages would be home for Christmas. However the end of the year passed and Carton, Fontaine and Kauffmann remained in captivity.

Throughout the period of cohabitation, the prospect of the coming election formed a constant backdrop to the relationship between Mitterrand and Chirac. The Prime Minister thought that two years in office would give him a decisive edge over his right-wing rival,

Raymond Barre. Mitterrand had made the opposite calculation: that after two years as Prime Minister, Chirac's appeal would wear thin. As the months passed, it looked more and more as if the President would be proved right.

But would Mitterrand stand for a second term?

As always, the President played his cards close to his chest. This time he had a good reason. The moment he confirmed that he would stand, he would lose the benefit of being above the fray. But if he ruled out a second term, he would be 'reduced to watching the trains go by'. So he sheathed himself in ambiguity, which, as he would have been the first to admit, was how he always felt most at ease. It was 'not his intention' to stand, he kept repeating, only to add: 'Will something happen to make me say, "Oh, that's a mistake"? I cannot suppose so.'

In retrospect it is clear that he made up his mind in stages. The first question – would he be in a position to win a second term? – was soon answered. Perhaps as early as August 1986, certainly by December that year, he was convinced that he could be re-elected if he wanted it. But the next question was: Did he want it? One of his oldest friends, Pierre Guillain de Bénouville, remembered: 'His hesitation went on for a long time. It was sincere. He said to me: "But Pierre, look at my age, my private happiness, my life . . ."'

Age was an excuse. Mitterrand would be 71 in May 1988. De Gaulle had won a second term at the age of 75. Clemenceau had been named Prime Minister when he was 76.

More serious was the question of Mitterrand's health.

He was still under treatment for prostate cancer. It had been in remission for six years and he told himself that he had been cured. His doctors, aware of the importance of 'positive thinking', did not disabuse him. But statistically, as Claude Gubler wrote later, the chances of his finishing a second term were close to nil. Already it was a medical miracle that he could finish his first term. What was the point of pushing his luck?

But the real problem lay elsewhere. Did he want to sacrifice the remaining years of his life to another presidential term? At 70, every man and woman knows that there is only a finite span ahead. The question of how to spend it is no longer a distant hypothesis but a binding choice. Mitterrand adored his daughter. If he stood again she would be thirteen, about to start out on the quicksands of adolescence when parents need to be more present than at any other period of their children's lives. As President he would have little time for her, for Anne, or for his 'official family'.

This was brought home to him in July 1987, in the middle of the crisis with Iran, when his younger son, Gilbert, and his two grand-daughters, Justine and Pascale, were involved in a car crash in northern Spain. The driver of the oncoming vehicle, a Spanish woman, was killed. Gilbert and his elder daughter escaped with light injuries. But Justine, then aged six, was in a critical condition with a fractured skull. The President and Danielle flew to Girona, where they arrived as the little girl was coming out of surgery. She survived. But Mitterrand was shattered. It was the same dilemma as had triggered his lament to Georges Dayan, forty years before: 'What is the point of working if you have no time for your private life?'

Family apart, he had other interests than politics. A shared love of rare books had created an improbable bond between him and Helmut Kohl. The Chancellor had given him a scarce original edition of poems by Apollinaire. Mitterrand had given him in return a seventeenth-century letter from the German-born Duchess of Orleans, pleading with the French War Minister, Louvois, to spare her birthplace, Heidelberg – a gift which Kohl, a native of that area, had particularly appreciated. Almost every day, accompanied by Attali or Patrice Pelat, the President would take an afternoon stroll through the Latin Quarter or along the banks of the Seine, browsing in his favourite bookshops. During Cabinet meetings, when a minister made a particularly tedious presentation, he annotated catalogues from antiquarian booksellers. Literature was an essential part of his being. No matter what else might be happening, he tried to read for two hours a day to 'oxygenate the mind'. When travelling he would sometimes send word to the pilot to circle round a couple more times before landing, so that he could finish a chapter.

Cohabitation had lightened his workload. He was able to play golf more often and to spend more time at Latche, where he took long walks in the forest, planted trees in the autumn and cared for his two donkeys, who reminded him of the mules of his childhood at Touvent. He had an almost carnal relationship with the soil, drawing energy and solace from the unchanging rhythms of the countryside.

'Why on earth would I want to stand again?' he asked a visitor to the book-lined sheepcote at Latche in the autumn of 1986. 'Look around you. What more do I need than I have here?'

For years he had collected walking sticks. 'He always used to say,' Danielle remembered, 'when I retire my dream is to sit on a bench in a town square, with my walking stick between my legs, and rest my chin on the handle and look at the people.' She tried hard to persuade him not to stand again.

But power is a drug. When you have it and you know you can keep it, it is hard to let go. 'It's a bit like the gamblers in a casino,' Mitterrand said later. 'After a while, it's not for money that they're there, glued to the table, it's simply that they like playing.' Dreams aside, sitting on a park bench and watching the world go by was not his style.

By the summer of 1987, he was persuaded not only that he could win but also that the next-best-placed Socialist, Michel Rocard, could not.[20] And in any case, would he have wanted Rocard, who irritated him beyond measure, to be his successor?

Only one question remained: did he want Jacques Chirac to become the next President of France?

Mitterrand's relations with Chirac's Cabinet, frigid in the first few weeks, had gradually thawed. The young Commerce Minister, Michel Noir, had inadvertently helped break the ice by complaining publicly that he had not been presented to the President. The following week, Mitterrand had gone up to him, held out his hand and, amid laughter, introduced himself: 'I'm François Mitterrand.' Not long afterwards, the President accidentally sat down in the Defence Minister's chair. When Giraud pointed out his error, 'You've taken my place, Mr President, and since I don't wish to take yours . . .', he shot back: 'You are the only one who doesn't.'

It was an exercise in seduction of the kind at which Mitterrand excelled. The more he could charm Chirac's ministers, the more he could divide the government and single out the Prime Minister as his primary opponent.

As his relationship with the Cabinet eased, so that with Chirac deteriorated. The Prime Minister's energy, which at first he had admired, he now found exasperating. 'He's like a spinning top which doesn't know why it turns,' Mitterrand complained. He detested the younger man's dissembling. Chirac's spokesman, Denis Baudouin, who had known him since they had worked together for Georges Pompidou, twenty years earlier, explained: 'Mitterrand never forgave Chirac his constant lying and his encroachments on the presidential prerogatives in foreign policy and defence. I imagine that Chirac, because I know how he is, always said yes to Mitterrand and did the opposite behind his back. It's his weakness.' Maurice Faure had a similar impression. Mitterrand 'realised that Chirac could not be relied upon', he said. 'He constantly went back on his word, from one day to the next, without even knowing that he was doing it.'

The Prime Minister's problem was that he did not know how to deal with Mitterrand. 'He was an amateur facing a professional,' said the Social Affairs Minister, Philippe Séguin. At Cabinet meetings François Léotard, the Culture Minister, recalled moments of 'distressing mediocrity', when Chirac 'behaved like a sub-lieutenant'. He was 'ill at ease' and 'obsequious'. His staff remembered that afterwards he always came back looking exhausted.

As time went by, Mitterrand's desire to settle scores with the Prime Minister grew stronger. 'Little by little,' Pelat recalled, 'he started to tell me that he hadn't completed everything he wanted to do and that the attacks [of the Right] were pushing him to take up the challenge.' Mitterrand told Attali: 'I've no desire to entrench myself, but the thought that my departure would give them so much pleasure would ruin my retirement.' Later he was more explicit: 'I never wanted to be a candidate again, but . . . Chirac and his people are a danger for democracy.' The Prime Minister, he said, was 'vulgar, loutish and wavering'. The RPR was set on gaining sole control of all the levers of power in the State.

In July 1987, Mitterrand summoned Dumas, Jospin, Joxe and Louis Mermaz to join him at Latche. 'I haven't yet taken a decision,' he told them, 'but you should now start working on the assumption that I may stand.' He left himself room for manoeuvre. The tentative campaign slogan they chose (and would later abandon) – 'The Mitterrand Generation' – could apply as well to Michel Rocard as to himself. But Rocard was informed that the President's candidacy was probable, if not yet certain, and from the autumn onward, in liaison with the Elysée, he occupied the terrain on Mitterrand's behalf, understanding that when the moment came he would step down in the President's favour.

At what point did Mitterrand's decision become irrevocable? Robert Badinter dated his resolution to a day in late December when the President, in Egypt for Christmas with Anne and Mazarine, decided that they should all ascend Mount Sinai, where Moses was said to have received the Ten Commandments. The direct path to the summit of the 7,000-foot mountain consists of 3,750 crude stone steps carved into the rock. Mitterrand's doctor, Claude Gubler, tried to dissuade him. 'We'll take our time,' the President assured him. 'We can stop and rest and, if it's too much, we'll come back down.' They took it slowly and reached the top well after dawn. Afterwards Badinter told his wife, Elizabeth: 'He's passed the test. He managed it. Now he'll stand.'

Others, more prosaic and perhaps more accurate, thought he based his decision on the evolution of the opinion polls in January and February 1988.[21] Initially Mitterrand was credited with 40 per cent of the vote in the first round, against Raymond Barre with 25 and Chirac with 20 per cent. But by the end of February, to the President's relief, Chirac and Barre were neck and neck. Barre, the President reasoned, would be much harder to beat in the second round because he was better able than Chirac to mobilise the Centre. But the former Prime Minister ran a lacklustre campaign and the UDF, which had been expected to back him, was divided and gave him little support.

On March 22, a Tuesday, three days before the deadline for candidates to register and four and a half weeks before Election Day, Mitterrand was asked on television whether he would seek a new term. 'Yes,' he replied.

The answer came out coyly, as though he enjoyed playing with the interviewer and was sorry the game had to end. But the harshness of the explanation which followed surprised everyone. 'I want France to be united,' he declared, 'and it won't be if it is in the hands of individuals who are intolerant, of parties which want to control every-thing, of clans and gangs [which] exercise domination over the entire country and risk tearing apart the social tissue and preventing social cohesion.' These 'clans, gangs and factions', he went on, in an allusion to Chirac and the RPR, were 'threatening civil peace'. One observer wrote that it was as though he were 'pouring out against the Prime Minister [all] the rancour that had built up' during the two years they had been forced to share power.

Next morning, Chirac and Mitterrand met as usual tête-à-tête before the Cabinet meeting. 'Your words last night were offensive to me,' the Prime Minister said. 'Over the last two years, your actions have sometimes been offensive to me,' the President replied.

It was an odd situation. Mitterrand and Chirac were expected to work together to run the country's affairs while engaged in a frontal struggle for power. In reality that was what they had been doing all along. The difference now was that it was out in the open.

The campaign was odd, too.

Chirac had declared his candidacy in mid-January, Barre three weeks later. The Prime Minister had the money and the electoral machine, the 'soldier-monks of the RPR', as Léotard had called them. Barre had neither but exuded a high sense of his own worth. 'A lot of people can see one [Barre] as Head of State,' Mitterrand commented, 'but he doesn't have the means to get there, while the other [Chirac] has the means, but people don't believe he can do it.'

Chirac's problem was, as it had been from the start, how to win back the extreme Right while retaining the support of middle-of-the-road voters. Michel Noir had written in *Le Monde*: 'Better to lose the presidential election than lose our soul treating with Le Pen and his ideas.' Chirac was furious but the opinion polls afterwards showed that a large majority of the electorate agreed.

Barre's problem was different and partly of his own making. He argued that, as de Gaulle had intended, a presidential election should 'hinge on the direct relationship between one man and the people'. Campaigning was pointless because 'either you are elected or you are not'. The fact that he was a poor public speaker no doubt comforted him in this view, but it was also a position of principle. 'To win the presidency,' he said a year later, 'you have to be ready to say and do just about anything. I did not want to do that.'

Mitterrand's position was different again. He was virtually certain of re-election and was reluctant to compromise the dignity of the presidency by plunging into the fray. For the first two weeks after declaring his candidacy, he refused to campaign at all, much as de Gaulle had done in 1965. Instead of advancing a political programme – 'a matter for political parties, not for a President of the Republic or someone who aspires to become one' – he wrote a 47-page 'Letter to all the French', intended as 'a sort of shared reflection, of the kind which happens among the family, around the table in the evening', covering 'all the big subjects which are worth discussing and mulling over between French men and women'.

He spent a week writing and polishing it, and the night before it was to be published stayed up till 3 a.m. at the printing press, correcting the proofs, like a neophyte brooding over a first novel. Two million copies were inserted as a supplement in national and provincial news-papers, and several million more printed for Socialist militants to distribute door to door.

The contrast with 1981 was striking. The '110 Propositions' had laid out a revolutionary programme for changing society. The 'Letter' was cautious and sage, offering middle-of-the-road nostrums to bandage society's ills. There would be 'neither nationalisations nor privatisa-tions'. The wealth tax, which Chirac had abolished, would be restored but its scope would be so narrow as to affect only the super-rich, and the revenue would be used to help the very poor.

The 'Letter' was 'very pale pink', one leading analyst wrote. *Le Monde* wondered when the President would bring himself 'to use the word, "socialism". Even "Left" would be a sensation.'

'There are two ways to keep the people amused,' Barre commented. 'One is to flood them with false promises: that was done in 1981. The other is to dull their senses by making them dream: that is what is being done today. Goodnight, little ones, sweet dreams! Tonton is looking after you . . .'

It was a non-campaign, 'smooth, without presence', focussed almost entirely on winning over the political Centre. Remaining neutral, keeping the Socialists at arm's length while encouraging them to direct their attacks at Chirac and the RPR, was a dual strategy. The goal was to label the Prime Minister a creature of the hard Right, ensuring that he would get through the first round at the price of alienating Barre's supporters, who would then be more likely to switch sides and vote for Mitterrand in the run-off.

Mitterrand had no alternative. The decline of the Communist Party meant that there was no longer a majority on the Left. The RPR, the UDF and the National Front together accounted for 52 per cent of voting intentions; the Socialists, Communists, Greens and extreme Left (not all of whom would vote for Mitterrand in the second round) made up only 48 per cent. To win, the President had to obtain the backing of at least part of the middle-of-the-road electorate which normally supported the Centre-Right.

This policy of 'opening', as Mitterrand called it, did not go down well with the Left, which made its views known in no uncertain terms at his first big rally at Rennes on April 8:

> Among the ranks of the opposition, there are worthwhile people, excellent people . . . *(No! No!)* . . . But yes, there are! . . . *(Boos, whistling, jeers . . .)* Believe me, there are! I even spend time with them sometimes . . . *(Redoubled booing)* We are not the [only] good ones, they are not [all] bad! . . . *(Whistles, shouts of 'Yes, they are!')* . . . even though they think that they are good and we are bad! *(Laughter, applause)*[22]

Mitterrand had extricated himself but drew two lessons from the crowd's reaction.

Staying neutral was not enough. To carry left-wing voters behind him, he would have to give them more encouragement and his overtures to moderate voters would need to be more discreet.[23] After Rennes, the direction of the campaign subtly altered, taking on a more socialist coloration.

It was acceptable to make cautious gestures towards Barre's supporters, who shared his distaste for the RPR's smash-and-grab tactics. It was acceptable for him to call for a large 'opening . . . as regards men and ideas' and to speak out against sectarianism. It was acceptable to promote Michel Rocard, by far the most popular Socialist leader, who represented the right wing of the Party, as a foretaste of what a second term might bring. Mitterrand had been cultivating Rocard for months, and ten days after the meeting in Rennes took him on a long, rain-drenched walk through the mountains of the Cévennes, in the Massif Central. Next day photographs of the two of them, in boots, raincoats and jerkins, and identical flat caps, were on the front pages of every newspaper in the country. They signalled to middle-of-the-road voters that if Mitterrand were re-elected, his second term would be very different from the first.

But to go further and suggest that right-wing ministers, even the most moderate among them, might participate in a left-wing government was a step too far.

It was the mirror image of the problem that Chirac was confronting.

But it was easier for Mitterrand to find common ground between the Centre and the Left than for the Prime Minister to reconcile the Centre and the extreme Right.

On Sunday, April 24, when the votes were counted, Mitterrand had 34 per cent, a little less than he had hoped for. But Chirac's support had collapsed. With 19.94 per cent, the Prime Minister had three percentage points less than he had been credited with in the polls. The reason for the missing numbers was clear: Jean-Marie Le Pen, who had been expected to get 12 per cent, had obtained almost 14.5 per cent of the vote. Far from winning back National Front voters, as he and Pasqua had hoped, a crucial part of Chirac's support had been siphoned off by the far Right. The Prime Minister was devastated. François Bujon de l'Estang said he was 'like a mechanical toy to which you've lost the key'.

Barre came in third, with 16.5 per cent, and offered his rival a poisonous endorsement: 'I support Jacques Chirac [and] I count on him [to] reject xenophobia, racism and all extremisms', those being precisely the reservations of Barre's supporters about the Prime Minister's campaign. But whatever Barre might have said, Chirac knew the game was over. To have any chance of winning he would need the support of the majority not only of Barre's supporters but also of Le Pen's. Arithmetically that was all but impossible.

To Chirac's credit, he fought on gamely 'to preserve the future', as he put it. But the next two weeks were a nightmare.

Four days after the first round, he and Mitterrand went head to head in the one televised debate of the campaign, lasting more than two hours, which was watched by 28 million people, three-quarters of the electorate. Mitterrand was on his dignity from the outset and his constant references to Chirac as 'Mr Prime Minister' soon got under his rival's skin:

CHIRAC: Allow me just to say that tonight, I am not the Prime Minister and you are not the President. We are two candidates who are equal and who are submitting ourselves to the judgement of the French people. You will permit me to call you Mr Mitterrand.
MITTERRAND: But you are absolutely correct, Mr Prime Minister.[24]

Chirac could call the President 'Mr Mitterrand' all he wanted. It did not make any difference. They were not at the same level.[25]

The climax of the debate came shortly afterwards. Chirac recalled that in 1981, Mitterrand, as part of the traditional amnesty which followed a presidential election, had released Jean-Marc Rouillan and Nathalie Ménigon, both leading figures in the extreme left-wing group, Action Directe. Some years later they had assassinated General René Audran, the Director of International Relations at the Defence Ministry, and Georges Besse, the head of Renault.* Did the President still defend such 'an indulgent, or as one would say today, lax policy in the realm of security'?

Mitterrand bristled. First he pointed out that Rouillan had at the time been charged only with a minor offence and that he had been freed under exactly the same conditions as those accorded in earlier amnesties by Pompidou and Giscard. Ménigon's case was more complicated. She had faced a charge of attempted murder but had been released on medical grounds. The government had hoped that a gesture of clemency might prevent the group from becoming radicalised and spare France the cycle of repression and violence which Italy had endured at the hands of the Red Brigades. Mitterrand did not go into that. Instead, attack being the best form of defence, he lashed out:

MITTERRAND: I have never freed terrorists. You, when you were Prime Minister [under Giscard in 1974], you freed a Japanese terrorist . . . A little later . . . you freed Abu Daoud [who had masterminded the killing of Israeli athletes at the Munich Olympics]. I am obliged to say that I remember the conditions under which you sent Mr Gordji back to Iran, after having explained to me, in my office, that the evidence against him was overwhelming and that his complicity in the terrorist attacks which had bloodied Paris at the end of 1986 was proven . . .

* General Audran was shot dead outside his home near Paris on January 25 1985, Georges Besse in similar circumstances on November 17 1986. By then Action Directe had established links with the Red Army Faction in West Germany, the Fighting Communist Cells in Belgium and dissident Palestinian groups in Lebanon. It was initially thought that both attacks, like other failed attempts to assassinate prominent French figures, were part of a strategy for West European revolution. However both Audran, who was in charge of French arms sales to Iraq, and Besse, who had headed the consortium to which Iran had made the disputed $1 billion loan, had roles which put them in conflict with Teheran. Rouillan and other members of Action Directe denied any Iranian connection, but French intelligence became convinced that Audran's murder, and probably that of Besse as well, had been manipulated by Iran.

CHIRAC: Mr Mitterrand, all of a sudden, in your concentrated fury, you have lost control of yourself . . . Look me straight in the eye and tell me, Mr Mitterrand: did I ever say to you that . . . we had proof that Gordji was guilty of complicity . . . in [these] acts? I always said that that was solely a matter for the investigating magistrate and that I did not know . . . what was in the dossier [against him] . . . Looking me in the eye, can you really contest my version of things?

MITTERRAND: To your face, I contest it. When Gordji was arrested [and] the Iranian Embassy was surrounded, with all the consequences that had in Teheran, it was because the government had provided us with what we thought were sufficiently serious [proofs] that he was one of those behind the terrorism at the end of 1986. And you know that very well.[26]

It was an electric moment. The President and Prime Minister of France were accusing each other of lying, live on television.

Which one was telling the truth?

Giscard said afterwards that he was sure that Chirac had been lying. 'Whenever he was going to serve me up some story that I didn't believe,' he told Mitterrand later, 'he always used to say: "I can promise you, looking you straight in the eye . . ."' The television audience gave the President the benefit of the doubt: 42 per cent found him convincing against 33 per cent for Chirac. In fact, both had taken liberties with the truth. Pasqua had indeed told Mitterrand that Gordji was behind the terrorist attacks. But three months before the Iranian was freed, the Prime Minister had warned him that they had very little evidence which would stand up in a court of law.

For the next week, Chirac clutched at straws. On May 4 the last three hostages in Lebanon – Marcel Carton, Marcel Fontaine and Jean-Paul Kauffmann – were finally released and flown to Paris, where the Prime Minister was once again on hand to greet them. The war with Iraq was drawing to a close. Teheran had decided that the problem with France had gone on long enough. It was later revealed that Chirac's intermediary, a Corsican named Jean-Charles Marchiani with a somewhat chequered past, had paid the trio's abductors a ransom of US $7 million.[27]

The following day came news of a different kind. In New Caledonia, French troops had stormed a redoubt where dissident members of the FLNKS had taken twenty-three policemen hostage on the small island of Ouvéa, 80 miles north of the mainland. Chirac had approved the operation in the hope that it would win him votes from National Front supporters. The hostages were freed, but two of the rescuers died and nineteen Kanaks were killed. It was discovered later that twelve had been executed with a bullet to the head. An official report spoke of 'acts contrary to military honour'.

'Twenty-one dead!' Mitterrand groaned. 'Baseness, perjury and lies . . . For 100,000 votes! You don't win votes with money and blood.'

Then on Friday, May 6, the government announced that one of the two French agents involved in the *Rainbow Warrior* affair, who was completing her sentence on the French Pacific atoll of Hao, was being repatriated because she was pregnant. 'Pregnant!' the President exclaimed. 'Since how many minutes?'

None of it helped.

On Sunday night, Mitterrand won 54 per cent of the votes, Chirac 46 per cent. It was established later that almost 20 per cent of Le Pen's supporters had voted for Mitterrand and 14 per cent of Barre's. The remainder went to Chirac or, in the case of the National Front, abstained. The Communists, the Greens and the extreme Left swung massively behind the President, who also outdid his rival in mobilising abstentionists from the first round. Mitterrand's slogan, *La France Unie* (United France), had succeeded better than even he had hoped. It was the worst result for the Right in a presidential election since the establishment of the Fifth Republic, almost thirty years earlier.

14

The Monarch

Mitterrand's second term began on a sour note. 'I have to lance the boil,' he told Michel Charasse. 'But it won't last more than six months.'

He was referring to Michel Rocard, whom he named Prime Minister on May 10, two days after the election, not because he wanted to but because he felt he had no alternative. 'People won't understand if I don't give him his chance. It's his turn,' he told Pierre Bérégovoy, who had hoped that this time the choice might fall on him. But he observed to Attali: 'Rocard has neither the ability nor the character for that post'.

Mitterrand's allergy to his new Prime Minister was intestinal. But politically he represented that 'opening' towards the Centre that the country seemed to want.

There was, however, a quid pro quo . . . or rather two.

Within the government Mitterrand surrounded Rocard with Socialist Party heavyweights loyal to himself, the 'elephants' as they were called: Bérégovoy, Roland Dumas, Pierre Joxe and the immovable Culture Minister, Jack Lang, all returned to the posts they had held two years earlier under Laurent Fabius. Jean-Pierre Chevènement was named Minister of Defence. Lionel Jospin became Education Minister and ranked second in the Cabinet hierarchy.

Within the Party, Mitterrand decided, Fabius, his dauphin-in-waiting, should become First Secretary in Jospin's place. It was the *sine qua non* of Rocard's nomination, he said later. If he was going to entrust the government to someone not from his own camp, he wanted to be sure that the Socialist Party was firmly in the hands of his allies.

But the President presumed too much.

To many in the Party, Fabius was like Mitterrand but without his master's charisma and charm. He was seen as cold, calculating and ambitious, with an aristocratic disdain for those he regarded as inferiors. Fabius might be on the Left, his critics argued, but if it served his ends to transform the Socialists into a French version of the US Democratic Party, a machine to win elections, without convictions and without a soul, he would not hesitate. His only interest in becoming party leader, they charged, was to add a paragraph to his résumé to further his own political career. Moreover he was not the only candidate available. Pierre Mauroy, having served as deputy party leader under both Mollet and Mitterrand was keen to have the post. The President tried to dissuade him, suggesting that he become Speaker of the National Assembly instead. But there was a spirit of revolt in the air. The antagonism between Fabius and Jospin, which had started with their dispute over precedence in the 1986 election campaign, was undiminished. Among the Party's 'Old Guard', who had been with Mitterrand since the days of the Convention in the 1960s, only one, Pierre Joxe, supported Fabius. The others spoke of 'an abuse of democracy', a 'monarchic' imposition of a candidate who was not wanted. The depth of the opposition to his protégé took Mitterrand by surprise. 'I would prefer Fabius,' he told them. 'But you must do as you wish. It's not my business, it's up to the Socialist Party.'

He was more shaken than he allowed it to appear.

That afternoon he telephoned Jospin: 'I've been thinking about this for a long time,' he said. 'My plan is to have you in government and Fabius at the head of the Party. As you well know, this isn't some spur-of-the-moment decision that I've just dreamed up. If it doesn't go through like that, you should be aware that I will cut the umbilical cord with the Party.'

Two days later, on Friday, May 13, when the members of the 'Mitterrandist' faction of the Executive Committee met to choose their candidate, Fabius was defeated by 63 votes to 54. Next day the full Committee confirmed Mauroy as party leader.

For the first time since 1971, Mitterrand had lost control of the Party he had spent so much effort putting together. The core around which it had been built – the alliance between the 'sabras' and the 'Old Guard' – had fissured. It would mark the beginning of a long period of Socialist decline.

One more task remained before the new team could start work.

Immediately after his victory, Mitterrand had decided to dissolve parliament and call legislative elections. It was a gamble. He had told his old ally, the Left-Radical leader, Maurice Faure, the previous autumn:

> Either I dissolve,. . . but then I risk losing everything and finding myself with the same balance of forces in parliament, in other words a right-wing majority, which would wipe out my victory – each one would go back to his own vomit, it would be the worst of all situations. Or I try to break up the Right, but political boundaries are always slow to rebuild. At the beginning the French would approve . . . But if I take that road, there's a big risk of bogging down.[1]

Had he been re-elected by a narrow margin, he would probably have left parliament as it was. But Mitterrand reasoned that the landslide which had given him a second term had generated sufficient momentum to produce a solid majority in the government's favour.

The Centrists had tried to dissuade him. Jacques Chaban-Delmas told Mitterrand he had 'a historic chance' to bring the French together. 'You can make 120 or 130 MPs switch sides, and the UDF and the RPR will explode,' he said.[2] Pierre Mehaignerie, the leader of Raymond Barre's followers within the UDF, thought '60 or 70 MPs and 110 Senators' would be willing to join a grand coalition of the Centre and the Left if Mitterrand gave the lead.

Once new elections had been called, that scenario was ruled out. The centrist parties' survival depended on their concluding electoral pacts with the Right. Any overture to the Left became impossible. For both sides it would now be a straightforward battle between Left and Right. Had Mitterrand accepted the implications of his decision, his gamble might have paid off. Instead he muddied the waters.

On Whit Sunday, which that year fell on May 22, he made, as every year, a pilgrimage to the hill of Solutré, a rocky bluff looking out over the vineyards of Burgundy, near Danielle's family home at Cluny. The tradition had started in 1946 as an annual reunion of members of the Resistance. After 1981 it had become an occasion for an informal conversation with journalists. That afternoon, in an attempt to reassure moderate voters, he said he wanted a Socialist victory because it would make it easier for him to open the door to the Centre, as he

had done in 1981 when the Socialists had had an absolute majority
but had nonetheless formed a coalition with the Communists. 'It's
not healthy that just one party governs,' he added. 'Political families
of other persuasions need to share in governing too.'

In the following morning's newspapers, the first part of his statement was forgotten. The headlines said it was wrong for a single party
to have a monopoly of power. What came across – although it was
not what Mitterrand had said and certainly not what he intended –
was that he did not want the electorate to give the Left a large parliamentary majority.

Whether because of these remarks, or because, after two years of
cohabitation, the French had decided they rather liked a balance of
power between Executive and Legislature, or simply because the
Socialists ran a lacklustre campaign, reflected in a record abstention
rate, the results were a cruel disappointment.[3] Mitterrand had been
banking on the Socialists getting about 300 seats, a dozen or so more
than the absolute majority. In the event they won 276, 13 fewer than
they needed.[4] The Communists obtained 25 seats, 10 fewer than in
the outgoing parliament; the right-wing parties and their affiliates,
273 seats; while the National Front was wiped out by the first-
past-the-post constituency system, which Chirac's government had
restored, obtaining only one seat despite having nearly 10 per cent
of the vote.

It was better than the 'worst of all situations' which Mitterrand
had envisaged with Maurice Faure, eight months earlier. But without
an overall majority, the Socialists were too weak to reach out to the
Centre in anything more than symbolic fashion.

Five weeks after a triumphal re-election, Mitterrand found himself
with a Prime Minister – Michel Rocard – whom he cordially detested;
a leader of the Socialist Party – Pierre Mauroy – who had been elected
against his wishes; and a parliament so divided that each time the
government wanted to pass legislation the Socialists would have to
form a temporary alliance with the Communists or parts of the
Centre-Right. It was a lot of stumbles in a short time.

Could it have been otherwise?

In the case of the Party, yes. Mitterrand had taken it for granted
that the Socialists would do his bidding. Had he brought Mauroy,
Fabius and Jospin together, spelt out what he wanted and put his own

Valery Giscard d'Estaing greeting Mitterrand at the Elysée on May 21 1981.

An uncooperative sitter. After eight sessions in 1982, the sculptor gave up in disgust before being persuaded to try again – this time successfully – a year and a half later.

Shaping government policy with his Prime Minister, Pierre Mauroy.

With Mikhail Gorbachev in Kiev a month after the fall of the Berlin Wall, December 1989.

Reconciliation with Germany: hand in hand with Helmut Kohl at Verdun, September 1984.

Even Margaret Thatcher
succumbed to the charm.

Despite their manifold
differences, Mitterrand
and Ronald Reagan
also struck up a
quizzical rapport.

In Sarajevo to break the siege by Bosnian Serbs, June 1992.

'God'…

… and his minions on earth below:

Fabius, the dauphin (left), and Rocard, the bête noire…

… Jacques Chirac (left) and Édouard Balladur.

With Rene Bousquet at Latche in the 1970s.

At Pierre Bérégovoy's funeral with his widow, Gilberte (centre), and Danielle in 1993.

In 1988 with Patrice Pelat, who was shortly afterwards charged with insider trading.

After the second operation for cancer in 1994.

Autumn 1995: one of Mitterrand's last public appearances.

Anne and Mazarine at his funeral at Jarnac, January 9 1996.

authority on the line, he would have been obeyed. Instead he told them it was their choice, allowing Jospin to say – truthfully – that the President did not want to get involved.

In part it was the sin of hubris. Mitterrand had been dazzled by the extent of his own victory, which he had obtained single-handed while keeping the Socialists offstage. If they were now back in power, they had him to thank for it. What right did they have to object to the dispositions he proposed? In part it was the old problem of Mitterrand's conception of the presidency. As Head of State, it was not his role to interfere in the day-to-day workings of a political party, even his own. In part it was his character. In domestic affairs – though not in foreign policy – ambiguity was always preferable to clarity. The reason was disarmingly simple: at home he could be himself, which meant he could duck and weave and tergiversate as he liked. Abroad he represented France, which meant he had to be straightforward.

Afterwards Mitterrand felt humiliated, complaining that he was being treated as a lame duck. 'They're dismembering my corpse and I've only just arrived,' he fumed. 'And those who were supposed to be closest to me were the ones who held the knives!' There was truth in that. But he could hardly blame those around him for thinking about his succession when he did so ceaselessly himself. He had wanted Fabius as party leader not simply as a counterweight to Rocard but to test the waters for the next presidential contest in seven years' time.

With hindsight his decision to call a snap election was probably correct. 'Are you sure,' he asked his ministers afterwards, 'that we would have had a [better] result if we had waited a few more months?' Everything in Mitterrand's experience told him that the centrist parties could not be relied upon. When push came to shove, they always threw in their lot with the Right.* But the President's refusal to campaign – he preferred to remain above the fray in the interests of an 'opening' which never came – was a mistake which cost his camp dear.

The outcome was a government that was neither fish nor fowl.

---

* A quarter of a century later, that judgement appeared to have been vindicated. By 2012, the centrist parties had all but disappeared from French politics. In that year's parliamentary elections, they obtained four seats and less than 5 per cent of the vote. Most of the former UDF had been swallowed up by the right-wing UMP, the successor to Chirac's RPR. French politics had become essentially bipolarised with adjuncts on the far Left and the far Right.

After the post-election reshuffle, Rocard found himself with forty-nine ministers, a record under the Fifth Republic. Half, on Mitterrand's instructions, were non-Socialists, among them six members of the UDF, including four who had been ministers under Giscard, recruited against the former President's wishes, and almost a dozen 'obscure personalities and media celebrities', as one historian put it, whose presence Mitterrand intended 'to show that the [Left] is not sectarian since it is governing with others'. The Socialist Party was not at all happy. 'Don't tell anyone I'm a Socialist because [if they don't know] I might have a chance of becoming a minister,' one party stalwart commented acidly.[5] It was not the 'opening' that the French had hoped for.

A year later, France was to celebrate the bicentenary of the Revolution. The G7 summit, which it was Mitterrand's turn to host, was convened to coincide. Neither the Americans nor the British realised the significance of the date, July 14 1989, and the French were careful not to mention that Heads of State from developing countries would also be invited. The symbolism was irresistible. Two hundred years after the storming of the Bastille, the leaders of the sans-culottes in the Third World would come to Paris as equal partners to attend the rich world's feast.

London and Washington, once they realised what was afoot, suggested changing the dates.[6] 'Human rights did not start in France,' Thatcher told Le Monde. 'For me, a British Conservative, the French Revolution was a utopian attempt to overthrow the old order . . . anticipating in large part the still more terrible Bolshevik Revolution of 1917.' In the end they came. But, like the extravaganza Mitterrand had organised seven years earlier at Versailles, the 1989 summit was rich in spectacle, short on substance. Half a million people lined the streets of Paris to watch the celebrations, which were broadcast live all over the world. The leaders of the industrialised countries, including for the first time George Bush, who had succeeded Reagan in January, approved new debt relief measures for the world's poorest countries. But that was as far as it went. Mitterrand's proposal that formal North–South summit talks should resume, on the model of Cancun, was heard out in silence and instantly dropped.

The Paris summit would be the last of its kind. As the Heads of

State and government savoured a *barigoule d'artichaut et homard* amid the nineteenth-century splendour of the Musée d'Orsay, a new revolution, as far-reaching as that in France two centuries before, was brewing in the world outside. The Soviet empire, with its roots in the Tsarist conquest of Central Asia and the Caucasus and Stalin's expansion into Eastern Europe after the Second World War, was beginning to crack apart.

It had started with Gorbachev's policies of *glasnost* and *perestroika*.

Not only had they brought an upsurge in ethnic tensions within the Soviet Union but they had weakened the hold on power of the national communist parties in all the satellite states. The first reports of unrest in Armenia and Azerbaijan, of strikes in Poland and anti-government demonstrations in Budapest and in Prague, a year earlier, were no more than straws in the wind. But in the West they had aroused disquiet. 'There is a risk of disorder in the Soviet empire,' Mitterrand had told the French Defence Council. 'For us, that disorder is probably not better than the order that has reigned there up to now.'

The other Western leaders shared that view.

Mitterrand, Thatcher, Reagan and Bush, even Helmut Kohl, whose nation, divided between the two blocs, was most directly affected, were torn by conflicting impulses. On the one hand, the changes in the East were positive. On the other they foreshadowed a potentially enormous shift in the geopolitics of Europe, which was inherently destabilising. A juggernaut had been set in motion, with unpredictable consequences. The one consolation, they all thought, was that it would happen gradually. Even if the Soviet empire was doomed to disintegrate, Mitterrand argued, it would take 'something of the order of a generation'.

Moreover the changes brought opportunities as well as alarm. Each one wanted his or her country to reap the benefits. A race began to see who would be boldest in challenging the established norms. 'We must return in force to Eastern Europe,' Mitterrand told the French Cabinet. Soon afterwards he met the Czech dissident, Václav Havel, newly released from prison in Prague. Thatcher went one better, visiting Lech Wałęsa – the leader of the banned Polish trade union, Solidarność – at the Gdansk shipyards. Both were 'firsts' by Western leaders.

Yet at the same time they all worried that the forces which Gorbachev had unleashed would eventually unseat him, and that the pendulum in Moscow would swing back to repression and confrontation. In New York in September 1988, Mitterrand confided his misgivings to Ronald Reagan. It was 'a very natural temptation', he said, for countries like Hungary and Poland to want to recover their freedom, but 'we must be prudent in encouraging [them] politically to assert themselves' because otherwise 'Mikhail Gorbachev will be in great difficulty'. To the Turkish Prime Minister, Turgut Ozal, later that year, he was even more explicit. 'The awakening of the different nationalities', he said, was 'an enormous obstacle' to Gorbachev and might cause him to fail. 'We must follow with the greatest attention what is happening in the [Soviet] republics . . . The fault line is already there.'

The Soviet leader himself gave no sign of such doubts but on the contrary forged ahead with ever greater determination. He consolidated his hold on power, becoming President, as well as party leader, and that winter amended the constitution to permit the first multi-candidate elections to the Soviet parliament. The following spring Hungary and Poland adopted multi-party systems, presaging the end of communist rule.

But the catalyst for the biggest change of all passed completely unnoticed.

On Tuesday, May 2 1989, Hungarian border guards began dismantling the electrified fence which, twenty years earlier, had replaced the minefields along the border with Austria. There was a technical explanation: the alarm system was so old that every time there was a storm it had to be switched off. The guards were told it needed to be replaced. But there was also a political reason. The reformists in the leadership in Budapest had decided to start removing the barriers that cut off Hungary from the West.

Two and a half weeks later, Mitterrand met George Bush at his summer retreat at Kennebunkport in Maine. The USSR and Germany were at the centre of their concerns. As the transcript of their conversation makes clear, neither had any idea that, even as they spoke, the Iron Curtain, rung down by Stalin fifty years earlier, was being stealthily raised:

MITTERRAND: The [West German] Social Democrats are idealistic dema-
    gogues. They want an agreement allowing German reunification. They
    are deluding themselves . . . The Soviets will never agree to that . . .

BUSH: As President of France, are you for [reunification]?

MITTERRAND: I'm not against it, given the changes that are happening in the East. If the German people want it, we won't oppose it. But the conditions are not yet [ripe]. I don't believe [they will be] for another ten years. [The Russians] will oppose it to the end, by force. There are only two possible causes of war in Europe: if West Germany gets nuclear weapons or if there's a people's movement pushing for the reunification of the two Germanies.[7]

Helmut Kohl did not know what was afoot either. But his intuition was more finely tuned. In the middle of June, less than four weeks after Mitterrand's conversation with Bush, Gorbachev visited Bonn. From his talks with the Soviet leader, Kohl said later, he sensed that Moscow's attitude to Germany was changing.

By then rumours had begun spreading on the East German grape-vine that border controls between Hungary and Austria might be relaxed. Hundreds of East German 'tourists', mainly young people, started camping out on the Hungarian side. On 19 August, the author-ities in Budapest made known unofficially that those who wished to leave might do so.[8] Several hundred East Germans entered Austria that day. A hundred thousand more would follow in the next two and a half months, heading for West Germany. In October, another exit route opened via Czechoslovakia. When the ageing East German leadership – the most resistant to reform in Eastern Europe – complained that their Warsaw Pact allies were doing nothing to help, Gorbachev warned icily: 'Life punishes those who react late.' East Germany's problems, he said, must be resolved by the East German leaders themselves.

On the night of November 9 1989, the Berlin Wall fell.

Throughout the West, it was a time of euphoria. To Mitterrand, it was a time of peril. He was convinced that if the Germans pushed for reunification, Gorbachev's days were numbered. When Rocard spoke enthusiastically of peace having been restored in Europe, the President exploded: 'Peace! How can he talk of peace? It's just the opposite that awaits us! . . . Gorbachev will never agree to go further and if he does, he'll be replaced by a hardliner. These people don't realise, but they are playing with world war.'[9]

To a greater or lesser extent, the rest of the G7 shared his fears.

During the Paris summit, four months earlier, Attali had noted in his diary: 'All of them think that in Moscow Gorbachev will fail and that the most hard-line communists will return to power.' Now Mitterrand told the Cabinet: 'Gorbachev cannot withstand the deterioration of his country's economy, tensions among the [Soviet] nationalities, loss of influence over his satellites and the calling into question of treaties and borders, all at the same time. To ask him to do that is to ensure his downfall.'

It is easy with hindsight to reproach Mitterrand for his lack of clairvoyance. A quarter of a century later the transcripts of the French President's discussions in the autumn and winter of 1989 – during the crucial six to nine months when Europe was being remade – convey a refusal to believe, a denial of what was happening in plain sight, because it flew in the face of everything that half a century of history had taught him.

In July he had told Bush: 'the USSR will never agree to lose control of Poland'. Five weeks later Poland had a non-communist Prime Minister. In January 1990 he told Thatcher that if Kohl continued pushing for reunification, the Russians 'will do to Dresden what they did to Prague'. They did nothing of the sort. The following month he told Kohl that if the Ukraine attempted to secede, 'it will be a case of civil war. Moscow will unleash terrible repression.' It did not. In March, he warned of a Soviet crackdown on Lithuania after its unilateral declaration of independence. That did not happen either.

Mitterrand was not alone. None of the Western leaders measured correctly the depth of the political earthquake shaking Europe. None realised the extent or, above all, the speed of the changes with which they were being confronted. All were locked into a vision of the Soviet Union and its policies which had held good throughout their lives and which it was impossible to imagine would suddenly be overturned.

Mitterrand's misjudgement was all the more striking because he had been among the first in Europe to recognise that German reunification was inevitable – one day. That, however, was in theory. It would probably happen before the end of the century, he had told a sceptical Helmut Schmidt, but 'not tomorrow'.[10] In practice, he argued, 'Gorbachev will never accept a united Germany inside NATO and the Americans will never agree to Germany leaving the Alliance.' 'So let's not worry,' he told Thatcher. 'The two superpowers will protect us from it.' The British Prime Minister was not so sure. 'Kohl . . . wants it and Gorbachev is weak,' she said.

The problem for Mitterrand was not so much the principle of reunification as the practical consequences that would result. A few days after meeting Thatcher he told the Cabinet that it was necessary to 'envisage coldly the possibility' that it would occur. But it risked leading to 'an economically and demographically powerful German bloc in the centre of Europe and that must be avoided'. De Gaulle, he recalled, had based French policy on François Mauriac's epigram: 'I love Germany so much that I am glad there are two of them.' If that were no longer possible, what was the alternative?

> All we can do is make the [European] Community more attractive so that an eventually reunified Germany will prefer the Community to balancing between East and West. You will say that West Germany plus East Germany plus Austria can make a formidable economic bloc. I'm going to tell you something . . . That prospect is causing great concern in Britain and Italy. History shows us that when a new force arises, it always provokes the emergence of another force to balance it. Europe has been rehearsing that old story for a thousand years.[11]

In public he kept repeating that the best response to Germany's desire for unity was 'to strengthen and accelerate the political construction of Europe'. But in private he accompanied that message with a blunt warning to Bonn. 'We are friends and allies,' he told the West German Foreign Minister, Hans-Dietrich Genscher in November, shortly after the Wall fell. 'But what you are doing is pushing us to a new Triple Alliance of France, Britain and Russia, exactly as in 1913 . . . You will be encircled and it will end in war.'

Anchoring Germany within the Community to prevent it striking out on its own and dominating Central Europe became the key to Mitterrand's thinking. European integration must come first, reunification, second. At first, Kohl seemed prepared to go along. But after the fall of the Berlin Wall, the Chancellor's attitude changed. On November 28, without informing even his own Cabinet, let alone Mitterrand as the Franco-German Treaty required, Kohl announced a 10-point programme for stage-by-stage unification. It would start with the 'fundamental transformation of the political and economic system' in East Germany, the holding of free elections and the release of political prisoners, to be followed by the creation of 'confederal structures' and eventually a German Federation.

Kohl set no timetable and maintained later that he had expected the European Union to be achieved long before Germany was united. But that was not how it looked to the others. A week later Mitterrand flew to Kiev to meet Gorbachev, whom he found seething over the Chancellor's initiative:

GORBACHEV: Your friend Kohl, your partner, is a hick from the countryside. Here even the humblest politician in the provinces thinks six moves ahead. Not him . . .

MITTERRAND: Between 1913 and 1989, we've seen a lot of things happen which weren't very happy. We must not start again.

[In] Germany . . . we are facing a contradiction. It's difficult not to take account of the strong political wishes of a people . . . On the other hand no one wants to see major changes in Europe as a result of German reunification without other measures being taken first . . . We need to work out agreements together on how Europe should evolve . . . so that the German problem is just one among many and not the most important one either. We must make progress in building the European Community so that the German problem is minimised . . . Achieving a balance in Germany cannot come before a balance in Europe . . .

The Europeans [are in agreement] that the German problem has been raised too quickly . . . Kohl's speech turned the order of things upside down and that was wrong . . .

GORBACHEV: I entirely agree . . . The 10-point plan was [like] a bull in a china shop . . . Help me to avoid German reunification! If you don't I will be replaced by a military [regime]. [Then] you will bear the responsibility for a war. Is that in the West's interest?. . . I told Genscher yesterday that Kohl's 10 points . . . amount to a political diktat . . . Shevardnadze [the Soviet Foreign Minister] told him: 'Even Hitler never used that kind of language!'[12]

Efforts to strengthen European unity had been underway since 1986, when the Twelve approved the Single European Act, committing themselves to increased political cooperation and to a single market by the end of 1992. Two years later West Germany proposed what it called 'a European monetary space', meaning a single currency. Britain, backed by the Netherlands, Portugal and Denmark, was hostile. The British government, Thatcher told Rocard that summer, 'neither wishes nor thinks possible the creation of a single currency and a central bank, even in the very long term'. But as the political landscape in Europe changed, British opposition diminished while it was the turn of the Germans to have second thoughts. Matters came to a head at the European summit at Strasbourg, on December 8 1989, two days after Mitterrand's meeting with Gorbachev in Kiev. After blowing hot and cold for a week, Kohl finally told his partners that Germany agreed to an intergovernmental conference on monetary union before the end of 1990. But in return he asked for a statement from the Twelve approving unification.

Thatcher, speaking for all of them, said Britain would refuse unless Kohl recognised the post-war border between East Germany and Poland, known as the Oder–Neisse line. For domestic political reasons, the Chancellor was determined to avoid that. Accordingly the Twelve approved a compromise. 'The German people,' they declared, 'will recover their unity by a process of free self-determination . . . with due respect for agreements and treaties and all the principles of [the] Helsinki [Conference] . . . and in the context of European integration.'

For the French President what mattered was that Kohl had committed himself to monetary union. It meant that he had chosen Europe, just as Mitterrand himself had done in 1983 by deciding that France would remain within the EMS. For Thatcher it was more difficult. She found herself between a rock and a hard place. Like Mitterrand, she was haunted by memories of the war – in her case as a teenager during the Blitz; in his through captivity and the Resistance. But where Mitterrand was convinced that the only way to ensure that Germany would never again seek to dominate its neighbours, as it had in 1914 and again in 1939, was through European integration, Thatcher saw that as jumping from the frying pan into the fire.

The result was an extraordinary conversation in the margins of the summit, in which both of them let down their guard and spoke frankly of their fears:

THATCHER: Kohl has no idea of the sensitivity towards reunification that prevails in Europe. Germany is divided because it was the Germans who imposed on us the most terrible of wars. Day by day, Germany is becoming more dominant . . .

MITTERRAND: Kohl is speculating on the natural impulses of the German people. He wants to be the one who encouraged that. Are there many Germans with the character to resist those urges? They have never fixed their borders . . .

THATCHER [*taking out of her handbag a map of Germany's pre-war borders and pointing to East Prussia, Pomerania and Silesia*]: They'll take all that and Czechoslovakia.

MITTERRAND: The way this is all speeding up is indeed very dangerous.

THATCHER: Kohl is going to encourage it. He's going to add fuel to the flames. We must put the Germans in a framework where it's kept under control. [As things stand now] they can make Berlin their capital again whenever they like.

MITTERRAND: Yes, and Gorbachev can't stop them any more . . .

THATCHER: The Americans don't even want to stop them. There's a strong pro-German lobby in America . . .

MITTERRAND: We no longer have the means to use force against Germany. We are in the position the leaders of France and Britain were in before the war, when they did not react to anything. We mustn't find ourselves in the same situation as at Munich! . . .

THATCHER: When East Germany has been a democracy for fifteen years, that will be the time to talk about reunification.

MITTERRAND: We should re-establish the entente between France and Britain, as in 1913 and 1938 . . .

THATCHER: The USSR has to change. It's now the only country in the East which doesn't have a multi-party system . . . Too many things are happening at the same time! [Imagine] if Germany takes power in Eastern Europe, as Japan did in the Pacific! . . . The rest of us must form an alliance to prevent that.[13]

The transcript of their discussion offers a rare glimpse of two of the world's most powerful leaders grappling with a problem, the solution of which escaped them and, uttering, in private, truths very far removed from the reassuring statements they were both making in public.

Mitterrand's fear that, by failing to take a stand against reunification, he would go down in history as having connived, like Chamberlain and Daladier, in the re-emergence of a German behemoth in Europe, was not feigned. Like Thatcher, he was worried about how far Germany's ambitions might go. Hence his constant demands that winter and the following spring, to the Chancellor's exasperation, that Germany commit itself irrevocably to its post-war frontiers. Kohl, he complained, always spoke of 'the unity of the German people' rather than reunification. 'What does that mean, "unity of the German people"?' he asked Attali. 'Does Kohl include in that the Germans in Polish Silesia or in the Czech Sudetenland?'

Shevardnadze, in talks with Dumas, expressed similar concerns. 'Kohl does not seek war,' he said, but 'the spirit of revenge lives on'.

Mitterrand's complicity with Thatcher proved short-lived. She soon realised that while the French President shared her anxiety, he considered reunification unstoppable. The only question was how long it would take. He no longer spoke of ten years. Vernon Walters, who had become Bush's Ambassador to Bonn, had suggested five years. Mitterrand now thought in those terms too.

In this uncertain context, five days before Christmas 1989, Mitterrand set out for East Berlin. The visit was a mistake. Most of his advisers had recommended that he call it off.[14] He persisted, partly out of curiosity to see for himself what East Germany was like and partly in a misguided attempt to slow the rush to reunification by showing that the moribund communist regime might still have a role to play.[15] If he gained anything from the visit, it was the realisation that East Germany was 'falling apart much more quickly than anyone had imagined'. Kohl, who had gone to Dresden the day before Mitterrand's arrival, had come away with a similar impression.

But between the French and West German leaders, relations had soured.

When the Chancellor proposed that Mitterrand join him for a symbolic crossing from East to West Berlin at the Brandenburg Gate, the President refused. Officially it was because he felt it was a German occasion and he would be out of place. In private he vituperated against Kohl's trickiness. 'He did not warn me about his 10-point plan. He refuses to recognise the Oder–Neisse line. And now he wants me to come and legitimise his grabbing East Germany. It's too crude. He can't really think I'll fall into a trap like that.'

At Latche at the beginning of January 1990, they held a dialogue of the deaf. Kohl assured his host that 'anchoring Germany in the European Community' was a 'prerequisite' for reunification – which in any case, he said, would probably take years. 'If I were German,' Mitterrand responded drily, 'I would be for reunification too . . . But being French, I don't feel the same passion.'

In East Germany that weekend hundreds of thousands of people demonstrated in favour of unity. 'Kohl's behind that,' Mitterrand fumed. 'He tells me that he hasn't done anything, but behind my back he's speeding things up.' The East Berlin regime was collapsing hour by hour. 'Three months ago,' he told the French Defence Council in mid-January, 'the great Soviet Union only had to frown and everyone bowed down. Now the Germans are starting to realise that the Soviet threat no longer exists.' A few days later, when Margaret Thatcher came to Paris to try to persuade him to join her in an attempt to slow the momentum, he told her it would be 'stupid and unrealistic to try to do so . . . No force in Europe seems able to prevent it.' In her memoirs she grumbled that he had 'a tendency to schizophrenia', saying one thing in public and another in private, but she admitted that on the fundamentals he had been right: the Germans were going to be reunited no matter what anyone did.

Over the next six months the remaining problems were ironed out.

After an icy two-week stand-off in March, when France joined forces with Poland to denounce Kohl's 'silence, heavy with ambiguities' on the recognition of the East German–Polish border and called for 'a legally binding commitment to be negotiated . . . before reunification', the Chancellor backed down. Mitterrand said later that it was 'the one disagreement which tested the two countries' friendship' over that period. Objectively, he maintained, French pressure had helped Kohl resist the irredentist demands of his more extreme supporters. Kohl felt that Mitterrand had underestimated his difficulties during what he called 'the most delicate time in my political career'.[16]

After the border issue was solved, the rift between them quickly healed.

In July Gorbachev removed the last obstacle by agreeing that the new unified Germany could remain in NATO if it wished, with the sole proviso that other NATO nations should not station troops on former East German territory after the withdrawal of Soviet forces.

A month later the two states signed a treaty of reunification and on 3 October 1990, German unity was proclaimed officially in Berlin.

To Helmut Kohl, the provincial lawyer from Bavaria, it was the realisation of an impossible dream.

The rest of Europe had very mixed feelings. Britain was hostile. Poland and Russia were viscerally opposed – 'It's in their genes,' Mitterrand told Thatcher. 'There's nothing you can do about that' – but powerless to intervene. So was France. The problem was not Kohl, Mitterrand said later, it was Germany: Kohl was not eternal; Germany would be there for ever. The day the Chancellor and Gorbachev reached agreement, Roland Dumas drafted a statement declaring that France was 'delighted' that there was no longer any obstacle to a united Germany 'with full rights and sovereignty'. That, Mitterrand accepted. But another sentence in the draft, stating that 'France regards this accord as a fortunate act for all Europeans', he crossed out.

For more than a year, the major powers had been struggling to find a framework within which to contain the political changes occurring within the Soviet bloc. The Cold War was not yet over, but everyone knew that its end was approaching. In the summer of 1989 Mikhail Gorbachev had spoken of 'a Common European Home', which he defined as 'a commonwealth of sovereign and economically interdependent nations' covering both the eastern and western halves of Europe. It was an attempt to preserve a semblance of Moscow's influence over its former satellites at a time when they were all adopting what one of Gorbachev's aides jokingly called 'the Sinatra doctrine', a reference to the words of the song, 'My Way'.[17]

Six months later, the Americans came up with an alternative. During a visit to Berlin in December, the US Secretary of State, James Baker, called for 'a new European architecture'. NATO, he proposed, should play an increased political role in relations with Eastern Europe and the USSR; the US and the European Community should strengthen their ties; and the Conference on Security and Co-operation in Europe (CSCE) should expand its activities across the whole of the emerging pan-European area. By then the Soviet Union's six Warsaw Pact partners had all, except East Germany, installed independent, non-communist governments.

To Mitterrand the common thread of Baker's proposals was the maintenance of American influence – or, as the State Department preferred to call it, 'leadership' – in Europe after the military threat from the Warsaw Pact had ceased.[18]

The French President had other ideas. Like Baker, he realised that if the Warsaw Pact disappeared, the role of NATO would have to change, if, indeed, it would still be needed at all.[19] But to him that meant it was time for the Europeans to start organising their own affairs. Accordingly, on December 31 1989, in a message of New Year greetings to the French people, he proposed a new political structure to bring together the European Community and the former communist states in the East:

> Europe will no longer be what we have known for half a century. [After having been] dependent on the two superpowers, she will return to her own history and geography, as one returns to one's own home. Either the tendency to break apart, to split into small pieces, will grow stronger and we will find again the Europe of 1919 . . . Or Europe will be built. She can do it in two stages. First thanks to the Community of the Twelve, which it is absolutely essential to strengthen . . . The second stage remains to be invented, [but] I expect to see in the 1990s the birth of a European Confederation in the true sense of the term which will associate all the states in our continent in a common, permanent organisation for trade, peace and security.[20]

To Mitterrand, creating a confederation was a way to affirm the common European identity of the former satellite states during what he saw as a lengthy transition period when their economic backwardness would preclude them from joining the European Community.

Gorbachev approved. Kohl was noncommittal. The EEC Commission President, Jacques Delors, was enthusiastic. The Americans were furious. Not only had Mitterrand put Moscow and Washington in the same basket as the 'two superpowers' which had kept Europe subservient, but the United States, not being part of Europe, was excluded from the proposed new arrangement.

At a meeting at Key Largo four months later, in April 1990, Mitterrand tried to mollify Bush, assuring his host that the idea of a European Confederation was 'for a distant future'. The idea that France was trying to exclude American influence was 'a fairy tale . . . another stupidity'. Bush chose to take him at his word. 'We understand that the Europeans need a space to talk among themselves,' he conceded, 'but at the same time we need to enlarge the role of the Alliance.'

In the end the proposal for a European Confederation turned out to be a red herring. Mitterrand's real goal had been to prevent the precipitate enlargement of the EEC. 'The Community already has difficulty settling its problems with just twelve members,' he said later. 'The danger is that with a large number . . . it will become no more than a free trade area.' That was what the British and the Dutch had always wanted: a common market without political commitments.

The French President was determined to avoid that. He told John Major, who had succeeded Thatcher as British Prime Minister the previous winter, that he did not want to see the East European states joining the Community for at least another twenty years. It was not only for fear that they would slow the pace of integration. Mitterrand was concerned that the entry of a mass of new members from East and Central Europe – traditionally Germany's sphere of influence – would strengthen still further German influence in a Community which it was already poised to dominate. The Confederation, in his view, would provide a halfway house, where potential new members of the EEC could wait until the Community's institutions were stronger and their own economies were more advanced.

The East Europeans saw through that. They interpreted his proposal, correctly, not so much as a stepping stone towards entry into the EEC but as a device to delay it. None of them wished to antagonise the United States, which they regarded as their best defence against the Soviet Union. And in any case, the CSCE, of which America was a member, already existed as a pan-European organisation. Why duplicate, unless the unspoken goal was to keep the Americans out?

In the end Mitterrand had to accept the logic of their position. In November 1990, he invited the thirty-four Heads of State and government of the CSCE to Paris, where they signed a 'Charter for a New Europe', marking the end of the Cold War. At the French President's urging, they also approved the creation of the European Bank for Reconstruction and Development to promote the transition of the former communist states to a market economy.[21] The US, which preferred such matters to be handled from Washington, was reticent. But Thatcher was enthusiastic and agreed that the bank should be based in London. The Franco-German Brigade, which Kohl and Mitterrand had agreed to set up two years earlier, became operational, providing a potential nucleus for broader measures of cooperation in European defence. The German Chancellor now proposed additional steps. To complement progress towards financial harmonisation, he said, the Community should start talks on strengthening cooperation in security and foreign policy. At first Mitterrand hesitated. France, like Britain, was jealous of its sovereignty. But the idea of closer political union as a counterweight to German reunification at a time when, throughout the former communist bloc, the old political structures were collapsing, had its attractions. In December 1990, a month after the CSCE meeting, France and Germany called for a common foreign policy and 'a genuine policy of common security leading in time to a common defence'. These would be discussed at an intergovernmental conference to be held in parallel with the conference on monetary union. The goal, the Twelve agreed, would be to transform the Community into a European Union – a term which now appeared for the first time – by the end of 1992.[22] The words 'federal Europe' were not pronounced, but it was a cautious step in that direction.

While Mitterrand focussed on the tectonic shifts occurring abroad, Michel Rocard got on with the business of government at home. He started well. Within weeks of taking office, he brokered an agreement between the Kanaks and the French settlers in New Caledonia, bringing peace to a territory which, two months earlier, had been on the brink of civil war. He introduced a government 'survival allowance' for what were called 'the new poor', the half-million or so families and individuals, without jobs and often without a home, who had no income of any kind. It was to be financed in part by the wealth tax, which the Socialists restored. No socialist government before had made a serious effort to aid those who, for whatever reason, had finished up on the scrapheap of society, or even, as Rocard now did, for those living on the margins, in tower blocks that had become slums, where, as he put it, 'everyday reality is made of elevators that don't work, broken letter boxes, dilapidated apartments . . .'

Even the President was impressed. 'Rocard is an enthusiast,' he commented. 'He believes in what he's doing and he's working at it.'

The plight of the millions of families who lived in squalid

low-income housing estates in the suburbs of the big cities had never been at the forefront of the Socialist Party's concerns. In the 1960s and '70s, the Communists represented the disinherited. When their influence collapsed, most of their clientele went to the extreme Right or the extreme Left. The Socialists' core support came from the working class and the bourgeois intelligentsia: teachers, civil servants, doctors, lawyers and other members of the liberal professions.

Christina Forsne, the left-wing Swedish journalist with whom Mitterrand had a long-standing liaison, wrote later that she could never make him understand that his failure to deal with the wretchedness of the 'new poor' was not only morally shaming but fraught with consequences for the future. He always replied that 'everything economically possible' was being done. Her criticisms were all the more striking because they came from a sympathetic source.

Under the presidency of François Mitterrand [she wrote], on the outskirts of [the big] cities there was real moral and material misery. The police no longer dared go there, families disintegrated, 90 per cent of the places in the kindergartens and schools were filled by immigrant children, there was violence, vigilantes and drugs. At the beginning of the '90s, in the worst-off districts, two out of three families lived in destitution. Under the long-drawn-out reign of a Socialist President, social marginalisation and poorly controlled immigration became a veritable time bomb . . .

I never felt that his heart bled for the suburbs . . . It was only when the violence spilled over – when racism started to kill – that he really became engaged . . . I used to pester him: 'Why are the Socialists deaf to all these problems?'. . . In return all I would get was a new speech about human rights . . . I would try to open his eyes, to ask him why he was incapable of communicating with these people who were struggling every day to survive, who couldn't look at things from the same perspective as he did . . . Weren't they, the 'little people', who were defenceless, the ones he should be helping and supporting first? . . .

I never understood how he could be so blind . . . After our long discussions, I used to be worn out. With the strange feeling that this President 'of all the French people', [as he used to describe himself,] admitted that in the end these [borderline] people would have to be written out of a future that was being built without them.[23]

It may be argued that she was merely opposing one form of left-wing idealism against another – the grass-roots social democracy of Olof Palme's Sweden against the intellectual socialism of the French. But she put her finger on a problem which no French leader, whether on the Left or the Right, was ever able to resolve – even if some, like Michel Rocard, tried harder than others: the blight of social decay in impoverished suburban 'zones', the French equivalent of the inner cities in Britain and the US, and the destruction of human dignity it entailed. She was right, too, about one of the causes. The mainstream leaders of the French Left were happy to trumpet their solidarity with the Third World, their defence of human rights, their championship of intellectuals persecuted by dictatorial regimes, but nothing could 'remove the scales from their eyes when it came to . . . the anger rumbling right beside them'.

The problem illustrated a key difference between the political approaches of Mitterrand and Rocard. The President looked for solutions that were principled, the Prime Minister for solutions that worked. 'Between us . . . it was the shock of two cultures,' Rocard said later. 'We were not made from the same wood.'

The 'honeymoon' between them, such as it was, did not last long. Mitterrand began to complain that Rocard was not 'Left' enough, conveniently forgetting that it was the Prime Minister's 'moderate' image and acceptability to the Centre that had made him choose him in the first place. That soon became an article of faith. No matter what Rocard did, Mitterrand was never satisfied. But the Prime Minister calculated that the longer he could stay at Matignon, the better his chances of contesting the presidential election in 1995, and he calibrated his attitude to Mitterrand accordingly. 'If you're hanging on to a bull by its tail,' he told his colleagues, 'the worst it can do is shit in your face. It can't throw you with its horns.'

Rocard was not Mitterrand's only domestic problem. The start of his second term had been tainted by financial scandals. In the summer of 1988, a group of investors – including Mitterrand's old friend, François Dalle, from l'Oréal; Samir Traboulsi, an influential Lebanese businessman close to the Finance Minister, Pierre Bérégovoy; and the Hungarian-American financier, George Soros – had made huge profits during a raid on the French bank, Société Générale, allegedly by insider trading.

A few months later the name of another member of Mitterrand's inner circle was cited in a similar case of financial skulduggery. Patrice Pelat, a friend since their days as PoWs together, was alleged to have profited illegally from a tip-off concerning a takeover bid by Pechiney, the state-owned French aluminium company. Pelat and Mitterrand were so close that he would enter the President's office without knocking. At the Elysée he was known jokingly as 'the Vice-President'. It was embarrassing enough that Dalle had been compromised. If Pelat was shown to have broken the law, it was getting dangerously near the centre of power. Moreover in both cases, the tip-offs from which they had benefited were said to have come from within the government.*

Pelat issued impassioned denials. But he was a rogue and Mitterrand knew better than to believe him. 'He says it's not true,' he told Fabius, 'but my intuition tells me that it is true, at least partly.' In February 1989 the President told a television interviewer that, if his old comrade were shown to be at fault, 'I cannot continue the same kind of friendship' as before. Three weeks later Pelat died of a heart attack. At his funeral, Mitterrand broke down and wept.

No one seriously claimed that he had been directly involved in leaking information. But the charges of malfeasance against two of his closest friends and the smear campaign that followed were impossible to lay to rest. The mud stuck. At well-heeled dinner parties all over France, no one could talk of anything but Mitterrand's hypocrisy in pretending that he had no interest in money while enriching his cronies.

Worse was to come. During the municipal elections that spring, a routine police investigation disclosed that the Socialist Party chief in Marseille, Michel Pezet, had been taking kickbacks from a prominent public works contractor. Normally matters of this kind were hushed up. Politicians on both Left and Right had to get their campaign funds from somewhere and, in the absence of public financing, false invoices

---

* In 1994, Traboulsi, who had acted as an intermediary in Pechiney's takeover of the American company, Triangle, and Bérégovoy's Chief of Staff, Alain Boublil, were sentenced to prison terms for insider trading. Ten years later, after one of the longest legal proceedings in French history, Soros was likewise convicted and fined 2.2 million Euros for his role in the raid on the Société Générale. Of the ten others accused in that case, eight, including Traboulsi and Dalle, were acquitted, and two benefited from an amnesty.

and kickbacks were the accepted method. This time, however, for reasons that were never explained, the investigation was allowed to continue.[24] In April a raid on the offices of Urbanet, a consultancy bureau whose official purpose was to advise Socialist town and provincial councils on public works contracts, turned up four spiral notebooks containing detailed accounts for the system of occult financing which had been set up for the Socialist Party by Pierre Mauroy on Mitterrand's instructions in the early 1970s. Over the previous seventeen years, the investigators discovered, Urbanet had brought the Socialists an average of 100 million francs (£10 million or US $16 million) annually in illegal funding.

The Right was certainly no less culpable. But the evidence found by the police dealt almost entirely with the malversations of the Left.

Mauroy insisted that the only answer was an amnesty. Otherwise, he told Mitterrand, thousands of Socialist elected officials could end up being charged. The President reluctantly agreed. But the outcry at this 'shameful attempt at self-whitewashing', as one magistrate described it, forced the government to think again. The amnesty was rewritten to cover businessmen who had provided illegal funds but MPs were excluded, which meant they could not be accused of whitewashing themselves. It was a breathtaking piece of hypocrisy – in practice there was no way that politicians could be charged for accepting illegal funds if those who provided them were amnestied – but it did the job. Early in the New Year the amnesty law passed. The Socialists breathed a collective sigh of relief.

But their troubles were not over.

Three months later, in March 1990, the Party held its biennial congress at Rennes in Brittany. Fabius was keen to try again for the post of First Secretary. Mitterrand did not dissuade him. But the Party split into three competing factions. Fabius and Jospin each had the support of 30 per cent of the delegates. Rocard, with 24 per cent, held the balance of power. They could agree on nothing and for the first time in the Party's history, the congress ended without being able to elect a new leader. A few days later, Mauroy was reappointed because there was no other choice.

For the second time in two years, Mitterrand had 'committed himself to Fabius not enough to make him win', as Jean-Louis Bianco put it, 'but enough to irritate everyone else and to end up making

Fabius's failure appear to be his own'. The Socialists were divided into warring clans. Still worse, the President's closest followers – the 'Mitterrandists' – were irremediably split. He said afterwards that he had underestimated the violence of the passions the contest had aroused. He was not being honest with himself. He had misjudged Rennes, just as he had misjudged the leadership election in 1988, because he was blinded by his antipathy towards Rocard and wanted to prevent him ever becoming his successor.

As if that were not enough, the row over the amnesty, which had seemed to have been laid to rest, flared up again more fiercely than ever. This time the target was the former Overseas Development Minister, Christian Nucci, who had been accused during Mitterrand's first term of misappropriating 7 million francs (£700,000 or US $1.2 million) which he had used for political expenses. Two weeks after the debacle at Rennes a panel of senior judges, who had been investigating the case, complained that the amnesty had been 'made to measure' to enable Nucci to escape trial. They were right. Mitterrand had insisted that the law be worded in such a way as to ensure that the ex-minister would be covered.

The accusations of 'self-whitewashing' resumed with a vengeance. Magistrates' associations, on the Left as well as the Right, denounced 'the cynicism of [the] political class'. In the provinces, angry judges, complaining of 'a two-speed justice system', ordered prisoners to be set free on the grounds that 'if stealing . . . millions of francs of government money does not trouble public order, why should stealing cars be a problem?' Three-quarters of those questioned in opinion surveys declared themselves scandalised by the amnesty for Nucci and two out of three thought the country's politicians were dishonest.

It had not been a good year. Mitterrand's reputation had been dragged through the mud. The congress at Rennes had confirmed his loss of control of the Socialist Party. The amnesty, which at first had seemed an elegant way to dispose of a problem which discredited the political class as a whole, had rebounded against the Left with a violence that left all of them reeling.

As usual, Mitterrand blamed his bête noire. 'Rocard is . . . behind all this hatred against Fabius,' he raged. 'What dwarves they are! . . . Rocard will pay dearly for this. I'll get rid of him. I have only to find a pretext.' In fact the Prime Minister was not remotely responsible for Fabius's defeat. Nor was he to blame for the amnesty. But the President needed to vent his spleen on someone and Rocard was his whipping boy. 'What a disaster!' he complained. 'Why did I listen to Rocard? He wanted this amnesty to protect his friends and keep the Socialist Party's support.' It was completely untrue. Rocard had been against the amnesty from the start but being, as he put it, 'a good soldier in a bad cause', had piloted the law through parliament under pressure from the Elysée and the Socialists.

Mitterrand was more lucid later when he said: 'the only thing that unites them is [the struggle for] my succession . . . They're all preparing for it . . . Since Rennes, the Socialists have not obeyed anyone, not Mauroy and not me. Each one thinks only of how to come out of it best for himself.'

After the spring of 1990, he was convinced that the Left would lose the parliamentary elections due in three years' time. It was the same pattern as in his first term – victory; disillusionment; defeat – but with much less reason. Once again, cohabitation loomed. The President described the amnesty as 'the worst error of my second term'. Rocard agreed. He said later it had cost the Socialists '150 seats in parliament and our honour'. But much as Mitterrand might try to blame those around him, the amnesty, like the Socialist Party's spectacular disunity at Rennes, was ultimately his doing. He had allowed them to happen where he had not actually encouraged them.

This time more was involved than just his habitual reluctance to lay down the law and compel others to obey. Some of his colleagues felt that, where domestic politics was concerned, he had become a spent force. He was disengaging, showing less interest and energy in the battles that would have to be fought to make his ideas prevail. Attali noted that, in contrast to his first term, now, when he criticised government policy, he rarely insisted that it be changed. 'He lets them do it as they wish,' Attali wrote. 'I have the feeling that apart from Europe and [a few other] big projects, all the rest bores him. He does his job as President on automatic pilot, as an observer rather than an actor.'

The two regions outside Europe that continued to hold Mitterrand's attention were the Middle East and Africa, which, in the French view, formed a unity.[25] The Middle East because of Israel, whose future he was convinced could be assured only by a peace settlement with the Palestinians, represented by the PLO; Africa because the raft of French-speaking territories which stretched from Mauritania to Madagascar remained an essential part of France's claim to greatness. Mitterrand's old dream of an empire 'from Flanders to the Congo' was gone, but 'Françafrique', the vast domain south of the Sahara in which Paris exercised special rights and responsibilities, lived on.

Throughout his first term, he had wrestled with a civil war in Chad, where a power vacuum had provided an opening for the Libyan leader, Colonel Gaddafi, to extend his influence southwards. Twice – in 1983 and again in 1986 – Mitterrand had sent troops to help the Chadian President, Hissène Habré, repel Libyan incursions. The aim was to show France's African allies that Paris could protect them. Six years later Mitterrand's firmness paid off. In 1987, Habré succeeded in quelling the Libyan-backed rebellion in the North. A peace agreement followed.* Socialist France had proved that it was a reliable suzerain.

Mitterrand's second term opened a new phase. The hopes born of independence had evaporated. 'Your continent is being marginalised,' Mitterrand told France's African partners at Casablanca in December 1988. The problem was bad leadership. But what could be done about it? Early on in his presidency Mitterrand had made timid attempts to 'moralise' the relationship between France and its former colonies. The African leaders had hated it. Later he had appointed his son, Jean-Christophe, who had been a journalist in Africa, to the 'African cell' at the Elysée. The opposition grumbled about nepotism and the French press nicknamed him *Papamadi* ('Papa-told-me'), but the African leaders were content. Jean-Christophe provided a family tie with the French President and that was what they wanted. When their regimes were under threat, France lent them its support. In return they maintained a privileged relationship with the former metropolitan power. Corruption, one-party dictatorship and the murder, imprisonment and torture of political opponents were passed over in silence.

By the beginning of 1990, this paternalistic approach was becoming

---

* France's problems with Libya did not end there. In September 1989, nine months after the destruction of a Pan Am airliner above Lockerbie, in Scotland, in which Libya later admitted it had been involved, a plane belonging to the French airline UTA was blown up over Niger. Libya afterwards acknowledged its implication in that attack too.

an anachronism. Africa had watched, mesmerised, as communism collapsed in Eastern Europe. The execution of the Romanian dictator, Nicolae Ceauşescu, had shown the African street that people could rise up and kill a tyrant. In South Africa, Nelson Mandela had been freed after twenty-seven years in prison. Érik Orsenna, who had been asked by Roland Dumas to reflect on African policy, warned that France was in danger 'of cutting itself off from the Africa of tomorrow, that of the rising generation'. Mitterrand, he said, should ask his African partners: 'What have you invested, Mr President, and you, Mr Minister, in your own country?' Coming shortly after a visit by Mobutu – who, on being reminded by a French minister that Zaire was tens of millions of dollars behind on its payments, had pulled out a UBS chequebook on a personal account in Switzerland, where he was estimated to have stashed away more than US $20 billion in ill-gotten gains, and asked: 'Who shall I make it out to?' – the question did not lack pertinence.

Mitterrand was not pleased. Like his right-wing predecessors, he had focussed on maintaining stable relations with the leaders of French Africa rather than promoting the welfare of their peoples.* Jean-Christophe explained his attitude by saying he did not want to be 'the White boss dictating to the former colonies'.

In June, after a tense meeting with his ministers at which the President had rejected their calls for a change of policy, Jean-Louis Bianco confronted him in his office. For the first time in the ten years they had worked together, he told Mitterrand he disagreed with him. France, he said, must channel aid where it was needed, not where African Presidents wanted it, and there must be more stress on human rights, democracy, pluralism and the fight against corruption.

Mitterrand was furious. 'You too! . . . It's idiotic,' he fumed. But he listened. At La Baule, in Brittany, on June 20, at a summit meeting with African Heads of State, he delivered a speech which he had worked on for days and rewritten half a dozen times. France, he told

---

* For the French Right there had been a quid pro quo. At election time, leaders like Omar Bongo in Gabon despatched emissaries with suitcases full of cash to finance the campaigns of the RPR and the UDF. It was the Gaullist version of Urbanet. Where the Socialists had taken kickbacks from corrupt public works contractors to whom their municipalities awarded contracts, the Right took kickbacks from corrupt African leaders. In return, Chirac, Giscard and their allies turned a blind eye to the dictators' turpitude.

them, had taken two centuries to achieve a democratic system and was in no position to give others lessons. But he went on,

> it is necessary for us to talk about democracy. It's a universal principle which the peoples of central Europe recently realised was so self-evident that, in a matter of weeks, regimes which had been considered very strong were overthrown. The people went out into the streets and the squares, and those in power, sensing their own weakness, ceased to resist, as though they had already known for a long time that their regimes were no more than an empty shell. And this people's revolution, the most important since 1789, is going to continue. [It] will go all round the world . . . There are not thirty-six different ways to democracy. [It means] a representative [political] system, free elections, a multi-party system, freedom of the press, an independent judiciary, no censorship . . . Some of you will say, 'we've tried that and we know the drawbacks'. But the drawbacks . . . are outweighed by the benefits of feeling that one is in an organised civil society . . . No matter what, that is the direction we must take. It is the path towards freedom on which you will travel at the same time as you travel along the path to development.[26]

Mitterrand went to immense lengths to avoid offending his listeners. Repeatedly he insisted that France was not interfering, it was merely offering an opinion. Nonetheless the speech raised hackles. Hassan of Morocco, Hissène Habré in Chad, Eyadéma in Togo found terms like 'democracy', 'people's revolution' and 'multi-party system' unacceptable.

At a news conference afterwards the French President drove home his point. 'French aid,' he said, 'will be lukewarm towards regimes which behave in an authoritarian fashion and do not accept progress towards democracy, and enthusiastic towards those who take the plunge with courage.'

The speech was not the turning point which Mitterrand's supporters claimed, but it did reflect a changing political climate. In the Ivory Coast and Gabon, there were multi-party elections. In Algeria, President Chadli Bendjedid legalised the opposition but then, two years later, confronted by the prospect of an Islamic fundamentalist victory in the elections, banned it again. In Morocco King Hassan agreed to release a number of political detainees and to make modest changes in his barbaric prison system. In Chad and Mali, dictators were overthrown bloodily, and in Bénin, peacefully. Elsewhere, African leaders either went through the motions of democracy while taking care to do nothing which might curtail their own power, or, like Eyadéma in Togo, refused to make any changes at all.

Mitterrand's promises of greater rigour, and of making aid conditional on democratic progress, remained a dead letter. Two years later, five of the most corrupt countries in the continent were still among those Paris was helping most.

To some that was a mark of pragmatism: Africa was not ready for democratic institutions; the only answer was to pay lip-service to democratic ideals.[27] 'La Baule?' Mitterrand said afterwards. 'It changes nothing.' To others it was a missed opportunity, the first sign that, in his mid-seventies, Mitterrand was beginning to show his age, losing touch with the way the world was evolving. There had been straws in the wind before. Attali remembered a Cabinet meeting on education at which the President had launched out on a long digression about the qualities of primary schools during his childhood in the 1920s. In the case of Africa, Mitterrand's ideas had been formed in the 1950s and had not changed greatly since. After La Baule, the ties between France and its former African colonies were still based, as before, on clientelism and patronage. Policy was decided when an African leader picked up the telephone and dialled the Elysée. The 'Africa of Papa', as de Gaulle would have called it, lived on. It would contribute to one of the continent's grimmest tragedies, the genocide in Rwanda.

In the Middle East, progress towards a peace settlement had been blocked since the mid-1980s. The reasons were multiple, but prominent among them were the intransigence of the Israeli Prime Minister, Yitzhak Shamir, who had succeeded Begin at the head of the Likud, and the Reagan administration's lack of interest.

Mitterrand received Shamir in Paris in January 1989 and said afterwards that it had been like talking to 'a block of granite'. The Israeli Prime Minister said no to everything: no negotiations with the PLO, no elections for a Palestinian administration in the occupied territories, no Palestinian State.[28] 'You say you want peace,' Mitterrand told him. 'But if you don't know who to talk to about peace, it's not much help . . . You offer nothing. You are denying the Palestinians the right to a homeland, the same right for which you yourselves fought.' Shamir's stonewalling convinced Mitterrand that the time had come for him to meet Yasser Arafat. The violence of the Israeli army's repression of the 'intifada' – a mirror image of David and Goliath, in which 120,000 Palestinians were arrested and more than a thousand killed – had dismayed Western opinion. The PLO National Council had for the first time conceded Israel's right to exist and Arafat had formally renounced the use of terrorism.

When the Israeli Premier learnt what Mitterrand intended, he sent an angry protest. The President did not reply. 'I am a friend of Israel,' he told his aides, 'but I haven't joined the extreme Right of the Likud.'

Arafat and Mitterrand met at the Elysée on Tuesday, May 2 1989, after much diplomatic hand-wringing over the niceties of protocol. This leader, unlike others, had the right to a red carpet but not an honour guard; to a greeting from the Chief of Protocol but not the Secretary-General. He was, however, allowed a Palestinian pennant, signifying sovereignty, on the armoured limousine which brought him from the airport. The President urged him to go further in making clear the PLO's willingness to recognise Israel and negotiate a lasting peace:

> In 1947, we recognised the State of Israel . . . We recognised a State, not necessarily its policies . . . You have been courageous . . . You have gone nine tenths of the way, the rest will cost you nothing . . . It would be to your advantage to say clearly that the [PLO] Charter [calling for Israel's destruction], will be abolished when there is peace . . . Israel needs to understand both that France is vigilant in matters affecting its security and that France recognises the right of the Palestinians, a people in exile, to return to their land . . . Historically Gaza has never been Jewish. They never wanted it. Shamir has more ambition than the [Old Testament] prophets.[29]

Arafat did more than he had been asked. That night he declared on French television that the offending articles in the Charter were 'null and void'.[30] It proved to be a key step in opening the way to an eventual Israeli–Palestinian agreement. But before that could happen, another problem intervened which led for a time to all other considerations being put aside. On the night of August 1 1990, the Iraqi army invaded Kuwait.

Iraq had ended its war with Iran with US $70 billion in debts and needing another $60 billion for reconstruction. Kuwait had 8 per cent of the world's oil reserves, which brought US $16 billion a year to a feudal and obscenely rich pro-American ruling family with little support among Arab states outside the Gulf. Saddam Hussein had calculated that the rest of the world would look the other way.

Next day Mitterrand told Roland Dumas: 'To make war on behalf of these billionaire potentates will be hard for us.' But he already knew that France would have no choice. '[My] intuition . . . is that this is just the beginning and the crisis is going to get worse,' he told a Cabinet committee that weekend. 'All these princes are too rich, they are too fat, they are afraid of losing the lifestyle to which they are accustomed. [But] we must be firm . . . We have to defend international law and solidarity.'

By August 9, the President's mind was made up.

That afternoon he asked the ministers most directly concerned to give their opinions. One after another, they expressed reluctance to see France join the United States in a war against Iraq. Jospin and Bérégovoy thought French intervention might be possible if the United Nations approved a military expedition. Joxe opposed military action of any kind. The Defence Minister, Jean-Pierre Chevènement, thought that if Saddam fell it would open the way to the spread of Iranian fundamentalism. Rocard agreed. For France to join 'a war of the rich countries', led by America, against 'a populous, poor, secular State' would be a grave mistake, damaging French relations with the rest of the Arab world. Others proposed that France should have a military presence on standby in the region but 'give ourselves some distance from the US' and allow time for sanctions to work. Mitterrand heard them out with ill-concealed irritation:

> When you shelter behind those arguments you're just reasoning in a vacuum! [Of course] we will pursue economic sanctions . . . And of course we must think of our relations with Iraq and with the Arabs. But the problem is this: are we going to let the Americans and the British act alone? . . . The Americans know that the French and the British are the only ones [in Europe] capable of taking action. If we don't respond, it means we are going to sit on the sidelines . . . If we say no, it means

we will not come to the aid of a country that has been threatened . . .
We can't follow two policies at the same time. If we evade that problem,
we've gathered here to no purpose. People will say France is out of
it . . . Iraq is an unscrupulous, bloody dictatorship, which is asphyxiating
the Kurds. In certain circumstances we are happy to have the Americans
with us. We are their allies . . . In this case we must be clear about our
solidarity. If we have to choose, I consider that we must fight against
[Saddam] Hussein, whatever the consequences may be. If we don't, we
are false brothers of the West.[31]

Ten days later he announced on television that 'as a result of the
actions of the Iraqi President, we are in a logic of war'.

In a context of Iraqi aggression, as with Argentina's invasion of
the Falklands in 1982 and the deployment of Pershing and cruise
missiles a year later, Mitterrand's instincts were sure. However much
he might equivocate on issues of domestic policy, or debate with
himself over the extent of change in the Soviet Union or in Africa,
here he was on familiar terrain. With Saddam it was a trial of strength.
From the late summer of 1990, French policy did not waver. To mollify
opinion at home, where a groundswell was developing on the Left
against French participation in an American-led coalition, and to show
the Arab States that France was sparing no effort to obtain a diplomatic
solution, Mitterrand went further than his partners, notably Thatcher
and Bush, in offering the Iraqi leader face-saving ways out. As he
expected, they led nowhere. At the end of August, he told Prince
Saud: 'we approve of all these peace initiatives, but we don't believe
in them'. A few days later, at a meeting with King Hussein of Jordan,
who had been urging a compromise with Saddam, he vented his
bitterness at the Iraqi leader:

Iraq violated the law. Until it says in one way or another that it is ready
to leave Kuwait, there will be a state of war . . . Iraq pays no attention
to what we have tried to do to save it [from its own folly] and treats
us like dogs. Saddam owes us 24 billion francs [£2.3 billion or US $4
billion] and he takes hostage all the French citizens [in Iraq]! It's an
unpardonable act of ingratitude. It's barbarous! Humanly speaking, in
seventy-four years and after fifty years in politics, I have never until
now seen a man dishonour himself like that! It's unworthy! . . . Is there

no gratitude, no appreciation, no respect for one's word in the Arab world?[32]

Two months later he spoke again of Saddam's duplicity in a conversation with George Bush. Both lamented that the ally of yesterday had become the enemy of tomorrow:

MITTERRAND: I used to get letters from the Emir of Kuwait and the King of Saudi Arabia [during the Iran–Iraq war], reproaching me for not giving Iraq enough arms!

BUSH: We, too – we used to give the Iraqis intelligence information.

MITTERRAND: We had only one idea in our heads: stopping Khomeini's Islamic revolution.[33]

The one faint hope, in Mitterrand's view, was to establish a link between Iraq's withdrawal from Kuwait and a resumption of the Middle East peace process, thus giving Saddam 'a pretext for yielding' because he would be able to portray his decision as a means to launch fresh negotiations between the Palestinians and Israel. Gorbachev was in favour. Saudi Arabia was not opposed. But the Americans were unenthusiastic and Saddam laid down as a precondition that the coalition must renounce the use of force, which made agreement impossible.

Mitterrand was still disgusted by the idea of going to war to save the Emir of Kuwait. 'How am I going to explain to the French peasants that I have imperilled the lives of their children to restore to power a billionaire?' he asked the US Secretary of State, James Baker. 'How can we be sure that using force won't just protect their bank accounts in Switzerland?' But the decision had been taken. Two days later, on November 20, he told Thatcher, in what proved to be their last meeting before her resignation, that, contrary to American predictions, he did not expect a long war. Iraq was less strong than it seemed.

It was Helmut Kohl who posed the question to which no one had an answer: 'Yes, but afterwards? Who is going to occupy the country? What's going to happen with the rest of the region?'

On the night of January 16 1991, Operation Desert Storm began. France had pre-positioned 10,000 ground troops, the third largest Western contingent after the US and Britain, as well as air and naval forces. It was more than a symbolic presence. The French General

Staff estimated that when ground combat began, they risked losing 100 dead and 300 wounded a day.

A week before the ultimatum to Saddam expired, an opinion poll found that 79 per cent of the French people opposed participation. But Mitterrand argued that, however unpopular the war might be, France had to take part to preserve its status in the world. 'If we are absent from the conflict, we will be absent from the settlement,' he told his ministers. 'What is more, we won't justify our role as a permanent member of the Security Council . . . Germany is still a political dwarf. The proof of that [is] that the Germans won't be there. As for the British, they are too much under the heel of the Americans.' It was a war, he told his critics, 'which touches both the conscience and the balance of the world . . . Were we not to participate militarily . . . people would speak of [our] decline.'

Not everyone agreed. On January 29, Chevènement resigned as Defence Minister to be replaced by Pierre Joxe. Chevènement had opposed the war from the outset, but Mitterrand had endeavoured to keep him in the government to silence the pacifist fringe of the Socialist Party, of which he was the spokesman. It proved a wise precaution. By the time the Defence Minister left, the coalition air bombardment was well under way and public opinion, in France as in America, had swung massively behind the government.

Three days after the launching of Desert Storm, both Bush and Mitterrand saw their popularity boosted by almost 20 per cent, among the sharpest rises ever recorded. Contrary to the predictions of the Pentagon that the coalition risked losing at least 100 aircraft a week, in the first seven days 21 planes were brought down by enemy fire. When the ground offensive started on February 24, in the 100 hours of combat before Saddam capitulated, France lost not hundreds of dead and wounded, as the Chiefs of Staff had predicted, but two soldiers dead and twenty-five wounded, all victims of American 'friendly fire'.

The Gulf War took Mitterrand back to the time, half a century earlier, when Britain, France and the United States had also fought together. When Bush telephoned him, five days before the land attack, and told him, 'You're the first I've called. Now I'll talk to Major', Mitterrand replied: 'We're a very small group of "happy few". I'm in touch with Major too. We think the same way.'

But the war did not produce the results that the French President had hoped for.

After Iraq's capitulation on February 28, the coalition felt it had no choice but to leave Saddam in power. Mitterrand regretted that. 'We could have continued for another two weeks,' he told Bush afterwards. 'But we did not.' The principle of non-aggression had been upheld – Kuwait had been returned to its ruling dynasty – but the mess the war had left behind was no better than what had gone before. Six weeks after hostilities ended, Bush confessed to him: 'The Gulf War was nothing compared to the problems we have now.'

The failure to complete the destruction of Saddam's forces had left the Iraqi leader free to crush dissent, which he did with characteristic brutality. In the South the Presidential Guard put down an uprising by Shiites, who had hoped the coalition would support them. In the North, at the end of March, it was the turn of the Kurds, who fled to Turkey and Iran. Bush was wary of further military action. 'We have no intention of getting involved in an Iraqi civil war that has been going on for years,' he told Mitterrand. The French President, whose wife, Danielle, was a passionate advocate of the Kurdish cause, urged him to do more. 'If necessary,' he insisted, 'military action must be envisaged':

> We have a moral duty and a political obligation to stop this man destroying and starving his own people. If we do nothing, we will undermine all the moral credit that has resulted from America's remarkable action [in the Gulf War]. It's a matter of avoiding genocide . . . It's not a legal issue. We cannot allow the civilian population to be punished because they believed in our victory . . . What's important is to put in place a temporary protection, which will last as long as necessary . . . so that in practice Saddam Hussein cannot attack his people . . . We have a right to do that because we won the war. [We did not do so] to abandon millions of people to government terrorism.[34]

A few days later a 'no fly' zone, patrolled by American, British and French aircraft, was created over northern Iraq, permitting the Kurds to establish de facto independence in October. A 'no fly' zone in the South followed a year later.

However, Mitterrand's overriding concern was not so much Iraq as the peace process between Israel and the Palestinians. One of the reasons he had insisted on French participation in the war was that he was convinced that it would help create the conditions for progress towards an Israeli–Palestinian settlement. There was now a window of opportunity, Mitterrand argued. Arafat, who, for reasons of internal Palestinian politics had felt obliged to support Saddam during the war, had seen his influence temporarily weakened. If an international conference were convened, the PLO would have to stay in the background, which would make it easier for Israel to take part. It was time for the United States to act.

The previous autumn Mitterrand had complained to the Defence Secretary, Dick Cheney, about what he said was a US double standard in the Middle East which undermined the West's authority in the region. Lebanon was a case in point. While Washington was taking a tough line with Iraq, it had done nothing to stop Syria exerting hegemony over its smaller neighbour. 'Lebanon is much more important to me than Kuwait,' the French President said. 'What help would the United States give us [there] if I asked for it? Compare that to the help France is giving [you] over Kuwait.' Cheney did not reply.[35] Then there was Israel. 'I defend their right to a secure existence,' Mitterrand had told the Defence Secretary, 'but not to the detriment of others. Their attitude is simply intolerable. So is their oppression of the Palestinians.'

Bush had in fact already decided that, after the Gulf War, he would make a fresh attempt to relaunch the peace process. During a lengthy discussion on the Caribbean island of Martinique, Mitterrand urged him to persevere:

MITTERRAND: The only real problem is that of the Palestinians. All the rest is relatively easy. I'm not talking about . . . Iraq. That's very important, but it's not the key issue . . . I don't want to apportion blame, but the latent war between Israel and Palestine will outlive both of us unless we have a resolute policy. You know my attachment to Israel . . . But I try to tell Israel the truth. By refusing every agreement, every compromise, Israel is equally responsible for the situation in the Near East . . . Unless America shows its determination, nothing will happen there.

BUSH: I know you think we have been the hostage of Israel. Well, if there's an American President who's been willing to try and do something about this problem, it's me. [But] they keep trying to use Congress to push us

beyond where it is reasonable for us to go . . . I realise our responsibility
. . . I can only say that with this government in Israel, it's not easy.

MITTERRAND: The main obstacle is the Israeli government. I'm not saying
you can tell them what to do . . . but we can't continue indefinitely [like]
this . . .

BUSH: I agree . . . [Palestinian] 'State'. That's the key word.

MITTERRAND I used to say before, 'state structure', 'homeland'. Then, when
I said, 'State', I got such a – forgive the expression – bollocking [from
Israel] that I started rather to enjoy it. It's curious how the human mind
works.[36]

Bush kept his word. He did try. Riding high in the opinion polls, he
was able for once to ignore the Jewish lobby and its allies in Congress.
In October 1991 the Madrid Conference consecrated the principle of
exchanging land for peace, leading three years later to the signing of
the Oslo peace accords and the establishment of the Palestinian
Authority. But France's role was limited. Mitterrand's gamble that
French participation in the Gulf War would ensure it a say in the
peace process did not pay off. To Shamir's Likud party, 'those who
are not with us are against us'. Mitterrand, who tried to be impartial,
was placed in the 'against us' camp. But above all, the United States,
having decided to take matters in hand, intended to run the show
itself. There was no place at the Middle East conference table for a
second-ranking European power.

Iraq's invasion of Kuwait allowed Michel Rocard's government to
survive until the spring of 1991 – Mitterrand could hardly change
Prime Ministers until the Gulf War was over – but it did not save
him. Since Rennes, his fate had been sealed. The only question was
who would replace him.

Many of the President's closest colleagues urged him to call a snap
parliamentary election to take advantage of the surge in his popularity
brought about by the war. It was not an easy decision. The moment,
he agreed, was 'politically propitious' but he was not convinced the
Socialists would prevail. Opinion polls commissioned by the Elysée
suggested that the Left was likely to do less well than in 1988, when
it had failed narrowly to win a majority. The public had followed him
in the Gulf, he told Fabius, 'but it doesn't follow me as solidly at home'.

After three years of strong growth, the economy had stalled; unemployment was rising again; and there had been an epidemic of rioting by disadvantaged youths in the suburbs. Mitterrand decided to wait.[37]

That made sense so long as there was a reasonable chance of doing better when the normal parliamentary term ended. But it would depend on the effectiveness of Rocard's successor. And there matters were more complicated, for the replacement of the Prime Minister had acquired such an emotional charge that the President's judgement had become skewed. There existed between them, Attali wrote, 'an incomprehension which had become dangerous for the functioning of the State'. The figures said it all. Seven years earlier, when Mauroy's popularity as Prime Minister was down to 25 per cent, Mitterrand had urged him to stay on. Now, with Rocard's popularity close to 60 per cent, he was determined to make him leave, no matter what the cost.

Naming Rocard, he told Attali, was 'my only mistake since 1988'. In fact his mistake had been to name Rocard and then to do everything in his power to make him fail. 'Mitterrand today,' the Prime Minister said a few weeks before he resigned, 'is cynicism in its purest state.'

It was the stance of a sovereign.

Like the French kings, Mitterrand had a favourite, Laurent Fabius, who enjoyed the monarch's esteem and affection, and a pretender, Michel Rocard, who risked disgrace and exile. Much of the President's energy in his second term was devoted to preventing Fabius's rival, Lionel Jospin, from forging an alliance with Rocard to unseat his young champion. The Elysée came to resemble the court of Louis XVI. Mitterrand's cultural adviser, Laure Adler, left an acid description of the 'agitated types of behaviour' which pervaded the 'château', as it was called – 'excesses of love, unflagging admiration [and] theatrical displays of fidelity':

> The Mitterrandist courtier . . . says 'Mr President' at least once in every phrase he utters, exclaims at the least word the President says, bursts out into inappropriate laughter [and] anticipates his desires . . . François Mitterrand, because he is President, lives at the Elysée as though in a bubble . . . Power is first and foremost, and perhaps solely, power over men. François Mitterrand knows that, he uses it and sometimes abuses it in his palace. By the affection he dispenses, he makes those around him hostages . . . To fill the distance between a

private life he can no longer have . . . and an official life which keeps
him in a straitjacket and prevents him being natural, a court has been
created – or he has created it – [which] is inherently unequal. He alone
can ask. Generally he gets what he wants, and when he doesn't . . .
he does not understand.[38]

Danielle said she could never work out why he wanted to surround
himself with such a hothouse atmosphere of flattery and intrigue.
'It's the one question to which I never found an answer. There were
people who – I used to ask myself – how could François put up with
them? [But when] I put it to him, "How can you keep someone like
that working beside you?", he'd evade the question and just say, "Oh,
you don't know him."'

The monarchical aspect of the Elysian court was only one facet of
Mitterrand's presidency, but it became steadily more pronounced.
André Rousselet recalled that over time it became harder to find a
way to tell him what he did not want to hear. That sovereign disdain
for the views of others helped to explain the choice he made in the
summer of 1991.

The obvious successor to Rocard was the Finance Minister, Pierre
Bérégovoy. He was a Mitterrand loyalist, a competent administrator
and had the confidence of the financial markets. He would represent
continuity. But Mitterrand wanted change. In 1984 he had chosen
Fabius as the country's youngest ever head of government. Now he
decided to appoint France's first woman Prime Minister.

Édith Cresson had worked with him since the days of the
Convention, almost thirty years earlier. She had guts. She had shown
herself to be a capable minister. To Mitterrand she was everything
that Rocard was not: energetic, passionate, trenchant, indiscreet, highly
political and willing to make waves. She had resigned as Minister for
European Affairs in October 1990, accusing Rocard of being afraid to
take unpopular decisions. 'I can no longer continue to be part of a
government where I find such an absence of will,' she told a weekly
magazine. It was unfair. If Rocard was reluctant to stick his neck out,
it was because he knew that Mitterrand was just waiting for an excuse
to chop his head off. But it was music to the President's ears. During
the winter he saw her frequently. Each time she distilled poison about
the Prime Minister's failings. By March he had decided that she would

be his choice. She told him that she would prefer to be Minister of Industry with Bérégovoy as Prime Minister. But Mitterrand insisted.

To prevent Rocard turning the tables on him and resigning of his own accord, as Chirac had done to Giscard in 1976, the President wanted to move fast. On May 10, at a private dinner at the Elysée to mark the 10th anniversary of his assumption of power, he went out of his way to make himself agreeable to Rocard and his wife, who had never previously been invited to such an occasion. The Prime Minister remembered Chirac's parting words to him when he had taken over three years earlier: 'Beware of Mitterrand when he smiles. It means there is a dagger in his hand.' Five days later, after the weekly Cabinet meeting, the Elysée announced that Cresson would take over as Prime Minister.

It proved a catastrophic decision.

Mitterrand was not wrong in thinking that the government needed a kick-start and that the time to do it was when his popularity as President was at a peak following the Gulf War. The Socialist Party was in the doldrums and, with Rocard on the way out, the government often seemed to be sleepwalking. But Édith Cresson, for all her verve and dynamism, was not the person to turn that around.

At the Elysée, Mitterrand's advisers were appalled. Most found her uncultured, brash and incompetent. Attali summed up the prevailing sentiment. The President, he wrote, had interpreted as a will to reform what was in fact Cresson's 'taste for novelty'. He had confused 'straight talking with boldness, disdain for others with freedom of judgement and an appearance of decision with decisiveness'. In part, that reflected the sour grapes of a predominantly male establishment mortified that 'Édith' had been considered a better choice than any of them. In part it was the frisson of a Latin country confronted with a woman who had dared to break the political glass ceiling. One young right-wing MP compared her to Louis XV's mistress, the marquise de Pompadour, an oblique reference to an affair Cresson had with Mitterrand in the 1960s. Rocard's Chief of Staff, Michel Huchon, nicknamed her Calamity Jane.

Public opinion was initially more positive. Seventy-seven per cent of those questioned said they were pleased that Mitterrand had named her.

But the President then repeated the same error that he had made with Rocard.

Cresson had wanted to replace the Socialist Party 'elephants' in the government – Bérégovoy at the Finance Ministry, Charasse at Budget, Jospin at Education, Joxe at Defence – with new faces so as to have her hands free to make the 'new start' Mitterrand wanted. He refused. The 'elephants' were furious that she had tried to get rid of them. As a result she had been fatally weakened even before she began. To add to her troubles, unlike her predecessors, she lacked the backing of a party faction. Mitterrand said afterwards it was one of the reasons he had chosen her. Her independence was 'a necessary virtue for the difficult period for which she was destined. She was not accountable to anyone except me.' But that was not enough to enable her to succeed. Instead of 'giving her the means to carry out her policy', Attali wrote later, 'he put her down like a cherry on top of the cake'.

Part of the damage that followed was self-inflicted. Cresson's outspokenness, disparaging the Japanese for 'working away like ants' and British men as 'mainly homosexuals', made the French smile but also cringe.

More serious was the economic downturn. Farmers, facing a reduction in subsidies from the EEC's Common Agricultural Policy, went on the rampage, attacking town halls and prefectures, burning trucks carrying imported agricultural produce and disrupting government meetings. There were strikes by dockers, nurses, steelworkers, truck drivers and public servants. As tax revenues declined, budget cuts loomed, forcing the government to reduce spending at what was politically the worst possible time.

By December Mitterrand had to admit that his protégée had failed.[39] To Jack Lang he complained that she had been unable to trigger 'the magic of power'. In fact, the problem was far more basic. Cresson had never been able to gain control of the government machine. Her staff at Matignon were ineffectual amateurs. Dominique Strauss-Kahn, then Minister of Industry, remembered the government being 'a total shambles'. Hubert Védrine, Mitterrand's diplomatic adviser, who had taken over from Bianco as Elysée Secretary-General, spoke of 'not spending a single day that was normal' as long as Cresson held office.

She had undone all the good that the Gulf War had brought Mitterrand. His support, in the country and in the Party, was slipping away. For the first time since his re-election his approval rating fell into negative territory. On the Left voices could be heard suggesting that he step down so as to trigger an early presidential election which Michel Rocard, whose popularity was undiminished, stood a good chance of winning against a quartet of right-wing leaders – Barre, Chirac, Giscard and Le Pen – who were quarrelling among themselves. Mitterrand was bitter. 'If they think I am going to resign before my term is up, they're wrong,' he told Fabius. 'If it would help, I would do it of my own free will. But for those who want to bury me, No!'

That winter Fabius was finally able to succeed Mauroy as Socialist Party First Secretary. But it was a pyrrhic victory. The quid pro quo was that Rocard would be the Party's candidate for the presidency in three years' time. Then, in March 1992, in a grim foretaste of the battles to come, the Socialists obtained only 18.3 per cent of the vote in elections for provincial councils in the *départements* and the regions. It was their worst result since the Party had been re-launched at Épinay twenty years earlier.

Less than a week afterwards, on Thursday, April 2, ten and a half months after Cresson's appointment, the President accepted her resignation.

It was a stunning rebuke.

He had insisted on installing a Prime Minister whom none of his colleagues wanted and who herself had opposed his decision, just as, two years earlier, he had tried to impose on the Socialists a First Secretary whom the majority of the Party did not want. In both cases he then failed to give them the support that might have allowed them to succeed. 'God', as the cartoonists now called Mitterrand, was becoming adept at setting in motion the pieces on the political chessboard and then watching from on high to see how the game played out. But he was not God, he was mortal. When they failed, he failed too. By the time Cresson resigned in April, 65 per cent of the French people said they were dissatisfied with him. Pierre Bérégovoy, whom he named to succeed her – not with any enthusiasm but because he was the only alternative – had just a year to turn things round before the parliamentary vote. Mitterrand had waited too long. The new Prime Minister had an impossible task.

François Mitterrand was not alone in misjudging the mood of his party and his country in the early 1990s. In Britain, Thatcher had been forced to resign. In the United States, George Bush would not be re-elected. In the USSR pressure was building on Gorbachev.

In January 1991, Soviet troops had tried rather half-heartedly to regain control of Lithuania and Latvia, which had declared unilateral independence a year earlier. The operation was an embarrassing failure. Gorbachev insisted afterwards that it had not been authorised by Moscow. To Mitterrand it suggested that the Soviet leader was losing control. When he met Bush in Martinique in March, he counselled prudence. 'It would be a mistake to force Gorbachev to go beyond the limit of what he can stand,' he said. 'I don't know what his chances are, but I don't want to make him lose . . . What's at stake is his international reputation, his authority in the world . . . Otherwise the Soviets will say to him: "You haven't been able to prevent an economic crisis, separatism, disarmament, the loss of Soviet influence . . . You must go!"' Bush agreed. From then on, the West tried discreetly to bolster Gorbachev's position. John Major invited him to attend the G7 summit in London. The Americans involved him in the Middle East peace talks. But five years of economic reforms had brought a sharp decline both in Soviet living standards and in Gorbachev's popularity at home. After the Baltic states, other Soviet republics demanded self-rule.[40] When Bush and Mitterrand met next, this time in Rambouillet, Gorbachev's future was once again at the forefront of their concerns:

BUSH: How is it going to work out between the Soviet Union and its constitutive republics? It's a huge problem . . .

MITTERRAND We need the world and the USSR to realise that Mr Gorbachev is their last chance before chaos. Up to now he's proved his strength – he has already ruled for longer than Lenin. [But] his economy is in agony . . . and we must not forget the problem of the generals in Moscow . . .

BUSH: On that point, our specialists have been saying for the last few weeks that there's less to fear from the Soviet army.

MITTERRAND: It's true that Gorbachev has been skilful there but he remains fragile.[41]

Five weeks later, on Monday, August 19 1991, shortly after 6 a.m., the Soviet news agency, Tass, announced that the Vice-President, Gennady Yanayev, had taken power because, 'for health reasons', Gorbachev was unable to fulfil his responsibilities. The trigger had been a proposal to increase the powers of the republics at the expense of the central Soviet government. Conservatives, led by the KGB Chairman, Vladimir Kryuchkov, foresaw that that would lead to the USSR's disintegration.

Mitterrand's first reaction was that the putsch would not succeed.

'Gorbachev appointed all those jerks [the coup leaders] in the winter to neutralise them,' he told Védrine. 'They are cretins. They won't bring it off because they represent only the past and are flying in the face of present-day Soviet realities.'

But in telephone conversations later with other Western leaders, he was much more prudent. To Major and to Bush, both of whom denounced the coup as unconstitutional, he said merely that the West should remind Moscow of 'the principles and criteria' – diplomatic codewords for democratic and economic reform – which the Soviet Union had to respect if it wished 'to have a dialogue with us'. To both men he gave the impression that he regarded the putsch as a fait accompli. Gorbachev was out of power and, like it or not, the West would have to deal with his successors. On television that night he conveyed the same message. France, he said, expected 'the new leaders' to honour their undertakings. 'If they are sincere and they want to preserve the chances of peace within the framework fixed by Gorbachev, there is no reason to worry. We shall soon know.' Only towards the end of the interview, in response to a question, did he say that he condemned what had happened in Moscow.

Dumas and Védrine listened with a sinking feeling to the President's acquiescence in the day's events. In the light of what followed, his comments looked even more inept.

Later that night Bush came out publicly in support of a call by Boris Yeltsin, the head of the Russian Federation, 'for the restoration of the legally elected organs of power and the return of Mikhail Gorbachev to his post of President'. Yeltsin had climbed on to a tank outside the Russian parliament building, urging a crowd of 20,000 protesters to resist the putsch and calling for a general strike. Images of his defiance, which, despite the regime's censorship, managed to find their way on to Soviet television, identified him for the Soviet people as the strongman around whom the coup's opponents would rally. The following night, KGB units, backed by tanks, were sent to storm Yeltsin's headquarters but backed off. The putsch leaders lacked the stomach for a fight. Next morning it was all over. Gorbachev was freed from house arrest in his villa in the Crimea, where he had been on holiday with his family when the plotters struck, and flew back to Moscow. Yanayev and his companions were arrested.

How could Mitterrand have misread the situation so badly?

He was not alone. The German Chancellor, Helmut Kohl, had reacted similarly. But Kohl had the excuse that he had to cope with German reunification.

Part of the explanation was that the French President had been expecting Gorbachev to be overthrown for so long that, when it happened, it seemed logical. Gorbachev himself had warned repeatedly that he might be unseated by a coup. Why question it, if that was his fate? Mitterrand thought he could 'read' Russia. The pendulum had swung too far and too fast in the direction of reform and now the inevitable correction had occurred.[42]

Moreover, as a European – and here he rejoined Kohl – his beliefs had been forged in the Second World War. Nationalism, to Mitterrand, was a perennial source of conflict. If the Soviet Union broke up, he had told Bush in March, 'we will have twenty more states in Europe [and] it's not going to help us at all . . . In Europe [nation-states] are permanent sources of war.' It was a nineteenth- as much as a twentieth-century view. Nationalism, Mitterrand believed, could be neutralised only if it were confined in a larger entity. That was the rationale for the European Community. Empires brought stability, whether they were communist, democratic or feudal. 'The Austro-Hungarian Empire,' he said, 'was actually rather convenient. We were wrong to get rid of it.'

It followed that if Gorbachev was unable to hold the Soviet empire together, it was better that he be replaced by a more conservative leadership which could. The President of the European Commission, Jacques Delors, made a similar judgement. A more orthodox Soviet leadership, he said, 'could have a positive side . . . Nationalist passions would be calmed.'

Once Bush had publicly backed Yeltsin, Mitterrand changed tack, 'firmly condemning the coup d'État' and demanding Gorbachev's return. After failing to reach the Soviet leader by telephone, he called Yeltsin to assure him of his support. On television on Wednesday night, after Gorbachev's safe return to Moscow, he insisted that he 'had always thought it would finish this way'.[43]

The following Saturday the Soviet leader resigned as the Communist Party's General Secretary and Yeltsin, now the real power-holder in Moscow, decreed the nationalisation of party property, followed by a total ban on Communist activities throughout the Russian Federation. The Ukraine – where a thousand years earlier the Rurikid dynasty had laid the foundations of the Russian State – declared itself independent. At a Cabinet meeting on August 28, Mitterrand spoke with mixed feelings. 'It would be nonsensical after having denounced the Soviet system for decades to complain now that at last it is changing. But as Head of State, I have to measure the consequences for us and for Europe.' He feared, he said, that the Union's collapse would 'bring grave threats for our continent . . . of anarchy and confrontations'.

In the Balkans and the Caucasus, that bleak assessment would be justified. But not in Russia itself. On December 8 1991, Yeltsin and the leaders of Belarus and the Ukraine formed a loose grouping which they called the Commonwealth of Independent States. By then, all fifteen Soviet republics had become independent. On Christmas Day, Gorbachev resigned as Soviet President. As Mitterrand had anticipated – prematurely – at the time of the putsch, four months earlier, his role was at an end. Next day the Soviet Union ceased to exist. Russia took over its nuclear arsenal, its permanent membership in the UN Security Council, its embassies abroad and the rest of its international obligations.

The disintegration of the Soviet empire, accompanied by the dissolution of its military arm, the Warsaw Pact, completed the end of the Cold War which had been officially proclaimed at the CSCE in Paris a year earlier. The 'new world order' announced by George Bush had become a reality. There was only one superpower: the United States of America.

France, like other medium-sized powers, found its influence sharply reduced. Its status as a maverick in the Western alliance counted for little when there was no latent conflict for that alliance to confront. The same was true of Britain and the 'special relationship' with America. Special relationship for what? In September 1991, Mitterrand had proposed a four-power summit of the US, the USSR, Britain and France, to discuss ways of securing the Soviet nuclear arsenal, parts of which were based in Belarus, the Ukraine and Kazakhstan. It would have been the first such meeting for more than thirty years.[44] Bush demurred. 'We mustn't give the impression of forming a club,' he told Mitterrand. 'You are right,' the President replied frostily. 'You will reach decisions with the Russians. If you don't want a four-power meeting, France will be all the freer . . . We will act according to our own interests.'

With the Middle East and East–West relations fenced off as Washington's preserve, France's sphere of activity was reduced to its own backyard: Africa and, above all, Europe. Mitterrand wanted the European Union, prefigured in the Single European Act, to be the crowning achievement of his second term, a European legacy to rival the accomplishments of de Gaulle.

The economic component – a single market and eventually a single currency – was relatively straightforward. Economics have the same laws everywhere.

Political cooperation was more difficult. Foreign and defence policy are at the core of national sovereignty. Mitterrand was as reluctant as anyone to give up national decision-making. But he foresaw that if Europe and, by extension, France were to have a voice in an increasingly globalised and multi-polar world, the continent would have to speak and act as one. The first question was whether the Europeans would be willing to surrender even a small part of their sovereignty for the greater power of all. It was the issue Churchill had raised at The Hague forty years earlier. The second was how to reconcile Europe's ambitions with the desire of the United States to retain a leading role in the continent's affairs.

Margaret Thatcher's departure had been an enormous stroke of luck for the French President. She and Mitterrand had got on well enough. But she would have done her damnedest to block progress towards a European Union. John Major, her successor, had made clear from the outset that he intended to take a more positive approach:

MAJOR: We want to play a meaningful role in Europe, it's in everyone's interests. We don't want to be considered as an island on the margins of Europe . . .

MITTERRAND: Europe has grown used to Britain's opposition, and to making plans without you in the belief that you would catch up with the train. That's what you always did . . . We used to have the impression that your country was somewhere else. What you are saying now is not necessarily more reassuring, but it is certainly much cleverer! . . .

MAJOR: I hope I shall spend more time in the driver's cabin than catching up with the train! There are areas where we have shared interests . . . We are not as far apart as you think.[45]

On the single currency, Major said he did not want it to be thought that 'we British were trying to block the process' but admitted that 'we have huge difficulties with parliament and our public opinion' and he could not commit himself to a firm starting date.

The real apple of discord was defence. In Mitterrand's view, the end of the Cold War meant that, sooner or later, the Americans would leave Europe. Major acknowledged that that was possible. Where they differed was over how Europe should respond. Mitterrand wanted to strengthen the Western European Union to serve as the nucleus of an autonomous European defence force which would operate alongside NATO. Major disagreed. 'I don't want to give the Americans a pretext to reduce their commitment,' he said. In any case, he added, apart from Britain, France, Germany and perhaps Italy, the other European armies had little credibility. Before there could be talk of European defence, the member states needed to show that they were willing to make the effort.

Mitterrand had clashed with George Bush on this issue at Key Largo in April 1990. The US President had argued that, for Americans, 'NATO is the only plausible justification for [our] military presence in Europe', and in the changed circumstances of the 1990s this meant that the Alliance had to have 'an expanded political role'.

MITTERRAND: I'd like to know what we're really talking about. If the American leaders would spell out what they mean by 'the political role of NATO' everything would be a lot easier . . .

BUSH [*struggling*]: Well, in a political situation that has changed, NATO's role will be different. Not just military, but more political . . . NATO will have to change gear . . . to get us through the critical period. We don't know who the enemy is any more.

MITTERRAND [*silkily*]: Yes, it's a nuisance not having an enemy.[46]

The proper role for NATO now that the Cold War was over would be the subject of increasingly dyspeptic exchanges throughout the rest of Bush's term in office. In Martinique, in March 1991, two months after his meeting with Major, Mitterrand assured the US President that he accepted that NATO was for the moment the only viable defence Europe had. 'I hope Europe will gradually acquire the means to defend itself,' he added. But that was not yet the case, so there was no reason for the Americans to be 'fearful of European unity':

There's no need to be . . . For the next twenty years, you must not put the question in terms of either/or . . . NATO and the idea of European defence should coexist: it's not one or the other . . . There will be progress on military matters when there's political progress. It will take a lot of time. Your British friend isn't very keen; nor are the Dutch; Ireland is neutral; and as for the Germans, since they've become big they no longer know what they're supposed to be doing.[47]

The US Senate, Mitterrand said, 'cannot have its cake and eat it': it could not both call for American troop reductions in Europe and oppose efforts by the Europeans to assume their own defence.

Four months later, in July, at Rambouillet, the tone had grown harsher. 'In the years ahead, your country will pull away from Europe,' he told Bush. 'It's inevitable. I have to take account of that to prepare for the future.' The US President winced. 'I want you to know,' he replied, 'that if Europe had any solution outside NATO, American opinion would immediately stop supporting both NATO and our presence in Europe'.

Two recent developments had upset the French leader. First, the Americans had begun speaking of making the CSCE the core of a new 'Euro-Atlantic community that extends east from Vancouver to Vladivostok', which brought back bad memories of Reagan's attempts at Williamsburg to extend NATO protection to Japan. Second, under American pressure, NATO's military command had agreed on the creation of a Rapid Reaction Force, which to Mitterrand was an attempt to forestall the creation of such a force by the Europeans. Shortly after his tetchy exchange with Bush, he laid out his concerns to Helmut Kohl:

The American presence is going to . . . enclose Europe in a structure that is totally dependent on Washington and stifle any desire for European defence . . . I am not going to send any divisions to defend the Kuriles islands [disputed between Japan and Russia]. Europe should not have agreed to capitulate like this in the middle of the battle. [It] amounts to accepting the status of an auxiliary force, like the foreign legion which imperial Rome, at the height of its power, used to levy from the countries it had subjugated.[48]

Mitterrand was less isolated than he seemed. Britain and Italy, the two European nations most determined to maintain the primary role of NATO, recognised the necessity for what was termed 'the emerging European identity in defence matters' lest one day budget pressures and changing priorities in Washington leave the Community unarmed. But Bush remained adamantly hostile. On October 23, after Kohl had agreed to upgrade the Franco-German Brigade to division strength, he wrote to Mitterrand in unusually sharp terms:

> I am concerned to see that the proposal which you and Helmut have made is causing serious divisions within the Alliance . . . We have avoided criticising publicly your idea of a European force, even though we are strongly opposed to anything which could be perceived as a wish to replace or to duplicate NATO. I wish only to ask you to confirm that it is not your intention, even in the long term, to propose a substitute to the Alliance.[49]

Mitterrand sent a soft answer. He understood Bush's predicament. 'We can't blame them [the Americans] too much for their attitude when they are the ones who are providing us with security,' he told the Spanish Prime Minister, Felipe González.

In the end a diplomatic compromise was found. In Rome, on November 7 1991, the sixteen NATO Heads of State and government noted the 'complementarity between . . . NATO and the Western European Union [and] between the Alliance and the European security and defence identity' and declared that 'multinational integrated European structures' would play 'a growing role . . . in strengthening the Allies' capacity to work together for their common defence'. It was a contorted formulation, but everyone was satisfied. To Bush it meant that European defence would develop under NATO tutelage. To Mitterrand it opened a space in which Europe could build a defence force of its own alongside moves to closer political and economic cooperation.

With that issue behind them, the European leaders gathered on Sunday December 8 in the small Dutch town of Maastricht, on the Meuse River not far from the German border, where an Allied paratroop attack towards the end of the Second World War had furnished the subject matter for a classic war film, A Bridge Too Far.

The political trade-off at the heart of the Maastricht negotiations had been agreed between France and Germany two years earlier. Mitterrand would back German reunification provided Kohl would commit a united Germany to Europe. As the details were inked in, a second trade-off followed. Kohl wanted a federal Europe on the German model with greater powers for the European Parliament. Mitterrand did not. They struck a compromise: Germany would moderate its federal ambitions and France would accept the German vision of monetary union. That meant a modest extension of the parliament's powers, an increase in the number of German MEPs, to take account of Germany's increased population, as Kohl wished, with, as a consolation to Mitterrand, agreement that parliament should continue to be based in Strasbourg. In return the future European Central Bank, which would oversee the common currency, would be modelled on the Bundesbank and independent of political control.

But agreement between France and Germany was one thing. Translating that into a new European treaty which the other ten members of the Community would accept was quite another.

The holdout, as always, was Britain.

Over lunch at Downing Street on December 2, the Monday before the Maastricht summit, John Major explained his difficulties to Mitterrand. The Conservative Party was deeply divided in its attitude to Europe. Parliament would not accept the single currency. To save face, Major told him, he needed an opt-out clause, not just for Britain – which would make it embarrassingly clear that London was isolated – but available to all the EEC member states.

MITTERRAND: That would amount to saying that we haven't made a final choice in favour of the single currency. Your position already carries risks for us. To have a generalised exemption clause would be going too far . . .

MAJOR: You have a Prime Minister in Great Britain who is more prepared to commit to Europe than you have ever had before! Don't put me in a position where I have to say no.

MITTERRAND: I know. You have been courageous. We ought to help you. But not by abandoning what we are meeting for [next week] in Maastricht. The point here is this: are we going to make an economic and monetary union? If we give ourselves a probationary period, that just creates uncertainty. Not to fix a date [for the passage to a single currency] would not be a concession, it would mean renouncing [our goal] altogether.[50]

They agreed to disagree. Mitterrand understood his host's position. 'If one day I need a lawyer,' he told Major, 'I'll ask you to act for me.' But there was no way the differences could be papered over.

Next day Kohl flew to Paris. He told Mitterrand that for Germany it was essential that the commitment to the common currency be irreversible. Britain, on the pretext of the special status of sterling, might be allowed to opt out, but no one else. The Chancellor thought a similar concession might be necessary on the Social Charter. Major had warned that if he agreed to it, the Thatcherite members of his Cabinet would probably resign, putting his government's survival at risk. The French President was reluctant. Not only would that mean that Britain could continue to adopt more flexible labour policies, with fewer protections for its workers, than the rest of the Community – making it potentially more attractive to multinational investors – but it would be another step away from the 'ever closer union' envisaged by the Single Act.

'There's a lot of nervousness in Europe,' Kohl summed up. 'We are going to have to go to work, François, and keep the ball between us for the 48 hours [the summit lasts]'.

And so they did.

At the opening session in Maastricht, on Monday morning, December 9, Mitterrand proposed that the timetable for the common currency be slightly amended. The Finance Ministers had suggested that it should be established by unanimous decision by the end of 1996 or, if that were not possible, by a majority vote before the end of 1998. Instead, Mitterrand said, the summit should fix an immoveable deadline so that the currency would automatically come into existence on January 1 1999. Kohl supported him. So did Jacques Delors and the Italian Prime Minister, Giulio Andreotti, whom he had sounded out the previous night.

At the time, it seemed no more than a marginal adjustment and it passed without debate. In fact it was the crucial decision of Maastricht. It meant that, whatever might happen in the meantime, within seven years, the Euro – or as it was then known, the Ecu (European Currency Unit) – would become a reality. The process had become unstoppable.

The rest of the morning was spent on Britain's demands for a generalised opt-out clause, which France and Germany refused. Major reserved his position. In the afternoon there was broad agreement on political cooperation and a common defence policy. It was agreed that EU citizens would be able to vote in local elections wherever they resided, and that cooperation on immigration, terrorism and drug-trafficking would be strengthened.

The other bone of contention remained the Social Charter. Every time Major raised objections, the Netherlands Prime Minister, Ruud Lubbers, who held the rotating presidency, proposed leaving the matter in abeyance, arguing that it should be dealt with 'later', by which he meant at a subsequent summit. 'The Dutch presidency isn't playing fair,' Mitterrand complained to Kohl. Next morning they agreed over breakfast that if Lubbers continued to evade the issue, they would have to force his hand. The moment of truth came a few hours later. Mitterrand proposed that Britain should be allowed to opt out not only from the common currency but from the Social Charter as well. Major refused, insisting that any opt-out clause – whether for the currency or the Charter – must apply to all the member states, not to Britain alone. The French President said that in that case he would return to Paris: there was no point staying in Maastricht if Britain intended to block any possibility of an accord. Faced with the prospect of the summit collapsing, Lubbers changed sides. All that evening, he, Kohl and Delors took turns trying to convince Major that, unless he compromised, Britain would be held responsible for the summit's failure. Shortly before 1 a.m. on Wednesday, December 11, the British Prime Minister yielded.

The Union Treaty was signed two months later and ratified by all twelve member states, although Denmark, where accession was initially rejected, required a currency opt-out similar to Britain's before it was approved at the second attempt. It came into force on November 1 1993.*

* In January 1999, when the time came for those members which met the Maastricht criteria to adopt the Euro, Austria and Finland, which had entered the EU in 1995, joined nine of the original Twelve in embracing the new currency. Greece was judged not to be ready. Sweden, which had joined at the same time, decided, like Britain and Denmark, to keep its own currency. It was not granted an opt-out but used a legal loophole to do so. Of the twelve new member states which had joined the EU by January 2013, five adopted the Euro while seven kept their own currencies. All except the original three holdouts – Britain, Denmark and Sweden – will be required to use the Euro as soon as they meet the entry criteria, which is expected to occur by 2020. The currency's biggest problems to date were caused by the admission of countries which had concealed the

In London, Mrs Thatcher denounced it as 'a treaty too far'. Had she remained in power, it would no doubt never have been agreed. In Paris, Mitterrand called it 'one of the most important developments of the last half-century'. The Euro, he declared, 'will be the strongest [currency] in the world, stronger than the dollar, because it will be much more stable and will allow Europe to assert itself as the first economic power on the planet'. Wishful thinking? History has yet to render a final verdict. But it was an accurate reflection of the euphoria of the time.* Whatever the travails of the common currency in the decades ahead, Maastricht opened the door to closer political, economic and fiscal harmony in the biggest industrialised region in the world.

As if German reunification, the Gulf War, the break-up of the Soviet empire and the establishment of the European Union were not enough to occupy the continent's leaders, the traditional powder keg, the Balkans, was about to explode into a war which they had thought consigned to another age.

In the early spring of 1991, the leaders of Croatia, Serbia and Slovenia had met secretly to discuss dividing up Yugoslavia on ethnic lines. Mitterrand already had an inkling of what was afoot. A few months before, the Yugoslav President, Borisav Jović, a close ally of the Serbian leader, Slobodan Milošević, had warned him that 'a fierce struggle' was under way to split up the country. 'It is not easy to delimit the territory between the different peoples,' he said, 'because we are all mixed together. There is a risk of civil war, [which would be] a tragedy for the Balkans and for Europe.' In April, the Krajina, the Serb-populated eastern frontier land of Croatia, declared secession. 'This is the beginning of the end,' Mitterrand told Attali. Like most of his colleagues,

---

true state of their finances. In 1999, Kohl was well aware that the Italians had falsified their accounts but insisted that, as one of the EU's founding members, Italy must be allowed to join as a matter of European solidarity. It set a disastrous precedent. Greece, whose finances were in an even more calamitous state, was admitted two years later.

* Mitterrand's statement was more accurate than the subsequent troubles of the Eurozone might make it appear. Within a year of the Euro first being circulated in January 2002, it exceeded parity with the dollar and has remained a stronger currency ever since, being valued at between US $1.05 and $1.61. According to the IMF, the EU's GNP reached US $17,611 billion in 2011 compared with $15,076 billion for the United States, making it, as he had predicted, 'the first economic power' in the world.

he favoured the maintenance of a federal Yugoslav state. John Major, facing the IRA insurgency in Northern Ireland, and Felipe González, confronted by Basque separatism, agreed. If Yugoslavia split, it would set a precedent for every other nationalist movement in Europe.

The one dissenting voice was that of Helmut Kohl. Until the First World War, Slovenia and Croatia had been part of the Austro-Hungarian Empire and thus under Germanic influence. When, at the end of June, the two countries declared independence, Kohl urged his partners to grant immediate recognition. The others refused and instead the EEC brokered a compromise. The Federal Government, now dominated by Milošević, agreed to suspend military operations against the breakaway republics in return for a three-month moratorium on independence during which negotiations would begin on a permanent settlement.

However the cessation of official hostilities did nothing to stop the fighting between the Croatian government and the Serb secessionists in the Krajina, who, notwithstanding Milošević's promises, continued to receive clandestine support from their allies in Belgrade. Mitterrand, like his partners, faced a dilemma. Should they intervene to separate the belligerents? Or stand by and do nothing?

The French went through the motions of drawing up contingency plans for a European peacekeeping force. To be effective it would require the deployment of 10,000 French troops and similar numbers from the other major countries. Mitterrand was unenthusiastic and it soon became clear that the others were too. Britain, in particular, was opposed. 'I am not sending my army anywhere,' Major told him. His Foreign Secretary, Douglas Hurd, assured Dumas that 'no British soldier will ever fight in Yugoslavia'. No one wanted to risk getting bogged down in the Balkan quagmire.

The diplomatic route was also doomed. Talks in The Hague, chaired by Lord Carrington, went nowhere.

But for Mitterrand there was a bigger problem. 'The break-up of Yugoslavia is a drama,' Dumas minuted him later that year. 'That of the Community would be a catastrophe.' The fear in Paris was that, at the very moment when Europe was preparing to proclaim its unity at Maastricht, France and Germany would find themselves on opposite sides in a European war. If the Germans backed the Croats and the French and the British, the Serbs, he told Kohl, only half in jest, they were heading for a replay of 1914. The Chancellor recognised the danger and agreed to delay any move to recognise Croatia until Maastricht was behind them.

On the other side of the Atlantic, the Americans watched with epicaricatic delectation the Europeans' predicament. The Bush administration, purred the Secretary of State, James Baker, thought it natural 'to let the European Community take responsibility for managing the crisis in the Balkans at a time when it wished to show that it was capable of acting as a united power'.

The problem, as the Community demonstrated over the coming months and years, was that it was capable of nothing of the sort. The comparison with the Gulf War was devastating. When Iraq invaded Kuwait, 3,000 miles away, Britain and France sent troops. When Serbian forces invaded Croatia, right in their own backyard, they sat on their hands. True, there was the small matter of oil being present in one case and not in the other. As Baker delicately put it, America's 'vital national interests were not at stake' in Yugoslavia. It was true, too, that Croatia's situation was much less clear-cut than that of Kuwait: its independence was opposed by the Serb minority within its own borders as well as by the Serbians in Belgrade. That alone made a Kuwait-style military intervention impossible, even had any of the outside powers been willing to contemplate it, which none was. However, the key difference lay elsewhere. In the Gulf War, America had provided leadership. In Yugoslavia, Washington was so wary of being drawn in that it blocked French and British attempts to get the UN Security Council to act lest that provide an opening for the Soviet Union to intervene. As a result the Europeans were left to cope on their own.

Not only were they unable to agree on a coordinated military response but diplomatically they were all over the place.

On December 23, less than a fortnight after the Twelve had agreed to establish the European Union and three days before the dissolution of the USSR, Kohl broke ranks and announced unilateral recognition of Croatia and Slovenia. Mitterrand had decided that there was no point fighting against it. The relationship between Paris and Bonn was more important than the war in the Balkans. On January 15 1992, Germany's partners tamely followed the Chancellor's lead.

By then a ceasefire, the 15th in six months, brokered by the former

US Secretary of State, Cyrus Vance, had finally taken hold in Croatia, opening the way for the UN to send peacekeepers. UNPROFOR, the United Nations Protection Force, would eventually include almost 40,000 men from several dozen countries, the largest contingents, ironically in view of their initial reluctance, being from France and Britain. That did not end the bloodshed. In the Krajina the Serbs pursued a systematic policy of ethnic cleansing. Television brought the horror of racial massacres into European living rooms. Increasingly, Serbia and its leader, Milošević, were perceived as the aggressors. Mitterrand rejected that argument. That winter he told the German newspaper, the *Frankfurter Allgemeine Zeitung*:

> You ask me which is the aggressor and which is the victim? I am inca-
> pable of saying. What I know is that the history of Serbia and Croatia
> has been filled with dramas of this kind for a very long time already,
> notably during the last world war, when the Serbs had many people
> killed in Croat [concentration] camps. You know that Croatia was part
> of the Nazi bloc. Serbia was not. As soon as [Marshal] Tito died, the
> latent conflict between Serbs and Croats was bound to reappear. It has
> done so.[51]

Historically, he was right. Croatian fascists had killed some 400,000 Serbs in the early 1940s, compared with an estimated 12,000 Croats who died in the 1990s. Croat atrocities had been so bestial that the Gestapo complained to Himmler that they were harming the Nazi cause. The Serbs had fought with the Allies. Mitterrand remained haunted by memories of Serb prisoners at the PoW camp at Ziegenhain, 'the most wretched, the poorest, the most badly beaten, and the only ones who resisted the Nazi divisions'.

But he was out of sync both with French public opinion and with the consensus emerging within the European Union. Milošević was not, as Mitterrand claimed, merely trying 'to establish a clearly delim-ited frontier and some kind of direct or indirect control over the Serbian minorities'. His goal, as Kohl argued, was to re-establish Greater Serbia, embracing all the Serb lands, with Kosovo, Montenegro and the Voivodina as vassals. The recognition of Croatia opened the way for the other ex-Yugoslav republics to demand independence. The result was another, far more terrible conflict: the war between the

Muslims and the Serbs in Bosnia-Herzegovina which, by the time it ended, would claim 200,000 lives.

Milošević's forces had withdrawn from Croatia only to throw their support behind the Bosnian Serbs. In April 1992, the Europeans recognised Bosnian independence. The secret agreements reached a year earlier between Milošević and the Croatian leader, Franjo Tudjman, which had remained in force despite the Croatian–Serbian war, then came into play, and the Serbs and Croats began to divide up Bosnia between them.

This time Mitterrand decided Milošević had gone too far. In a series of messages to Belgrade, he asked the Serbian leader to put pressure on his Bosnian Serb ally, Radovan Karadžić, to reopen the airport at the Bosnian capital, Sarajevo, which the Serbs were blockading, to permit an airlift of food and other vital supplies. For weeks nothing happened. Then, on June 23, he received a message from the Bosnian President, Alija Izetbegović, whom he had met in Paris at the beginning of the year. 'We've reached the end of the road,' Izetbegović told him. 'We have neither food nor arms nor hope. It is the Warsaw ghetto all over again. Will you, yet again, allow the Warsaw ghetto to die?' The message was delivered by Bernard-Henri Lévy, a flamboyant French literary heavyweight who had just returned from Sarajevo. He compared Izetbegovic's situation to that of Salvador Allende, the left-wing Chilean President killed in an army coup twenty years earlier, whom Mitterrand had greatly admired.

Later that week, the Twelve met in Lisbon for their first summit since Maastricht and warned that if the Serb blockade were not lifted, the use of 'military means to attain humanitarian objectives', a reference to possible air strikes, was no longer excluded. It was an empty threat but it marked a change of tone.

The following afternoon Mitterrand left for home. But instead of heading for Paris, his plane turned east towards Yugoslavia.

The siege of Sarajevo by Serb militias had tightened. The airport was surrounded by Serb armour and, even if the runways could have been cleared, a landing in darkness was impossible. The President spent the night at Split, on the Croatian coast, and next morning flew to the Bosnian capital by helicopter. Dumas had warned Milošević and, through him, the Bosnian Serbs, that a French delegation was about to arrive, but had not disclosed that Mitterrand was leading it. He was driven into the city in an armoured troop carrier but insisted on getting out to walk through the streets, where he was given an ecstatic welcome. People leaned out of the windows of their apartments, cheering and throwing bouquets of flowers, while among the crowds that gathered as he passed, handwritten signs were held up: 'Merçi, Monsieur'. He laid a rose outside the baker's shop where, a month earlier, twenty-two people had been killed by a mortar shell, and visited the injured in one of the city's hospitals. Afterwards, at a news conference with President Izetbegović, he explained why he had come:

> I believe in the symbolic force of acts. I hope to seize the world's conscience to come to the aid of a population in danger, because what is happening is not acceptable. Since the start of the conflict in former Yugoslavia, both sides have committed wrongs. But one cannot put back to back those who fire on an unarmed city and those who are their victims . . . The people of Sarajevo are truly prisoners, condemned to murderous blows, and I feel an overpowering sense of solidarity with them . . . This city is shut off, closed and isolated from the rest of the world, and all the while it is being subjected to practically constant gunfire that is destroying its vital centres and killing many of its people. This is not acceptable.[52]

Like his journey to Beirut eight years earlier, after a car bomb killed fifty-eight French soldiers, Mitterrand's decision to fly to Bosnia showed unusual courage. He was 75 years old. His cancer, in remission for a decade, was showing signs of returning. 'Throughout his visit,' the New York Times reported, 'the city was under almost continuous artillery, mortar and sniper fire'. The President's escort helicopter was hit by rifle fire as they landed, and on the way out he was trapped in the airport terminal, where he was to meet Karadžić and other Bosnian Serb leaders, by a fire fight between Serbian tanks, on the perimeter a few hundred yards away, and Bosnian snipers. 'The talks [with Karadžić],' the Times correspondent wrote, 'in which the Serbs presented their fighters as blameless in Sarajevo, were drowned out at times by volleys of fire from their tanks and machine guns. As they have for weeks past, Serbian gunners fired directly at apartment buildings in [the nearby suburb of] Dobrinja.' When eventually the President was able to leave, after spending six hours in the city, it was judged that the shelling made it too risky to use a fixed-wing aircraft and he left by helicopter flying at treetop level.

The visit was a success in that the Bosnian Serbs announced that night that they would turn over control of the airport to the UN peacekeepers, permitting a resumption of the airlift of relief supplies, which started arriving at the rate of 150 tons a day. It was a success, too, in that it silenced, at least for a time, charges from the French opposition, and from the Left, that Mitterrand was soft on the Serbs and should have been threatening military action to bring the conflict to an end.

But it did not fundamentally change the President's reading of the situation. The Serbs, he now accepted, were aggressors. But they and the Croats were the victors. Bosnia was a fiction. 'Look at the map,' he told the Cabinet. A Muslim power had been established there to rule over a collection of scattered districts, but its existence, apart from an ephemeral medieval kingdom, had no historical reality. Instead of trying to acquire arms and internationalise the conflict, the Bosnians should accept the situation and seek a negotiated settlement.[53] Britain felt the same. When Mitterrand said that arming the Bosnians would just 'add war to war', Major wrote to tell him: 'I am in complete agreement.' The Bush administration was even more determined not to get involved. At the State Department the Under-Secretary, Lawrence Eagleburger, was quoted as saying: 'This conflict is a tribal war. If these people can't live together without killing each other, it is difficult for us to end [it].'

Humanitarian aid, they all agreed, was desperately needed, not least to mollify opinion at home. But military intervention, even indirectly by making arms available, was ruled out. To Mitterrand it was a war in which all sides were at fault, fuelled by ancient hatreds and old alliances. 'As long as I live,' he said, 'never – mark my words well – never will France make war on Serbia.'

But events were moving in a way that Western governments would be powerless to resist.

While Mitterrand had been in Sarajevo, Izetbegović had spoken to him of Serb 'extermination camps'. The French Humanitarian Affairs Minister, Bernard Kouchner, who was present, thought the Bosnian leader was exaggerating. But before long the first television images appeared showing Serbian death camps. Public opinion was revolted.

In all the European countries and in the United States, where Bush was fighting an uphill battle for re-election against Bill Clinton, pressure for action grew exponentially. People were sickened that their governments were doing nothing in the face of horrors which recalled the rise of Nazism in the 1930s. Mitterrand might tell the Cabinet, 'Milošević is not Hitler', but neither the public, nor the press, nor the politicians were ready to continue listening. 'Non-intervention,' Jacques Chirac declared, 'is in fact to make ourselves complicit in a war of territorial conquest and in the atrocities which are taking place day after day.' Fabius demanded that a war crimes tribunal be established to try the Serbian leaders for crimes against humanity. Both called for the bombing of Serbian military targets.

In October 1992, under US pressure, the UN Security Council imposed a 'no fly' zone over Bosnia. Britain and France dragged their feet. Both countries had several thousand soldiers in the peacekeeping force and feared Serb reprisals if Serbian planes were shot down. The French General Staff, like the British, opposed direct military intervention, warning that it could result in 'a Vietnamese-style escalation, like that under Johnson, [leading] in time to public opinion swinging back in favour of withdrawal'. But by then the momentum towards a tougher position was unstoppable. European Union leaders, meeting at Edinburgh that month, for the first time explicitly designated Serbia as the aggressor. Three days later Mitterrand agreed to send twelve French aircraft to help enforce the 'no fly' zone. 'If we absolutely must I will accept the bombing [of Serb targets] in Bosnia,' he said. '[But] I oppose any bombing in Serbia, because it would amount to a declaration of war and of that there is no question.'

It was a very strange double standard.

To Mitterrand it was acceptable to use force in Kuwait to safeguard France's status as a player in world affairs, but not to prevent the butchery of tens of thousands of Europeans in a genocidal war a few hundred miles down the Mediterranean coast. It was true that the circumstances were different. To send ground forces to fight in a country tailor-made for guerrilla combat amid a patchwork of ethnic pockets spitting hatred at each other would have been insane. On the other hand, to bomb Serb artillery positions and airfields would have been a simple way to put pressure on Belgrade and carried little risk.[54]

Nonetheless, for eighteen months, from July 1991 to December

1992, Britain, France, Germany, Italy and the United States, not to mention the smaller European countries, were united in their refusal to do so. Mitterrand's stance was not the exception but the rule.

It was a failure of leadership by everyone concerned – not only by Mitterrand but by Bush and by Kohl and Major and all the other Europeans. Above all it was a failure of Europe. Mitterrand had said early on that 'Europe does not have the means to impose its views'. That was a misstatement. Europe did not have the *will* to impose its views.

The lesson of the Balkans was that all Europe's talk of 'political union', implying the coordination of foreign and defence policy for common goals, was just that: talk. To require political cooperation before economic unity was putting the cart before the horse. With hindsight, Maastricht would have two achievements to its credit. It had made a huge stride towards harmonising economic policy. But it had also shown that, at the present stage of European integration, a pooling of sovereignty in foreign affairs and defence was a pipe dream. For America that was the silver lining. Washington now knew it no longer had to worry about the Europeans striking out on their own. They were incapable of doing so. Even the Eurocorps, conceived by Mitterrand and Kohl as a force of 60,000 men with, as its nucleus, the Franco-German brigade, which Bush and Cheney had fretted about when it was first announced,[55] was seen for what it was: an idea that existed largely on paper and would have a marginal impact over the coming decades.[56] In the meantime American primacy in the Old World would continue unchallenged.

By the summer of 1992, there was no longer any doubt. Mitterrand's cancer was back. Two years earlier he had told his doctor, Claude Gubler, that he wanted to prepare public opinion for the possibility that he might have to resign. But on that occasion it had been a false alarm. The complications of his two families had caught up with him. Mazarine, then fifteen, was having an adolescent crisis and Danielle had chosen that moment to leave the family home at Latche in a fit of depression without saying where she had gone. Four days later the GSPR tracked her down in the Pyrenees. The episode had left the President shaken. He asked himself once again whether this second term was worth it if it meant that he was unable to care for those he loved.

This time the relapse was not only real but took a much more acute form than he had experienced before.

Mitterrand was 'irritable, his face drawn, emaciated and tired', a visitor to Latche reported in August. 'He was eating almost nothing and found it hard to stand upright.' The President told Dumas that he was exhausted, he had 'to get up at night almost every hour to piss'. At the end of that month, Steg was flown down to examine him. Surgery was necessary, the professor told him, and it could not be delayed. On September 3, against his doctors' advice, Mitterrand took part in a three-hour-long television debate on the ratification of the Maastricht Treaty, which was then hanging by a thread. Eight days later, Steg operated. It was announced that cancerous tissue had been found and that the President would be treated accordingly. Nothing was said about any earlier condition. Medical experts estimated that a man of his age, newly diagnosed with an early-stage cancer, had at least five years and possibly longer ahead of him.[57] Only it was not early-stage cancer. He had had it for eleven years and it was already a miracle that he had survived so long.

Asked, as he left hospital on September 16, whether he intended to resign, he shot back: 'I don't think they removed a lobe of my brain. It wasn't up there that it happened.' It was a matter, he said, of 'waging an honourable battle against oneself'. Less than 48 hours later he was back at work.

The Maastricht Treaty was approved by a narrow margin – 51 to 49 per cent – opening the way for Denmark and, finally, Britain to complete ratification in the summer of 1993. But the uncertainty carried over into the financial markets. The previous week, on Black Wednesday, speculation against sterling had forced Britain to leave the European exchange rate mechanism, earning George Soros, the most prominent of the currency speculators, the title of 'the man who broke the Bank of England'. The next target was the franc.

In a narrative that would be repeated with variations over the next twenty years, the fiercely independent Chairman of the Bundesbank, Helmut Schlesinger, refused to lower German interest rates. Two days later, Mitterrand received Kohl at the Elysée. He was still suffering from his operation – his economic adviser, Guillaume Hannezo, remembered that, during the meeting, he had to leave the room every quarter of an hour to relieve himself – but the urgency of the threat to Europe focussed his mind. 'If Germany does not react,' he warned the Chancellor, 'it's the end of everything that . . . you and I have accomplished over the last ten years.' Kohl saw the danger. But Schlesinger, who was in Washington for an IMF meeting, dug in his heels. 'The two governments can do what they like,' he told his French counterpart. 'Me, I won't sign.' Kohl telephoned him and, in Hannezo's words, with the full weight of his 6 feet 5 inches, 260 lb, bulk, 'sat on the independence of the Bundesbank'. Schlesinger signed. However next morning, September 23, as the French Cabinet met, it seemed that even Germany's support was not going to be enough. At midday, Pierre Bérégovoy told Hannezo that France would have to follow Britain and Italy and leave the EMS. Three hours later the speculation mysteriously stopped. 'It was totally irrational,' Védrine said afterwards. 'As if by a miracle, on the very edge of the abyss, the [attacks] died away.'

The success of the Maastricht referendum and the defence of the franc helped the government in the opinion polls. But it would take more than that to pull the Left out of the political morass to which the errors of the previous three years had condemned it.

Bérégovoy had got off to a good start. Public opinion found him capable and down to earth. But in the autumn the outlook had darkened. Laurent Fabius, who was to have led the Socialist campaign for the parliamentary elections, now six months away, was charged with manslaughter in connection with the use by hospitals of blood contaminated by the AIDS virus while he had been Prime Minister. The charge was frivolous but it disqualified him as the Socialists' champion.* Bérégovoy then took over. But he too would unexpectedly stumble.

On February 3, seven weeks before the first round of voting, the *Canard enchaîné* revealed that in 1986 the Prime Minister had accepted an interest-free loan of one million francs (£85,000 or US $140,000) from Mitterrand's friend, Patrice Pelat, to buy a small flat in Paris. At the time he had not been a member of the government, so there was

---

* In 1999, when the case was eventually heard, Fabius and the Social Affairs Minister, Georgina Dufoix, were acquitted of all charges. The Health Secretary, Edmond Hervé, was convicted of 'failing to observe the obligation of security or prudence' but not sentenced, on the grounds that pre-trial publicity had affected his right to the presumption of innocence. The court noted that Fabius, against the advice of government medical specialists, had insisted in July 1985 on the immediate introduction of HIV testing and by so doing had probably saved hundreds of lives.

no direct conflict of interest, and the fact that, after a lifetime in politics, he needed a loan to buy a modest apartment was testimony enough to his probity. But Pelat's subsequent involvement with a member of Bérégovoy's private office in the insider trading scandal over Pechiney had left a whiff of scandal. Bérégovoy, it was claimed, had returned the favour of the loan by helping to further Pelat's interests after he had been returned to office two years later.

The accusation had been cunningly framed. It had been leaked to the *Canard* by a right-wing magistrate, Thierry Jean-Pierre, who for years had been waging a fanatical anti-Socialist crusade. In the fevered climate of the campaign, when even to answer such a charge would have been taken as an admission of guilt, it was impossible to disprove.

Even without the discrediting of the Socialists' two standard-bearers, the Party was in a mess. 'Each one falls back on his own calculations or those of his clan,' Védrine had written to Mitterrand. 'The leaders are tearing each other to pieces. No one has any proposals for the future. In short, the Socialists are going to rack and ruin.' The succession of scandals, exacerbated by the amnesty; the collapse of the Communist Party and the rise of the National Front; the failure of Édith Cresson's prime ministership; and the rise in unemployment, which for the first time exceeded three million, meant that once again the only uncertainty was over how badly the Left would lose. There was no way it could obtain a majority. The 'opening' to the Centre had failed. The Greens, who the opinion polls predicted would get 15 per cent of the vote, had rejected the Socialists' approaches. The problem was insoluble. Mitterrand's party was too discredited to be a useful ally.

A little over a month later, on March 21 1993, the Socialists and Left-Radicals won just over 20 per cent of the vote, the Communists 9 per cent. It was the worst result for the Left since 1958. Even Mitterrand was surprised. 'I knew we were going to be in a minority, but not to that extent,' he said that night.

Afterwards he blamed himself for not having insisted that the government reintroduce proportional representation. The Socialist Party leaders had refused to do so because they thought it would look like an electoral manoeuvre and it would have brought about the election of some sixty National Front MPs. 'I should have imposed it,' he said afterwards, 'even against our own side . . . I should have broken [their resistance] to prevent us having to go through this.'

But that had been the problem throughout Mitterrand's second term. He had consistently failed to enforce his will – whether it was within the Socialist Party or within the government.

The outcome of the second round of voting the following weekend was that the Right won 480 out of 577 seats. The Socialists had 67, less than a quarter of their strength in the outgoing parliament, and the Communists 23. Among those who lost their seats were Rocard and Jospin, the Left's leading candidates for the presidential elections two years later. It was the most true blue, conservative parliament France had had since 1815, when Louis XVIII returned to power following the fall of Napoleon after the battle of Waterloo. Never in France in modern times had the disavowal of a ruling party been more complete.

The election had a tragic postscript.

On May 1 1993, Pierre Bérégovoy killed himself.

For years afterwards, rumours would circulate about the circumstances of his death. The autopsy established that he had shot himself in the head with a pistol which his police bodyguard had left in the glove compartment of his car. Conspiracy theorists – the same people who cast doubt on the reality of Patrice Pelat's heart attack – whispered that Mitterrand had had the former Prime Minister killed to ensure his silence, since he no doubt knew secrets which the President wished to hide.

The truth, of course, was otherwise. Bérégovoy had been in a black depression. He blamed himself for the Socialists' defeat. Above all, he blamed himself for having accepted Pelat's loan which had cost him his honour. Pelat had been a generous and very wealthy friend who had helped him for years while asking nothing in return. But it had been imprudent. Bérégovoy, whose career had begun as a sixteen-year-old lathe operator in a textile factory, felt he had betrayed his class and his roots. One of his closest aides, Olivier Rousselle, remembered him repeating, over and over again, 'Socialism is screwed in this country. We'll never be able to lift our heads. It needs something dramatic . . . If I disappeared, that would suit everyone. That would be the act which would wash all the sins away.' The day before he died, Michel Charasse had warned Mitterrand: 'I'm afraid he's going to kill himself.' The President said he would arrange a lunch the following week. But whether because he had been through the same thing after the Observatory Affair in 1959, and thought Bérégovoy would pull through, as he himself had done, or simply because he was convinced that the former Prime Minister had nothing for which to reproach himself, he left it too late. '[He] was obsessed by this loan which had completely obliterated all the best side of his personality,' the President said later. 'He could talk of nothing else. It was as though it had paralysed him, even though he had nothing to be guilty about . . . I tried to cheer him up, telling him: "You're exaggerating, you're depressed. It's a bad time but it will pass". [But] he did not stop talking about it.'

On May 4, a Tuesday, at the cathedral in Nevers, where Bérégovoy had been mayor, Mitterrand delivered a corrosive funeral oration, denouncing those who had hounded him to death. 'All the explanations in the world,' he said, his voice shaking with anger, 'cannot justify throwing to the dogs the honour and finally the life of a man at the price of a double dereliction, on the part of his accusers, of the fundamental laws of our Republic which protect the dignity and freedom of each of us.' His targets were the right-wing judge, Thierry Jean-Pierre, who had selectively – and illegally – leaked the results of his investigations in order to foment a smear campaign, and the journalists and editors who had abetted it without considering, or sometimes caring, whether what they wrote was true.[58] But it was also a lament for a political culture in which, half a century after *Gringoire* and *Le Crapouillot* had driven Roger Salengro to suicide, depressingly little seemed to have changed.

15

The Survivalist

The cohabitation which began in the spring of 1993 was very different from that seven years earlier. Then Mitterrand's goal had been to position himself for re-election. Now his concern, cancer permitting, was to complete his second term.

For that he needed a prime minister who, unlike Chirac, would be ready to cooperate with him, to respect his prerogatives in matters of defence and foreign policy and to avoid gratuitous clashes of authority. Barre and Giscard were possibilities. But Chirac's RPR again formed the largest parliamentary group and logically the new prime minister should come from its ranks. Édouard Balladur, who had been Finance Minister during the first cohabitation, was the obvious choice.

Precisely because Balladur's nomination seemed self-evident, Mitterrand jibbed. But as with Rocard, five years earlier, he saw no alternative. 'It was not in my interests,' he said afterwards, 'to oppose the trend of public opinion.' Accordingly, the morning after the second round, he sent Védrine to meet Balladur in secret at the Plaza-Athenée hotel, a palatial establishment on the Avenue Montaigne, the other side of the Champs-Elysées. The prospective Prime Minister gave the assurances Mitterrand wished to hear. 'I would do nothing,' he told Védrine, 'which might detract from the functions of the presidency.' There would be no repetition of the Chirac years, 'no competition between us at summit meetings . . . I will not be responsible for seeing the dignity of our country infringed. We cannot make a spectacle of ourselves and I will do what is needed to ensure that we arrive at common positions.' On Europe they had no major disagreements. At home, he promised to try to avoid exacerbating social tensions. The fact that he did not intend to stand for the presidency in 1995 – it having been agreed that Chirac would be the RPR's candidate – would make that easier, he said.

That evening Mitterrand announced that he had chosen Édouard Balladur to head the new government, both for 'his ability to unite the different elements of the majority behind him [and] for his competence'.

The new Prime Minister was the antithesis of Chirac. Where one was brash, earthy, impetuous and trenchant, a product of Harvard and the *Grandes Écoles*, brimming with the energy and the appetites of a raffish country squire, the other was suave, urbane and pompous. Mitterrand had learnt to appreciate Balladur during the first cohabitation, when the Minister used to pass him caustic notes at Cabinet meetings during long-winded speeches by his colleagues. But he was as vain as a peacock, insisting on the full honours due to his station, and was depicted by cartoonists in a brocade jacket, periwig and court pumps, being carried about in a sedan chair by beribboned flunkeys.

The following day, March 30, Balladur proposed Alain Juppé, the Secretary-General of the RPR, as Foreign Minister; Charles Pasqua at the Interior; and François Léotard, who led the Republican Party, part of the UDF, at Defence. Seven years earlier, when Chirac had put forward Léotard's name as Defence Minister, Mitterrand had demurred. 'He's capable of declaring war without either of us even noticing,' he had commented. This time he made no objection. That evening a list of thirty ministers was announced from the Elysée, among them an up and coming politician named Nicolas Sarkozy, then in his late thirties, as Minister of the Budget. Roughly half were drawn from the RPR, the remainder from the array of parties that made up the Centre-Right. At their first Cabinet meeting, on Friday, April 2 – it having been thought better to avoid April Fool's Day – both sides emphasised harmony. They were there together, Mitterrand said, 'because the people wished it'. It was an unusual situation, Balladur responded, 'which in the end is becoming usual . . . All those who are here will try to make [it] work as well as possible.'

If the President and the Prime Minister were on the way to finding a modus vivendi, that was not true within the Socialist Party. The following day, Saturday, when the Executive Committee met, the knives were out for Fabius. He had been discredited by the scandal over the contaminated blood. He had raised hackles by packing the Secretariat and key party committees with his own supporters. He had helped lead the Socialists to a disastrous defeat and now, when a mea culpa might have saved him, he insisted that he had no reason to step down because whatever might have befallen others, he had retained his parliamentary seat.

The President's protégé was roundly booed. That night, when the matter was put to a vote, not only Rocard and Jospin and their supporters but many of Mitterrand's own faction joined forces against him. Fabius and his supporters were ousted and the leadership confided to a provisional directorate, headed by Michel Rocard, which was charged with preparing an emergency congress in the autumn.

Mitterrand was furious. He was still exercised by the Socialists' refusal to make Fabius party leader in 1988. Now, after Fabius had spent only fourteen months in the post, they had rejected him again.

'Do you realise what you've done?' he stormed at Claude Estier, one of his most loyal supporters. 'You've given the Party to Rocard!' Guy Mollet had used similar words, twenty-two years earlier at Épinay, when he had realised that he was losing control of the Party to Mitterrand. The President's resentment of the former Prime Minister knew no bounds. Jean Glavany, who had been Mitterrand's Private Secretary at the Elysée in his first term, remembered a lunch at the home of Henri Emmanuelli, another Mitterrand loyalist who lived not far from Latche, at which they had tried to persuade him to change his mind. 'We kept telling him he was the one who had put Rocard in Matignon and that since then his criticisms of Rocard, however he phrased them, didn't convince anyone any more. We told him that Fabius, his favourite, had screwed up as party leader . . . He went pale. He almost got up and left.'

By the autumn, when Rocard was confirmed as First Secretary, the President was ready to declare a truce. But it was an armed stand-off, not a cessation of hostilities. The Socialist Party was in disarray. Mitterrand decided he would leave it to its own devices. He and the Party no longer had the same priorities. His overriding goal was to survive the rest of his term. He was not going to put himself out on a limb for them, least of all when they were led by a man he regarded as the bane of his existence. Instead, just as he had when Rocard had been Prime Minister, he watched, raptor-like, waiting to swoop down at the first mistake.

*

Mitterrand's influence in the final two years of his presidency was limited both by the necessity of sharing power with a right-wing government and by the cancer which was slowly destroying him.

His one unquestioned success came on the only issue over which, perhaps not coincidentally, he engaged in a real trial of strength with Balladur's government.

A year earlier, in April 1992, he had written to the leaders of the four other declared nuclear powers – Britain, China, Russia and the United States – to announce that France would suspend nuclear weapons testing for a year. He had urged them to follow suit. It was a peace dividend from the end of the Cold War – each nuclear test at Mururoa cost about 100 million francs (£12 million or US $18 million) – and a recognition that the nature of the threat had changed. Rather than a nuclear conflict, Mitterrand argued, Europe was more likely to face regional wars like those in the Balkans. The French General Staff strongly disagreed. So did the right-wing parties, which claimed that a moratorium would weaken French defence. None of the other four leaders responded and by the summer Mitterrand had concluded that, as he had feared might be the case, his appeal had fallen on deaf ears.

But then, in October, George Bush announced that the United States, too, would suspend testing. Britain followed. Russia gave a similar undertaking. The only holdout was China.

In July 1993, three months after Balladur took office, Bush's successor, Bill Clinton, wrote to Mitterrand and, after paying tribute to the French leader's 'international authority and sense of History', said he had decided that 'a complete ban on testing would increase the security of the United States and of the world' and asked France to join America in working on a new test ban treaty. A week later, at the G7 Summit in Tokyo, Mitterrand promised his support.

For the French Right the issue became a *casus belli*. Chirac attacked the President for endangering French independence and betraying the heritage of de Gaulle. At the technical level, the question was whether France could develop computer simulation and laboratory testing to a point where actual explosions became unnecessary. Mitterrand thought yes. The military thought no. But from the start the argument had been essentially political. Chirac used it to undermine Balladur, whom he was starting to see as a potential rival for the presidency, by suggesting that the Prime Minister was not tough enough to stand up to Mitterrand. The President used it as an occasion to affirm his power. At Chirac's urging, Balladur toyed with the idea of going over Mitterrand's head and ordering the tests to resume without the President's agreement. He quickly realised that the army would not obey. 'It was a classic case,' Mitterrand said later, 'of a situation where you can't trigger a crisis unless you are willing to resign.' Balladur was not. The moratorium continued until the end of Mitterrand's second term, by which time the French Atomic Energy Commission had concluded that simulation techniques were sufficiently advanced to make further tests unnecessary.*

The other key challenge which Mitterrand faced concerned Rwanda. Among those who had pledged, with varying degrees of conviction, to introduce a more democratic system after his speech at La Baule was the Rwandan President, Juvenal Habyarimana, an army officer who had seized power in a coup eighteen years earlier and headed the country's only legal political party. In the early period of his rule, Habyarimana had pursued a policy of national reconciliation between his own domi-nant Hutu tribe, which made up 85 per cent of the population, and the minority Tutsis, who had been treated by the Belgian colonial admin-istration as a privileged aristocracy. But in the 1980s Rwanda had been confronted by a collapse in the price of its main export, coffee, and a land shortage caused by a rapidly growing population. Habyarimana's popularity had slumped. In such circumstances, Rwandan politicians returned to the one value which they knew would never let them down: ethnicity. In the 1960s and '70s, Habyarimana's predecessor, Grégoire Kayibanda, had rallied Hutu support by whipping up racial fears which culminated in massacres. In each case upwards of 10,000 Tutsis had died and several hundred thousand more fled into exile in Burundi, Uganda and Zaire. By 1990 the stage was set for a repetition.

Mitterrand's speech introduced a new element into the equation.

* In June 1995, shortly after his election to the presidency, Chirac announced that a final series of six tests would nonetheless be carried out at Mururoa before the switch to laboratory simulations. The decision was symbolic. The Right expected it, and having argued so strongly that tests were essential, to have failed to follow through would have been an embarrassment. Early in 1996, the tests were completed. Later that year all five nuclear powers signed the Comprehensive Test Ban Treaty. Since then only India and Pakistan (in 1998) and North Korea (in 2006, 2009, 2012 and 2013) have tested nuclear warheads.

Urging African leaders to adopt a multi-party system, which meant creating a space for their political opponents, risked reigniting dormant regional and ethnic tensions. That had been one of the reasons why, at La Baule, he had addressed the issue so gingerly. But it was a risk that was inherent in any democratic transition. Exactly the same situation had arisen in former Yugoslavia. Once the dead hand of Tito's dictatorship was lifted, ethnic nationalism exploded.

In October 1990, three months after Habyarimana announced the legalisation of opposition parties, the Rwandan Patriotic Front (RPF), a Tutsi exile organisation based in Uganda, sent a small guerrilla force, numbering about a hundred men, into northern Rwanda, hoping to take the government by surprise and trigger an uprising. Two weeks later, France and Belgium sent 800 soldiers, ostensibly to protect their citizens in Rwanda. The rebel incursion was halted about 60 miles north of the capital and the guerrillas scattered into the mountains. There is no evidence that French troops took part directly. But the message that their presence conveyed was that France had decided to back Habyarimana's regime.

Over the next three years, it became clear that the Rwandan dictator had no intention of paying more than lip-service to democracy. In such circumstances, Mitterrand had warned at La Baule, France would reduce its aid. Instead French military and economic assistance not only continued but increased. Habyarimana, an American diplomat commented, concluded that 'he could do anything he liked, militarily and politically . . . France would stick behind him no matter what.'

Mitterrand never explained why he adopted this attitude. But, apart from his reluctance, shared by the rest of the French political establishment, to be seen as a neo-colonialist, telling his African partners what to do, there were a number of factors specific to Rwanda.

The country was a useful listening post to observe neighbouring Zaire (now the Democratic Republic of the Congo), which, because of its wealth of natural resources, was of enormous interest to all the Western powers. Mitterrand did not want to lose that. Moreover he had promised the African leaders at La Baule: 'Each time an external threat arises . . . France will be there beside you.' The RPF incursion could be said to fit the definition of an external threat because it had been launched from Uganda. Finally, there was what the French call 'the Fashoda syndrome', named after a village in what is now South

Sudan where French and British troops faced off in 1898 in a struggle for control of the Nile Valley. The British had won. To men of de Gaulle's and Mitterrand's generations, that defeat was a symbol of the need to resist British encroachments in the continent wherever they might occur. Rwanda lay on the divide between anglophone and francophone Africa. The RPF leader, Paul Kagame, had lived in Uganda, a former British protectorate, since the age of four. He had been trained as a soldier in the United States and had served in the Ugandan army as Chief of Military Intelligence. Habyarimana was a francophone with close ties to Paris. To Mitterrand that alone was enough to justify his support.

At the outset no one could have foreseen the repercussions of that decision. Neither Mitterrand nor anyone else imagined that by supporting Habyarimana's regime he was putting his hand into an infernal mechanism which would lead, four years later, to his being accused of complicity in the Rwandan genocide.

But as the months passed there were warning signs that should have alerted him. In February 1993, the DGSE reported that 'veritable ethnic massacres' were being carried out by militias associated with the President's party against 'Tutsis, people married to Tutsis and [moderate] Hutus from the South'. Other foreign observers filed similar reports. The picture which emerged was of Habyarimana's entourage, known as the Akazu or 'private council', led by his wife, Agathe, fomenting racial hatred to solidify support behind the ruling group. Hutu villagers were encouraged to kill their Tutsi neighbours, whom the authorities accused of colluding with the *inyenzi*, the 'cockroaches', as the RPF were called. Thousands died in small-scale pogroms orchestrated by local officials. A refugee would later tell a French parliamentary commission, 'It was less risky to kill a Tutsi than it would have been to steal a chicken.'

While a peace accord, providing for a transitional government of Hutus and Tutsis, was signed in Arusha in August 1993, grenades, assault rifles and machetes were already being distributed to Hutu militiamen for use against 'the enemy within': Tutsis and Hutu moderates. Scattered across the green mountains of some of the most exquisite countryside in Africa, where the long-horned cattle of the Tutsi herders grazed on the mountainsides as though stuck on with drawing pins, the towns and villages were tinder-dry, waiting to catch fire.

The spark was provided on April 6 1994. Habyarimana's plane was hit by a missile as it came in to land at the capital, Kigali. The Rwandan leader; the President of Burundi, who was travelling with him; several government ministers and the French crew were all killed. For years afterwards, there would be argument about who had been responsible. Kagame's RPF, dissatisfied with the peace terms? Or, more plausibly, the Hutu extremists of the Akazu who feared that under the arrangements agreed at Arusha they would lose their power? In the end it hardly mattered. Habyarimana's assassination, regardless of who was behind it, was the trigger for the worst genocide of the late twentieth century. In the next 100 days an estimated 800,000 people, almost all of them Tutsis, were slaughtered.

Whether it would have made a difference if Mitterrand had withdrawn the French military in 1991 or 1992, when it became clear that the conflict was not a foreign invasion but the beginning of a civil war, is unclear. Pierre Joxe had urged him to do so. His military adviser, General Christian Quesnot, acknowledged that the RPF would have taken power sooner had there been no French military presence. In that case the genocide might have been forestalled. But it is also possible that the prospect of the RPF's victory would have made the Akazu unleash the killings earlier. There is no way of telling.

That France continued to support the Hutu government for more than a year after the President had been briefed about massacres by Hutu extremists is harder to explain. But until the spring of 1994 no one in Paris recognised the nature of the evil that was at work in Rwanda. It may be argued that they should have done so: the massacres in neighbouring Burundi in 1972 and again, just six months earlier, after the assassination by a Tutsi of Burundi's Hutu President, where each time more than 100,000 people had died, were proof enough of the ethnic hatreds smouldering beneath the surface. But it is easy to be wise after the event. If the RPF had agreed to take part in a transitional government under Habyarimana, despite the continuing murders of Tutsis in the countryside, why should France place the bar higher? Non-interference in internal affairs was the cornerstone of policy towards its former African colonies.

Where Mitterrand's attitude became problematic was over what happened after Habyarimana's assassination. A new government was formed by Hutu extremists from the Akazu. Within a week the French

Air Force evacuated most of Rwanda's European residents. But for the next two months, while more than half a million Africans were being killed, France did nothing. Nor did anyone else. The bulk of the 2,500-man UN force which had been stationed in Rwanda to monitor the Arusha accords was withdrawn. The five permanent members of the UN Security Council – Britain and the United States as well as France, Russia and China – refused to classify the massacres as genocide because that would have required them to intervene. America had just been forced into a humiliating withdrawal from Somalia after the 'Black Hawk down' incident in Mogadishu. Britain thought the quickest way to end the killing would be for the RPF to take power. China and Russia had no interest in the area. The UN Secretariat, under Boutros Boutros-Ghali, had its hands full with the conflict in former Yugoslavia.

In Paris, where Mitterrand's adviser, Bruno Delaye, noted that 'the French silence is deafening', Balladur opposed any intervention, even humanitarian. Mitterrand's speech at Cancun, thirteen years earlier, in which he had denounced 'non-assistance to a people in danger' as too serious 'a moral and political fault for us to continue to commit', seemed to be from another age. The French military, which had trained the Hutu army, remained locked into a mindset which – a full eight months after the Arusha accords – held the RPF to be rebels, based abroad, and the Hutu government the legitimate power. Three weeks after the genocide had begun, at a time when there were already 200,000 Tutsi dead, Quesnot compared the RPF to the Cambodian Khmer Rouges – the 'Black Khmers', he called them – and insisted that they were 'the most fascist party [he had] ever encountered in Africa'. It was an extraordinary inversion of reality. If anyone in Rwanda bore comparison with the Khmer Rouges it was the Hutu extremists of Habyarimana's inner circle, the very people whom France was supporting.[1]

Mitterrand was little better. Over breakfast with Kohl, at the end of May, he dismissed as 'one-sided' the idea that only Tutsis were being killed.[2] If it was an attempt to distance himself from a murderous regime, it was singularly unconvincing. Did he really not understand what was happening in Rwanda? Or was it realpolitik at its worst, an attempt to salvage something, regardless of the human cost, from a mistaken commitment to a Hutu leadership which had turned out to be genocidal – a commitment that had irreversibly antagonised its victorious rivals, the RPF and its leader, Paul Kagame?

Two weeks later the French President abruptly changed his position. On June 15, he called for the establishment of safe areas outside Kigali and other towns where those fleeing the massacres would find protection. Balladur was reluctant, but Mitterrand insisted and a week later, with UN backing, Operation Turquoise, as it was called, got under way. From a base at Goma, just across the Zairean border, 2,550 French soldiers, backed by a token African force, were deployed to northern and south-western Rwanda. Some of the Tutsi refugees who had escaped the massacres were saved. But the vast majority of those the French protected were Hutus, among them many of the Hutu militiamen who had been carrying out the killings and who fled to the French-held areas after Kagame's troops occupied the capital. Shortly afterwards, Mitterrand told his colleagues at the G7 summit in Naples that if the French contingent left without UN peacekeepers being sent to take their place, 'there will be a second genocide, this time the other way round'. He offered no evidence to back up that assertion, nor did any mass killings of Hutus occur.

The timing of Operation Turquoise, just as the RPF was about to take power, has given rise to persistent suspicions in France that it was a political, rather than a humanitarian operation, a rearguard action to save the Hutu regime which France had been supporting. Pierre Favier and Michel Martin-Roland, who chronicled Mitterrand's presidency, were given access to some, though perhaps not all, of the confidential records of meetings of Cabinet committees and communications from the General Staff, and wrote that they could find no trace in the archives of any political motive behind 'Turquoise' other than a belated attempt to redeem 'French honour', as Mitterrand put it, by preventing further slaughter in Rwanda. However, a map attached to a note from Quesnot, dated May 6 1994, showed Rwanda divided into 'Hutuland' and 'Tutsiland', the former corresponding to what would become the French safe areas. If, six weeks before 'Turquoise' began, there was already talk at the Elysée of creating a rump Hutu state, it lent credence to the view that the operation had an ulterior motive.[3] Other elements supported that thesis. Senior French generals continued to maintain, as late as the end of June, that it was impossible to determine who was massacring whom. French soldiers participating in 'Turquoise' were told that, while France had to remain neutral, the main threat to the population came from the RPF. Only after their deployment did they discover, amid the stench of charnel houses and the excavation of mass graves, that the murderers were all Hutus, acting with the encouragement or on the orders of the local administration, while almost all the victims were Tutsis.

Mitterrand's supporters have argued that the situation at the time was much less clear than hindsight made it appear and that all leaders sometimes make bad decisions in good faith. Nonetheless, the succession of coincidences is troubling. Why did France change policy not in April or May, when the massacre of the Tutsis was in full spate, but – without explanation – in mid-June, when the Hutus were at risk? Why did French troops make no effort to arrest senior Hutu officials linked to the genocide? Why did Mitterrand not realise that by allowing the Hutu extremists to escape into Zaire, he was enabling the creation of rebel bastions which would destabilise the entire region for decades to come? Why afterwards did successive French governments drag their feet over putting on trial those implicated in the genocide who had sought asylum on French soil?[4] Why, finally, did both Mitterrand and his successors systematically ostracise Kagame's government? None of that is evidence that France was 'responsible' for the slaughter. The cause of the genocide was endemic to Rwanda. To each of those questions, taken individually, answers can be attempted. But, taken together, they form an indictment. Not only was Mitterrand perceived as having connived with a genocidal regime for political ends but even on the most cynical interpretation his policy was a failure. When the Hutu regime fell, France lost all influence in Rwanda, which quickly became part of the anglophone camp.

There was a disturbing parallel between Mitterrand's response to events in Rwanda and to the developing war in Bosnia. In the one, he was confronting genocide, in the other, ethnic cleansing, a distinction which is largely semantic.

In both cases he refused to intervene: in Rwanda because, 'How do you tell the difference between Hutus and Tutsis? . . . Everyone is killing everyone else'; in Bosnia because, 'Where would you intervene anyway? Down there, they are fighting everywhere, in each village.' In both cases he declined to identify the aggressor. In Rwanda, it had been the Hutu government; in Bosnia it was the Serbs and, by extension, Milošević's regime in Belgrade. In both cases, between the lines, there was an unstated disdain for the underdog. Serbia was a 'real' country, an ancient nation with its own history, he kept saying; Bosnia was 'a fiction'. The Hutus were the main force in Rwanda; the Tutsis a minority most of whose leaders were in exile. In both cases, he expected the end result to be partition: in former Yugoslavia, a cluster of small Balkan republics; in Rwanda, 'Hutuland' in the west, adjoining francophone Zaire, and 'Tutsiland' in the east, adjoining anglophone Uganda and Tanzania. In both cases, Mitterrand, like other Western leaders, was reduced to standing by helplessly as the slaughter raged. Only at the margins, through Operation Turquoise in Rwanda and participation in the UN peacekeeping force in Bosnia, was France able to make its influence felt.

The difference was that in the Balkans Mitterrand's possibilities – not to speak of responsibility – were much more limited than in the Rwandan tragedy.

Aside from his surprise visit to Sarajevo in 1992, the goal of which, he insisted, was 'humanitarian . . . without any ulterior political motive', the French President's main concern had been all along to avoid getting sucked into the Balkan morass. His underlying analysis remained unchanged. The Serbs and the Croats had won and the Bosnians would have to accept it. The use of ground troops, other than UN peacekeepers, was ruled out. Airstrikes would have limited effect. Lifting the arms embargo – which would allow the Bosnians to acquire heavy weaponry – would internationalise the conflict, with the risk that the whole region might go up in flames: Serbia and its ally, Russia, would throw their weight behind the Bosnian Serbs; the Islamic world would support the Bosnian Muslims. Although he did not put it so bluntly, he was convinced that the West could do nothing and would just have to stand by and watch. In January 1993, he told George Bush:

> I do not believe in a military solution. The Serbs and the Croats occupy three fifths of the territory [of Bosnia-Herzegovina] and they will not leave. It may last a long time and the [television] images will create a political situation which is hard to stomach. I am as outraged as anyone else, but if I send 10,000 men, I can have a thousand of them killed in the passes through the mountains before they even reach their

objective. In democracies, such losses turn public opinion. So I certainly won't do it. We can only envisage selective, limited actions like liberating the camps under the UN mandate, the neutralisation of Sarajevo and [enforcing the no fly zone].[5]

Bill Clinton, who was sworn in later that month, wanted to succeed where his predecessor had failed. In Geneva, where a new round of peace talks had begun, Cyrus Vance and his British counterpart David Owen had unveiled a proposal to divide Bosnia into ten provinces based on the ethnicity of the majority of their inhabitants. Over the next four months, while the murderous charade of 'ethnic cleansing' continued – 50,000 Bosnian women had been raped 'on the orders of the Serb hierarchy', a French diplomat reported – one side after the other accepted and then rejected the plan in a minuet of constantly changing intentions. Clinton threatened airstrikes if the Serbs blocked a settlement. In May, Mitterrand asked the US Secretary of State, Warren Christopher, whether the new President had thought through what that would involve:

> France has been on the ground since the first day [and] now has nearly 5,000 men under the UN Command . . . The Serbs are not easily intimidated. I approve your approach of threats and dissuasion. But . . . we need to look coldly at what will follow . . . Bombing without ground support won't solve the problem . . . Bosnia is not Iraq. No matter what the original intention, you will inevitably be sucked into a spiral of violence. Not to mention the problem of the soldiers who are now present there and who do not have the means to wage war against the Serbs whose attitude will change once they are attacked.[6]

The last point was crucial. The Americans, who had no ground forces in former Yugoslavia, could bomb Serb positions with impunity. France and Britain could not.

On May 15 1993, the Bosnian Serbs rejected the Vance–Owen plan. The same day the Security Council approved the creation of 'security zones' in six Muslim-populated areas of Bosnia. Clinton rowed back, agreeing that there would be no bombardment of Serb positions and that the arms embargo against Bosnia should remain in force. Public opinion in both the United States and France judged the decision harshly. 'Mr Clinton has failed to deliver on his promises, talking loudly and leaving his stick on his shoulder,' wrote the *New York Times*. 'The next time he voices threats, they will have less credibility.' Bernard Kouchner denounced 'a Munich of the spirit'.

Mitterrand was relieved. 'No one will make war,' he told the Cabinet's Defence Committee. But no one would make peace either.

The fundamental problem was that none of the major powers was ready to take decisive action. Washington was willing to launch airstrikes, 'from a height of 10,000 metres' as the French Defence Minister put it; it authorised the CIA to parachute arms to the Bosnian Muslims to circumvent the embargo; but it 'refused categorically' any steps which might lead to the direct involvement of American soldiers. At the NATO summit in January 1994, where Mitterrand pushed the US President to take a tougher stance, Clinton agreed to support the latest European peace plan for the partition of Bosnia and to approve airstrikes when Serb forces attacked UN personnel. But when the Russians dug in their heels in support of their Serbian allies, he refused to follow through.

In the meantime the UN force was paralysed. 'The Bosnians are using the security zones to reinforce and train their troops,' the UN Commander, General Briquemont, complained, 'the Croats are threatening to intervene if the Muslims don't stop attacking, and the Serbs are carrying out a massacre a day.' At that point France, like Britain, came close to pulling out and abandoning Bosnia to its fate.

That winter Mitterrand had written to Milošević, warning that 'a veritable genocide' threatened Sarajevo and other Bosnian towns unless the Serbs allowed relief supplies to pass and urging him to help end this 'tragic and dishonourable story'. For two weeks the convoys were able to get through. Then they were halted again. 'This is madness!' the French leader exclaimed. He became increasingly convinced that the only way to change the situation was for the United States, the European Union and Russia to impose a solution on all three parties – Serbs, Croats and Bosnians – without seeking to judge who was right and who was wrong. But Clinton refused. In the American view, it was for the Serbs, not the Bosnians, to make concessions. Védrine summed up the French government's frustrations:

> The American attitude is completely cynical . . . I am afraid [they] have
> no vision of the future and no idea how to lead these unfortunate

peoples to coexist in peace tomorrow and rebuild their countries. They are encouraging the Bosnians to fight to the last Bosnian, just as [in 1956] they encouraged the Hungarians to rise up against the Soviets, [just as] they armed the Afghan resistance against the same Soviets – which doesn't stop them being completely indifferent to the chaos into which Afghanistan has [since] fallen. Today they are taking an interest in the good Bosnian Muslims because it's a way to fight the communist, fascist Serbians . . . The American attitude is no doubt the second reason – after the relentless determination . . . of the three parties to the conflict – that the war has continued so long. There is no reason for the European leaders to share that responsibility with them. Since there is already a European–American malaise on this point, perhaps we should openly provoke a crisis [which] could force the United States to change its attitude?[7]

To the short-termism of the Americans, which Washington saw merely as a reflection of its national interests, Mitterrand opposed a long-termism which was scarcely less one-sided. Throughout the Balkan conflict, he had complained that 'the mistake was to have created Bosnia . . . That country is a historical nonsense.' Europe, he maintained, should never have recognised the Sarajevo government. He told Warren Christopher:

> Europe has always lived under empires . . . Some European peoples have never known democracy. Others have never been independent or never existed as nations . . . Now every ethnic group thinks it should have its own special status. We haven't seen that since the start of the Middle Ages.[8]

From opposite starting points, both the United States, by focussing exclusively on immediate goals, and France, by situating events in the historical perspective of past centuries, had arrived at a form of detachment which blunted their determination to force a resolution of the problems they now faced.

At the beginning of February the complacency of the Western powers was shattered by the explosion of a 120mm mortar shell at the market at Sarajevo, killing sixty-six people and wounding 200 others. The attack attracted worldwide condemnation. France, after consulting the United States and Britain, called for a muscular response: the lifting of the siege of the Bosnian capital and the impounding by UNPROFOR of all heavy weapons within a 20-kilometre radius of the city. Four days later, on February 9, NATO issued an ultimatum: if the Serbs did not comply by midnight on Sunday, February 20, airstrikes would be launched to enforce it. The deadline was met. But during the negotiations a new player emerged: Russia. It was pressure from Yeltsin that persuaded Milošević and his Bosnian Serb allies to agree. Mitterrand congratulated the Russian President on the success of his diplomacy and two months later wrote to Bill Clinton to propose yet again that 'the United States, Russia and the European Union speak with the same voice and exert pressure together on all the protagonists'. This time Clinton agreed. At the end of April 1994, the British, French, Russian and US Foreign Ministers met in London and agreed to form a Contact Group to coordinate policy in the Balkans.

That spring NATO had intervened militarily for the first time, shooting down four Serbian fighters which violated the 'no-fly zone' and launching airstrikes in support of UNPROFOR forces. A stalemate set in. 'There isn't a real war any more,' Mitterrand told Clinton in June. 'There are only local conflicts, so that's progress. It shows we are on the right track.' But if there was no war, there was no peace either. Progress towards a diplomatic settlement remained blocked.

It would take another eighteen months before the Dayton accords, negotiated by the US Assistant Secretary of State, Richard Holbrooke, and signed by the Bosnian, Croat and Serbian leaders in Paris in December 1995, brought the conflict to an end. By then Serbian power was ebbing. Yeltsin had made clear the limits of Russian support. During the summer, Croatian forces had recovered the Krajina and then gone on to occupy Serb-controlled areas in western Bosnia. The American Congress had voted to lift the arms embargo. Clinton, facing re-election a year later, was determined to deny the Republicans a chance to accuse him of weakness abroad. Mitterrand had left the scene and a new administration had taken office in Paris, more united than its predecessor and keen to show its mettle by helping to bring the war to an end. The Europeans and the Americans, with Russian acquiescence, finally resolved to use force to impose a settlement. In the first three weeks of September, NATO aircraft flew more than 3,500 sorties against 338 targets in Serb-controlled regions of Bosnia.

The inevitable question, as in Rwanda, was: could it not have been done sooner? Had massive airstrikes been authorised at a much earlier stage, would the butchery have ended more quickly? Perhaps. But no one – in France, in Britain, in the US or in Russia – was prepared to take that risk. In the Balkans, Mitterrand was one player among many and even had he brought all his weight to bear in favour of immediate intervention – which he showed no desire to do – Clinton would certainly not have agreed. Moreover airstrikes in the initial stages of the conflict might well not have had the same effect. By 1995, the circumstances were finally in place for a combination of force and diplomacy to succeed. That had not been the case earlier.

Rwanda and Bosnia notwithstanding, political life in France continued. In June 1994, elections were due for the European Parliament. Michel Rocard, as First Secretary, was to lead the Socialist campaign. It would be a trial run before the presidential election eleven months later.

The field was even more fragmented than usual. The Left-Radicals, which in the previous two European elections had joined forces with the Socialists, this time campaigned separately. Their standard-bearer was Bernard Tapie, a controversial businessman who had served briefly as a minister under Mitterrand in 1992. Mitterrand admired Tapie. He was bright, charismatic, curious and had had a dozen different careers – racing driver, pop singer, actor, football club manager and corporate raider, among others – all undertaken with the unquenchable determination of those from humble backgrounds who have pulled themselves up by their own bootstraps. Precisely because of his unorthodox background, the Socialist leaders loathed him. In the spring of 1994, he was embroiled in a court case involving allegations of corruption – for which he would later be sentenced to two years' imprisonment – linked to Olympique de Marseille, the city's football club of which he was President. When he approached Rocard on behalf of the Left-Radicals to discuss a joint campaign, the First Secretary refused to see him. So he decided to head a slate of candidates for the Left-Radicals alone. Mitterrand, always pleased to be able to put a spoke in Rocard's wheel, quietly encouraged him.

Tapie was not Rocard's only problem. Bernard-Henri Lévy, who had fallen out with the President over his refusal to lift the arms embargo against Bosnia, organised what he called a 'Sarajevo list' to

campaign for increased European support for Izetbegovic's government. Initially Lévy and his allies were credited with 12 per cent of
voting intentions, much of it drawn from the Left. Rocard decided
that they, rather than the Left-Radicals, were the main threat and
made clumsy attempts to win them over. It was a fatal error. When
the results came in on June 12, the 'Sarajevo list' won a paltry 1.5 per
cent. Tapie won 12.3 per cent. The Socialists, who under Fabius and
Jospin had won well over 20 per cent, saw their support collapse to
14.5 per cent. Rocard's presidential ambitions were over. The following
weekend he was replaced as First Secretary by Henri Emmanuelli.

Mitterrand was delighted to see him go. He was not directly to
blame for Rocard's defeat: his old adversary had obligingly destroyed
himself by running a terrible campaign. But it left him with the
problem of who would carry the Left's colours in 1995. Jacques Delors
was the obvious choice. He was popular, competent, capable of
winning the support of the Centre-Right, a *sine qua non* for victory at
a time when Communist support was hovering around 6 per cent,
and he would shortly complete his term as President of the European
Commission. 'He could win,' Mitterrand said a few weeks later, 'but
the question, the only question, is whether he really wants to. Having
spoken to him, I don't think he does.' He was right. Delors was flattered, he adored the attention which his new status as potential champion of the Left brought him, but he had no stomach for the battles
that a presidential election would entail. On December 11, he
announced on television that he would not stand.

That left the Party floundering. Rocard was out of the race. Fabius
was entangled in the row over contaminated blood. Emmanuelli was
unknown beyond the Socialist Party faithful. Mitterrand had realised
months before that if Delors bowed out, the only other possibility
was Fabius's rival, Lionel Jospin, who had withdrawn from active
politics a year earlier. He had mixed feelings about Jospin. The strait-
laced, schoolmasterly party militant, who had risen through the ranks
to become First Secretary in 1981, was 'psycho-rigid' in his eyes. But
the previous summer he had married his mistress, Sylviane Agacinski,
a philosophy teacher, and Mitterrand, remembering his own experience with Anne Pingeot, had recognised the surge of energy in the
younger man. 'It was a pleasure to see him,' he said after the ceremony.
'He looked blooming and that's something which counts too.' Then

in the autumn they had become estranged again. Jospin had criticised him publicly, saying that he would have preferred that Mitterrand's past were 'simpler and clearer', a reference to his record during the war which had once again come under scrutiny. Nonetheless, there was no alternative. At the beginning of February, two and a half months before Election Day, Jospin received the Party's nomination.

The last ten months of Mitterrand's presidency were a nightmare. Both physically and mentally he was under attack. Physically from his cancer, mentally by ghosts from his past.

The previous year the hormone treatment he had been having was judged insufficient and he began a course of chemotherapy. It weakened him and failed to stop the cancer progressing. By the spring of 1994 it was clear that a second operation would be necessary. Mitterrand hesitated. His brother, Robert, who had recovered from prostate cancer without surgery, advised against it. 'How many more times will I have to do this?' Mitterrand asked Gubler plaintively.

Week after week he kept putting off the decision. The Rwandan genocide was raging and France had just announced the launch of Operation Turquoise. On July 4 he flew to Cape Town, becoming the first European Head of State to visit Nelson Mandela after his election to the presidency. From July 8 to 10 he attended a G7 summit in Naples. On the 14th, with Helmut Kohl beside him, he presided over the Bastille Day parade in which, for the first time, German soldiers marched alongside French troops. The following day there was a European summit in Brussels. For a very sick man nearing his 78th birthday it was an impossible schedule. Finally, on the evening of Sunday, July 17, he entered hospital, where Steg operated the next day.

The second operation was more difficult than the first. Mitterrand was suffering from a blockage of both kidneys. Steg succeeded in inserting a catheter into one but was unable to place the second. They decided to leave it. 'You can live with one good kidney,' Gubler said. 'He would never forgive us if [he had to wear] a permanent urine pouch.' As it was, he added, 'Steg and I thought [his] life expectancy would be a matter of months.' Ten days later he was back at the Elysée, chairing a Cabinet meeting. But the second operation marked the beginning of an ineluctable decline. 'Everywhere,' Védrine remembered, 'people were saying that he would not last until the end of the year.'

Like many others in such circumstances, Mitterrand experimented
with alternative medicine, including a homeopathic treatment from
a controversial 'healer' who had been banned from practising medicine
a few months earlier. Gubler and Steg were alarmed until one day
Mitterrand's driver, Pierre Tourlier, was persuaded to steal a sample
from the presidential briefcase and tests showed that it was harmless.[9]
Tourlier remembered the President being surrounded by 'a swarm of
pseudo-doctors and charlatans, all promising a miracle cure'. But he
continued to receive treatment by more orthodox methods, resuming
chemotherapy in the autumn, followed in November by radiation
treatment five times a week. Gubler and Steg found an ally in Mazarine,
then a few weeks short of her twentieth birthday. When her father
threatened to stop the radiotherapy, she upbraided him, 'You never
follow your choices through to the end!' and took him aside to tell
him, out of earshot of the others, that there was no question that he
had to continue. Gubler, who was present, remembered that she was
the only one who was able to talk to him like that.

For four months after the operation, Mitterrand was in constant
pain. He arrived at the Elysée each morning at around 10 a.m. and
went immediately to his private quarters to retire to bed and read the
newspapers. Anne Lauvergeon, who had succeeded Attali, recounted
that whenever she came to discuss the day's business, Mitterrand used
the same words: 'I'm sorry to present you with such a wretched
spectacle.' If he had no official duties, he would get up at lunchtime
and dine at the Elysée or at a restaurant outside. On a good day, he
would take a walk. On a bad day, he returned to bed. One frequent
visitor to the Elysée that autumn recalled: 'I had the feeling of coming
face to face with death . . . He was already on the other side.'

There were highs and lows, often in quick succession. In mid-
October, for the first time since the operation, he was able to play
golf. But two days later, during a Defence Committee meeting on
Bosnia, his body seized up. 'It was as though he was suffocating,'
Védrine remembered. 'For two interminable minutes he was unable
to get out a word. Then he made a sign to me and whispered to call
a doctor. By the time I got back he was talking [normally] again.' The
same thing happened when the Cabinet met a week later. 'He rested
his head in his hands and remained frozen for a long time without
speaking,' a minister recalled. Then he got control of himself and the

meeting continued. That afternoon he was due to receive the Lithuanian President. The visit had to be delayed for an hour but he refused to cancel it. In the evening, at a farewell for one of his aides-de-camp, he appeared, 'livid and walking with extreme difficulty', and shook everyone's hand. Next day he was at Blois in Normandy, where Jack Lang was mayor, to inaugurate a bridge over the Loire. The ceremony left him exhausted. 'He lay prostrate in the drawing room,' Lang recalled. 'I thought he was going to die. Then he joined us at table and talked for more than two hours.' Pierre Tourlier remembered journeys when he would vomit and they would have to stop to let him lie down by the side of the road. 'It's like having the Gestapo inside me,' he complained after a particularly violent attack. His son, Gilbert, said that the only time his father felt comfortable was when he was curled up in a foetal position.

That winter Gubler, who had been Mitterrand's doctor for twenty-five years, was replaced. Amid the intrigues and rivalries of the President's court, Gubler's frank assessments of his condition were not what he wanted to hear. Jean-Pierre Tarot, who succeeded him, had helped several of Mitterrand's friends, likewise stricken with cancer, through the last months of their lives, and was as discreet as Gubler had been flamboyant. Until his arrival, Mitterrand had adamantly rejected painkillers. Anne Lauvergeon thought it was partly 'a peasant attitude, regarding drugs as poison' and partly his Christian upbringing which led him to equate pain with an act of redemption. Tarot was able to persuade him to take carefully dosed injections of morphine.

The four months from August to November, when Mitterrand was physically weakest, coincided with a political onslaught against him of rare violence, dredged up out of the turpitudes of French behaviour during the Second World War.

The previous year, Pierre Péan, a French investigative journalist, had asked him to cooperate on a book about his life in the 1930s and '40s, covering his time at Vichy and in the Resistance. The President had agreed. At the end of August 1994, six weeks after the operation, Péan's book, *Une jeunesse française* ('A French Youth'), was published with a photograph of Mitterrand and Pétain on the cover – the same photograph that de Gaulle had refused to use against him in the 1965 election campaign. It was a scrupulously balanced account of a deeply troubled period, describing the conflicting wartime pressures to which young men of Mitterrand's generation had been subjected. But that was not how the press and the political class received it. All the old accusations from the 1950s and '60s roared back into life: Mitterrand had been a member of the Cagoule; he had frequented the extreme Right; he was anti-Semitic; he had been at Vichy and was therefore a collaborator; Pétain himself had awarded him the *francisque*. This time it was not the Right but the Left that was up in arms. Many of the comments showed the ignorance of the younger generation of French politicians about a time which none had experienced and most preferred to view through the comforting prism of Gaullist myth. But another factor was also at work. The ageing monarch was enfeebled and nearing the end of his reign. The revelation of his supposed perfidy was the perfect opportunity for the Socialists to turn the page, putting Mitterrand behind them and making a new virginity for themselves as the champions of political morality.

The firestorm that erupted over Péan's book showed how much the memory of collaboration in France remained an open wound.

Two issues, in particular, fuelled the attacks.

Since September 1984, when Mitterrand and Kohl had sealed the Franco-German reconciliation at Verdun, the President had each year sent a wreath to be laid at Pétain's tomb on the Île d'Yeu off the coast of Brittany. De Gaulle, Pompidou and Giscard had done the same, though less regularly. To Mitterrand, it was not just a matter of honouring the hero of the First World War but of trying to reconcile the two halves of France: those who had supported Pétain and those who had fought with de Gaulle. As he would learn to his cost, that was wildly premature. In July 1992, the President attended a memorial ceremony on the 50th anniversary of the round-up by French police of 13,000 Jews for deportation to Auschwitz. As he rose to speak he was greeted with boos and whistles. The Justice Minister, Robert Badinter, whose father had died in the gas chambers in Poland, berated the crowd: 'You make me ashamed. Shut up, or leave this place of sorrow! You dishonour the cause you think you serve.' The protests were against Mitterrand's refusal to apologise publicly for the anti-Semitism of the Vichy regime. Like de Gaulle, he argued that Pétain's government had usurped the powers of the French State, and those who had spent the war fighting against it could not now be expected to accept responsibility for its misdeeds. To his Jewish critics, that amounted to defending Pétain's policies, the proof being the wreath laid each year at his tomb.

The following year the wreath-laying ended. Emotions were still too raw. But Mitterrand drew the line at an apology. There was no question, he said, of 'France going down on its knees . . . and apologising for Vichy's crimes. I tell you solemnly, I will never accept that because it is wrong.'*

The other neuralgic issue awakened by Péan's book was Mitterrand's relationship with René Bousquet, the Vichy police chief responsible for the round-up.

Until the late 1970s, Bousquet had been a respected member of the Paris establishment. He had been cleared by the Special Court, amnestied by René Coty, and his *Légion d'honneur* had been restored. His circle of friends included men like Jacques Chaban-Delmas, Edgar Faure, Pierre Mendès France and Henri Queuille, a representative selection of the great and the good. As well as helping to run the Banque d'Indochine, he was a board member of the French airline, UTA, chaired by Antoine Veil, whose wife, Simone, an Auschwitz survivor and prominent member of the French Jewish community, was Giscard's Health Minister. As such he was a frequent guest at the Veils' table. Attali claimed to have been at a lunch in 1977, attended by Bousquet as well as Henri Frenay and other former leaders of the Resistance, at which Mitterrand said: 'Without him, none of us would be here today'. Not everyone was won over. Roland Dumas, to whom Mitterrand introduced Bousquet in 1968, saying he was 'a very decent fellow', found him 'Odious! Arrogant!' But Mitterrand liked him, appreciated his wit and respected his intellect. 'Had it not been for the war,' he told Dumas, 'he would have been a minister, maybe Prime Minister.'

In 1978, the façade of respectability began to crack. The former Commissioner for Jewish Affairs at Vichy, Louis Darquier de Pellepoix, who had been living in Spain since the war under the protection of

---

* In 1995 Jacques Chirac, who had been a child during the war, offered the apology the Jewish community was waiting for. Raymond Barre, who supported Mitterrand's position, probably came closest to the truth when he said that while the French people had been guilty, the Republic – in other words, France as a country – had not. Had Mitterrand found those words, the issue would have been defused. But, as Barre noted, that was 'a question of generations'.

one of Franco's generals, gave an interview to *l'Express* in which he accused Bousquet of having been in charge of the Jewish deportations. The Veils refused to see him again and he was removed from the UTA board. Afterwards a Jewish researcher, Serge Klarsfeld, found further evidence of Bousquet's involvement in the persecution of Jews. Mitterrand then also broke off their relations. Finally, in 1989, a Jewish deportees' association initiated court proceedings against him for crimes against humanity.

Political opinion was divided. Simone Veil and Chaban-Delmas, among others, thought that a trial would merely reopen old wounds. So did Mitterrand. In February 1990, he wrote that he was 'extremely reticent' about letting the case go forward. 'Things that happened nearly half a century ago, no matter how tragic they were, should not be stirred up again today . . . The great events which have torn apart our country have always been followed by amnesties or a necessary forgetfulness, for a nation cannot keep on simmering its resentments.'

In this, Mitterrand followed de Gaulle. To both men, reconciliation was more important than retribution. Not only after the Second World War but also after the war in Algeria. In 1982, over howls of protest from the Socialist Party, the President had insisted on an amnesty for the former leaders of the OAS, Salan and Jouhaud, and six other generals who had participated in the attempted putsch in 1958. 'We must know how to forgive,' he had told Pierre Joxe. 'It is time to close the Algerian chapter. [They] have the right to have the French flag on their coffins.'

He had made an exception for Klaus Barbie, the former Gestapo chief of Lyon, whom US intelligence had helped to escape to South America after the war in order to use his 'anti-communist expertise'. Barbie had been arrested in January 1983 in Bolivia, which offered to extradite him to France. Mitterrand at first hesitated. Badinter insisted that morally there was no choice. 'In the name of what would we refuse this offer?' he asked, 'and so grant Barbie an unjustifiable impunity.' Mitterrand was persuaded. Barbie, after all, was not French. But the Gestapo chief's conviction and sentence of life imprisonment for crimes against humanity in 1987 broke a decades-long taboo on war crimes trials in France. Two years later Paul Touvier, a leader of the pro-Nazi Milice, who had been protected for years by the Catholic

Church, was arrested and became the first Frenchman to be convicted of crimes against humanity. Bousquet never stood trial. He was shot dead in the doorway of his home in 1993 by an unstable young man who apparently wanted to use the case to win publicity for himself. But Maurice Papon, the Paris police chief under de Gaulle and afterwards a minister under Giscard, was later imprisoned for his role in the deportation to death camps of some 1,500 Jews from the area around Bordeaux.

Apart from Barbie, all these men were in their eighties. That alone made Mitterrand reluctant. 'I have no sympathy for Touvier,' he said. '[But at that age] it's juridically absurd . . . I call that hounding people . . . They are more relentless now than fifty years ago. We were the ones who suffered and perhaps that's why we were not as harsh.' He had a point. 'Men are neither black nor white, they are grey,' he said. The most unforgiving were those who came after, unable to accept that an idealised past should have been sullied by the weakness of their forebears. 'You're too young,' he told the journalists who questioned him. 'You can't understand because you didn't live in that time. It belongs to those who lived it.'

Ten days after the publication of Péan's book, Mitterrand decided that the fallout was such that he would have to intervene directly. He agreed to a live discussion on television on Monday, September 12 1994, after the evening news. That day, Anne Lauvergeon remembered, 'he was at his worst, lying in bed, barely able to speak . . . He had a nosebleed caused by the chemotherapy. The doctors wanted him [to cancel], fearing that his nose would start bleeding again on camera.'

Few of those who watched the broadcast were unmoved by the spectacle of a very ill, elderly man attempting, sometimes at the limits of coherence but with a dignity and conviction which grew stronger as the interview progressed, to convey *his* truth about a period of French history which fascinated and appalled his compatriots.

What he said added little in terms of fact. He misremembered the anti-Jewish legislation under Vichy, claiming that it affected only foreign Jews whereas in fact it covered French Jews as well. He stubbornly refused to condemn Bousquet, who, he said, was now dead and could not answer his accusers. He reiterated the Gaullist position that France had no reason to apologise for the crimes that Vichy had committed. But the significance of the broadcast lay elsewhere. Even though the

President told his brother, Robert, next morning, that he had made a hash of it, his appearance drew a line under the affair. When Pierre de Bénouville proposed that a statement be issued by the surviving leaders of the Resistance – Passy, Rol-Tanguy, Dechartre and Chaban-Delmas among others – vouching for Mitterrand's bona fides, he rejected the idea. 'I don't need anyone to defend me,' he said. 'I've done nothing wrong, I don't have to apologise. That would be to play the other side's game . . . These accusations are an extraordinary, immense . . . hypocrisy. In the end, nothing will remain of them.'

A few days afterwards, letters began arriving at the Elysée. Soon they came by the sackful, several hundred each day. Altogether 12,000 people from all sides of the political spectrum wrote to Mitterrand in the weeks that followed, the great majority to assure him of their support and urge him not to give up. The tide of public opinion was turning. But not yet the political class and the press. The former Defence Minister, Jean-Pierre Chevènement, described the President that autumn as a quarry which had been cornered and whose carcass the hunters were preparing to throw to the dogs.

As though Mitterrand's cancer and the furore over Vichy and Bousquet were not enough, other 'revelations' followed.

His friendship with Patrice Pelat came back from the grave to haunt him. In 1982, Pelat had sold his company, Vibrachoc, to Alsthom, which was then State-owned, for 110 million francs, nearly twice its true value. At the end of 1993, Thierry Jean-Pierre, the magistrate whose leaks to the press about Pelat's loan to Bérégovoy had provoked the former Prime Minister's suicide, had given selected journalists copies of a lengthy report – in principle protected by judicial confi-dentiality – recounting the late businessman's dealings. In it he charged that, on Mitterrand's instructions, the State had overpaid Pelat as a recompense for financial favours the President had received before he came to power. The following September, when the frenzy about Bousquet was at its height, one of the magistrate's allies, an extreme right-wing journalist named Jean Montaldo, published a polemical tract entitled *Mitterrand and the Forty Thieves*, which purported to show that, on this and other occasions, Mitterrand had misused State funds. Montaldo was an amusing mischief-maker and made his case by innuendo. The book was a runaway bestseller.

The mainstream press, led by *Le Monde* and the weekly news

magazines, *l'Express* and *Le Point*, fearing to be left behind, adopted the same tone and tactics as its less reputable rivals.

One of Montaldo's sources had been François de Grossouvre, Mazarine's godfather, who, after many years as a wealthy, aristocratic factotum to the President, had become estranged from him. In 1994, de Grossouvre was in the throes of what in other times would have been called a nervous breakdown. Then in his 77th year, he was obsessed by his age and declining virility. His young mistress had just left him. He was torn between hatred of his former patron and an obsessive desire to be restored to favour. He had loathed Pelat, whom he had seen as a rival, and had been happy to give Montaldo, and anyone else who would listen, snippets of gossip about Pelat's relationship with Mitterrand. On the evening of April 7, he blew out his brains with a .357 Magnum in his office at the Elysée. Before long it was rumoured that, like Bérégovoy, de Grossouvre had been murdered at Mitterrand's behest to silence him. As in the earlier case, the supposed plot took on a life of its own.

Another lame duck came home to roost in December 1994 when court proceedings began against Christian Prouteau, who had headed the anti-terrorist cell at the Elysée in the 1980s, and Gilles Ménage, Mitterrand's security adviser and afterwards Chief of Staff, for their role in tapping the telephones of the writer, Jean-Edern Hallier and others to protect the President's private life. Again there were selective leaks to the press designed to cause the maximum embarrassment.

By then the object of this protection, Mitterrand's second family, was no longer a secret. On Thursday, November 3, *Paris Match* published a photo-spread showing the President and his daughter leaving a restaurant together. Mitterrand had known for some weeks that the pictures existed and had sent word that he would prefer them not to appear. But the magazine's editors told him they felt obliged to publish and he did not try to prevent them.

Afterwards it would be said that Mitterrand had organised the 'coming out' of Mazarine, just as he had allegedly 'encouraged' Péan to write about his years at Vichy, in order to clear the decks before he left power. In neither case was that true. The photographs showing the President with Mazarine were taken from 500 metres away with a high-powered telephoto lens by two paparazzi who had been awaiting an opportunity for months. Péan had approached Mitterrand to ask for his help on a book about the Vichy years, not the other way round. Nonetheless, both disclosures had a positive side. If his past were to be raked over, better that it happen now, while he was there to correct the most egregious errors, rather than after he had gone, when there would be no one to speak for him. Mazarine was 'not enthusiastic', he said later, and Anne, an intensely private person, 'took it very badly'. But in the end he was not displeased. It was better for both of them, he felt, that it should come out while he was still alive.

Paris Match was widely criticised for breaking the unwritten rule that the private lives of politicians should remain private. Nicolas Sarkozy, then Balladur's Budget Minister, who would later have his own problems with paparazzi when he became President, said the coverage was 'lamentable'. Pasqua deplored it. Giscard regretted it. But the public was unfazed. Few were shocked that the French President should have a second, unofficial family. 'It's a pity I don't have one or two more daughters in reserve,' Mitterrand said wryly. 'It would have helped me climb back further in the opinion polls.'

Paradoxically, the turmoil of the previous months had also had a silver lining. It had left him exhausted but had given him something to fight against. 'What does not kill you makes you stronger,' he used to say to his colleagues. That autumn, he acknowledged, there had been times when he felt he would not see the end of the year. But by December the radiation treatment began to have an effect. 'You've seen my new haircut?' he asked mischievously. 'Rather than having a few stray hairs waving about ridiculously, it would be better to . . . have it all cut off!' Mentally he was back on form. For the first time since his operation, he invited a group of friends for a lunch of oysters, crab and roast duck in his private apartments. Physically he was still extremely weak. When he had no official engagements, he worked in his bedroom in a specially made reclining chair which eased the pain. But the months when he had been at rock bottom were behind him.

On March 30 1995, a Thursday, seven weeks before his presidency was to end, Mitterrand inaugurated the new National Library which would bear his name. All French Presidents have tried to put their stamp on the architecture of Paris: de Gaulle began construction of the city's ring road, the *périphérique*, and decreed the removal to the suburbs of its 'belly', the food market at Les Halles; Richard Rogers and Renzo Piano were commissioned to build the 'Pompidou Centre' nearby; Giscard transformed the Gare d'Orsay railway station into a museum of nineteenth-century art. Leaving a legacy in stone was part of a monarchical tradition which went back to Louis XIV, who had built a palace at Versailles to perpetuate his glory as Sun King, and beyond that to the sovereigns of medieval times. But Mitterrand did more than any of his immediate predecessors, changing the face of Paris as no one else had done since Napoleon III ordered Baron Haussmann to build the majestic boulevards through which the life of the city runs today.

Fittingly, in view of the President's love of literature, the library, built in an abandoned industrial zone in the south of Paris, the French equivalent of London's Canary Wharf, was the last major architectural undertaking of his fourteen years in power. Spread out over six hectares between four glass towers, shaped like half-open books, the reading rooms are disposed about a subterranean cloister, replicating in minimalist, late twentieth-century fashion the ambulatory of a medieval monastery. Like the Grand Louvre, the world's biggest museum, with its classical glass pyramid, designed by the Chinese-American architect, I.M. Pei, it was one of his more successful projects. Not all Mitterrand's forays into bricks and mortar would work out so well. The opera house in the Place de la Bastille, the site of the French Revolution, conceived as a way to make available to the masses classical music, opera and ballet, was technically at the summit of its art but aesthetically a disaster, resembling an enormous public lavatory. Nonetheless, to Mitterrand they were all essential parts of the heritage that he left behind. 'I appreciate architecture more than music,' he wrote. 'For me it is the first of the arts.'

Attali felt that in his last years, architecture was the only thing, apart from Europe, which held his interest. The two had coalesced in a project which had a historical importance beyond all the rest combined: the Channel Tunnel linking France to Britain. It had been under discussion for almost 200 years, had been agreed between Mitterrand and Thatcher in 1986 and was opened by the French President and the Queen in 1994. For a British Prime Minister steadfastly opposed to European integration it might seem an odd decision. But it was in keeping with the two countries' history. In the 1960s, de Gaulle, who was even more opposed than Thatcher to Britain's presence in Europe, had joined Macmillan in launching the Anglo-French supersonic jet, Concorde. For both, bilateral amity between Britain and France – the Entente Cordiale – was to be encouraged. Britain's role in Europe was not. To Mitterrand, for whom Europe was primordial, that was a historical reality to be reckoned with. If the British were unwilling to join the continentals in a Europe-wide adventure, at least with France they could make progress as a twosome.

But by the spring of 1995, the time for laying down legacies was drawing to a close. The presidential election campaign was already under way. For the first time, Mitterrand was a spectator. In a few weeks' time it would be someone else's responsibility to make a contribution, literally and metaphorically, to the architecture of France and Europe.

Chirac, on Mitterrand's advice, had declared his candidature early. Balladur, who had initially insisted that he had no intention of standing, waited until mid-January, two weeks after Jospin. The opinion polls gave the Prime Minister such a comfortable lead that *Le Monde* reported that most of the electorate thought the race was already decided. But then a scandal developed over what appeared to be an attempt by Balladur's office to embroil one of Chirac's allies in corruption allegations. By the end of February, the positions had been reversed. Chirac was ahead in the polls and the Prime Minister was trying desperately to catch up. Mitterrand, like everyone else, was surprised. But he recognised Balladur's problem. To win a presidential election you had to make people dream. Balladur, like Raymond Barre, was unable to do that.

On Sunday, April 23, when the results of the first round came in, Jospin was in the lead with 23.3 per cent and Chirac second with 20.8. The Prime Minister, in third place with 18.5 per cent, was eliminated.

The balance was weighted in Chirac's favour. As well as Balladur's followers, he could count on the support of a good part of the 15 per cent of the electorate which had voted for the National Front candidate, Jean-Marie Le Pen. Jospin refused Mitterrand's offer to campaign on his behalf. 'I did not want to be the shadow cast by someone else. I wanted to be a candidate off my own bat, not the son or the lieutenant of François Mitterrand,' he said. When Jospin's colleagues demurred, he dug in his heels. 'You don't campaign looking into the rear-view mirror,' he told an interviewer, 'but with the headlights focussed on the future.' It was not very elegant. On Sunday, May 7, Chirac was elected with 52.6 per cent of the vote.

Ten days later the handover took place. As a gesture to his successor, Mitterrand had had his office restored to the same state, with the same furniture, as when General de Gaulle had occupied it, twenty-five years earlier. He handed Chirac the nuclear codes, asked him to find posts for two of his aides, as Giscard had done almost fourteen years earlier, and recommended to his care the pair of mallards which had taken up residence in the Elysée gardens. Shortly after midday, Mitterrand left the palace for the last time. Since the French Revolution, only King Louis-Philippe and the Emperor Napoleon III had held power for longer.

16

The Testament

François Mitterrand retired not to the house which he shared with Danielle in the rue de Bièvre but to a nondescript official apartment put at his disposal by the State, on the Left Bank of the Seine in the rue Frédéric Le Play, named after a nineteenth-century economist who had studied the living conditions of the European working class. His visitors were often surprised that he chose such a 'clinical, impersonal' place. But it was a stone's throw from the Champ de Mars, the formal gardens which stretch out southwards for almost half a mile from the Eiffel Tower, where he could walk Baltique, the black Labrador bitch who was his inseparable companion, and it meant that Anne could continue living with him, which would have been difficult had they remained at the quai Branly and impossible at the rue de Bièvre. It was not 'home', however, as their other apartment had been. It was the place in which he had chosen to die.

The entrance hall was laid out like a doctor's waiting room with black leather settees and a huge charcoal portrait of Mitterrand on one wall. On either side of the long white corridor which led from it were rooms occupied by his bodyguards and a small secretariat. Further on lay his private office, furnished as it had been at the Elysée, with a designer writing table in pale blue lacquered metal and leather and the specially made reclining chair where he could lie and work. Beyond, on the other side of a double door, were the living quarters. Anne was away at work during the day, returning discreetly in the evening through the service entrance in order not to draw attention.

Life after the presidency revolved around lunch with friends – often at a local restaurant, D'Chez Eux, behind the École Militaire, which specialises in the hearty fare of the south-west and reminded him of his childhood – followed by an hour's walk in the gardens or along the banks of the Seine. At the end of May, he fell, opening a cut above his eye, the first of many such mishaps, often occasioned by Baltique – 'the worst brought up dog in France' – whose displays of affection made him lose his balance. In June he went to Cluny, where, on Whit Sunday, he attempted the annual ascent of the escarpment of Solutré. This year he did not make it. He had just had a new catheter and was still suffering from its insertion. But trying to live normally – to do the things he had always done – was a way to dominate his cancer. And until the end of the summer, Mitterrand seemed to be succeeding. 'Death?' he said to Pierre Favier. 'You need to think about it and get ready for it every day . . . But it's not death that frightens me; it's not living any more.'

Quietly he began to make his farewells. A last visit to the Nièvre to vote in the municipal elections. A trip to Venice with Anne, to stay with an old friend, the Slovenian painter, Zoran Mušić, and his wife, Ida Barbarigo, in their palatial apartment beside the Grand Canal. In August, after giving Dr Tarot the slip, a last surreptitious journey with Anne to Touvent.

But Mitterrand's principal goal, in the months that remained, was to burnish the image he would leave behind. He had made a first attempt the previous winter with the Nobel laureate, Elie Wiesel, in a book of conversations entitled *Mémoire à deux voix* ('Memoir for Two Voices'), published shortly before he left office. His aim, he said, was to use the written word 'to give a sense of order to one's life'. But the 'Memoir' became mired in the controversy about René Bousquet. Privately at first and then publicly Wiesel taxed the former President with anti-Semitism. Mitterrand, he alleged, 'never mentioned Vichy. Today I can't stop asking myself: why?' Afterwards, in his autobiography, the Holocaust survivor accused his old friend of 'refusing to investigate the Nazi past of certain Frenchmen', of 'links with former Cagoulards and other collaborators', of 'secretly' having had a wreath laid at Pétain's tomb – even, supreme malice, of 'making it a habit to surround himself with Jews' – to insinuate, without ever accusing him directly, that he was and had always been a closet anti-Semite. Such an amalgam of half-truths, untruths and innuendo said more about Wiesel and those for whom he was the self-appointed spokesman than about Mitterrand or France. But above all it showed the difficulty of discussing dispassionately, even fifty years after the event, what remained – and remains – an emotionally uncontrollable issue.

Despite the squabble with his co-author, *Memoire à deux voix* was an illuminating book. But it was not the record Mitterrand wished to leave behind. He decided to try again with a young left-wing journalist named Georges-Marc Benamou, who also happened to be Jewish. This time he wanted a book structured around the continuities and contrasts between himself and de Gaulle. But as the months passed, the same arguments over Bousquet and Vichy resurfaced. Mitterrand was appalled by what he saw as the younger man's simplistic view of history. 'He asks questions an ape wouldn't ask,' he complained, 'and he knows nothing about Gaullism.' Benamou was Wiesel bis minus the literary talent.[1] The book which resulted, entitled *Mémoires inter-rompus* ('Interrupted Memoirs') and completed in December, also disappointed him. Ever the perfectionist, Mitterrand had reworked the original material again and again, sometimes rewriting the same answer as many as five times. But he was too ill to correct it as he would have wished and almost a third of the manuscript had to be scrapped because he was too weary to go through it.

Mémoires interrompus was a testament in the sense that it offered a considered account of some of the most contentious periods of his life. But he had wanted something else – a reflective coda to the *Coup d'état permanent* as a verdict on the unspoken rivalry with his giant predecessor which had fired the whole of his political career. That had been beyond Benamou's powers and, by the closing months of 1995, it was beyond Mitterrand's too.

Mitterrand also worked that summer on a book about Germany. On May 8, the day after Chirac's election, he had travelled to Berlin to commemorate the 50th anniversary of VE Day. Abandoning his prepared text, he spoke of German history being 'indissolubly linked to France [in a] strange, cruel, beautiful and powerful adventure' and of Europe being built on 'ruins, disasters and death'. He went on:

> Are we celebrating a defeat? Or is it a victory? And if so, what victory? No doubt it is the victory of freedom over oppression. But to my eyes it is above all – and this is the only message I want to leave you with – a victory of Europe over itself . . .

I did not come here to celebrate the victory in which I rejoiced for my own country in 1945. I did not come to rub in a defeat because I have known [from my own experience during the war] the strength of the German people, its virtues and its courage. The uniforms of those soldiers, who died in such great numbers, and even the ideas in their heads, matter little to me. They were brave. They accepted that they would die. In a bad cause, but to them their actions had nothing to do with that. They loved their motherland. We must reckon with that. We are making Europe and we also love our countries. Let us remain true to ourselves.[2]

The speech was applauded in Germany but highly controversial in France. To suggest that uniforms – SS uniforms? – and ideas – Nazi ideas? – mattered little, even with the caveats that Mitterrand attached and in the context of European reconciliation, was going too far. As always, when challenged, he refused to retract. In Moscow, next day, he told Yeltsin that he had 'never considered the German [soldiers] as enemies'. Like the French, they had fought because it was their duty, without asking questions about why they were fighting.

It was essentially the same problem as over Bousquet and Vichy. Jean Daniel of *Le Nouvel Observateur*, who had known Mitterrand for forty years, commented that the priority he attached to reconciliation, whether within France or beyond, was out of step with an age which sought moral absolutes.[3] But the issue went deeper. Half a century later, France was still unable to accept the way most of its people had behaved during the Occupation. Anything which touched on the ambiguities of those years, remembered by those who had lived through them as a time of national shame, risked triggering an excessive, irrational reaction.

'I work in shades of grey,' Mitterrand told the novelist, Jean d'Ormesson. 'There are black threads and white threads. I weave them together and with that I make grey'.

France did not want to be reminded of the grey in its past.

De l'Allemagne, de la France ('About Germany, about France'), which Mitterrand completed shortly after *Mémoires*, was both a hymn to Franco-German reconciliation and an attempt to justify his reticence towards German reunification. Like *Mémoires*, it was riddled with small errors which he was too ill to correct and included a long section on foreign reactions to his election in 1981, which had nothing to do with

Germany and seemed to have been tacked on to make the volume more substantial.

But it gave him a sense of purpose. Defending his record helped him fight against his cancer.

The same combination of reasons prompted him to accept an invitation from George Bush to join four other retirees – himself, Gorbachev, Thatcher and the former Canadian Prime Minister, Brian Mulroney – for a conference in October at Colorado Springs on the end of the Cold War. During the summer the argument over whether or not France should apologise for Vichy's role in the deportation of Jews in 1942 had been reignited by Lionel Jospin, who contrasted Mitterrand's refusal with the gesture made in Poland in 1970 by Willy Brandt, who had fallen to his knees before the monument to the Warsaw Ghetto. Mitterrand had been furious. 'There's no comparison,' he snapped. 'France was not Germany, Pétain was not Hitler.' The episode persuaded him not to pass up the opportunity to put on the record once again, this time among his peers, far from the petty quarrels which exercised the political class in France, the views on East–West relations for which he preferred to be remembered.

Until the end of September it was not certain that his health would allow him to attend. He lunched that month with his unofficial chroniclers, Pierre Favier and Michel Martin-Roland. 'Don't sit too close,' he greeted them drily, 'I'm more radioactive than Mururoa':

> I'm at 106 grays [the standard unit of radiation absorbed by body tissue] when the maximum is supposed to be around 60. Now the cancer is in the bones. It started at the bottom of the spinal column, then it went up into [my neck] which they treated before the summer. That burnt my gullet. [This evening] they are going to do the left shoulder. Every time they do it, it leaves you exhausted. I have difficulty standing up, I'm unsteady on my legs, I lose my balance. Up to now, each time they have managed to stop it spreading further. But if it gets into the marrow, the spinal cord, I shall be paralysed.[4]

Having dealt with his clinical condition – a ritual to which all his visitors were subjected – he perked up. 'You didn't come to hear the groans of a dying man,' he said, 'so let's talk about the things you are interested in.' Helmut Kohl telephoned him regularly, he told them, adding with a chuckle, 'though not as often as Arafat'. Then he launched into a searing portrait gallery of his colleagues. Michel Rocard: 'A mistake to appoint him . . . He did nothing.' Jacques Chirac: 'How he used to lie to me! Today I wonder if he even realised it.' Raymond Barre: 'Likeable, but a loser.' Giscard: 'Completely old-fashioned.' Michel Debré: 'A mediocre person.' Jacques Delors: 'Zero.' Nicolas Sarkozy: 'A talent for biting and betraying. But that's not enough.'

The venom was also a ritual. He had told the writer Franz-Olivier Giesbert that Rocard was 'just good enough to be a junior minister for Posts and Telegraphs, or something like that'. As for Édouard Balladur, 'I've rarely met anyone worse than myself, but [can he really be] as bad as that?' Balladur, he said, warming to his subject, was 'such a horrible person . . . that it makes me feel I'm not so bad after all and even, relatively speaking, quite sincere. If you cut his skin with a knife, you'll see there's only poison underneath.' Paul Quilès, with whom he had lunch two months later, found his judgements 'so acerbic that I promised myself I would never repeat them'.

Playing Jupiter, hurling lightning bolts at the mortals in the world below, consoled him in his pain. Like his meticulous descriptions of the progress of his cancer, recounted 'vertebra by vertebra, like a general addressing his troops', as Jean Glavany put it, it was a way to give himself the strength to continue.

On Saturday October 7, he boarded a Concorde for New York, accompanied by Dr Tarot and two bodyguards, and then travelled on to Denver and the Rocky Mountains, where the conference was to be held in the ballroom of the Broadmoor Hotel, a Gatsby-era palace emulating the grandeur of St Moritz and Gstaad. Bush had organised it to raise funds for his presidential library.

During the debate on Sunday afternoon, Mitterrand spoke frankly of his qualms about German reunification. 'The question,' he said, 'had been whether [it] was a certainty or whether it could be avoided.' His conclusion, he told the audience of American multimillionaires, had been that it was not avoidable. Afterwards, in a television interview, he drove home that point. 'The problem was not whether one liked [the idea of reunification] or whether one did not like it. It was to know whether there was any force on earth – other than brutal Soviet military force – which could stop [it].' Gorbachev, he said, had had neither the will nor the ability to do so, and as a result it had taken place peacefully.

Mitterrand was glad he had come. 'It was a pleasure talking to George Bush,' he said afterwards, 'and even more with Margaret Thatcher . . . She's a character, a real character. There's a complicity between us which can only be explained by the difference in our beliefs.' His relationship with 'Dear Mrs Thatcher', as he called her, always made him smile:

> Her inimitable mixture of firmness and tactical flexibility . . . consisted of presenting her setbacks in a glorious light. That is how the philosopher's stone works today. [It] transforms a political failure into success. It was all the easier for her because she was an accomplished practitioner of this kind of alchemy, to which she gave herself every time she returned from a European summit so that in her own country her ideas, which were always rejected [by her partners], won her, after a proud speech before the House of Commons, a Roman triumph.[5]

But the journey had exhausted him. In New York, on the way back, he was tempted to stay an extra day for a last look at a city whose architectural purity he adored. However, after 15 minutes walking among the skyscrapers, near the Waldorf Astoria, his strength gave out. His bodyguards found him a seat in the atrium of a bank where it took him three-quarters of an hour to summon up the energy to go back.

On his return to Paris, Mitterrand, as de Gaulle had done before him, approved the creation of a historical foundation which would bear his name, the Institut François Mitterrand, financed – like Bush's library – by wealthy benefactors. But his heart was still set on a book to define his image for posterity, the book which Benamou had been unable to write. Serge July called it his 'passion for rectification . . . Everything which he or those around him thought had been wrongly understood – which meant by and large everything which had been understood correctly but which might give him a bad image – he tried to rectify or reshape, and when it was necessary he would reshape it ten times.' He would have preferred to oversee the whole process himself. But since it was too late for that, it was a matter of finding someone to write it that he could trust.

Earlier that year Jean Lacouture, who had written an unsurpassed biography of de Gaulle, had approached him to ask whether he would consider cooperating on the story of his life. Mitterrand had hesitated. Lacouture was not from his political camp. But at the end of September, when it was clear that *Mémoires* would not do the job, he invited him to come round.

A month later, after his return from America, when Lacouture made his next visit, Mitterrand's condition had changed for the worse. The writer was escorted through a double door to a small, bare, white room, where he found Mitterrand 'sunk into his bed, very pale, with his head, like white marble, buried amid the sheets'. It was a measure of his decline, Lacouture reflected, that such a proud, fastidious man would allow himself to be seen in such a state.

Mentally he was alert. 'So? What are you going to write about me?' he asked. Lacouture replied that he envisaged a book placing his life in the context of 'France and the French, with their faults and their qualities'. Mitterrand made a feint: 'Yes, I'm French, but I'm from Aquitaine.' However, the idea pleased him and the following month he gave his consent. Lacouture was as good as his word. Three years later he entitled his biography, *Mitterrand: une histoire de Français* ('A Frenchman's story'). It was an excellent book, balanced, curiously affectionate and scrupulously fair. But Mitterrand would probably have been disappointed. It did not have quite the same magic as Lacouture's relation of the life of Charles de Gaulle, partly, perhaps, because the material was not the same. One was the stuff of Shakespearian drama, the other of Racine. The two men had lived their lives by very different scripts. Even beyond the grave, the rivalry lingered.

The end of October 1995 marked the start of Mitterrand's 80th year. He celebrated quietly at home with Anne. A week later he flew to Latche for the delayed anniversary of his wedding with Danielle.

Throughout November he continued to work on *Mémoires* and *De l'Allemagne, de la France*. But his strength was slowly ebbing away. There were better days and worse days. One weekend he was well enough to visit André Rousselet at Beauvallon, across the water from St Tropez, where he had spent the first Christmas after his escape in 1941. In December he made a last trip to Gordes. At other times he was barely able to stand. For his daily promenade in the Champ de Mars, one of his bodyguards carried a folding stool so that if he could not get from one park bench to the next, he could sit down between. Often he turned back after only a few minutes. He told Marie de Hennezel, a psychologist specialising in help for the terminally ill, who had become a friend: 'We are each of us in an aircraft which one day will finish by crashing into a mountainside. Most people forget about it. Me, I think about it every day. But perhaps that is because I already glimpse the mountain through the window.'

By then he had come to terms with the fact that he was not going to be cured. The only question, he wrote, was 'how to die?' 'Dying is as easy as being born,' de Hennezel assured him. 'The body is ready. It understands [both].'

But in his case there was a second, more delicate question: where to be buried? Danielle had wanted him to be interred in the cemetery at Cluny, her family home. He had refused. That would be too much of a slap in the face for Anne. The best answer would be the family crypt at Jarnac, where only a single place remained.[6] But how to arrange that without upsetting Danielle, who had told him that she wanted to be buried at his side? He resorted to a pirouette. She had proposed buying a plot of land on Mount Beuvray in the Nièvre, where Vercingetorix was said to have united the Gauls against Rome in 52 BC. He agreed and the contract was signed in May. Three months later all hell broke loose. The proposed burial plot, 10 metres square, was on a protected archaeological site and had been made over to them illegally by the local Socialist mayor. If Mitterrand did not organise the leak that triggered the scandal, it certainly served his purpose. Once it was splashed across every front page, he could tell Danielle with a straight face that he 'wanted to sleep peacefully' and at Mount Beuvray that would no longer be possible.[7] Burial at Jarnac was the only solution.

Just as the apartment in the rue Frédéric Le Play was in theory neutral ground, but in fact Anne lived there, so the family crypt, where Danielle could not follow, was also a gesture in Anne's direction. Danielle might be his wife, the gesture said, but even in death, she did not own him.

One more challenge remained. Marie de Hennezel had told him that the best way for a terminally ill person to cope with the approach of death was to set a series of goals to be accomplished beforehand. Mitterrand's last goal was to return to Egypt, where, almost every winter since the 1980s, he had spent Christmas at the Old Cataract

Hotel at Aswan on the Nile. Dr Tarot encouraged him. The journey was suicidal for a dying man – but better that he should spend his final weeks living the life he wished. Mitterrand had no desire to end like his friend, Jean Riboud, who had spent his last ten months in a wheelchair after his cancer metastasised into his spine. 'I'm counting on you to make sure that no one will ever see me shrivelled up like a vegetable, mindless and bedridden,' he told Michel Charasse. 'You must do everything to spare me that.'

The tests he had had in mid-December had been inconclusive. But he knew that he did not have much time left. He told his brother, Robert, 'I don't think I shall keep going for another two months'. When his publisher, Odile Jacob, informed him that she was planning a launch party for *Mémoires* in February, he smiled and said, 'I shan't be there any more.' De Hennezel was another frequent visitor that month. 'It's not a big deal,' he told her. 'But it takes so long, this business of dying.'

On Christmas Eve, Mitterrand, accompanied by Anne and Mazarine, Jean-Pierre Tarot and his family, the Rousselets and four others, boarded an airliner sent by the Egyptian President, Hosni Mubarak, to fly to Aswan. At the Old Cataract, the Presidential Suite, which Mitterrand occupied, boasted a spacious private terrace, the only one in the hotel, with a view across the Nile to Elephantine Island, an old ivory-trading centre on the border between Egypt and Lower Nubia. The sight of the river seemed to put fresh vigour into him and, to Rousselet's amusement, Mitterrand found the energy to flirt with his friend's young wife, Anouchka.

They spent Christmas Day on a felucca, sailing among the islands. Mitterrand, in a deckchair in the shade of the single lateen sail, was lost in reveries. But the effort was too much for him. The following days he remained cloistered in his suite. He had originally intended to stay on until the New Year. But on Friday morning, December 29, he telephoned Mubarak to apologise for not being able to join him for lunch and explained that he would have to return to France. His physical weakness, coupled with Mazarine's desire to get back to Paris to be with her boyfriend, had got the better of him. That afternoon the Egyptian President's jet carried them back to Biarritz.

Two days later, at Latche, Danielle organised a New Year's Eve dinner. There were twenty at table. At Mitterrand's request, Henri Emmanuelli had managed to find some ortolans – small buntings, which are drowned in Armagnac and pan-roasted – a centuries-old delicacy in south-western France which has since been outlawed, the birds having been declared a protected species. It was not the orgiastic last supper which subsequent accounts alleged.[8] Mitterrand arrived from his sheepcote after all the others and sat apart, in an armchair, with a low table beside him and an ottoman where his guests came, one by one, to sit and talk. The meal was lavish – oysters, foie gras and capon, as well as the ortolans – and he tried everything. But unlike the previous year, when he had joined them at table and eaten the small birds whole in the traditional manner, so hot that the eater has to hide his mouth behind a napkin, this time Jack Lang had to help him, cutting one up into small pieces. Shortly before 11 p.m., he left, supported by Tarot, after sweeping the table with a long, silent gaze which re-echoed like an adieu.

The following day, Monday, he would only drink tea and, in the evening, a bowl of soup. He refused his medicine. Next day he had nothing to eat either. He told Jean Munier he felt the cancer was becoming general. In the afternoon Tarot chartered a plane to fly him to Paris for new tests. The results confirmed that it had metastasised to his brain.

Back at the apartment he cloistered himself in his monk's cell of a room, agreeing only to a glucose drip so that it could not be said that he had starved himself to death. 'He stopped fighting,' Tarot said. Jean-Christophe, whom he called back from a business trip to the Middle East, found him in bed, wrapped in the sheets, with his eyes closed. When he asked how he was feeling, his father replied: 'Sick as a dog.' Then, opening his eyes, he corrected himself: 'As sick as two dogs.'

The final days were spent arranging Mitterrand's affairs. Apart from the houses at Latche and in the rue de Bièvre, he and Danielle had less than 250,000 francs (£30,000 or US $45,000) in the bank and nothing in stocks, an inheritance so paltry that one might have thought it would have silenced those in France who maintained that he had abused his position to salt away hidden wealth.* He worried that she

---

* Afterwards, Danielle recounted, her banker called her. 'He said to me, "Madame Mitterrand, there's a bit of money in your account. It's a pity not to put it to work." I told him, "It's lazy, that money, it does not want to work." He said, "But it would bring you some income." I told him, "I don't need it." Then he said to me, "They warned me that that might be your reaction. You must admit, it's not very common".'

would not have enough to live on – unnecessarily, because, as he must have been well aware, the French State is generous to the widows of former presidents. Danielle inherited his pension and the royalties from his books. To Mazarine he bequeathed his library. She also became his literary executor. Anne had long been independent. She owned her apartment in the Latin Quarter and she had her career as a curator at the Musée d'Orsay. François left her the little house amid the olive trees at Gordes.

There were also spiritual matters to settle.

Two days before his death, when André Rousselet tried discreetly to enquire whether he wanted a religious service at his funeral, he answered, 'I still have time to think about all that'. In fact he had already thought about it. In his will, drawn up at the time of his first operation, three years earlier, he had written equivocally, 'a Mass is possible'. But what kind of Mass and where? Should he take extreme unction, as his devoutly Catholic sister, Geneviève, urged him? Did he want the government to proclaim a period of national mourning? Even as the end approached, he tried to put off the moment when he would have to commit himself.

In the last months, Anne remembered, 'death was a real problem for him. [It sometimes made him] very stressed. He kept asking himself questions. So many questions . . .'

Mitterrand was an agnostic. 'I don't know whether I believe or I don't believe,' he wrote, 'but it's a problem which intrigues me.' Ever since his faith had faltered as a PoW at Ziegenhain, he had, in his own words, 'walked around the subject'. Years earlier he had written,

---

Money, she said, 'only serves to fatten the fortunes of those who produce nothing'. It was not logical: Danielle was happy to accept donations for the Third World NGOs she had founded without asking her benefactors embarrassing questions about the source of the wealth which allowed their generosity. But it reflected a genuine disdain which she and François Mitterrand shared: so long as money was available for essentials – in the sense in which Oscar Wilde would have understood that term – it was not something either of them wished to think about. Five years later, when Jean-Christophe was charged with illegal arms dealing in Angola, of which he was afterwards acquitted, she borrowed five million francs (£500,000 or US $700,000) from friends for his bail. In 2013, the courts were still trying to establish whether she had ever paid it back. She auctioned off many of François's possessions – including his clothes, the gifts he had received and the wine in his cellar – to raise money for charitable work in the developing world.

'I was born a Christian and no doubt I will die one. But in between?'
In fact he was deeply ambivalent: he both believed in God and did
not. 'I have a mystical soul and a rationalist brain, and . . . I am incapable of choosing between them,' he had told Giesbert the previous
spring.

He had been close all his life to certain clerics whose spirituality
he admired and had been a regular visitor to Taizé, an ecumenical
monastic community in Burgundy which preached simplicity and
reconciliation. But the Catholic hierarchy was another matter. Christ
had been an agitator, he had told Elie Wiesel. If He were to return
today to preach in France, 'the local bishop would contact the authorities and ask them to move Him on somewhere else.'

On the wall of his bedroom in the rue Frédéric-Le-Play were
pictures of Francis of Assisi and Thérèse of Lisieux, a young
nineteenth-century nun who had become, with Joan of Arc, one
of the four patron saints of France. At the beginning of December,
her remains were brought in a gilded reliquary to the Church of
St Francois Xavier, near the Invalides, as part of a procession across
France to mark the coming centenary of her death. When the
cortège left for Normandy, it made a detour to the building where
Mitterrand lived so that he could stand on the pavement, resting
his hands on the casket, for a few moments of meditation. It was
not her sainthood that attracted him. He had once written that
'there is more charity in the heart of Louise Michel [a social activist
and heroine of the Paris Commune] than in all the Communion
of Saints of the Church of Rome.' But Francis and Thérèse were
eccentric, transcendent figures. Transcendence was what Mitterrand
sought from religion.

He believed fervently in prayer. There were times when he disappeared and would be found on his knees in a village church or behind
a pillar in a cathedral, lost in contemplation. But at the same time,
he was sceptical. People pray when they are in trouble and forget
to do so when they are happy, he told Wiesel. 'That seems to me
suspect.' And to whom should one pray? He had no answer. When
he prayed, he said, it was not because he expected to be heard. It
was 'to communicate with a transcendent world'. Marie de Hennezel
had encouraged him to read the Bardo Thodol, the Tibetan Book
of the Dead, which teaches that once the flesh is left behind the

soul need have no fear. He was intrigued by the death rites of ancient Egypt. His discussions with the astrologer, Elizabeth Teissier, sought to pierce the veil which separates the here and now from what might lie beyond.

All his life, since the death of his grandmother when he was fourteen years old, Mitterrand had been fascinated by death as a moth is fascinated by a candle. Her last words, he told de Hennezel, had been: 'Oh! The Light! So it was true!' Every night, before he slept, he said, he had a thought for those who had died: his parents, his closest friends, the old Jesuit who had been his companion in the *kommando* at Schaala and who, paralysed and speechless after a stroke, had had 'all the light of the world in his eyes'. Mitterrand approved the view of one of Marie de Hennezel's patients, who felt God was the invention of man rather than the other way round but nonetheless insisted that life could not be reduced to a packet of atoms. 'He who dies, will see,' she had written. For himself, he said in an interview with *l'Express*, shortly after leaving office, 'I am not fixated on death, but rather on the immense question mark that death represents. Is it nothingness? That's possible. But if it is not nothingness, what an adventure!'

The time for philosophising was drawing to a close.

On Sunday evening, January 7 1996, when Danielle and Gilbert came to see him, Tarot told them he had left word that he did not wish to be disturbed. He had asked Tarot to say 'those who love me will understand'. Danielle went in anyway but Mitterrand was drifting between consciousness and sleep. Gilbert thought afterwards that it was 'partly that he did not want to be seen in such a state, but also that he wanted to confront death alone'. In fact, there was another reason of which neither of them was aware. In the early hours of Sunday morning, Mitterrand had been restless and had awakened Anne. 'He wanted to get up,' she said, 'but he wasn't supposed to because he had all kinds of tubes and things attached. So at three o'clock in the morning I telephoned Tarot. I explained to him: "I've told him not to [move], but he doesn't understand what I say to him any more". Tarot didn't come over but I think he grasped what that meant. François had always said: "When it reaches my brain, you should finish me off. I don't want to end in that state." In the morning, when Tarot came, he said I could leave. I went back to the rue Jacob.

I was exhausted and that night I slept there . . . That was when [Tarot] must have given him an injection to end it all. I feel I was the one who condemned him. But he absolutely rejected the idea of being incapacitated – and that I understand very well.'

Any form of euthanasia is illegal in France and Tarot has never commented on suggestions that he might have eased Mitterrand's death. He gave a different account of the final hours. Tarot was Jesuit-educated. After Danielle and Gilbert left, he said, Mitterrand asked him to administer the last rites, giving him absolution for his sins.[9] At dawn, with Tarot beside him, he died in his sleep. A year earlier, he had been asked: 'When you appear before God, what will you say to him?' 'At last I know,' he had replied.

The doctor called Anne and then Danielle. President Chirac was informed and came at once to offer his condolences. For the next two days, an unending procession made its way to the small, blank room where Mitterrand's body lay in a dark grey suit, under a white coverlet, small and frail, his face an ivory mask. Giscard came, to pay tribute to the man who had defeated him in 1981; Michel Rocard, to the man who had helped destroy his political career; and Fabius, to the man who had failed, not for want of trying, to anoint him as his political heir.

Mitterrand's comrades from the Resistance – Jean Munier, Chaban-Delmas, Pierre Guillain de Bénouville – made the journey. So did his old mistresses, whom Pierre Tourlier, his driver, who knew all his secrets, gently turned away. De Bénouville, Roland Dumas and Mitterrand's sister, Geneviève, took turns to watch through the night beside him.

On Tuesday, January 9, the coffin was sealed in the presence of Danielle and Anne. After thirty years when neither family had acknowledged the existence of the other, they now grieved together. Roger Hanin had proposed that the body lie in state, to allow the people of Paris to pay their last respects, at the Trocadéro, on the Right Bank of the Seine, where the UN General Assembly had adopted the Universal Declaration of Human Rights in 1948. But Gilbert objected to his father being 'lugged about' and it was decided instead that the Socialist Party would organise a memorial ceremony the following evening at the Bastille. The party faithful gathered under a fine rain to light candles. In his will Mitterrand had said he wanted no speeches. A recording was played of his New Year wishes to the French people a year earlier, which he had concluded with the words, 'I believe in the forces of the spirit. I will not leave you.' Then Barbara Hendricks sang *Le Temps des Cerises* ('Cherry Time'), a nineteenth-century ballad associated with the destruction of the Paris Commune, where the 'cherries' were the drops of blood of the revolutionaries.

Next morning there was not one Mass but two.

The coffin was escorted to the military airport by an arrowhead formation of police motorcyclists in white uniforms, like a skein of geese, followed by the cortège of family and friends. Flags all over France were flown at half-mast. At 11 a.m., there was a minute of silence. At Jarnac, Anne and Mazarine waited in the church beside Jean-Christophe, Danielle, Gilbert and the grandchildren. Charasse stood outside, holding Baltique on a leash. The disparate circles of friends, which all his life Mitterrand had carefully kept apart, had come together at his death.

De Gaulle, twenty-five years earlier had chosen a similar arrangement: a simple, private ceremony at Colombey and a formal Mass at Notre Dame. For the General, eighty Heads of State and government had attended. Sixty came for Mitterrand, a comparison which would probably not have pleased him. For the homily of Cardinal Lustiger, Fidel Castro was placed next to Prince Rainier of Monaco while Prince Charles, representing the Queen, sat beside the Togolese dictator, Gnassingbé Eyadéma. Arafat, Shimon Peres and Mitterrand's recent host, Hosni Mubarak, were there. So were the Russian President, Boris Yeltsin, Al Gore, representing Bill Clinton, Juan Carlos of Spain and King Sihanouk of Cambodia. But the image that remained fixed in the minds of the millions who watched on television that day was of a tear rolling down the cheek of a colossus. Helmut Kohl, who had grasped Mitterrand's hand at Verdun, mourned the passing of his friend.

On the night of Mitterrand's death, Jacques Chirac found the words to transcend the country's political divisions and voice a tribute to which the nation could relate. He spoke of what Mitterrand had bequeathed to France – 'a modern, calm democracy, thanks notably to the experience of alternating political power which we mastered

[and] which has made our institutions stronger' – and of his commitment to social justice; to humanism, through the abolition of the
death penalty; and to 'a Europe in which France, working with a
Germany with which she is reconciled, has a place in the first rank'.
He went on:

> François Mitterrand . . . was the reflection of his century . . . The war.
> The Resistance . . . Life in dark times and in glorious ones . . . My
> position is peculiar because I was [his] adversary. But I was also his
> Prime Minister and today I am his successor. All that creates a special
> bond, in which there is respect for the statesman and admiration for
> the man who struggled in private against his illness with remarkable
> courage . . . From our relationship, the lessons I have retained are that
> courage is strong when it is supported by willpower; and that we must
> place man at the centre of all we do . . . At this moment, when François
> Mitterrand is becoming part of history, I wish us to meditate on the
> message he left behind.[10]

It was a generous speech. Two years later, when the emotion of the
moment had passed and politics reclaimed its rights, Chirac was more
circumspect, speaking rather of his predecessor's faults – his having
encouraged, for electoral reasons, the growth of the extreme right-
wing National Front; his lack of 'solid convictions'; his attitude to
France, which 'he loved . . . with his head, not with his guts'; his
'archaic views'; even, surprisingly, that 'if he knew France, he did not
know the world outside' – and expressing regret at having given the
impression that Mitterrand could be held up as an example.

The Left, too, would express growing reservations about its former
champion.

Even before Mitterrand's death, Lionel Jospin had called for a 'right
of inventory', by which he meant that the Socialists should pick and
choose what they wanted to retain from his years in power and jettison
the rest.

Like Chirac, Jospin condemned his mentor for having encouraged
the National Front. History would prove them both wrong.
Mitterrand had gambled that bringing the extreme Right into the
open, rather than forcing it underground, would help to neutralise
its venom, just as respectability had accelerated the Communists'

decline. Twenty years later the National Front – having become no more, if no less, extreme than the right wing of the Republican Party in America – was well on the way to becoming part of the mainstream of French politics, while in Britain, and elsewhere in Europe, the growth of anti-immigrant sentiment among the electorate, finding no other outlet, fuelled the emergence of diehard racist parties.

The Left professed to be offended in its virtue by the ambiguities of Mitterrand's past, by the monarchical aspects of his reign (which the Socialist Party's courtiers had assiduously served) and by the use of state funds to protect his second family. That, too, would be forgotten. Sixteen years after his death, 90 per cent of left-wing voters and 60 per cent of the whole electorate viewed his presidency positively. François Hollande, who, in 2012, became the next Socialist to enter the Elysée, was seen, according to opinion polls, as the left-wing candidate who most resembled him and during his campaign worked assiduously to portray himself as Mitterrand's heir. To later generations, the anomalies which had troubled Mitterrand's contemporaries – Bousquet, Vichy and the flirtation with the far Right – no longer seemed so important.

Mitterrand never liked discussing his legacy. He preferred to quote the epitaph on Willy Brandt's tombstone: 'I did what I could.' Yet of all the twentieth-century French leaders, only he and de Gaulle left France a changed country. One had consoled it for its humiliations and its loss of empire, bringing stability and strong leadership. The other cajoled it into entering the modern world. De Gaulle had closed one chapter of French history; Mitterrand had opened another.

During his fourteen years in power, France, which had defined itself for the previous two centuries by reference to the Revolution of 1789, began a slow and painful accommodation to the economic and political realities of the world outside. The French are change-averse and the transformation is incomplete. Mitterrand may be reproached for not putting the French Socialists more firmly on the road to become a reformist, social democratic party, able to confront the challenges of the coming century rather than wallowing in the illusions of the last. But there is a limit to what one lifetime can achieve. 'Ideas ripen like fruits and men,' Mitterrand wrote. 'All works – artistic, aesthetic, philosophical, practical, political – are unfinished.' The construction of Europe and the quest for social justice, the two great causes which had sprung from Mitterrand's experience as a prisoner of war, and modernisation, which had imposed itself as a necessity during his time in office, must be legacy enough.

Acronyms

ASALA L'Armée secrète arménienne de libération de l'Arménie (Armenian Secret Army for the Liberation of Armenia) was founded in Beirut in 1975 by members of the Armenian diaspora, led by Hagop Hagopian, to press Turkey to recognise the Armenian genocide. By 1988, when Hagopian was assassinated in Athens, it had carried out more than 80 attacks, mainly against Turkish targets, killing 46 people. Its last known actions were in the 1990s.

BCRA Le Bureau Central de Renseignement et d'Action (Central Bureau of Intelligence and Operations) was the Gaullist intelligence service, created in London in July 1940 and headed by André Dewavrin, better known as Colonel Passy. In November 1943, it was merged with the Giraudist special services to become the Bureau de Renseignement et d'Action de Londres (BRAL) and placed under the authority of Jacques Soustelle.

CERES Le Centre d'études, de recherches et d'éducation socialiste (Socialist Education, Study and Research Centre) was founded by Jean-Pierre Chevènement and others in 1966 as a left-wing pressure group. Unlike the Militant tendency in the British Labour Party – which in some ways it resembled – CERES formed part of the mainstream of the French Socialist Party until 1991, when it broke away in protest against French participation in the coalition against Iraq.

CFDT La Confédération française démocratique du travail (French Democratic Confederation of Labour) is the country's main non-communist trade union organisation. Unlike the Trades Union Congress in Britain, it has no organic link to any political party.

CGT La Confédération générale de travail (General Labour Confederation), founded in 1895, is the largest French trade union movement, historically dependent upon and directed by the French Communist Party.

CHAN Centre Historique des Archives Nationales (French National Archives).

CNPG Le Comité national des prisonniers de guerre (National Committee of Prisoners of War) was a PoW movement, controlled by the French

Communist Party, founded in the autumn of 1943. Nine months later it became part of the MNPGD.

COCOM The Western Coordinating Committee for Multilateral Export Controls was set up in the 1940s after the onset of the Cold War to prevent the sale of military or dual-use technologies to communist countries. It ceased to operate in 1994.

CSCE The Conference on Security and Co-operation in Europe approved the Helsinki accords on East–West cooperation in 1975. Renamed the Organisation for Security and Cooperation in Europe (OSCE), it now has 57 member states. Not to be confused with the Commission of the same name, which is an emanation of the United States Congress.

CSPPA Le Comité de soutien avec les prisonniers politiques arabes et du Proche-Orient (Support Committee for Arab and Middle Eastern Political Prisoners) waged a terrorist campaign in France from 1986 to 1987 on instructions from Teheran to try to obtain the release of Anis Naccache and four accomplices, who had attempted to assassinate the former Iranian Prime Minister, Shapour Bakhtiar, in Paris.

DGSE La Direction générale de la sécurité extérieure (General Directorate of External Security) is the French equivalent of the CIA and MI6 and answers to the Ministry of Defence. Before 1982 it was known as the SDECE (Service de documentation extérieure et de contre-espionnage).

DST La Direction de la surveillance du territoire (Directorate for Territorial Surveillance) is under the Interior Ministry and is tasked with counter-espionage within France. Its role is similar to that of the FBI and MI5.

EMS The European Monetary System, created in 1979, had at its core an exchange rate mechanism (ERM) which allowed member states' national currencies to fluctuate against a weighted average by a maximum of 2.25 (later 15) per cent. After 1998 it was superseded by the Eurozone.

ETA Euskadi ta askatasuna (Basque Homeland and Freedom) is a Basque separatist organisation, formed under Franco's dictatorship in 1958, which was responsible for more than 800 deaths in terrorist attacks in Spain. In October 2011 it announced that it was abandoning armed struggle.

EUREKA The European Research Coordination Agency was established in 1985 on the initiative of Mitterrand and Kohl to ensure European independence in research and development. It has 40 members, including all EU member states.

FARL Les Fractions armées révolutionnaires libanaises (Lebanese Armed Revolutionary Fractions), a small left-wing urban guerrilla group formed by Maronite Christians from northern Lebanon, carried out a series of terrorist attacks against Israeli and American diplomats in France in the early 1980s. After the arrest of its leader, Georges Ibrahim Abdallah, who was sentenced to life imprisonment in 1987, its activities largely ceased. Abdallah was freed, over American objections, in March 2013.

FGDS La Fédération de la gauche démocrate et socialiste (Federation of the Democratic Socialist Left) was founded in 1965 to unite the non-communist Left ahead of that year's presidential election. It played a key role in the success of left-wing candidates in the 1967 parliamentary elections but broke up a year later because of rivalry among its leaders.

FLN Le Front de libération nationale (National Liberation Front) launched the Algerian war of independence in October 1954 and later, under Ahmed Ben Bella, became Algeria's ruling party, remaining the country's dominant political force until a military coup in 1992.

FLNKS Le Front de libération nationale kanak et socialiste (Kanak Socialist National Liberation Front) was founded in 1984 by Jean-Marie Tjibaou to bring together the Kanak nationalist parties in a single movement for New Caledonian independence. Following the negotiation of a power-sharing arrangement between the FLNKS and the main French settlers' party, the two communities agreed that, for the time being, the islands should remain French.

FNPG La Fédération nationale de prisonniers de guerre (National Federation of Prisoners of War) was created in 1945 by a merger of the MNPGD and the prisoners' mutual aid centres set up by the Vichy administration.

GIGN La groupe d'intervention de la Gendarmerie nationale is an elite counter-terrorist force of the French police which intervenes in hijackings and hostage-taking. Its counterparts elsewhere include the Delta Force in the United States, the SAS in Britain and the German KSK.

GSPR Le Groupe de sécurité de la présidence de la République (Presidential Security Group) is a police unit, analogous to the US Secret Service, charged with the protection of the French President and his family.

IFM Institut François Mitterrand.

MNPGD Le Mouvement nationale de prisonniers de guerre et déportés (National Movement of Prisoners of War and Deportees) resulted from a merger of the communist CNPG; Mitterrand's movement, the RNPG; and Michel Cailliau's MRPGD. It was subsumed into the FNPG a year later.

MRPGD Le Mouvement de résistance de prisonniers de guerre et déportés (Resistance Movement of Prisoners of War and Deportees) was headed by Michel Cailliau, de Gaulle's nephew and Mitterrand's bitter rival. Also known as the 'Charette network', it was smaller than Mitterrand's movement, the RNPG, with which it eventually merged.

OAS L'Organisation de l'armée secrète (Secret Army Organisation), created in 1961 by French ultra-nationalists determined to prevent Algerian independence, made more than a dozen attempts to assassinate de Gaulle and was responsible for at least 2,000 murders, mainly of Algerians. Its leaders, including Georges Bidault, Jacques Soustelle and General Raoul Salan, were amnestied in 1968.

ORA L'Organisation de résistance de l'armée (Army Resistance Organisation) was formed in January 1943 after the German occupation of southern France. Initially loyal to General Giraud, it later joined forces with its Gaullist counterpart, the Armée secrète, to become the backbone of the Forces françaises de l'intérieur, the Gaullist resistance army in France.

PSA Le Parti Socialiste Autonome (Autonomous Socialist Party) broke away in 1958 from the SFIO, as the Socialist Party was then called, in protest against its support for the return of General de Gaulle. Two years later it merged with several other small left-wing groups to form the PSU.

PSU Le Parti Socialiste Unifié (Unified Socialist Party), whose leading members included at different times Charles Hernu, Gilles Martinet, Michel Rocard and Alain Savary, represented an idealistic, intellectual, anti-colonial strain of the French Left, advocating worker self-management and a revolution in education. After Mitterrand won control of the Socialist Party in 1971, the PSU's influence declined. It was dissolved in 1990.

RDA Le Rassemblement démocratique africain (African Democratic Rally) was founded in 1946 by Félix Houphouet-Boigny, later President of the Ivory Coast. Originally a pan-African movement, bringing together nationalist parties in ten French African colonies, its raison d'être disappeared after 1958, when the idea of a pan-African federation was abandoned in favour of national independence.

RNPG Le Rassemblement national de prisonniers de guerre (National Rally of Prisoners of War), also known as Pin'–Mitt', was a resistance movement founded by Mitterrand, Maurice Pinot and others who had worked for the Vichy administration in 1942.

RPF Le Rassemblement du peuple français (Rally of the French People) was founded by de Gaulle in 1947. It was anti-communist and opposed to the institutions of the Fourth Republic. After initially attracting a wide following, it split and became inactive after 1954.

RPF The Rwandan Patriotic Front was formed in 1987 by Tutsi exiles in Uganda, led by Paul Kagame, now Rwanda's President. It won power seven years later during the Rwandan genocide, in which an estimated 800,000 Tutsis and moderate Hutus were massacred by Hutu extremists. Today it plays a key role in Kagame's ruling coalition.

RPR Le Rassemblement pour la république (Rally for the Republic), established by Jacques Chirac in December 1976 as a vehicle for his political ambitions, was the last in a long line of political parties, stretching back to the RPF, which claimed to uphold the banner of Gaullism. In 2002 it merged with other Centre-Right and right-wing parties to form the Union for a Presidential Majority (UMP), afterwards renamed the Union for a Popular Movement, now the country's main right-wing political force.

SALT The Strategic Arms Limitation Talks between the United States and the Soviet Union, launched in 1969, led in the 1990s to the conclusion of bilateral treaties cutting back the American and Russian nuclear arsenals.

SDI The Strategic Defence Initiative, popularly known as 'Star Wars', unveiled by President Reagan in March 1983, proposed using land- and space-based laser weapons to create an anti-missile shield protecting the United States from nuclear attack. By 1987 the administration had been forced to recognise that the scheme was not a practical proposition.

SOE Britain's Special Operations Executive, set up by Churchill in 1940 to conduct espionage, reconnaissance and sabotage in German-occupied Europe.

Super-NAP A branch of the resistance movement, Noyautage des Administrations Publiques (Infiltration of the Public Administration), which recruited informants in the Vichy government. Super-NAP was charged with introducing resistance agents into the top levels of the civil service.

UDF L'Union pour la démocratie française (Union for French Democracy) was created in 1978 as an umbrella movement for a number of centrist and Centre-Right parties which supported the then President, Valéry Giscard d'Estaing. As French politics became increasingly polarised after the 1990s, the majority of its members joined the neo-Gaullist UMP In 2007, what remained of the movement was absorbed into the MoDem (Democratic Movement) led by François Bayrou.

UDSR L'Union démocratique et socialiste de la Résistance (Democratic Socialist Union of the Resistance) was founded after the war as a broad-church centre-left party for ex-members of the non-communist Resistance. Mitterrand became its President in 1953. It participated in almost every government under the Fourth Republic and was dissolved in 1964.

UNPROFOR The United Nations Protection Force, charged with peace-keeping in Croatia and Bosnia from 1992 to 1996.

Bibliography and Sources

In France, more than 500 books have been published wholly or partly about François Mitterrand – a larger number than for any other historical figure except Charles de Gaulle. In English, the available literature can almost be counted on the fingers of one hand: there are two scholarly political biographies, both by American academics – *Mitterrand*, by Wayne Northcutt of Niagara University, New York (Holmes and Meier, 1992) and *François Mitterrand: The Last French President*, by Ronald Tiersky of Amherst College (St Martin's Press, 2000) – and a small number of monographs on policy. In addition, Catherine Nay's French-language biography, *Le noir et le rouge*, which is excellent on Mitterrand's early years but ends with his accession to the presidency in 1981, has been translated as *The Black and the Red: François Mitterrand, the Story of an Ambition* (Harcourt Brace Jovanovich, 1987), as have two of Mitterrand's own books: *La paille et le grain*, with a preface by his friend, William Styron, published under the title, *The Wheat and the Chaff* (Seaver Books, New York, 1982); and *Mémoire à deux voix*, with Elie Wiesel, which appeared in America as *Memoir in Two Voices* (Little, Brown, 1996). Franz-Olivier Giesbert's sensitive account of Mitterrand's meditations on death, *Le vieil homme et la mort*, is also available in English under the title *Dying without God* (Arcade Publishing, 1998). But no substantial new work has appeared for almost fifteen years, which is alone sufficient reason to look again at a major world leader, and an unusually complicated human being, whom the passage of time now allows us to see more clearly than was the case when he lived.

Since almost all the sources of information about Mitterrand are in French, I have resisted – with some help from my publishers, who understand book economics infinitely better than I do – the temptation to give an exhaustive list of references which to most readers would be inaccessible. The notes which follow are therefore limited to explanatory material, intended to elaborate on the text or to clarify controversial issues, and to sources for extracts cited *in extenso*. For those requiring more detailed references, a complete list of sources and accompanying notes is available on request by email from mitterrandbiography@free.fr.

That said, it may be helpful to give a brief survey of the published materials, as well as archival and other resources, on which I have relied. There are two major French-language biographies of Mitterrand, which tower over all the rest: Giesbert's *Mitterrand: une vie* (Seuil, 1996) and Jean Lacouture's two-volume *Mitterrand: une histoire de Français* (Seuil 1998). Both authors had extensive interviews with Mitterrand – in Giesbert's case stretching back over twenty years – as well as with his contemporaries, and had privileged access to his personal papers. Serge July's *Les années Mitterrand* (Grasset, 1986) also provides useful insights, while Roland Cayrol's *François Mitterrand, 1945-1967* (Fondation nationale des sciences politiques, 1967), the earliest biographical study, offers an interesting portrait of Mitterrand at a time when his national destiny was not yet assured.

For the early years there are four main published sources: Mitterrand's own reminiscences in *Mémoire à deux voix*, with Elie Wiesel, and *Mémoires interrompus*, with Georges-Marc Benamou (Odile Jacob, 1995 and 1996); the autobiography of his brother, Robert, *Frère de quelqu'un* (Robert Laffont, 1988); and Pierre Péan's meticulously researched study, *Une jeunesse française* (Fayard, 1994), which covers Mitterrand's life up to the end of the war. Stéphane Trano's book, *Une affaire d'amitié* (l'Archipel, 2006) and Laure Adler's *l'Année des adieux* (Flammarion, 1995) contain unpublished letters from Mitterrand to his best friend, Georges Dayan. Like *Mitterrand: portrait total* (Carrere, 1986) by Pierre Jouve and the psychoanalyst Ali Magoudi, they also contain anecdotes that he recounted about his life before he became a politician. An essential source for his relationship with Marie-Louise Terrasse is *Catherine Langeais: la fiancée des Français* (Fayard, 2003), written by her nephew, Jean-Marc Terrasse, which reproduces many of the letters in which Mitterrand poured out his passion for her.

His articles in the 1930s in the *Revue Montalembert* and *l'Echo de Paris* have been preserved, as have his writings in captivity for the PoW journal, *l'Ephémère*, and at Vichy for *France: revue de l'État Nouveau*. Many, though not all, have been reprinted in the two volumes of *Politique* (Fayard, 1977 and 1981), which offer Mitterrand's own selection of his work from 1938 to 1981. Among the efforts he preferred to omit were a long poem entitled *Pluie amie* ('Friendly Rain'), describing life at the front during the 'phoney war', and an unpublished erotic novel, *Plein accord* ('Full Harmony'), written when he was 23 and madly in love with Marie-Louise Terrasse.

After the war, Mitterrand's reflections on his experiences as a PoW and in the Resistance were published as *Les Prisonniers de guerre devant la politique* (Éditions du Rond Point, 1945) and *Leçons des choses de la captivité* (Grandes Éditions Françaises, 1947). He returned to the subject in *Ma part de vérité* (Fayard, 1969) and *La Paille et le grain* (Flammarion, 1978). With Marguérite Duras in *Le bureau de poste de la rue Dupin et autres entretiens* (Gallimard,

2006), he recounted the Gestapo raids which almost cost him his life in June 1944. Other key sources for the period are Jean Védrine's *Dossier PG-Rapatriés 1940-1945* (privately printed, Asnières, n.d. but 1981), a two-volume compilation of war memoirs and related documents which offers the most complete account to date of the PoW movement in France; and Christopher Lewin's *Le Retour des prisonniers de guerre français: naissance et développement de la FNPG, 1944-1952* (Sorbonne, 1986). Michel Cailliau, in *Histoire du 'M.R.P.G.D.'* (privately published, 1987), gave a fiercely hostile account of Mitterrand's activities, to which Cailliau's colleague in captivity, Charles Moulin, offered a corrective in *Mitterrand intime* (Albin Michel, 1982). Mitterrand's articles for *l'Homme libre* and its successor, *Libres*, are also informative.

For the Fourth Republic, from 1946 to 1958, Georgette Elgey's monumental six-volume series, *La Quatrième République* (Fayard, 1993-2008, the sixth volume yet to be published) and the diaries of President Vincent Auriol (*Journal du septennat, 1947-1954*, Vols 1-7, Tallandier, 2003) are indispensable. Mitterrand's career in the UDSR is described in a monograph by Eric Duhamel: *L'UDSR ou la genèse de François Mitterrand* (CNRS Éditions, 2007). On the colonial problem, which was then among Mitterrand's principal concerns, his views are set out in *Aux frontières de l'Union Française* (Julliard, 1953) and *Présence française et abandon* (Plon, 1957). François Stasse (*La Morale de l'Histoire, Mitterrand – Mendès France, 1943-1982*, Seuil, 1994) provides a sensitive account of Mitterrand's complex and often uneasy relationship with Pierre Mendès France, while François Malye and Benjamin Stora have explored his much-criticised attitude towards Algerian independence (*François Mitterrand et la guerre d'Algérie*, Calmann-Lévy, 2010). Danielle Mitterrand's recollections appear in two books, *En toutes libertés* (Ramsay, 1996) and *Le livre de ma mémoire* (Jean-Claude Gawsewitch, 2007).

The Observatory Affair – recently the subject of a full-length study by Patrick Lestrohan (*L'Observatoire, l'affaire qui faillit emporter François Mitterrand: 16 octobre 1959*, Coédition Scrineo, 2012) – can best be understood from the archival materials held by the Institut François Mitterrand, which contain not only the complete files of the investigating magistrate and the police but also Mitterrand's handwritten notes as he tried desperately to extricate himself from the trap which his enemies had sprung.

The years which followed were marked by the proliferation of political clubs, recounted by Jean-André Faucher in *Les clubs politiques en France* (Éditions John Didier, 1965), and by Mitterrand's efforts to unify the Left, of which first-hand accounts are given by Claude Estier (*Journal d'un fédéré*, Fayard, 1970); Louis Mexandeau (*Histoire du Parti Socialiste*, Tallandier, 2005, and *François Mitterrand: le militant*, Cherche Midi, 2006); and Jean Poperen

(*L'unité de la gauche*, Fayard, 1975). Contrasting perspectives are offered by Gilles Martinet (*Cassandre et les tueurs*, Grasset, 1986), from the standpoint of the PSU, and Etienne Fajon (*L'union est un combat*, Éditions Sociales, 1975), from the Communist Party. Jean-Michel Cadiot (*Mitterrand et les Communistes*, Ramsay, 1994) also offers useful insights. Mitterrand's own version is given in *La rose au poing* and *L'abeille et l'architecte* (Flammarion, 1973 and 1978), in *Ici et maintenant* (Fayard, 1980), and in his articles for the Socialist Party journal, *l'Unité*, for his constituency newspaper, *le Courrier de la Nièvre*, and for the left-wing magazines *la Nef* and *Dire*.

For Mitterrand's years as President, from 1981 to 1995, two immense, and extraordinarily detailed, sources are available: the four volumes of *La décennie Mitterrand* (Seuil, 1990-1999) by Pierre Favier and Michel Martin-Roland, two journalists from the French news agency, AFP, who were accredited to the Elysée and won Mitterrand's trust; and the three volumes of *Verbatim* (Fayard, 1993-1995) by the President's Special Adviser, Jacques Attali. Their value for the biographer, apart from the exhaustive relation they provide of Mitterrand's time in office, lies in the confidential documents they contain – verbatim transcripts of meetings with Reagan, Gorbachev, Thatcher and other world leaders; minutes of French Cabinet and Defence Council meetings; discussions at the G7 and at European Union summits – all of which, by law, should have remained out of public view for thirty years or, in some cases, longer.

Favier and Martin-Roland had Mitterrand's authorisation to publish these documents and appear to have been scrupulous in the use they made of them. Attali took a scissors-and-paste approach which led even Mitterrand to complain that he seemed 'more concerned with the number of readers than with historical truth'. As a result, while the three volumes of *Verbatim* provide fascinating insights into Mitterrand's reasoning, they cannot be relied on. In some cases, moreover, what are presented as official transcripts of conversations with foreign leaders differ significantly from the texts held by the National Archives. Therein lies the rub, for most of these transcripts, and all of the Cabinet minutes, remain officially sealed. Accordingly the only versions available are those which have been 'leaked' (in other words, published in violation of government regulations) and which may, or may not, be accurate.

It is a very French problem – a double standard which allows those in privileged positions to flout the law, even if the result is to give currency to false information, just as French investigating magistrates leak the results of their investigations with impunity, even if, as in the case of Pierre Bérégovoy, the result is to drive a former Prime Minister to suicide.

For Mitterrand's presidential archive, there are additional complications. The sheer volume of material held by the National Archives from the fourteen years that he was in office – some 15,000 box-files occupying nearly *two kilometres* of shelves – is such that, at the present rate of progress, it will be another fifty years before it has all been catalogued (and until it has been catalogued, it cannot be consulted). Part of the problem is that Mitterrand's style of rule, favouring written analysis, led to an explosion of paper just before the advent of electronic word processing began to allow archives to be stored and searchable digitally. But over and above that, Mitterrand's tendency to complicate further whatever was complicated already led him to introduce a double-key system for archival access. As well as authorisation from the National Archives, permission to consult presidential documents has to be obtained from Mitterrand's nominee, Dominique Bertinotti, who worked at the Elysée as an archivist in the 1990s and has since become a Cabinet minister.

France being France, a way was eventually found to circumvent this cumbersome process. The Institut François Mitterrand possesses copies of many of the more important presidential documents and makes them available to bona fide researchers. But bureaucrats being bureaucrats, that has led to a monumental turf fight over who should have the right to control access to the presidential papers. None of the protagonists is at fault. But the result, as Mitterrand no doubt intended – in a last sideways jab at History – is that access to the presidential archive is an unalloyed nightmare.

The transcripts of official conversations and Cabinet documents cited in this book have, wherever possible, been verified, either with the originals in the National Archives or with persons privy to the discussions.

Besides *Verbatim* and *La décennie Mitterrand*, three other published works draw extensively on the presidential archive: *L'œil du pouvoir* (Fayard, 1999-2001), a massive three-volume series by Mitterrand's security adviser, Gilles Ménage, describing the French government's counter-terrorism strategy from 1981 to 1986; *François Mitterrand: les années du changement* (Perrin, 2001), papers presented at a colloquium, held in 1999, on the first three years of Mitterrand's presidency; and *Mitterrand et la réunification allemande* by Tilo Schabert (Grasset, 2002), discussing French attitudes towards Germany and Mitterrand's negotiations with Kohl on German reunification.

Contemporary documents are the stuff of which history, and therefore biography, is made, because, unlike memoirs, they have not been reinterpreted – consciously or unconsciously – after the event. Mitterrand's private papers, held by the Institut, clarify certain aspects of his military service. The National Archives, when not hobbled by restrictions on access to presidential files, contain useful material on Mitterrand's captivity as well as the complete archives of the UDSR, deposited by Laurence Soudet after the party was wound up in 1964. The archives of its successor, the FGDS, have also been preserved (at the Office Universitaire de Recherche Socialiste in Paris). Contemporary newspaper articles are another valuable resource. Even when factually wrong, they reflect the perception of events at the time and often provide the only reliable guide to their chronology, without which any interpretation of history is impossible.

Where contemporary evidence is not available, analysis and reminiscence must suffice. Among the former, Robert Schneider's magisterial account of the disconnect between Mitterrand and Michel Rocard, *La haine tranquille* (Seuil, 1993), provides a convincing explanation of why Mitterrand consistently sidelined the socialist leader best placed to succeed him. Hubert Védrine, who was Mitterrand's diplomatic adviser before becoming Secretary-General at the Elysée, gives a (sometimes overly defensive) account of the President's foreign policy in *Les mondes de François Mitterrand* (Fayard, 1996). Alain Duhamel, who collaborated with Mitterrand on *Ma part de vérité*, explores the unspoken rivalry with de Gaulle in *De Gaulle – Mitterrand: la marque et la trace* (Flammarion, 1991).

The memoirs of those who worked with Mitterrand and of members of his inner circle and his family are so numerous as to daunt the most assiduous reader. Some are more illuminating than others, among them *François* (Seuil, 1996), by Christina Forsne, a Swedish journalist with whom Mitterrand had a lengthy affair; *Lettre à un ami mystérieux* (Grasset, 2001) by his brother-in-law, Roger Hanin; Roland Dumas's two books, *Le fil et la pélote* (Plon, 1996) and *Coups et blessures* (Cherche-midi, 2011); Laurent Fabius's autobiographical essay, *Les blessures de la vérité* (Flammarion, 1995); Charles Salzmann's *Le bruit de la main gauche* (Laffont, 1996), which includes a fascinating recollection of Mitterrand's journeys to the Soviet Union; and Michel Charasse's *55 faubourg St Honoré* (Grasset, 1996), about his time at the Elysée. Mitterrand's chauffeur (and confidant), Pierre Tourlier, offers a different perspective on the President in *Conduite à gauche* (Denoël, 2000) and *Tonton* (Éditions du Rocher, 2005), as does one of Mitterrand's bodyguards, Daniel Gamba, in *Interlocuteur privilégié* (JC Lattès, 2003). Robert Badinter, Jack Lang, Pierre Mauroy and many others have also written instructive memoirs. But the list goes on and on and will no doubt be extended by a fresh avalanche of reminiscence to mark the centenary of Mitterrand's birth in 2016. The interest of French readers in their enigmatic leader appears to be inexhaustible.

The last months of his life were chronicled minutely (albeit, in places, with a tendency to be excessively judgemental) by Christophe Barbier (*Les dernier jours de François Mitterrand*, Grasset, 1997) and, less reliably, by Georges-Marc Benamou in *Le dernier Mitterrand* (Plon, 1996). *Le grand secret* (Plon, 1996), the publication of which Mitterrand's family tried to prevent, is an account by his doctor, Claude Gubler, of the President's cancer and the measures taken to conceal it.

My other major source for this book has been interviews with Mitterrand's family and inner circle. Jean Lacouture and Patrick Rotman recorded some two dozen interviews in 1999 and 2000 for their television documentary series, *Mitterrand: le roman du pouvoir*, which provided the basis for a book of the same title (Seuil, 2000). The transcripts, large parts of which are unpublished, have been generously placed at the disposal of researchers at the Institut François Mitterrand. I subsequently undertook a number of longer interviews, some extending over many hours, with Jean Balenci (Danielle Mitterrand's long-term partner); Édith Cahier (Robert Mitterrand's first wife); Roland Dumas; Georges Fillioud; Dominique Hernu (Charles Hernu's widow); Jacques Maroselli, who joined Mitterrand in the FGDS; Louis Mermaz; Anne-Marie Mitterrand (the wife of his nephew, Olivier); Danielle Mitterrand; Jacques Mitterrand; Guy Penne, another companion of the 1960s; Anne Pingeot; André Rousselet and Laurence Soudet. Without their help this book would be the poorer. Oral history cannot replace documentary sources, but it often provides the essential context that allows them to be interpreted correctly.

In the notes which follow, IFM stands for Institut François Mitterrand; CHAN denotes the French National Archives.

Notes

Prologue

1. Afterwards he had an armoured door installed. But he continued to receive letters containing death threats, and colleagues in the Senate, where he represented the Nièvre, a rural constituency in central France, warned him of rumours that he would be the next victim.

2. In the early 1960s, the future archbishop of Paris, Monsignor Veuillot, used to telephone Pope John XXIII from the brasserie's basement because, as he put it, 'here I can be at ease, I know that no one is listening in'.

3. 'Audition verbale de M. Mitterrand à son domicile', October 17 1959, IFM carton 41.

4. This was the sense of the article in *Paris-Presse* which Mitterrand had read that evening. The writer, Lucien Neuwirth, had been one of the leaders of the Committee of Public Safety, set up in Algiers to demand de Gaulle's return in May 1958. 'There is mistrust and anguish,' he warned. 'Why? De Gaulle has committed himself personally. He has rejected [Algerian] independence. The people and the army have confidence in him. So what is missing? [The problem is the] government . . . When a government shows its authority, doubts disappear . . . In a democracy, when there is danger, the powers-that-be need to be made to face up to their responsibilities. To re-establish public confidence, the Fifth Republic must prove its authority . . . and the promises it made must be kept.'

5. Although Bourgès-Maunoury reported Pesquet's overtures to the police, he, too, withheld Pesquet's name.

6. Pesquet approached Bourgès-Maunoury's office on August 18 and met him three weeks later, on September 12. The Interior Minister was informed of the contact on October 22. Puzzled by the government's silence, Bourgès-Maunoury contacted the investigating magistrate, Edgar Braunschweig, on November 3.

7. The giveaway lines in the letter were: 'When [Mitterrand] reaches the Avenue de l'Observatoire, he will pretend to panic, drive his car to the left side of the

road, get out and run off into the night'. Pesquet might, as Mitterrand claimed, have guessed what route he would take (although even that is a stretch, for a man discovering he is followed may head in any direction to throw off his pursuers). He might even have written several letters, to cover various possible routes, releasing only the one which fitted the facts most closely. But unless it had been agreed beforehand, he could not possibly have foreseen, in terms that were almost word for word those which Mitterrand later used to the police, exactly what his victim would do when the attack occurred.

8.   The General described Mitterrand as a *chargé de mission*, which can mean 'adviser', 'officer' or, as in this case, 'representative'.

9.   There were a very few exceptions, almost all of them friends from his childhood and time at college; fellow prisoners; and comrades in the Resistance, with whom the use of *tu* was an unwritten but ironclad rule. Even a close friend of forty years' standing, André Rousselet, used *vous* to Mitterrand.

10.   Mazarin, Cardinal Jules, *Bréviaire des politiciens*, Arléa, 1997.

1: A Family Apart

1.   Mitterrand, François and Wiesel, Elie, *Mémoire à deux voix*, Odile Jacob, 1995, pp. 11, 12, 15, 17 & 19.

2.   Mitterrand told this story so often that, even though it was true, it came to sound like an alibi against accusations of anti-Semitism.

3.   Hence the term, *coup de Jarnac*, signifying a clever and unexpected winning thrust. The Catholics then used one of their own: in 1771, the Jesuits, in the *Dictionnaire de Trévoux*, rewrote the definition to mean a tricky, disloyal blow. A century later, the error was corrected, but by then the new meaning had stuck. Mitterrand's opponents used it against him throughout his political career.

4.   The Edict of Nantes in 1598 ended the 'Wars of Religion' and proclaimed religious tolerance. In 1685, it was revoked by Louis XIV, who unleashed such a wave of anti-Protestant terror that more than 200,000 Huguenots fled the country, most of them to the Netherlands, Britain and Germany. Discrimination against Protestants did not end completely until the Revolution, a hundred years later.

5.   The pastor's concern was that if young people of both confessions played tennis together, it might lead to 'mixed' marriages.

6.   According to Franz-Olivier Giesbert, Mitterrand at the age of fourteen dreamed of entering a seminary.

7.   In his book, *Ma part de vérité*, Fayard, 1969. François Mitterrand also used the word, 'unclassifiable'.

8.   Édith Cahier wondered: 'Did François suffer because of that? . . . Perhaps he

became what he was out of a desire for revenge, a desire to be first? There's always a motive for everything.' Pierre de Bénouville also remarked that the Mitterrands were *vinaigriers* crushed by the great men of cognac' and asked himself whether that explained François's 'rancour against money and capitalism'.

9. François Dalle, interview with Jean Lacouture, c. 1999, IFM typescript.

10. Towards the end of François's schooldays, discipline at St Paul's eased. On special occasions, students would be allowed an exeat to spend a weekend at home.

11. In a letter dated January 30 1927, Robert informed his parents that François 'who, as you know, was down in the dumps' and had had a difficult first term, was back to normal again.

12. Despite Chardonne's wartime collaboration, de Gaulle was also among his admirers.

13. François's recollection was different. He told Charles Moulin that the first film he saw was one of the earliest French 'talkies', *Un trou dans le mur* ('A Hole in the Wall'), directed by René Barbéris in 1930.

14. The brothers spent two summers at Westgate, in 1929 and 1930.

15. Mitterrand and Wiesel, *Mémoire à deux voix*, pp. 43–4.

16. In January 1933, at the age of sixteen, François won an oratory contest for children from Catholic schools with a speech about the role of priests during the First World War. Like Churchill, when he was a boy, he had a tendency to stammer.

17. In an interview towards the end of his life, Mitterrand put his 'entry into *seconde*' (the fifth year of secondary education which in France marks the transition to *lycée* or senior high school) on a par with the death of his grandmother and the sale of Touvent as one of the three great shocks of his early life. The following year, in *première*, he failed the English oral in the bac. By his own account, he was paralysed by shyness: 'I couldn't put three words together . . . I was frozen inside'. He failed two attempts at the oral that summer but scraped through a year later. Robert, who jumped a class, spent six years at the college and obtained his bac at the unusually young age of fifteen. Jacques got his bac after seven years, François after eight, both passing the exam in the summer of 1934.

18. Jacques Mitterrand had a similar recollection: 'We were impregnated with [the teachings of] the Church. So for us it was out of the question.'

19. After the Second World War, Charles Maurras, who had collaborated with the Nazis, was condemned as a fascist. The leaders of the other right-wing leagues, including de la Rocque, who had fought for the Resistance, were unjustly tarred with the same brush. 'De la Rocque was neither fascist nor anti-Semitic,' Mitterrand said later. 'To me he was appealing . . . I was won over by [his] open character.'

20. De Bénouville acknowledged that 'in those days my life was organised around

that group [the Cagoule]', but stopped short of saying that he was a member. Two others of Mitterrand's friends, Claude Roy and André Bettencourt, who also lived at the hostel, supposedly 'hung out' with members of the Cagoule, but there is no evidence that either of them participated in its activities.

21. Bouvyer was the lover of Marie-Josèphe, the second-oldest of François's sisters, who married and subsequently divorced a young Breton aristocrat, the marquis of Corlieu. Their affair lasted from 1942 to 1947.

22. Among them, Jean Delage, who employed the epithet 'Negroid' to describe Gaston Jèze and afterwards recruited Mitterrand to write for *l'Écho de Paris*.

23. Le Sillon was founded in 1894 by Marc Sangnier, who later brought the Youth Hostel movement to France. It campaigned for the ending of class differences, and for political, economic and intellectual emancipation for all, notably in the workplace. François's father, Joseph, who shared some of his brother-in-law's ideas, introduced a system of worker participation in the family vinegar business, a revolutionary idea for the time which earned him the disapproval of conservative employers in the region.

24. According to François Dalle, 'he scraped through. It's not that he couldn't have done well, but he didn't do any work . . . His interests were elsewhere . . .'

25. Mitterrand was preparing his thesis for a doctorate in law when the war intervened.

26. In later life, under the name Catherine Langeais, Marie-Louise Terrasse became one of France's best-loved television presenters.

27. Letter of May 28 1938, in Terrasse, Jean-Marc, *Catherine Langeais, la fiancée des Français*, Fayard, 2003, pp. 121–3.

28. Throughout the late summer of 1938, François pleaded with her to agree to a formal engagement. Her refusal did not deter him. On January 4 1939, he wrote to Marthe to say that 'Marie-Louise and I love each other . . . and we would like our situation to be made clear'. That led nowhere either.

29. 'Thus far and no further', *Revue Montalembert*, April 1938, in Mitterrand, François, *Politique*, Vol. 1, Fayard, 1977, pp. 3–6.

30. The first mention of the international situation in Robert's diary for 1938 was on March 4, when he received a letter from his father who was 'worrying about Hitler'. On the 16th, another letter: 'Very much affected by the *Anschluss*, he sees the future in black'. Two days later a third letter: 'he is really worried'.

31. Details of Mitterrand's naval aspirations are fragmentary. He told his brother, Robert, that he had passed the *concours* for the Merchant Marine, but did not explain why, leaving Robert to wonder in his diary whether he was 'planning to find a way to make his military service pleasanter?' Jean-Marc Terrasse, evidently quoting Marie-Louise, wrote that he had intended to apply to the 'Commissariat of the Naval Reserve', an apparent reference to the École des officiers du commissariat de la marine at Brest, where naval administrators were trained.

32. The 'Higher Military Preparation' (Préparation Militaire Supérieure, or PMS) lasted three weeks. In a letter to Marie-Louise's father on April 25 1940, Mitterrand confirmed that he had attempted the PMS, but had 'followed [the course] irregularly and very much neglected it, with the result that I was placed on the third list . . . [meaning] no admission to the officers' training school'.

33. On October 4 1939, Robert wrote in his diary: 'If he has chosen not to seek a deferment, at the end of which he could have been sent to the provinces as an officer cadet in reserve, it's because he prefers to remain in the region around Paris. He seems to have good reason not to wish to leave . . . But he is going . . . to pay for it dearly, for the life of a foot-soldier doesn't have much in common with that of an officer cadet.' He was evidently unaware that François had already tried, and failed, to obtain a place as an officer cadet.

34. François finally introduced Marie-Louise to Robert in December 1938.

35. *Libres*, June 22 1945.

36. Magoudi, Ali and Jouve, Pierre, *Mitterrand: portrait total*, Carrère, 1986, p. 73.

37. Mitterrand and Wiesel, *Mémoire à deux voix*, p. 139.

38. In his letter of August 6 1940, he wrote that 'I'm leaving now, for where? Germany no doubt . . .' He arrived at Ziegenhain two days later, not at the beginning of September as he remembered.

2: The Captive

1. His account, entitled 'Pilgrimage in Thuringia', published in the Pétainist magazine, *France, revue de l'État nouveau*, No. 5, 1942 (reprinted in Mitterrand, *Politique*, Vol. 1, pp. 11–14), conflated two different journeys: from Lunéville to Ziegenhain (Stalag IXA), a distance of some 500 kilometres; and from Ziegenhain to Bad Sulza (Stalag IXC). The latter segment, of 200 kilometres, through Eisenach, Gotha, Erfurt and Weimar, lies east of Ziegenhain and could not therefore have been on the route from France.

2. *L'Ephémère*, August 15 1941, reprinted in Mitterrand, *Politique*, Vol. 1, pp. 9–10.

3. Danielle Mitterrand remembered: 'He didn't like to expose himself to the sun. He didn't like sand . . . I think he liked walking on the sand, but he didn't take off his shoes. No, he didn't like nudity.' I am unaware of any published photograph of him shirtless or in a bathing costume.

4. Although Mitterrand registered at Stalag IXA, his PoW number was for Stalag IXC, presumably because, like many others at Ziegenhain, he was destined for a *kommando* there.

5. Mitterrand, François and Benamou, Georges-Marc, *Mémoires interrompus*, Odile Jacob, 1996, pp. 13–14.

6. The chronology of Mitterrand's stay at Ziegenhain is contradictory. He stated

repeatedly that the rule of the gangs lasted three months. But he left Ziegenhain for Bad Sulza after only eight weeks, so it must have ended sooner.

7. *L'Expansion*, July–August 1972. At the end of his life he wrote that 'it was in captivity that I started fundamentally to call into question the criteria by which I had lived until then'.

8. Pierre Péan, in his book, *Une jeunesse française* (Fayard, 1994), maintained that Ziegenhain was 'different . . . It was heaven compared to other camps'. In fact the majority of the Stalags and Oflags – with certain exceptions like Stalag IXB, near Frankfurt, and the so-called disciplinary camps, Rawa Ruska and Kobierzin in the Ukraine and eastern Poland, where repeat offenders were sent – afforded the inmates facilities to keep them occupied outside working hours. There was no comparison between the PoW camps and death camps like Auschwitz.

9. Cited in Péan, p. 135.

10. *L'Ephémère*, September 1 1941.

11. In the early months he had to put his plans on hold because, until December 1940, his wounded arm was too stiff to move without difficulty.

12. In addition to Stalags IXA and IXC and the disciplinary camp, IXB, the region contained four Oflags where allied officers were imprisoned.

13. In what order, and for how long, he worked at which job is unclear. Paul Charvet wrote in his diary that Mitterrand began work at the hay station on November 11 1940. Mitterrand himself remembered working for the carpenter for six months. But since his entire stay at Schaala lasted only five months – from early October 1940 to March 5 1941 – and in that period he did many other jobs, that was impossible. He probably worked at the carpenter's shop for a few weeks, although at the time no doubt it seemed much longer.

14. They were captured on March 23 1941 and were still in Spaichingen on Easter Day (April 13), when their jailer announced to them the fall of Yugoslavia. Mitterrand completed his three-week sentence at Bad Sulza and was sent back to Ziegenhain in May. Marie-Louise Terrasse's parents received a letter from him on May 20 (or, more likely, dated May 20), informing them that he had just returned there.

15. He wrote to André Terrasse in July 1941 that his efforts to escape were 'only for her [Marie-Louise]'. Towards the end of his life, he acknowledged that although he had suffered from the loss of liberty, 'I had adapted to my lot pretty well, and I wasn't the only one. Force of habit prevented many escapes. I didn't want to leave my companions. I got used to living in the places where I was put. I no longer wanted to change all that. The idea of escaping, the need to escape, stems from other impulses. Even today I couldn't tell you what they are.' Elsewhere he wrote that the arrival of a parcel from home, containing a pair of slippers, almost made him change his mind and call off the escape.

16. Letter written in early July 1941, cited in Terrasse, *Catherine Langeais*, pp. 230–34.

17. Medical orderlies were sometimes repatriated as escorts for seriously ill PoWs

who were sent home under the accords the Vichy government had negotiated with the Germans.

18. *L'Ephémère*, November 15 1941.

19. His estrangement from the Church was gradual and incomplete. As late as the summer of 1960, he still sometimes attended services, and even when he ceased religious practice altogether, his faith was not entirely lost: he doubted and asked questions but did not find answers.

20. It was the first and last escape by prisoners crossing the perimeter fence of Stalag IXA during the five years the war lasted.

21. Mitterrand wrote later that he had crossed the demarcation line on December 15 1941. In fact, that appears to have been the date of his arrival in Mantry (after spending three nights hiding in Boulay, which he left with the owner of the newspaper shop, Maya Baron, at 5 a.m. on December 13; that night crossing into the Occupied Zone; and the following night in a hayloft in the Free Zone). Marie-Claire Sarrazin remembered him spending three days at Mantry, which is consistent with his having applied for demobilisation on December 18 at Lons-le-Saunier. He was given two months' leave of absence, starting on December 20, and his demobilisation was made effective by the regional centre in Bourg-en-Bresse on February 20 1942.

3: *Schisms of War*

1. The description is that of Maurice Pinot, Commissioner for Prisoners of War at Vichy.

2. When Mitterrand registered for demobilisation on December 18, he gave his address as c/o the Levy-Despas, which means that Robert must have visited him before that date. He arrived in St Tropez shortly before Christmas, probably on December 23, and travelled on to Jarnac on January 1.

3. By comparison, a print worker in Paris that year earned 4,250 francs a month; a staff member at a Mutual Aid Centre, 2,000 francs.

4. Letter of April 22 1942 to Marie-Claire Sarrazin, cited in Péan, *Une jeunesse française*, p. 188.

5. Favre de Thierrens's service was 'attached' to the Legion, rather than being an integral part of it, but that was splitting hairs: in practice they were one and the same thing.

6. The article was to have been published in a Pétainist journal in March 1943, but never appeared.

7. Letters of March 13 and April 22 1942, cited in Péan, pp. 179 & 188.

8. The phrase is from Jacques Bénet but it also represented Mitterrand's thinking.

9. It is impossible to ascertain exactly when Mitterrand joined the counterfeiting operation or even when it began. It may not have started until June, but a May

date is plausible. Mitterrand had known Roussel since March. The latter was in charge of the workshop and trusted him enough to take him in mid-June to meet Antoine Mauduit at Montmaur to discuss more active resistance activities. A *terminus ad quem* is provided by Bénet, who visited Mitterrand in July by which time the counterfeiters 'were already in action'.

10. Mauduit rented the Château de Montmaur in June 1942. He founded 'the Chain' three months later.

11. The *maquis* of the Vercors, in the mountains 40 miles further north, created in the winter of 1942, is usually regarded as having been the first in France. However the *maquis* of Montmaur, in the area known as the Duvelloy, was contemporaneous and possibly earlier. Mitterrand, who returned there in November 1942 and again in early 1943, remembered seeing Mauduit communicating with his men by field telephone and 'wearing a curious outfit that was half-civilian, half-military, with an alpine chasseur's beret on his head'.

12. He obtained the post through Jean-Albert Roussel, who said later that Mitterrand had also been offered a job at the Commissariat for Jewish Questions, which would have paid three times more, but had turned it down. Mitterrand himself denied that.

13. Mutual Aid Centres, often associated with Maisons de Prisonniers (Prisoners' Bureaux), were set up in the Occupied Zone from the winter of 1941. In the Free Zone, the first Aid Centre opened in July 1942.

14. The exact date is unclear. Jean Védrine wrote that the group around Barrois 'which would become the Aid Centre' started forming in March–April 1942; Pierre Coursol remembered the Aid Centre being formally established in late September.

15. Mitterrand wrote later that this second Montmaur meeting, on August 15 1942, appointed an executive committee comprising, in addition to the 'three Ms', Barrois, Gagnaire and Guy Fric, and 'immediately constituted a network' covering much of south-eastern France. It did not. He was describing history as it should have been, rather than as it was.

16. Letter of June 16 1942, cited in Péan, *Une jeunesse française*, p. 197.

17. Simon Arbellot de Vacqueur was from the Charente and knew Mitterrand's family. Gabriel Jeantet commissioned articles from Mitterrand in the winter of 1942.

18. Apart from his trip to Paris to meet Marie-Louise Terrasse in January 1942, before the wearing of yellow stars became obligatory, there is no evidence that Mitterrand travelled to the Occupied Zone before November 1942, when the demarcation line was abolished. He would not therefore have seen Jews wearing yellow stars until that month or possibly later, by which time his views about Vichy had already changed. He is known to have visited the capital in January 1943, and his brother, Robert, remembered another trip the following spring.

19. The December 1942 issue of Jeantet's journal, *France, revue de l'État nouveau*, in which one of Mitterrand's articles appeared, also contained a violently anti-Semitic report by Noël de Tissot, one of the founders of the pro-Nazi Milice, later an officer in the Waffen-SS; and an essay by Lazare de Gérin-Ricard, a pillar of Action Française, describing methods to stop the 'Hebrew invasion'. Questioned towards the end of his life about his collaboration with the journal, Mitterrand replied: 'I wanted very much to write for a magazine . . . I didn't ask myself what ideas that magazine was conveying, or the kinds of people who wrote for it . . . Perhaps I should have paid more attention.' The explanation, however inadequate it may seem today, has the ring of truth. Had Mitterrand wished to, he could have claimed plausibly that writing for an extreme right-wing publication was part of his cover at a time when he was organising a clandestine movement. He did not.

20. Edgar Morin remembered a clandestine press service run by Gilles Martinet (the Agence d'Information et de Documentation, or AID) issuing a thick dossier on Auschwitz, but that could not have been earlier than April 1944. The first detailed report to Allied governments on December 10 1942, entitled 'The mass extermination of Jews in German-occupied Poland', drawing on information from Jan Karski and Witold Pilecki, both members of the Polish Resistance, had been published early in 1943. But Karski had not had access to the death camps and Western leaders were reluctant to believe him. Pilecki escaped from Auschwitz in April 1943, but when he provided an eyewitness account of the gas chambers it was thought that he was exaggerating. Not until the winter of 1944, when the Russians liberated Auschwitz and other camps in Poland, did the Allies finally face up to the reality of what had been happening there.

21. Neither General de Gaulle in his speeches nor his spokesman, Maurice Schumann (himself of Jewish origin) in his BBC radio broadcasts, addressed directly the persecution of the Jews. To the extent that they were mentioned at all, they were included with communists, Freemasons and Gaullists as victims of reprisals by the Germans and their collaborationist allies.

22. Letter of January 26 1943, cited in Péan, *Une jeunesse française*, pp. 251 & 253–4.

23. Pinot was opposed to armed struggle until a general uprising became feasible, arguing that premature action would only provoke needless reprisals.

24. A note on the state of public opinion in France, issued over Cailliau's signature on February 1 1944, said that Jews and Freemasons should be kept out of a future French government. Cailliau insisted afterwards that that did not reflect his personal views and in the 1970s he won a court case against Mitterrand for suggesting otherwise.

25. Pierre Merli's group in Nice started sabotage activities in February 1943 and Munier and Pelat in the autumn of that year.

26. According to Dechartre, the meeting, which he recalled as having taken place on May 28 1943, was arranged because 'there were three movements . . . the Gaullist movement, the communist movement and a movement which was a bit more bizarre which was born out of the Mutual Aid Centres . . . The General said, "three movements, that's two too many" . . . so I was given the mission to prepare what was afterwards called the fusion [of the three movements].' In that account, given long afterwards, he apparently conflated two different discussions, for the communist prisoners' movement was not launched until the end of 1943. He was also mistaken about Mitterrand's moustache and slicked-back hair, a disguise which the latter adopted on his return from Algiers in January 1944. In an earlier version, given to his close friend, Charles Moulin, in the 1970s, Dechartre also conflated different encounters but not in the same sense. To Moulin he claimed that at Lyon they only 'exchanged three words' and that their first serious discussion took place in Paris in March 1944. That is not plausible either. Dechartre's recollections are important and their substantive accuracy is not in dispute: the only uncertainty is over the timing of their conversations. In this section I have cited only those remarks which I feel were likely to have been made at Lyon, leaving to subsequent chapters those parts which the internal chronology indicates must have been made later.

27. Dechartre used the term, 'Bakerfix', which was a popular brillantine pomade for women marketed by Mitterrand's future hostess in Marrakesh, the music hall star, Josephine Baker.

28. Philippe Dechartre, interview with Jean Lacouture, c.1999, IFM typescript.

29. Jacques Bénet said the Committee appointed in February 1943 had seven members: Barrois, Bénet, Mauduit, Mitterrand, de Montjoye, Pilven and Pinot. In February that could not have been so, but the seven names may well have corresponded to the membership of the Committee in the late spring of 1943, after the departure of Michel Cailliau in April and of Jean-Albert Roussel. It is unclear exactly when the initials RNPG were first used. In November 1943, Mitterrand used the term MNPG (National Movement of Prisoners of War). The name by which it would later be known, RNPG, appears to have been coined later that winter for the discussions on a merger with Cailliau's movement. Before that it was referred to as Pin'–Mitt', or simply, 'the movement'.

30. Letter to Marie-Claire Sarrazin, July 17 1943, cited in Péan, *Une jeunesse française*, pp. 322–3. As often in Mitterrand's private correspondence during this period, he indulged in flights of fancy which are misleading if taken literally. Here the sentence which I have paraphrased as 'I am not in that league' actually stated: '[As for me], I can only be a leader by scheming or by terror, or by virtue of the ruthless networks of [all that is] inhuman . . .' His intention was to draw a distinction between his own lesser talents and those of the truly 'great men' who were able both to move the masses and to love them as individuals, but

that was not how he wrote it. The imagery may have been drawn subconsciously from the struggle between the Resistance and the Gestapo.

31. In a note on December 13 1943, Captain Lejeune attested that 'Monnier' (Morland) 'belongs to the [paramilitary] Service d'Action of the DSS [Giraudist Special Services], incorporated into the BRAL [London Intelligence and Action Bureau, set up in November 1943]'.

32. That Bousquet, from 1943 onwards, aided the Resistance, or its individual members, is not in doubt, though his reasons for doing so are open to question. Mitterrand did not meet him until 1949. He was on record as saying that Bousquet had 'saved lives' during the war and, during Bousquet's trial that year, authorised Jean-Paul Martin to testify that 'Bousquet had rendered great services to the Resistance, and that I [Mitterrand] would vouch for that'. Martin, who had been Mitterrand's informant in the police department, said later that Bousquet and Mitterrand had been the two most important influences in his life. André Rousselet, for decades part of Mitterrand's inner circle, said he was convinced that Mitterrand's support for Bousquet was in part 'for services rendered'.

33. The award was almost certainly made between February and mid-April 1943. Mitterrand later maintained that he did not receive the medal in person, having already left for London when the awards ceremony was scheduled, some seven to nine months later. That seems not to have been true. Some of his friends remembered him wearing the *francisque* in the summer of 1943.

34. Jean Pierre-Bloch, who in 1943 was with the BCRA in London, wrote that members of the Resistance were instructed to accept decorations from Vichy because refusal would attract suspicion. He added that in Mitterrand's case, the BCRA had been informed and advised him not to refuse. André Ullmann, who had belonged to Cailliau's movement and was therefore in principle a hostile source, confirmed that.

35. Jacques Bénet dated the beginning of 'permanent and methodical resistance' to 'the first days of March 1943 . . . That marked the real start of the RNPG.'

36. Mitterrand obtained admission to the meeting using a pass provided by an ex-prisoner working for Masson's Commissariat.

37. This is taken from Maurice Schumann's account on the BBC French service on January 12 1944.

38. Another version holds that he was helped by a communist militant named Piatzook, who ordered the doors to be opened as the Milice were coming to arrest him so that he could escape. Since that makes a better story, it is hard to understand why Mitterrand never told it himself if it were true.

39. Pierre Péan quoted an unnamed friend of Mitterrand as saying that, after the Wagram incident, some of Pétain's aides considered offering Mitterrand Masson's job. At that time the entourages of the Marshal and of Pierre Laval, the Prime Minister, were locked in a struggle for influence. The appointment

of Mitterrand, a *maréchaliste*, to replace Laval's man, Masson, would have marked a victory for Pétain's group. Mitterrand himself, in this account, decided the moment for such an initiative was past. The suggestion is intriguing, for, if founded, it would show that, even after Wagram, Mitterrand had not completely burnt his boats with Vichy and could still consider returning to the *maréchaliste* fold. But it does not ring true. Masson's post was not vacant – he reportedly offered his resignation, but it was refused and he remained in office until the following January – and even if it had been, there is no reason to think that Laval would have accepted Mitterrand, known as an ally of Maurice Pinot, as his replacement.

40. A few weeks earlier, Dobrowolsky had run off with the movement's treasury. Jean Munier and Pol Pilven had tracked him down and brought him back to face Mitterrand, who had decided to spare his life. When arrested, in August 1943, he was on his way to North Africa where, on Mitterrand's instructions, he was to join the Free French forces.

41. Miller was arrested in October.

42. Mitterrand told Jean Warisse in London a month later that d'Astier had provided his movement with money and arms.

43. Bettencourt quoted Mitterrand as saying that Lenin and Trotsky had also thought about 'getting themselves up' for power. Captain Lejeune of the ORA who received him in London, claimed many years later that Mitterrand often said during this period, 'When I shall be a Minister . . .' By then, however, Lejeune had fallen out with Mitterrand and his account must be read accordingly.

44. Ginette Munier offered an alternative version of these events, in which she and Jean Munier went together to the station and, finding Mitterrand and André Bettencourt in one of the carriages, warned them not to descend. The four of them then travelled on to Clermont-Ferrand, where they stayed with one of Bettencourt's friends. The two versions are not necessarily contradictory: Fanny Pfister, Jean Munier and Ginette may well all have been at the station that day. Ginette, Mitterrand and Munier returned briefly to Vichy soon after to try to get news of Pilven and Jean Renaud, but Jean-Paul Martin told them the Gestapo had already taken them away.

45. In his book, *Ma part de vérité*, Mitterrand wrote that on arrival in London he had been asked to sign a register acknowledging de Gaulle's leadership and, when he refused to do so, was denied clean clothes and accommodated in 'a room with neither door nor window' – an unfortunate phrase which prompted his opponents to ask how he had got in. But that was written twenty-five years later when he was at loggerheads with the Gaullists and, like much of what he said at such moments, was invective rather than history. De Gaulle could be equally cavalier with the truth when the mood took him.

   In fact, the BCRA financed Mitterrand's stay in London from the day he arrived. Whatever reservations he may have had about the Gaullists were quickly dispelled and soon after his return to France, his movement publicly proclaimed its loyalty to the General.

His failure to register the RNPG as a resistance organisation under the BCRA, in the same way that Cailliau had registered the 'Charette network', did cause problems in one respect, however. When the war ended, its members were denied the benefits that other, officially recognised, movements obtained. The fact that the MNPGD (which succeeded the RNPG) was integrated into de Gaulle's FFI, the French Forces of the Interior, in 1944 was not regarded as sufficient proof of their status. Recognition was finally accorded almost half a century later, in 1991.

Mitterrand's own position as an officer in the FFI was confirmed in 1945 by General Koenig, the Military Governor of Paris, who, in another citation for the *Croix de guerre* – Mitterrand's third of the war – described him as 'Lieutenant-Colonel in the FFI' and wrote: 'Animated by the deepest patriotic feelings. Extremely active and with an inflexible will, took the initiative to create . . . all over France the Resistance Movement of Prisoners and Deportees. By untiring activity and despite great dangers . . . he organised a clandestine intelligence service for the Allies [and] sustained and animated Resistance in the most diverse forms – sabotage of railways and factories, punctual attacks and false identity papers.'

46. 'Interrogation of Pepe and Monier, 23rd November 1943', SOE archives, London.
47. This corresponded to the 'Committee of Seven' described by Bénet as leading the movement in the summer of 1943, allowing for the withdrawal of Mauduit and de Montjoye to run the *maquis* at Montmaur and the replacement of Pol Pilven by Munier following his arrest on November 11. The main difference was that Mitterrand now placed himself at the movement's head while Maurice Pinot ranked third.
48. The relative strengths of the two groups was shown when, after the merger of March 1944, the RNPG was given control of nine of the 12 military regions, while the MRPGD and the communist CNPG shared the other three between them.
49. Mitterrand's incorporation into the Gaullist ranks was backdated to 15 November, the day of his arrival at Tangmere. He was appointed to the BRAL's 'Action Service' on December 1.
50. Mitterrand and Benamou, *Mémoires interrompus*, pp. 129–31. To Pierre Merli in 1944, he said, 'It was not pleasant'; to Benamou, fifty years later, that 'it went less badly than has been reported'. Merli's conclusion, that it was 'tough but not negative' is probably a fair summation.
51. Letter from Frenay to 'Vergennes' (Michel Cailliau), March 18 1944, in IFM carton 7.
52. That Schumann was acting on instructions from Algiers was shown by his

(premature) announcement in the same broadcast that the three prisoners' movements had already merged: 'It is a wonderful piece of news that I have the privilege of announcing to the country: from now on there is one – I say again, *one* – prisoners' movement in France', a point which he repeated no fewer than four times.

53.   Following his remarks in November to Marie-Claire Sarrazin ('making my entrance into the century') and Bettencourt ('doing something once the war is over'), this phrase – in a letter to Dayan written from London in February 1944 – was a further sign of Mitterrand's nascent political ambition.

54.   While in Algiers, Mitterrand was offered a post with the Consultative Assembly – which de Gaulle had set up to buttress his role as supreme representative of the nation and to prepare the transition to a provisional government – but turned it down.

55.   Mitterrand, *Ma part de vérité*, p. 23.

56.   Having appointed Mitterrand to head the prisoners' movement, de Gaulle had no reason to prevent him returning to take up his post. Michel Cailliau later acknowledged that 'if the General had given orders to keep Mitterrand in Algiers . . . he could not have left'. It was Cailliau himself, using his uncle's name, who persuaded his Gaullist friends to block Mitterrand's departure. According to Colonel Passy, Jacques Soustelle, whom de Gaulle had appointed to head the combined Gaullist and Giraudist special services, was among those whom Cailliau misled. As a result Mitterrand turned to the Giraudists, whom Cailliau could not influence, to get him a flight out.

57.   Mitterrand, François, *La paille et le grain*, Flammarion, 1975, pp. 164–6.

58.   Mitterrand arrived in Marrakesh on December 29. He reached London on January 2 from Prestwick, where Montgomery's plane had landed. Five days later he was given a new code name, 'Merchant', by the SOE in preparation for his return to France.

59.   Mitterrand thought Colonel Passy had used his influence with the SOE to arrange his return. The MGB502 was captained by Lieut.-Cmdr. Philip Williams, not, as Mitterrand remembered, by David Birkin (whose daughter, the singer, Jane Birkin, later made her home in France); David Birkin was the vessel's navigator.

60.   These details are from the account of John Motherwell, a Canadian officer who made an identical crossing exactly a month before.

61.   According to Pierre Péan, the 7.65mm automatic had one more surprise in store. Mitterrand, who had no use for weapons, gave it to Jean Munier, who was astonished to find that the first bullet in the chamber was a blank. Had he tried to use it to defend himself in a firefight, he would probably have been killed. A simple mistake? Or a parting shot from one of Cailliau's friends in London?

62.   They were hidden with Jean's brother, Georges Munier, at Levallois. Mitterrand had told Jean Warisse in London the previous November that Colonel

Buckmaster had promised to organise parachute drops of 60 containers of weaponry for the use of the prisoners' movement. They were to be delivered the following month at a dropping zone at St Laurent du Pont, just north of Grenoble, where Patrice Pelat was active. Whether Buckmaster followed through is not known.

63. After the liberation of Bergen-Belsen, Mauduit refused repatriation until his fellow prisoners could also return. Mitterrand sent Pelat and Finifter to bring him back to France, but when they arrived on May 11 they found he had died two days earlier after contracting pleurisy.

64. According to Charles Moulin, who had been in Stalag XIB with Cailliau, the decision to set up the CNPG was taken in June 1943 by a small group of communist prisoners from that camp. Four months later Cailliau asked a colleague, Jacques Bourgeois, to negotiate a merger between the CNPG and his own network. In a letter to de Gaulle on February 1 1944, he referred specifically to the communist movement as one of the three which were to come together. Mitterrand and Frenay, in letters to Cailliau on January 26 and February 16, mentioned only the fusion of *two* movements – Mitterrand's RNPG and Cailliau's MRPGD. De Gaulle was already aware of the CNPG's existence when they met in December, yet the collegial leadership which the General approved – Mitterrand, Bénet and Cailliau – did not include a communist representative, and when Frenay realised that a communist had been added he blamed Mitterrand for allowing it. The likeliest explanation is that both Frenay and de Gaulle had been led to believe that Cailliau's movement and the communists were already in the process of becoming a single organisation and therefore Cailliau would represent both.

65. Until early February 1944, Cailliau hoped to persuade de Gaulle to reverse the decision – for which Cailliau blamed Frenay – to appoint Mitterrand, Bénet and himself to a collegial leadership. In his letter to his uncle on February 1, which was not received until mid-March and to which the General did not deign to reply, he demanded that Pinot and Mitterrand be excluded from the new unified organisation; denounced Mitterrand as a Pétainist, a collaborator and a follower of Charles Maurras; declared that his own movement 'refuses to obey [the decision communicated by] Frenay'; and requested the General to arbitrate. After Frenay's telegram of February 16, he was forced to accept that de Gaulle's decision was final.

66. Michel Cailliau had initially proposed meeting at the Observatory, near the gardens where, fifteen years later, Mitterrand's career would risk coming to a premature end. Charles Moulin suggested a more discreet venue, the studio of the painter, Georges Goës, at 117, rue Notre-Dame-des-Champs.

67. In the autumn of 1943, Mitterrand had become an advisory member of the National Resistance Council's Social Commission, headed by Maxime Blocq-Masquart.

68. Védrine, Jean, *Dossier PG-Rapatriés 1940– 1945*, privately printed, Asnières, n.d. but 1981, Vol. 2, pp. 544–5. These extracts are from a tract issued in August 1944, shortly before the liberation of Paris. According to Védrine, the MNPGD had been urging its members to take up arms against the Germans since April that year.

69. Bénet wrote later that they had been detained for a month in Spain and reached Algiers only in mid-June. Mitterrand asked them to stay on to represent the MNPGD at the Consultative Assembly, but they refused because they wanted to get back to France. However Cailliau, still determined to thwart Mitterrand in any way he could, used his influence to prevent their return until after Paris had been liberated.

70. Munier originally said his repatriation was ordered by 'the authorities of the German Army' rather than by Hitler personally. Afterwards he amended his account to bring it into line with Mitterrand's version. Whatever signature was on the document, it was sufficiently impressive to make the German patrol back off.

71. Many aspects of this episode remain unclear. Marguerite Duras reworked her diary entries of that year into a semi-autobiographical book, *La Douleur*, published in English as *War: A Memoir*, in which the character named Rabier represents Delval. After the liberation of Paris, opinion within the MNPGD was divided about the guilt of Bourgeois and Médina. Philippe Dechartre and Georges Beauchamp believed they were innocent, and accused Duras of having spread false charges against them. Edgar Morin concluded, probably correctly, that Bourgeois had been careless but not a traitor, but Médina's case was more difficult. Mitterrand was also unsure. Other than circumstantial elements, the main grounds for suspecting them were that their apartment had been searched by the Gestapo and placed under seal shortly before the June 1 raids. In an interview in the 1990s, Médina told Pierre Péan that he found, when he returned there surreptitiously some days later, that photographs had been taken. Delval told an investigating magistrate in the autumn of 1944 that 'lists' containing complete information about the movement (not photographs, as Médina maintained) had been found by the two German agents who had carried out the search. At other times, Delval gave different versions. In *La Douleur*, Duras quoted him as saying there was 'a traitor' in Mitterrand's movement who had talked under threat of deportation. To Dionys Mascolo, in September 1944, he said there were two traitors in the movement. At his trial in December, he spoke again of 'one traitor'. Delval was executed in January 1945, having been convicted on the basis of testimony from Duras, who wrote later that she had wanted to see him dead (apart from Delval's role in her husband's arrest, her lover, Mascolo, was by then having a passionate affair with Delval's wife, Paulette: both women bore Mascolo's children a year later). Delval may have invented the story of 'traitors', initially as part of the game of seduction he

was playing with Duras in the summer of 1944, and later, at his trial, to minimise his own guilt: had they really existed, it would have been in his interest
to give a much more detailed account. But the claim that compromising documents were found in the two men's apartment is plausible. The Gestapo had
to have obtained its information from somewhere, and the chronology is
suggestive: as well as the two raids on June 1, the Gestapo's arrival the following
day at the apartment where Munier had hidden arms, the arrest on June 7 of
Steverlynck's contact, Jakub Scheimowitch, who had worked closely with
Médina, and the killing of Steverlynck on June 8, all came in quick succession
after the apartment had been searched. Médina left Paris, apparently without
telling his colleagues, shortly before the city was liberated and for a time disappeared from sight, leaving behind conflicting versions of what he had been
doing. When Péan questioned him in the 1990s, he found him 'ill at ease',
becoming more so as the conversation progressed. Perhaps the likeliest explanation is that Médina did indeed have papers at home which put the Gestapo
on Mitterrand's trail, but failed to tell his comrades exactly what they were,
making it a case of imprudence, exacerbated by concealment, rather than
outright betrayal.

72. Parodi held the rank of Commissioner in his own right as well as being
Secretary-General for the Liberated Territories pending the arrival of François
Billoux, who reached Paris with de Gaulle. Including Parodi, there were sixteen
secretaries-general.

73. Mitterrand and Wiesel, *Mémoire à deux voix*, p. 213.

74. *L'Homme libre*, August 22 1944, reprinted in Mitterrand, *Politique*, Vol. 1, pp.
18–19.

75. This speech, with de Gaulle's appeal of June 18 1940, is remembered in France
as one of the two emblematic addresses of the war years. The text is available
at http://www.charles-de-gaulle.org/pages/espace-pedagogique/le-point-sur/
les-textes-a-connaitre/discours-de-lrsquohotel-de-ville-25-aout-1944.php

76. In a speech in the 1980s at a banquet hosted by Jacques Chaban-Delmas,
Mitterrand asserted that Chaban, not de Chevigné, had been his companion
that night. He confessed later that the original version was correct. It had been
a case of not letting the facts get in the way of a good story.

77. Mitterrand wrote later: 'There was good humour and a kind of smile in his
remark. It could have been meant to say, "Hmmm. You really aren't easy to
get rid of!"'

78. Mitterrand, *La paille et le grain*, pp. 11–13.

79. On August 31. The official handover took place on September 5.

80. Frenay's account was written years later, when his relations with Mitterrand
had cooled. At the time he had no problem with Mitterrand's refusal, inviting
him and Maurice Pinot to dinner that night to discuss the Ministry's future.

4: Loose Ends, New Beginnings

1. Danielle liked to tell this story but Mitterrand himself denied it.

2. The description, Don Juan, is from André Rousselet.

3. Marie-Louise had seen Mitterrand again during the war, when he was with Marie-Claire Sarrazin, but their new relationship as 'intimate friends' appears to have dated from 1945, after his marriage to Danielle.

4. In the English marriage ceremony, the vow is 'for better *or* for worse'. The French, more realistically, say 'for better *and* for worse'.

5. The French historian, Robert Aron, in his three-volume *Histoire de l'épuration*, estimated that between 30,000 and 40,000 alleged collaborators were killed without judicial process after the war. It is now widely accepted that that figure is too high.

6. *L'Homme libre*, September 6 1944, reprinted in Mitterrand, *Politique*, Vol. 1, pp. 20–21.

7. Cartier provided the Resistance with 43 million francs (more than US $1 million, equivalent to $16 million at 2013 rates) in 1943–44.

8. Writing in *Libres* in February, Mitterrand sympathised with Frenay's 'solitude'. Six weeks later he paid tribute to 'the immense work of clearing up and reconstruction' that the Minister had undertaken.

9. *Libres*, May 28 1945.

10. Danielle Mitterrand, interview, March 19 2009. Elsewhere she wrote that her last moments of unblemished happiness were in May 1945.

11. Pascal Mitterrand was born on June 10 and died on September 17 1945.

12. In Neuilly the Mitterrands had had an apartment in the Boulevard Maurice Barrès at the northern end of the Bois de Boulogne. The move to rue Guynemer in the winter of 1946 provoked a short-lived scandal. The house had belonged to the Vatican before the war and during the Occupation had been requisitioned by the Germans. In 1945 it was taken over by a deportees' association led by Germaine Tillion and Geneviève de Gaulle. The following year the Vatican demanded it back with a view to dividing it into apartments for commercial letting. The association petitioned the government to intervene on its behalf. But either the government failed to state its case with sufficient vigour or the Vatican's agents turned a deaf ear. The association was forced to pack its bags, only to discover, a few weeks later, that among the new tenants were Henri Frenay and François Mitterrand. From there it was but a short step to insinuate that the deportees had been pushed out to make way for the ex-Minister and his colleague. For decades after, Gaullists held up the episode as an example of Mitterrand's lack of morality. The truth was simpler: the Vatican wished to recover its property and put it to commercial use in order to replenish Church funds. Could Frenay or Mitterrand have prevented that? The interim Prime Minister, Léon Blum, had been approached a month earlier and had been

unable, or had failed, to intervene. Was it an error of political judgement to rent an apartment which had come on to the market in such circumstances? In retrospect, the answer was yes. But morally there were no grounds for reproaching either Mitterrand or Frenay.

13. Bugeaud, Pierre, *Militant prisonnier de guerre*, l'Harmattan, 1990, p. 98.

14. Mitterrand and Benamou, *Mémoires interrompus*, pp. 155–6.

15. Mitterrand told Georges-Marc Benamou that, for the Lewis mission, the General's 'choice fell on me'. That was deliberately misleading. The government – whether in the person of de Gaulle or Frenay is unclear – sent a three-man delegation from the FNPG, two of whose members, Bénet and Bugeaud, also belonged to the Provisional Consultative Assembly, which exercised some of the functions of a parliament pending elections under a new constitution. The Americans liberated both Dachau and Landsberg on April 29. The French delegation visited on May 1.

16. A number of SS guards were killed by the prisoners and others by US troops before or, in a few cases, after they surrendered, which prompted a US army investigation. But that occurred in the first 24 hours after the camp was liberated.

17. 'What are principles? Banalities! Marvellous banalities!' (Mitterrand, speaking in April 1980).

18. Although Mitterrand had a law degree, he could not practise because he had not passed the *certificat d'aptitude à la profession d'avocat* which was necessary to join the Bar. In 1954 the law was changed to allow lawyers who had obtained their degree before 1941 to practise without the additional qualification.

19. Mitterrand, François, *Les Prisonniers de guerre devant la politique*, Editions du Rond Point, 1945, pp. 36–7.

20. This can be inferred from Mitterrand's letter to Georges Dayan in January 1946, in which he stated that he had 'almost stood' in the Vosges, and then went on to deliver a litany of complaints against the Socialist Party. The implication appears to be that he considered standing on a moderate left-wing list, which included Socialists. He does not say why he did not do so, but throughout his career he was adept at judging which seats were *'jouable'* (feasible) and which were not: in this case, presumably, he decided that the seat was not.

21. *Libres*, October 26 1944.

22. The party I have described as 'Christian Democrat' was the MRP, the 'People's Republican Movement', whose leading figure was Georges Bidault. The MRP was in the tradition of Le Sillon of Marc Sangnier, who had become the party's honorary president in 1944.

23. Philippe Dechartre, interviewed in the 1990s, spoke at length of Mitterrand's views about the Communists, quoting him as saying, during their meeting in Lyon in May 1943: 'It's true, I am not a commie. Far from it . . . But everything we are doing is for our country . . . [both for now and] for what will come

after, for rebuilding France, to enable us to have a role in the great political debate that will take place after the war. And we can do nothing there unless we take account of communist arithmetic.' Dechartre continued: '[That was] in '43. In '43! It was stupefying. The image of François saying that, in a completely relaxed manner but with absolute certainty, has always stayed with me. [To him] it was as ineluctable as an equinox.' The problem is that their conversation must have taken place later, because the issue that triggered it was Mitterrand's attitude to the communist CNPG, which was not formed until October 1943. It is plausible that Mitterrand spoke in these terms after his return from London in 1944. At that time he talked often of 'rebuilding France' and his remarks about 'communist arithmetic' were little different from what he wrote in *Les prisonniers de guerre* eighteen months later. However recognising the role of the Communists was one thing; working out how to deal with them was another. Nothing in his conversation with Dechartre or in his writings of this period indicated a willingness to unite with them. To describe his remarks as 'stupefying' was to read far more into them, with the benefit of knowing what happened in the succeeding decades, than they actually contained. In 1945, Mitterrand was on the same wavelength vis à vis the Communists as the rest of the political mainstream. As he told Dayan, he preferred to fight them.

24   The UDSR was initially conceived by Frenay – under the provisional name, 'Labour Union of Liberation' – as a means of uniting the whole of the non-communist Resistance in a broad-church political party. However the left wing of Frenay's group, led by d'Astier de la Vigerie and Pascal Copeau, split off to form a rival movement, and in practice the UDSR drew most of its strength from Combat and Franc-Tireur. It became the party of choice for moderate non-communists from the Resistance and obtained 31 seats in the 1945 elections.

25.   Each *département* contained several 'sectors', corresponding to constituencies. Votes were counted at the level of the *département*, but lists of candidates were established by sectors. The list on which Mitterrand figured represented the Rassemblement de gauches républicaines (RGR), or Rally of Left-wing Republicans, which despite its name catered to moderate right-wing voters. It included the Radical Party, the UDSR and five small Centre-Right or right-wing parties.

26.   Barrachin's list came fourth, which meant he retained his seat but by a narrow margin. Mitterrand's list received 25,580 votes, mainly from Barrachin's supporters.

27.   According to Danielle, Queuille advised him to seek a seat either in the Nièvre or the Vienne. She said he chose the former 'because the Vienne was dyed-in-the-wool conservative and in the Nièvre there was the legacy of the Resistance'. In later years, Mitterrand spoke of Queuille's patronage but never mentioned Barrachin, probably because a connection with the Radicals sat better with his subsequent career as a socialist.

28.   The five parties were the Republican Freedom Party or PRL (to which Barrachin

belonged); the Gaullist Union; the Peasant Party; the UDSR and the Radicals. His only right-wing rival was a Christian Democrat.

29.   Although Mitterrand secured one of the two seats the Communists had formerly held in the Nièvre, he did so, as Barrachin and Queuille had foreseen, not by winning communist votes but by uniting a substantial part of the right-wing electorate behind him. The other three seats went to a Communist, a Socialist and a Christian Democrat.

5: The Staircase of Power

1.   Blum was elected on December 12 1946 with the support of the UDSR after both the outgoing MRP Prime Minister, Georges Bidault, and the Communist Party leader, Maurice Thorez, had been unable to obtain a majority.

2.   The Commission on the Press was important both to the Radicals and to the UDSR, for which the defence of press freedom against the Communists and other interest groups was a key priority.

3.   The average life of governments in the Third Republic was 9 months and 15 days, compared with 6 months and 16 days in the Fourth Republic. One government in ten in the Third Republic remained in power for two years or more; in the Fourth Republic, fewer than one in ten lasted one year, the record of longevity being held by Guy Mollet, who held office for sixteen months in 1956–57.

4.   Georges Beauchamp, who had known Ramadier before the war, also promoted Mitterrand's candidacy.

5.   Paul Ramadier was invested by the National Assembly as *Président du Conseil* (Prime Minister) on January 21 1947 and his government was sworn in a week later.

6.   This was of course also true of Mitterrand's membership in the insurrectional government headed by Alexandre Parodi in August 1944, but that had been a provisional body.

7.   Moulin, Charles, *Mitterrand intime*, Albin Michel, 1982, pp. 73–4.

8.   By one account the dispute with the strikers was resolved after Mitterrand had warned Thorez at the previous week's Cabinet meeting, on January 29, that unless a solution were found he would order the police to evacuate the Ministry by force. Thorez's intervention is plausible and may have paved the way for Zimmermann's acceptance of the mediation committee which Mitterrand proposed.

9.   Auriol, Vincent, *Journal du Septennat*, Vol. 2, Armand Colin, 1974, p. 319 (September 2 1948).

10.   Mitterrand was named Secretary of State for Information in the government of the Radical, André Marie, which lasted 33 days from July to August 1948. He kept the same post, with a slightly different title, under Queuille.

11.   It is not clear exactly what the landowner, Baron Louis Thénard, hoped to obtain from Mitterrand. He owned the main newspaper in Dijon, *Le Bien Public*, and may have been seeking an interest in the *Journal du Centre* in the Nièvre, which was then controlled by the Socialists.

12.   In 1946, the Public Works Minister, Jules Moch, was dressed down by Auriol for using the familiar *tu* to the President. In 1981, the Defence Minister, Charles Hernu, committed an identical faux pas. As a minister, Mitterrand was also called to order on occasion. Auriol told Marcel Haedrich: 'Your friend Mitterrand intervenes all the time at Cabinet meetings and I am obliged to tell him: "Mr Mitterrand, you will speak when I ask you to do so."'

13.   Mali was at that time known as French Sudan and Bénin as Dahomey.

14.   Mitterrand, François, *Aux frontières de l'Union Française*, Julliard, 1953, reprinted in *Politique*, Vol. 1, pp. 67–8.

15.   The distinction was analogous to that between Pétainists and *maréchalistes*. But whereas the *maréchalistes* eventually abandoned the Marshal and, in most cases, joined the Resistance, the 'sentimental Gaullists' all subsequently rallied to the General's cause.

16.   According to Louis Deteix, in the autumn of 1950, Mitterrand and a group of friends met at Cluny to discuss how to speed up the adhesion of former PoWs to the party.

17.   The two right-wing parties backing Mitterrand this time were the RGR, the Rally of Left-wing Republicans, and the UIPRN, the Union of Independents, Peasants and National Republicans. Although the names were different, they covered the same part of the political spectrum as the right-wing parties which had supported him five years before.

18.   Under the Fourth Republic, the holding of legislative elections did not automatically entail the government's resignation. In March 1951, Pleven had been replaced as Prime Minister by Henri Queuille, who maintained essentially the same Cabinet, including Mitterrand as Minister of Overseas Territories. After the elections on June 17, Queuille's government had remained in office, unaffected by the changes in parliament, until July 10, when it lost a vote of confidence. Pleven was then asked to form a new government and was sworn in a month later, on August 11 1951.

19.   Mitterrand had been sniping at two of Pleven's allies in the Party – the Secretary-General, Joseph Lanet, and an influential conservative, General Chevance-Bertin, who had estates in Africa and supported the settlers' views.

20.   In 1946, the party won 23 seats with four affiliates; in 1951, 13 seats with five affiliates. The RDA joined the UDSR group in January 1952. In the late 1940s, when the 'dedicated Gaullists' were preparing their departure, the UDSR's parliamentary strength fell below 14, the minimum required to form a group, and it had to affiliate briefly with the Radicals in order to maintain its membership of parliamentary commissions.

21.   In the winter of 1946, when France was still hesitating over whether to seek a military or a political solution in Indochina, de Gaulle had strongly advised Léon Blum, who was interim Prime Minister, to support the High Commissioner, Admiral Thierry d'Argenlieu, who advocated the use of force. Three months later d'Argenlieu was dismissed for insubordination. By then it was too late: the war was under way. The historian, Georgette Elgey, has described it as one of de Gaulle's worst misjudgements.

22.   The text is available at http://www.cvce.eu/obj/Address_given_by_Winston_Churchill_at_the_Congress_of_Europe_in_The_Hague_7_May_1948-en-58118da1-af22-48c0-bc88-93cda974f42c.html

23.   The Western European Union (WEU) was created by Britain, France and the Benelux countries as a mutual defence organisation two months before the Congress at The Hague in May 1948. The treaty was modified in October 1954, when Italy and Germany joined. The organisation was dissolved in 2011.

24.   Among those helping Mendès that day was Edgar Faure, a fellow Radical whom he had known since they had been law students together. Two and a half years earlier, Faure, who had been invested as Prime Minister and had named Mitterrand his Minister of State, was about to announce the list of the new Cabinet to the press when Mitterrand stopped him and suggested that he look at it again. Sure enough, when Faure redid his calculations, he found that the Radicals and the CNIP were over-represented. Another minister who was present, Édouard Bonnefous, remembered how impressed Faure had been by Mitterrand's mastery of the subject.

25.   The list which Mitterrand helped to draw up named six Radicals to the Cabinet (plus three junior ministers); five Gaullists (plus four); two UDSR (plus two); two Christian Democrats (plus one); and one CNIP (plus two).

26.   In July 1950, Auriol considered Mitterrand as a possible Prime Minister but ruled him out, presumably on the grounds that he was too young and lacking in experience. Three years later, when Mitterrand resigned from the government of Joseph Laniel in September 1953, in protest against its policies in North Africa, he was already seen as destined for higher things. His colleague, Édouard Bonnefous, wrote: 'If [next time round] a Socialist would be unable to get enough support to head a left-wing majority, might it not be possible to call on someone from the UDSR? In that case, François Mitterrand could legitimately aspire to . . . play a leading role'.

27.   The demonstrators who died had been carrying banners calling for Algerian independence.

28.   According to Robert Mitterrand, the alleged discovery of the arms stockpile and the printing of the tracts were among the reasons which Baylot gave Mitterrand that week to justify banning the July 14 demonstration.

29.   Mendès was also kept awake all night by telephone calls, including one from President Coty, urging him not to remove Baylot. He reportedly told Mitterrand

next morning: 'I wasn't sure whether you were right to want Mr Baylot's departure. Now, after all these interventions on his behalf, I know you were right. Do it straight away.'

30. Mitterrand, Robert, *Frère de quelqu'un*, Robert Laffont, 1988, p. 306.

31. The Cabinet met on July 10, a Saturday. Baylot was dismissed the following Monday, July 12.

32. According to Robert Mitterrand, Mendès cited pressure of work when he tried to explain to Mitterrand afterwards why he had failed to inform him of the accusations against him.

33. The boutique rejoiced in the name *La Colombe Blanche* ('The White Dove').

34. When the case came to court in 1956, Mitterrand acknowledged having 'a doubt' about the nature of Baylot's role.

35. An independent right-wing MP, Jean-Louis Vigier, was told by Dides of Mitterrand's alleged involvement at the same time as Fouchet. Vigier informed Coty and selected journalists.

36. *Journal officiel*, 3 December 1954.

37. Pierre Nicolay, then Mitterrand's Chief of Staff, remembered Mitterrand being 'sickened' by Mendès's conduct. Pierre Charpy, who saw him often during this period, described him as 'completely demoralised'. Thirty years later, in 1983, Mitterrand told Catherine Nay: 'He betrayed me'. In the last years of his life, in the 1990s, Mitterrand played down the importance of the rift, telling François Stasse that 'it didn't count for much' and Georges-Marc Benamou that claims that he had resented Mendès's attitude were 'false'.

38. Thus, on September 19, the day after Dides's arrest, when Mendès visited the Nièvre to inaugurate a war memorial to members of the Resistance, he spoke affectionately of his 'good friend, François Mitterrand'. Six weeks later, in a speech to the UDSR, Mitterrand returned the compliment, praising the Prime Minister's 'talent and authority'. In December, Mendès spoke in parliament of the 'esteem, affection and confidence' he bore Mitterrand, and sent him personal letters of encouragement during the crisis. Still more significant was Mendès's defence of Mitterrand during the Observatory Affair five years later.

39. There was a curious coda. In January 1955, Dides sent André Dubois, Baylot's successor as chief of police, a letter retracting all his allegations against Mitterrand and acknowledging the Minister's 'patriotic sentiments'. For reasons that were never fully explained, Dubois did not inform Mitterrand but instead transmitted the letter to Mendès France, who regarded it as insincere because it was written at a time when Dides, who had been suspended, was trying to win reinstatement. In another disastrous misjudgement, the Prime Minister decided not to make it public. Had it been published, the arguments of the Right would have been exposed as hollow. Mitterrand did not learn of its existence until many years later.

40. Mitterrand also thought it possible that the Gaullists had mounted the affair in an attempt to destabilise the Fourth Republic.

41. Georgette Elgey, whose research on this period is unequalled, speculated that Dides might initially have reported the leaks in good faith after having himself been deceived by Baranès. Roland Dumas, who represented Mitterrand when he gave evidence at the trial in 1956; André Rousselet, who worked with Jean-Paul Martin in Mitterrand's private office; Baylot's successor, André Dubois; and even Pierre Mendès France, all, to varying extents, shared that view, which Mitterrand himself angrily rejected. If they were right, it would mean there was no political conspiracy at the outset, merely a series of misunderstandings which created a muddle which others subsequently exploited for their own political ends. The theory is beguiling: muddle is much more common in politics than conspiracy. The problem is that it ignores two salient and irrefutable facts. Firstly, when Baranès gave Dides information about the leak of the Defence Council meeting in May, the latter immediately reported it to the then Interior Minister, a conservative Radical politician named Léon Martinaud-Duplat; but when the second leak occurred, he bypassed his own minister and went to Fouchet instead. He claimed to have done so because he thought Mitterrand might be the leaker, even though he must have known that to be false, or, at least, extremely improbable, since the leak in May had occurred at a time when Mitterrand had no government post. Why did he denounce a man whom he knew was almost certainly innocent? Secondly, and even more damning, in his conversation with Fouchet, Dides kept silent about the leak in May. The only logical reason for him not to mention it was that he had an ulterior motive.

Elgey suggested that he might have approached Fouchet because Jean-Paul Martin, representing Mitterrand, refused to see him when he sought a meeting with the Minister after Baylot's dismissal, which had led to the disbanding of the anti-communist 'intelligence network' which Dides had created. But that is standing chronology on its head. Baylot was fired on July 12; Dides had approached Fouchet ten days beforehand. On July 2, Dides had no obvious reason to wish to harm Mitterrand, absent a political motive.

There remains, therefore, a prima facie case that the attack was mounted for political (or, conceivably, unexplained personal) reasons. Whether it was the work of Dides alone, of Dides and Baylot, or of a larger group, may never be known. But once it was under way, it was exploited to the hilt by right-wing politicians who saw it as a bludgeon with which to beat the government. As with most political 'affairs' in France, the initial cause was less important than the use that was made of it.

6: Requiem for Empire

1. *Journal officiel*, June 4 1953.
2. The conference was to have been held in June 1954.

3. The FLN's decision to launch armed struggle, as Mitterrand later acknowledged, was a direct consequence of the French defeat at Dien Bien Phu. If the Viet Minh could outfight the French army, Ben Bella and his colleagues reasoned, there was no reason why Arabs could not do so too.

4. On October 30 Mitterrand sent instructions to the Governor-General to carry out 'the necessary arrests'. By the time the order reached Algiers, the attacks had already occurred.

5. In the three months to February 1955, 67 civilians and 46 soldiers died, almost all of them Algerians. The strength of the armed forces during the same period rose from 57,200 to more than 80,000 men. Naval and air force units were also reinforced.

6. *Journal officiel*, November 12 1954.

7. The reforms were discussed by the Cabinet on January 5 1955. Mendès France's government fell on February 6.

8. 'For a political leader,' Mitterrand said, 'there is only one ambition: to rule. Those who aspire merely to be Under-Secretaries of State are not political figures, they are just bit players.'

9. *France Observateur*, January 13 1955.

10. He was quoted as saying: 'During the parliamentary campaign of 1956, everyone thought I was tired or even ill. In fact, I was suffocated by rage that I was still not Prime Minister.' One may wonder whether he spoke quite so bluntly, but he certainly had high hopes of being invited to form a government. Whatever the cause of his malaise, it was serious enough for Georges Dayan's brother, Jean, a doctor, to have to give him an injection through the seat of his trousers before he mounted the tribune to speak at election meetings.

11. Under the Fourth Republic, the Justice Minister was normally second in order of protocol after the Prime Minister. As Interior Minister under Mendès France, he had ranked third in the Cabinet.

12. The rebels killed 123 men, women and children at Philippeville, of whom 71 were French nationals, the remainder, alleged 'collaborators'. By the French army's account, 1,273 Arabs died in the reprisals. The FLN put the figure at 12,000.

13. The journalist, Françoise Giroud, who saw Mitterrand often at that time, said he realised that by signing the decree authorising military courts he had made his position untenable but he could see no good way out.

14. Malye, François and Stora, Benjamin, *François Mitterrand et la guerre d'Algérie*, Calmann-Lévy, 2010, pp. 116 & 119.

15. Mitterrand did protest, however, when a few days later the police searched the home of a distinguished professor, Henri Marrou, who had attacked Mollet's policies in *Le Monde*.

16. François Stasse quoted members of his entourage describing him as 'sullen and ill at ease' during this period.

17. 'Speech to the USDR Congress', October 27 1956. Mitterrand's position on Algerian self-government had begun to change shortly before Suez, largely because of pressure from within the party. But it was a slow and reluctant conversion. Not until June 1957 did he fully embrace the idea that Algeria should be self-governing,

18. Bourgès-Maunoury responded that 'to dishonour those who have the task of carrying out military operations . . . is infamous'. To demonstrate his willingness to punish military abuses, he summoned the commander-in-chief in Algeria, General Salan, to Paris in April and asked him to put an end to brutal interrogations and the pillaging of Arab shops. Salan replied: 'If the political authorities think we have carried out [our work] badly, they have only to relieve us of police duties.' After a long silence, Bourgès-Maunoury told him to keep on as before. The arm-wrestling between Bourgès and Mitterrand continued. Later that month, the Defence Minister asked Mitterrand to help stop the 'campaigns of denigration' against the army, which, he said, were being orchestrated by the FLN, a none too subtle hint that the Justice Ministry was playing into the hands of the rebels. When Reliquet obtained Robert Lacoste's agreement to try the most notorious offenders, Bourgès-Maunoury objected that 'the complaints against the soldiers are unfounded'.

19. Even within the confines of the Cabinet, Mitterrand appears to have said little. Gaston Defferre claimed that he denounced the use of torture, but other ministers had no memory of his having done so.

20. Both *Le Monde* and *France Observateur* listed Mitterrand as among the possible candidates for the prime ministership, and *l'Express*, on June 7 1957, wrote that he was not merely a possible but the best candidate for the post. Édouard Bonnefous remembered Mitterrand's 'great disappointment' at being passed over.

21. The sticking point was apparently Bourgès's insistence on retaining Robert Lacoste as governor.

22. Bidault abandoned his attempt to form a government on April 22. Mitterrand's meeting with Coty must therefore have taken place on April 23. The President approached Pleven later the same day. In subsequent accounts, Mitterrand conflated their discussion with a second exchange at the end of May, after it was already clear that Coty would name de Gaulle.

23. Mitterrand wrote: 'The accusations being made against me find an echo at the Elysée . . . [Pleven] has been called to help resolve the crisis, while I myself am marked with suspicion.'

24. Coty vouchsafed this information to Roger Duchet, the Secretary-General of the CNIP, the main right-wing party, to which the President also belonged. Duchet, although hostile to Mitterrand, speculated in his memoirs that, had Mitterrand been appointed, he 'would no doubt have named a Cabinet of a new style' and the Fourth Republic might have evolved differently.

25. Lacouture, Jean, *Mitterrand: une histoire de Français*, Vol. 1, Seuil, 1998, p. 193. The meeting took place on the morning of May 31. See also *Le Quotidien de Paris*, October 26 1977 (reprinted in Mitterrand, François, *Politique*, Vol. 2, Fayard, 1981, p. 9), where Mitterrand alluded to what appears to have been another, unpublicised meeting with the President, on or around May 10, at which, he claimed, Coty had again raised the possibility of his forming a government. (According to Mitterrand, Coty said to him when they met on May 31: 'I told you three weeks ago that I was going to designate you.') That would be consistent with the President's remarks to Roger Duchet. But no other source confirms a meeting in the second week of May and, speaking twenty years afterwards, Mitterrand may have confused the sequence of events.

26. Both Coty's assistant, Francis de Baecque, and René Pleven took the view that if Coty did not call on Mitterrand to form a government, it was because the President doubted his fitness to be Prime Minister. Others blamed the influence of Coty's Military Adviser, General Ganeval. Mitterrand himself, wrongly, accused Guy Mollet for blocking his nomination.

27. Not only was Felix Gaillard two years younger than Mitterrand, but following his fall, Coty had invited three other Radicals, René Billières – who had been a junior minister only once – Jean Berthoin and 36-year-old Maurice Faure to try to form a government. All had declined.

28. Mitterrand himself later recognised this. In his closing speech to the UDSR congress on February 1 1959, he accused the former President of bearing the primary responsibility for blocking change, leading the system to collapse. The 'decadence' of the Fourth Republic, he said, was 'situated first and foremost at the pinnacle of the State'.

29. In *Paris-Presse* at the end of February, Georgette Elgey had written that de Gaulle was planning to return, 'preferably by statutory legal means'.

30. Elgey, Georgette, *Histoire de la 4ème République, 5ème Partie: La Fin – La République des Tourmentes, troisième tome, 1954–1959*, Fayard, 2008, p. 773.

31. De Gaulle admitted as much to Pflimlin. When the Prime Minister urged him to disavow the sedition, he refused to do so, saying, 'after all, these people want things to change. They think the [present] regime is bad. I cannot say they are wrong.' If he spoke out before this change occurred, he said, 'I will lose to no purpose all the credit I might have'.

32. At his press conference of May 19, de Gaulle said: 'I understand very well the attitude and the action of the military command in Algeria . . . The Army . . . is normally the instrument of the State and it should remain so. But for that, there has to be a State.'

33. On the morning of May 27, de Gaulle's emissary, the same Colonel Paillole whose services had helped Mitterrand to leave Morocco with Montgomery in January 1944, asked Massu to postpone the operation, which had been scheduled for the following day. However, that evening the Socialist group in parliament

voted to oppose de Gaulle's investiture. On May 28, at the General's request, Salan's Chief of Staff, General André Dulac, who had flown from Algiers during the night, arrived at Colombey to discuss the situation. According to Dulac, after hearing a detailed briefing on 'Resurrection', de Gaulle gave the plan his approval, insisting, however, that within a few days of the operation being completed he must be 'called in as an arbiter, a man of reconciliation'. Dulac quoted de Gaulle as saying: 'It would have been immensely preferable that my return to office take place by a [regular] process . . . But we must save the ship.' That night, de Gaulle met the President of the National Assembly, André le Troquer, who reiterated the Socialist group's rejection of his candidature. 'If parliament follows you,' the General replied, 'there will be nothing else for me to do but let you explain yourself to the parachutists while I nurse my sorrows in my retirement.' 'Resurrection' was finally launched on the afternoon of May 29, but, according to the Air Force Commander, General Jouhaud, it was countermanded in view of Coty's speech after the aircraft had already taken off from Algiers. Significantly, de Gaulle had written to his son that morning: 'According to the information I have, action is imminent from the South towards the North . . . It is infinitely probable that nothing more can be done under the present regime.' The best reading of this dramatic and extremely confused period is that, while de Gaulle did not want the military to intervene, he had decided to resign himself to it if there were no other choice.

34. Mitterrand, *Ma part de vérité*, pp. 39–40.

35. Mitterrand also told Charles Hernu that they faced twenty years out in the cold. He made a 'very brief' journey to the Nièvre with Jean Pinel on Friday, May 30, having been in Paris on May 28 and 29, and returned in the early hours of Saturday, in time to meet Coty that morning and de Gaulle at 3 p.m. According to Pinel, Mitterrand made his decision to vote against de Gaulle on the evening of May 30. Mitterrand himself dated it to the afternoon of May 29. He probably revisited the issue constantly throughout this period.

36. In March 1981, Mitterrand told Pinel: 'You remember I told you it would take twenty years. I was wrong. It will have been twenty-three.'

37. There are three extant versions of Mitterrand's remarks: Duveau's notes, taken at the time, cited in Giesbert, Franz-Olivier, *Mitterrand: une vie*, Seuil, 1996, p. 179; Mitterrand's account to Georges-Marc Benamou, thirty-five years later (in *Mémoires interrompus*, pp. 180–90); and an article in *Combat* on October 22 1962, which contains no direct quotation. This extract conflates the first two.

38. *Journal officiel*, June 1 1958.

39. Mitterrand's friend, Charles Moulin, remembered him saying that in the Berry, the area of central France from which his paternal grandparents hailed, the local peasants were always puzzled when a traveller stopped to ask the way.

'In our country,' they said, 'you don't start out on a journey unless you know where you are going and how to get there.'

40.   Jean Pinel, to whom Mitterrand had predicted that the Gaullists would remain in power for the next twenty years, quoted him as having said at the same time 'I'll do three things: I will bring the Communists down to 10 per cent; I will "hang a saucepan" on to the Right; and I will govern from the centre.' The goal of bringing communist support down to 10 per cent was not new: he had said the same thing to Georges Beauchamp in 1947. 'Hanging a saucepan on to the Right' described perfectly the way Mitterrand would use the National Front of Jean-Marie Le Pen to bite into the electorate of the mainstream right-wing parties after 1986, but there was no way he could have known that in 1958. If Pinel's memory was accurate, Mitterrand presumably had in mind some other means of eroding the Right's support, but it is not clear what. The one prediction that was not realised was that he would 'govern from the centre'. When he became President in 1981, Mitterrand governed from the Left.

41.   Lefranc, Pierre, *Avec qui vous savez*, Plon, 1979, p. 129.

42.   The concept of the 'reserved domain', initially called the 'presidential sector', was first put forward in September 1959 by Jacques Chaban-Delmas, at that time President of the National Assembly.

7: Crossing the Desert

1.   'Speech to the National Council of the UDSR', May 18 1957, in CHAN, carton 412AP15 [2UDSR15 Dossier 2].

2.   The General proposed that a vote be taken four years after the fighting 'ended' – that being defined as meaning fewer than 200 deaths from terrorist attacks a year.

3.   Both Mitterrand and Bourgès-Maunoury had voted against de Gaulle's return to power and against the new constitution. When Pesquet met Bourgès, he identified himself as a supporter of 'French Algeria' and told him that a wave of assassinations of prominent Gaullists and Fourth Republic leaders – including de Gaulle, Debré, Chaban Delmas and others – was imminent. He had come to warn him to take precautions, he added, because he approved of Bourgès's anti-Gaullist stance. There was no discussion of faking an assassination attempt. Pesquet afterwards minimised the importance of their meeting, claiming, untruthfully, that he had wanted to see Bourgès on a matter unrelated to the political situation. Why Pesquet sought out the former Prime Minister has never been satisfactorily explained. The most plausible theory is that it was a trial run to see how a prominent politician, and the authorities, would react to a specific threat against named individuals. But it is also possible that it was

a separate initiative, relating instead to some other projected machination which was afterwards abandoned.

4. In his speech, Mitterrand alluded to the fact that the government had concealed for two weeks Bourgès-Maunoury's meeting with Pesquet – a dissimulation which, if not ordered by Debré, certainly had his approval. 'For my part,' Mitterrand told the Senate, 'I will not qualify the government's omission [to inform the magistrate] as "contempt of court", because I, unlike [Mr Debré], do not make accusations before I have made enquiries.'

5. That day Debré told reporters: 'Mr Mitterrand lied, yet again.' A week later he offered a different version: it was true that they had met, he said, but he had not requested the meeting and it had taken place at the Senate, not the Ministry of Justice. He repeated this under oath three years later at the trial of General Salan, stating that in the course of their discussion Mitterrand 'reassured me and told me that he would easily dispose of these accusations'. In his memoirs, written in the 1980s, he reverted to his initial denial, insisting that no meeting had ever taken place.

6. According to Pesquet, Adolphe Touffait, the prosecutor for the *département* of the Seine, which included Paris, was a family friend. By his account, Touffait, allegedly at the request of Jean-Louis Tixier-Vignancour, designated André Braunschweig, who had served in the army with Pesquet in 1939, to be the investigating magistrate.

7. If it is accepted that Debré's motive was not the Bazooka Affair, the only other possible reason for him to have set Pesquet on to Mitterrand would have been the desire to humiliate a political opponent. But Mitterrand, in 1959, at a time when the government was facing enormous problems in Algeria, was hardly important enough to warrant such attention. He was a gadfly, but no more. Moreover, if Debré was manipulating Pesquet with a view to discrediting the opposition, why was Bourgès-Maunoury – a man who was in no way a threat to the government – the initial target? Such a scenario is too improbable to take seriously.

8. More than ten years later, President Georges Pompidou declared an amnesty for this and other cases, which finally brought the proceedings to a close.

9. Pesquet told Alain Simon, who by 1965 had replaced Braunschweig, that Tixier-Vignancour had manipulated him throughout. Later he claimed that while Tixier had been involved in the plot, the principal authors were Debré and his close aide, Christian de la Malène. Pesquet's variable-geometry accusations, each more improbable than the one before, read like pulp fiction. Where Baranès, the initiator of the 'Leaks Affair', was a confidence trickster primarily interested in money, Pesquet was a mythomaniac. But his claim that Tixier had been the mastermind is plausible.

10. There were other troubling coincidences. Tixier's name had been cited in the 'Leaks Affair' in 1954. Another protagonist of that period, the former police

commissioner, Jean Dides, knew that the 'assassination attempt' had been faked on Tuesday, October 20, at least 36 hours before Pesquet made it public. So did Jean-Marie Le Pen, a former parachutist in Algeria who had known Pesquet when they were both Poujadist MPs. The first public reference to Pesquet's role appeared in *l'Aurore* on the morning of Wednesday, October 21, which meant the newspaper must have had the information at the latest the previous evening. Pesquet testified before Braunschweig on Thursday, October 22, and gave a press conference the same day.

11. The term 'Young Turk' was originally applied to those, including Mendès France, who tried to rejuvenate the Radical Party in the 1930s. Hernu and others of the succeeding generation sought to do the same in the 1950s. Mitterrand contributed to the journal, *Le Jacobin*, which Hernu launched in 1951, but the two men became close only after 1959.

12. André Rousselet and Charles Moulin remembered a similar, smaller meeting having been held in a hotel at the Place de la République in Paris some time before the gathering at Poigny.

13. *L'Express*, January 11 1996.

14. When Queen Elizabeth II visited Paris in 1957, Danielle was commissioned to undertake the gilded leather binding for a presentation volume commemorating her stay.

15. Robert Schneider, in a carefully researched account of Mitterrand's family, claimed that in the late 1950s Danielle had told François that she wanted a divorce, but that he had refused for fear that it would harm his career. When I asked her about Schneider's assertion, she answered immediately: 'Oh, no. No. I haven't read that book, but I never said that to [François]. Nor did he ever ask me [for a divorce].' Given the openness with which she addressed their decision to 'live separate lives' and the fact that the only two people who knew for certain what was said between them were Danielle and François themselves, I see no reason to disbelieve her.

16. He wrote after his return that, whatever precautions the Chinese authorities might have taken, 'it would be inconceivable that, if a murderous famine existed in the interior provinces, there would be no sign of it in the big cities and the over-populated countryside of the eastern seaboard. No matter how powerful the Communist Party may be, it is incapable of keeping a starving population behind some latter-day Great Wall in order to deceive the guests it invites . . . While I saw nowhere euphoria or prosperity, nor did I see anywhere physiological misery and the horrible marks of hunger.' Twenty years later, after Mao's death, China acknowledged that the famine had indeed claimed tens of millions of lives, which the Communist Party had hidden from foreign visitors.

17. Years later, Anne suggested calling their daughter Pascale. Mitterrand rejected the name but did not explain why. Afterwards she learnt by chance from a

mutual friend of his first son's death. Mitterrand never spoke of it to her, but when, in 1977, his first granddaughter was born, she was named Pascale in his memory.

18.   Lacouture, Jean, *De Gaulle*, Vol. 3, Seuil, 1986, p. 167.

8: De Gaulle Again

1.   John Clark of the Labour Party's International Department recognised early on the importance of the French clubs and became friendly with Charles Hernu. In the early 1960s, he organised a visit to London by a delegation including Hernu and Mitterrand, who spoke at a conference attended by Labour Party luminaries at the House of Commons. The President of the LCR, Ludovic Tron, was one of the few senators who had voted against lifting Mitterrand's parliamentary immunity in November 1959.

2.   *Journal officiel (Sénat)*, July 17 1962.

3.   A number of presidential candidates, including Mitterrand in 1981, promised constitutional revisions, but the only changes to date were made in 2000, when Jacques Chirac reduced the presidential term from seven years to five, and in 2008, when Nicolas Sarkozy managed, by the slimmest of margins – a single vote – to pass a series of largely symbolic measures whose stated purpose was to make the constitution more modern.

4.   The Council's ruling against the Military Court caused, in its own words, '[such] very strong tension [with] General de Gaulle . . . that it seemed for a moment to be threatened, if not in its existence, at least in its role and attributions'. Likewise after Gaston Monnerville had spoken out against de Gaulle's constitutional revision, the General refused to shake hands with him, banned him from visiting the Elysée and ordered the government to keep its dealings with the Senate to a minimum until Monnerville stepped down, six years later. Such pettiness did not enhance de Gaulle's reputation, but it was part of the package that made up his character, just as duplicity was part of Mitterrand's. In another example involving the Council of State, the Culture Minister, André Malraux, had tried in 1959 to dismiss the director of the national theatre, the *Comédie Française*. When the Council ruled the dismissal illegal, Malraux changed the theatre's statutes and tried again to dismiss the director, only to be told that his actions were once again illegal, because he was 'trying to allow the government to escape the authority of the courts'.

5.   De Gaulle underwent a successful prostate operation in April 1964.

6.   The General's references to mortality were legion, from his angry retort to Mitterrand in May 1958, 'You want my death!' to his proposal on September 20 1962 that 'if death or illness interrupt my mandate' the next President

should be elected by direct suffrage. They became almost obsessive after the death of his brother, Pierre, to whom he had been extremely close, in 1959.

7. The text of Saint-Just's speech was posted up in towns all over France. He was guillotined with Robespierre and other Jacobins in 1794.

8. Mitterrand, François, *Le Coup d'État permanent*, Plon, 1964, pp. 29–31 & 47.

9. Ibid., pp. 153–7.

10. Passeron, André, *De Gaulle parle, 1962– 1966*, Fayard, 1966, p. 92.

11. Mitterrand, *Le Coup d'État permanent*, pp. 74 & 106.

12. *Journal officiel*, April 24 1964.

13. Franz-Olivier Giesbert, whose study of this period is the most complete to date, has raised the intriguing question of whether Mitterrand was already in 1958 looking ahead to the possibility of a United Front between the Communists and the non-communist Left. There were certainly straws in the wind pointing in that direction. Maurice Thorez had been calling since May 1958 for a government of union with communist participation. That same year the extreme Right – as ever! – accused Mitterrand of favouring such an arrangement. The avant-garde of the non-communist Left was also discussing, in coded language, the possibility of a Union of the Left. Moreover Mitterrand's puzzling conversation with René Coty on May 31 1958 would be much more understandable if Coty's question had been, 'Will you accept communist *ministers*?' However, every version Mitterrand ever gave of their discussion referred not to ministers but to *votes*. All that can be said is that there is no convincing evidence that Mitterrand was thinking in 'United Front' terms before 1962. Most of the elements which would eventually lead him to an alliance with the Communists were already present in 1958. But he seems not to have reached a firm conclusion until three or four years later.

14. *Courrier de la Nièvre*, September 28 1963.

15. Claude Estier recalled Mitterrand telling him at the beginning of 1965, when Defferre's campaign was already faltering, that he was thinking of standing as a candidate that year. Mitterrand himself wrote afterwards that 'since 1962, that is to say, since it was decided that the election of the President of the Republic would be conducted by universal suffrage, I knew that I would be a candidate. When? How? I could not foretell.'

16. Mitterrand first sounded out the Party's intentions in June through a communist lawyer, Jules Borker, who was a member of Colloques Juridiques, a political club of which Charles Hernu was Secretary-General. Other contacts followed in July and August, notably between Claude Estier and Waldeck Rochet.

17. Mitterrand wrote later that, before announcing his candidature, he had received assurances from both Maurice Faure and Daniel Mayer that they would not stand against him. Mayer came out publicly in support of Mitterrand on

September 25. Faure's name was still being mentioned as one of Guy Mollet's preferred candidates at the beginning of October.

18. Unknown to Mollet, Mitterrand had had a meeting with Pinay on September 15, arranged by his brother, Robert, at which he persuaded the former Prime Minister that, if he stood, he risked being eliminated in the first round.

19. *Le Nouvel Observateur*, October 27 1965.

20. Mendès's son-in-law and biographer, François Stasse, attributed his reluctance to work actively for Mitterrand's election – other than by giving verbal support, most notably in his interview with the *Nouvel Observateur* – to the fact that Mitterrand had no clear programme and that, in Mendès's view, policies were more important than personalities. That may have been a factor. But was it sufficient to explain his extraordinary behaviour between the two rounds of voting, when he refused to attend Mitterrand's campaign rallies on the pretext of previous engagements? Twenty years later, long after Mendès's death, that still rankled with Mitterrand. Laurence Soudet, who had worked with Mendès for almost a decade before joining Mitterrand's campaign team, insisted that, despite the two men's differences, Mendès was 'totally behind [him] in 1965. Totally . . . He told me: "Work for him full-time." All of Mendès's team, or at least [most of it], worked on the campaign.' But apparently, for Mendès, putting all his resources at Mitterrand's disposal and campaigning personally were two different things.

21. Mitterrand, *Ma part de vérité*, p. 47.

22. According to Laurence Soudet, the office in the rue du Louvre had originally belonged to the UDSR but after the party collapsed in the early 1960s, Mitterrand had sublet it to her to produce Mendès's journal, *Les Cahiers de la République*. Mitterrand took it back for the duration of the campaign.

23. Alain Peyrefitte, the Information Minister, had tried hard to prevent it, telling the heads of French television and the radio stations, all of which were under state control, that 'the General, considering that he already has historical legitimacy, has decided not to campaign on radio or television . . . In order to maintain equality of chances, you are asked not to broadcast the voices of any of the other candidates.' Threatened with a strike, Peyrefitte backed down. Each candidate was allowed two hours of air time. Georges Fillioud, then editor-in-chief of the radio station, Europe 1, was among those who rejected Peyrefitte's proposal. After the election he was fired on the instructions of de Gaulle's communications adviser, Pierre Lefranc.

24. At a Cabinet meeting on December 8, de Gaulle acknowledged: 'I was mistaken. It was I, and I alone, who confused election and referendum.'

25. There could have been no greater contrast with the attitude of Pierre Mendès France, who in 1954 had announced that he would refuse the Communists' support, even if they voted for him, because he disagreed with their policies. Mitterrand said afterwards he felt Mendès had been wrong: the Communists

had asked for nothing in return, so why reject their votes? His attitude to the extreme Right in 1965 was the same. Jean Lacouture wondered whether he lost more votes from 'democrats' – meaning those from the Centre and the Centre-Left – than he gained from Tixier's supporters, but the results appeared to show that he did not. The episode gave André Malraux the occasion for a quip at Mitterrand's expense, deploring that he was 'the candidate of the three Lefts, one of which is on the extreme Right'.

26.   The 'seven fundamental options' of Mitterrand's campaign, announced at his press conference on September 21 1965, included 'genuine democracy; expansion and progress; the building of the European Community; social justice; and basic freedoms'. It would be hard to be more bland.

27.   In the parliamentary elections in 1962, left-wing candidates had received 8.15 million votes, equivalent to 10.2 million in 1965 had the abstention rates been the same; in 1967, the total would be 10 million with a slightly lower turnout, equivalent to 10.4 million with the same abstention rate. Mitterrand in 1965 received 7.7 million in the first round (and 10.6 million in the second round, when he benefited from the votes of the anti-Gaullist Centre and Right). The first-round shortfall, 2.5 or 2.7 million, or three million by an alternative calculation based on individual constituencies, represented the number of left-wing voters who stayed at home, cast blank votes or supported de Gaulle. The last group were estimated at 500–800,000.

28.   To this end Mitterrand proposed the creation of a shadow Cabinet on the British model to provide spokesmen who would counter Gaullist policies in parliament and put forward alternatives. Guy Mollet on behalf of the Socialists and René Billères for the Radicals reluctantly agreed on condition that they had the final say over the naming of the shadow ministers. The result was a dosage of posts – Mollet as shadow Foreign and Defence Minister; a Radical Party leader for Planning and Public Works; a member of Mitterrand's Convention for Economic Affairs – that was lampooned in the press as a return to the bad old ways of the Fourth Republic. There was another, more fundamental reason why the shadow Cabinet was a flop. Such a system worked when the opposition, as in Britain, was united. The Federation was not.

29.   The first time had been in July 1934, when the Socialists and the Communists signed a unity pact against fascism which led two years later to the formation of the Popular Front. The pact collapsed at the end of 1938.

30.   When Mauroy suggested, at the meeting on March 16, that the components of the Federation fuse into a single party, Mollet whispered to Mitterrand, 'Don't take that seriously. He's young, he has no authority to say that.' Charles Hernu commented: 'The Federation is dead.'

31.   Anne Pingeot, interview, March 25 2013.

32.   When Mitterrand bought it in 1965, the gallery, or loggia, led to an attic under the eaves, hardly tall enough to stand up in. Danielle kept the gallery, installing

a television set and a couple of easy chairs, but opened up the rest to give the house more volume.

33. Since their marriage, they had lived at Auteuil, at Neuilly and in the Latin Quarter, each time in comfortable, standard-issue bourgeois Parisian apartments. The small seaside villa they had built at Hossegor was practical but characterless. Latche was a real home.

34. This sometimes took absurd forms. Anne called it Latché, with an accent on the final syllable, which was how the locals had referred to it before the Mitterrands took possession. Danielle insisted that it should be Latche, with no accent (which is how it is spelt here on the grounds that, whatever the etymology, the owner has the final say over what a house should be called). In the abundant literature in France on the Mitterrands' retreat, half the authors – including Danielle's brother-in-law, Roger Hanin – use the accent; the other half do not. (Similar controversy, though for different reasons, surrounds the spelling of Touvent. The road sign by the hamlet says 'Toutvent'; the Mitterrands called it Touvent. Such discrepancies, stemming from the differences between the old southern and northern languages, the langue d'oc and the langue d'oï, are not unusual in France.)

35. They stayed at l'Ombrellino in 1970, to celebrate Anne's passing the *concours* to become a museum curator, and returned frequently to Italy thereafter.

36. The figure of one million was given by the CFDT. The police estimated 300,000. Two and a half weeks later, on May 30, the Gaullists claimed a million participants in their counter-demonstration while the police estimated a third of that number.

37. Mitterrand addressed meetings at Vichy on May 5, at Chambéry on May 10 – the night when the worst rioting occurred and Charles Hernu urged him, without success, to return to Paris at once – and then in Gap, Digne, Niort, and Château-Chinon. He claimed later that in these speeches (of which no texts survive) he spoke of the social and political changes which the agitation portended, adding that while 'youth is not always right, . . . society is always wrong to strike back'.

38. At a meeting on the evening of May 13, Cohn-Bendit denounced a long list of politicians, including Mitterrand, before adding: 'but that one might at a pinch be useful to us'.

39. Mendès maintained that he had not been informed beforehand. Claude Estier, however, remembered having been sent to Mendès's home on the morning of May 28 to give him an advance copy of the statement Mitterrand would make.

40. François Flohic wrote afterwards that Massu's intervention was 'decisive'.

41. Jean Lacouture's interpretation was that de Gaulle flew to Baden Baden in order to 'take everyone by surprise'. The General himself later acknowledged that he had had several options in mind: to resign his post and retire; to withdraw for a time and reflect while seeing how France would react; and to use Massu as

a sounding board to evaluate his choices. But 'creating a surprise' was not among them: the surprise was incidental, not the purpose of the manoeuvre.

42.   On May 13 1958, the night of the barricades in Algiers paved the way for de Gaulle's return to power. On May 13 1968, ten days of student demonstrations peaked with a million-strong march across Paris. On May 29 1958 Coty summoned de Gaulle from retirement; he was sworn in on June 1. On May 30 1968, the demonstrations on the Champs-Elysées signalled that de Gaulle was back in control; a month later he obtained an unassailable parliamentary majority.

43.   In an interview some months later, Mitterrand maintained: 'I have never been against [the movement]. If I was outraged by certain errors of leadership on the part of the students' chiefs, I never dreamed of being against the youth as others were, on the Right.'

44.   Gaullist propaganda, he wrote, had 'lied about the events of May as no one has been able to lie since Goebbels'. The June elections were no more honest than 'elections under Franco.'

9: Union of the Left

1.   Mitterrand, *Ma part de vérité*, pp. 163–8.

2.   Mitterrand wrote in 1969: 'Over twenty-five years, as I observed our society, I often believed that under the pressure of rival interests it was changing. *Today* I have to admit that nothing whatever has changed anything . . . This implacable [resistance to change] is a constant of capitalist society.' (Emphasis added)

3.   'Speech to the Socialist Party Congress', June 13 1971, in Mitterrand, *Politique*, Vol. 1, pp. 531–42.

4.   Ibid.

5.   Under an agreement signed in February 1968, the Communists and the FGDS undertook 'to examine together measures to be taken to prevent attempts of whatever kind to stop a government of the Left from implementing its programme'. Despite the convoluted wording, it was the first time the Communists and the non-communist Left had gone beyond a simple electoral accord and it marked an important step towards an eventual alliance – or would have done, had it not been overtaken by the events of May and the Soviet invasion of Czechoslovakia.

6.   Giesbert, *Mitterrand: une vie*, p. 260 and Poperen, Jean, *l'Unité de la gauche (1965–1973)*, Fayard, 1975, p. 393.

7.   Cited in Nay, Catherine, *Le noir et le rouge*, Grasset, 1984, p. 203.

8.   In 1969 Guy Mollet's party claimed to have some 87,000 members, a figure reduced to 70,000 during the preparatory negotiations for Épinay. The Convention claimed 10,000 members. In reality, according to Mitterrand, the Socialists had 56,000 members at Épinay and the Convention, 8,000. The new

party born of their merger claimed more than 80,000 members at the end of 1971 and 100,000 a year later.

9.   Roland Dumas offered a similar judgement: 'I do not know whether François Mitterrand was at the bottom of his heart a man of the Left,' he wrote, 'but I can testify that, in politics, he behaved like a man of the Left.'

10.   *L'Expansion*, July–August 1972.

11.   According to Roland Leroy, who was present that night, Mitterrand was 'shattered' by the result. When he arrived at the Tour Montparnasse his first words were 'Those who no longer believe may leave.'

12.   Mitterrand had announced that, if elected, he would name a Socialist Prime Minister. Defferre, as a known moderate with plenty of government experience behind him, was the obvious choice to reassure opinion ahead of the parliamentary elections which would have to follow. The same logic made Mendès France an ideal candidate for the Foreign Ministry. Marchais had made clear that the Communists would not ask for any of the four key ministries – Defence, Foreign Affairs, Interior or Justice – but, like the Socialists' other allies, they would expect a role appropriate to their status.

13.   Cited in Giesbert, *Mitterrand: une vie*, p. 277.

14.   Ibid., pp. 295–6.

15.   Mitterrand formed a limited partnership with Roland Dumas to acquire the house and subsequently bought him out. Danielle, in her account of the purchase, did not mention Dumas's participation. A simple oversight? Or did François omit to tell her that he had had to seek help from his wealthy friend and colleague?

16.   Anne bought the apartment for 60,000 francs (£5,600 or US $13,000) in 1973, when prices were at rock bottom during the first Oil Shock. Her parents, who had at first been furious over her relationship with Mitterrand, were by then reconciled to the arrangement. She and François started building the house at Gordes in 1972.

17.   Madeleine Séchan, a country doctor in the Luberon whom François and Anne met through Laurence Soudet, delivered the baby and declared the birth at the town hall the following day. One other couple were in on the secret: Charles Salzmann, who pioneered psephological analysis in France and would later become one of Mitterrand's political advisers, and his wife, Monique.

18.   Roland Dumas gave a vivid account of having met Mitterrand one day, when Mazarine was about a year old, pushing her in a pram along the banks of the Seine. 'Solemnly, like a patriarch from the provinces,' he recounted, 'he showed me a small bundle wrapped up against the cold. [After a while] he raised his hat and went on his way. He did not say it was his daughter but I understood at once.' The story is revealing not because it was true – Anne Pingeot demolished it in a few well-chosen words: 'Are you out of your mind? Pushing a pram? In Paris? Never! That would be completely out of character' – but

because so many of Mitterrand's colleagues liked to pretend afterwards that they had been in on the family secret. In reality, very few were.

19. Mexandeau dated their conversation to the first half of June. That month Mitterrand resumed his duties as First Secretary, which Pierre Mauroy had been carrying out on an acting basis. It is hard to pinpoint exactly when he decided to continue: it probably happened gradually in the course of the summer. By September, if not before, his mind was made up.

20. Mitterrand wrote later that relations between the two parties began to go downhill three or four months after the 1974 election. In fact the Communist Party had been divided from the outset on the usefulness of the alliance. One group in the leadership, headed by Marchais's deputy, Roland Leroy, had made no secret of its hopes that Mitterrand's election bid would fail. Leroy's face 'lit up', Mitterrand remembered, when he learnt that the Left had obtained only 43 per cent of the vote in the first round, 'not enough to win, just enough to believe it possible'. Marchais's position was more difficult to decipher. He had put his weight as Secretary-General behind the Common Programme while making clear privately to his Politburo colleagues that he had doubts about the alliance. He apparently felt that he could turn the situation to his advantage regardless of whether Mitterrand won or lost.

21. Lucien Sève had written in l'Humanité before the second round that 'each one [should] determine his position by himself in the voting booth', thus implicitly authorising communist voters to ignore the Party's official directive to support the candidate of the Union of the Left.

22. Giesbert, Mitterrand: une vie, pp. 280–81.

23. Robrieux was speaking in December 1977, but his conclusion, that 'for the first time since 1917 Soviet Russia is afraid of a socialist experience developing on the [European] continent which will have the support of the Communists and will be able to invent a model of society different if not contrary to its own', was the same as Mitterrand had brought back from Moscow two and a half years earlier.

24. The description, 'rotund and orotund', I owe to my friend, Stephen Jessel, who covered Barre's premiership for the BBC in the late 1970s.

10: Politics is War

1. The expression fin de règne which I have translated here as 'the end of a reign' is usually rendered in English as 'the end of an era', but in the context in which Mauroy was speaking, he plainly intended the literal implication that Mitterrand's 'reign' was drawing to a close.

2. The original 'sabras' were Jews born in Israel who had never known any other home. Mitterrand's 'sabras' were Socialist Party members who had never belonged to any other movement. Technically that was not the case of Jospin,

who had been a member of a Trotskyist group and of the PSU, but it was true of Fabius and Quilès.

3.   In Beijing, where I was then working, that was the explanation current among the French community, made up at that time mainly of diplomats and journalists. The word from the French Embassy was that the visit was Mitterrand's swansong. In one of those petty acts of vengeance which politicians or their acolytes are often unable to resist, the Ambassador, Claude Chayet, who had grown up in China and had won his spurs in the negotiations which ended the Algerian war, was afterwards blamed for the defeatist mood and sent to vegetate for the rest of his career at the Law of the Sea Conference in New York. Had Giscard won a second term, the sceptics would no doubt have been proved right. Mitterrand would have ended his career, like Guy Mollet before him, as a back-bench MP.

4.   Philippe Dechartre in http://www.gaulliste.org/documents/dechartre_1981. pdf.

5.   Giscard asked Mitterrand to give the day's rate for the franc against the mark. He told friends next day he had had the riposte on the tip of his tongue – 'And the rate for diamonds, can you tell me that?' – but had bitten back the words in order not to lower the tone of the debate.

11: *The Novitiate*

1.   Edward Luttwak, a Georgetown University professor and one of Reagan's foreign policy advisers, had met Mitterrand during the campaign and, on his return to Washington, had also vouched for his anti-Soviet credentials.

2.   In the United States, this is not regarded as a handicap. In European democracies with parliamentary systems, an up-and-coming politician is usually expected first to win election as an MP; then to serve an apprenticeship as a junior minister; and only some years later to aspire to senior ministerial office. When François Hollande was elected in 2012, he became the first French President not to have been either a minister or an MP beforehand.

3.   The Wednesday lunches, attended by Bérégovoy, Defferre, Estier, Fabius, Jospin, Joxe, Mauroy, Mermaz, Mexandeau, Poperen, Quilès, and sometimes Edith Cresson, Charles Hernu and Jack Lang, ended in November 1982.

4.   After the June 1981 elections, Mitterrand enjoyed a majority in the National Assembly on a scale seen only three times before in 200 years – in 1815, 1919 and under de Gaulle in 1968. In the General's case, moreover, although the elections marked a triumph for the Right, they coincided with a serious weakening of his personal position.

5.   Meeting with Vice-President George Bush, June 24 1981, in CHAN, carton 5AG4 CD4.

6.   Ibid.

7. Despite the DST's claims to the contrary, it appears that Reagan had been informed by William Casey, the CIA Director.

8. According to Ménage, it was not proved conclusively until much later that the Russians were responsible for bugging the fax machines: in the meantime, the possibility that another intelligence service, perhaps even the CIA, might have been involved, could not be ruled out. The expulsion of the forty-seven Soviet diplomats was a consequence of Farewell's revelations. The discovery of the bugging played an indirect role by convincing French officials, notably at the Foreign Ministry, which until then had been reluctant, that tough measures against the Russians were justified.

9. A small number of Soviet diplomats were also expelled from Britain and the United States and several American and British citizens were arrested for espionage on the Russians' behalf. In France, some twenty Soviet agents were identified. Some were double agents who were left in place, but twelve were sent for trial or otherwise neutralised, among them a general in the engineering corps working on nuclear warheads for French submarine-launched missiles. Similar waves of arrests took place in West Germany, where a senior official at Messerschmitt, who had been working for the KGB since 1954, was among those detained, as well as in six other Western countries.

10. Was there more to it than that 'official' version suggested? 'It's a crazy story,' Mitterrand said later. 'I don't have the key. But the way it ended seemed to me so singular that I stopped believing such nonsense.' His suspicions that it might all have been a manipulation on the part of the CIA were mistaken. It was not a Soviet manipulation either. While it is possible that Vetrov's end may have been different from that described, the account is coherent with everything that is known about his character: a womaniser, a romantic taking suicidal risks, an idealist. No one has ever produced a convincing reason to doubt it.

11. Mitterrand, Speech to the Bundestag, January 20 1983, in http://discours.vie-publique.fr/notices/847900500.html

12. The quotation is often rendered incorrectly as 'The pacifists are in the West, the Euromissiles in the East': in fact he said, 'Pacifism, and all that it condemns, is in the West . . .'

13. Kissinger telephoned Attali on January 26, six days after the speech; Reagan wrote on January 28.

14. Mitterrand, Speech at Cancun, October 20 1981, in http://discours.vie-publique.fr/notices/817144500.html

15. De Gaulle's comment was made at a news conference in November 1967. He condemned Israel for launching the war and said France would have condemned the Arab states had they initiated the hostilities. Israel's military victory, he added, would inevitably be followed by 'repression, oppression and expulsions' in the occupied territories which would accelerate the spiral of violence and do nothing to bring Israel peace.

16. 'Discours de François Mitterrand à la Knesset, 4 mars 1982' in http://discours. vie-publique.fr/notices/827006800.html

17. Shultz telephoned Cheysson on September 19, the day after the massacre became known, to say that if France did not agree to send back its troops within 24 hours, the US Marines would go in alone. Diplomatically Cheysson refrained from reminding him that it had been the US administration, fearing American casualties, which had insisted on leaving in the first place.

18. 'As long as Begin is there,' he told his entourage in the summer of 1982, 'nothing will be possible. His idea of "Greater Israel" makes all negotiation vain. There's nothing to be negotiated.'

19. Bernard Vernier-Palliez, November 16 1984, valedictory telegram, in CHAN, 5AG4 CD74, Dossier 1.

20. Gilles Ménage, Mitterrand's deputy Chief of Staff in 1982–88 with special responsibility for anti-terrorist measures, described the Israeli invasion as 'the major event which started to change everything, . . . the final shock in a fatal chain of cause and effect whose terrible consequences would unfold over several years . . . The Israeli invasion of June 1982 created . . . lasting conditions for the birth, structuring and development of the nebula of Middle Eastern terrorism of which France would be the principal victim from 1982 to 1987.'

21. Ménage wrote that 'no one [in 1981] had understood the extent of the facilities Lebanon offered at that time for every kind of terrorism . . . [The country was] an arsenal of weapons, [with] numerous training camps and large numbers of specialists, all accustomed to working underground, in rigidly compartmentalized groups, experienced in the most sophisticated techniques for handling explosives, not to mention financial means [and] ways of procuring false identities [and] passports . . . Beirut in 1981 was ready and waiting to be the crossroads of international terrorism.'

22. Nixon's 'limited incursion' into Cambodia in May 1970 had exactly the same effect, giving a breathing space to US forces in Vietnam and helping to create the conditions for their withdrawal, but spreading the Vietcong, whom it had it been intended to eradicate, throughout Cambodia. That created the conditions for the Khmers Rouges to seize power. Begin's invasion appeared to be more successful in the short term. It neutralised the PLO and blocked the peace process for the next decade. But the price was to spread Lebanese-based terrorism throughout the Western world. Moreover, as Yitzhak Rabin, later Israel's Prime Minister, noted, the PLO's place was soon taken by the Shiite Hezbollah, the 'Party of God', leaving Israel's position in the region no more secure than before.

23. From 1970 to 1979, fatal attacks by Palestinian terrorists occurred in Austria, Belgium, Britain, Italy, West Germany, Norway, Switzerland and the US. In France, several attacks took place in the early 1970s, including two at Orly Airport in January 1975. But from then until 1980, only one major incident

occurred on French soil: a shooting at the El Al counter at Orly on May 20 1978 in which four people, including the three Palestinian terrorists, were killed.

24.   On March 29 1982, the 'Organisation for Arab Armed Struggle', a name some-times used by Carlos and his associates, claimed responsibility for a bomb explosion on a train between Toulouse and Paris which killed five people and injured twenty-seven. A month earlier, the Venezuelan terrorist had written to the Interior Minister, Gaston Defferre, seeking the release of two members of his group, Bruno Breguet and Magdalena Kopp, who had been arrested in France in possession of arms and explosives. The French learned only much later that Kopp was Carlos's wife. On April 15, the day the pair was due to appear in court, a French diplomat and his wife were assassinated in Beirut. The opening of Breguet and Kopp's trial a week later coincided with the explosion outside *Al watan al arabi*.

25.   Here and elsewhere French acronyms are used for the 'Secret Army for the Liberation of Armenia' and the 'Armed Revolutionary Lebanese Fractions' since neither operated in English-speaking countries and both are best known by their French initials. In April 1982, the latter group, an extreme left-wing offshoot of Waddi Haddad's branch of the Popular Front for the Liberation of Palestine, to which Carlos had at one point belonged, assassinated an Israeli diplomat, Yacov Barsimantov (actually an agent of Mossad) in Paris. Four months later two French policemen were killed trying to defuse a bomb placed by the FARL under an American diplomat's car. In August 1982 the group blew up a car belonging to an Israeli diplomat, injuring him and his two passengers as well as more than forty pupils from a nearby secondary school. At the beginning of the year the FARL had assassinated an American deputy military attaché in Paris. The same group may also have been responsible for an unsuc-cessful attempt to kill the American chargé d'affaires, Christian Chapman, in November 1981.

26.   The various terrorist campaigns peaked in different countries at different times. In Britain, IRA bomb attacks, which had reached a high point in the early 1970s, resumed from 1982 to 1984. In France tensions were at their height in the summer of 1982 and from late 1985 to 1986.

27.   The attack in the rue Copernic was organised not by Abu Nidal's Fatah–Revolutionary Council as such but by a related organisation, the Popular Front for the Liberation of Palestine–Special Command, led by Selim Abu Salem. Almost thirty years later, France sought the extradition from Canada of a Lebanese sociology professor, Hassan Diab, who it alleged had carried out the attack. The Canadian government approved the extradition order on April 4 2012, but Diab entered an appeal.

28.   Ménage wrote later that it was 'difficult to date with precision' the moment when the government understood the significance of the attacks on Jewish interests in 1980 and 1982, but that at the time everyone concerned – political

authorities, specialists on the Middle East, intelligence services – were 'a hundred leagues away' from appreciating the forces at work.

29. Ménage acknowledged afterwards that 'the authorities in Teheran . . . were right to complain about this violation of the rules concerning the right of asylum' because 'the assurances we gave them ad nauseam to convince them of our determination to reduce their opponents to silence remained a dead letter'.

30. On May 24 1982, eleven people were killed and twenty-two injured by a car bomb at the French Embassy in Beirut. Responsibility was claimed by 'Al Jihad', apparently an early version of 'Islamic Jihad'. The motive for the attack was never explained, but the explosion occurred two weeks after Anis Naccache and his companions were sentenced. If, as seems likely, the two events were related, no one in France – not even Ménage, writing fifteen years later – made the connection.

31. Shortly afterwards, ASALA claimed responsibility for two failed car bomb attacks on French diplomats in Teheran. The French press at the time speculated on the possibility of a Libyan role.

32. The name Islamic Jihad had first been used six months earlier, when a suicide bomber detonated a ton of explosives in a delivery van, killing more than sixty people at the US Embassy in Beirut in April 1983. There had been two previous attacks using this technique, both unsigned: against the Iraqi Embassy in Beirut in 1981, killing sixty-one people including the Ambassador; and against an Israeli Army base at Tyre in November 1982, killing seventy-four people.

33. Cabinet minutes, October 26 1983, in Ménage, Gilles, L'œil du pouvoir, Vol. 3, Fayard, 2001, pp. 207–8.

34. The Americans were equally at sea. A CIA report received by the French on October 26 said the attacks had been organised jointly by pro-Syrian Palestinians, opposed to Arafat, and pro-Iranian Shiites – a finding which subsequent investigations confirmed – but added that the responsibilities of the Syrian (and Iranian) authorities 'cannot be clearly established'.

35. The full story of Arafat's extraction from Tripoli has yet to be written. Mitterrand persuaded Reagan to put pressure on Israel to allow the convoy to leave. He also provided French good offices for an exchange on November 23 of 4,600 Palestinian prisoners held by Israel for six Israeli soldiers captured by the PLO whose lives were increasingly imperilled as Arafat's position became more precarious. It is tempting to assume that the two events were linked, but the evidence is lacking. It was learnt later that the Soviet Union had exerted pressure on Assad to allow Arafat's forces to leave, though whether it did so out of fear that a direct clash with the French might ignite a larger conflagration or because Moscow, too, recognised that Arafat was worth preserving, is not clear.

36. Only the Director of the Criminal Investigation Department, Michel Guyot, was eventually granted a reprieve.

37. As though that were not enough, Mitterrand appointed Joseph Franceschi, who had been his unofficial adviser on security matters before 1981, to second Gaston Defferre as Secretary of State for Security. It was not a good idea. Defferre, concentrating on his decentralisation programme and spending half of each week in Marseille, where he was mayor, failed conspicuously to bring the police to heel yet, jealous of his prerogatives, refused to allow Franceschi to do so either. The diarchy at the head of the Interior Ministry was allowed to continue for almost two years, ending only when both men were assigned new portfolios in a reshuffle in July 1984.

38. Less than ten days after Prouteau's nomination, in August 1982, his deputy at the GIGN, Captain Paul Barril, announced with great fanfare the arrests of three Irish 'terrorists' in the Paris suburb of Vincennes. It soon emerged that some of the evidence against them had been fabricated. Barril, who benefited from a long friendship with Prouteau, was later banned from the Elysée on Mitterrand's orders, but not before he had managed to embarrass the government in another case, this time related to Corsica.

39. Gamba, Daniel, *Interlocuteur privilégié: J'ai protégé Mitterrand*, JC Lattès, 2003, pp. 86–8.

40. Valéry Giscard d'Estaing likewise announced during the campaign of 1974 that he would publish regular health bulletins but after his election changed his mind.

41. Emblematic of the well-intentioned but slightly loopy side of the Socialists' early forays into mass culture, it fell victim to budget cuts in 1983.

42. Jacques Attali quoted Mitterrand as saying in June 1981: 'At this stage, what I am doing is politics. [For the rest] we will see later.'

43. In November 1981, a business survey found that 83 per cent of managers of small and medium-sized companies had no intention of taking on extra workers in the coming six months and 56 per cent ruled out any new investment.

44. Nonetheless, Mitterrand went further than he needed to. He insisted, over Mauroy's objections, on reducing the working week from 40 to 39 hours without loss of pay, which was understandably popular with workers but nullified the effect of the measure in terms of job creation; and he decided – against the advice of Rocard and Badinter – that the State should take a 100 per cent stake, rather than 51 per cent, in the nationalised enterprises and banks. Both decisions were economically counter-productive.

45. The writer was among the 300 journalists present that day and must confess that, like his colleagues, he failed to recognise Mitterrand's underlying message.

46. 'The choice of the Socialists is to share wealth,' Mauroy observed, 'but socialism amid penury doesn't make much sense.'

47. Mitterrand's adviser on international economic affairs, Elizabeth Guigou, remembered: 'When he arrived at the Elysée, [he] was not as familiar with

monetary techniques as Giscard d'Estaing might have been. He sought to multiply his contacts to the maximum and hear all points of view. He did not want to be the prisoner of just one school of thought . . . He wanted to be sure he could explain things in simple terms.'

48. Unemployment passed the two million mark in May 1982 but then appeared to stabilise just above that level until the autumn of 1983.

49. The argument is as follows: had France left the EMS in March 1983, the French and German economies would have diverged; Mitterrand and Kohl would have followed different national policies; the British budget quarrel would at best have been papered over at Fontainebleau in 1984 and the EEC's subsequent enlargement to include Spain and Portugal would have been delayed. By staying in the EMS, Mitterrand not only strengthened the Franco-German relationship as the locomotive of European unity but made possible the agreements at Fontainebleau and the Single European Act that followed. Beyond that it is impossible to speculate: there are too many variables at work. But, had France left the Exchange Rate Mechanism, it is hard to see how Maastricht, or its equivalent, could have come about. And without Maastricht, or something like it, there would have been no Euro.

50. It is often claimed that Mitterrand had reached his decision well before the municipal elections but allowed the actors to play out their roles, as in a piece of theatre, until the denouement became clear. That is giving him too much credit. On February 21, Elizabeth Guigou had sent him a memorandum summing up the effects of a withdrawal from the EMS in terms almost identical to those Michel Camdessus would use to Fabius three and a half weeks later. To reinforce the message, the Elysée's new Secretary-General, Jean-Louis Bianco, who had succeeded Bérégovoy, had minuted: 'Mr President, leaving the EMS will put us in the hands of the IMF.' If Mitterrand had accepted that judgement, the manoeuvring of the following weeks would have been unnecessary. Instead he continued to hope for a different outcome. The cacophony at the economists' lunch on February 28 comforted him in the belief that an alternative might yet be possible.

51. Cited in Lacouture, Jean, *Mitterrand: une histoire de Français*, Vol. 2, Seuil, 1998, p. 63.

52. Jacques Toubon, an RPR MP with close ties to Chirac, noted that the change had been managed 'without big difficulties. It's very striking . . . Mitterrand can be grateful to Jospin for having got him through this turn without [much] pain. It was a masterstroke on the part of the Socialists.'

53. In 1974, the burden of direct and indirect taxation in France was 36.3 per cent. By the time Giscard left office in 1981, it had reached 42.9 per cent. In 1983 it was 44.7 per cent. By comparison, according to the OECD, the level in the USA in 1985 was 25.6; in West Germany, 36.1; in Britain, 37.6; and in Sweden, 47.8 per cent. In 1986, the tax burden in France fell back below 44 per cent and

remained there for the following five years, only to climb again under the right-wing government of Édouard Balladur in 1993, reaching a peak in 1999 of nearly 48 per cent.

12: *The Sphinx*

1. Jacques Attali, who gave a less credible, variant – 'the eyes of Stalin and the voice of Marilyn Monroe' – claimed that Mitterrand was speaking after a meeting with Thatcher in London on September 10–11 1981 in which she had shown herself intransigent about the plight of the Irish hunger strikers.

2. Britain received a rebate of 1.175 billion euros in 1980 and 1.41 billion in 1981.

3. The Euro was not created until 1999, but its predecessors, the MEUA, or European Unit of Account, and the Ecu, or European Currency Unit, which were used for internal accounting among EEC countries, had the same value against national currencies. I have therefore used the term Euro throughout.

4. Attali quoted him as having said as early as May 1982: 'The question of Britain's presence in the Community is now raised.'

5. Attali, Jacques, *Verbatim*, Vol. 1, *1981–86*, Fayard, 1993, pp. 641–2.

6. The memorandum on which the plan was based was prepared by Elizabeth Guigou at the Elysée.

7. Howe made the comment during a discussion with a group of British journalists in Paris, the writer among them, shortly after the Fontainebleau summit.

8. With the passage of time, Thatcher herself began to believe that she had triumphed. At a banquet in Buckingham Palace on October 23 1984, she told the French President, 'I thank you for yielding to me at Fontainebleau because that enabled us to open the way for Europe . . .', to which Mitterrand replied, 'I don't wish to argue with you over the word "yield": what matters is that you believe it.'

9. Meeting with Helmut Kohl, October 4 1982, cited in Schabert, Tilo, *Mitterrand et la réunification allemande*, Grasset, 2002, p. 88.

10. Mitterrand always insisted that the gesture had been spontaneous. Christina Forsne, who questioned him at length about it, wrote that the decision had been taken some months earlier.

11. Modest attempts had been made to increase the powers of the conseils généraux and town councils in 1871 and 1884, but important decisions remained subject to approval by the *préfet*, which meant that in practice they were taken by the central government.

12. Savary's family certainly thought so. At his death in February 1988, they let it be known that Mitterrand would not be welcome at the funeral. When the Elysée sought clarification, his widow allowed that 'the presence of the President of the Republic would be an honour', meaning that if Mitterrand insisted on

attending, which he did, it would be in his role as Head of State not as a former colleague.

13. Cabinet minutes, December 21 1983, cited in Favier, Pierre and Martin-Roland, Michel, *La décennie Mitterrand*, Vol. 2, Seuil, 1991, pp. 110–12.

14. In November 1983, Mitterrand told Monseigneur Vilnet, the President of the Episcopal Conference: 'We will let the normal parliamentary and ministerial procedures play out, but there is no question of allowing private or Catholic schools to be stifled. Count on me, I am watching!' The following December and January, he told Cardinal Lustiger that he did not think Savary's proposals would become law.

15. A new law was necessary because the decentralisation programme, enacted in 1982, devolved greater powers to the communes, which could no longer be obliged by administrative fiat to subsidise private schools in their jurisdictions.

16. Mitterrand behaved callously towards Savary, giving him no advance notice of his announcement on July 12 and refusing to receive him after he formally confirmed the withdrawal of the schools bill two days later. It is difficult to interpret that as anything other than small-minded revenge for Savary's slights in the 1960s. The Minister told Mauroy on July 13 that he intended to resign. He sent Mitterrand his resignation letter on the 16th. Mauroy and the rest of the government followed suit on the evening of July 17.

17. At the time of his appointment, Fabius had a 60 per cent approval rating, and his rating remained above or close to 50 per cent until November 1985. Mitterrand's popularity was in negative territory from June 1983 to March 1986, falling to 26 per cent in November 1984. By comparison, de Gaulle consistently obtained an approval rating of more than 50 per cent (with one brief drop to 49 per cent in 1963), while Pompidou had even higher ratings until his death in 1974. Giscard was in positive territory until the last four months of his presidency, when his approval rating fell to 42 per cent. Mitterrand's successors were even more unpopular than he had been: Jacques Chirac fell in 2006 to 16 per cent of favourable opinions and Nicolas Sarkozy, in 2010, to 20 per cent.

18. This became more marked after Fabius took over in July 1984. According to Jean-Louis Bianco, Mitterrand thought it necessary to stress the Prime Minister's independence because of his youth and their previous relationship as mentor and protégé. This was not without risks. In December 1985, the President, without informing Fabius beforehand, decided to receive the Polish leader, General Jaruzelski, who had been execrated in the West since he had declared martial law four years earlier. The Prime Minister was furious and told parliament he was 'troubled' by the President's action, an open breach of protocol which provoked a political crisis and ended with him offering his resignation. Mitterrand, then travelling in the French West Indies, responded with a fable. There were two monkeys in a laboratory, he said, an old monkey and a young one. Both were given electric shocks. The young monkey, who received them

rarely, yelped each time in distress and soon died. The old monkey, who received them constantly, thought it was normal and lived for years.

19.   De Gaulle was also a master of 'giving time to time', retiring to Colombey-les-Deux-Églises for a decade to write his memoirs while awaiting the call to return to power.

20.   *Le Monde*, April 6 1984.

21.   The catastrophic performance of Marchais's list in 1984 almost caused his downfall. But Charles Fiterman, the Communist Transport Minister, whom the Secretary-General's opponents on the liberal wing of the Party saw as a potential successor, refused to come out openly against him. After ten days of uncertainty, Marchais was able to reassert his authority and the last chance of bringing the French Communist Party into the modern world was definitively lost.

22.   Meeting with President Reagan, Washington, March 22 1984, in CHAN 5AG4 CD74, dossier 1.

23.   Meeting with Konstantin Chernenko, Moscow, June 21 1984, cited in Attali, *Verbatim*, Vol. 1, pp. 654–5.

24.   According to Charles Salzmann, who took notes, the subject was raised 'in passing, almost discreetly'.

25.   Attali, *Verbatim*, Vol. 1, pp. 654–5 and Favier and Martin-Roland, *La décennie Mitterrand*, Vol. 2, p. 226.

26.   The participants' memories of this conversation differ. According to Salzmann, Mitterrand asked Chernenko about the state of Soviet agriculture and Gorbachev replied in his place. Favier and Martin-Roland give a different version in which Mitterrand, rather than Chernenko, asks: 'Since when?' The version quoted here is taken mainly from Attali, whose account in this instance appears the most reliable. All three agree on Gorbachev's reply.

27.   Recalling their conversation, more than six years later, Mitterrand said that that was the impression Gorbachev had given him 'between the lines'. Neither the words he quoted nor anything similar appears in the lengthy account of the conversation given by Attali, who had access to the official transcript. While it is possible that Mitterrand's memories of the meeting were coloured by later events, Gorbachev wrote afterwards that he was already convinced before Chernenko's death that the Soviet system could not continue as it was and that what would become known as *perestroika* and *glasnost* would be necessary to change it.

28.   The regularity with which the hand of the CIA appeared in press leaks, going back to 1983, designed to deepen the hostility between Paris and Moscow, is hard to explain as anything other than a deliberate campaign of disinformation – of the kind which all intelligence services engage in, but which, because of the importance of the media in America, has become more developed there than elsewhere.

29. The Americans claimed that Mitterrand dismissed Bonnet because he was convinced that Farewell's materials had been planted by the CIA and blamed the DST for failing to discover the supposed manipulation. The chronology does not hold up. Bonnet had been appointed in November 1982 – many months after Farewell had fallen silent – and could therefore have had nothing to do with any supposed CIA plot. He was fired for leaking information about the case without political authorisation. Among the 'collateral damage' resulting from the *Le Monde* report was Mitterrand's decision to place Edwy Plenel, the investigative reporter who broke the story, under surveillance by Prouteau's 'cell' at the Elysée. There was no legal basis for doing so and when it came to light, some years later, it triggered a long-running scandal about politically motivated phone-tapping.

30. Attali, *Verbatim*, Vol. 1, pp. 806–7.

31. Cabinet minutes, cited in Favier and Martin-Roland, *La décennie Mitterrand*, Vol. 2, p. 248.

32. Mitterrand acknowledged as much to Gorbachev when they met: 'France is a country which is proud of its independence. Of course we know how the world and the balance of forces in it have evolved, and the pre-eminent weight of the United States and the USSR. But we have preserved our autonomy in decision-making'.

33. Attali, *Verbatim*, Vol. 1, pp. 857–61.

34. Ibid.

35. At a Cabinet meeting after Gorbachev's departure, Mitterrand wondered aloud about the possibility of a looser relationship between Moscow and its east European satellites: 'It could mark the start of a revolution which would also be a relief [to the Soviet Union]. Certainly the Russians exploit the eastern European countries, but it has to be said that these countries also cost them a lot.'

36. The DGSE (at that time, the SDECE) began regular surveillance of Greenpeace's activities around Mururoa in 1972. From 1976 until 1984 there was relatively little activity. But in September 1984, the DGSE sent Hernu and Fabius an 'information note' on Greenpeace, describing the organisation's alleged links with pro-Soviet interests and concluding that it posed a danger to French interests 'because of its capacity for investigation and propaganda work'.

37. The possibility of 'anticipating' the Greenpeace campaign was first discussed on November 12 1984 at a meeting attended by Fabius, Hernu and Admiral Henri Fages, the Commander of the French fleet in the Pacific.

38. Lacoste stated afterwards that, on March 19 1985, Hernu ordered him to 'arrange for the DGSE to stop Greenpeace carrying out its plans to intervene against the French nuclear testing programme at Mururoa'. The Minister talked to Lacoste about it again on May 6, insisting on the importance of putting the *Rainbow Warrior* out of action. Lacoste wrote in his memoirs that Hernu had

confirmed the decision at a meeting on the morning of July 4, six days before the vessel was blown up.

39. Lacoste said afterwards that during the meeting with Mitterrand, 'Without entering into detail, I referred to Mr Hernu's intentions.'

40. The threat of a French boycott of New Zealand produce proving insufficient, the following year the Foreign Trade Minister, Michel Noir, threatened to block the renewal of New Zealand's trade privileges with the whole of the EEC. That forced the New Zealand Prime Minister, David Lange, to agree to arbitration by the UN Secretary-General, Javier Perez de Cuellar. Under the 'arrangement' which Perez de Cuellar worked out, the two agents were transferred to Hao, in French Polynesia, in July 1986, after serving only a year in a New Zealand prison.

41. Hernu admitted as much to Roland Dumas in late July or at the beginning of August, telling him: 'Yes, it was a wartime operation that went wrong, like many others.'

42. Mitterrand did not lie. He was never asked point blank whether he had ordered the attack on the *Rainbow Warrior* and, had that question been put to him, he could have answered in all honesty that he had not. But he deliberately misled the country by making it appear that he had no knowledge of what had happened.

43. Nonetheless, Mitterrand defended Hernu to the end. He told Attali on the eve of his 'resignation': 'Hernu must go. He had nothing to do with it, but that's how it is.' Six days later, when Fabius publicly ascribed to Hernu the responsibility for ordering the attack, Mitterrand shook his head and said, 'he merely covered up for it'. Why did Mitterrand try to hide, even in private, the extent of Hernu's implication, when he knew very well that Hernu had been at the origin of the affair? One can only surmise that he was embarrassed at having had to sacrifice a loyal friend to protect his own position.

44. According to Gilles Ménage the crucial information about the 'third team' came from an indiscretion by an adviser at the Elysée. Lacoste thought that Pierre Joxe had authorised the leak to *Le Monde* through his press adviser, Guy Perrimond, in order to force Mitterrand to confront Hernu and bring the affair to an end.

45. Ménage, *L'œil du pouvoir*, Vol. 3, pp. 316 & 318.

46. Note from Robert Badinter to Mitterrand, *c.* October 24 1985, cited in ibid., p. 363.

47. Marie Seurat, cited in ibid., pp. 604–5.

48. The first US hostage to be freed as a result of the 'Irangate' arms shipments, an American pastor, was released on September 14 1985. A few days later the Lebanese press quoted 'diplomatic sources' as saying that it was the result of an arms deal between the US, Israel and Iran. The White House immediately issued a denial. Two other US hostages were freed in 1986. When the French

discovered what Reagan had been up to, they were outraged. 'This double game,' Ménage wrote, 'is not only a dereliction of the solidarity and morality which they [the Americans] proclaim from the rooftops. It's going to end by convincing the kidnappers – the fundamentalist groups and their Iranian bosses – that they can obtain more and more from the "Great Satan" – and how much more from the "Little Satan" – provided they turn up the pressure ever more harshly.' In what way Reagan's decision to exchange American hostages for arms was different from Mitterrand's subsequent decision to exchange – albeit with certain face-saving conditions – French hostages for an Iranian assassination squad, Ménage did not explain.

49. Curiously neither Mitterrand nor his advisers drew a parallel between the role of the Syrian government in the 1982 attack on the *Al watan al arabi* newspaper in Paris and the possible role of the Iranian government in the hostage-taking and related bomb attacks three years later. In French eyes, it was one thing for a government to seek to neutralise domestic opponents on foreign soil and quite another for it to use terror as an adjunct to diplomacy in dealings with foreign governments. To Iran, as to Libya and Syria, the two were exactly the same.

50. Assad's emissary, Dr Iskandar Louka, arrived in Paris on September 24. Mitterrand replied the following day.

51. Mitterrand's revised offer was contained in a telegram from the French Foreign Ministry to the Ambassador in Damascus, Henri Servant, on December 25 1985.

52. Badinter to Mitterrand, January 3 1986, cited in Favier and Martin-Roland, *La décennie Mitterrand*, Vol. 2, pp. 512–13.

53. The chronology was as follows: on January 2, Mohamed Sadegh, an Iranian representative, spoke of Iran's desire for clearer assurances from Mitterrand but did not give the impression that the exchange was in any way threatened; on January 5, Assad told Mitterrand that a difficulty had arisen but the deal should still go through; the following day the French felt that the Syrians were pulling back; on January 7, Sadegh was told by Teheran that the exchange was off; on January 10, Islamic Jihad issued a statement in Beirut, admitting a 'sharp deterioration' in the health of one of the hostages, 'which could threaten his life'. Jean-Paul Kauffmann later reported that in mid-January there was unusual agitation among the kidnappers, after which he no longer heard Seurat coughing in a nearby cell. On February 6, GCHQ Cheltenham in Britain intercepted a message to Teheran from the Iranian Ambassador in Damascus in which he spoke of 'a bird who has flown his cage'. The French specialists who analysed the intercept assumed that one of the hostages had died but assumed wrongly that it was Marcel Carton, who suffered from heart disease. It was not until a month later that Seurat's death was confirmed. The inference is that the kidnappers' handlers in Teheran must have been told that Seurat was dying at some point between January 2 and 4. Assad was clearly unaware of

it when he wrote to Mitterrand on January 4. Syrian intelligence was probably informed shortly afterwards, between January 6 and 10.

54. The Iranians claimed that Dr Reza Raad, a Lebanese-born Frenchman from Chirac's RPR party who had acted as an intermediary between the French government and unnamed 'associates' of the kidnappers, had told them the opposition might agree to exchange the hostages against *Naccache and all his companions*, instead of against Naccache alone with the other four to follow later. Neither this nor other Iranian accounts can be taken at face value and Raad afterwards strongly denied them. However, Chirac himself confirmed on several occasions that he had 'intervened a lot' to try to secure the hostages' release and told Mitterrand some months after: 'I thought in January that I would be able to bring them back and I was getting ready to telephone you to tell you.' That does not prove that Chirac's emissaries undercut the government's negotiations, but it undermines his claim that his emissaries engaged only in 'exploratory' discussions.

55. In August 1981, Mitterrand described his programme as 'radical social-democracy'. Two years later the word 'radical' had dropped from his vocabulary.

56. Most serious studies have concluded that voters rarely moved directly from the Communist Party to the National Front. Instead, scholars claimed, ex-Communists switched their votes to the Socialists, to the extreme Left, to the RPR and in a few cases to centrist parties, while mainstream right-wing voters – notably the shopkeepers and artisans who twenty-five years earlier had supported Pierre Poujade – shifted to the National Front. There are reasons to question that. Until very recently, opinion polls systematically underestimated the Front's electoral support because a sizeable proportion of those questioned were unwilling to admit voting for what was seen as a racist party. The proportion of ex-Communists voting National Front was almost certainly greater than the surveys showed.

57. Mitterrand at Lille, February 7 1986, in http://miroirs.ironie.org/socialisme/www.psinfo.net/entretiens/mitterrand/1986lille.html

58. Islamic Jihad pretended that the 'execution' was in reprisal for the expulsion to Baghdad on February 19 of two Iraqi dissidents, opponents of Saddam Hussein, who had been arrested in France a week earlier. The expulsions were the result of a series of bureaucratic errors. An incorrect report by Amnesty International that one of the two had been executed gave Islamic Jihad the pretext it had been looking for to announce Seurat's death. Under intense pressure from Paris, and veiled threats to cut off arms supplies, Saddam Hussein agreed a week later to pardon the two men, who were later discreetly returned to France.

59. A French newspaper report that Mitterrand might resign if the Right won the elections by a large margin also made the Iranians hesitate. It had been inspired by the Elysée to mobilise left-wing voters. But in Teheran it raised questions

about Mitterrand's promise to free the other four members of the commando before the end of his mandate.

60. In the autumn of 1986, the left-wing newspaper, *Le Matin*, accused Chirac of having deliberately sabotaged the negotiations in Teheran in March 1986 by sending word to the Iranians that they would get much more favourable terms if they waited until the new government was in place. The reports were based on diplomatic telegrams quoting statements by the Iranian negotiators. Chirac denied what he called these 'lying allegations', but after the full text of one of the telegrams was published — having been leaked by Roland Dumas, evidently with Mitterrand's agreement — the RPR journal, *La Lettre de la Nation*, retorted on the Prime Minister's behalf that the Iranians must have considered 'the leaders of the opposition more credible'. It was an unfortunate turn of phrase, giving the impression that in the final days before the election — and not just in January, as he had acknowledged before — Chirac had indeed intervened. Pierre Joxe insisted: 'There is proof, and one day it will be made known.' Mitterrand was more cautious, saying only: 'It is certain that the RPR sent envoys to Damascus, Baghdad, Teheran and Beirut, but what they said is less so.' In Chirac's defence, it should be added that no convincing evidence was ever produced to back up the charge that the opposition had encouraged the Iranians to delay the hostages' release.

13: *The Florentine*

1. Cited in Favier and Martin-Roland, *La décennie Mitterrand*, Vol. 2, p. 503.

2. This claim was questionable. Between 1982 and 1985, the enterprises national-ised by Mitterrand had sold off dozens of subsidiaries to foreign interests. However, Mitterrand could have argued that the sale of subsidiaries was not the same as allowing whole sectors of strategic industries to pass into foreign hands and Chirac would probably have found it difficult to convince public opinion of the contrary.

3. Attali, Jacques, *Verbatim*, Vol. 2, Fayard, 1995, pp. 123–4.

4. An opinion poll published on June 18 showed that three voters out of five were dissatisfied with the government and that Chirac's own popularity rating had fallen below 50 per cent.

5. Meeting with Margaret Thatcher, October 16 1986, cited in Attali, *Verbatim*, Vol. 2, pp. 179–83.

6. Cabinet minutes, March 4 1987, cited ibid., p. 271.

7. Meeting with Thatcher, October 16 1986, ibid.

8. Cited in Favier and Martin-Roland, *La décennie Mitterrand*, Vol. 2, pp. 643–4.

9. Meeting with Thatcher, January 29 1988, cited in Attali, *Verbatim*, Vol. 2, p. 449. Mitterrand had told her fifteen months earlier: 'I don't attach importance to

the American presence in Europe. It pushes the Russians to be warlike . . . Everything depends on the Americans' resolution . . . If they don't have it, the presence of their soldiers on the continent won't give it to them.'

10. According to the French National Employment Agency, l'ANPE, unemployment was 2.4 million in March 1986 and 2.3 million in May 1988.

11. Cabinet minutes, October 3 1984, cited in Favier and Martin-Roland, *La décennie Mitterrand*, Vol. 2, p. 277.

12. The connection between these events was questionable. Chirac had opened a second line of negotiation through Lebanese businessmen in West Africa, through whom a ransom of 10 million francs (£1 million or US$ 1.5 million) was reportedly paid to the hostage-takers. Nonetheless the government took the view that the normalisation of ties with Iran had helped.

13. A sixth bomb, left in an underground train, failed to explode.

14. When the Elysée got wind of the DST report in July, Pasqua denied that it existed.

15. Diplomatic relations were broken on July 17. Four days earlier, the French cargo ship, *Ville d'Anvers*, had been attacked in the Gulf. It was announced on July 29 that the aircraft carrier *Clemenceau* would be sent to the area.

16. After July 1987, six westerners were taken hostage in Lebanon: a UN officer, Lieutenant-Colonel William Higgins, who was later executed; an elderly Briton, Jackie Mann; two German relief workers and two Swiss citizens. In none of those cases could the order be traced back directly to Teheran. The last Western hostages were freed in 1992, by which time, with the encouragement of the Iranian President, Ali Khamenei, the Hezbollah had moderated its revolutionary goals and begun playing a role in mainstream Lebanese politics.

17. He told Thatcher at the end of that month: 'The situation is frozen for a long time to come. It could be like the situation of Cardinal Mindszenty in Budapest', a reference to the Hungarian churchman who spent fifteen years in the US Embassy there.

18. Cited in Attali, *Verbatim*, Vol. 2, p. 372.

19. After the Cabinet meeting on July 8, Mitterrand told Pasqua: 'If the dossier against Gordji is as weak as you think, we have not got off to a very good start.' The Interior Minister replied: 'We don't know. It's difficult to predict what the magistrate will do.' Gilles Ménage told Mitterrand later that he believed the magistrate had more than enough evidence to prefer charges.

20. In July 1987, he told Jospin: 'I'm going to [stand] for one fundamental reason. If anyone can win, it's me. If I thought that someone else, including Rocard, could win instead and ensure the continuation [of the Left], I wouldn't be a candidate.'

21. Claude Estier thought that Mitterrand had set himself a deadline of February 10 to make up his mind. Mitterrand himself said later: 'I didn't take any irrevocable decision until the spring of 1988.'

22. Lacouture, *Mitterrand*, Vol. 2, p. 278. See also Favier and Martin-Roland, *La décennie Mitterrand*, Vol. 2, p. 727.

23. According to Attali, opinion surveys commissioned by the Elysée showed that 'voters [were] disorientated by the absence of a campaign' by Mitterrand as candidate of the Left. On April 12 and 13, the President asked both his own campaign headquarters and the Socialist Party leadership to be more aggressive against Chirac and the RPR while continuing to spare Raymond Barre.

24. 'Debate between François Mitterrand and Jacques Chirac', April 28 1988, complete transcript in http://discours.vie-publique.fr/notices/887013300.html

25. This was the judgement of Franz-Olivier Giesbert. I cannot put it better.

26. 'Debate between François Mitterrand and Jacques Chirac', April 28 1988, *supra*. Mitterrand accused Chirac of having released the Japanese terrorist following a grenade attack carried out by Carlos on the Publicis Drugstore in St Germain on September 15 1974 in which two people died and 34 were injured. In fact the man, 25-year-old Yutaka Furuya, a member of the Japanese Red Army, was flown to Amsterdam on Friday, September 13, after a Red Army commando, in liaison with Carlos, took over the French Embassy in The Hague, holding the Ambassador and ten others hostage. The hostages and the Japanese commando, together with Furuya, were flown to Damascus on the night of September 16. Abu Daoud was briefly arrested and then released in January 1977, by which time Raymond Barre was Prime Minister, Chirac having resigned in July 1976.

27. Mitterrand and Roland Dumas were convinced that Chirac had also given a verbal undertaking to pardon Anis Naccache and his accomplices if he were elected. Both Marchiani and his Iranian interlocutors confirmed that that had been part of the deal. The Prime Minister denied it.

14: *The Monarch*

1. Conversation with Maurice Faure, October 6 1987, cited in Giesbert, *Mitterrand: une vie*, p. 536.

2. Cited ibid, p. 546.

3. The opinion polls had predicted that the Socialists and Left-Radicals would do at least as well as in the parliamentary landslide of 1981. In fact they won 35.9 per cent in the first round compared with 37.4 per cent seven years earlier.

4. The Socialists obtained 275 seats but could count on the support of a dissident, Claude Miquieu in the Hautes-Pyrenées, who had been excluded from the Party for standing against its official candidate.

5. Favier, Pierre and Martin-Roland, Michel, *La décennie Mitterrand*, Vol. 3, Seuil, 1996, p. 42.

6. Ibid., pp. 102–3.

7. Meeting with President George Bush, Kennebunkport, May 20 1989, in Attali, Jacques, *Verbatim*, Vol. 3, Fayard, 1998, p. 241.

8. The border was officially declared open on September 11 1989. That day East Germans started arriving in West Germany via Austria, after crossing from Hungary, at the rate of two hundred an hour.

9. Five days earlier Mitterrand had warned that German reunification would force Britain, France and the USSR to react and that 'war would be certain in the 21st century'.

10. Mitterrand was still saying that reunification was 'not for tomorrow' in mid-October 1989, less than a month before the Berlin Wall came down.

11. Cabinet minutes, October 18 1989, in Attali, *Verbatim*, Vol. 3, pp. 322–3.

12. Meeting with Gorbachev, December 6 1989, cited ibid., pp. 360–67.

13. Meeting with Thatcher, December 8 1989, cited ibid., pp. 368–70.

14. Shortly before the Strasbourg summit, Caroline de Margerie, who was charged with preparing the visit, advised Mitterrand to cancel. On December 9, to test the waters, the President told Helmut Kohl he was wondering whether to maintain the trip. According to Kohl's adviser on European affairs, Joachim Bitterlin, the Germans were not in favour, but 'it was impossible for [the Chancellor] to tell the President directly: "It's not your trip, Tintin, it's mine."'

15. The only version of his talks with the East German Prime Minister, Hans Modrow, to have been made public is from the former East German archives. The French transcripts were sent directly to the National Archives in Paris and no French or German historian has been allowed access to them. According to the East German version, Mitterrand stressed the need to take reunification slowly and to do nothing which might upset the existing balance in Europe. During the visit he signed five cooperation agreements covering the period 1990–94 and spoke of the two countries 'still having much to do together', adding that East Germany might yet have 'an important place' in Europe in the future. It is hard to believe that he would have done that had he not believed – like most of his partners – that the regime would survive, perhaps not for five years, as Vernon Walters had predicted, but at least for a few years more.

16. Kohl said later, 'I had an immense problem of internal politics which people like Mitterrand could not imagine.'

17. The term was first used by Gorbachev's spokesman, Gennadi Gerasimov, during an appearance on *Good Morning America* in October 1989.

18. Baker acknowledged in his memoirs that his decision to visit East Germany on December 12 – a week before Kohl and eight days before Mitterrand – was 'in order to show American leadership by going there first'. The Bush administration wanted NATO to be the main player in future pan-European relations because American influence in the alliance was preponderant.

19. Hubert Védrine said Mitterrand felt that 'the military alliances were losing their *raison d'être*'.

20. Cited in Jean Musitelli, 'François Mitterrand, architecte de la Grande Europe' in http://www.mitterrand.org/Francois-Mitterrand-architecte-de.html.

21. Agreement was reached to set up the EBRD in May 1990. The bank opened for business in April 1991 with 36 members, including Australia, Egypt, Japan, Korea and Morocco from outside the CSCE area. Four other non-CSCE states, Israel, Jordan, New Zealand and Tunisia, joined later. As of 2013, the bank had 57 member countries.

22. On March 28 1990, Kohl proposed that the Twelve should convene an inter-governmental conference on political union. Three weeks later he and Mitterrand suggested a parallel conference on monetary union. On April 28, the Dublin Summit called for the conclusion of Economic and Monetary Union by the end of 1992.

23. Forsne, Christina, *François*, Seuil, 1997, pp. 225, 228 & 232.

24. Normally it would have been up to the Interior Minister, Pierre Joxe, to decide whether or not the investigation should proceed. However, given the political sensitivities surrounding the case, it is hard to believe that Mitterrand was not informed. The Socialist Party in Marseille was split between Pezet's supporters and those of Robert Vigouroux, who had succeeded Gaston Defferre as the city's mayor upon the latter's death in 1986. The Party leadership in Paris backed Pezet. Mitterrand's sympathies were with Vigouroux, who he thought had a better chance of being elected. Did the rivalry between them play into the decision to allow the investigation to continue? Whatever the reason, it soon became clear that it was a seriously bad idea.

25. In this, as much else concerning Africa, French and British attitudes differ. The French, whose possessions included Arab territories in North Africa – notably Algeria, Morocco and Tunisia – recognise a continuity between the Arab and African worlds. The British, whose possessions were all in sub-Saharan Africa (except Egypt and Sudan, which had condominium or protec-torate status), regard Africa and the Middle East as being essentially separate regions.

26. Mitterrand, Speech at La Baule, June 20 1990, in http://www.rfi.fr/actufr/articles/037/article_20103.asp.

27. Jacques Chirac, who insisted that Mitterrand did not understand what he called 'the African mentality', said in a speech in Abidjan that year that 'the multiparty system is a political error,. . . a luxury which these countries do not have the means to offer themselves'.

28. Two months later, George Bush nicknamed him 'Mr No'.

29. Meeting with Yasser Arafat, May 2 1989, in Attali, *Verbatim*, Vol. 3, pp. 226–30.

30. The Palestine National Council did not formally confirm the nullity of those parts of the Charter which rejected Israel's right to exist until April 24 1996.

31. Minutes of Cabinet committee discussion, August 9 1990, cited in Attali, *Verbatim*, Vol. 3, pp. 556–61.

32. Meeting with King Hussein, September 3 1990, ibid., pp. 584–6.

33. Transcript of conversation with Bush, November 18 1990, ibid., pp. 637–9. It was a pattern repeated in Afghanistan, where the Americans armed the Mujahideen to fight the Soviet Army only to find that they had nurtured the Taliban who provided bases for al-Qaeda.

34. Meeting with President Bush, April 11 1991, transcript in CHAN 5AG4 CD75, dossier 1.

35. Mitterrand did not use the term 'double standard', but made clear that was what he meant. 'I ask the United States,' he told Cheney, 'to adopt comparable positions towards all the problems that arise in the Arab world.' The meeting took place after Mitterrand had just spent a year trying to save a Lebanese Christian General, Michel Aoun, whose forces had rashly challenged Syrian suzerainty. It was the last time France would try to play a significant role in Lebanese affairs. Describing France's problems with Syria over Lebanon, he later told George Bush: 'For [Assad], the Lebanon is part of Syria, Israel is part of Syria, Jesus Christ was Syrian.' The US President commented: 'That's not bad!'

36. Meeting with President Bush, March 14 1991, Martinique, in CHAN 5AG4 CD75, dossier 1.

37. In 1988, French GNP grew by 4.3 per cent, in 1989 by 3.9 per cent and in 1990 by 2.4 per cent. In 1991, growth was forecast to be almost 2 per cent but actually came in at 0.8 per cent. From mid-1990 to mid-1991, unemployment grew by 8.3 per cent, from 2.5 to over 2.7 million.

38. Adler, Laure, *L'année des adieux*, Flammarion, 1995, pp. 110–12.

39. In June, 49 per cent of those questioned approved of Cresson's performance and 35 per cent disapproved. A month later the proportions were reversed. Her popularity declined steadily until, by the following summer, 78 per cent were dissatisfied with her and only 22 per cent approved.

40. The weakening of the links between Moscow and the republics did not occur tidily. Lithuania declared independence in March 1990 and Latvia in May, but neither was recognised internationally until the following year. Estonia had declared itself sovereign in 1988 – the first Baltic country to do so – and from 1990 onwards progressively rejected Soviet control. But, like Latvia and Armenia, which announced its secession in August 1990, its independence was not recognised until the autumn of 1991. The Russian Federation and Moldova declared themselves sovereign in June 1990, followed by the Ukraine in July, marking the beginning of a jurisdictional dispute with the central Soviet government which then spread to other republics. Georgia declared independence in April 1991.

41. Meeting with President Bush, July 14 1991, cited in Favier, Pierre and Martin-Roland, Michel, *La décennie Mitterrand*, Vol. 4, Seuil, 1999, pp. 50–51.

42. The flaw in Mitterrand's reasoning – which, I confess, at the time, I shared – with

much less justification than he had because I had recently spent two months in Moscow – was his failure to realise that the coup leaders lacked the confidence to take decisive measures against their opponents. It is true that it was an extraordinary turnaround: that the KGB, whose Chairman, Kryuchkov, was among the plotters, would prove reluctant to crush opposition, flew in the face of seventy years of Soviet history. Even after five years of Gorbachev's reforms, it seemed inconceivable that the Soviet State would be impotent in the face of an unarmed crowd, all the more so since, two years earlier, in June 1989, the Chinese leadership, facing a similar situation when protesters occupied Tiananmen Square, had sent in troops who opened fire leaving more than two thousand dead. To Mitterrand (and to me), it seemed obvious that Gorbachev had gone too far, the inevitable reaction had ensued and there would now be a breathing spell while the new Soviet leadership worked out how to proceed. We both misread the situation completely.

43.   Curiously the French public approved of the President's stance. An opinion poll found that 58 per cent, including 40 per cent of right-wing voters, expressed confidence in his handling of the situation. In other polls taken the same week, fewer than half of those questioned said he should have taken a tougher line. Six weeks later, Gorbachev's book, *The August Coup: The Truth and the Lessons*, revealed the Soviet leader's irritation at Mitterrand's lack of support. 'From Foros [the Crimean resort where his villa was situated], I had a conversation with President Bush,' Gorbachev wrote. 'François Mitterrand should have called me. He did not and I still regret that today.' It was later claimed that this passage – which appeared only in the French, Italian and Finnish language editions of the book – was a translation error. In fact, according to his press secretary, Andrei Grachev, Gorbachev indeed felt that Mitterrand had 'abandoned him too quickly'. The offending line was changed in the English-language edition to avoid making too big an issue of it. At the end of October, the Gorbachevs stayed with the Mitterrands at Latche, at which point both Presidents denied that there had been any change in their relations.

44.   Britain, France, West Germany and the United States held summit meetings in London and in Guadeloupe in 1977 and 1979, but the last meeting of the 'Big Four' nuclear powers had taken place in Paris in 1960. It was attended by De Gaulle, Eisenhower, Khrushchev and Macmillan.

45.   Meeting with John Major, January 14 1991, cited in Attali, *Verbatim*, Vol. 3, pp. 691–3.

46.   Meeting with President Bush, April 19 1990, Key Largo, ibid., pp. 468–70, and transcript of lunch discussion the same day in CHAN 5AG4 CD74, dossier 1.

47.   Meeting with President Bush, March 14 1991, Martinique, in CHAN 5AG4 CD75, dossier 1.

48.   Meeting with Helmut Kohl, Bad Wiessee, July 23 1991, in Favier and Martin-Roland, *La décennie Mitterrand*, Vol. 4, pp. 201–2.

49. Letter from Bush to Mitterrand, October 23 1991, ibid., p. 207.

50. Meeting with John Major, London, December 2 1991, ibid., pp. 223–4. The opt-out allowed Britain to seek parliamentary approval before adopting the principle of the single currency, which meant that in practice it could delay a decision as long as it wished.

51. *Frankfurter Allgemeine Zeitung*, November 29 1991.

52. Favier and Martin-Roland, *La décennie Mitterrand*, Vol. 4, p. 301 and *New York Times*, June 29 1992.

53. This was Mitterrand's argument to Kohl when they met in Berlin on December 3 1992: 'we must reason as if the Serbs and Croats have won. The solution is to seek a consensus of the three communities.'

54. Some of the arguments advanced by the French military to avoid committing troops, or even enforcing a 'no fly' zone, were risible. The Serbs, the French General Staff warned, might try to provoke Western aircraft into 'shooting down civilian airliners or planes transporting the wounded', and there would be an increased risk of Serb terrorist attacks in France. Why there had not been an increase in terrorist attacks during the Gulf War – which had been waged against a country much more experienced in matters of terrorism than Serbia – was not addressed.

55. Mitterrand's conversation with Bush at Munich on July 5 1992 (transcript in CHAN 5AG4 CD75) was revealing in this regard. It was the last such argument between the two men. By the time Clinton took office in January 1993, European defence was no longer an issue:

> MITTERRAND: Any organisation developing in parallel to NATO seems suspect [to you]. You have the same reaction to the Eurocorps . . . It's a force which has political value vis-a-vis Germany, which has been for so long our enemy . . . It's a matter of Franco-German reconciliation . . . It will be very difficult to take it further. Other countries aren't ready yet. [In any case], I don't expect American troops to leave for a very long time. I'll be dead before that happens . . .
>
> BUSH [*unconvinced*]: I'd understand better if you thought we were about to withdraw. What's this Eurocorps going to do? . . . It's reviving [isolationist] feelings in the USA. How many differences can we stand? CSCE, COCOM [and now] the Eurocorps!
>
> MITTERRAND: I don't feel obliged to say yes to everything you decide without having been consulted . . . I don't want to discover what's happening by reading the newspapers. It's true that you [Bush] are good enough to write to me just beforehand, [but unlike Reagan] you are a special case . . . If the Eurocorps serves no purpose, why is it a problem for you? . . . France is part of NATO

but not of the integrated command. We want to maintain that distance. That's why the Eurocorps cannot be part of the integrated command. But this is all theory. [In practice] the Corps cannot act outside NATO. You are treating as antagonistic things which are in fact complementary . . . This Corps is the embryo of what in 25 years' time will be a means for Europe to ensure its own security. [But] I've gone as far as I can. I won't take any further steps.

JAMES BAKER: The problem is if one day this embryo is going to duplicate NATO . . .

ROLAND DUMAS: For the last 12 months, NATO has been unwilling to concern itself with Yugoslavia. The Europeans can have their own problems. In certain areas, they [should] be able to act off their own bat.

MITTERRAND: The creation and development of the Eurocorps is worrying American diplomacy. Why?

BUSH: Our problem is that the message received in the United States is that NATO's defensive mission is no longer necessary . . .

MITTERRAND: So what are we supposed to do? Let the American government take all the decisions?

56. The Eurocorps became operational in 1995 with a permanent staff of 1,000 officers and men, based in Strasbourg. Belgium, Luxembourg and Spain are permanent members, as well as France and Germany. Other countries have also contributed. The Corps has taken part in peacekeeping operations in Bosnia and Kosovo and with the NATO-led security force in Afghanistan.

57. *Paris Match*, in its issue of September 24 1992, quoted Gubler as saying that the cancer was 'in its initial stages' and had not metastasised into the bone. In fact metastasis, as he well knew, had already been well advanced ten years earlier. Professor Bernard Debré, the Chief of the Urology Department at Cochin Hospital, where the operation took place (and the son of Mitterrand's nemesis, Prime Minister Michel Debré), estimated that the President had 'from five to 15 years' before him.

58. That may seem unduly harsh, but after more than forty years spent working for a variety of broadcasting organisations, newspapers and magazines, it is a judgement I am ready to defend. Journalism is a difficult business, but editors' insistence on matching every story that their competitors manage to obtain leads to a suspension of critical faculties. In France, during the campaign against Bérégovoy – which had been launched for political purposes by Judge Jean-Pierre and his associates – no serious writer, whether on the Left or the Right, stood up to ask whether there was any substance to the accusations. The limitations of the medium make such false unanimity hard to avoid, notwithstanding the integrity of the journalists concerned. As for those who do not care whether what they write is true – and

they are legion – their role is indissociable from Western democratic practice in which the right to disseminate false views is a necessary part of freedom of speech. It is part of the job description of politicians that they be able to withstand campaigns of calumny. For men like Bérégovoy and Salengro, that proved not to be the case.

15: The Survivalist

1. While it was certainly not Mitterrand's intention to support the Hutu extremists, France's consistent opposition to the Tutsi-led RPF meant that objectively it was on the side of the Hutus, whether under Habyarimana or the Akazu leadership which took his place.

2. That Mitterrand knew this to be untrue was confirmed six weeks later when he spoke of the risk of a second genocide. By late May a wealth of information was available about the massacres, including a report from the French Health Minister, Philippe Douste-Blazy, who had returned a few days earlier from a visit to Rwandan refugee camps in Zaire during which he had estimated the number of dead at 500,000.

3. Quesnot first used the term 'Tutsiland' in a note on April 29, in which he charged that Uganda's President Yoweri Museveni was aiming to create a Tutsi state in Rwanda.

4. In April 2013, investigating magistrates from the Paris High Court ordered a former Rwandan army captain, Pascal Simbikangwa, who had allegedly been a member of the Akazu, to be sent for trial on charges of 'complicity in genocide' and 'complicity in crimes against humanity' relating to massacres carried out between April and July 1994. Unless the magistrates' decision is overturned on appeal, it will be the first such trial held in France – almost twenty years after the event.

5. Message to President Bush, January 3 1994, cited in Favier and Martin-Roland, *La décennie Mitterrand*, Vol. 4, p. 497.

6. Meeting with Warren Christopher, May 4 1993, in CHAN 5AG4 CD75.

7. Hubert Védrine, Note to Mitterrand, January 25 1994, cited in Favier and Martin-Roland, Vol. 4, p. 512.

8. Meeting with Warren Christopher, January 24 1994, in CHAN 5AG4 CD75.

9. Pierre Tourlier situated this episode later and wrote that he intervened at the request of Gubler's successor, Dr Jean-Pierre Tarot. According to Gubler, Mitterrand's use of alternative medicines began in the autumn of 1994.

16: The Testament

1. After Mitterrand's death, Benamou published two further books, *Le dernier Mitterrand*, recounting the last two and a half years of his life, and *'Jeune homme,*

vous ne savez pas de quoi vous parlez'. The latter – a systematically hostile account – employed the same amalgam of innuendo and half-truth as the references to Mitterrand in Wiesel's autobiography.

2. Mitterrand, François, *De l'Allemagne, de la France*, Odile Jacob, 1996, pp. 241–7.

3. Cited in Sylvie Thiéblemont-Dollet, 'François Mitterrand: une mise en scène télévisuelle ou la reconstruction d'une image déconstruite', in *Discours audio-visuels et mutations culturelles: actes du colloque organisé par l'AFECCAV, Bordeaux, 28, 29, 30 septembre 2000*, L'Harmattan, 2002, p. 341.

4. Favier and Martin-Roland, *La décennie Mitterrand*, Vol. 4, p. 624.

5. Mitterrand, *De l'Allemagne, de la France*, pp. 42 & 143.

6. According to Christophe Barbier, Mitterrand told the Mayor of Jarnac, Maurice Voiron, in March 1995, well before the purchase of the plot at Mount Beuvray, that it was his intention to be buried in the family crypt.

7. In a conversation with Georges-Marc Benamou at the end of August, Mitterrand referred to the fate of Louis XI, whose tomb at Cléry-St-André, near Orleans, was repeatedly profaned.

8. Notably that of Benamou, in *Le dernier Mitterrand*. Christophe Barbier collated the accounts of almost all those present. The two most credible witnesses were his son, Gilbert, who said, 'He tasted everything, which was already extraordinary', and Jack Lang, who remembered that he ate modestly. Benamou had been brought by Pierre Bergé with Danielle's agreement but without the knowledge of Mitterrand, who had been displeased to learn of his presence.

9. In a book entitled *Le dernier tabou: Révélations sur la santé des présidents* (Pygmalion, 2012), two journalists, Denis Demonpion and Laurent Léger, claimed – without citing their source – that, 'at his express request', Mitterrand was given a lethal injection during the night of January 7–8. That assertion is questionable. It is very unlikely that Mitterrand, at that stage, was in any state to make such a request. For the same reason, one may legitimately wonder whether Mitterrand authorised Tarot to administer the last rites that night or whether he had already expressed his wishes earlier. But the doctor was well aware that Mitterrand wished to die with dignity. The only person who knows for certain what happened is Tarot himself. For the last six hours of Mitterrand's life, he was alone in the apartment with him. It is worth remembering, however, that once a cancer metastasises to the brain, death often follows very rapidly. It is possible, therefore, that Mitterrand died a natural death. Ambiguity, the constant companion of his life, was with him to the end.

10. Jacques Chirac, 'Intervention télévisée', January 8 1996, in http://www.jacqueschirac-asso.fr/fr/wp-content/uploads/2010/04/D%C3%A9c%C3%A8s-de-Fran%C3%A7ois-Mitterrand.pdf

Picture credits

Protesting against 'the Wog invasion' (© Keystone-France/Gamma-Rapho); Marie-Louise Terrasse, aged 20 (Collection Jean-Marc Terrasse); with Henri Frenay (© AFP); in the government of Pierre Mendès France (© Keystone-France/Gamma Rapho); big game hunting (© Pierre Vals/Paris Match/Scoop); at the Cannes Film Festival (rue des Archives); Jean-Christophe Mitterrand's 19th birthday (© AFP); Anne and François (Jean-Loup Salzmann); Valéry Giscard d'Estaing greeting Mitterrand at the Elysée (© Jean Gaumy, Magnum Photos; and © Archive/AFP); sitting for the sculptor, Daniel Druet (© Guy le Querrec, Magnum Photos); with Pierre Mauroy (© Guy le Querrec, Magnum Photos); with Mikhail Gorbachev in Kiev (Philippe Janin); at Verdun with Helmut Kohl (DPA); with Margaret Thatcher (Lionel Cironneau/AP/PA Images); with Ronald Reagan (© Bettmann/Corbis); in Sarajevo to break the siege by Bosnian Serbs (© Christophe Simon/AFP); campaigning for a second term (© Raymond Depardon, Magnum Photos); Laurent Fabius and Michel Rocard (© Jean-Michel Turpin/Sygma/Corbis); Jacques Chirac and Édouard Balladur (© Derrick Ceyrac/AFP); with Rene Bousquet at Latche (Julien Quideau); at Pierre Bérégovoy's funeral (© Michel Gangne/AFP); with Patrice Pelat (© Frank Perry/AFP); after the second cancer operation (Dominique Aubert); Anne and Mazarine at the funeral (© Derrick Ceyrac/AFP).

Index

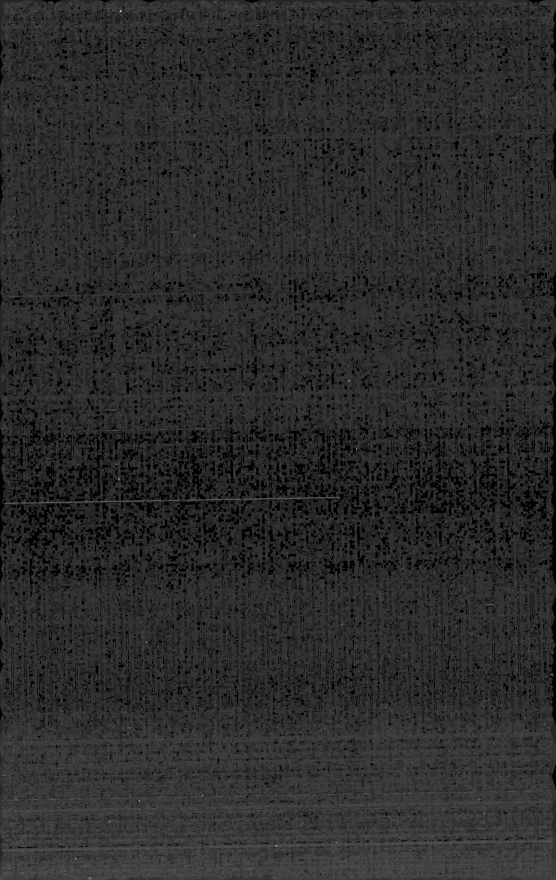